What's New in This Edition

Sams Teach Yourself Database Programming with Visual Basic 6 in 21 Days teaches you all the techniques necessary to build a complete database solution. In this edition, we have concentrated on improving on our Visual Basic 5 efforts. You'll find the following new features/improvements in this edition:

- All exercises and code examples take advantage of new Visual Basic 6 features.

- Four entirely new chapters have been added to cover the new Microsoft Data Environment Designer, Microsoft Report Designer, ActiveX Data Objects, and Attached Tables.

- Several chapters have been revised to take advantage of the new ADO and OLE DB features of Visual Basic 6.0, including data graphs, data bound lists, and securing your database applications.

- The SQL-VB utility has been updated again. This handy scripting utility now sports an Explorer interface and built-in editor, and has a new feature that enables you to inspect the database schema while you edit the script. SQL-VB can also manage data in all Microsoft Jet–supported database formats, including HTML data sources.

Curtis L. Smith

Michael C. Amundsen

SAMS

Teach Yourself

Database

Programming

with Visual Basic® 6

in 21 Days

SAMS

A Division of Macmillan Computer Publishing
201 West 103rd St., Indianapolis, Indiana, 46290 USA

Sams Teach Yourself Database Programming with Visual Basic ® 6 in 21 Days

Trademarks

Warning and Disclaimer

EXECUTIVE EDITOR
Chris Denny

ACQUISITIONS EDITOR
Sharon Cox

DEVELOPMENT EDITOR
Tony Amico

MANAGING EDITOR
Jodi Jensen

PROJECT EDITOR
Nancy Albright

INDEXER
Bruce Clingaman

PROOFREADER
Cynthia Fields

TECHNICAL EDITORS
Doug Mitchell
Jeff Perkins

TEAM COORDINATOR
Carol Ackerman

SOFTWARE DEVELOPMENT SPECIALIST
Dan Scherf

INTERIOR DESIGNER
Gary Adair

COVER DESIGNER
Aren Howell

LAYOUT TECHNICIANS
Michael Dietsch
Ayanna Lacey
Heather Hiatt Miller

Contents at a Glance

Contents

About the Authors

Curtis Smith

Curtis Smith has been working in the computer industry for many years. He has a financial background, which helps to bring a practical real-world flair to *Sams Teach Yourself Database Programming with Visual Basic 6 in 21 Days*. Curtis has worked in the federal government, and in the banking, transportation, and pharmaceutical industries. He has significant experience implementing financial, project management, inventory, and maintenance software applications. Curtis holds a BA degree from Muskingum College (New Concord, Ohio), an MBA from Miami University (Oxford, Ohio), and is a Certified Public Accountant. He is currently the Manager of Business Systems for Kendle International Inc., a Contract Research Organization located in Cincinnati, Ohio.

Mike Amundsen

Mike Amundsen works as an IS Consulting and Training Specialist for Design-Synergy Corporation, a consulting and project management firm specializing in information technology services. He travels the U.S. and Europe teaching and consulting on Windows development topics.

Mike's other book projects include authoring the two previous editions of *Sams Teach Yourself Database Programming with Visual Basic;* the MAPI, SAPI, and TAPI Developer's Guide published by Sams Publishing, and contributing to a number of books on Visual Basic, Visual InterDev, and other topics. Mike has contributed to a number of periodicals, including several editions of *Cobb Journal, Visual Basic Programmers Journal,* and *VB Tech* magazine.

When he's not busy writing or traveling to client sites, Mike spends time with his family at his home in Kentucky. You can reach Mike at

tysdbvb@amundsen.com

or visit his Web site at

www.amundsen.com.

Dedications

To my wife Chris, my friends, acquaintances, and relatives who have supported me through this effort.
—Curtis Smith

To Scott Ivey, thanks for your continued support and encouragement.
—Mike Amundsen

Acknowledgments

There are a number of folks who helped us complete this edition. Many students, colleagues, and volunteers spent time poring over the book and providing us with feedback on how we could improve our work. To all those who devoted their time and energy to helping us find gold among the bits of dirt and coal, we thank you.

We also thank all those who sent us email and visited our Web site in order to help us continue to improve the book—even after the first printing of the second edition was on the shelf. Many of you went out of your way to send us friendly suggestions and tips on how to clarify examples and remedy problems in the book. If this edition is better, it is due in large measure to your help.

Of course, the folks at Sams Publishing deserve a great deal of thanks for their continued support and assistance. Much of the work of publishers goes unnoticed and sometimes unappreciated. The authors and the staff at Sams both know that this book would not be in your hands today without the diligent and relentless efforts of the people at Sams Publishing.

Although there are several people at Sams who deserve special thanks for helping us complete this edition, we want to especially thank Doug Mitchell for his untiring work. His attention to detail and insistence on accuracy have added immensely to this edition. The work of a technical editor is a tedious, and often thankless, task. If you find the coding examples in this edition clearer and more helpful, it is due in large measure to Doug's efforts.

Tell Us What You Think!

As the reader of this book, *you* are our most important critic and commentator. We value your opinion and want to know what we're doing right, what we could do better, what areas you'd like to see us publish in, and any other words of wisdom you're willing to pass our way.

As the Executive Editor for the Visual Basic Programming team at Macmillan Computer Publishing, I welcome your comments. You can fax, email, or write me directly to let me know what you did or didn't like about this book—as well as what we can do to make our books stronger.

Please note that I cannot help you with technical problems related to the topic of this book, and that due to the high volume of mail I receive, I might not be able to reply to every message.

When you write, please be sure to include this book's title and author as well as your name and phone or fax number. I will carefully review your comments and share them with the author and editors who worked on the book.

Fax: 317-817-7070

E-mail: vb@mcp.com

Mail: Chris Denny, Executive Editor
           Visual Basic Programming team
           Macmillan Computer Publishing
           201 West 103rd Street
           Indianapolis, IN 46290 USA

Introduction

Welcome to Database Programming in Visual Basic 6

Welcome to *Sams Teach Yourself Database Programming with Visual Basic 6 in 21 Days*. You cover a lot of ground in the next 21 lessons, from developing fully functional input screens with fewer than 10 lines of Visual Basic code and working with Visual Basic components, to handling complex user security and auditing in multiuser applications, to creating online help files for your Visual Basic programs, and much more. Whether you are a power user, a business professional, a database guru, or a Visual Basic programmer, you'll find something in this book to help you improve your Visual Basic and database skills.

Each week you focus on a different aspect of database programming with Visual Basic. In Week 1, you learn about issues related to building simple database applications using the extensive collection of data controls available with Visual Basic. In Week 2, you concentrate on techniques for creating database applications using Visual Basic code. In Week 3, you study advanced topics, such as multiuser applications, locking schemes, database integrity, and application-level security. You also learn techniques for creating ODBC- and OLE DB–enabled Visual Basic applications.

Database Design Skills

This book helps you develop your database design skills, too. Each week covers at least one topic on database design. Day 1 covers Visual Basic database data types, and Day 6 covers the use of the Visdata program to create and manage databases. Day 7 teaches you to use SQL SELECT statements to organize existing data into usable datasets. On Days 12 and 14, you learn advanced SQL data definition and manipulation techniques, and on Day 15 you learn the five rules of data normalization.

ActiveX DLLs and Custom Controls

Throughout the book, we show you how to use and develop DLLs and custom controls that you can reuse in all your future Visual Basic programs. This includes components for input validation, error trapping, graphing data, creating ADO-based input forms, user login/logout, program security features, and audit trails. All these components can be added to existing and future Visual Basic programs with very little, if any, modification. After you build these libraries, you can modify them to fit your specific needs and even add new libraries of your own.

Who Should Read This Book

This book is designed to help you improve your database programming skills using Visual Basic. You do not have to be a Visual Basic coding guru to use this book. If you are a power user who wants to learn how to put together simple, solid data entry forms using Visual Basic, you'll get a lot from this book. If you have some Visual Basic experience and want to take the next step into serious database programming, you'll find a great deal of valuable information here, too. Finally, if you are a professional programmer, you can take many of the techniques and code libraries described here and apply them to your current projects.

What You Need to Use This Book

Most of the code examples in this book were built using Microsoft Visual Basic 6, Professional Edition (the Remote Data Control and Remote Data Objects can be used only with the Enterprise edition of Visual Basic 6). Most of the examples work using Visual Basic 5, Professional Edition, but some do not. Version 6 of Visual Basic has several new features not available with version 5. If you are using Visual Basic 5, you can still get a great deal out of this book, but we strongly encourage you to upgrade to Visual Basic 6. There are lots of new features in Visual Basic 6, and you'll be glad you upgraded.

If you have Visual Basic 6, Enterprise Edition, you can take advantage of some new features not available in the Professional Edition, but this is not a necessity.

Visual Basic 6 is available only in a 32-bit version. That means you need to run Visual Basic (and its completed projects) under Windows 95/98 or Windows NT.

Quick Course Summary

Here is a brief rundown of what you accomplish each week.

Week 1: Data Controls and Microsoft Jet Databases

In the first week, you learn about the relational database model, how to use the Visual Basic database objects to access and update existing databases, and how to use the Visdata program to create and maintain databases. You also learn how to design and code data entry forms (including use of the Visual Basic bound data controls), and how to create input validation routines at the keystroke, field, and form levels. You learn how to use the Visual Basic Data Report Designer report writer to design and display simple reports. Lastly, you learn how to use Structured Query Language (SQL) to extract data from existing databases.

When you complete the work for Week 1, you will be able to build Microsoft Jet databases, create solid data entry forms that include input validation routines, and produce printed reports of your data.

Week 2: Programming with the Microsoft Jet Database Engine

Week 2 concentrates on topics that are of value to developers in the standalone and workgroup environments. You explore a wide variety of topics, including the following:

- What the Microsoft Jet engine is, and how you can use Visual Basic code to create and maintain data access objects
- How to create data entry forms with Visual Basic code
- How to use the Microsoft graph control to create graphs and charts of your data
- How to use data-bound list boxes, data-bound combo boxes, and data-bound grids to create advanced data entry forms
- How to make applications more solid with error handling
- How to create and update databases with Structured Query Language (SQL).

When you complete the lessons for Week 2, you will be able to build advanced database structures using the SQL language and create complex data entry forms using Visual Basic code, including bound lists and grids and error-handling routines.

Week 3: Advanced Database Programming with SQL and ODBC

The third and final week covers several very important topics. This week's work focuses on the database issues you encounter when you develop database applications for multiple users and/or multiple sites. You learn the five rules of data normalization and how applying those rules can improve the speed, accuracy, and integrity of your databases.

You explore Visual Basic database locking schemes for the database, table, and page levels. You also learn the advantages and limitations of adding cascading updates and deletes to your database relationship definitions. You learn how to use the Visual Basic keywords `BeginTrans`, `CommitTrans`, and `Rollback` to improve database integrity and processing speed during mass updates.

We show you how to write data entry forms that use the Remote Data Control, Remote Data Objects, the new ADO Control, and ActiveX Data Objects to link directly with the ODBC interface to access data in registered ODBC data sources.

You review application-level security schemes, such as user login and logout, program-level access rights, and audit trails to keep track of critical application operations.

You also learn how to use the Microsoft Replication Manager to establish and maintain database replication schemes to protect and update your mission-critical distributed data.

When you finish the final week of the course, you will be able to build solid multiuser applications that include database locking schemes, cascades, and transactions; OLED DB and ADO interfaces; and application security and audit features. And you will be able to manage distributed data through replication.

What's Not Covered in This Book

Although there is a lot of good stuff in this book, there are some important topics we don't cover in these pages. For example, we don't talk in detail about Visual Basic coding in general. If you are new to Visual Basic, you might want to review the book *Sams' Teach Yourself Visual Basic in 21 Days*. This is an excellent introduction to Visual Basic.

Although we discuss issues such as connecting to back-end databases such as SQL Server and Oracle, we do not cover the specifics of these systems. We focus on techniques you need for connecting your Visual Basic applications to remote databases, and not on how to operate remote databases.

We also do not cover any third-party controls or add-ins for Visual Basic. That isn't because we don't think they are useful. There are literally hundreds of new and existing third-party products for Visual Basic, and many of them are very good. Because we wanted the book to be as accessible as possible to all our readers, we use only those controls or add-in products that are included in the Visual Basic 6 Professional Edition.

What's on the CD-ROM?

In the back of this book, there is a CD-ROM that contains lots of Visual Basic code, sample and demonstration programs, and handy utilities. Following is a brief description of the contents of the CD-ROM. Refer to the installation directions on the last page of the book for details on how to install and run these programs.

Chapter Projects and Examples

All examples and exercises mentioned in this book are stored in the TYSDBVB6 directory of the CD-ROM. You can copy these files directly to your workstation hard disk or enter them from the listings in the book.

About the DLLs and Custom Controls

All reusable DLLs and Custom Controls mentioned in the text are also included on the CD-ROM. If you want to save yourself some typing, you can simply add these libraries to your Visual Basic projects. You can also copy these libraries to your workstation hard drive and modify them for your own use.

Several projects in the text use these custom components. In order for these projects to work, load and compile the components on your machine. This will make sure they are properly registered on your workstation and compiled with the most recent version of Visual Basic. You may need to change the directory location of some of these components, too. The key thing to remember is to load and compile these components before attempting to load the programs that *use* the component.

Online Resources

We encourage you to keep in touch with us electronically. You can visit our Web site at

`www.amundsen.com/books`

and email us at

`tysdbvb@amundsen.com`

and

`curtis-smith@worldnet.att.net`

WEEK 1

At a Glance

This week, you learn the basic skills of Visual Basic 6 database application development. You design and implement complete data entry forms, work with bound controls, write input validation routines, create reports, construct database files, and work with SQL statements.

Day 1: You learn basic controls and write a complete Visual Basic database data entry application using no more than three lines of Visual Basic code. You also learn the basics of relational database theory, including databases, data tables, and fields. You learn the database data types recognized by Visual Basic and how to use them in your Visual Basic applications.

Day 2: You learn what the Visual Basic database objects are and how to use them to read and write data tables. You learn the basics of the DAO database access model—the classic data access interface for Visual Basic and Microsoft Windows applications.

Day 3: You learn how to design and build quality data entry forms using Visual Basic bound data controls. You also learn how to design forms that conform to the Windows 95/98 style specifications.

Day 4: You learn the fundamentals of input validation for data entry forms. You learn how to write keyboard filters and field-level and form-level validation routines. You also work with a Visual Basic custom control, Vtext, that contains validation routines you can use in any Visual Basic application.

Day 5: You learn how to create reports with the Visual Basic 6 Data Report. You learn that this is an easy-to-use tool for displaying data to the screen, printer, or Web page.

1
2
3
4
5
6
7

Day 6: You use the Visual Data Manager (Visdata) to perform database operations to create and maintain your applications. This includes designing databases, building tables, and creating SQL statements.

Day 7: This is the first of three days devoted to one of the most important topics in database programming: Structured Query Language (SQL). After learning in general terms what SQL can do for you, you learn the basics of this powerful and simple language. You learn about SQL clauses you can use to select and sort records from your databases. You also learn SQL keywords, such as SELECT, ORDER BY, WHERE, DISTINCTROW, TOP N, TOP[]PERCENT, and GROUP BY. You also study SQL aggregate functions (SUM, AVG, and so on), joins, unions, and crosstab queries.

DAY 1

Database Programming Basics

Your project today is to create a completely functional data entry program using Visual Basic 6. The program you create will be able to access data tables within an existing database; it will also enable users to add, edit, and delete records.

You also work through the definition of a relational database, as well as the basic elements of a database, including data table, data record, and data field. You learn the importance of establishing and maintaining data relationships. These are some of the key elements to developing quality databases for your applications.

Finally, you learn Visual Basic database field types, including their names, storage sizes, and common uses. Along the way, you create a programming project that explores the limits, possibilities, and common uses of Visual Basic database field types.

Sound like a lot for one day? Not really. You will be amazed at how quickly you can put together database programs. Much of the drudgery commonly associated with writing data entry programs (screen layout, cursor control, input editing, and so on) is automatically handled using just a few of Visual Basic's input controls. In addition, with Visual Basic's data controls it's easy to add the capability of reading and writing database tables.

So let's get started!

Starting Your New Visual Basic Project

If you already have Visual Basic up and running on your PC, select File | New Project to create a new project. If you haven't started Visual Basic yet, start it now. Select Standard EXE and click OK in the dialog that appears. Now you're ready to create the data entry screen.

Adding the Database Control

The first thing you need to do for the database program is open the database and select the data table you want to access. To do this, double-click the data control in the Visual Basic toolbox (see Figure 1.1). This places a data control in the center of the form. When this is done, the form is ready to open a data table. At this point, your screen should look something like the one in Figure 1.1.

 Tip

Are you not sure which of those icons in the toolbox is the data control? You can press F1 while the toolbox window is highlighted to display a help screen describing each of the Visual Basic tools.

You can also get help on a particular control in the toolbox by clicking its icon and pressing F1 to activate Visual Basic help.

Tool Tips are also available in Visual Basic 6. Simply rest the mouse pointer on any icon to view a pop-up description of that item. This option can be toggled on and off by selecting Tools | Options, choosing the General tab, and then checking the Show ToolTips check box.

Next, you need to set a few of the control's properties to indicate the database and data table you want to access.

Setting the `DatabaseName` and `RecordSource` Properties

You must first set the following two properties when linking a data control to a database:

DatabaseName   Selected database

RecordSource   Selected data table in the database

Label   TextBox   CommandButton

FIGURE 1.1

*The data control as it
appears when you first
add it to your project.*

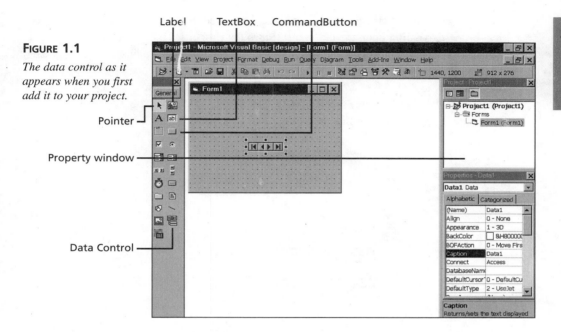

Pointer

Property window

Data Control

The BOOKS6.MDB database will be used in the exercise that follows. This database can be
found in the TYSDBVB6\SOURCE\DATA directory created by the CD-ROM that shipped with
this book.

Caution

Make sure that you run through the installation program on the CD-ROM to
copy the exercise files onto your hard drive. Do not simply copy the files
from the CD-ROM to your hard drive. The copy method will give you read-
only files that will make many of your exercises malfunction.

Tip

If you do not see the Properties dialog box, press F4 or select View |
Properties Window from the menu, or click the properties icon on the Visual
Basic toolbar at the top of the screen.

To set the DatabaseName of the data control, first select the data control by single-
clicking the control. (The data control will already be selected if you did not click anywhere else on the form after you double-clicked the data control in the toolbox.) This
forces the data control properties to appear in the Visual Basic Properties dialog box.

Locate the `DatabaseName` property (properties are listed in either alphabetical or categorical order, depending upon the tab you select in the Properties box), and click the property name. When you do this, three small dots (. . .), the properties ellipsis button, appear to the right of the data entry box. Clicking the ellipsis button brings up the DatabaseName dialog box. You should now be able to select the `BOOKS6.MDB` file from the list of available database files (`\\TYSDBVB6\SOURCE\DATA\BOOKS6.MDB`). Your screen should look something like the one in Figure 1.2.

FIGURE 1.2

Using the Visual Basic File | Open dialog box to see the `DatabaseName` *property.*

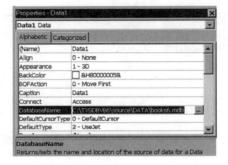

When you have located the `BOOKS6.MDB` file and selected Open, Visual Basic inserts the complete drive, path, and filename of the database file into the input area, linking the database and your program together. Always double-check this property to make sure that you correctly selected the desired database.

Note

> People often use the words database and data table interchangeably. Throughout this book, *data table* is used to refer to a single table of data, and *database* is used to refer to a collection of related tables. For example, the Titles table and the Publishers table are two data tables in the BOOKS6 database.

Now that you know what database you will use, you must select the data table within that database that you want to access by setting the `RecordSource` property of the data control. You can do this by locating the `RecordSource` property in the Properties window, single-clicking the property, and then single-clicking the small down arrow to the right of the property input box. This brings up a list of all the tables in the `BOOKS6.MDB` database, as shown in Figure 1.3. For the first database program, you will use the Titles data table in the `BOOKS6.MDB` database.

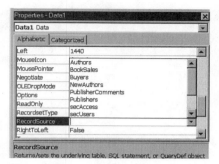

FIGURE 1.3

Setting the RecordSource *property to the Titles table.*

To select the Titles table from this list, simply click on it. Visual Basic automatically inserts the table name into the RecordSource property in the Properties window.

Setting the Caption and Name Properties

You need to set two other data control properties in the project. These two properties are not required, but setting them is a good programming practice because it improves the readability of the programming code. Here are the optional properties:

Caption   Displayed name of the data control

Name   Program name of the data control

Setting the Caption property of the data control sets the text that displays between the record selection arrows on the data control. (Please note that you will need to expand the width of the data control to read this text.) It is a good habit to set this to a value that makes sense to the user.

Setting the Name property of the data control sets the text that will be used by the Visual Basic programmer. This is never seen by the user, but you should set the Name to something similar to the Caption to make it easier to relate the two when working on your program.

For your program, set the Caption property of the data control to Titles and the Name property of the data control to datTitles. Now that you've added the Caption property, use the mouse to stretch the data control so that you can see the complete caption. Your form should look like the one in Figure 1.4.

FIGURE 1.4

A data control stretched to show the Captions *property.*

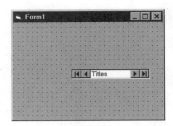

Note

The name of the data control (datTitles) might seem unusual. It is, however, a logical name if you remove the first three letters, *dat*. This prefix is added to designate this object as a data control. The three-character-prefix naming convention is Microsoft's suggested nomenclature for Visual Basic 6 and is used throughout this book.

Use the search phrase Object Naming Conventions in Visual Basic 6 Online Help to find a complete listing of the suggested object prefixes.

Saving Your Project

Now is a good time to save your work up to this point. To save this project, select File | Save Project from the main menu. When prompted for a filename for the form, enter DATCNTRL.FRM. You will then be prompted for a filename for the project. Enter DATCNTRL.VBP.

Note

FRM is the default extension given to Visual Basic 6 forms, and VBP is the default extension given to Visual Basic 6 projects.

It's always a good idea to save your work often.

Note

This, and all other projects that you complete from this book, can be found in the directories that were created by the Setup program on the CD-ROM included with this book.

> **Tip**
>
> One way to make sure you keep an up-to-date copy of your project saved on disk is to set the `When a program starts:` environment variable to Save Changes. You can do this by selecting Tools | Options and choosing the Environment tab. Then select either the Save Changes option or the Prompt to Save Changes option.

Adding the Bound Input Controls

Now that you've successfully linked the form to a database with the data control and selected a data table to access, you are ready to add input controls to the form. Visual Basic 6 supplies you with input controls that can be directly bound (connected) to the data table you want to access. You merely place several input controls on the form and assign them to an existing data control.

NEW TERM   Associating a control on a form to a field in a data table is referred to as *binding* a control. When they are assigned to a data source, these controls are called *bound input controls*.

Let's add the first bound input control to the Titles table input form. Place an input control on the form by double-clicking the TextBox control in the Visual Basic 6 toolbox. This inserts a TextBox control directly in the center of the form. When the control is on the form, you can use the mouse to move and resize it in any way you choose. You could add additional input controls by double-clicking the text box button in the toolbox as many times as you like. Set the `Name` property of this control to `txtTitle`. Add a label to describe this control by double-clicking the label control. Set the label's `Name` property to `lblTitle`, and the `Caption` property to `Title`. Refer to Figure 1.1 if you have any problems finding a particular Visual Basic control.

> **Tip**
>
> When double-clicking controls onto a form, each instance of the control is loaded in the center of the form. When you add several controls in this manner, each control is loaded in exactly the same place on the form, like a stack of pancakes. It looks as though you still have only one, but they're all there! You can view each of the controls you loaded on your form by using the mouse to drag and drop the topcontrol to another portion of the form.

Setting the `DataSource` and `DataField` Properties

You must set two text box properties in order for the TextBox control to interact with the data control. These are the two required properties:

DataSource   Name of the data control

DataField   Name of the field in the table

A relationship is established between a field (the DataField property) in a table (the DataSource property) and a bound control when you set these two properties. When this is done, all data display and data entry in this input control is linked directly to the data table/field you selected.

Setting the DataSource property of the TextBox control binds the input control to the data control. To set the text box DataSource property, first select the TextBox control (click it once), and then click the DataSource property in the Property window. By clicking this property's down arrow, you can see a list of all the data controls currently active on this form. You have added only one data control to this form, so you see only one name in the list (see Figure 1.5). Set the DataSource value to datTitles by clicking the word datTitles in the drop-down list box.

FIGURE 1.5

Setting the DataSource property of a bound text box.

The second required property for a bound input control is the DataField property. Setting this property binds a specific field in the data table to the input control. Set the DataField property of the current input control by single-clicking the DataField property in the Property window and then single-clicking the down arrow to the right of the property. You now see a list of all the fields that are defined for the data table that you selected in the DataSource property (see Figure 1.6). Click the Title field to set the DataField property for this control.

Now that you have the general idea, finish up the data entry form by adding bound input controls for the remaining fields in the Title data table. Refer to Table 1.1 for details.

While you're at it, add label controls to the left of the TextBox controls and set their Caption properties to the values shown in Table 1.2. Size and align the controls on the form, too. Also, size the form by selecting its borders and dragging to a desired shape. Your form should look something like the one in Figure 1.7 when you're done.

FIGURE 1.6

Selecting the DataField *property of the TextBox control.*

FIGURE 1.7

The completed data entry form for Titles.

TABLE 1.1 THE INPUT CONTROL DataSource AND DataField PROPERTIES FOR THE TITLES FORM

Textbox	DataSource	DataField
txtISBN	datTitles	ISBN
txtTitle	datTitles	Title
txtYearPub	datTitles	YearPub
txtPubID	datTitles	PubID
txtDescription	datTitles	Description
txtNotes	datTitles	Notes
txtSubject	datTitles	Subject
txtComments	datTitles	Comments

TABLE 1.2 THE LABEL CONTROL Caption PROPERTIES FOR THE TITLES FORM

Label	Caption
lblISBN	ISBN
lblTitle	Title
lblYearPub	Year Published
lblPubID	Publisher ID
lblDescription	Description
lblNotes	Notes
lblSubject	Subject
lblComments	Comments

You can now run the program and see the data control in action. Select Run | Start (or press F5) to compile and run your program. You can walk through the data table by clicking the left and right arrows on the data control at the bottom of the form. The left-most arrow (the one with the bar on it) moves you to the first record in the data table. The rightmost arrow (which also has a bar) moves you to the last record in the data table. The other two arrows simply move you through the data table one record at a time.

You can make any changes permanent to the data table by moving to a different record in the table. Try this by changing the data in the Title input control, moving the record pointer to the next record, and then moving the pointer back to the record you just edited. You will see that the new value was saved to the data table.

Now let's include the capability of adding new records to the data table and deleting existing records from the data table.

Adding the New and Delete Command Buttons

Up to this point, you have not written a single line of Visual Basic code. However, in order to add the capability of inserting new records and deleting existing records, you have to write a grand total of two lines of Visual Basic code: one line for the add record function, and one line for the delete record function.

The first step in the process is to add two command buttons labeled Add and Delete to the form. Refer to Table 1.3 and Figure 1.8 for details on adding the command buttons to your form.

FIGURE 1.8

The form layout after adding the Add and Delete command buttons.

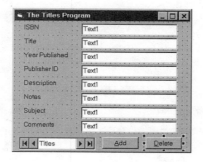

TABLE 1.3 COMMAND BUTTON PROPERTIES FOR THE TITLE FORM

Name	Caption
cmdAdd	&Add
cmdDelete	&Delete

Note

Adding an ampersand (&) to the Caption of a command button causes the letter immediately following the ampersand to be underlined. The under-lined letter (also known as a shortcut key or hot key) serves as a prompt to the user to indicate that it can be pressed in conjunction with the Alt key to execute the procedure that the button contains.

Double-click the Add button to bring up the Visual Basic code window to add code behind the Add command button. You see the subroutine header and footer already entered for you. All you need to do is add a single line of Visual Basic code between them:

```
Private Sub cmdAdd_Click()
datTitles.Recordset.AddNew   ' add a new record to the table
End Sub
```

Note

Visual Basic automatically creates the Sub_End Sub routines for each new procedure you create. When you are performing the exercises in this book, insert the code only between these two lines (in other words, don't repeat the Sub_End Sub statements, or your code will not work properly).

Now open the code window behind the Delete button and add this Visual Basic code:

```
Private Sub cmdDelete_Click()
datTitles.Recordset.Delete  ' delete the current record
End Sub
```

RUNTIME AND DESIGN-TIME PROPERTIES

RecordSet is a runtime-only property of the data control. This property is a reference to the underlying data table defined in the design-time RecordSource property. The RecordSet can refer to an existing table in the database or a virtual table, such as a Visual Basic Dynaset or Snapshot. This is covered in more depth on Day 2, "Visual Basic Database Objects." For now, think of the RecordSet property as a runtime version of the RecordSource property you set when you designed the form.

In the two preceding code snippets, you used the Visual Basic methods AddNew and Delete. You will learn more about these and other Visual Basic methods in the lesson on Day 3, "Creating Data Entry Forms with Bound Controls."

Save the project and run the program again. You can now click the Add button and see a blank set of input controls for data entry. Fill them all with some data (refer to Figure 1.9 for an example of a new record) and then move to another record in the table. The data is automatically saved to the data table. You can also use the Delete button to remove any record from the table. First, find the record you just added (it's the last record in the table) and then click the Delete button. Now move to the previous record in the table and try to move forward again to view the record you just deleted. You can't. It's not there!

FIGURE 1.9

Example data filling in blank fields after clicking the Add button.

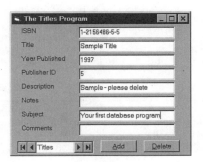

Note

When you entered data into this form, you may have noticed that the tab sequence didn't follow a logical progression. This happened because you added the txtTitles control first, but placed the txtISBN control in the first position on the form. Visual Basic defines the tab order of controls in the sequence they are placed on the form.

To correct this problem quickly, select the last control you want in your tab sequence (in this case, the Delete button) and enter 0 in its `TabIndex` property. Next, select the second-to-last control in the tab sequence (the Add button) and enter 0 in its `TabIndex` property. Continue to set all the `TabIndex` values to 0 for all controls in your tab sequence by moving backward through the form. Complete the process by setting the `TabIndex` value of the txtISBN control to 0.

The `TabIndex` property of a control is incremented by 1 each time a lower value is entered in another control. Therefore, by setting the `TabIndex` property of the txtISBN control to 0, you reset the value of the `TabIndex` property of txtTitle to 1, txtYearPub to 2, and so on.

If you didn't enter data into the data entry form that you created in this exercise in quite the same way as Figure 1.9 (for example, you incorrectly entered characters in the Year field, which only accepts numbers), you might have received an error message from Visual Basic 6 saying that you have invalid data in one of the fields. This is supposed to happen! Visual Basic 6 (more precisely, the Microsoft Jet Engine) verifies all data entries to ensure that the correct data type is entered in each field. Input validation routines, a means of restricting data entry even further, are covered in depth on Day 4, "Input Validation," and error trapping is reviewed in the lesson on Day 13, "Error Handling in Visual Basic 6." You can skip over these messages for now.

Now that you have completed your first Visual Basic 6 database program, it's time to discuss the structure of a relational database.

What Are Relational Databases?

Before looking at the individual components of relational databases, let's first establish a simple definition. For the purposes of this book, a relational database is defined as a collection of data that indicates relation among data elements; or, to put it even more directly, a relational database is a collection of related data.

In order to build a collection of related data, you need three key building blocks. These building blocks are (from smallest to largest)

- Data fields (sometimes called data columns)
- Data records (also known as data rows)
- Data tables

Let's look at each of these elements in more depth.

Data Fields

The first building block in a relational database is the data field. The data field contains the smallest element of data that you can store in a database, and each field contains only one data element. For example, if you want to store the name of a customer, you must create a data field somewhere in the database and also give that field a name, such as `CustomerName`. If you want to store the current account balance of a customer, you must create another field, possibly calling it `AccountBalance`. All the fields you create are stored in a single database (see Figure 1.10).

FIGURE 1.10

Examples of data fields in a database.

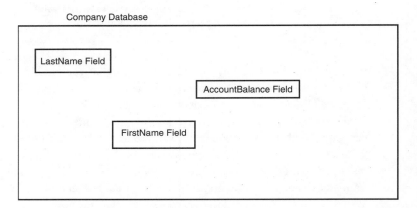

Although it is possible to store more than one data element in a single field (such as first and last name), it is not good database practice to do so. In fact, storing more than one data element in a field can lead to problems when you or other users try to retrieve, update, or sort data.

This concept seems simple in theory, but it's not so easy in practice. The CustomerName field discussed earlier is a good example. Assume that you have a database that contains a list of your customers by name, and you need to sort the list by last name. How would this be done? Can you assume that each CustomerName data field contains a last name? Do some contain only a first name? Some might contain both first and last names, but in

---

Note In formal database theory, a data field is often referred to as a "data column." Throughout this book, the terms *data field* and *data column* are used interchangeably.

what order—last name, first name or first name, last name? When you look at this situation, you discover that you're actually storing two data elements in the CustomerName field (first name and last name). For this reason, many databases contain not just the CustomerName data field, but data fields for LastName and FirstName.

When you begin constructing your database, spend time thinking about the various ways you (and your users) need to retrieve useful data. The quality and usefulness of your database rests on the integrity of its smallest element: the data field.

Data Records

Data records are a collection of related data fields. To use the example started earlier, a Customer Record could contain the fields LastName, FirstName, and AccountBalance. All three fields describe a single customer in the database.

Note

> Formal database theory refers to a data record as a "data row." *Data record* and *data row* are used interchangeably throughout this book.

A single data record contains only one copy of each defined data field. For example, a single data record cannot contain more than one LastName data field. Figure 1.11 shows the Company Database with a Customer Record defined. The Customer Record (row) contains three fields (columns).

FIGURE 1.11

An example of a data record in a database.

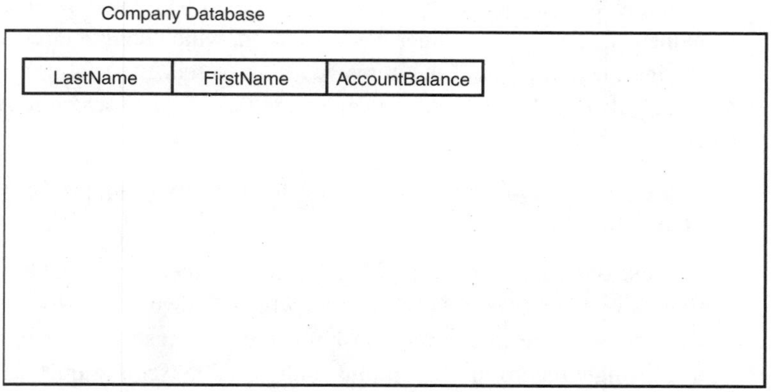

Company Database

LastName	FirstName	AccountBalance

Data Table Rows and Columns

By combining data fields and data records, you create the most common element of relational databases: the data table. This element contains multiple data records, and each data record contains multiple data fields (see Figure 1.12).

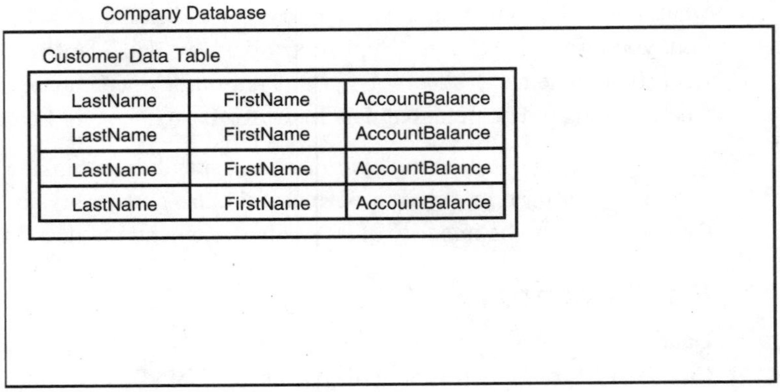

FIGURE **1.12**

An example of a data table in a database.

Company Database

Customer Data Table

LastName	FirstName	AccountBalance
LastName	FirstName	AccountBalance
LastName	FirstName	AccountBalance
LastName	FirstName	AccountBalance

Just as each data record contains related data fields (LastName, FirstName, and AccountBalance), each data table contains related records. Data tables have meaningful names (CustomerTable or tblInvoice, for example) in the same way that data fields have meaningful names (LastName, FirstName, AccountBalance, and so on). These names help you and other users remember the contents of the elements (table elements and field elements).

Database Relationships

Just as a data record can contain several related data fields, a database can contain several related tables. Using relationships is a very efficient way to store complex data. For example, a table storing customer names could be related to another table storing the names of items the customer has purchased, which could be related in turn to a table storing the names of all the items you have to sell. By establishing meaningful relationships between data tables, you can create flexible data structures that are easy to maintain.

You establish relationships between data tables by using pointer or qualifier fields in your data table.

You use qualifier fields to point to records in other tables that have additional information. Qualifier fields usually describe what's known as one-to-one relationships. A good example of a one-to-one relationship is the relationship between a single customer record and a single record in the shipping address table (see Figure 1.13).

You use pointer fields to point to one or more records in other tables that have related information. Pointer fields usually describe what are known as one-to-many relationships. A good example of a one-to-many relationship is the relationship between a single customer master record and several outstanding customer orders (see Figure 1.14).

Figure 1.13

An example of a one-to-one relationship between tables.

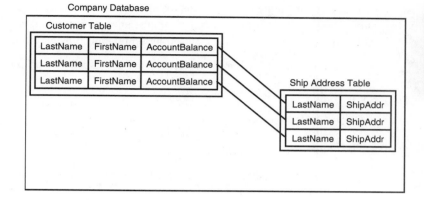

Figure 1.14

An example of a one-to-many relationship between tables.

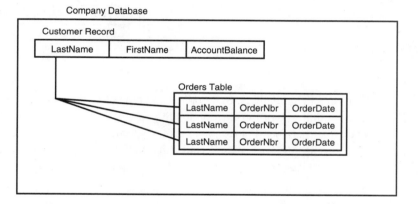

One-to-One Relationships

One-to-one relationships are used to link records in a master table (such as the Customer Table) to a single related record in another table.

For example, assume you have two types of customers in your Company Database: retail and wholesale. Retail customers get paid commissions on sales, so you need to add a Commission field to the Customers table. Wholesale customers, however, purchase their products at a discount, so you also need to add a Discount field to the Customers table. Now your database users have to remember that, for Retail customers, the Discount field must be left empty, and for Wholesale customers, the Commission field must be left empty. You must remember these rules when adding, editing, and deleting data from the database, and you must remember these rules when creating reports.

This might seem to be a manageable task now, but try adding a large number of additional data fields (along with the exceptions), and you have quite a mess on your hands!

Instead of establishing all data fields for all customers, what you need is a way to define only the fields you need for each type of customer. You can do this by setting up multiple tables in a single database and then setting up relationships between the tables.

In the example illustrated in Figure 1.15, you have added an additional data field: Type.

FIGURE 1.15

Using a qualifier field to establish a one-to-one relationship.

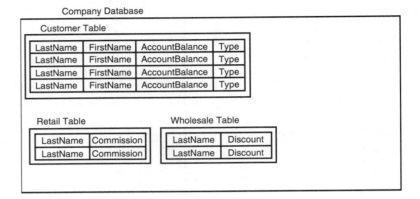

This data field qualifies, or describes, the type of customer stored in this data record. You can use this type of information to tell you where to look for additional information about the customer. For example, if the Type field is set to Retail, you know you can look for the customer in the Retail Table to find additional information. If the Type field is set to Wholesale, you can find additional information in the Wholesale Table.

By creating the RecordType field, you can establish a one-to-one relationship between records in the Customer Table and the Retail and Wholesale Tables.

One-to-Many Relationships

One-to-many relationships are used to link records in a master table (such as the Customer Table) to multiple records in another table.

For example, you can keep track of several orders for each customer in your database. If you were not creating a relational database, you would probably add a data field to your customer table called Order. This would contain the last order placed by this customer. But what if you need to keep track of more than one outstanding order? Would you add two, four, or six more order fields? You can see the problem.

Instead, you can add an additional table (the Orders Table) that can contain as many outstanding orders for a single customer as you need. After you create the Orders Table, you can establish a relationship between the Customer Table and the Orders Table using the

LastName field (refer to Figure 1.13). The LastName field is used as a pointer into the Orders Table to locate all the orders for this customer.

You can use many different approaches to establish relationships between tables. They are usually established through a key field. Key fields are covered in depth in the next section.

Key Fields

Usually, at least one data field in each data table acts as a key field for the table. Key fields in relational databases are used to define and maintain database integrity and to establish relationships between data tables. You create keys in your data table by designating one (field) or more in your table as either a primary key or a foreign key. A data table can have only one primary key, but it can have several foreign keys. The primary key is used to control the order in which the data is displayed. The foreign key is used to relate fields to fields in other (foreign) tables in the database.

Note

Key fields are sometimes referred to as "index fields" or "indexes." *Key fields* and *index fields* are used interchangeably throughout the book. It is important to note that in most PC databases (Xbase, Paradox, Btreive, and so forth), indexes are used only to speed processing of large files and play only a minor role in maintaining table relationships. The Visual Basic database model (.mdb files) and other true relational database models use key fields to establish database integrity rules as well as to speed database search and retrieval.

As mentioned earlier, a data table can have only one primary key. The primary key is used to define a unique record in the data table. In the Customer table, the LastName field is the primary key field for the data table. This means that no two records in that table can have exactly the same value in the LastName fields (see Figure 1.16). Any attempt to add more than one record with an identical primary key would result in a database error.

Tip

The main role of the primary key is to maintain the internal integrity of a data table. For this reason, no two records in a data table can have the same primary key value. Many companies with large customer bases use Social Security numbers or area codes and telephone numbers, because they know they are likely to have more than one customer with the same name. In these cases, the SSN or phone number would be the primary key field.

FIGURE **1.16**

The LastName field is the primary key key field in the Customer table.

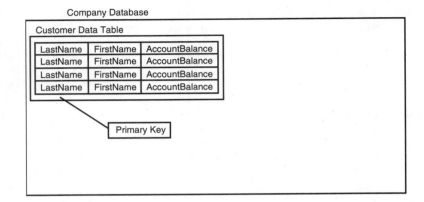

A data table can have more than one foreign key. It can also have no foreign key at all. In the Orders Table, the LastName field would be defined as a foreign key field. This means that it is a nonunique field in this data table that points to a key field in an external (foreign) table. Any attempt to add to the Orders table a record that contains a value in the LastName field, which does not also exist in a LastName field in the Customer Table, would result in a database error. For example, if the Customer table contains three records (Smith, Amundsen, and Jones), and you try to add a record to the Orders Table by filling the LastName field of the Orders Table with Paxton, you get a database error. By creating foreign key fields in a table, you build data integrity into your database. This is called referential integrity.

The main role of a foreign key is to define and maintain relationships between data tables in a database. For this reason, foreign key fields are not unique in the data table in which they exist.

Database integrity and foreign keys are covered in depth on Day 15, "Database Normalization," and Day 16, "Multiuser Considerations."

Now that you've worked through the basics of database elements in general, let's look at specific characteristics of Visual Basic data fields.

Visual Basic Database Field Types

Visual Basic stores values in the data table in data fields. Visual Basic recognizes 14 different data field types that you can use to store values. Each data field type has unique qualities that make it especially suitable for storing different types of data. Some are used to store images, the results of check box fields, currency amounts, calendar dates, and various sizes of numeric values. Table 1.4 lists the 14 database field types recognized by Visual Basic.

The first column contains the Visual Basic data field type name. This is the name you use when you create data tables using the Visual Data Manager from the Toolbar. You learn about using this tool in Day 6, "Using the Visdata Program."

The second column shows the number of bytes of storage taken by the various data field types. If the size column is set to V, the length is variable and is determined by you at design-time or by the program at runtime.

The third column in the table shows the equivalent Visual Basic data type for the associated database field type. This column tells you what Visual Basic data type you can use to update the database field.

TABLE 1.4 VISUAL BASIC DATA FIELD TYPES

Data Field Type	Size	VBType	Comments
BINARY	V	(none)	Limited to 255 bytes
BOOLEAN	1	Boolean	Stores 0 or -1 only
BYTE	1	Integer	Stores 0 to 255 only
COUNTER	8	Long	Auto-incrementing Long type
CURRENCY	8	Currency	15 places to left of decimal, 4 to right
DATETIME	8	Date/Time	Date stored on left of decimal point, time stored on right
DOUBLE	8	Double	
GUID	16	(none)	Used to store Globally Unique Identifiers
INTEGER	2	Integer	
LONG	8	Long	
LONGBINARY	V	(none)	Used for OLE objects
MEMO	V	String	Length varies up to 1.2 gigabytes
SINGLE	4	Single	
TEXT	V	String	Length limited to 255

Note

It is important to understand the difference between the Visual Basic data field types and the Visual Basic data types. The data field types are those recognized as valid data types within data tables. The data types are those types recognized by Visual Basic when defining variables within a program. For example, you can store the value 3 in a BYTE field in a data table, but you store that same value in an Integer field in a Visual Basic program variable.

Even though it is true that Visual Basic enables programmers to create database applications that can read and write data in several different data formats, all database formats do not recognize all data field types. For example, xBase data fields do not recognize a CURRENCY data field type. Before developing cross data-engine applications, you need to know exactly what data field types are needed and how they are to be mapped to various data formats. The various data formats are covered in Day 8, "Visual Basic, DAO, and the Microsoft Jet Engine."

A number of items in Table 1.4 deserve additional comment:

- LONGBINARY data fields are for storing images and OLE objects. Visual Basic has no corresponding internal data type that maps directly to the LONGBINARY data field types. This information is usually stored as character data in Visual Basic. For example, a bitmap image would be stored in a LONGBINARY data table field, but it would be stored as a string variable in a Visual Basic program. Double-clicking a data-bound LONGBINARY field automatically invokes the local application that is registered to handle the stored OLE object.

- The BOOLEAN data field type is commonly used to store the results of a bound check box input control. It stores only a -1 (True) or 0 (False). For example, if you enter 13 into the input box, Visual Basic stores -1 in the data field. To make matters trickier, Visual Basic does not report an error when a number other than 0 or -1 is entered. You should be careful when using the BOOLEAN data type, because any number other than 0 entered into a BOOLEAN data field is converted into -1.

- The BYTE data field type accepts only input ranging from -0 to 255. Any other values (including negative numbers) result in a runtime error (error number 524) when you attempt to update the data record.

Caution

This behavior is changed from previous versions of Visual Basic. In the past, Microsoft Jet would automatically convert the invalid value to a byte value and not report an error. For example, if you enter the value 255 (stored as

1

FF in hexadecimal), Visual Basic stores 255 in the data field. If you enter 260 (stored as 0104 in hexadecimal—it takes two bytes!), Visual Basic stores a decimal 4 in the data field, because the rightmost byte is set to hexadecimal 04.

- The COUNTER data field type is a special case. This is an auto-incrementing, read-only data field. Any attempt to write a value to this data field results in a Visual Basic error. Visual Basic keeps track of the integer value to place in this field; it cannot be altered through the input controls or through explicit programming directives. The COUNTER field is often used as a unique primary key field in sequential processing operations.

- MEMO and TEXT data field types both accept any character data as valid input. MEMO data fields are built with a default length of 0 (zero). The physical length of a MEMO field is controlled by the total number of characters of data stored in the field. The length of a TEXT field must be declared when the data field is created. The Visual Data Manager that ships with Visual Basic allows the TEXT field to have a length of 1 to 255 bytes.

- GUID data field types are used to store a special type of 128-bit number: the Globally Unique Identifier. This value is used to identify ActiveX components, SQL Server remote procedures, Microsoft Jet replication IDs, and other objects that require a unique identifier. For more on Microsoft Jet replication, see Day 20, "Database Replication."

Building the Visual Basic 6 Field Data Types Project

The following project illustrates how different Visual Basic data field types store user input. You also see how Visual Basic responds to input that is out of range for the various data field types. Use the following steps:

1. Begin by creating a new Visual Basic project (select File | New Project). Using Table 1.5 and Figure 1.17 as guides, populate the Visual Basic form.

Caution

Notice that you are creating a set of four buttons with the same name, but different Index property values. This is a control array. Control arrays offer an excellent way to simplify Visual Basic coding. However, they behave a bit differently than nonarrayed controls. It is important that you build the controls exactly as described in this table.

FIGURE 1.17

The form for the Visual Basic data field types project.

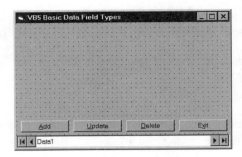

TABLE 1.5   CONTROLS FOR THE VISUAL BASIC DATA FIELD TYPES PROJECT

Control	Property	Setting
Project	Name	prjFieldTypes
Form	Name	frmFieldTypes
	Caption	VB6 Basic Data Field Types
CommandButton	Name	cmdBtn
	Caption	&Add
	Height	300
	Index	0
	Width	1200
CommandButton	Name	cmdBtn
	Caption	&Update
	Height	300
	Index	1
	Width	1200
CommandButton	Name	cmdBtn
	Caption	&Delete
	Height	300
	Index	2
	Width	1200
CommandButton	Name	cmdBtn
	Caption	E&xit
	Height	300
	Index	3
	Width	1200

Control	Property	Setting
DataControl	Name	datFieldTypes
	DatabaseName	FIELDTYPES.MDB (include correct path)
	RecordSource	FieldTypes

2. Now add the code behind the command button array. Double-click the Add button (or any other button in the array) to bring up the code window. Enter the code from Listing 1.1 into the cmdBtn_Click event.

LISTING 1.1 CODE FOR THE cmdBtn_Click EVENT

```
 1: Private Sub cmdBtn_Click(Index As Integer)
 2: '
 3: ' handle button selections
 4: '
 5: On Error GoTo LocalError
 6: '
 7: Select Case Index
 8: Case 0 ' add
 9: datFieldTypes.Recordset.AddNew
10: Case 1 ' update
11: datFieldTypes.UpdateRecord
12: datFieldTypes.Recordset.Bookmark = _
      datFieldTypes.Recordset.LastModified
13: Case 2 ' delete
14: datFieldTypes.Recordset.Delete
15: datFieldTypes.Recordset.MovePrevious
16: Case 3 ' exit
17: Unload Me
18: End Select
19: Exit Sub
20: '
21: LocalError:
22: MsgBox Err.Description, vbCritical, Err.Number
23: '
24: End Sub
```

There may be several things in this code segment that are new to you. First, different lines of code are executed based on the button that is pushed by the user. This is indicated by the Index parameter that is passed to the Click event. Second, some error-handling code has been added to make it easy for you to experiment with the data form. You learn more about error-handling in Day 13. Don't worry if this code segment looks a bit confusing. For now, just enter the code that is shown here.

Now is a good time to save the project. Save the form as `FieldTypes.frm` and the project as `FieldTypes.vbp`. Run the project to make sure that you have entered all the code correctly up to this point. If you get error messages from Visual Basic, refer to Table 1.5 and the preceding code lines to correct the problem.

Testing the BOOLEAN Data Type

Now you can add a text box input control and a label to this form. Set the caption of the label to `Boolean:`. Set the `DataSource` property of the text box to `datFieldTypes` and the `DataField` property to `BooleanField`. Set the `Text` property to blank. Refer to Figure 1.18 for placement and sizing.

FIGURE 1.18

Adding the BOOLEAN data type input control.

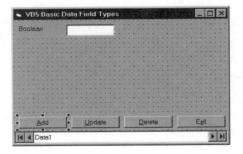

Now run the program. If this is the first time you've run the program, you should see an empty field. Press the Add button to create a new record, and then press the Update button to save that record. You see that the first value in the input box is a `0`, the default value for BOOLEAN fields. Enter the number `13` in the text box and click the Update button. This forces the data control to save the input field to the data table and update the display. What happened to the `13`? It was converted to `-1`. Any value other than `0`, when entered into a BOOLEAN data type field, is converted to `-1`.

Testing the BYTE Data Type

Now let's add a label and input control for the BYTE data type field. Instead of picking additional controls from the Toolbox Window and typing in property settings, Visual Basic enables you to copy existing controls. Copying controls saves time, reduces typing errors, and helps keep the size and shape of the controls on your form consistent.

To copy controls, use the mouse pointer, with the left mouse button depressed, to create a dotted-line box around both the label control and the TextBox control already on your form (in this case, the label Boolean and its text box). When you release the left mouse button, you see that both controls have been marked as selected. Now click Edit I Copy to copy the selected controls to the Clipboard. Use Edit I Paste to copy the controls from the Clipboard back onto your form.

At this point, Visual Basic asks whether you want to create a Control Array. Say yes, both times. You then see the two controls appear at the top left of the form. Use your mouse to position them on the form (see Figure 1.19).

FIGURE 1.19

Copying controls on a form.

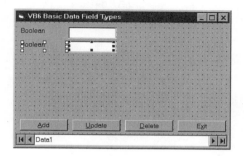

> **Tip**
>
> The text box and label controls on this form are part of a control array. Because using control arrays reduces the total number of distinct controls on your forms, it reduces the amount of Windows resources your program uses. You can copy controls as many times as you like—even across forms and projects!

You just created duplicates of the BOOLEAN input control. Now change the label caption to Byte and the text box DataField property to ByteField, and you have two new controls on your form with minimal typing. Your form should look like the one in Figure 1.20.

FIGURE 1.20

Adding the BYTE data type to your form.

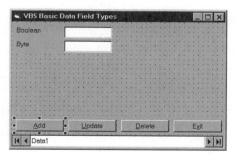

Save and run the program. This time, after pressing the Add button, enter the value 256 into the Byte input control and press the Update button. You see that when Visual Basic attempts to store the value to the data table, a runtime error is reported. Byte data fields can accept only positive values between 0 and 255. Trying to save any other value in this data field causes the Microsoft Jet data engine to report an error to Visual Basic.

Testing the CURRENCY Data Type

Copy the label and TextBox control again using the mouse to select the controls to be
copied and the Copy and Paste commands from the Edit menu. Change the label
Caption property to Currency and the text box DataField property to CurrencyField.
Refer to Figure 1.21 for spacing and sizing of the controls.

FIGURE 1.21

*Adding the CURRENCY
data type to your form.*

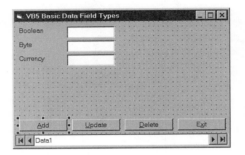

Save and run the program and test the CURRENCY data type text box. Press the Add button,
enter the value 1.00001, force Visual Basic to save the value to the data table (press the
Update button), and see what happens. Try entering 1.23456. When storing values to the
CURRENCY data type field, Visual Basic stores only four places to the right of the decimal.
If the number is larger than four decimal places to the right, Visual Basic rounds the
value before storing it in the data field. Also, you notice that Visual Basic does not add a
dollar sign ($) to the display of CURRENCY type data fields.

Testing the DATETIME Data Type

The Visual Basic DATETIME data type field is one of the most powerful data types. Visual
Basic performs extensive edit checks on values entered in the DATETIME data type field.
Using DATETIME data type fields can save a lot of coding when you need to make sure
valid dates are entered by users.

Create a new set of label and TextBox controls by copying the label and TextBox controls again. Change the label Caption property to DateTime and the text box DataField
property to DateTimeField. Your form should look like the one in Figure 1.22.

Save and run the program. Try entering 12/32/95. As you can see, Visual Basic gives
you an error message when you enter an invalid date. Now enter 1/1/0 into the Date text
box. Notice that Visual Basic formats the date for you.

How does Visual Basic decide what date format to use? The date format used comes
from the settings in the Windows 95 Control Panel Regional Settings applet. While you
have this program running, experiment by calling up the Windows 95 Regional Settings

applet. (From the taskbar, select Start | Settings | Control Panel and then select Regional Settings.) Change the date format settings and return to your Visual Basic program to see the results.

FIGURE 1.22

Adding the DATETIME *data type to your form.*

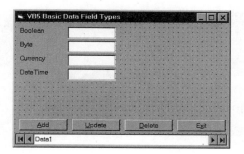

Tip

The Visual Basic DATETIME data type should always be used to store date values. If you install your program in Europe, where the common date display format is DD-MM-YY instead of the common U.S. format of MM-DD-YY, your program will work without a problem. If you store dates as strings in the format MM/DD/YY or as numeric values in the format YYMMDD, your program will not be able to compute or display dates correctly across international boundaries.

Testing the COUNTER Data Type

Now let's test a very special database field type: the COUNTER data type. This data type is automatically set by Visual Basic each time you add a new record to the data table. The COUNTER data type makes an excellent unique primary key field, because Visual Basic is able to create and store more than a billion unique values in the COUNTER field without duplication.

Note

Actually, the Counter data type is not a true database field type. Instead, the Counter data type is a Long data field with its Attribute property set to AutoIncrField. You won't find the Counter data type listed in the documentation, but you will see references to auto-incrementing fields and see a "Counter" type as an option when you build data fields with the Visual Data Manager.

Copy another label/TextBox control set onto the form. Change the label `Caption` property to `Counter` and the text box `DataField` property to `AutoIncrField`. See Figure 1.23 for guidance in positioning and sizing the control.

FIGURE 1.23

Adding the COUNTER *data type to your form.*

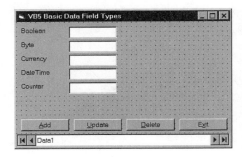

Now save and run the program one more time. Notice that the `COUNTER` data type already has a value in it, even though you have not entered data into the field. Visual Basic sets the value of `COUNTER` fields; users do not. Add a new record to the table by pressing the Add button. You see a new value in the `COUNTER` input control. Visual Basic uses the next available number in sequence. Visual Basic is also able to ensure unique numbers in a multiuser setting. If you have three people running the same program adding records to this table, they will all receive unique values in the Counter text box.

Caution

> You should never attempt to edit the value in the COUNTER text box! If Visual Basic determines that the counter value has been changed, it displays a Visual Basic error message, and you cannot save the record. Even if you reset the value in the COUNTER data field back to its original value, Visual Basic refuses to save the record.

Additional Visual Basic Data Types

The rest of the Visual Basic data types (INTEGER, SINGLE, DOUBLE, TEXT, MEMO, BINARY, LONGBINARY, and GUID) are rather unspectacular when placed on a form. The following are some notes on the various Visual Basic data types that you should keep in mind when you are designing your data tables:

- Visual Basic returns an error if you enter more than the maximum number of characters into a TEXT data field.

- The LONGBINARY data field is used to store graphic image data and enables any alphanumeric data to be entered and saved. The storage of graphic data is covered later in the book (see Day 10, "Displaying Your Data with Graphs").

- Check the Visual Basic online help under Visual Basic Data Types for additional information on the high and low ranges for DOUBLE, INTEGER, and SINGLE data fields.

- BOOLEAN data fields allow you to enter values other than 0 or -1 without reporting an error. Notice that Visual Basic alters the data you entered into these data fields without telling you!

- The CURRENCY data field stores only the first four places to the right of the decimal. If you enter values beyond the fourth decimal place, Visual Basic rounds the value to four decimal places and gives you no message.

- The DATETIME data field has some interesting behavior. Visual Basic does not let you store an invalid date or time in the data field; you receive a "Type mismatch" error instead. Also, the display format for the dates and times is determined by the settings you choose in the Windows Control Panel (through the International icon). In fact, when valid data is stored in a DATETIME data field, you can change the display format (from 12-hour time display to 24-hour time display, for example), and the next time you view that data record, it reflects the changes made through the Control Panel.

- The GUID data field type is used to store special 128-bit numbers called Globally Unique Identifiers, which uniquely identify Windows 95 Registry entries.

- The BINARY data field type allows from 0 to 255 bytes of data storage and has only limited uses. If you are using the Visual Data Manager, you see a "Binary" field type—this is actually the LONGBINARY field.

- The MEMO and LONGBINARY data field types are known as "large value" data fields, because they can hold up to 1.2 gigabytes of data in a single field. If you are working with large data fields, you need to move data between your program and the data table using the GetChunk and AppendChunk methods. You learn more about these methods on Day 8.

- The Visual Basic 6 documentation describes several other data field types recognized by Microsoft Jet (Big Integer, Char, Decimal, Float, Numeric, Time, TimeStamp, and VarBinary). However, these other data field types cannot be created using the Visual Data Manager or using Visual Basic code. These additional data field types may be returned by data tables built using other database tools, including Microsoft SQL Server or other back-end databases.

Summary

In today's lesson you learned the following database application concepts:

- You learned how to use the data control to bind a form to a database and data table by setting the `DatabaseName` and `DataSource` properties.
- You learned how to use the text box bound input control to bind an input box on the form to a data table and data field by setting the `DataSource` and `DataField` properties.
- You learned how to combine standard command buttons and the `AddNew` and `Delete` methods to provide add record and delete record functionality to a data entry form.

You also learned the following about relational databases:

- A relational database is a collection of related data.
- The three key building blocks of relational databases are data fields, data records, and data tables.
- The two types of database relationships are one-to-one, which uses qualifier fields, and one-to-many, which uses pointer fields.
- There are two types of key (or index) fields: primary key and foreign key.

In addition, you learned the 14 basic data field types recognized by Microsoft Jet and Visual Basic. You constructed a data entry form that enables you to test the way Visual Basic behaves when attempting to store data entered into the various data field types.

Quiz

1. What are the two properties of the data control that must be set when you link a form to an existing database and data table?
2. What property must you set if you want the data control to display the name of the data table in the window between the record pointer arrows?
3. What are the two properties of the TextBox control that must be set when you bind the input control to the data control on a form?
4. How many lines of code does it take to add a delete record function to a Visual Basic form when using the data control?
5. What environment setting can you use to make sure that Visual Basic will automatically save your work each time you attempt to run a program in design mode?
6. What are the three main building blocks for relational databases?

7. What is the smallest building block in a relational database?

8. A data record is a collection of related _____.

9. What is the main role of a primary key in a data table?

10. Can a data table have more than one foreign key defined?

11. List all the possible values that can be stored in a BOOLEAN data field.

12. What is the highest value that can be stored in a BYTE data field?

13. What happens when you attempt to edit a COUNTER data field?

14. How many places to the right of the decimal can be stored in a CURRENCY data field?

15. What Windows Control Panel Applet determines the display format of DATE data fields?

Exercises

1. Add the caption "The Titles Program" to the data entry form created in this chapter.

2. Place an additional command button labeled Exit on the data entry form in the DATCNTRL.VBP project. Add code behind this command button to end the program when it is clicked.

3. In the DATCNTRL.VBP project, modify the Add button to move the cursor to the first input control (txtISBN) on the data entry form. (Hint: search for SetFocus in the Visual Basic online help.)

4. Answer questions A, B, and C based on the data in this table:

SSN	Last	First	Age	City	St	Comments
123-45-6789	Smith	Mark	17	Austin	TX	Trans. from New York.
456-79-1258	Smith	Ron	21	New York	NY	Born in Wyoming.
987-65-8764	Johnson	Curt	68	Chicago	IL	Plays golf on Wed.

A. How many records are in the data table?

B. Which field should you select as the primary key?

C. Identify each data field, its Data Field Type, and its VISUAL BASIC Type.

5. Modify the Visual Basic Data Field Types example from this lesson by creating a check box and placing the results in the existing BOOLEAN text box.

DAY 2

Visual Basic Database Access Objects

On Day 1, "Database Programming Basics," you learned how to create simple data entry forms using some of the data-bound controls and the various data field types. Today, you learn about the programmatic data objects of Visual Basic. Data objects are used within a Visual Basic program to manipulate databases, as well as the data tables and indexes within the database. The data objects are the representations (in program code) of the physical database, data tables, fields, indexes, and so on. Throughout today's lesson, you create small Visual Basic programs that illustrate the special features of each data object.

Every Visual Basic program that accesses data tables uses data objects. Even if you are using only the data-aware controls (for example, the data control and bound input controls) and are not writing programming code, you are still using Visual Basic data objects.

About the Data Access Object (DAO) Model 3.51

Today, you use the Microsoft DAO 3.51 data access object model. This is the default object model of the Data Control that you commonly use to bind inputs to forms on Windows dialogs. The DAO model is optimized for accessing Access-style ISAM databases over local area network connections. Visual Basic 6 ships with two DAO libraries for your programs:

- DAO 3.51 Object Library (the most current version)
- DAO 2.5/3.51 Compatibility Library, which allows use of obsolete DAO 2.5 objects in your Visual Basic 6 programs

Note

In previous versions of DAO, the Recordset object types were available as unique data objects (Dynaset, Table, and Snapshot). These objects can still be used when working with the older (version 2.5) data access object model, but it is not recommended. All data access object models now support the Recordset object types and that is the object you should use in all new Visual Basic programs.

Visual Basic can also use a number of other object models to access data. Later in this book, you learn about two other object models for accessing data. The Remote Data object (RDO) model is optimized for accessing RDBMS databases over local area network. The Active Data Object (ADO) Model is designed to enable access to databases over intranet and Internet connections, along with providing a viable alternative to RDO.

It's All About the Recordset

The primary data object used in DAO-based programs is the Recordset object. This is the object that holds the collection of data records used in your Visual Basic programs. There are three different types of Recordset objects. They are

- Dynaset-type
- Table-type
- Snapshot-type

Any one of these Recordset objects can be used to gain access to an existing data table in a database. However, each has unique properties and behaves differently at times. Today, you learn how these three types of Recordset data objects differ and when to use these objects in your programs.

You also learn about another data object today: the Database object. You can use the Database object to get information about the connected database. Today, you learn about the general properties and behaviors of the Database object of the data control and how you can use them in your programs.

> **Note**
>
> You learn more about the Database object in Day 8, "Visual Basic and the DAO Jet Database Engine."

2

Dataset–Oriented Versus Data Record–Oriented

Before you learn about Visual Basic data objects, you should first learn some basics of how data object models in Visual Basic operate on databases in general. When you understand how Visual Basic looks at databases, you can better create programs that meet your needs.

The database model behind the Microsoft Access database and other SQL-oriented databases is quite different from the database model behind traditional PC databases, such as FoxPro, dBASE, and Paradox. Traditional PC databases are record-oriented database systems. Structured Query Language (SQL) databases are dataset-oriented systems. Understanding the difference between record-oriented processing and dataset-oriented processing is the key to understanding how to optimize database programs in Visual Basic.

In record-oriented systems, you perform database operations one record at a time. The most common programming construct in record-oriented systems is the loop. The following pseudocode example shows how to increase the price field of an inventory table in a record-oriented database:

```
ReadLoop:
    If EndOf File
       Goto EndLoop
    Else
       Read Record
       If Record.SalesRegion = 'Northeast' Then
          Price=Price*1.10
          Write Record
       End If
    EndIf
Goto ReadLoop
EndLoop:
End Program
```

Processing in record-oriented systems usually involves creating a routine that reads a single data record, processes it, and returns to read another record until the job is completed. PC databases use indexes to speed the process of locating records in data tables. Indexes also help speed processing by enabling PC databases to access the data in sorted order (by LastName, by AccountBalance, and so on).

In dataset-oriented systems, such as Microsoft Access, you perform database operations one set at a time, not one record at a time. The most common programming construct in set-oriented systems is the SQL statement. Instead of using program code to loop through single records, SQL databases can perform operations on entire tables from just one SQL statement. The following pseudocode example shows how you update the price field in the same inventory file in a dataset-oriented database:

```
UPDATE Inventory
   SET Price=Price*1.10
   WHERE Inventory.SalesRegion = 'Northeast'
```

The UPDATE SQL command behaves with SQL databases much like keywords behave with your Visual Basic programs. In this case, UPDATE tells the database that it wants to update an entire table (the Inventory table). The SET SQL command changes the value of a data field (in this case, the Price data field). The WHERE command is used to perform a logical comparison of the SalesRegion field to the value Northeast. As you can see, in dataset-oriented databases, you create a single statement that selects only the records you need to perform a database operation. After you identify the dataset, you apply the operation to all records in the set. In dataset systems, indexes are used to maintain database integrity more than to speed the location of specific records.

Visual Basic and Data Access Objects

Visual Basic database objects are dataset-oriented. Visual Basic programs generally perform better when data operations are done with a dataset than when data operations are done on single records. Some Visual Basic objects work well when performing record-oriented operations; most do not. The Visual Basic Table-type Recordset object is very good at performing record-oriented processing. The Visual Basic Dynaset- and Snapshot-type Recordset objects do not perform well on record-oriented processes.

A common mistake made by database programmers new to Visual Basic and DAO programming is to create applications that assume a record-oriented database model. These programmers are usually frustrated by Visual Basic's slow performance on large data tables and its slow response time when attempting to locate a specific record. Visual Basic's sluggishness is usually due to improper use of the data object model—most often because programmers are opening entire data tables when they need only a small subset of the data to perform the required tasks.

Dataset Size Affects Program Performance

Unlike record-oriented systems, the size of the dataset you create affects the speed at which Visual Basic programs operate. As a data table grows, your program's processing speed can deteriorate. In heavily transaction-oriented applications, such as accounting systems, a dataset can grow quickly and cripple your application's capability of processing information. If you are working in a network environment where the machine requesting data and the machine storing the data are separated, sending large datasets over the wire can affect not only your application, but all applications running on the network. If you are working in an intranet or Internet environment, the wait times can be even worse. For this reason, it is important to keep the size of the datasets as small as possible. This does not mean you have to limit the number of records in your data tables! You can use Visual Basic data objects to select the data you need from the table instead.

For example, you might have a data table that contains thousands of accounting transactions. If you want to modify the payment records in the data table, you can create a data object that contains all the records (quite a big set), or you can tell Visual Basic DAO to select only the payment records (a smaller set). Or, if you know that you need only to modify payment records that have been added to the system in the last three days, you can create an even smaller dataset. The smaller the dataset, the faster your program can process the data. Visual Basic data objects give you the power to create datasets that are the proper size for your needs.

The Dynaset-type Recordset Data Object

The Visual Basic Dynaset-type Recordset data object is the most frequently used data object in Visual Basic database programs. It is used to dynamically gain access to part or all of an existing data table in a database—hence the name Dynaset. When you set the `DatabaseName` and `RecordSource` properties of a Visual Basic data control, you are actually creating a Visual Basic Dynaset-type Recordset. You can also create a Dynaset-type Recordset by using the `CreateDynaset` method of the Database object.

When you create a Visual Basic Dynaset-type Recordset, you do not create a new physical table in the database. A Dynaset exists as a virtual data table. This virtual table usually contains a subset of the records in a real data table, but it can contain the complete set.

Because creating a Dynaset does not create a new physical table, Dynasets do not add to the size of the database. However, creating Dynasets does take up space in RAM on the machine that creates the set (the one that is running the program). Depending on the number of records in the Dynaset, temporary disk space can also be used on the machine requesting the dataset.

Strengths of the Dynaset-type Recordset Object

There are several reasons to use Dynasets when you access data. In general, Dynasets require less memory than other data objects and provide the most update options, including the capability of creating additional data objects from existing Dynasets. Dynasets are the default data objects for the Visual Basic data control, and they are the only updatable data object you can use for databases connected through Microsoft's Open Database Connectivity (ODBC) model. The following sections provide more details of the strengths of the Dynaset data object.

Dynasets Are Really Key Sets

Visual Basic Dynasets use relatively little workstation memory, even for large datasets. When you create a Dynaset, Visual Basic performs several steps. First, Visual Basic selects the records you requested. Then, it creates temporary index keys to each of these records and sends the complete set of keys to your workstation along with enough records to fill out any bound controls (text boxes and/or grid controls) that appear on your onscreen form. This process is illustrated in Figure 2.1.

FIGURE 2.1

Dynasets contain key sets that point to the actual data.

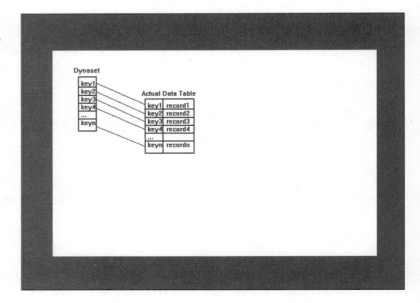

> **Note**
>
> The actual data request engine used by Visual Basic is called the Microsoft Jet data engine. In pure SQL systems, all requests for data result in a set of data records. Data requests to the Microsoft Jet engine result in a set of keys that point to the data records. By returning keys instead of data records, Microsoft Jet engine is able to limit network traffic and speed database performance.

The set of keys is stored in RAM and—if the set is too large to store in RAM alone—in a temporary file on a local disk drive. As you scroll through the dataset, Visual Basic retrieves actual records as needed from the physical table used to create the Dynaset. If you have a single text box on the form, Visual Basic retrieves the data from the table one record at a time. If you have a grid of data or a loop that collects several records from the table in succession, a small set of the records in the dataset is retrieved by Visual Basic. Visual Basic also caches records at the workstation to reduce requests to the physical data table, which speeds performance.

If the Dynaset is very large, you might end up with a key set so large that it requires more RAM and temporary disk space than the local machine can handle. In that case, you receive an error message from Visual Basic. For this reason, it is important that you use care in creating your criteria for populating the dataset. The smaller the dataset, the smaller the key set.

Dynasets Are Dynamic

Even though Dynasets are virtual tables in memory created from physical tables, they are not static copies of the data table. After you create a Dynaset, if anyone else alters the underlying data table by modifying, adding, or deleting records, you see the changes in your Dynaset as soon as you refresh the Dynaset. Refreshing the Dynaset can be done using the `Refresh` method. You can also refresh the Dynasets by moving the record pointer using the arrow keys of the data control or using the `MoveFirst`, `MoveNext`, `MovePrevious`, and `MoveLast` methods. Moving the pointer refreshes only the records you read, not the entire Dynaset.

Although the dynamic aspect of Dynasets is very effective in maintaining up-to-date views of the underlying data table, Dynasets also have some limitations and drawbacks. For example, if another user deletes a record that you currently have in your Dynaset and you attempt to move to that record, Visual Basic will report an error.

> **Note** You'll learn more about handling database errors in Day 13, "Error Handling in Visual Basic 6."

Dynasets Can Be Created from More than One Table

A Dynaset can be created using more than one table in the database. You can create a single view that contains selected records from several tables, update the view, and therefore update all the underlying tables of the data at one time. This is a very powerful aspect of a Visual Basic Dynaset data object. Using Visual Basic Dynasets, you can create virtual tables that make it easy to create simple data entry screens and display graphs and reports that show specialized selections of data.

Use Dynasets to Create Other Dynasets or Snapshots

Often in Visual Basic programs, you need to create a secondary dataset based on user input. The Dynaset data object is the only data object from which you can create another Dynaset.

You can create additional Dynasets by using the Clone method or the `CreateDynaset` method. When you clone a Dynaset, you create an exact duplicate of the Dynaset. You can use this duplicate to perform lookups or to reorder the records for a display. Cloned Dynasets take up slightly less room than the original Dynaset.

Let's put together a short code sample that explores Dynasets. You do this all in Visual Basic code, too, instead of using the Visual Basic data control.

First, start a new Visual Basic Standard EXE project. Be sure to add a reference to the Microsoft DAO 3.51 Object Library before you begin coding. To do this, Select Project | References from the Main menu (see Figure 2.2).

FIGURE 2.2

Adding the Microsoft DAO 3.51 reference to a Visual Basic project.

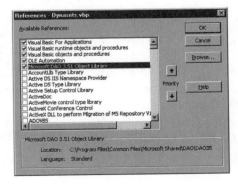

Now double-click the form to open the code window to the Form_Load event. You will write the entire example in this procedure.

When you open a Dynaset using Visual Basic code instead of using the data control, you must create two Visual Basic objects: a Database object and a Recordset object. Listing 2.1 shows how you create the objects in Visual Basic code.

LISTING 2.1   CREATING A DATABASE OBJECT AND A RECORDSET OBJECT

```
1: Private Sub Form_Load()
2: '
3: ' creating Dynaset-type recordsets
4: '
5: Dim db As Database ' the database object
6: Dim rs As Recordset ' the recordset object
7: '
8: End Sub
```

You must initialize these objects with values before they can access data. This process is similar to setting the properties of the data control. To initialize the values, you first create two variables that correspond to the DatabaseName and RecordSource properties of the Visual Basic data control. The code sample in Listing 2.2 shows how it is done.

Tip

> The code sample in Listing 2.2 uses the App.Path Visual Basic keywords. You can use the Path method of the App object to determine the drive letter and directory from which the program was launched. In most projects throughout this book, you find the databases are stored in a folder called DATA in the same directory tree as the sample projects. By using the App.Path method as part of the database name, you always point to the correct drive and directory for the required file. Be sure to change this path in your example to point to the proper location of the BOOKS6.MDB file on your workstation.

LISTING 2.2   DECLARING DATABASE AND DATA TABLE VARIABLES

```
1: Private Sub Form_Load()
2: '
3: ' creating Dynaset-type recordsets
4: '
5: Dim db As Database ' the database object
6: Dim rs As Recordset ' the recordset object
```

continues

LISTING 2.2   CONTINUED

```
 7: '
 8: ' create local variables
 9: Dim strDBName As String
10: Dim strRSName As String
11: '
12: ' initialize the variables
13: strDBName = App.Path & "\..\data\books6.mdb"
14: strRSName = "Titles"
15: '
16: End Sub
```

> **Tip**
>
> Notice that you created two string variables, and both variable names start with the letters str, which stand for string type. This is the prefix of the variable name. The prefix of the name tells you what type of data is stored in the variable. This is common programming practice. Adhering to a consistent naming convention makes it easier to read and maintain your programs.

Before you continue with the chapter, save this form as DYNASETS.FRM and save the project as DYNASETS.VBP.

Now that you have created the data objects, created variables to hold database properties, and initialized those variables with the proper values, you are ready to actually open the database and create the Dynaset-type Recordset. The code in Listing 2.3 shows how to do this using Visual Basic code.

LISTING 2.3   OPENING THE DATABASE AND CREATING THE DYNASET

```
 1: Private Sub Form_Load()
 2: '
 3: ' creating dynaset-type recordsets
 4: '
 5: Dim db As Database ' the database object
 6: Dim rs As Recordset ' the recordset object
 7: '
 8: ' create local variables
 9: Dim strDBName As String
10: Dim strRSName As String
11: '
12: ' initialize the variables
13: strDBName = App.Path & "\..\data\books5.mdb"
14: strRSName = "Titles"
```

```
15: '
16: ' create the objects
17: Set db = DBEngine.OpenDatabase(strDBName)
18: Set rs = db.OpenRecordset(strRSName, dbOpenDynaset)
19: '
20: End Sub
```

There are two added lines in Listing 2.3. The first (line 17) opens the BOOKS6.MDB database and sets the Visual Basic database object db to point to the database. This gives your Visual Basic program a direct link to the selected database.

> **Tip**
>
> Note that this database object was created using the OpenDatabase method of the DBEngine object. The DBEngine object is covered in greater detail on Day 8.

Now you can use the db data object to represent the open database in all other Visual Basic code in this program. The second line (line 18) in Listing 2.3 creates a Dynaset-type Recordset object that contains all the records in the Titles table. The Visual Basic rs object is set to point to this set of records. Notice that the OpenRecordset method is applied to the db Database object.

> **Tip**
>
> Notice that these last two lines of code use the Set keyword. This Visual Basic keyword is used to initialize all programming objects. You might think that you could perform the same task using the following code line:
>
> Rs = db.OpenRecordSet(strRSName,dbOpenDynaset)
>
> However, this does not work. In Visual Basic, all objects must be created using the Set keyword.

The code in Listing 2.3 is all that you need to open an existing Microsoft Access database and create a Dynaset-type Recordset ready for update. However, for this project, you want to see a bit more. Let's add some code that tells you how many records are in the Titles data table.

You need one more variable to hold the record count. You also use the MoveLast method to move the record pointer to the last record in the Recordset. This forces Visual Basic to touch every record in the collection, and therefore gives you an accurate count of the total number of records in the table. You get the count by reading the RecordCount property of the Recordset. When you have all that, you display a Visual Basic message box that tells you how many records are in the Recordset. Listing 2.4 contains the code to add.

LISTING 2.4 COUNTING THE RECORDS IN A DYNASET

```
 1: Private Sub Form_Load()
 2:     '
 3:     ' creating dynaset-type recordsets
 4:     '
 5:     Dim db As Database ' the database object
 6:     Dim rs As Recordset ' the recordset object
 7:     '
 8:     ' create local variables
 9:     Dim strDBName As String
10:     Dim strRSName As String
11:     Dim intRecs As Integer
12:     '
13:     ' initialize the variables
14:     strDBName = App.Path & "\..\..\data\books6.mdb"
15:     strRSName = "Titles"
16:     '
17:     ' create the objects
18:     Set db = DBEngine.OpenDatabase(strDBName)
19:     Set rs = db.OpenRecordset(strRSName, dbOpenDynaset)
20:     '
21:     ' count the records in the collection
22:     With rs
23:         .MoveLast ' move to end of list to force a count
24:         intRecs = .RecordCount ' get count
25:     End With
26:     MsgBox strRSName & " :" & CStr(intRecs), vbInformation, _
           "Total Records in Set"
27:     '
28: End Sub
```

Save the form (DYNASETS.FRM) and project (DYNASETS.VBP) again and run the program. You see a message box telling you how many records are in the Recordset. Figure 2.3 shows the results of a typical run. Your record count may be different—that's OK.

FIGURE 2.3

Displaying the Record Count *of a Recordset.*

You can use the OpenRecordset command on an existing Recordset to create a smaller subset of the data. This is often done when the user is allowed to create a record selection criterion. If the dataset returned is too large, the user is allowed to further qualify the search by creating additional criteria to apply to the dataset.

Let's modify DYNASETS.VBP to create a smaller Dynaset-type Recordset from the existing Recordset. You need to create a new Recordset object and a new variable called strFilter to hold the criteria for selecting records. The code in Listing 2.5 shows how to add the object and variable to the existing DYNASETS.VBP project.

LISTING 2.5 ADDING A NEW RECORDSET OBJECT AND STRING VARIABLE

```
 1: Private Sub Form_Load()
 2:     '
 3:     ' creating dynaset-type recordsets
 4:     '
 5:     Dim db As Database ' the database object
 6:     Dim rs As Recordset ' the recordset object
 7:     Dim rs2 As Recordset ' another recordset
 8:     '
 9:     ' create local variables
10:     Dim strDBName As String
11:     Dim strRSName As String
12:     Dim intRecs As Integer
13:     Dim strFilter As String
14:     '
15:     ' initialize the variables
16:     strDBName = App.Path & "\..\..\data\books6.mdb"
17:     strRSName = "Titles"
18:     strFilter = "YearPub>1990"
19:     '
20:     ' create the objects
21:     Set db = DBEngine.OpenDatabase(strDBName)
22:     Set rs = db.OpenRecordset(strRSName, dbOpenDynaset)
23:     '
24:     ' count the records in the collection
25:     With rs
26:         .MoveLast ' move to end of list to force a count
27:         intRecs = .RecordCount ' get count
28:     End With
29:     MsgBox strRSName & " :" & CStr(intRecs), vbInformation, _
            "Total Records in Set"
30:     '
31: End Sub
```

Now that you have the object and the variable (lines 7, 13, and 18 in Listing 2.5), you can add code that creates a new Recordset. First you set the Filter property of the existing Recordset using the variable you just created. Then you create the new Recordset from the old one. See lines 32 and 33 of the code in Listing 2.6.

LISTING 2.6 USING THE Filter PROPERTY TO CREATE A RECORDSET

```
 1: Private Sub Form_Load()
 2:      '
 3:      ' creating dynaset-type recordsets
 4:      '
 5:      Dim db As Database ' the database object
 6:      Dim rs As Recordset ' the recordset object
 7:      Dim rs2 As Recordset ' another recordset
 8: '
 9:      ' create local variables
10:      Dim strDBName As String
11:      Dim strRSName As String
12:      Dim intRecs As Integer
13:      Dim strFilter As String
14:      '
15:      ' initialize the variables
16:      strDBName = App.Path & "\..\..\data\books6.mdb"
17:      strRSName = "Titles"
18:      strFilter = "YearPub>1990"
19:      '
20:      ' create the objects
21:      Set db = DBEngine.OpenDatabase(strDBName)
22:      Set rs = db.OpenRecordset(strRSName, dbOpenDynaset)
23:      '
24:      ' count the records in the collection
25:      With rs
26:          .MoveLast ' move to end of list to force a count
27:          intRecs = .RecordCount ' get count
28:      End With
29:      MsgBox strRSName & " :" & CStr(intRecs), vbInformation, _
             "Total Records in Set"
30:      '
31:      ' create filtered collection
32:      rs.Filter = strFilter
33:      Set rs2 = rs.OpenRecordset
34:      '
35: End Sub
```

Now that you've created the new Recordset from the old one, you can get a count of the selected records. You can add the same code you used earlier: Move to the end of the Recordset, get the RecordCount, and show it in a message box. Listing 2.7 shows the completed program.

LISTING 2.7 DISPLAYING THE RECORD COUNT OF THE FILTERED RECORDSET

```
 1: Private Sub Form_Load()
 2:     '
 3:     ' creating dynaset-type recordsets
 4:     '
 5:     Dim db As Database ' the database object
 6:     Dim rs As Recordset ' the recordset object
 7:     Dim rs2 As Recordset ' another recordset
 8:     '
 9:     ' create local variables
10:     Dim strDBName As String
11:     Dim strRSName As String
12:     Dim intRecs As Integer
13:     Dim strFilter As String
14:     '
15:     ' initialize the variables
16:     strDBName = App.Path & "\..\..\data\books6.mdb"
17:     strRSName = "Titles"
18:     strFilter = "YearPub>1990"
19:     '
20:     ' create the objects
21:     Set db = DBEngine.OpenDatabase(strDBName)
22:     Set rs = db.OpenRecordset(strRSName, dbOpenDynaset)
23:     '
24:     ' count the records in the collection
25:     With rs
26:         .MoveLast ' move to end of list to force a count
27:         intRecs = .RecordCount ' get count
28:     End With
29:     MsgBox strRSName & " :" & CStr(intRecs), vbInformation, _
            "Total Records in Set"
30:     '
31:     ' create filtered collection
32:     rs.Filter = strFilter
33:     '
34:     ' count the records in the collection
35:     Set rs2 = rs.OpenRecordset
36:     With rs2
37:         .MoveLast ' move to end of list to force a count
38:         intRecs = .RecordCount ' get count
39:     End With
40:     MsgBox strFilter & " :" & CStr(intRecs), vbInformation, _
            "Total Records in Set"
41:     '
42: End Sub
```

Save and run the code to check the results (see Figure 2.4). Notice that the first record count (the full dataset) is larger than the second record count (the filtered dataset).

FIGURE 2.4

Displaying the Record Count *of the filtered recordset.*

It is also important to notice that the second Recordset object was created from the first Recordset object. This a very powerful feature of Visual Basic. When you want to get a smaller dataset, you don't have to reload the data from the database; you can use an existing Recordset as the source for a new dataset.

> **Tip**
>
> Creating subsets of a Recordset in this manner can sometimes be slower than simply creating a new Recordset from the database itself. The exception to this rule is when your database is stored at a distant server. In cases where your source data is far away and possibly available only over a slow network connection, using the Filter property to create subsets of data can be faster.

Now let's make one more series of changes to DYNASETS.VBP that illustrates the Clone method for Recordsets. Cloning a Recordset makes a duplicate of the set. Add another data object (rs3), and add the Clone Recordset program code in Listing 2.8.

LISTING 2.8 CLONING A NEW RECORDSET

```
 1: Private Sub Form_Load()
 2:      '
 3:      ' creating dynaset-type recordsets
 4:      '
 5:      Dim db As Database ' the database object
 6:      Dim rs As Recordset ' the recordset object
 7:      Dim rs2 As Recordset ' another recordset
 8:      Dim rs3 As Recordset ' for cloning
 9:      '
10:      ' create local variables
11:      Dim strDBName As String
12:      Dim strRSName As String
13:      Dim intRecs As Integer
14:      Dim strFilter As String
15:      '
16:      ' initialize the variables
17:      strDBName = App.Path & "\..\..\data\books6.mdb"
```

```
18:        strRSName = "Titles"
19:        strFilter = "YearPub>1990"
20:        '
21:        ' create the objects
22:        Set db = DBEngine.OpenDatabase(strDBName)
23:        Set rs = db.OpenRecordset(strRSName, dbOpenDynaset)
24:        '
25:        ' count the records in the collection
26:        With rs
27:            .MoveLast ' move to end of list to force a count
28:            intRecs = .RecordCount ' get count
29:        End With
30:        MsgBox strRSName & " :" & CStr(intRecs), vbInformation, _
               "Total Records in Set"
31:        '
32:        ' create filtered collection
33:        rs.Filter = strFilter
34:        '
35:        ' count the records in the collection
36:        Set rs2 = rs.OpenRecordset
37:        With rs2
38:            .MoveLast ' move to end of list to force a count
39:            intRecs = .RecordCount ' get count
40:        End With
41:        MsgBox strFilter & " :" & CStr(intRecs), vbInformation, _
               "Total Records in Set"
42:        '
43:        ' clone the recordset
44:        Set rs3 = rs.Clone ' clone it
45:        With rs3
46:            .MoveLast ' move to end
47:            intRecs = .RecordCount ' get count
48:        End With
49:        MsgBox "Cloned Recordset: " & CStr(intRecs), vbInformation, _
               "Total Records in Set"
50:        '
51: End Sub
```

Line 8 and lines 43 through 49 are the new lines in the Form_Load method. Notice that to clone a Recordset, you use the Clone method to load a new Recordset object variable. When you run the program this time, you see that the Recordset created using the Clone method contains the same number of records as its parent.

Dynasets Can Use Bookmarks, Filters, and Sorts

Dynaset-type Recordsets can use the Bookmark, Filter, and Sort properties to reorder data for display (Sort) or create a subset of the Recordset (Filter). Using the Visual Basic Find method on a Recordset forces Visual Basic to start at the first record in the collection and read each one until a match is found. When the selected record is found, your user may want to return to the record that was displayed before the search began. That's what Visual Basic Bookmarks do. They remember where you were.

When you search for a record in the dataset using one of the Find methods, you should set Bookmarks before your search to remember where you started. This is especially handy if your Find criteria results in a null record. When a FindFirst method fails to locate the desired record, the record pointer is set to the first record in the collection. If you have saved the bookmark before starting the search, you can reset the Visual Basic Bookmark and return the user to the place from which the search started.

Let's build a quick project to demonstrate the use of Bookmarks. Use the information in Table 2.1 to create a small form with a data control, two bound input controls, two label controls, and a single command button.

TABLE 2.1   CONTROLS FOR BOOKMARKS.FRM

Control	Property	Setting
VB.Form	Name	FrmBookMarks
	Caption	"Bookmark Demonstration"
	ClientHeight	1320
	ClientLeft	60
	ClientTop	345
	ClientWidth	4605
	StartUpPosition	2 'CenterScreen
VB.CommandButton	Name	CmdSaveBookmark
	Caption	"&Save Bookmark"
	Height	300
	Left	2760
	Top	180
	Width	1695
VB.Data	Name	DtaBookMarks
	Align	2 'Align Bottom
	Caption	"Data1"
	Connect	"Access"
	DatabaseName	C:\TYSDBVB6\SOURCE\ DATA\BOOKS6.MDB

Control	Property	Setting
	RecordsetType	1 'Dynaset
	RecordSource	"Authors"
VB.TextBox	Name	TxtName
	DataField	"Name"
	DataSource	"dtaBookMarks"
	Height	300
	Left	1440
	Top	600
	Width	3015
VB.TextBox	Name	TxtAUID
	DataField	"AUID"
	DataSource	"dtaBookMarks"
	Height	300
	Left	1440
	Top	180
	Width	1215
VB.Label	Name	LblName
	BorderStyle	1 'Fixed Single
	Caption	"Author Name"
	Height	300
	Left	120
	Top	600
	Width	1215
VB.Label	Name	LblAUID
	BorderStyle	1 'Fixed Single
	Caption	"Author ID"
	Height	300
	Left	120
	Top	180
	Width	1215

Refer to Figure 2.5 as a guide for sizing and locating the controls on the form.

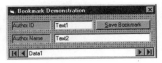

FIGURE 2.5

Laying out the Bookmark Demonstration form.

When you have completed the form layout, add the following code behind the command button. The code in Listing 2.9 is a toggle routine that saves the current place in the table by reading (and storing) the Bookmark, or restores the previous place in the table by reading (and updating) the Bookmark.

LISTING 2.9   CODING THE cmdSaveBookmarks_Click EVENT FOR BOOKMARKS.VBP

```
 1: Private Sub cmdSaveBookmark_Click()
 2:     '
 3:     ' show how bookmarks work
 4:     '
 5:     Static blnFlag As Boolean
 6:     Static strBookmark As String
 7:     '
 8:     With dtaBookMarks.Recordset
 9:         If blnFlag = False Then
10:             blnFlag = True
11:             cmdSaveBookmark.Caption = "&Restore Bookmark"
12:             strBookmark = .Bookmark
13:             MsgBox "Bookmark Saved", vbInformation
14:         Else
15:             blnFlag = False
16:             cmdSaveBookmark.Caption = "&Save Bookmark"
17:             .Bookmark = strBookmark
18:         End If
19:     End With
20: End Sub
```

Tip

Listing 2.9 uses two Static variables. Static variables keep their value even after the procedure ends. Using Static variables in your program is an excellent way to keep track of flag values even after procedures or functions exit. The only other way to make sure that variables maintain their value after exit from a routine is to place them in the declaration area of the form. The problem with placing them at the form-level declaration is that they now can be altered by routines in other procedures or functions on the same form. Declaring Static variables within the procedures in which they are used follows good programming practice by limiting the scope of the variable.

Save the form as BOOKMARKS.FRM and the project as BOOKMARKS.VBP, and then run the program. The program opens the BOOKS5.MDB file, creates a Dynaset-type Recordset of all the records in the Authors data table, and presents the first record on the form. Note that the command button caption says Save Bookmark. Click the command button to create a Bookmark that points to this record of the collection. The caption changes to Restore Bookmark. Now use the arrow buttons on the data control to move to another record on the form. Click the command button. You see that the record pointer has been returned to the first record in the collection. This is because the Recordset Bookmark property was reset to the value you stored earlier.

Dynasets and ODBC

If you are accessing data from an ODBC data source, the only Visual Basic data object you can use to update the underlying data table is a Dynaset-type Recordset. You learn more about ODBC-connected databases on Day 9 , "Creating Database Programs with the Data Environment Designer," and on Day 18, "Using the ActiveX Data Objects (ADO)."

Limitations of the Dynaset-type Recordset Data Object

Although the Dynaset is an excellent data object, it has a few drawbacks that must be considered. Chief among these is that Dynasets do not allow you to specify an existing index, and you cannot use the Visual Basic Seek method to quickly locate a single record in the Dynaset. Also, errors can occur when displaying records in a Dynaset if the records in the underlying data table have been altered or deleted by another user.

Dynaset Access and Seek Limitations

Dynasets cannot make use of Index objects that exist in a database because the Index is built to control the entire data table and not just a subset of the data. Because Dynasets could be subsets of the data table, the Index is useless. Also, because you cannot specify an Index object for a Dynaset, you cannot use the Visual Basic Seek method on a Dynaset.

These are only minor limitations. If you have defined an Index in the underlying table with the Primary flag turned on, the Visual Basic data engine uses the primary key index when creating the Dynaset. This usually puts the Dynaset in optimal order. Even though you cannot use the Seek method on a Dynaset, you can use the FindFirst, FindNext, FindPrevious, and FindLast methods. Even though they are not true index searches, they are fast enough for operations on small- to medium-sized Dynasets.

Dynamic Membership-Related Errors

If your program opens a database and creates a Dynaset from an underlying table while another user has also opened the same database and created a Dynaset based on the same underlying data table, it is possible that both users will attempt to edit the same data record. If both users edit the same record and both attempt to save the record back to the underlying table, the second person who attempts to save the record receives a Visual Basic error.

When the second person tries to save the record, Visual Basic discovers that the original record in the underlying data table has been altered. In order to maintain database integrity, Visual Basic does not allow the second person to update the table.

When to Use the Dynaset-type Recordset Data Object

The Dynaset object should be used in most database programs you write. In most cases, the Visual Basic Dynaset data object is the most effective data access object to use. It offers you a way to create a dynamic, updatable subset of data records in one or more data tables. The Dynaset object is the default object created by the bound data control and is the only updatable data object you can use to access ODBC data sources.

The Dynaset is not a good data object to use when you need to do a great deal of record-oriented processing on large datasets, such as index look-ups on large transaction files. If you have a Visual Basic program that uses Dynasets and is showing slow database performance, look for places where you can limit the size of Dynasets by narrowing the selection criteria.

Using the Find Methods with Dynasets

Before completing the review of Dynaset objects, it is important to spend a bit more time on the Find methods. In this section, you'll build a sample project that shows you how to use the Find methods to locate records in the record set.

Tip

> The Find methods can be applied to DAO Dynaset and DAO Snapshot datasets. However, you cannot apply the Find methods to DAO Table datasets.

Dyansets do not have indexes applied to them. In other words, you cannot perform a "seek" action to locate a specific record. However, Dynasets will allow sequential searches for an individual record. To handle this, Dynasets support the four Find methods:

- FindFirst starts the search from the first record in the dataset, begins searching forward, and returns the first record that matches the search criteria.

- FindLast starts the search from the last record in the dataset, begins searching backward, and returns the first record that matches the search criteria.
- FindNext starts the search from the current record in the dataset, begins searching forward, and returns the first record that matches the search criteria.
- FindPrevious starts the search from the current record in the dataset, begins searching backward, and returns the first record that matches the search criteria.

As you can see from the list, there are two possible search directions: forward and backward. There are also three possible search-starting locations: the first record in the set, the last record in the set, or the current record in the set.

The basic syntax of the Find methods is

```
FindFirst "<fieldexpression><operator><value>"
```

The fieldexpression can be a simple name (MyID) or a combination of fields (CustID & InvoiceNumber). The <operator> can be any of the valid comparators (=, <>, >=, <=, and so forth). Finally, the <value> portion of the statement can be any value of the proper type that might be found in the <fieldexpression>, such as ID0009, CUST99INV203, and so forth.

Here are a few completed examples of valid Find statements:

```
FindNext "Amount>1000"
FindLast "MyIDCode='ID909'"
FindFirst "CustID & InvoiceNumber = 'CID101INV909'"
```

You should notice that the Find methods use a single string as a parameter and that you must use single quotation marks when the search value is a string instead of a number.

The most commonly used method is the FindFirst method. This provides the same results as an indexed "seek." You can use FindFirst to return the first record in the collection that matches your criteria. However, FindLast is also quite handy. For example, you might want to know the date of the last invoice that was issued for a particular customer:

```
With Me.dtaInvoiceData.Recordset
   .FindLast "CustID='C1003'
   msgbox .Fields("IssueDate").Value
End With
```

Now that you have an idea of how the Find methods work, it's time to build a sample project to show them in action. First, create a new Visual Basic 6 Standard EXE project.

Now, using Figure 2.6 and Table 2.2, lay out the test form with one data control, three labels, three text boxes, and three command buttons.

FIGURE 2.6

Laying out the dsFind form.

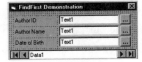

TABLE 2.2 CONTROLS FOR THE DSFIND FORM

Control	Property	Setting
VB.Form	Name	frmFind
	BorderStyle	3 'Fixed Dialog
	Caption	"FindFirst Demonstration"
	ClientHeight	1575
	ClientLeft	45
	ClientTop	330
	ClientWidth	3990
	Name	"System"
	Size	9.75
	MaxButton	0 'False
	MinButton	0 'False
	ShowInTaskbar	0 'False
	StartUpPosition	3 'Windows Default
VB.CommandButton	Name	cmdFindDOB
	Caption	"..."
	Height	31
	Left	3480
	Top	840
	Width	315
VB.CommandButton	Name	cmdFindName
	Caption	"..."

Control	Property	Setting
	Height	315
	Left	3480
	Top	480
	Width	315
VB.CommandButton	Name	cmdFindAUID
	Caption	"..."
	Height	315
	Left	3480
	Top	120
	Width	315
VB.TextBox	Name	Text3
	DataField	"DOB"
	DataSource	"Data1"
	Height	315
	Left	1560
	Text	"Text1"
	Top	840
	Width	1875
VB.TextBox	Name	Text2
	DataField	"Name"
	DataSource	"Data1"
	Height	315
	Left	1560
	Text	"Text1"
	Top	480
	Width	1875
VB.TextBox	Name	Text1
	DataField	"AUID"
	DataSource	"Data1"
	Height	315
	Left	1560
	Text	"Text1"

continues

2

TABLE 2.2　CONTINUED

Control	Property	Setting
	Top	120
	Width	1875
VB.Data	Name	Data1
	Align	2 'Align Bottom
	Caption	"Data1"
	Connect	"Access"
	DatabaseName	"I:\tysdbvb6
		\source\data\
		books6.mdb"
	DefaultCursorType=	'DefaultCursor
	Exclusive	0 'False
	Height	345
	Left	0
	Options	0
	ReadOnly	0 'False
	RecordsetType	1 'Dynaset
	RecordSource	"Authors"
	Top	1230
	Width	3990
VB.Label	Name	Label3
	Caption	"Date of Birth"
	Height	255
	Left	180
	Top	900
	Width	1275
VB.Label	Name	Label2
	Caption	"Author Name"
	Height	255
	Left	180
	Top	540
	Width	1275

Control	Property	Setting
VB.Label	Name	Label1
	Caption	"Author ID"
	Height	255
	Left	180
	Top	180
	Width	1275

After completing the form layout, save the form as rsFind.frm and the project as prjFind.vbp before you begin adding code to the project.

Using Find to Locate a Unique Numeric Value in the Dataset

You can use the FindFirst method to locate a single record in the dataset. This would give you the same results as if you were using a table index. You can do this by using the equals operator (=) in the find clause:

```
FindFirst "MyField = 'BGATES'"
```

As an example, add the code from Listing 2.10 to the cmdFindUAID_click event.

LISTING 2.10   ADDING CODE TO THE cmdFindAUID_click EVENT

```
 1: Private Sub cmdFindAUID_Click()
 2:      '
 3:      ' find a single numeric value
 4:      '
 5:      Dim varAUID As Variant
 6:      Dim strBkMark As String
 7:      '
 8:      varAUID = InputBox("Enter AUID code:", "Find Author", 13)
 9:      If varAUID = "" Then
10:          Exit Sub
11:      End If
12:      '
13:      With Me.Data1.Recordset
14:          strBkMark = .Bookmark
15:          .FindFirst "AUID=" & varAUID
16:          If .NoMatch = True Then
17:              .Bookmark = strBkMark
18:              MsgBox "Unable to find AUID [" & varAUID & "]", _
                     vbCritical, "Find Error"
19:          End If
20:      End With
21:      '
22: End Sub
```

Notice that this routine first retrieves an author ID number from the user (line 8) and then attempts to locate a record in the dataset with the same value (line 15). If the record is found, the pointer is moved to that record and the display is updated automatically. If, however, it is not found, the pointer is first restored (line 17) and a message box appears (line 18).

Now save this project and press F5 to test it. When you press the browse button next to the Author ID field, you'll see a sample input dialog. If you enter a valid value, the form will automatically move the data pointer to the requested record and update the display (see Figure 2.7).

FIGURE 2.7

Locating an Author
ID in the dataset.

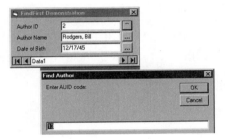

Using Find to Locate the First Occurrence of a String Value

You can also use the Find method to perform wildcard searches of dataset fields. You use the LIKE operator and pass a valid wildcard string to the Find method.

> **Tip**
>
> The Microsoft Access database uses the asterisk (*) as the wildcard character for searches. However, other SQL-type databases (SQL Server and Oracle, for example) use the percent sign (%) instead.

Add the code from Listing 2.11 to the cmdFindName_click event.

LISTING 2.11 ADDING CODE TO THE cmdFindName_Click EVENT

```
1: Private Sub cmdFindName_Click()
2:     '
3:     ' find the first record that matches
4:     ' using wildcard string search
5:     '
6:     Dim varName As Variant
7:     Dim strBkMark As String
8:     '
9:     varName = InputBox("Enter Search Criteria for Author Name:", _
```

```
               "Find Author", "*sm*")
10:        If varName = "" Then
11:            Exit Sub
12:        Else
13:            varName = "'" & varName & "'" ' fix for string
14:        End If
15:        '
16:        With Me.Data1.Recordset
17:            strBkMark = .Bookmark
18:            .FindFirst "Name LIKE " & varName
19:            If .NoMatch Then
20:                .Bookmark = strBkMark
21:                MsgBox "Unable to find Name LIKE [" & varName & "]", _
                       vbCritical, "Find Error"
22:            End If
23:        End With
24:        '
25: End Sub
```

You should notice that this routine wraps the string search value in single quotation marks (line 13). This is an important step in using the Find methods. All string values must be wrapped in single quotation marks. Also note the use of the LIKE keyword as the comparison operator. This enables you to use wildcard markers in the search value.

When you save and run this project, you'll be able to find the first record in the dataset that meets the wildcard search.

Using Find to Locate a Record in a Date Range

In the last Find method example in this project, you see how you can use date-type data to search for a record within a range of dates. To do this, you must accept a start and end date from the user and incorporate those dates into a valid search clause. Listing 2.12 shows how this can be done. Add this code to the cmdFindDOB_Click event.

LISTING 2.12 USING Find WITH DATE RANGES

```
1: Private Sub cmdFindDOB_Click()
2:     '
3:     ' find the first record that is in a date range
4:     '
5:     Dim varDateS As Variant
6:     Dim varDateE As Variant
7:     Dim strBkMark As String
8:     '
9:     varDateS = InputBox("Enter Start Date for DOB:", "Find Author", _
```

continues

LISTING 2.12   CONTINUED

```
                  Format("01/01/50", "short date"))
10:       If varDateS = "" Then
11:           Exit Sub
12:       Else
13:           varDateS = "#" & varDateS & "#" ' fix for date
14:       End If
15:       '
16:       varDateE = InputBox("Enter End Date for DOB:", "Find Author", _
17:        Format(Now(), "short date"))
18:       If varDateE = "" Then
19:           Exit Sub
20:       Else
21:           varDateE = "#" & varDateE & "#" ' fix for date
22:       End If
23:       '
24:       With Me.Data1.Recordset
25:           .FindFirst "DOB>=" & varDateS & " AND DOB<=" & varDateE
26:           If .NoMatch = True Then
27:               .Bookmark = strBkMark
28:               MsgBox "Unable to find DOB in Range " & varDateE & _
29:                   " to " & varDateE, vbCritical, "Find Error"
30:           End If
31:       End With
32:       '
33: End Sub
```

Just as you must surround string search values in single quotation marks, you should surround date search values with the # sign. This tells the DAO search engine that the value
is a date-type.

Caution

> Some RDBMS systems will not accept the # as a valid date-wrapper. If you
> are having trouble with Find methods and dates, you should check your
> database documentation to learn the proper way to send date-type search
> values.

After adding the code from Listing 2.12, save and run your project. You can now search
for a record within a specified date range.

The Table-type Recordset Data Object

The Visual Basic Table-type Recordset data object is the data object that gives you access
to the physical data table, sometimes referred to as the "base table." You can use the

Table object to directly open the table defined by Data Manager (or some other database definition tool). The chief advantage of using the Table object is that you can specify search indexes and use the Visual Basic Seek method. Like Dynasets, Tables take a limited amount of local workstation memory.

The Table-type Recordset data object also gives you instant information on the state of the data table. This is important in a multiuser environment. As soon as a user adds or deletes a record from the table, all other users who have the data table open as a Visual Basic Table object also see the changes.

Visual Basic Table objects have their drawbacks, too. You cannot use a Select statement to initialize a Table object, and you cannot combine data tables to create unique views of the database when you create Table objects.

You cannot use Bookmarks, create Filters, or sort the table. Furthermore, you cannot use the Table data object to access ODBC data sources. Only Dynasets and Snapshots can be used with ODBC data sources.

Strengths of the Table-type Recordset Data Object

The real strength of Table objects is that you can specify Index objects to use when searching for specific records in the table. Table objects also use limited workstation memory and offer instant updates whenever that data in the table changes.

Data Pointers and Instant Membership Notification

Like Dynasets, Table objects use limited workstation memory because Visual Basic caches pointers to the actual records at the workstation instead of loading all the records into workstation memory. This gives your programs the fastest access speed of all the data objects when you are searching for a single record.

Unlike Dynasets and Snapshots, Table objects are not subsets of the data table. They contain all the records in the table at all times. As soon as a new record is added to the data table, the record is available to the Table object. Also, as soon as a user deletes a record from the table, the Table object is updated to reflect the deletion.

Table-type Recordset Objects, Indexes, and the Seek Method

The Visual Basic Table-type Recordset data object enables you to specify an index to apply to the data table. You can use indexes to order the data table for displays and reports and to speed searches using the Seek method.

The following project (TBSEEK.VBP) demonstrates the use of Visual Basic Table-type Recordset objects, indexes, and the Seek method. It opens the Titles table of the

BOOKS6.MDB database and gives you the ability to select one of three indexes. When the index is selected, the program loads the records from the table into a list box. When you click the Search button, you are prompted to enter a search value to use in the Seek method on the table.

Use the information in Table 2.3 to build a new Standard EXE project that demonstrates the use of Visual Basic Table objects, indexes, and the Seek method.

TABLE 2.3 CONTROLS FOR THE TBSEEK.VBP PROJECT

Control	Property	Setting
VB.Form	Name	frmTbSeek
	BorderStyle	3 'Fixed Dialog
	Caption	"Table Index and Seek Demonstration"
	ClientHeight	2895
	ClientLeft	45
	ClientTop	330
	ClientWidth	6630
	MaxButton	0 'False
	MinButton	0 'False
	ShowInTaskbar	0 'False
	StartUpPosition	3 'Windows Default
VB.CommandButton	Name	cmdExit
	Caption	"E&xit"
	Height	300
	Left	5220
	Top	2520
	Width	1200
VB.CommandButton	Name	cmdSeek
	Caption	"&Seek"
	Height	300
	Left	3360
	Top	2520
	Width	1200

Control	Property	Setting
VB.CommandButton	Name	cmdPublisher
	Caption	"&Publisher"
	Height	300
	Left	1380
	Top	2520
	Width	1200
VB.CommandButton	Name	cmdISBN
	Caption	"&ISBN"
	Height	300
	Left	120
	Top	2520
	Width	1200
VB.ListBox	Name	lstRecordset
	FontName	"Terminal"
	FontSize	9
	FontCharset	255
	FontWeight	400
	FontUnderline	0 'False
	FontItalic	0 'False
	FontStrikethrough	0 'False
	FontHeight	2040
	Left	120
	Top	360
	Width	6315
VB.Label	Name	lblIndex
	BorderStyle	1 'Fixed Single
	Height	255
	Left	120
	Top	60
	Width	6315

2

Refer to Figure 2.8 as a guide for placement and positioning of the controls listed in Table 2.3.

FIGURE 2.8

*Laying out the
TbSeek form.*

 Note

> Because you again create data objects in Visual Basic code in this exercise, you need to load the Microsoft DAO 3.51 Object Library for this project (refer to Figure 2.2).

After you have placed the controls on the form and sized them, you need to place the code from Listing 2.13 in the declaration section of the form. This code declares several variables that you use throughout the form.

LISTING 2.13   DECLARATION CODE FOR THE TBSEEK.VBP PROJECT

```
 1: Option Explicit
 2: '
 3: ' form-level variables
 4: '
 5: Dim db As Database
 6: Dim rs As Recordset
 7: '
 8: Dim strDBName As String
 9: Dim strRSName As String
10: Dim strIndex As String
11: Dim strField As String
```

Next, place the code from Listing 2.14 in the Form_Load event of the form. To do this, double-click anywhere on the form space to open the Visual Basic code window. Then select Form from the drop-down list on the upper left and Load from the drop-down list on the upper right.

The code in Listing 2.14 opens the BOOKS6.MDB database and opens the Titles table. Be sure to adjust the path used in line 4 of Listing 2.14 to point to the location of the BOOKS6.MDB database on your workstation.

LISTING 2.14 CODING THE FORM_LOAD ROUTINE OF TBSEEK.VBP

```
 1: Private Sub Form_Load()
 2:     '
 3:     ' set vars
 4:     strDBName = App.Path & "\..\..\Data\Books6.mdb"
 5:     strRSName = "Titles"
 6:     '
 7:     ' open database and table
 8:     Set db = DBEngine.OpenDatabase(strDBName)
 9:     Set rs = db.OpenRecordset(strRSName, dbOpenTable)
10:     '
11: End Sub
```

Now, add the procedure shown in Listing 2.15 in the declaration section. This is the procedure that sets the table index and loads the list box in the proper order.

LISTING 2.15 CODING THE LoadList ROUTINE OF TBSEEK.VBP

```
 1: Public Sub LoadList()
 2:     '
 3:     ' load data collection into list box
 4:     '
 5:     On Error Resume Next ' in case we get null fields
 6:     '
 7:     Dim strLine As String
 8:     '
 9:     lstRecordset.Clear ' dump the old local data
10:     '
11:     ' add data to the list control
12:     With rs
13:         .Index = strIndex
14:         .MoveFirst
15:         '
16:         Do While Not .EOF
17:             strLine = Space(60)
18:             Mid(strLine, 1, 20) = .Fields("Title")
19:             Mid(strLine, 22, 4) = CStr(.Fields("YearPub"))
20:             Mid(strLine, 28, 15) = CStr(.Fields("ISBN"))
21:             Mid(strLine, 47, 5) = CStr(.Fields("PubID"))
22:             lstRecordset.AddItem strLine
23:             .MoveNext
24:         Loop
25:     End With
26:     '
27:     ' update the caption
```

continues

LISTING 2.15   CONTINUED

```
28:        lblIndex.Caption = "Titles Table - Indexed by [" & strField & "]"
29:        '
30: End Sub
```

The LoadList procedure is an example of a way to load a standard Visual Basic list box with data from a table. The routine first clears out the list box (line 9). Then the Index property of the table object is set based on the user's input and moves to the first record in the table (lines 13 and 14).

Now the fun starts. The Do While..Loop construct reads each record in the table and creates a single line of text (strLine) that contains each of the fields separated by a single space. Notice that you need to use the CStr() function to convert the numeric fields in the data table (YearPub, ISBN, and Pub_ID) into string values before you can add them to strLine. After the line is built, the strLine is added to the list box using the lstRecordset.AddNew method (line 22). After the item is added to the list box, the record pointer is advanced using the rs.MoveNext method. This goes on until there are no more records in the table (line 23).

The following two code segments go behind the appropriate command button to set the indexes. They set values for selecting the index, setting the display, and calling the routine to load the list box.

Place this code in the cmdISBN_Click event:

```
Private Sub cmdISBN_Click()
    '
    ' set for ISBN index
    '
    strIndex = "PrimaryKey"
    strField = "ISBN"
    LoadList
    '
End Sub
```

Place this code in the cmdPublisher_Click event:

```
Private Sub cmdPublisher_Click()
    '
    ' set for PubID index
    '
    strIndex = "PubID"
    strField = "PubID"
    LoadList
    '
End Sub
```

The Seek routine shown in Listing 2.16 calls an input box to prompt the user for a search value, performs the seek, and reports the results of the search. The routine first checks to see whether the user has filled the list box by selecting an index. If the list box contains data, the routine calls the Visual Basic InputBox function to get user input and then invokes the Seek method of the table object. If the record is not found, you see a Seek Failed message. If you entered a record that is on file, you see a Record Found message.

LISTING 2.16 CODING THE Seek ROUTINE FOR TBSEEK.VBP

```
 1: Private Sub cmdSeek_Click()
 2:      '
 3:      ' perform table seek
 4:      '
 5:      Dim strSeek As String
 6:      '
 7:      ' must set index first!
 8:      If lstRecordset.ListCount = 0 Then
 9:          MsgBox "Select an Index First!", vbExclamation, _
             "Missing Index"
10:      End If
11:      '
12:      ' perform the indexed seek
13:      With rs
14:          strSeek = InputBox("Enter a Seek value for " & strField)
15:          .Seek "=", strSeek
16:          If .NoMatch = True Then
17:              MsgBox strSeek & " not in table", vbCritical, _
                 "Seek Failed"
18:          Else
19:              MsgBox "Title: " & .Fields("Title"), vbInformation, _
                 "Record Found"
20:          End If
21:      End With
22:      '
23: End Sub
```

Of course, every project should have an Exit button. Enter the following line for the Exit button:

```
Private Sub cmdExit_Click()
     '
     ' end program
     '
     rs.Close
     db.Close
     Set rs = Nothing
     Set db = Nothing
```

```
     ¦
     Unload Me
     ¦
End Sub
```

When you have completed the coding, save the form as TBSEEK.FRM and the project as TBSEEK.VBP, and then run the program. Click the ISBN or Publisher buttons to set the index and load the list box. Note that each time you select a different button, the list is loaded in a different order. After the list is loaded, click the Seek button to perform an indexed search on the data table. If you enter a value that is in the index, the program reports the title of the book in a message box; otherwise, you see an error message. See Figure 2.9 for an example.

FIGURE 2.9

Testing the TbSeek Demonstration project.

Limitations of the Table-type Recordset Data Object

Even though the Visual Basic Table-type Recordset object provides the fastest search speed of any of the data objects, it also has certain drawbacks. You cannot sort a table, you can't use the Table object when accessing ODBC data sources, and you can't use the Visual Basic data control to access a Table object.

Tables Cannot Use Bookmarks, Sorts, or Filters

Unlike Dynasets and Snapshots, Visual Basic Table objects cannot be sorted, filtered, or have Bookmarks set. Instead of sorting the data, you can use Index objects to establish the order of the data in the table. If you need to filter the table (usually because it is a large table), you need to create a Dynaset or Snapshot that contains a subset of the data in the table.

Table objects can't use Bookmarks, so you can't mark your place in a table, move around, and then return to the location using Visual Basic Bookmarks. You can, however, save the table index value instead. The table must have an index declared, and you must know the fields used in the declared index. You can get this information from the Design form of Data Manager, or you can get it at runtime by reading the `Index.Name` and `Index.Fields` properties of the Table object. Refer to the section on the Database data object for an example of how to read the `Index.Name` and `Index.Fields` properties of a data table.

ODBC Data Source Limitations

If you plan to do any work with ODBC data sources, you have to forget using the Visual Basic Table object. It does not matter whether the ODBC source is a SQL Server data source or a spreadsheet on your local workstation. You cannot define a Table object to access the data. You must use a Dynaset or Snapshot object for ODBC data requests.

The reason for this limitation is that the ODBC driver gives Visual Basic access to virtually any type of data. There is no requirement that the data source comply with the Visual Basic data engine data table format. Because the Table object is designed specifically to provide direct access to Visual Basic data tables, it can be used only to access a data table that exists as a data table in a Microsoft Access database.

When to Use the Table-type Recordset Data Object

The Visual Basic Table-type Recordset object is the best choice when you need to provide speedy searches of large data tables. As long as you do not need to access ODBC data sources, and you do not need to get a set of data for processing, the Table object is an excellent choice.

If, however, you need to process sets of data instead of single records, the Table object does not work as easily or as quickly as a Dynaset or Snapshot object.

The Snapshot-type Recordset Data Object

Visual Basic Snapshot-type Recordset objects are almost identical to Dynaset-type Recordsets in behavior and properties. However, there are two major differences between Snapshot objects and Dynaset objects. These two differences are the most important aspects of Snapshots:

- Snapshots are stored entirely in workstation memory.
- Snapshots are read-only and nonupdatable objects.

Instead of reviewing strengths and limitations of the Snapshot data object, let's look at these two properties of Snapshots in depth.

Snapshot-type Recordset Storage

You need to consider several things when using Snapshot data objects. For example, unlike Visual Basic Dynasets, Snapshot objects are stored entirely at the workstation. If you create

a Snapshot that contains 500 data records, all 500 records are sent from the data table directly to your workstation and loaded into RAM memory. If the workstation does not have
enough RAM available, the records are stored in a temporary file on a local disk drive.

Because all the requested records are loaded on the local machine, initial requests for data can
take longer with Snapshots than with Dynasets. However, when the data records are retrieved
and stored locally, subsequent access to records within the Snapshot object is faster than with
the Dynaset object. Also, because all records must be stored locally, you must be careful not
to request too large a dataset; you might quickly run out of local RAM or disk space.

Snapshots are static views of the underlying data tables. If you request a set of data
records in a Snapshot object, and then someone deletes several records from the underlying data table, the Snapshot dataset does not reflect the changes in the underlying table.
The only way you can learn about the changes in the underlying data tables is to create a
new Snapshot by making a new request.

Snapshot-type Recordsets Are Read-Only Data Objects

Visual Basic Snapshots are read-only data objects. You cannot use Snapshots to update
data tables. You can only use them to view data. This is because Snapshots are actually a
copy of the data records created at your local workstation.

The project in Listing 2.17 illustrates the static aspect of Snapshot data objects compared
to the dynamic aspect of Dynaset and Table data objects. Start a new Standard EXE project. There are no controls in this project, so be sure to add the Microsoft DAO 3.51
Object Library to access the data objects.

The entire source code is listed. Enter it into a single form and save it as SNAPSHOTS.FRM
and SNAPSHOTS.VBP.

LISTING 2.17 COMPARING SNAPSHOT-TYPE AND DYNASET-TYPE RECORDSETS

```
 1: Option Explicit
 2: '
 3: ' form level variables
 4: '
 5: Dim db As Database
 6: Dim rsDynaset As Recordset
 7: Dim rsSnapshot As Recordset
 8: Dim rsTable As Recordset
 9: '
10: Dim strDBName As String
11: Dim strRSName As String
12: Dim varRecords As Variant
```

```
13: Dim intReturned As Integer
14: Dim intColumns As Integer
15:
16: Private Sub Form_Activate()
17:      '
18:      ' main control routine
19:      '
20:      strDBName = App.Path & "\..\..\Data\books6.mdb"
21:      strRSName = "Titles"
22:      OpenFiles
23:      '
24:      ' show title
25:      Me.Cls
26:      Me.Print "Comparing Recordset Types (Dynaset, Snapshot, & Table)"
27:      Me.Print
28:      '
29:      ' show first compare
30:      Me.Print ">First Pass"
31:      CountRecs rsDynaset, "Dynaset"
32:      CountRecs rsSnapshot, "Snapshot"
33:      CountRecs rsTable, "Table"
34:      Me.Print
35:      '
36:      ' save rec, delete it, count
37:      SaveDynasetRec
38:      DeleteDynasetRec
39:      Me.Print ">After Dynaset Delete"
40:      CountRecs rsDynaset, "Dynaset"
41:      CountRecs rsSnapshot, "Snapshot"
42:      CountRecs rsTable, "Table"
43:      Me.Print
44:      '
45:      ' restore rec and count
46:      RestoreDynasetRec
47:      Me.Print ">After Dynaset Restore"
48:      CountRecs rsDynaset, "Dynaset"
49:      CountRecs rsSnapshot, "Snapshot"
50:      CountRecs rsTable, "Table"
51:      Me.Print
52:      '
53: End Sub
54:
55: Public Sub OpenFiles()
56:      '
57:      ' open database and
58:      ' populate objects
59:      '
60:      Set db = DBEngine.OpenDatabase(strDBName)
61:      '
```

2

continues

Listing 2.17   CONTINUED

```
62:        With db
63:            Set rsDynaset = .OpenRecordset(strRSName, dbOpenDynaset)
64:            Set rsSnapshot = .OpenRecordset(strRSName, dbOpenSnapshot)
65:            Set rsTable = .OpenRecordset(strRSName, dbOpenTable)
66:        End With
67:        '
68: End Sub
69:
70: Public Sub CountRecs(rsTemp As Recordset, strType As String)
71:        '
72:        ' count records in the object
73:        '
74:        Dim intCount As Integer
75:        '
76:        With rsTemp
77:            .MoveFirst
78:            .MoveLast
79:            intCount = .RecordCount
80:        End With
81:        '
82:        Me.Print vbTab, "Total for " & strType & ":"; intCount
83:        '
84: End Sub
85:
86: Public Sub SaveDynasetRec()
87:        '
88:        ' save a single record
89:        '
90:        With rsDynaset
91:            .MoveFirst
92:            varRecords = .GetRows(1)
93:        End With
94:        '
95: End Sub
96:
97: Public Sub DeleteDynasetRec()
98:        '
99:        ' remove first record in the collection
100:        '
101:        With rsDynaset
102:            .MoveFirst
103:            .Delete
104:        End With
105:        '
106: End Sub
107:
108: Public Sub RestoreDynasetRec()
109:        '
```

```
110:        ' add saved rec back in
111:        '
112:        Dim intLoop As Integer
113:        '
114:        With rsDynaset
115:            .AddNew
116:            For intLoop = 0 To UBound(varRecords, 1)
117:                .Fields(intLoop).Value = varRecords(intLoop, 0)
118:            Next
119:            .Update
120:        End With
121:        '
122: End Sub
```

2

Although there is not a lot of new code in this example, there are a few things worth pointing out. First, you see extensive use of the `With..End With` construct in Listing 2.14. This construct was introduced in Visual Basic 4.0 and is very useful when working with Visual Basic objects. Using the `With..End With` construct is faster than naming the same objects several times in code.

Also, notice the use of the `GetRows` method of the `Recordset`. This method fills a variant data variable with the contents of one or more records from the `Recordset`. This is a very efficient way to read several records into memory without using the slower `For..Next` loops.

When you run the `SNAPSHOTS.VBP` program, you see three record count reports. The first report occurs right after the data objects are created. The second count report occurs after a record has been removed from the Dynaset object. The last count report occurs after the record has been restored to the Dynaset object. Note that both the Table and the Dynaset objects reflect the changes in the data table, but the Snapshot does not (see Figure 2.10).

FIGURE 2.10

Comparing Dynasets, Snapshots, and Tables.

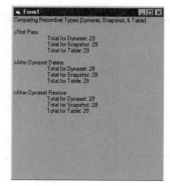

When to Use the Snapshot Data Object

Visual Basic Snapshot-type Recordset objects work best if you have a small set of data that you need to access frequently. For example, if you have a list of valid input values for a particular field stored in a control table, you can load these valid values into a Snapshot and refer to that dataset each time you need to verify user input.

If the dataset is not too large, Snapshots are very good for use in creating calculated reports or graphic displays. It is usually a good idea to create a static dataset for use in calculating reports. This way, any changes in the dataset that might occur in a multiuser environment from the time you start the report to the time you end it will not confuse any calculations done by the report.

 Tip

> It's a good idea to keep your Snapshots to less than 64KB in size. You can estimate the eventual size of your Snapshots by calculating the number of bytes in an average data record and estimating the average number ofrecords you can expect in your Snapshot. You can refer to Day 1 for information on the size of Visual Basic data types.

The Data Control Database Data Object

The Database object of a Visual Basic data control gives you access to all the properties and methods associated with the database underlying the data control. By using the related data objects, TableDefs, Fields, and Indexes, you can get information about all the tables in the database, all the indexes in the database, and all the fields in each table. Also, you can get additional information about the field types and index parameters.

The Data Control Database data object is most useful when you are developing generic database routines. Because the Database object gives you access to all the field names and properties, you can use this information to write generic data table display and update routines instead of having to write routines that have hard-coded field names and data types. TableDefs objects are covered in more detail on Day 8. For now, though, let's write a short routine that lists all the tables, fields, and indexes in the BOOKS6.MDB database.

First, start a new Standard EXE project in Visual Basic and load the Microsoft Jet DAO 3.51 Object Library. Use the information in Table 2.4 to set up the form.

TABLE 2.4   CONTROLS FOR THE Database.vbp PROJECT

Control	Property	Setting
VB.Form	Name	frmDatabase
	Caption	"Database Object Demo"
	ClientHeight	4605
	ClientLeft	60
	ClientTop	345
	ClientWidth	6090
	StartUpPosition	3 'Windows Default
VB.TextBox	Name	Text1
	Height	1275
	Left	420
	MultiLine	-1 'True
	ScrollBars	2 'Vertical
	Top	540
	Width	2355
VB.Data	Name	Data1
	Exclusive	0 'False
	Height	345
	Left	0
	Options	0
	ReadOnly	0 'False
	RecordsetType	1 'Dynaset
	Top	4260
	Width	6090

Be sure to set the Visible property of the data control to false. It is there only to give you access to the various database properties that you print on the form itself. You won't need to see it or use it in this example. Also, don't worry about the placement of the text box. You'll add some code that will resize the box at runtime.

First, add the code from Listing 2.18 to the Form_Resize event. This will resize the text box to always fill the entire form during runtime.

LISTING 2.18 RESIZING THE TEXT BOX AT RUNTIME

```
 1: Private Sub Form_Resize()
 2:      '
 3:      With Me.Text1
 4:          .Left = 0
 5:          .Top = 0
 6:          .Width = Me.ScaleWidth
 7:          .Height = Me.ScaleHeight
 8:      End With
 9:      '
10: End Sub
```

Now enter the program code in Listing 2.19 in the Form_Activate event. This is the code that does all the "real work."

LISTING 2.19 LISTING DATABASE OBJECTS

```
 1: Private Sub Form_Activate()
 2:      '
 3:      ' show high-level database objects
 4:      '
 5:      Dim tb As TableDef
 6:      Dim fl As Field
 7:      Dim ix As Index
 8:      '
 9:      Data1.DatabaseName = App.Path & "\..\..\data\books6.mdb"
10:      Data1.Refresh
11:      '
12:      With Me.Text1
13:          .Text = "Table Info:" & vbCrLf
14:          For Each tb In Data1.Database.TableDefs
15:              .Text = .Text & vbTab & tb.Name & vbCrLf
16:              For Each fl In tb.Fields
17:                  .Text = .Text & vbTab & vbTab & fl.Name & vbCrLf
18:              Next
19:          Next
20:          '
21:          On Error Resume Next ' in case there's no index
22:          .Text = .Text & vbCrLf & "Index Info:" & vbCrLf
23:          For Each tb In Data1.Database.TableDefs
24:              .Text = .Text & vbTab & tb.Name & vbCrLf
25:              For Each ix In tb.Indexes
26:                  .Text = .Text & vbTab & vbTab & ix.Name & " "
27:                  .Text = .Text & "[" & ix.Fields & "]" & vbCrLf
28:              Next
29:          Next
30:      End With
31:      '
32: End Sub
```

After you enter the code, save the form as DATABASE.FRM and the project as DATABASE.VBP, and then run the program. You see a list on the screen showing all the high-level objects in the connected database, including the names of the base tables and their fields along with the names of the indexes and the index field names. Your screen should look something like the one in Figure 2.11.

FIGURE 2.11

Viewing database object information.

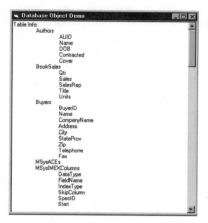

2

> **Note**
>
> You may see several tables that start with MSYS. These are system tables used by the Microsoft Jet database engine and are not used for data storage or retrieval. You should also notice that each Index object consists of a unique name and one or more fields (displayed in brackets). You do not see a data table associated with the index because the Microsoft Jet engine does not store that information in a manner you can easily see (it's actually in one of those MSYS tables!)

Summary

In today's lesson, you learned that there are three main types of Visual Basic Recordset data objects:

- Table-type objects are used when you have a large dataset and need to do frequent searches to locate a single record. You can use the Visual Basic Seek method and use Visual Basic Indexes with the Table object.

- Dynaset-type objects are used in most cases when you need read and write access to datasets. The Dynaset uses little workstation memory and enables you to create virtual tables by combining fields from different tables in the same database. The Dynaset is the only data object that enables you to read and write to ODBC data sources.

- Snapshot-type objects are used when you need fast read-only access to datasets. Snapshot objects are stored in workstation memory, so they should be kept small. Snapshots are good for storing validation lists at the workstation or for small reports.

You also learned about another data object: the Database object. You can use the Database object to get a list of tables in the database, a list of indexes associated with the tables, and a list of fields in each of the tables.

Quiz

1. Are Visual Basic Database objects dataset-oriented or record-oriented?

2. What is the most common Visual Basic data object?

3. Do Dynasets use a relatively large amount or small amount of workstation RAM? Why?

4. What are the weaknesses of using a Dynaset object?

5. What are the main advantages of using the Table data object?

6. Do you use the `Refresh` method with the Table data object?

7. What is the difference between a Snapshot and a Dynaset data object?

8. Whch data object do you use to extract table and field names from a database definition?

Exercises

1. You need to open a connection to a Microsoft Access database for read and write capability. Assume it is a very large table and that you have only limited memory resources on your client workstations. Which data object type should you use (Snapshot, Dynaset, Table)? Write the code to open the appropriate data object type on an existing Access database. Assume that the database name is `C:\DATA\ACCTPAY.MDB`, with your desired table named Vendors.

2. Given the same data source as in Exercise 1, write the code to open a data object to be used in the generation of a report. In this example, you need only the

records where the column OverDueAmount is greater than $1000. (Assume the RAM memory is adequate on the machine running the program.)

3. Given the same data source as in Exercise 1, write the code that opens the data object so that you can access the data often in a multiuser environment to search for single records.

2

DAY 3

Creating Data Entry Forms with Bound Controls

Today's lesson is a review of all the bound data controls that are shipped with Visual Basic Professional. You'll review the special properties, events, and methods that relate to database programming, and you'll create short examples to illustrate how each of the bound controls can be used in your database programs.

You'll also review general rules for designing quality forms for Windows programs, covering alignment, font selection, control placement and spacing, and color choices.

Finally, you'll create a short project that establishes customizable color schemes for your application. This project will show you how to use the Windows Control Panel Color applet to set colors for your applications.

What Are Bound Data Controls?

Before you get into the details of listing the properties, events, and methods of Visual Basic bound data controls, let's review what a bound control actually is and why it's so useful.

NEW TERM   *Bound data controls* are the same as any other Visual Basic control objects, except that they have been given additional properties, events, and methods that enable you to "bind" them directly to one or more data tables. This binding makes it easy to create data-aware input and display objects that you can use to perform data input and display with very little program code.

Using bound controls simplifies your programming chores a great deal. Most bound controls automatically handle the various chores related to processing data entry and display for databases. The bound controls make it easy to write Visual Basic programs that handle all (or nearly all) of the following processes:

- Loading data from the database into a Visual Basic data object
- Selecting the data record(s) requested by the user
- Loading form controls with values in the requested record(s)
- Trapping simple user input errors
- Enforcing database integrity rules
- Updating the data object with modified data from the form controls

You do not need to use bound data controls in your database programs. In fact, as you will see in the lessons next week, there are times when it is better to use unbound controls in your programs. However, when you use unbound controls, you need to take responsibility for handling all the processes outlined in the preceding list. Although this is not an insurmountable task, it's a good idea to take advantage of the power of bound data controls whenever possible. Using the prebuilt and tested bound controls helps you create solid, functional database entry forms in a short period of time.

Using the Data Control

The Visual Basic data control is the control used to gain access to database tables. The data control enables you to establish a link to a single Dynaset data object in a database. You can have more than one data control in your program and more than one data control on a single form.

Like all Visual Basic controls, there are properties, events, and methods associated with the data control. Because this book is about databases, this lesson will focus on the properties, events, and methods that are important in dealing with database activity. In the process, you will build a small program that illustrates these database-related aspects of the Visual Basic data control.

Data Control Properties

There are five data control properties that deserve special attention:

- DatabaseName
- Exclusive
- Options
- ReadOnly
- RecordSource

There is a sixth data control property that is used only for data access: the Connect property. The Connect property is used when you are accessing non-Microsoft Access databases. You'll learn more about using the Connect property in the lesson on Day 8, "Visual Basic and the DAO Jet Database Engine."

Setting DatabaseName and RecordSource Properties

The DatabaseName and RecordSource properties were discussed on Day 2, "Visual Basic Database Access Objects." The DatabaseName property contains the name of the database you want to access. In Microsoft Access databases, this is the complete drive, path, and filename of the Microsoft Access database file. For example, to connect to the BOOKS6.MDB Microsoft Access database located in the C:\DATA directory, you set the DatabaseName property to C:\DATA\BOOKS6.MDB. You can do this through the Property box at design-time or through Visual Basic code at runtime.

Let's start a project to illustrate the data control properties, events, and methods. Load Visual Basic and start a new project. Drop a data control on a blank form. For this project, accept the default data control name property of Data1.

On Day 2, you set the DatabaseName and RecordSource properties at design-time using the Visual Basic properties window. Visual Basic enables you to set most control properties at runtime (that is, while the program is running). The advantage of setting properties at runtime is that you can build programs that enable users to decide what database and data table they want to access. For this project, you set these properties at runtime using Visual Basic code.

NEW TERM   *Design-time* refers to the time when you are designing your Visual Basic application. *Runtime* refers to the time when your finished application is running.

You set these data control values in a separate procedure called OpenDB. To create a new procedure in Visual Basic, double-click anywhere on the form in order to bring up a Visual Basic code window. Now select Add Procedure from the Visual Basic Tools menu. You see a dialog box that asks you for the name of the procedure (see Figure 3.1).

FIGURE 3.1

Creating a new Visual Basic procedure.

Enter OpenDB. Make sure the radio button for Sub is selected and then click OK. You now see the new Visual Basic procedure header and footer, ready for you to enter your program code.

The following procedure sets the DatabaseName property of the data control on the current form. Please note where I have entered the location of the BOOKS6.MDB file. You may need to substitute a different path if you installed the database elsewhere on your system.

Note

If you install your data files in the same directory as your program files, you can use the App.Path command to identify the data file location. App.Path can be used as part of the database name to identify the database location without having to know the name of the directory in which it is stored. The Path property of the App object returns the drive and directory in which the project has been stored.

This methodology is useful when building applications that will be distributed across an organization or to multiple organizations. App.Path enables you to utilize setup programs that enable the user to select the directory in which to install the program files. Your data files will be found as long as they are stored with the program files.

As an illustration, if you had installed your BOOKS6.MDB file in the same directory as you saved the current project, you could substitute

```
cDBName = App.Path + "\books6.mdb"
```
for the line:
```
cDBName = "c:\tysdbvb6\source\data\books6.mdb"
```

This would enable you to move and store your programs in any directory without having to worry about changing the pointer to your database.

Place the following code in the general declarations section of your form:

```
1: Public Sub OpenDB()
2: Dim cDBName As String      ' declare a string variable
3: '
4: cDBName = "c:\tysdbvb6\source\data\books6.mdb" ' point to database
5: '
6: Data1.DatabaseName = cDBName ' set database property
7: '
8: Data1.Refresh ' update data control properties
9: End Sub
```

Tip

When you enter Visual Basic program code, Visual Basic looks for typing errors automatically. Each time you press the Enter key, Visual Basic scans the line, capitalizes Visual Basic reserved words (if everything has been typed correctly), adds spaces between the equal signs, and so on. When you enter code, don't try to capitalize or space properly; let Visual Basic do it for you. That way, if you finish a line and press the Enter key and then notice that Visual Basic has not "edited" for you, you'll know that there is probably something on that line that Visual Basic didn't understand. Now you'll catch your typing errors as you code!

3

The last line in the procedure forces the data control to update all the new properties that have been set in the routine. Any time you use Visual Basic code to change data control properties, you must invoke the Refresh method to update the data control. This is just one of the data control methods. Other data control methods are discussed throughout today's lesson.

Tip

Notice that in the code example you declare a variable, set the variable to a value, and then set the data control property with the variable. This could all be done in a single line of code. Here's an example:

```
Data1.DatabaseName= C:\TYSDBVB6\SOURCE\DATA\BOOKS6.MDB"
```

By declaring variables and using those variables to set properties, you create a program that is easier to understand and modify in the future.

When you set the DatabaseName property, you are telling Visual Basic the database you are using. However, at this point, Visual Basic does not know what data table you want to use with the data control. Use the RecordSource property to indicate the data table you want to access.

Now, modify the OpenDB procedure you created earlier by adding code that sets the RecordSource property of the data control to access the Authors data table. Be sure to declare a variable, initialize it to the correct table, and then use the variable to set the data control property. When you are finished, your procedure should look like the one shown in the following code example:

```
 1: Public Sub OpenDB()
 2: Dim cDBName As String     ' declare a string variable
 3: Dim cTblName As String    ' declare a string variable
 4: '
 5: cDBName = "c:\tysdbvb6\source\data\books6.mdb" ' point to database
 6: cTblName = "Authors" ' point to authors table
 7: '
 8: Data1.DatabaseName = cDBName ' set database property
 9: Data1.RecordSource = cTblName ' set recordsource property
10: '
11: Data1.Refresh ' update data control properties
12: End Sub
```

Before you get too far into the project, you should save your work. Save the form as BNDCTRL1.FRM and the project as BNDCTRL.VBP.

Setting the ReadOnly and Exclusive Properties

There are two more data control properties that you need to set in this example: ReadOnly and Exclusive. The ReadOnly and Exclusive properties are Boolean (True/False) properties that you can use to limit access to the database. When you set the Exclusive property to True, you are opening the database for your use only. In other words, no one else can open the database (or any of the tables in the database) while you have it open. This is handy when you want to perform major updates or changes to the database and do not want anyone else in the file at the same time.

For the example, open the database for exclusive use. Modify the OpenDB procedure so that it sets the Exclusive property to True. Your code should look like the following:

```
 1: Public Sub OpenDB()
 2: Dim cDBName As String     ' declare a string variable
 3: Dim cTblName As String    ' declare a string variable
 4: Dim bExclusive As Boolean ' declare true/false var
 5: '
 6: cDBName = "c:\tysdbvb6\source\data\books6.mdb" ' point to database
 7: cTblName = "Authors" ' point to authors table
 8: bExclusive = True ' set to exclusive open
 9: '
10: Data1.DatabaseName = cDBName ' set database property
11: Data1.RecordSource = cTblName ' set recordsource property
12: Data1.Exclusive = bExclusive
13: '
14: Data1.Refresh ' update data control properties
15: End Sub
```

Caution

> When you open the database with Exclusive set to True, no other programs that access the database can be run without errors until you close the database. Use the Exclusive property sparingly!

The ReadOnly property opens the database with read rights only. You will not be allowed to make any changes, additions, or deletions in any table while you have the database open in read-only mode. This is handy when you are using the data for creating a report or for display purposes only. (Read-only mode is faster, too.)

Note

> Don't confuse the Exclusive property and the ReadOnly property. They are not the same! The Exclusive property makes sure that no one else can access the database while you have it open. The ReadOnly property makes sure that your program cannot update the database while you have it open. The Exclusive property affects everyone who wants to access the database. The ReadOnly property affects only the person running your program

3

Again, for this example, you open the file as read-only. Make changes to the OpenDB procedure to include variables that set the ReadOnly property to True. When you are done, your code should look something like the following:

```
 1: Public Sub OpenDB()
 2: Dim cDBName As String     ' declare a string variable
 3: Dim cTblName As String    ' declare a string variable
 4: Dim bExclusive As Boolean ' declare true/false var
 5: Dim bReadOnly As Boolean  ' declare true/false var
 6:
 7: cDBName = "c:\tysdbvb6\source\data\books6.mdb" ' point to database
 8: cTblName = "Authors" ' point to authors table
 9: bExclusive = True ' set to exclusive open
10: bReadOnly = True ' set to read only
11: '
12: Data1.DatabaseName = cDBName ' set database property
13: Data1.RecordSource = cTblName ' set recordsource property
14: Data1.Exclusive = bExclusive
15: Data1.ReadOnly = bReadOnly
16: '
17: Data1.Refresh ' update data control properties
18: End Sub
```

Save your work before entering more Visual Basic code.

Setting the Options Property

All the properties you have set in the previous code relate to the database that Visual Basic is accessing. The Options property of the Visual Basic data control enables you to establish the properties of the Dynaset opened in the RecordSource property of the data control. There are several options that can be set in the Options property of the data control. In today's lesson, you learn about the three most commonly used options.

Here are the three Options values for the data control that is covered today:

- dbDenyWrite
- dbReadOnly
- dbAppendOnly

These three options are actually Visual Basic constants that are predefined in the language. They are like Visual Basic variables, except that they have a single, set value that cannot be changed. Table 3.1 shows the three constants and their numeric values.

TABLE 3.1 DYNASET OPTION VALUES

Dynaset Option	Numeric Value
dbDenyWrite	1
dbReadOnly	4
dbAppendOnly	8

Setting the dbDenyWrite option prevents other users from changing the data in the Dynaset while you have it open (similar to the Exclusive database property). The dbReadOnly option prevents you from changing the data in the Dynaset (similar to the ReadOnly database property). The dbAppendOnly option enables you to add new data to the Dynaset but does not let you modify or delete existing records.

Setting the dbReadOnly option speeds processing of the Dynaset and is handy for generating displays or reports. The dbDenyWrite option is useful when you want to make major changes to the Dynaset and want to prevent other users from accessing the records in the Dynaset until you are done making your changes. Using the dbAppendOnly option enables you to create data entry routines that limit user rights to adding records without deleting or modifying existing ones.

Now you add the code that sets the Options property of the data control. Notice that you do not have a property for each of the three options. How do you set them individually? You do this by adding up the constants and placing the result in the Options property of the data control.

For example, if you want to open the Dynaset for only appending new records, set the Options property of the data control to dbAppendOnly. If you want to open the Dynaset to deny everyone the right to update the database and to allow read-only access for the current user, set the Options property to dbDenyWrite + dbReadOnly.

For now, set the data control options to DenyWrite and ReadOnly. When you are done, your procedure should look like this:

```
 1: Public Sub OpenDB()
 2: Dim cDBName As String     ' declare a string variable
 3: Dim cTblName As String    ' declare a string variable
 4: Dim bExclusive As Boolean ' declare true/false var
 5: Dim bReadOnly As Boolean  ' declare true/false var
 6: '
 7: cDBName = "c:\tysdbvb6\source\data\books6.mdb" ' point to database
 8: cTblName = "Authors" ' point to authors table
 9: bExclusive = True ' set to exclusive open
10: bReadOnly = True ' set to read only
11: '
12: Data1.DatabaseName = cDBName ' set database property
13: Data1.RecordSource = cTblName ' set recordsource property
14: Data1.Exclusive = bExclusive
15: Data1.Options = dbDenyWrite + dbReadOnly
16: Data1.ReadOnly = bReadOnly
17: '
18: Data1.Refresh ' update data control properties
19: End Sub
```

You have now completed the procedure for opening the BOOKS6.MDB database and creating a Dynaset from the Authors table. The database and the Dynaset will be opened exclusively for read-only access. Only one thing is missing: You must first make sure the OpenDB procedure is executed! Place the following code line in the Form_Load procedure:

```
Private Sub Form_Load ()
OpenDB ' open the database, set dynaset
End Sub
```

Now save the project and run the program. If you get an error report, review the code examples and then make the necessary changes before going on to the next section, where you add a few more routines that illustrate how data control methods work.

Data Control Methods

Most Visual Basic controls have associated methods. Each method can be thought of as a function or process that you can tell the program to run. The Visual Basic data control has several methods, but only three are database-related. Here's a list of them:

- `Refresh`
- `UpdateControls`
- `UpdateRecord`

You have used the `Refresh` method in today's example already. This method is used any time you change any of the properties of the data control. Using the `Refresh` method updates the data control and forces it to rebuild the Dynaset. This refresh updates not only the behaviors and properties of the Dynaset but also the records in the set. If records are added to the table by another user after your program has created its Dynaset, invoking the `Refresh` method makes sure that your Dynaset contains the most recent records.

The `UpdateControls` method is used to update any bound input controls. Invoking the `UpdateControls` method is the same as reading the current record and putting the values in the fields of the data table into the input controls on a form. This happens automatically each time you press the arrow buttons on the data control. But you can force the update to occur any time during the data entry process. It's especially handy if you want to undo user changes to a data record.

Now, add a single field to the form and test the `UpdateControls` method. Add a text box control to the form and set the `DataSource` property to `Data1`. You'll set the `DataField` property using Visual Basic code in a moment; leave it blank for now. Refer to Figure 3.2 for positioning and sizing the control.

FIGURE 3.2

Adding the bound text box control.

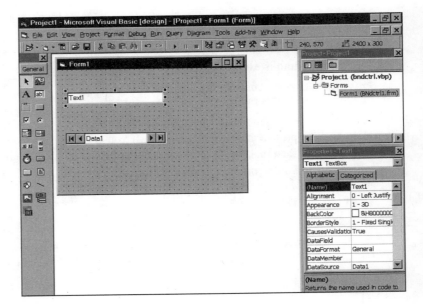

Now add the following new procedure (BindControls) to your form. Remember, to insert a procedure you need to use the Add Procedure command from the Tools menu after you have double-clicked the form. This new procedure links the text box to the field in the Dynaset using the DataField property of the text box:

```
Public Sub BindControls()
Dim cField1 As String
'
cField1 = "Name"
'
Text1.DataField = cField1
End Sub
```

Now, add the BindControls procedure to the Form_Load event to make sure it gets called when the program starts. Your Form_Load event should look like this:

```
Private Sub Form_Load ()
OpenDB ' open the database, set dynaset
BindControls ' link controls to data fields
End Sub
```

You need to add a command button to the form to activate the UpdateControls method. Place a single command button on the form and set its Name property to cmdRestore and its caption to &Restore. Also, add the following code line behind the cmdRestore_Click event:

```
Private Sub cmdRestore_Click()
data1.UpdateControls ' restore textbox values
End Sub
```

Your form should look like the one shown in Figure 3.3.

Now save and run the project. When the first record comes up, edit the field. Change the name or add additional information to the field. Before you click an arrow button, press the Restore button. You'll see that the data in the text box reverts to the value initially read into it when you first started the program.

Now, add a button that invokes the UpdateRecord method. The UpdateRecord method tells Visual Basic to save the values of the bound input controls (the text box in this project) to the Dynaset. Refer to Figure 3.4 for sizing and positioning the button.

3

FIGURE **3.3**

*Adding the Restore
button to the form.*

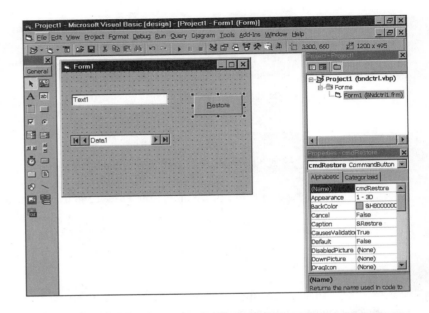

FIGURE **3.4**

*Adding the Update
button to the form.*

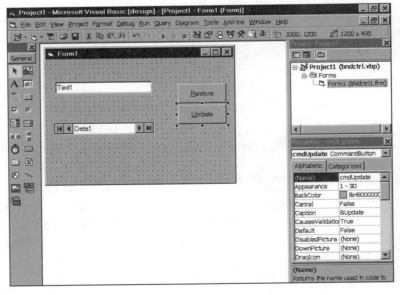

Using the UpdateRecord method updates the Dynaset without moving the record pointer.
Now, add a command button to the form, set its Name property to cmdUpdate and its
Caption property to &Update, and then place the following code line behind the button in
the cmdUpdate_Click event:

```
Private Sub cmdUpdate_Click()
data1.UpdateRecord 'write controls to dynaset
End Sub
```

 Note

> It is important to remember the difference between the UpdateControls method and the UpdateRecord method. The UpdateControls method reads from the data object and writes to the form controls. It updates the controls. The UpdateRecord method reads from the form controls and writes to the data object. It updates the record.

Save and run the project again. This time, after you edit the text box, click the Update button. Now, move the record pointer forward to the next record and then back to the record you edited. What do you see? The record was not updated! Remember, in the OpenDB procedure you set the ReadOnly property of the database to True and turned on the ReadOnly value of the Options property. Now modify the OpenDB procedure and change the ReadOnly property to False and drop the dbReadOnly and dbDenyWrite constants from the Options property by setting the Options property to 0.

When you rerun the program, you can now edit the text box, restore the old value with the Restore button, or save the new value with the Update button. You can also save the new value by moving the record pointer.

This last behavior of the data control can cause some problems. What if you changed a field and didn't want to save the changes, but instead of clicking the Restore button, you moved to the next record? You would change the database and never know it! In the next section, you use one of the data control's events to help you avoid just such a situation.

Data Control Events

All Microsoft Windows programs contain events. These events occur each time the computer senses that a user clicks a button or passes the mouse over an object on the form, or when any other process occurs. When an event takes place, the Windows operating system sends a message that tells all processes currently running that something has happened. Windows programs can then "listen" for messages and act, based on their programming code, when the right message comes along.

In Visual Basic, you can create program code that executes each time a specific event occurs. There are three data control events that relate to database functions:

- Reposition
- Validate
- Error

The Reposition event occurs each time the data control moves to a new position in the Dynaset. The Validate event occurs each time a data control leaves the current record. The Error event occurs each time a database error occurs when the arrow buttons on the data control are used to move the record pointer. Visual Basic automatically creates procedure headers and footers for all the events associated with a control. When you place a data control on your form, Visual Basic creates the procedures Data1_Reposition, Data1_Validate, and Data1_Error.

Now, add some code to the project that will tell you when an event occurs. First, you need to get a message box to pop up each time you reposition the record pointer using the arrow buttons on the data control. To do this, place the following code in the Data1_Reposition event:

```
Private Sub Data1_Reposition()
MsgBox "Repositioning the pointer..."
End Sub
```

Next, to get a message box to pop up each time you leave a record using the data control's arrow buttons, place the following code in the Data1_Validate event:

```
Private Sub Data1_Validate(Action As Integer, Save As Integer)
MsgBox "Validating Data..."
End Sub
```

Now save and run the project. Notice that the message from the Reposition event is the first thing you see after the program begins. This is because the pointer is positioned on the first record in the Dynaset when the Dynaset is first created. (See Figure 3.5.)

FIGURE 3.5

The Reposition
event at the start
of the program.

After you click the OK button in the message box, you see the Visual Basic form with the data control. Click one of the arrow buttons. You'll see that the message from the Validate event pops up. This message is sent before Visual Basic leaves the current record. (See Figure 3.6.)

FIGURE 3.6

The Validate
event message.

After you click the OK button in the message box, you see the message from the `Reposition` event again. This is the event message sent when Visual Basic reads the next record.

You might have noticed that the header for the `Validate` event contains two parameters: `Action` and `Save`. These two parameters can be used to learn more about what action is currently being attempted on the data control and can give you control over whether the user should be allowed to save the new data to the Dynaset. These parameters are set by Visual Basic while the program is running. You can read the values in these parameters at any time during the program. For now, you'll explore the `Action` parameter. The next set of code adds a routine to the `Validate` step that pops up a message box each time the arrow buttons of a data control are clicked.

Just like the `Options` property constants, Visual Basic also provides a set of predefined constants for all the possible `Action` values reported in the `Validate` event. Although these constants are handy, they are not very useful to users of your programs. The following code example shows you how to translate those constants into a friendly message using a string array. Add the following line to the general declarations section of the form:

```
Option Explicit
Dim VldMsg(4) As String ' declare message array
```

Now add the following procedure, which loads a set of messages into the array you declared previously. These messages are displayed each time the corresponding action occurs in the `Validate` event. Notice that you are using the predefined Visual Basic constants:

```
Public Sub MakeVldMsgArray()
VldMsg(vbDataActionMoveFirst) = "MoveFirst"
VldMsg(vbDataActionMovePrevious) = "MovePrevious"
VldMsg(vbDataActionMoveNext) = "MoveNext"
VldMsg(vbDataActionMoveLast) = "MoveLast"
End Sub
```

Update the `Form_Load` event to call the `MakeVldMsgArray` procedure. You can see that `MakeVldMsgArray` has been added at the start of the event. Here's the code:

```
Private Sub Form_Load()
MakeVldMsgArray ' create message array
OpenDB ' open the database, set dynaset
BindControls ' link controls to data fields
End Sub
```

Now you need to add the one bit of code that will be executed each time the `Validate` event occurs. This code displays a simple message each time you click the arrow buttons of the data control. The actual message is determined by the `Action` value that Visual

Basic passes to the Validate event. The Action value is, of course, determined by the arrow button on the data control that you click while the program is running.

Now you have to replace the Validating data message that you entered in the previous example. Here's the new code:

```
Private Sub Data1_Validate(Action As Integer, Save As Integer)
MsgBox VldMsg(Action) ' message based on user action
End Sub
```

Save and run the program to see a message box that tells you what you probably already know! There are several other actions that can occur during the Validate event. You'll explore these actions on Day 4, "Input Validation."

For the rest of the project, comment out the Validate event code and the Reposition event code. Now you'll concentrate on adding additional Visual Basic bound controls to the project.

Adding the Bound Text Control and the Bound Label Control

There are no database-related methods or events associated with the bound text control or bound label control. And there are only two properties of the bound text control and the bound label control that are database-related:

- DataSource
- DataField

The DataSource property is the name of the data control that maintains the link between the data table and the text or label control. The DataField property identifies the actual field in the data control Dynaset to which the text box or label control is bound. You cannot set the DataSource property at runtime—it's a design-time–only property. You can, however, set the DataField property at either runtime or design-time.

Bound text controls give you the ability to add input fields to your data forms that automatically link to the Dynaset defined in the data control. Bound label controls are handy when you want to display information without letting users update it. You've already added a bound text control to the project, so now add a bound label control, too.

You add the label control to display the AuID (the author ID) field of the Authors table. This gives users the chance to see the author ID but not update it. Add a label control to the form and set its DataSource property to Data1. Also, set the BorderStyle property to Fixed Single to make it look similar to a text box control. Refer to Figure 3.7 for positioning and placement.

FIGURE 3.7

*Adding the bound
label control.*

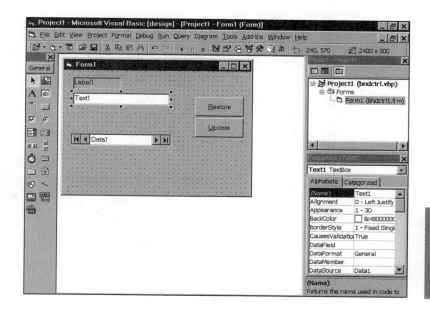

Now update the `BindControls` procedure to set the `DataField` property of the label control. Your code should look like this:

```
Public Sub BindControls ()
Dim cField1 As String
Dim cField2 As String
'
cField1 = "Name"
cField2 = "AuID"
'
Text1.DataField = cField1
Label1.DataField = cField2
End Sub
```

Now save and run the project. You see that the label control contains the values stored in the AuID field of the Dynaset. As you move through the Dynaset using the arrow buttons, the label control is updated just as the text control is updated.

Adding the Bound Check Box Control

The bound check box control is basically the same as the text control. It has no special database-related events or methods and has the same two database-related properties: `DataSource` and `DataField`. The difference between the text box control and the check box control is in how the data is displayed on the form and saved in the Dynaset.

Check boxes are linked to Boolean data type fields. Remember that these fields can hold only -1 or 0. Check boxes do not display -1 or 0. They display an empty box (0) or a checked box (-1). By clicking the display of the check box, you can actually update the Boolean value of the bound Dynaset field.

Using Figure 3.8 as a guide, add a check box control to the form. Set its `DataSource` property to `Data1` and its `Caption` property to `Under Contract`. You do not need to set the `DataField` property at this time. This will be done by modifying the `BindControls` procedure.

FIGURE 3.8

Adding the bound check box control.

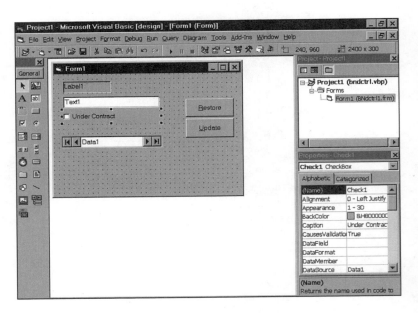

Now, update the `BindControls` procedure to link the check box control to the Contracted field in the Authors table. When you are done, your `BindControls` procedure should look like this:

```
Public Sub BindControls ()
Dim cField1 As String
Dim cField2 As String
Dim cField3 As String
'
cField1 = "Name"
cField2 = "AuID"
cField3 = "Contracted"
'
Text1.DataField = cField1
Label1.DataField = cField2
Check1.DataField = cField3
End Sub
```

Save and run the project. You will see that some check boxes are turned on and some are turned off. You now have a bound check box control!

Adding the Bound OLE Control

The Visual Basic OLE control has no database-related events or methods and only two database-related properties:

- DataSource
- DataField

Like the bound check box control, the OLE control has unique behaviors regarding displaying bound data. The OLE control is used to display OLE objects that are stored in an MDB file by Microsoft Access. This control cannot be used to display binary pictures saved directly to an MDB file by an application other than Access.

Now, let's add an OLE control to the form and bind it to a field in the Authors table. Drop an OLE control on the form and select the Cancel button in the Insert Object dialog box when you are prompted for the Object Type. Now, set the OLE control's DataSource property to Data1, and its SizeMode property to 1 - Stretch. Refer to Figure 3.9 for control sizing and placement. You will bind this control to the Cover field with Visual Basic code in the following section, so leave the DataField property empty.

FIGURE 3.9

Adding the bound OLE control.

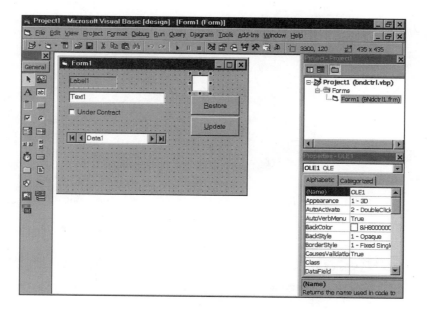

After you add the control to the form, update the `BindControls` procedure to bind the OLE control to the Cover field in the Authors table. When you're done, the procedure should look like this:

```
Public Sub BindControls ()
Dim cField1 As String
Dim cField2 As String
Dim cField3 As String
Dim cField4 As String
'
cField1 = "Name"
cField2 = "AuID"
cField3 = "Contracted"
cField4 = "Cover"
'
Text1.DataField = cField1
Label1.DataField = cField2
Check1.DataField = cField3
OLE1.DataField = cField4
End Sub
```

Save and run the project. You now see icons displayed in the top-right corner of the form (only for the first few records). These icons are stored in the binary data type field of the database. Note that you don't have to do any fancy "loading" of the picture into the OLE control, because the data control binding handles all that for you!

When you run your completed project, it should look like the one shown in Figure 3.10.

FIGURE 3.10

The completed project.

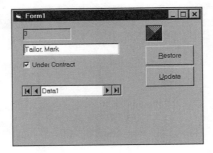

You have just completed a form that contains bound controls for handling text, numeric, Boolean, and OLE object data types stored in a database.

General Design Rules for Quality Forms

Now that you know how to use the Visual Basic data controls, it's time to learn about form design. Microsoft encourages developers to adhere to a general set of guidelines when designing the look and feel of their programs. In this project, you focus on the layout and design of quality forms. You will explore guidelines for the following aspects of form design:

- Control placement and spacing
- Label alignment
- Standard fonts
- Use of colors

The guidelines set here will be used throughout the remainder of the projects in this book.

Note

The style guidelines used in this book adhere to the look and feel of Microsoft Windows 95. Even if you are still using Windows 3.1 or Windows for Workgroups, we encourage you to adopt the Windows 95 layout standards.

Guidelines for Win95-Style Forms

There are a few general guidelines for developing Win95-style forms. The primary areas to consider are listed in Table 3.2. This table describes the standard measurements Microsoft recommends for form controls. It also contains recommended spacing for these controls. Refer to Figure 3.11 when reading this section. This figure shows an example of a data entry form that is built using the Windows 95 standards described in this section.

TABLE 3.2 CONTROL SPACING AND SIZING

Form Control	Size/Spacing
Control height	300 twips
Command button width	1,200 twips
Vertical spacing between controls	60 twips for related items 90 twips for unrelated items
Border widths (top, bottom, and side)	120 twips

FIGURE 3.11

A Win95-style input form.

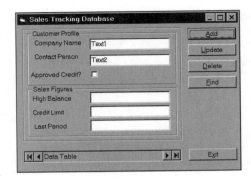

The Default Form Color

When you first start your form, set its BackColor property to light gray. Set the BackStyle property for labels to Transparent so that the background color can show through. For controls that do not have a BackStyle property (such as check box controls and radio button controls), set the BackColor property to light gray. The gray tones are easier to read in varied light. Using gray tones also reduces the chance that a user who experiences colorblindness will have difficulty with your input screens.

Using the Frame Control to Lift Input Areas off the Page

Use the Frame control to create a palette on which to place all display and input controls. Do not place buttons or the data control on the palette unless they act as part of the input dialog box (refer to Figure 3.11). Use only one palette per form. This makes it easy for the user to see that these controls are grouped together and that they deserve attention.

The Default Font

Use 8-point sans serif, regular (not bold) as the default font for all controls. If you want to use larger type in a title, for example, do so sparingly. Keep in mind that the default font is a proportionally spaced font. The space taken up by the letter *W* is greater than the space taken up by the letter *j*. This can lead to difficulty aligning numbers and columnar data. If you are doing a lot of displays and lists that include numeric amounts or other values that should line up, you should consider using a monospaced font such as Courier or FixedSys.

Input Areas and Display Areas

Use the color white to indicate areas where the user can perform input. If the field is for display purposes only, set it to gray (or to the form color if it is not gray). This means that all labels should appear in the same color as the form background (such as gray labels for gray forms). Also, make all display-only areas appear recessed on the palette. All text boxes that are active for input should appear white. This makes the action areas of your form stand out to the user. By keeping to the standard of white for input controls and gray (or form-colored) for display-only controls, users will not be so quick to attempt to edit a read-only control.

Using the Frame Controls to Group Related Information

When placing controls on a form, you should group related items together by enclosing them within a frame control. This frame control is sometimes called a group box because it boxes in a group of related controls. The frame caption is optional, but it is recommended. Using the frame control to group related items helps the user to quickly understand the relationship between fields on the form.

Alignment of Controls on the Form

All controls should be left-justified on the form. Show a clean line from top to bottom. This makes it easy to read down a list of fields quickly. Try to avoid multicolumn labels. If you must have more than one column of labels and input controls, be sure to left-align the second column, too.

Standard Sizing and Spacing for Controls

All controls should have standard height, spacing, and width where appropriate. Microsoft publishes its Win95 spacing standards in pixels or DLU (dialog units). Because Visual Basic controls work in twips instead of pixels, you need to know that one pixel equals 15 twips. Table 3.2 shows the recommended spacing and sizing for various controls on a form. Use these as a guide when creating your forms.

Notice that the height of all controls is the same. This makes it easy to align controls on a form regardless of their type (command buttons, text boxes, check boxes, and so on). The recommended spacing between controls seems quite wide when you first begin designing forms with these standards. However, you'll find that once you get the hang of these numbers, you'll be able to put together very clean-looking forms in a short amount of time.

Colors

Color standards for Win95 are quite simple—use gray! Although Microsoft recommends the gray tones for all forms, the color settings are some of the most commonly customized GUI properties in Windows programs. In this section, you learn two ways you can approach adding color to your applications: system colors and custom colors.

First, put together a simple form, using Table 3.3 and Figure 3.12 as a guide. Remember that you are building a Win95-style form! You won't spend time linking the input controls to a data control right now—just concentrate on building the form and adding color-switching capabilities.

Tip

Here are a few suggestions to help you build the form:

- Before you begin placing controls on the form, set the Grid Height and Grid Width properties on the General tab in the Tools|Options menu item to 60 each. This will give you a smaller grid to work with and will make it easier to place controls on the form.

- Place the Frame you will use for your palette on the form first. Then place all other controls directly on the palette. Do not place controls on the palette by double-clicking the tool in the tools window or by using the Copy command. Click the control icon once and then paint the control on the palette with the mouse. This sets the control as a "child" of the palette. Now, any time you move the palette, the controls will move along with it.

- Place the bound command buttons on the palette one after the other without setting any properties. When you want to set the command button properties, click one of the command buttons and then hold the Shift key while you click each of the other three. Now you can use the properties window to set values for all four of the controls at once. Set the command button's FontBold, Height, and Width properties this way to save time.

- You can easily set border widths if you remember that the grid dots appear every 60 twips on the form. All border widths should be set at 120 twips. This Microsoft standard makes it easy to distinguish separate controls and keeps a nice border around the form and around palettes and frames. Because border widths should be set at 120 twips, make sure that you can see two grid dots between the edge of the form and the edge of any other control (panel, command button, and so on).

- Remember that controls should be separated from each other by at least 90 twips. The value of 90 twips is an odd value when compared to the 60 twips between items and the 120 twips between borders. This odd spacing causes the user to break up the sections of the form a bit. This makes it easy for the user to see the separation between controls. When placing controls in a vertical line, use the Top property to determine where the control appears on the form. Because each control is 300 twips in height and the controls must be 90 twips apart, add 390 twips (300 + 90) to the Top value to determine where the next control should appear underneath.

FIGURE 3.12

The color switching project.

TABLE 3.3   CONTROLS FOR THE COLOR-SWITCHING PROJECT

Control	Property	Setting
Form	Caption	Color-Switching
	Name	frmColor
Frame	Caption	(set to blank)
	Name	Frame1
Text Box	Name	txtOneLine
	Font	MS Sans Serif, Regular, 8pointFalse
	Height	300
	Width	1800
Text Box	Name	txtDisplayOnly
	Font	MS Sans Serif, Regular, 8pointFalse
	Height	300
	Width	1800
	Caption	Display Only
Label	Caption	Prompt1:
	Font	MS Sans Serif, Regular, 8 point
	BackStyle	2 - Transparent
Label	Caption	Prompt2:
	Font	MS Sans Serif, Regular, 8 point
	BackStyle	2 - Transparent
Data Control	Caption	Data1
	Font	MS Sans Serif, Regular, 8 point
	Height	300
	Width	1800

continues

3

TABLE 3.3 CONTINUED

Control	Property	Setting
Command Button	Name	cmdDefault
	Caption	&Default
	Font	MS Sans Serif, Regular, 8 point
	Height	300
	Width	1200
Command Button	Name	cmdSystem
	Caption	&System
	Font	MS Sans Serif, Regular, 8 point
	Height	300
	Width	1200
Command Button	Name	cmdCustom
	Caption	&Custom
	Font	MS Sans Serif, Regular, 8 point
	Height	300
	Width	1200
Command Button	Name	cmdExit
	Caption	E&xit
	Font	MS Sans Serif, Regular, 8 point
	Height	300
	Width	1200

Save the form as COLORS.FRM and the project as COLORS.VBP. You have built a form that has three command buttons: Default, System, and Custom. You add code to the project that makes each of these buttons change the color scheme of the form. First, you add the code that sets the colors to the Win95 default: light gray.

Standard Colors

First, create a Visual Basic constant to represent the hex value for light gray, white, and black. Here's the code:

```
Option Explicit
'
' constant for colors
Const LIGHT_GRAY = &HC0C0C0
Const WHITE = &HFFFFFF
Const BLACK = &H0
```

Next, add a new procedure, SetColors, that sets the colors of the form. Because you'll be using this code to set more than one color scheme, add a parameter called nSet to the procedure header. You have only one set right now, but you'll add others soon. The following code sets the BackColor property of the form and data control to light gray:

```
Sub SetColors (nSet As Integer)
'
' set to default colors
If nSet = 0 Then
txtDisplayOnly.BackColor = LIGHT_GRAY
Frame1.BackColor = LIGHT_GRAY
frmColor.BackColor = LIGHT_GRAY
Data1.BackColor = LIGHT_GRAY
'
txtOneLine.BackColor = WHITE
txtOneLine.ForeColor = BLACK
End If
End Sub
```

Finally, add a single line of code to the Default command button to execute the SetColors procedure.

```
Sub cmdDefault_Click ()
SetColors 0
End Sub
```

Save and run the project. You now see that the background for the form and the data control are set to light gray when you click the Default button. The form now meets the default color standards for Win95 forms.

Custom Colors

You may want to set your own customized colors for your form. The following code will do just that. Suppose you want the background to appear in red and the text to appear in blue.

First, add the constants for blue and red to your declaration section:

```
Option Explicit
'
' constant for colors
Const LIGHT_GRAY = &HC0C0C0
Const WHITE = &HFFFFFF
Const BLACK = &H0
Const BLUE = &H800000
Const RED = &H80
```

Next, modify the SetColors procedure to include your new colors. Notice that you now need to set both the ForeColor and the BackColor properties of all the controls along with the `BackColor` of the form itself. This time, you set the colors to the custom set if the parameter is set to 1. Here's the code:

```
Sub SetColors (nSet As Integer)
'
' set to default colors
If nSet = 0 Then
txtDisplayOnly.BackColor = LIGHT_GRAY
Frame1.BackColor = LIGHT_GRAY
frmColor.BackColor = LIGHT_GRAY
Data1.BackColor = LIGHT_GRAY
'
txtOneLine.BackColor = WHITE
txtOneLine.ForeColor = BLACK
End If
'
' set to custom colors
If nSet = 1 Then
txtDisplayOnly.BackColor = RED
Frame1.BackColor = RED
frmColor.BackColor = RED
Data1.BackColor = RED
'
txtOneLine.BackColor = WHITE
txtOneLine.ForeColor = BLUE
End If
End Sub
```

Now, add the following code to the Custom button:

```
Sub cmdCustom_Click ()
SetColors 1
End Sub
```

Save and run the program to see the results. Not such a good color scheme, you say? Well, some may like your custom setting; some may want to keep the default setting. Now you can select the scheme you want with a click of the mouse!

System Colors

As you can see in the previous code example, some color schemes can be less than perfect. Many programmers add routines to enable users to customize the color scheme to their own taste. The easiest way to do this is to let Windows set the color scheme for you. The code example that follows uses the color scheme selected through the Windows 95 Display applet. This is an excellent way to give your users the power to customize their application color without writing a lot of Visual Basic code.

There are several Windows constants for the system colors that are set by the Control Panel program. For this example, you use only three. The following code shows a modified declaration section with the Windows system color constants added:

```
Option Explicit
'
' constant for colors
Const LIGHT_GRAY = &HC0C0C0
Const WHITE = &HFFFFFF
Const BLACK = &H0
Const BLUE = &H800000
Const RED = &H80
'
' windows system color values
Const WINDOW_BACKGROUND = &H80000005      ' Window background.
Const WINDOW_TEXT = &H80000008            ' Text in windows.
Const APPLICATION_WORKSPACE = &H8000000C  ' Background color of MDI apps
```

Next, you add code to the SetColors routine that sets the colors to the Windows system colors:

```
Sub SetColors (nSet As Integer)
'
' set to default colors
If nSet = 0 Then
txtDisplayOnly.BackColor = LIGHT_GRAY
Frame1.BackColor = LIGHT_GRAY
frmColor.BackColor = LIGHT_GRAY
Data1.BackColor = LIGHT_GRAY
'
txtOneLine.BackColor = WHITE
txtOneLine.ForeColor = BLACK
End If
'
' set to custom colors
If nSet = 1 Then
txtDisplayOnly.BackColor = RED
Frame1.BackColor = RED
frmColor.BackColor = RED
Data1.BackColor = RED
'
txtOneLine.BackColor = WHITE
txtOneLine.ForeColor = BLUE
End If
'
' set to system colors
If nSet = 2 Then
txtDisplayOnly.BackColor = APPLICATION_WORKSPACE
Frame1.BackColor = APPLICATION_WORKSPACE
frmColor.BackColor = APPLICATION_WORKSPACE
Data1.BackColor = APPLICATION_WORKSPACE
'
txtOneLine.BackColor = WINDOW_BACKGROUND
txtOneLine.ForeColor = WINDOW_TEXT
End If
End Sub
```

3

Finally, add this line of code to the System button to activate the system color scheme:

```
Sub cmdSystem_Click ()
SetColors 2
End Sub
```

Save and run the program. When you click the System button, you see the color scheme you selected in the Control Panel as the color scheme for this application. Now, while the program is still running, start the Control Panel application and select a new color scheme for Windows. Your Visual Basic program instantly changes its own color scheme!

Summary

Today you have learned about creating data entry forms with Visual Basic bound data controls. The Visual Basic data control has five database-related properties. Three refer to the database and two refer to the Dynaset:

- The database properties of the Visual Basic data control are DatabaseName, which is used to select the database to access; Exclusive, which is used to prevent other users from opening the database; and ReadOnly, which is used to prevent your program from modifying the data in the database.
- The Dynaset properties of the Visual Basic data control are Recordsource, which is used to select the data table within the database, and Options, which is used to set ReadOnly, DenyWrite, and AppendOnly properties to the Dynaset.

The Visual Basic data control has three database-related methods:

- Refresh updates the data control after setting properties.
- UpdateControls reads values from the fields in the Dynaset and writes those values to the related form controls.
- UpdateRecord reads values from the form controls and writes those values to the related fields in the Dynaset.

The Visual Basic data control has three database-related events:

- Reposition occurs each time the record pointer is moved to a new record in the Dynaset.
- Validate occurs each time the record pointer leaves the current record in the Dynaset.
- Error occurs each time a database error occurs.

The Visual Basic bound form controls can be used to link form input and display controls to data fields in the database:

- The bound text box control is used for data entry on character and numeric data table fields.

- The bound label control is used for display-only character and numeric data table fields.

- The bound check box control is used for data entry on the Boolean data type field.

- The bound OLE control is used to display OLE objects stored directly in an MDB file by Microsoft Access.

- The Three-D panel control behaves the same as the label control; the Three-D check box control behaves the same as a standard check box control.

You have also learned the following general rules for creating Visual Basic forms in the Windows 95 style:

- The default color is light gray for backgrounds.

- The Frame control is used to create a palette on which to place all other controls.

- The default font is 8-point sans serif, nonbold.

- Input areas should have a white background, and display areas should have a light gray background. Also, display areas should be recessed into the input palette.

- Frame controls are used to group related items on a form.

- All controls, including field prompts, should be left-justified. Field prompts should be written in mixed case and followed by a semicolon.

- The standard spacing and sizing of common controls should be as follows:

  The control height is 300 twips.

  The command button width is 1200 twips.

  The vertical spacing between controls is 60 twips for related items and 90 twips for unrelated items.

  The border widths (top, bottom, and side) should be 120 twips.

Finally, you learned how to write code that sets control colors to the Windows 95 default colors, how to create your own custom color scheme, and how to link your control colors to the color scheme selected with the Windows Control Panel Color applet.

3

Quiz

1. How do you establish a database name for a data control using Visual Basic code?

2. What property do you set to define a table in Visual Basic code?

3. What is the main difference between the `UpdateControls` and the `UpdateRecord` methods?

4. What two values can a bound check box produce?

5. What property do you use to bind a control to a field in a table?

6. What is the standard form color for Windows 95 applications? What is the standard color of the input areas? What is the standard color of display-only text? How are labels aligned?

Exercises

1. Write Visual Basic code to set the properties to open a database (named `STUDENTS.MDB`) for a data control named `Data1`.

2. Modify the code you wrote in the first exercise and set the properties to open a table (Addresses) in `STUDENTS.MDB`.

3. Modify the code you wrote in the second exercise by binding controls to the data fields in the Addresses table. Include fields for StudentID (which you should declare as `cField1`), Address (`cField2`), City (`cField3`), State (`cField4`), and Zip (`cField5`).

DAY 4

Input Validation

Today, you learn about one of the most important aspects of database programming: input validation. Validating user input before it is written to the database can improve the quality of the data stored in your tables. Good validation schemes can also make your program user friendly and, in many cases, can increase the speed at which users can enter valid data.

You explore several specific topics on input validation, including the following:

- Field-level validation versus form-level validation
- How to speed data entry by filtering keyboard input
- How to use input masks to give users hints when entering data
- How to limit user choices and speed input with validation lists
- How to handle required field inputs in Windows forms
- How to handle conditional field input validation in Windows forms

After you learn how to develop input validation routines, you learn how to use a custom OCX control containing seven valuable validation routines that you can use in your projects throughout the book. You can also use the custom controls in any project you build in the future.

Before you get into the details of how to perform input validation, let's first talk about what input validation is and why it is so important to good database application design.

What Is Input Validation?

Input validation is the process of checking the data entered by the user before that data is saved to the database. This is sometimes referred to as *client-side validation*. This is because the validation action happens at the client's workstation—before data is sent to the database at the server.

Input validation is a proactive process; it happens while data is being entered. Input validation is not the same thing as error trapping. Error trapping is a reactive process; it happens after the data has been entered. This is an important point. Input validation should be used to prevent errors. If you have good input validation schemes, you have fewer errors to trap! You learn more about the reactive process on Day 13, "Error Handling in Visual Basic 6."

Input validation can be used to give users guides on how to enter valid data. The best example of this kind of input validation is the use of a validation list. A validation list is a list of valid inputs for a field. If the user has only a limited number of possible valid choices for an input field, there is much less chance of a data entry error occurring. Good validation schemes give the user a list of valid input from which to choose while performing data entry.

Input validation can automatically edit data as the user enters it, instead of telling the user to fix invalid entries. For example, if the data entered in a field must be in all capital letters, the program should automatically convert lowercase characters to uppercase, instead of waiting while the user enters mixed case and then reporting an error and forcing the user to reenter the data.

Input validation reaches beyond the individual keystroke and field. It is also important to validate data at the form level. Input validation schemes should make sure that all required fields on a form are completed properly. If you have several fields that must be filled with valid data before the record can be saved to the database, you must have a method for checking those fields before you allow the user to attempt to save the record.

Conditional input fields must be validated, too. A conditional field is slightly different from a required field. Conditional fields usually occur when a user has checked a Yes/No box and then must enter additional data to complete the process. For example, if the user indicates on a form that the customer requests all products to be shipped instead of picked up, input validation should make sure that valid data has been entered into the shipping address fields. Another example of conditional field validation is when entering a value in one field requires that the value in another field be within a certain range. For example, if the customer's credit limit is above $50,000, you must enter a valid credit-worthiness code of 5 or above. In this case, the two fields must be checked against one another and verified before the user can save the record to the database.

As you can see from the preceding examples, input validation is more than just making sure the data entered in a field is correct. Input validation should be viewed as a set of rules to ensure that quality data is entered into the system. Before you begin writing your data entry forms, you should spend time developing a comprehensive set of validation rules. After you develop these rules, you are ready to start creating your data entry form.

Common Input Validation Rules

Almost every field in your database requires some type of input validation. Before you design your form, put together a list of all the fields you need on the form and answer the following questions for each input field:

- Must data be entered in the field? (Is it a required field?)
- What characters are valid/invalid for this field (numeric input only, capital letters only, no spaces allowed, and so on)?
- For numeric fields, is there a high/low range limit (must be greater than zero and less than 1,000, can't be less than 100, and so on)?
- Is there a list of valid values for this field? (Can user enter only Retail, Wholesale, or Other; Name must already be in the Customer table, and so on.)
- Is this a conditional field? (If users enter Yes in field A, they must enter something in field C.)

Even though each data entry form is unique, you can use some general guidelines when putting together input validation schemes:

- If possible, limit keystrokes to valid values only. For example, if the field must be numeric, don't allow the user to enter character values. If spaces are not allowed, make sure the Spacebar is disabled. Help the user by limiting the kinds of data that can be entered into the field.
- Limit input choices with lists. If there is a limited set of valid inputs for a field, give the user a pick list or set of radio buttons to choose from.
- Inform the user of range limits. If a field has a high or low range limit, tell the user what the limits are.

4

- Point out required fields on a form. Mark required fields with a leading asterisk (*) or some other appropriate character. Possibly change the background color of required fields.
- Group conditional fields together on the form. If entering Yes in one field means that several other fields must be completed, put the additional fields close to the Yes/No field to help the user. Keep conditional fields of this type disabled until the Yes/No flag has been set. This helps the user see that new fields must be entered.

Field-Level Validation

The first level of validation is at the field level. This is the place where you can make sure the user is entering the right characters in the field, entering the data into the field in the proper format, and entering a valid value based on a list of possible choices.

For the rest of this section, you will be building a sample application that illustrates the various input validation methods this chapter covers. If you haven't done so already, start up Visual Basic 6 and create a new Standard EXE project. Set the Caption property of the form to Input Validation and the Name of the form to frmValidation. Set the project Name property to Validation and save the form as VALIDATION.FRM; save the project as VALIDATION.VBP.

Filtering Keyboard Input

One of the easiest ways to perform input validation is to filter keyboard input. Filtering keyboard input requires capturing the keystrokes of the user before they appear on the screen and filtering out the keystrokes you do not want to appear in the input controls. You can filter invalid or undesirable keystrokes by creating a beep for the user each time an invalid key is pressed (for example, a beep each time a letter is pressed in a numeric field). You can also convert the invalid key to a valid one (for example, change lowercase to uppercase). Or you can simply ignore the keystroke completely and prevent the invalid values from ever appearing in the input control.

 Tip

Keep in mind that not all your potential users may be able to hear an audible beep and could become confused at the inability to input data. Windows operating systems all have several useful Accessibility Options that you may want to review, including the use of message boxes for hearing-impaired users.

Discarding Unwanted Keystrokes

For the first keyboard-filtering example, you set up a textbox control that accepts only numerals zero through nine. First, add a label control and a textbox control to the form. Set the Caption property of the label control to Numbers. Set the Name property of the textbox control to txtNumber and set the text property to blank. Your form should resemble the one in Figure 4.1.

FIGURE 4.1

Adding the Numbers *input control.*

Save and run the program. You can enter any type of data in the textbox that you wish—numbers, letters, spaces, and so on. Now you add a small bit of code that filters out all but the numerals zero through nine. You do this by using the textbox control KeyPress event.

The KeyPress event occurs each time a user presses a key while the field has the focus. Each time a key is pressed while the cursor is in the textbox control, the ASCII value of the key is sent to the KeyPress event where you can evaluate it and act accordingly.

> **Note**
>
> Each key on the keyboard has an ASCII (American Standard Code for Information Interchange) numeric value. Your Visual Basic 6 documentation has a list of the ASCII codes for each key on the keyboard.

In this example, you want to ignore any keystroke that is not a 0, 1, 2, 3, 4, 5, 6, 7, 8, or 9. To do this, you need to add a small bit of code (see Listing 4.1) to the KeyPress event of the txtNumbers textbox.

LISTING 4.1 LIMITING DATA ENTRY IN THE KeyPress EVENT

```
1: Private Sub txtNumber_KeyPress(KeyAscii As Integer)
2:    '
3:    Dim strValid As String
```

continues

LISTING 4.1   CONTINUED

```
 4:    '
 5:    strValid = "0123456789"
 6:    '
 7:    If InStr(strValid, Chr(KeyAscii)) = 0 Then
 8:        KeyAscii = 0
 9:    End If
10:    '
11:    End Sub
```

In Listing 4.1, you declared a string variable that holds the list of valid keys. The next line loads the string with the valid keys for this field, and the next line checks to see whether the key pressed is in the string of valid keys. It does this by converting the numeric value passed by Visual Basic 6 in the KeyAscii parameter (the ASCII value of the key pressed) into a readable character using the Visual Basic 6 Chr function and searching for the result in the list of valid keys in the cValid string. If the key pressed is not in the cValid string, the keystroke is set to 0. Setting the keystroke to 0 is telling Visual Basic 6 to pretend nothing was ever typed!

Now save and run the program. No matter what keys you type, only the numerals 0 through 9 appear in the textbox. You have filtered out everything but numerals. You may also notice that keystrokes, such as the Backspace and Delete keys, no longer work! You've told Visual Basic 6 to ignore them. You can fix that by adding a statement that checks to see whether the keystroke is a control code. Control codes are used in Visual Basic 6 to indicate that the key the user pressed was not a printable character but a keyboard control character. Common control characters are the Esc key, the Enter key, the Backspace key, and so on.

You can also add any other characters to the validity list if you like. For example, you probably want to be able to enter a minus sign, a plus sign, and a decimal point in this number field. To do this, you add those three characters to the strValid string. Your program code should now look like Listing 4.2.

LISTING 4.2   THE KeyPress EVENT WITH CONTROL CHARACTERS

```
1: Private Sub txtNumber_KeyPress(KeyAscii As Integer)
2:     '
3:     Dim strValid As String
4:     '
5:     strValid = "0123456789+-."
6:     '
7:     If KeyAscii > 26 Then ' if it's not a control code
8:         If InStr(strValid, Chr(KeyAscii)) = 0 Then
```

```
 9:              KeyAscii = 0
10:         End If
11:     End If
12:     '
13: End Sub
```

Notice that in Listing 4.2, you first tested to see whether the key pressed was greater than 26. ASCII code 26 is the last Visual Basic 6 control code. The routine in Listing 4.2 now skips over filtering of control codes. When you save and run the program, you can pass the plus, minus, and decimal point characters into the textbox, too.

Converting Keystrokes

Now let's create validation code that accepts only uppercase characters. This is a bit trickier. Instead of ignoring lowercase input, you convert it to uppercase and then pass it through to the textbox.

First add another label and textbox control. Set the label Caption property to Uppercase. Set the Name property of the textbox to txtUpper and set the text property to blank. Your form should look like the one in Figure 4.2.

FIGURE 4.2

Adding the Uppercase *control and label to the form.*

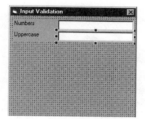

The code needed for the txtUpper KeyPress event is in Listing 4.3. Even though there's only one line of code in this routine, there's a lot going on. This line of code (reading from the inside function outward) first converts the KeyAscii value into a printable character, converts that character to uppercase, and then converts the character back to an ASCII numeric value. Notice that instead of setting the Visual Basic 6 KeyAscii parameter to 0 (discarding it), this routine converts it to an uppercase value. This works no matter what key is pressed.

4

LISTING 4.3   THE KeyPress EVENT TO FORCE LETTERS TO UPPERCASE

```
1: Private Sub txtUpper_KeyPress(KeyAscii As Integer)
2:     '
3:     KeyAscii = Asc(UCase(Chr(KeyAscii))) ' change to uppercase
4:     '
5: End Sub
```

When you save and run the program, you see that any letter key you enter converts to an uppercase letter and passes through to the textbox.

The two types of keyboard filters illustrated here (discard or convert) can be combined to form a powerful input validation tool. Let's create a validation example that allows only uppercase letters A through Z, or numerals 0 through 9—no spaces or any other characters.

First add a new label/textbox control pair. Set the label `Caption` property to `Combined`. Set the textbox `Name` property to `txtCombined` and the text property to blank. Refer to Figure 4.3 for positioning and sizing information.

FIGURE 4.3

Adding the Combined field to the form.

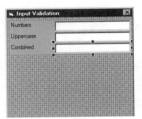

Listing 4.4 shows how to combine a check against a valid list and a conversion of keystrokes into a single input validation.

LISTING 4.4   A SINGLE KeyPress EVENT TO CHECK FOR VALID ENTRY AND FORCE UPPERCASE

```
 1: Private Sub txtCombined_KeyPress(KeyAscii As Integer)
 2:     '
 3:     Dim strValid As String
 4:     '
 5:     strValid = "0123456789ABCDEFGHIJKLMNOPQRSTUVWXYZ"
 6:     '
 7:     KeyAscii = Asc(UCase(Chr(KeyAscii)))
 8:     '
 9:     If KeyAscii > 26 Then ' if it's not a control code
10:         If InStr(strValid, Chr(KeyAscii)) = 0 Then
11:             KeyAscii = 0
12:         End If
```

```
13:      End If
14:      '
15: End Sub
```

Input Masking

It is very common to have fields on your form that require special input formats. Examples of special formats are telephone numbers, government or employee identification numbers, hour/minute time entry, and so on. Visual Basic 6 ships with a bound data control that handles special input and display formatting: the MaskedEdit control. The MaskedEdit control works like the standard Visual Basic 6 textbox control, with a few added properties that make it a powerful tool for your input validation arsenal.

Before you start using the MaskedEdit control, you may need to add it in your Visual Basic 6 toolbox. The MaskedEdit control is not automatically included in the default Visual Basic 6 toolbox. To add it to your toolbox window, first select Project| Components from the Main menu. Next, scroll down the list to find the Microsoft Masked Edit Control 6.0 item. This adds the MSMASK32.OCX to your toolbox.

Let's add a phone number input field to the form. Add a new label to the form and set its Caption property to Phone Number. Now add a MaskedEdit control to the form. Set its Name property to mskPhone, the Mask property to (###) ###-#### (the U.S. phone number format) and the PromptInclude property to False.

> **Tip**
>
> It is essential that you set the PromptInclude property to False when using the MaskedEdit control as a bound control. If the PromptInclude property is set to True, you get a database error each time you add a new record to the table or attempt to save or read a record that has a null value in the data field linked to the MaskedEdit bound control.

Your form should resemble Figure 4.4.

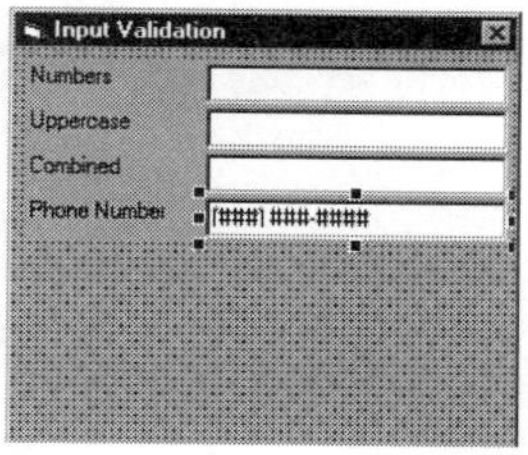

FIGURE 4.4

Adding the MaskedEdit Phone Number *control to the form.*

4

You do not need to add any additional filtering to the control because the MaskedEdit control makes sure that only digits are entered and that the input is limited to 10 digits formatted as a standard U.S. phone number.

Save and run the program. You can see that when the control is initialized, the phone number mask is displayed. When the MaskedEdit control receives the focus, a series of underlines appear as an input guide for the user. The underlines disappear when control is given to an object other than the MaskedEdit control.

Note

The formatting characters of the MaskedEdit control are not saved to the database field when the PromptInclude property is set to False. This means that in the previous example, only the phone number digits would be saved to the data table, not the parentheses or the dash.

The Visual Basic 6 MaskedEdit control offers an extensive set of input masking tools. It ships with several input masks predefined, including dollar amounts, U.S. phone numbers, and several date and time formats. To view these formats, select the MaskedEdit control, click the right (alternate) mouse button, and select Properties from the menu that appears. You find the formats on the General tab.

You can also create custom input format masks for inventory part numbers, email addresses, and so on. Although you won't look at all the possibilities here, there is one other MaskedEdit format option that you illustrate on your form in this lesson, because it is very useful when displaying dollar amounts.

The MaskedEdit control gives you the power to add a display mask in addition to an input mask. Up to this point, you have been using the input mask capabilities of the MaskedEdit control. Now let's add a control that shows the display capabilities, too.

Add another label control and another MaskedEdit control to the form. Set the label Caption property to Dollars. Set the MaskedEdit control Name property to mskDollars and the format property to $#,##0.00;($#,##0.00).

Tip

The MaskedEdit display property actually has three parts, each separated by the semicolon (;). Part one determines how positive values are displayed. Part two determines how negative values are displayed. Part three determines how zero values are displayed.

This property affects the *display* of the data, not the input, so you do not see any input guides when you set the format property or when you save and run the program. Your form should look like the one in Figure 4.5.

FIGURE 4.5

Adding the Dollars *control to the form.*

Now run the program and enter a numeric value in the Dollars textbox. When you leave the textbox to go to another control, you see the MaskedEdit control format the display of the amount you entered. Your screen should resemble Figure 4.6. Please note that two decimal places always appear to the right of the decimal.

FIGURE 4.6

The display results of the MaskedEdit *control.*

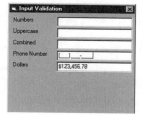

Validation Lists

One of the most common field-level validation routines is the use of a validation list. The list contains a set of possible inputs for the field—usually displayed in a list box or a drop-down list control. Instead of having to guess at a valid value, the user can simply scan the list and click on the proper choice. Validation lists require a bit more programming to use, but the rewards far exceed the effort. Using validation lists virtually guarantees that you will not have a data entry error occur on the input field.

Before you can use a validation list for input validation, you must first have a list. It is usually a good idea to load any validation lists you need for a form at the time you load the form. This means that validation lists should be loaded in the Form_Load event. Let's add some code to your project that loads a drop-down list box with a list of possible customer types.

First, add another label and a drop-down combo box control to the form. Set the label Caption property to Customer Type, set the drop-down combo box Name property to cboCusType, and set the Style property to 2DropDown List. Your form should look like the one in Figure 4.7.

FIGURE 4.7

Adding the DropDown List *control to the form.*

> **Note**   You can't change the height of the combo box control in Visual Basic 6. It is set at 315 twips and cannot be updated.

Now add Listing 4.5 to load the list box with valid values.

LISTING 4.5   ADDING THE Form_Load EVENT TO LOAD A LIST BOX

```
 1: Private Sub Form_Load()
 2:     '
 3:     ' load dropdown list box
 4:     With cboCustType
 5:         .AddItem "Retail"
 6:         .AddItem "Wholesale"
 7:         .AddItem "Distributor"
 8:         .AddItem "Other"
 9:     End With
10:     '
11: End Sub
```

In Listing 4.5, you are adding values directly to the list using program code. Each AddItem method adds an additional valid selection to the list. You could also load the control with values from a data table. This would give you a more dynamic list of valid values. For now, stick to the direct load example here; later in this book, you add validation lists loaded from data tables.

Save and run the program. You can now click the down arrow of the drop-down list box and see the list of valid values. Now the user can't help but pick a correct item for the input field.

Notice that when you first start the form, the combo box shows an empty value. This indicates no selection has been made. You can add some code to your form that selects a default item from the list, too. Listing 4.5b shows a modified version of Listing 4.5. Notice that line 9 now contains the ListIndex =.

LISTING 4.5B   ADDING ListIndex TO THE COMBO BOX

```
 1: Private Sub Form_Load()
 2:     '
 3:     ' load dropdown list box
 4:     With cboCustType
 5:         .AddItem "Retail"
 6:         .AddItem "Wholesale"
 7:         .AddItem "Distributor"
 8:         .AddItem "Other"
 9:         .ListIndex = 0 ' set default value to first item in the list
10:     End With
11:     '
12: End Sub
```

Now when the form starts, you see that the first value in the list has already been selected.

Up to this point, you have been developing methods for handling field-level validation. The next step is to add validation routines at the form level.

Form-Level Validation

Form-level validation is an essential part of designing a good validation scheme for your form. Although many input errors can be caught and corrected at the field level, there are several validation steps that can be performed well only at the form level.

Although field-level validation is performed at the time a key is pressed or at the time a field loses focus, form-level validation is performed at the time the user presses Enter, or clicks the OK or Save button. These are validations that are done after the user has entered all fields, but before any attempt is made to store the values to a data table.

Form-level validation can be divided into three groups:

- Independent content validation
- Required field validation
- Dependent field validation

Let's look at each type of form-level validation.

Independent Content Validation—High/Low Ranges

A common form-level validation routine is one that checks the upper and lower values of a numeric entry and makes sure the value is within the high/low range. This is very useful on all types of forms that have preset minimum or maximum values for dollar amounts or unit counts.

> **Note**
>
> Although it might seem that this kind of validation should be done at the field level, it is better to perform it at the form level. If a user enters a value that is not within the acceptable range, the field that contains the invalid data must be given focus so that the user can correct the entry. Setting the control's focus is best done outside of any other control's GotFocus or LostFocus event. Also, because a user can use the mouse to skip over any field on the form, placing independent content validation routines within the controls' events means that users may skip important validation steps in the process.

To set up the form-level validation, first add a single command button to the form. Set its Name property to cmdOK and its Caption property to &OK. Now add another label/textbox pair to the form. Set the label Caption to High/Low. Set the textbox Name property to txtHighLow and the text property to blank. Refer to Figure 4.8 for sizing and placement information.

FIGURE 4.8

Adding the High/Low *control and OK button to the form.*

It is best to add a routine to each form that will contain all the form-level validation. This adds a level of organization to your forms and keeps all the related code in a single location. An added benefit to keeping all form-level validation code in the same place is that you can easily reuse the code. For example, you could use form validation routines when the user presses the OK button or when the user attempts to exit the form entirely. By placing the validation code in one routine, you can call it from the OK routine or from the Form_Unload event if needed.

So, first add the code from Listing 4.6 to the cmdOK_click event. This will call a general form validation routine and, upon return, display a message, if it exists.

LISTING 4.6   CALLING THE FORM-LEVEL VALIDATION ROUTINE FROM THE cmdOK_click EVENT

```
 1: Private Sub cmdOK_Click()
 2:     '
 3:     Dim strMsg As String
 4:     '
 5:     strMsg = ValidateForm()
 6:     '
 7:     If strMsg = "" Then
 8:        Unload Me ' all went fine
 9:     Else
10:        MsgBox strMsg, vbExclamation, "Validation Error"
11:     End If
12:     '
13: End Sub
```

As you can see in Listing 4.6, a custom function called ValidateForm will be used to handle all the dirty work of form-level validation (see line 5). If any errors occur during the validation process, a string will be returned that contains the error message. If the string returned is empty, you know that no errors were detected during form-level validation.

Now, create the ValidateForm method. First, select Tools | Add Procedure from the Main menu. Next, enter Validate Form for the Name property. Be sure the Function and Public radio buttons are selected before you press the OK button.

Add the code in Listing 4.7 to the ValidateForm routine.

LISTING 4.7   THE FORM-LEVEL VALIDATION ROUTINE TO CHECK FOR VALUES IN A RANGE

```
 1: Public Function ValidateForm() As String
 2:     '
 3:     ' validate this form and return an error message if needed
 4:     '
 5:     ' vars for high/low validation
 6:     Dim intHigh As Integer
 7:     Dim intLow As Integer
 8:     Dim strHighLowMsg As String
 9:     '
```

continues

LISTING 4.7   CONTINUED

```
10:    Dim strSendMsg As String
11:    '
12:    ' values for high/low check
13:    intHigh = 100
14:    intLow = 1
15:    strHighLowMsg = "High/Low field must contain a value between " & _
16:    CStr(intLow) & " and " & CStr(intHigh)
17:    '
18:    strSendMsg = ""
19:    '
20:    ' check high/low field
21:    With txtHighLow
22:        If Val(.Text) < intLow Or Val(.Text) > intHigh Then
23:            strSendMsg = strSendMsg & vbCrLf & strHighLowMsg & vbCrLf
24:            .SetFocus
25:        End If
26:    End With
27: '
28:    ValidateForm = strSendMsg
29:        '
30: End Function
```

The code in Listing 4.7 establishes the integer variables for the high and low in the range, sets them to 100 and 1 respectively, and then checks the value entered into the txtHighLow text control. If the value is out of the allowed range, the return message is set, and the input cursor is moved back to the field that contains the invalid data. Notice that the message not only tells the user that the data is invalid, it also tells the user what values are acceptable. If the data entered is within range, the return message is left blank—an indication that no error was encountered.

Now save and run the program. If you skip to the OK button without entering data or enter data outside the allowed range, you see the validation message.

Independent Content Validation—Min/Max Field Lengths

Another common form-level validation step is to make sure that character strings meet the minimum or maximum length requirements. This is done in the same way numeric values are checked for high and low ranges.

Let's add input validation to ensure that the Uppercase textbox you placed on the form earlier is no longer than 10 characters, and at least 3 characters in length. You just need to modify the ValidateForm method shown in Listing 4.7 to match the one in Listing 4.8.

LISTING 4.8   ADDING THE FORM-LEVEL VALIDATION CODE TO CHECK THE LENGTH OF FIELDS AND A VALID RANGE OF VALUES

```
 1: Public Function ValidateForm() As String
 2:     '
 3:     ' validate this form and return an error message if needed
 4:     '
 5:     ' vars for high/low validation
 6:     Dim intHigh As Integer
 7:     Dim intLow As Integer
 8:     Dim strHighLowMsg As String
 9:     '
10:     ' vars for min/max len validation
11:     Dim intMinLen As Integer
12:     Dim intMaxLen As Integer
13:     Dim strMinMaxMsg As String
14:     '
15:      Dim strSendMsg As String
16:     '
17:     ' values for high/low check
18:     intHigh = 100
19:     intLow = 1
20:     strHighLowMsg = "High/Low field must contain a value between " & _
21:     CStr(intLow) & " and " & CStr(intHigh)
22:     '
23:     ' values for length check
24:     intMinLen = 3
25:     intMaxLen = 10
26:     strMinMaxMsg = "Upper field must be between " & _
27:     CStr(intMinLen) & " and " & CStr(intMaxLen) & " long."
28:     '
29:     strSendMsg = ""
30:     '
31:     ' check high/low field
32:     With txtHighLow
33:         If Val(.Text) < intLow Or Val(.Text) > intHigh Then
34:             strSendMsg = strSendMsg & vbCrLf & strHighLowMsg & vbCrLf
35:             .SetFocus
36:         End If
37:     End With
38:     '
39:     ' check upper field
40:     With txtUpper
41:         If Len(.Text) < intMinLen Or Len(.Text) > intMaxLen Then
42:             strSendMsg = strSendMsg & vbCrLf & strMinMaxMsg & vbCrLf
43:             .SetFocus
44:         End If
45:     End With
46:     '
```

4

continues

LISTING 4.8   CONTINUED

```
47:     ValidateForm = strSendMsg
48:     '
49: End Function
```

In Listing 4.8, you added variables for the minimum and maximum length of the entry field and a new message variable. Notice that the strSendMsg variable has filled in such a way as to allow both messages to be sent to the user. This way, the user gets all the validation error messages at once, instead of one at a time.

Save and run the form to test the validation rule. You see that now both form-level validation rules must be met before the form unloads.

 Note The txtUpper field has both field-level and form-level validation rules applied to it. The field-level routine executes when data is entered into the field. The form-level validation routine executes when this data record is saved. It is perfectly acceptable, and sometimes recommended, having both field-level and form-level validation for the same control.

Required Fields

Almost every form has at least one field that is required input. Some forms may have several. Checking for required input fields is done at the form level. Let's add code to the ValidateForm method that makes sure that users fill out the Combined field every time.

You validate that the txtCombined field contains valid data. Listing 4.9 shows how you can modify the ValidateForm method to get this done.

LISTING 4.9   MODIFYING THE FORM-LEVEL VALIDATION ROUTINE TO CHECK FOR REQUIRED FIELDS

```
 1: Public Function ValidateForm() As String
 2:     '
 3:     ' validate this form and return an error message if needed
 4:     '
 5:     ' vars for high/low validation
 6:     Dim intHigh As Integer
 7:     Dim intLow As Integer
 8:     Dim strHighLowMsg As String
 9:     '
10:     ' vars for min/max len validation
11:     Dim intMinLen As Integer
```

```
12:       Dim intMaxLen As Integer
13:       Dim strMinMaxMsg As String
14:       '
15:       Dim blnOK As Boolean
16:       Dim strSendMsg As String
17:       '
18:       ' values for high/low check
19:       intHigh = 100
20:       intLow = 1
21:       strHighLowMsg = "High/Low field must contain a value between " & _
22:       CStr(intLow) & " and " & CStr(intHigh)
23:       '
24:       ' values for length check
25:       intMinLen = 3
26:       intMaxLen = 10
27:       strMinMaxMsg = "Upper field must be between " & _
28:       CStr(intMinLen) & " and " & CStr(intMaxLen) & " long."
29:       '
30:       blnOK = True
31:       strSendMsg = ""
32:       '
33:       ' check high/low field
34:       With txtHighLow
35:          If Val(.Text) < intLow Or Val(.Text) > intHigh Then
36:             strSendMsg = strSendMsg & vbCrLf & strHighLowMsg & vbCrLf
37:             .SetFocus
38:          End If
39:       End With
40:       '
41:       ' check upper field
42:       With txtUpper
43:          If Len(.Text) < intMinLen Or Len(.Text) > intMaxLen Then
44:             strSendMsg = strSendMsg & vbCrLf & strMinMaxMsg & vbCrLf
45:             .SetFocus
46:          End If
47:       End With
48:       '
49:       ' check the combined field
50:       With txtCombined
51:          If Len(Trim(.Text)) = 0 Then
52:             strSendMsg = strSendMsg & vbCrLf & _
53:             "Combined field is a required field" & vbCrLf
54:             .SetFocus
55:          End If
56:       End With
57:       '
58:       ValidateForm = strSendMsg
59:       '
60: End Function
```

4

The only change you made is to add lines 49–57 to the routine. This code checks the length of the string in the `txtCombined` textbox. If the result is zero, an error message is displayed. Notice the use of the `Trim` function to remove any trailing or leading spaces from the `txtCombined` string. This makes sure that users who enter blank spaces into the field do not get past the validation step.

Conditional Fields

NEW TERM   There are times when entering a value in one field of the form means that other fields on the form must also contain valid data. Fields of this type are called *conditional fields*. A good example of conditional field validation can be found in an order tracking system. For example, when a user enters `Yes` in the Ship to Site? field, he or she must then enter a valid value in the Shipping Address field. The Shipping Address field is a conditional field because its validation is based on the condition of the Ship to Site? field.

Now add a conditional validation to the `ValidateForm` method. For this example, make the field CustType conditional to the field Upper. In other words, if the Upper field contains data, the CustType field must contain data. See Listing 4.10 for an example of how to do this in the `ValidateForm` method (see lines 61–68).

LISTING 4.10   ADDING THE FORM-LEVEL CONDITIONAL VALIDATION ROUTINE TO THE `ValidateForm` METHOD

```
 1: Public Function ValidateForm() As String
 2:     '
 3:     ' validate this form and return an error message if needed
 4:     '
 5:     ' vars for high/low validation
 6:     Dim intHigh As Integer
 7:     Dim intLow As Integer
 8:     Dim strHighLowMsg As String
 9:     '
10:     ' vars for min/max len validation
11:     Dim intMinLen As Integer
12:     Dim intMaxLen As Integer
13:     Dim strMinMaxMsg As String
14:     '
15:     Dim blnOK As Boolean
16:     Dim strSendMsg As String
17:     '
18:     ' values for high/low check
19:     intHigh = 100
20:     intLow = 1
21:     strHighLowMsg = "High/Low field must contain a value between " & _
22:     CStr(intLow) & " and " & CStr(intHigh)
```

```
23:    '
24:    ' values for length check
25:    intMinLen = 3
26:    intMaxLen = 10
27:    strMinMaxMsg = "Upper field must be between " & _
28:    CStr(intMinLen) & " and " & CStr(intMaxLen) & " long."
29:    '
30:    blnOK = True
31:    strSendMsg = ""
32:    '
33:    ' check high/low field
34:    With txtHighLow
35:       If Val(.Text) < intLow Or Val(.Text) > intHigh Then
36:          strSendMsg = strSendMsg & vbCrLf & strHighLowMsg & vbCrLf
37:          blnOK = False
38:          .SetFocus
39:       End If
40:    End With
41:    '
42:    ' check upper field
43:    With txtUpper
44:       If Len(.Text) < intMinLen Or Len(.Text) > intMaxLen Then
45:          strSendMsg = strSendMsg & vbCrLf & strMinMaxMsg & vbCrLf
46:          blnOK = False
47:          .SetFocus
48:       End If
49:    End With
50:    '
51:    ' check the combined field
52:    With txtCombined
53:       If Len(Trim(.Text)) = 0 Then
54:          strSendMsg = strSendMsg & vbCrLf & _
55:          "Combined field is a required field" & vbCrLf
56:          blnOK = False
57:          .SetFocus
58:       End If
59:    End With
60:    '
61:    ' check conditional upper/custtype fields
62:    If Len(Trim(txtUpper)) <> 0 And Len(Trim(cboCustType)) = 0 Then
63:       strSendMsg = strSendMsg & vbCrLf & _
64:       "If Upper field contains data then " & _
65:       "the Customer Type field must also contain data" & vbCrLf
66:       blnOK = False
67:       cboCustType.SetFocus
68:    End If
69:    '
70:    ValidateForm = strSendMsg
71:    '
72: End Function
```

4

Save and run the program. Now you must enter valid data in both fields before the form unloads. You have probably also found out that each time you click the OK button, all the form-level validation steps are performed. It is good programming practice to deliver all the validation results to the user at once. It can be very frustrating to fill out a form, receive an error message, and then fix the message, only to receive another one, and another one, and so on.

Using the VText Custom Control

The input validation routines you created today cover most of the situations you are likely to encounter when designing data entry forms. In fact, after you design one or two of these forms, you begin to see that you are writing the same validation code over and over. Instead of repeatedly writing the same code, or even constantly performing cut, copy, and paste operations, Microsoft Visual Basic 6 gives you the power to create your own custom controls that have new properties and methods for input validation. After you build these new controls, they can be used in all your data entry programs.

 In this last part of today's lesson, you learn how to use a custom OCX called VText that contains all the validation methods discussed in this chapter. This OCX was written using Visual Basic 6, and you can find the source code for this control on the CD-ROM in the VText folder in the SOURCE section. The Vtext control is a very basic implementation of validation routines, but it gives you a good framework with which to develop your own custom control to handle common validation chores for your Visual Basic 6 applications.

 Caution

> Before you can use the Vtext control, you need to add the source code for the control project into your Visual Basic IDE. In a production application, you use the installed and compiled OCX. However, using the source code in this case will give you a better chance to see how the OCX works. You can compile it and install it later for future use in other Visual Basic projects. An example project that uses the Vtext source code is included on the CD-ROM. You can find it in SOURCE\CHAP04\VBGCHAP04.VBG.

The Vtext Control Properties and Methods

The Vtext control works very much like the hand-coded validation routines covered earlier in this chapter. There are seven types of validation you can control with the Vtext custom control:

- UpperCase
- Digits only (0 through 9)
- Numeric only (0 through 9, +-)

- Required
- InRange (high & low)
- CheckSize (min length, max length)
- Conditional Input

Each of the corresponding validation types has a Boolean flag (on/off), an associated method (CheckRequired, CheckInRange, and so forth), and an associated error event (CheckRequiredError, and so forth). You can use the custom property page to set the various values of the Vtext control (see Figure 4.9).

FIGURE 4.9

Setting the properties of the Vtext *control using the Property Pages dialog.*

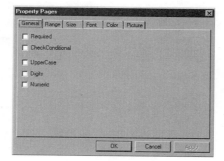

Laying Out the ValText Data Form

Start a new Standard EXE project with Visual Basic 6 and add the source code to the Vtext custom control project to your project group. To do this, select File | Add Project from the main menu and locate the TYSDBVB6\SOURCE\CHAP04\VTEXT\VTEXT.VBP project. Click on Open to add this project to your group. You now have both your new Standard EXE project and the Vtext OCX project loaded in the Visual Basic IDE.

Now, using Figure 4.10 and Table 4.1, complete the design layout of the test form. Be sure to add the Frame control first, and then draw the two Vtext controls and the Data Control directly on the frame. This will make sure the Vtext and Data Controls are child controls of the frame.

FIGURE 4.10

Laying out the test form.

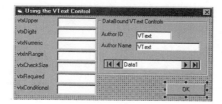

4

TABLE 4.1   CONTROLS FOR THE VALTEXT TEST FORM

Control	Property	Setting
VB.Form	Name	frmTest
	BorderStyle	3 'Fixed Dialog
	Caption	"Using the VText Control"
	ClientHeight	2715
	ClientLeft	45
	ClientTop	330
	ClientWidth	6135
	MaxButton	0 'False
	MinButton	0 'False
	ShowInTaskbar	0 'False
	StartUpPosition	3 'Windows Default
ValText.VText	Name	vtxUpper
	Height	315
	Left	1320
	Top	60
	Width	1215
	UpperCase	-1 'True
	Text	" "
VB.Frame	Name	Frame1
	Caption	"DataBound VText Controls"
	Height	1815
	Left	2580
	Top	60
	Width	3435
ValText.VText	Name	VText2
	DataField	"Name"
	DataSource	"Data1"
	Height	255
	Left	1200
	Top	780
	Width	1995

Control	Property	Setting
ValText.VText	Name	VText1
	DataField	"AUID"
	DataSource	"Data1"
	Height	255
	Left	1200
	Top	420
	Width	1095
VB.Data	Name	Data1
	Caption	"Data1"
	Connect	"Access"
	DatabaseName	"I:\tysdbvb6\ source\data\ books6.mdb"
	DefaultCursorType=	'DefaultCursor
	DefaultType	2 'UseODBC
	Exclusive	0 'False
	Height	345
	Left	180
	Options	0
	ReadOnly	0 'False
	RecordsetType	1 'Dynaset
	RecordSource	"Authors"
	Top	1320
	Width	3060
VB.Label	Name	Label8
	Caption	"Author ID"
	Height	255
	Left	120
	Top	420
	Width	1095

continues

4

TABLE 4.1   CONTINUED

Control	Property	Setting
VB.Label	Name	Label9
	Caption	"Author Name"
	Height	255
	Left	120
	Top	780
	Width	1155
VB.CommandButton	Name	cmdOK
	Caption	"OK"
	Height	375
	Left	4740
	Top	2160
	Width	1215
ValText.VText	Name	vtxDigits
	Height	315
	Left	1320
	Top	420
	Width	1215
	Digits	-1 'True
	Text	""
ValText.VText	Name	vtxInRange
	Height	315
	Left	1320
	Top	1140
	Width	1215
	CheckRange	-1 'True
	LowValue	"50"
	HighValue	"100"
	Text	""
ValText.VText	Name	vtxCheckSize
	Height	315
	Left	1320
	Top	1500

Control	Property	Setting
	Width	1215
	CheckSize	-1 'True
	MinLength	5
	MaxLength	10
	Text	" "
ValText.VText	Name	vtxRequired
	Height	315
	Left	1320
	Top	1860
	Width	1215
	Required	-1 'True
	Text	" "
ValText.Vtext	Name	vtxConditional
	Height	315
	Left	1320
	Top	2220
	Width	1215
	CheckConditional=	'True
	Text	" "
ValText.Vtext	Name	vtxNumeric
	Height	315
	Left	1320
	Top	780
	Width	1215
	Numeric	-1 'True
	Text	" "
VB.Label	Name	Label1
	Caption	"vtxUpper"
	Height	315
	Left	60
	Top	60
	Width	1215

4

continues

TABLE 4.1   CONTINUED

Control	Property	Setting
VB.Label	Name	Label2
	Caption	"vtxDigits"
	Height	315
	Left	60
	Top	420
	Width	1215
VB.Label	Name	Label3
	Caption	"vtxNumeric"
	Height	315
	Left	60
	Top	780
	Width	1215
VB.Label	Name	Label4
	Caption	"vtxInRange"
	Height	315
	Left	60
	Top	1140
	Width	1215
VB.Label	Name	Label5
	Caption	"vtxCheckSize"
	Height	315
	Left	60
	Top	1500
	Width	1215
VB.Label	Name	Label6
	Caption	"vtxRequired"
	Height	315
	Left	60
	Top	1860
	Width	1215

Control	Property	Setting
VB.Label	Name	Label7
	Caption	"vtxConditional"
	Height	315
	Left	60
	Top	2220
	Width	1215

After you've completed the form and set the various custom properties of each of the Vtext controls, save the form (TEST.FRM) and the project (VALTEXT.VBP) before continuing to the next section to add the code behind the form.

Adding Code to the TEST.FRM Form

Because the Vtext custom control handles most of the details of form-level and field-level validation, you don't need to add much code to your TEST form. However, you do need to add some. Most of the code you add is code that responds to error events fired by the VTEXT control. However, you also add a bit of code to perform validation when someone clicks the OK button.

Listing 4.11 contains all the code you need to add to the form to respond to error events fired by the Vtext control. Add this code to your project in the appropriate locations.

LISTING 4.11 ADDING CODE THAT RESPONDS TO THE Vtext ERROR EVENTS

```
 1: Private Sub vtxCheckSize_CheckSizeError(vValue As Variant)
 2:     '
 3:     MsgBox "Invalid Entry Length! [" & CStr(vValue) & "]", vbCritical, _
        "vtxCheckSize"
 4:     '
 5: End Sub
 6:
 7: Private Sub vtxCheckSize_ConditionalError(strMsg As String)
 8:     '
 9:     MsgBox strMsg, vbCritical, "vtxCheckSize"
10:     '
11: End Sub
12:
13: Private Sub vtxDigits_DigitsError(KeyAscii As Variant)
14:     '
15:     MsgBox "Enter Digits only! '0123456789'", vbCritical, "vtxDigits"
16:     '
```

continues

LISTING 4.11   CONTINUED

```
17: End Sub
18:
19: Private Sub vtxInRange_InRangeError(vValue As Variant)
20:     '
21:     MsgBox "InRange Error Reported!", vbCritical, "vtxInRange"
22:     '
23: End Sub
24:
25: Private Sub vtxNumeric_NumericError(KeyAscii As Variant)
26:     '
27:     MsgBox "Enter Numeric data only! '0123456789.+-'", vbCritical, _
          "vtxNumeric"
28:     '
29: End Sub
30:
31: Private Sub vtxRequired_RequiredError()
32:     '
33:     MsgBox "This is a required field!", vbCritical, "vtxRequired"
34:     '
35: End Sub
```

As you can see from Listing 4.11, the VTEXT control will automatically fire off error events if the validation settings you established in the properties dialog are not met.

The only other item of business is to add some validation code to the cmdOK_click event. This will fire off validation checks when a user attempts to leave the form. Add the code from Listing 4.12 to your project.

LISTING 4.12   CALLING VALIDATION ROUTINES FROM THE cmdOK_click EVENT

```
 1: Private Sub cmdOK_Click()
 2:     '
 3:     ' perform form-level validation
 4:     '
 5:     If vtxInRange.CheckRange = True Then
 6:         vtxInRange.InRangeValidate
 7:     End If
 8:     '
 9:     If vtxCheckSize.CheckSize = True Then
10:         vtxCheckSize.CheckSizeValidate
11:     End If
12:     '
13:     If vtxConditional.CheckConditional = True Then
14:         vtxConditional.ConditionalValidate vtxConditional, vtxUpper
15:     End If
16:     '
17: End Sub
```

You should notice that no message-handling code is added here. That is because any messages that will be displayed are handled in the _error events of the controls (see Listing 4.11).

After adding the code to the form, save the form and project again and press F5 to run the project. You should now be able to exercise all the validation rules established for the form and see messages displayed when you violate those rules (see Figure 4.11).

FIGURE 4.11

Testing the VALTEXT *project.*

Summary

Today, you learned how to perform input validation on data entry forms. You learned that input validation tasks can be divided into three areas:

- Key filtering: preventing unwanted keyboard input
- Field-level validation: validating input for each field
- Form-level validation: validating input across several fields

You also learned that you should ask yourself a few basic questions when you are developing validation rules for your form:

- Is it a required field?
- What characters are valid/invalid for this field (numeric input only, capital letters only, no spaces allowed, and so on)?
- For numeric fields, is there a high/low range limit (must be greater than zero and less than 1,000, can't be less than 100, and so on)?
- Is there a list of valid values for this field? (Can the user enter only Retail, Wholesale, or Other; Name must already be in the Customer table, and so on.)
- Is this a conditional field? (If users enter Yes in field A, they must enter something in field C.)

You learned how to write keyboard filter validation functions using the Visual Basic 6 KeyPress event. You learned how to write field-level validation functions that check for valid input ranges, input that is part of a list of valid data, and input that is within minimum and maximum length requirements. You also learned how to write validation functions that make sure dependent fields have been filled out properly.

Finally, you learned how to use the VText custom control, which incorporates all the validation techniques you learned in this chapter. You can use this ActiveX control in all your future Visual Basic projects.

Quiz

1. What is the difference between input validation and error trapping?
2. What Visual Basic event occurs every time a key is pressed on your keyboard?
3. Do characters in a validation list need to be entered in any particular order?
4. What does the following code mean?

   ```
   If Len(Trim(txtUpper)) <> 0 then
   ```
5. Should conditional field validation be performed at the field level or the form level?
6. When should you load validation lists?
7. What do the three sections of the format property of the MaskedEdit control represent? What character separates these sections?

Exercises

1. Write code to allow entry of only capital letters in a field. The user should be able to enter control codes, but not numbers or symbols.
2. Write the format property for a MaskedEdit control that rounds the entered number to the nearest hundredth, includes commas in all numbers, and places an en dash (–) in front of negative numbers.
3. Write a form-level validation routine that requires that entry to be made into a field named txtDate before a record can be saved by pressing a button named cmdOK.
4. Write the code to fill a combo box named cboEmployees with your employees' last names of Smith, Andersen, Jones, and Jackson. What property do you set in the combo box control to sort these names alphabetically?

DAY 5

Writing Reports For Visual Basic 6 Applications

Today, you learn how to create reports using a new report writer to Visual Basic 6: The Data Report. Doing the exercises in this chapter, you learn

- How to connect to data sources using the Data Environment, a new tool in Visual Basic 6 that enables the user to quickly make data connections at design-time
- How to bind a report to a Data Environment
- How to add fields to a report
- How to format a Data Report
- How to call a Data Report from within a Visual Basic 6 project
- How to export data using the Data Report

Understanding Report Writing

Report writing is the method by which data is pulled from your database and displayed in a printed format, Web page, or text file. A printed report is, in many situations, the ultimate product of your database application. With the release of Visual Basic 6, Microsoft has included the Data Reporter for creation of data reports. This tool uses the ADO Data Environment to extract data from a data source (multiple data sources of varying data types if you like) as a basis for the report.

Creating a Report with the Data Report Designer

There are three main steps in creating a Data Report. The first is to define the connection to your data by building the Data Environment. The second step in creating the report is to bind the report to the Data Environment and add fields and other objects. The third and final step is to call the report from within your Visual Basic 6 program, using the SHOW method.

Let's now look at each of these steps as you build the first project today.

Starting the Data Project

Start your project by opening Visual Basic 6 and selecting Data Project from the New Project dialog. The Project Explorer shows that a Data Project starts with two designers—a Data Environment and a Data Report—and a data entry form.

To create a Data Report, you must first identify the data that will be in the report. This is the function of the Data Environment.

Creating the Data Environment and Establishing the Connection

In your exercise, you do not have to create a Data Environment, because one is created by the Data Project. You can, however, insert a Data Environment into an existing project by selecting the Project | Add Data Environment menu item. Please note that you may need to select Project | More Active X Designers | Data Environment if you have more than four designers in your project.

You create the Data Environment to store the definition of the dataset to be used in the report. Double-click on the Data Environment designer in the Project Explorer window to bring up the Data Environment designer. Now, click on DataEnvironment1 in the window that appears and then look at the Properties window. Set the Name property to deBook6. See Figure 5.1.

FIGURE 5.1

The Data Environment.

Next click on Connection1 and change its `Name` property to `cnnAuthors`. In the Data Environment designer window, right-click on the `cnnAuthors` connection and select Properties from the menu that appears. You should now see the Properties dialog. See Figure 5.2.

FIGURE 5.2

The cnnAuthors Properties window.

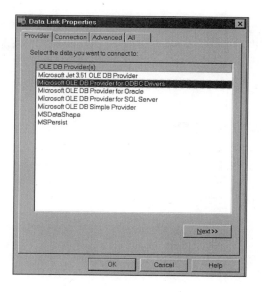

To create the connection, click on the Next button at the bottom of the Provider tab while Microsoft OLE DB Provider for ODBC Drivers is selected. This brings up the Connection tab. Select the second option, Use Connection String and then its Build button. Select the New button that appears on the Machine Data Source tab. Select System Data Source on the next dialog. Select the Next button and then Microsoft Access in the list box that appears, and then click Next and then Finish. When you click the Finish button, you will be prompted with a screen similar to Figure 5.3.

FIGURE 5.3

The ODBC definition dialog.

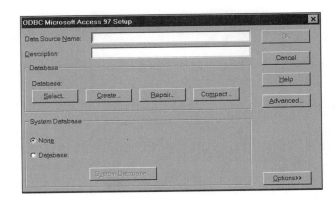

To define the data source, click on the Select button in the database section of the dialog. Find the file \\TYSDBVB6\SOURCE\DATA\BOOKS6.MDB when the file find dialog appears. When done, click on the Database Name field and enter BOOKS6.MDB. Select OK to keep your definition.

Now open the Use Data Source Name combo box and select BOOKS6.MDB. Test your connection by selecting the Test Connection button at the bottom-right of the Connection tab. When successful, click OK to store your connection definition.

It is now time to save your work. Save the form as frmDatRpt, the Designer file as deBOOK6.DSR, the Data Report designer as drBOOKS6.DSR, and the project as datRPT.VBP.

Creating the Command Object

After you have defined the Data Environments Connection, you can define the Command. The Command stores the connection to the table and the fields that are used on the report. Right-click on Commands in the Data Environment designer and select Add Command. You should see a dialog similar to Figure 5.4.

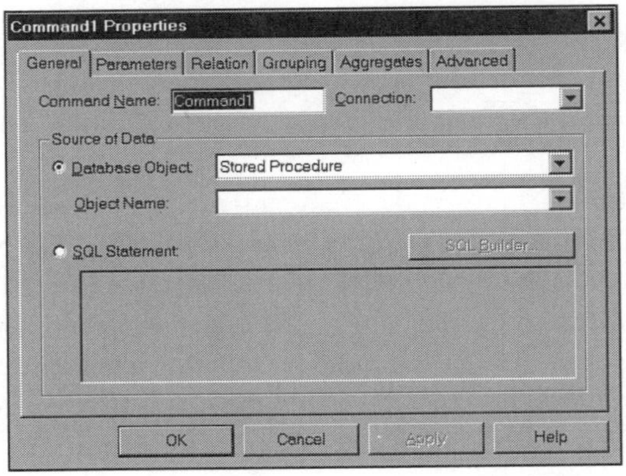

FIGURE 5.4

A Data Environment Command definition screen.

Note The Data Environment can also be used to build data entry forms. See Day 9, "Creating Database Programs with the Data Environment Designer," for a more detailed look at the Data Environment.

Set the Command Name to comAuthors. Open the Connection combo box and select cnnAuthors. You are asked whether you want to make this change. Answer Yes to that question. You want to use a database object for your first report, so make sure the Database Object option is selected. Then select Table from that combo box.

When you open the Object Name combo box, the connection to the BOOKS6.MDB database is made, and all the tables contained within it are displayed. For this exercise, select the Authors table and click the OK button when you are done.

Notice that the Data Environment designer has a new command named comAuthors with a plus sign next to it. Open this object and you will see all the fields that are contained within the table.

You have now completed all the Data Environment work necessary to create a simple list report. Your next step is to build the report to display the connection information.

Building a Simple Data Report

Now it's time to create the report to display the data defined in the Data Environment. To do this, first double-click on the DataReport1 object in the Project Explorer window. This displays a data report screen. Find the Name property in the Properties window and set it to drAuthors. Next set the DataSource property to deBook6 and the DataMember property to comAuthors.

Note The DataSource and DataMember properties are the only two properties that must be set in a Data Report. These properties bind the report to the Data Environment.

You can now add fields to the Data Report. To do this, you display the Data Environment by double-clicking on it in the Project Explorer window. Next close all but the Data Environment and the Data Report windows and select Window | Tile Horizontally. You need as much screen real estate as possible when laying out a data report.

You now can simply click and drag fields from the Data Environment (the window titled DataProject - deBook6 (DataEnvironment)) to the Data Report (the window titled DataProject - drAuthors (DataReport)). For this exercise, click and drag the AUID, Name, and DOB fields from the Data Environment to the Detail section of the drAuthors. Your screen should look similar to Figure 5.5 when you are done.

Note

When you drag fields onto the Data Report, you may also get a label. This option of the Data Environment can be changed to prevent this from happening. To do this, right-click on the topmost object in the Data Environment window (in this case, deBook6) and select Options, or simply select the Options icon at the top of the Data Environment. There is a check box under the Field Mappings tab that reads Drag and Drop Field Captions. Uncheck this box to remove the automatic addition of labels to your report.

FIGURE 5.5

Building the Data Report.

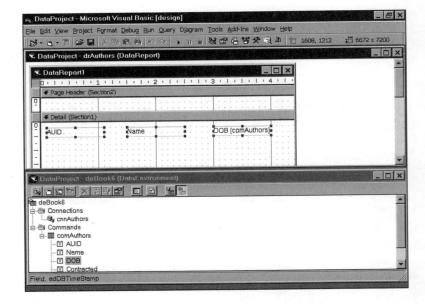

Note

Select all the appropriate objects and make ample use of the Align, Horizontal Spacing, and Vertical Spacing options on the Alternate mouse button menu. These features will save you a great deal of time and give your reports a more "polished" look.

Displaying Your Report

The SHOW method is used from within your Visual Basic 6 application to display your report to the screen. Save your project at this point, close all windows, and then open the Project Explorer. Double-click on the frmDatRpt object and set its Name property to frmDRProject.

Now let's add a menu to this form. Do this by selecting Tools | Menu Editor. For the first menu item, enter &File in the Caption field and mnuFile in the Name Field. Click the Next button and then the right-pointing arrow (indent). Enter the Caption of E&xit and a Name of mnuExit. Press Next to move on.

> **Note**
> The Menu Editor is available only when a form is selected. It will not display as available if either the Data Environment or Data Report is the selected item when the Tools menu is opened.

> **Note**
> The ampersand (&) is used to identify the letter to be underlined in the display of the menu at runtime. This underlined letter can be used in conjunction with the Alt key as a hotkey for the menu item.

Now click the left-pointing arrow (outdent) and add &Reports to the Caption field and mnuReports to the Name field. Press Next to add this menu item.

Add one last menu item. The Caption property should be &Authors Listing and the Name property should be mnuAuthorsListing. When done, your menu designer should look like Figure 5.6.

5

FIGURE 5.6

Building a menu for the Data Report project.

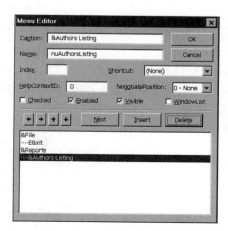

To call the report, you need one short line of code. To enter the code, select the menu option Reports|Authors Listing from `frmDatRpt.FRM` to display the code window. Now enter the code from Listing 5.1.

LISTING 5.1   CODE TO DISPLAY A DATA REPORT

```
1: Private Sub nuAuthorsListing_Click()
2:      drAuthors.Show
3: End Sub
```

You see from line 2 of Listing 5.1 that you simply add the `Name` property of your report, followed by a period and the word `Show` to display any report.

Enter the code in Listing 5.2 to the `Click` event of `mnuExit`. This code stops execution of the program when the Exit menu item is selected.

LISTING 5.2   CODE TO STOP EXECUTION OF THE PROGRAM

```
1: Private Sub mnuExit_Click()
2:      Unload Me
3: End Sub
```

Save and execute your project. Click on the Reports|Authors Listing menu option to display your data report. Take note of the printer icon. Send your report to the printer. Also take note of the Export icon. The Data Report can be used not just to display data, but also to extract data or to publish Web pages. You learn about exporting later in this chapter.

Finally, take note of the spacing of the records and the lack of column headers in your report. The next section of this chapter focuses on cleaning up the report and adding the necessary headings.

Formatting Your Report

The packaging of your reports is often just as important as the information contained within. Users give greater credibility to reports that have a polished look. The focus of this section is on making your reports look good.

Note

Never underestimate the importance of the printed reports coming from your application. To many, it is the only thing they will see regarding the application. It is quite common for excellent applications to be deemed failures simply due to their lack of quality reporting.

Defining Row Spacing on Your Report

In the previous section, your report had a large amount of whitespace between records. The Data Report designer uses the amount of space in the Detail section of the report to gauge spacing between records. To reduce the amount of space between records, you drag and reduce the size of the Detail section. Do this now, and use Figure 5.7 as a guide.

FIGURE 5.7

Reducing the size of the Detail section reduces the line spacing between records.

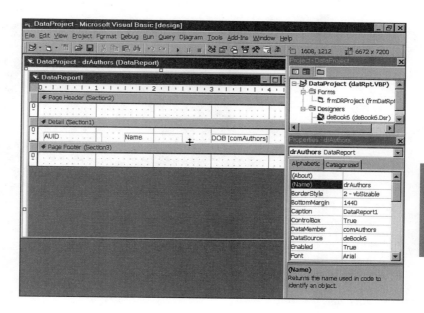

Inserting Column Headings on Your Report

Of course, just putting data fields on your report is not too useful to the header of the report. Therefore, the Data Report enables you to place Headers at the tops of each column.

Open the data report you created in the previous exercises. Next, make sure your Toolbox is displayed on screen (View|Toolbox). Double-click on the RptLabel control.

Drag the control into the Page Header section of your report just above the AUID field. Set its Caption property to Author ID, its Name property to Label1 and its Font property to Arial, Bold 8 pt.

Now add RptLabels to function as column headings for the other two columns. Use Table 5.1 and Figure 5.8 as a guide.

FIGURE 5.8

Adding column headings to your report.

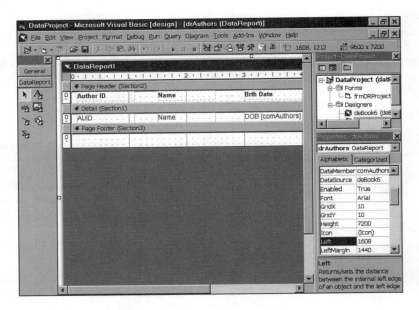

TABLE 5.1   ADDING COLUMN HEADINGS TO YOUR REPORT

Control	Property	Setting
RptLabel	Name	Label2
	Caption	Name
	Font	Arial, Bold 8 pt.
RptLabel	Name	Label3
	Caption	Birth Date
	Font	Arial, Bold 8 pt.

Save and run your project. You can see how the report is starting to look better, but you still have some work to do to complete it. Let's add some headers and footers.

Inserting Headers and Footers

All good printed reports have certain characteristics. First, the data is relevant to the audience that is to use it. Second, the report is laid out in a neat, logical manner. Finally, the report is self-documenting. That is, the name of the report, date created, and page numbers are all clearly displayed. These items are best placed in the Report Header and Report Footer sections of your report.

You need to add the Report Header section to your report at this time. To do so, simply right-click on the report and select Show Report Header/Footer. Two new sections are then created. These sections will appear at the very beginning and the end of the printed report. They differ from the Page Header, which appears on every page.

Now add a `RptLabel` to the Header Section. Set its `Name` property to `lblHeading`, its `Caption` property to `Author Listing`, and its `Font` property to `Arial, Bold 12 pt`. You also need to expand the size of the control to enable it to display the entire caption.

Now, expand the size of the Report Header Section and insert a second label below the Author Listing label. Use the same font size as previously and set its `Caption` property to display your name.

Inserting Controls into Your Report

To finish the Report Header, right-click inside the Report Header section and select the Insert Control | Current Date (Long Format) menu option. Align your control with the other two controls in the header; set its `Font` property to `Arial, Bold 12 pt`. and its `Width` property to `3600 twips`.

Note   One twip is approximately 1/1440-inch.

Leave a little space below the date field in the Report Header section to allow for separation from the Report Heading and the Page Headings on the printed report. Use Figure 5.9 as an example.

5

FIGURE 5.9

*Adding the Report
Header section of
the data report.*

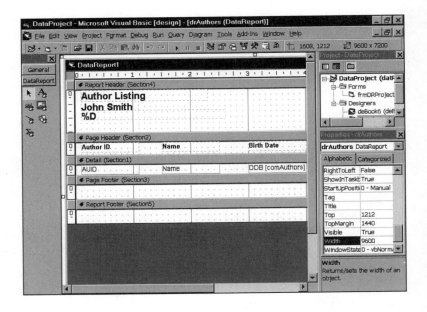

Note   Report writing with a tool such as the Microsoft Data Report is an iterative
process. You should always expect to run many tests of a new report and
make adjustments that best meet your needs.

Run your report and take a look at the heading. Make sure that the date is displayed
fully. You may have to increase the size of the control if it is not.

Let's now put a page number in the lower-left corner of each page. To do this, right-click
in the Page Footer section of the report and select Insert Control | Current Page Number.
Left-align this control with those in the Report Header.

To finish this report, you add one more feature. It should be obvious to the users that
they have received all the pages of the report. The best way to do this is to put an end-of-
report marker on each report you generate. For this example, add a label in the Report
Footer section. Set its `Caption` property to `***END OF REPORT***` and its `Font` property
to `Arial, Bold 12 pt`. You need to enlarge the size of the control to accommodate the
larger font.

When you are done, run the project and review the report. It should look similar to the
one in Figure 5.10.

FIGURE 5.10

*Your first completed
Data Report.*

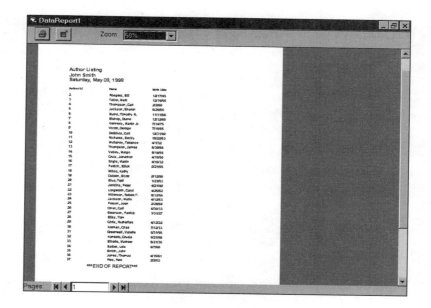

FIGURE 5.10

*Your first completed
Data Report.*

Creating Reports Using SQL Statements

The Data Reporter enables you to create reports using SQL statements as the basis for
the Command object. In this section, you use a SELECT statement to extract and ORDER
data for the report you created in the previous section.

Open the DATRPT.VBP project you completed in the previous section. Double-click on the
Data Environment object in the Project Explorer window. Right-click on the Command
comAuthors and select Properties. On the General tab of the Properties dialog, select the
SQL Statement option.

You could now either type your SQL statement in the dialog that appears or use the SQL
Builder to construct the statement. For this example, type the following statement:

```
Select AUID, Name, DOB from Authors ORDER by Name
```

Click OK and then run your project. Display the Authors Listing report. Note how the
report is now sorted by the name of the author rather than by the Author ID as was
previously the case.

Note

Please see Day 9 for a more thorough discussion on the Data Environment
and use of the SQL Builder.

Building More Complex Data Reports

In the previous section, you built a simple list report. In this section, you concentrate on building a more complicated report with aggregate functions and groupings.

To start this report, open the project you started earlier today. Insert a new Data Environment into the project and name it deSales. Create a Connection, cnnSales, that uses an ODBC data source that connects to \\TYSDBVB6\SOURCE\DATA\BOOKS6.MDB. If you want, you can reuse the connection BOOKS6.AUTHORS used in the previous report.

Now add a new Command to the Data Environment and call it comSales. Use cnnSales as the connection and link to the BookSales table.

Add a new Data Report to the project by selecting Project | Add Data Report. Set the DataSource property of this Data Report to deSales, the DataMember property to comSales, and the Name property to Drsales. Save the project and save the Data Environment as DESALES.DSR and the Data Report as DRSALES.DSR.

Arrange your desktop so that only the DESALES Data Report and Data Environment are visible. Tile the windows horizontally to make them easier to work with. Add all the fields in the BookSales table at one time by selecting comSales Command and dragging it into the Detail section of the Data Report. With all the fields still selected, right-click your mouse and select Horizontal Spacing | Make Equal. Right-click once again and select Align | Tops. Finally, give yourself a little room to work by right-clicking and selecting Horizontal Spacing | Increase.

You need to modify the menu on FRMDATRPT.FRM to call this new report. Open this form and go to the Menu Editor. Add the item Sales Report beneath, and at the same level as, Author Listing. Set its Name property to mnuSalesReport.

Enter the code in Listing 5.3 into the mnuSalesReport Click event to call the report when that menu item is selected.

LISTING 5.3   DISPLAYING THE SALES REPORT

```
1: Private Sub mnuSalesReport_Click()
2:     drSales.Show
3: End Sub
```

Next, add a report heading, page headings, page footings, and report footings in accordance with Table 5.2. Use Figure 5.11 as a guide.

FIGURE 5.11

Laying out the Quarterly Sales Report.

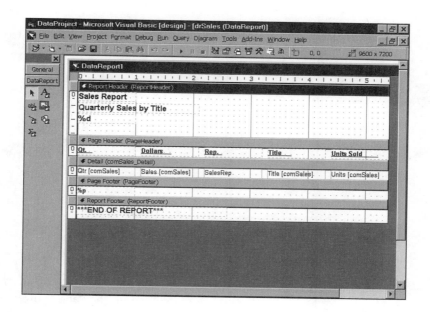

TABLE 5.2   LAYOUT OF THE SALES REPORT

Control	Property	Setting
(Insert the following into the Report Header)		
RptLabel	Caption	Sales Report
	Font	Arial, Bold, 10 pt.
	Left	0
	Name	lblTitle
RptLabel	Caption	Quarterly Sales by Title
	Font	Arial, Bold, 10 pt.
	Left	0
	Name	lblQTSales
RptLabel	Caption	%d
	Font	Arial, Bold, 10 pt.
	Name	lblDate
(Insert the following into the Page Header)		
RptLabel	Caption	Qt.
	Font	Arial, bold, 8 pt. underlined
	Name	lblQT

continues

5

TABLE 5.2 CONTINUED

Control	Property	Setting
RptLabel	Caption	Dollars
	Font	Arial, Bold, 8 pt. underlined
	Name	lblDollars
RptLabel	Caption	Rep.
	Font	Arial, Bold, 8 pt. underlined
	Name	lblRep
RptLabel	Caption	Title
	Font	Arial, Bold, 8 pt. underlined
	Name	lblBookTitle
RptLabel	Caption	Units Sold
	Font	Arial, Bold, 8 pt. underlined
	Name	lblUnitsSold

(Insert the following into the Page Footer)

Control	Property	Setting
RptLabel	Caption	%p
	Font	Arial, Bold, 8 pt.
	Name	lblPageNo

(Inset the following into the Report Footer)

Control	Property	Setting
RptLabel	Caption	***END OF REPORT***
	Font	Arial, Bold, 10 pt.
	Name	lblEOR

Save and run this report. When you do, you will notice two things. First, notice the numbers under the dollar caption. Some formatting needs to be done to turn these numbers into dollars. Second, notice how the records are sorted by quarter. It would be more helpful to see the records sorted and grouped by title.

To resolve the dollar column formatting, stop execution of the report and return to the report designer. Click on the txtSales field and change its DataFormat property to Currency. Accept the 2 decimal place default. Also, change the Alignment property to 1 - rptJustifyRight. To clean things up, right-justify the heading for this column. Finally, drag all the controls to the right of this column further to the right to separate the sales dollars from the Sales Rep field. See Figure 5.12 for an example of how your report should now look.

FIGURE 5.12

Modifying the layout to handle column formatting.

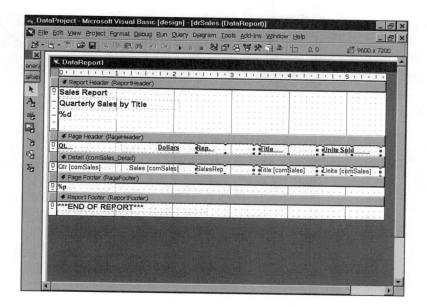

Add a grouping in the Data Environment to enable you to group the report by titles. To do this, double-click on the deSales Data Environment designer in the Project Explorer window. Next, right-click on the comSales Command and select Properties. Check the Group Command Object check box on the Grouping tab. Click on Title in the Fields in Command list box and move it to the Fields used for Grouping list box. Select OK when you are finished.

Notice how the grouping information has been added to your Data Environment. See Figure 5.13.

You are not quite done getting the grouping to display on your report. Change the DataMember property of the DRSALES report to identify the grouping and not the original command. Open the data report, click on the report title bar, and change the DataMember property to comSales_Grouping. Finally, right-click on the data report and select Insert Group Header/Footers. Run your project and now examine the data on your report.

This grouping is nice, but you are not quite done. You really want the data grouped and totaled by quarter for each title. Adding aggregate functions to do this is the subject of the next section.

5

FIGURE 5.13

The Data Environment after a grouping has been added.

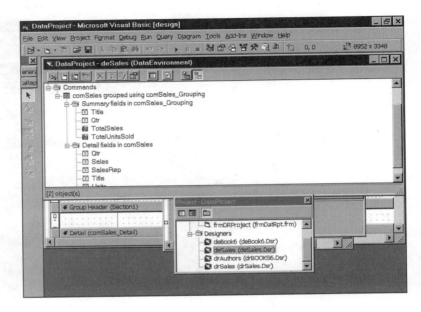

Adding Aggregate Functions to a Report

Aggregate functions can be added to a Data Environment and dragged onto a data report to do most basic math functions, including average, count, maximum, minimum, standard deviation, and sum. As you will see in the next portion of this exercise, it is quite easy to add aggregate functions such as summations to your report.

Note

> A Data Environment aggregate function is used to perform mathematical calculations on attached data. Functions that can be performed include Average, Count, Maximum, Minimum, Standard Deviation, and Sum.

You now add two aggregate functions to your project. The first will sum the dollar sales, and the second will total the unit sales for each title. Begin by opening the properties for the comSales Command and clicking on the Aggregate tab. Select the Add button and complete the screen, using the parameters from Table 5.3 to add two aggregate sum functions.

TABLE 5.3   ADDING SUM AGGREGATE FUNCTIONS

Aggregate	Setting	Value
TotalSales	Name	TotalSales
	Function	Sum
	Aggregate on	Grouping
	Field	Sales
TotalUnitSales	Name	TotalUntSales
	Function	Sum
	Aggregate on	Grouping
	Field	Units

When you are finished, select OK and then save your work. Now position your screens and drag the TotalSales aggregate function into the Group Footer just below the Sales field in the Detail section. Set its alignment right-justified and its DataFormat to Currency. Do the same for the TotalUnitSales function, but place it in the Group Footer under the Units field. Make sure its alignment is also right-justified, but don't change its DataFormat property.

Run the report once again. That's all there is to adding an aggregate function to your report. See Figure 5.14.

FIGURE 5.14

Displaying the aggregate functions.

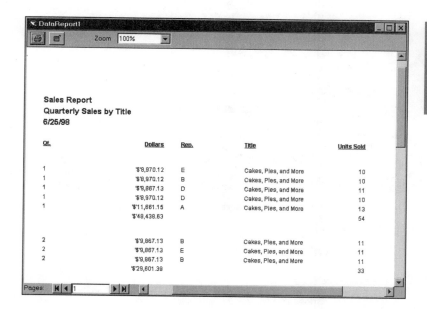

5

Exporting Data

The Data Report is also a good tool for extracting data to other applications or for publishing information to a Web page. After the report is generated, you have the choice of saving it to HTML and Text formats. Try this by generating the Sales Report once again. When the print preview of the report appears, select the Export icon at the top of the screen. Save the report in HTML format.

After the report is saved to your hard drive, open Windows Explorer, find the report, and double-click on it. The .HTM extension should be associated with a browser, and the report should automatically appear.

FIGURE 5.15

The Sales Report as viewed through a browser.

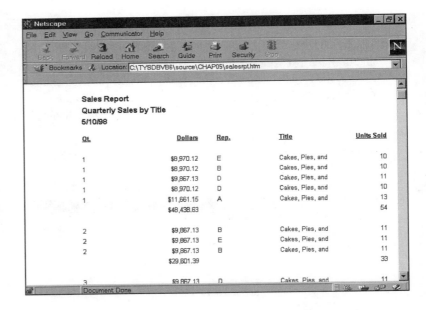

Note

Data can also be extracted into ASCII text from within a data report. Simply follow the same procedure as you did to extract data in the HTML format, but select Text in the Save As Type combo box that appears on the Export dialog.

Creating Data Reports from Joined Tables

To this point you have concentrated on writing reports with data from just one data table. Due to the design of relational databases, however, this is not likely to be the case for all reports you write in the real world. One of the strong points of using the Data Environment is that you can join tables within the designer and even join tables from separate databases. This joined data can be then placed on your data report.

The focus of this section is to create a Data Report from a Data Environment that joins two tables. If you are familiar with the BOOKS6.MDB database used throughout this text, you will know about two tables ideal for this example. They are the Authors table and the Titles table.

Here are the fields that are contained within these tables:

Author	Titles
AUID	ISBN
NAME	Title
DOB	AUID
Contracted	Year Published
Cover	PubID
	Description
	Notes
	Subject
	Comments

You will notice that these tables have the AUID field in common, so you will use it to join these two tables in your new Data Environment.

Let's start a new Data Project and build a new Data Environment. Create a new Connection and name it CNNBOOKS6. Create a new ODBC data source and call it BOOKS6. This data source should be defined as a System data source with a Microsoft Access Driver and access the \\TYSDBVB6\SOURCE\DATA\BOOKS6.MDB database.

Now create a new command and call it comTitle. Use the cnnBooks6 connection and then select the Table database object of Titles. Click OK to save your work.

Next, right-click on comTitles in the Data Environment designer and choose the option Add Child Command. This brings up the screen that enables you to identify the table and key on which to join these tables.

5

Enter the name of `comAuthors` and select the Authors table as the Source of Data. Now move to the Relations tab and click on Relate to a Parent Command Object. The Parent Command of `comTitles` should automatically appear, and the parent and child relation fields should default to AUID. Click the Add button to complete the relation. Your screen should look similar to Figure 5.16.

FIGURE 5.16

Defining a Relation in a Data Environment.

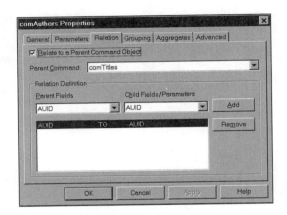

Click OK to complete the definition. Check your Data Environment designer against Figure 5.17.

FIGURE 5.17

The Data Environment.

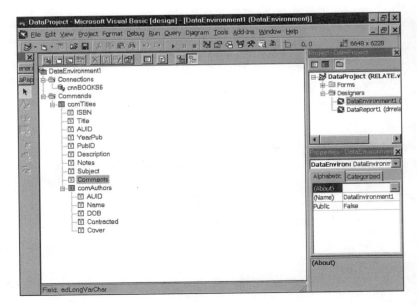

Note

> Do not try to create two children to a single parent command at the same level, because the data report can show only one child at a time.

Make sure you save your work. Save the data form as RELATE.FRM, the Data Environment as DERELATE.DSR, the Data Report as DRRELATE.DSR, and the project as RELATE.VBP.

As you can see, it is quite easy to join two tables in a Data Environment. In the next section, you use this information to build a report.

Using Related Tables to Build a Data Report

Let's now begin the design of the report using the Data Environment created in the previous section. Open the Data Report. Do you remember what properties need to be set to bind the report to the Data Environment? You're correct if you said the DataSource and the DataMember. Set these values to DataEnvironment1 and comTitles, respectively.

Now open the Data Report and right-click on it. Select the Retrieve Structure menu item. This function will read the Data Environment that the report is bound to and insert the appropriate sections into the report.

Note

> Be careful when using the Retrieve Structure command, because it will delete any previous modifications your have made to your data report.

Drag the Title field from the Titles table (comTitles) onto the Group Header of the report. Next, drag AUID and YearPub from comTitles onto the detail section. Finally, drag Name and DOB from the comAuthors command onto the report retail section. Add a report header, a page footer, and a report footer. Use Figure 5.18 as a guide.

You won't use the SHOW method to execute this report. Instead, change the Startup object in the properties of the project. Do this by selecting Project|DataProject Properties and by selecting DataReport1 as the Startup object.

Now run your report and take a look at it. Notice how the title appears above the data and that the data from two separate tables appears together within the detail section under each title.

5

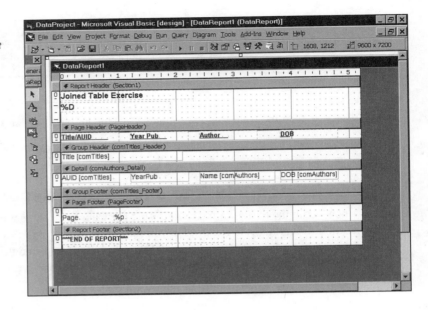

FIGURE 5.18

The data report layout for the joined table exercise.

Summary

Today, you learned that creating a Data Environment is the first step in creating a Data Report. To create a Data Environment, you first must define the Connection and then define the Command(s). You learned that Commands can exist in a hierarchy and define relationships between different data tables.

You also learned how to set the `DataSource` and `DataMember` properties of the Data Report to bind it to the Data Environment. The `DataSource` stores the name of the Data Environment, and the `DataMember` stores the name of the Command that will be used on the report.

You learned that dragging and dropping fields from the Data Environment onto the Data Report is a fast way to build a report.

You also learned how to format a data report. This includes changing fonts, adding headers and footers, and inserting aggregate functions.

You learned how easy it is to export data from a database into an HTML document. The Data Report thus makes it easy for you to develop reports that can be placed on the Web.

Finally, you learned how to build relationships among tables in the Data Environment. You learned that you need to use the `Retrieve Structure` command to insert the appropriate headers and footers into your report. You learned that the hierarchy of the commands in the data environment design dictates where fields can be placed on a data report.

Quiz

1. Why do you define a Command in a Data Environment?
2. What two properties of a Data Report need to be set in order to bind it to the Data Environment?
3. How do you define row spacing for a data report?
4. Can SQL statements be used in data reports?
5. How do you display a Data Report from within a Visual Basic 6 program?
6. What SQL SELECT clause can be used to sort a report?
7. What property of the Data Report needs to be changed if a grouping is added to a report?
8. Can an aggregate function be defined that returns the median of a data column?
9. Can a data report be exported directly into a Microsoft Excel format?

Exercise

1. Create a data report that uses the BOOKS6.MDB database that was installed from the CD-ROM that shipped with this book. On your report, include a listing of all authors and the name of their publishers. (Note: In order to produce this report, you relate the Authors table to the Titles table and the Titles table to the Publishers table.)

5

DAY 6

Using the Visdata Program

Today you learn everything you need to know about using one of the most valuable sample programs that is shipped with Visual Basic 6: the Visdata sample application. You learn how to use the Visdata sample application to maintain your database files, including creating and modifying database tables, performing simple data entry on existing tables, and using Visdata to make backup copies of existing databases.

Note

This lesson does not cover the source code for Visdata or talk about how Visdata works. You can, however, learn a great deal by bringing the Visdata project up within Visual Basic 6 and studying the modules and forms. Studying Visdata in this manner is an excellent way to learn how to create dynamic data entry forms, handle SQL processing, and link your Visual Basic 6 programs to back-end database servers using ODBC drivers.

Using Visdata to Maintain Databases and Tables

Visdata is an excellent tool for constructing and managing databases for your Visual Basic 6 applications. You can use it to create new databases, add or modify tables and indexes, establish relationships, set user and group access rights, test and store SQL query statements, and perform data entry on existing tables.

Visdata can present dynamic data entry forms in page format or grid layout format. You can add, edit, or delete records in any table using Visdata. You can connect to Microsoft Access databases, as well as versions of dBASE, FoxPro, and Paradox. You can even access data from Excel spreadsheets, delimited text files, and ODBC-connected databases. Visdata is a great tool for building sample tables and entering test data for your Visual Basic 6 applications. It is also a good tool for compacting, repairing, and managing user and group access rights for Microsoft Jet databases.

Visdata enables you to test SQL queries and save them in your Microsoft Jet database as stored queries that you can access from your Visual Basic 6 programs. You can also use Visdata to copy records from one table to another—even to copy whole data tables from one database to another. This capability gives you the power to create backups of selected information from your existing databases.

Finally, you can use Visdata to inspect the properties of Microsoft Jet data objects such as fields, relationships, tables, and indexes. You can learn a great deal about how the Microsoft Jet database engine operates by using Visdata to peek under the hood to see the heart of the Visual Basic 6 data access engine.

The Visdata Opening Screen

 If you don't already have Visdata running, start it now. You can start Visdata by selecting Visual Data Manager from the Add-Ins menu. After it is started, select File | Open Database | Microsoft Access and then open the \\TYSDBVB6\SOURCE\DATA\BOOKS6.MDB database that was installed by the CD-ROM included with this book. Your screen should look like Figure 6.1.

FIGURE 6.1

The Visdata main screen.

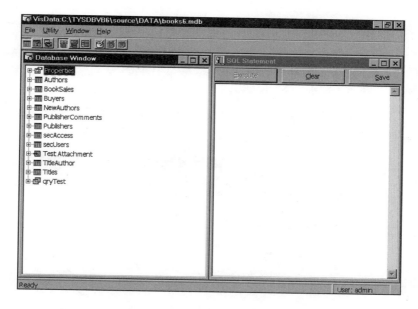

This MDI form is "Data Central" for the Visdata application. All database activity starts from this screen. Four major components of this screen deserve attention:

- The Main Menu — This menu gives you access to all the features of Visdata. This menu also expands when you open a database.
- The Database Window — This window shows all the properties and table objects present in the database you currently have open.
- The SQL Statement Window — This window enables you to write and execute standard SQL statements against the database you currently have open.
- The Toolbar — You use this to determine the type of data objects you want to work with.

Now let's go through each of the four components of the Visdata main screen in a bit more depth.

The Main Menu

The Visdata main menu contains four menu items: File, Utility, Window, and Help. The Utility menu item is enabled only after a database is opened.

The Visdata Main Menu gives you access to all the features and options of the program. You'll learn each menu option in depth later, but first, let's explore the File menu options just a bit.

6

The File | Open Database option, which you used in the preceding section, enables you to open an existing database. This database can be one of several formats. The most common database format you'll probably deal with is the Microsoft Jet format (also known as the Microsoft Access database format). For practice, let's use Visdata to open an existing Microsoft Jet database.

Select File | Open Database | Microsoft Access. The Visdata program presents you with an Open Microsoft Access Database dialog box (see Figure 6.2).

FIGURE 6.2

Opening a Microsoft Access database.

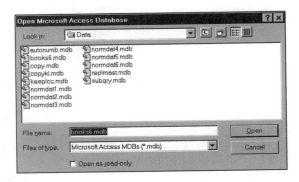

 Locate and select the BOOKS6.MDB database that can be found in the \TYSDBVB6\SOURCE \DATA directory (which was created by the CD-ROM that ships with this book). Click the Open button to load the database. After the database is loaded, Visdata updates the Database window to show all the primary data access objects in the currently opened database. Your screen should now look something like Figure 6.3.

You can close the database by selecting File | Close from the Visdata main menu.

The Database Window

The Database window shows all the major data access objects in the currently opened database. You go to the Database window to add new tables to the database and modify the design of one of the current tables. You can also open existing data tables to add records to them. If you click the alternate mouse button within the Database window while you have a table highlighted, you see several other table management options.

 Note

We use the term "alternate mouse button" to avoid any confusion between left-handed and right-handed users. If you have your mouse set for left-handed use, the alternate button is the left button; if you have your mouse set for right-handed use, the alternate button is the right button.

FIGURE 6.3

Visdata with an open database.

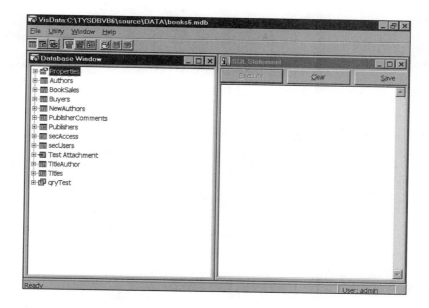

Properties

The Properties object shows the various properties of the opened database. With the
BOOKS6.MDB database open, click the plus sign (+) sign next to the Properties object. Your
screen should look like Figure 6.4.

FIGURE 6.4

Viewing the database properties.

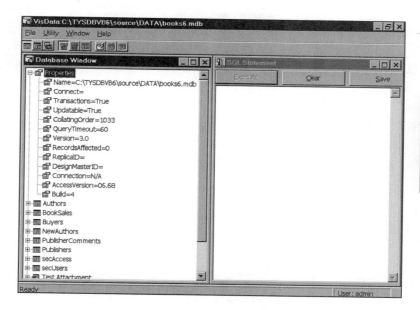

6

Note

> Many of the properties listed on this screen are available only in the version 3.0 Microsoft Jet MDB format. Don't be alarmed if your screen has several empty fields. You learn more about the difference between the various MDB formats later.

Open

The Open alternate mouse option loads the selected table. It performs the same function as double-clicking the table name.

Design

The Design option brings up the table Structure design dialog. You can view, edit, and add fields and indexes from this screen. Try this with a few tables so you can get a feel for the information available in the Design dialog.

Rename

The Rename option enables you to rename the highlighted table without deleting the data. Highlight the Authors table by clicking it once with the primary mouse button. Now click the alternate mouse button to bring up the context menu. Select Rename from the menu, enter MoreAuthors as the new name, and then press Enter. Your screen should look like Figure 6.5 as you rename the Authors table.

FIGURE 6.5

Renaming a data table.

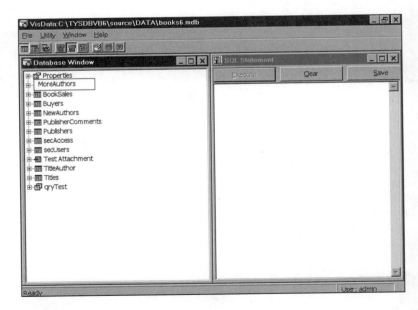

Before you continue with the project, change the MoreAuthors table back to Authors using the same technique previously described.

Delete

The Delete option enables you to delete the highlighted table and all its contents. To delete a table and all its contents, select the table you want to delete, click the alternate mouse button, and then select Delete.

Copy Structure

The Copy Structure option enables you to copy the highlighted table's field layout and design, with or without existing data, to a different database. Select the Authors table and click the alternate mouse button to bring up the context menu. Select Copy Structure from the menu list, and you see a dialog box like the one in Figure 6.6.

FIGURE 6.6

Copying a table.

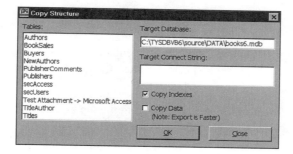

Notice that you can enter a new database name and connect string in the dialog box. This capability means you can copy the structure to an entirely different database. Leave the database name and connect string alone for now. Check the Copy Indexes and Copy Data check box, click on the Authors table in the Table list box, and click OK. You are then prompted for a table name. Enter MoreAuthors and click OK. A message from Visdata appears, telling you that the new table has been created. When you exit the dialog by clicking Close, Visdata refreshes the Window List automatically. You should now see a new table in the list: MoreAuthors.

Refresh List

The Refresh List option updates the window to reflect changes in the data access objects that are part of the database. Usually, Visdata refreshes the Database window each time you take an action that affects the contents of the list. Some actions, however, do not automatically update the window. For example, if you use the SQL window to enter SQL statements to create a new data table in the database, Visdata does not automatically refresh the Database window.

6

To refresh the Database window, simply click anywhere in the Database window and then click once with the alternate mouse button to bring up the context menu. Select Refresh List from the list. Visdata refreshes the Database window to reflect the current state of the data access objects in the opened database.

New Table

This option displays the Table Structure dialog, which can be used to construct a new table or index. You work on building new tables in the section entitled "Adding Tables and Indexes to the Database," later in this chapter.

New Query

This option displays the Visdata Query Builder, which can be used to help build SQL statements. You learn about the Query Builder when you explore the Utility menu later in this chapter.

The SQL Statement Window

The SQL Statement window enables you to enter and execute standard SQL statements against the opened database. You can save the SQL query for later use in your Visual Basic 6 programs.

Select the SQL Statement window by clicking the top border of the window one time. Now enter the following SQL query into the text window:

```
SELECT * FROM Authors
```

Now, select the Execute button in the SQL Statement window to run the query. This is not an SQL Passthrough query, so answer No when prompted with this question.

This statement selects all the data in the Authors table and presents it to the screen. Your screen should look similar to the one in Figure 6.7.

FIGURE 6.7

Results of an SQL query.

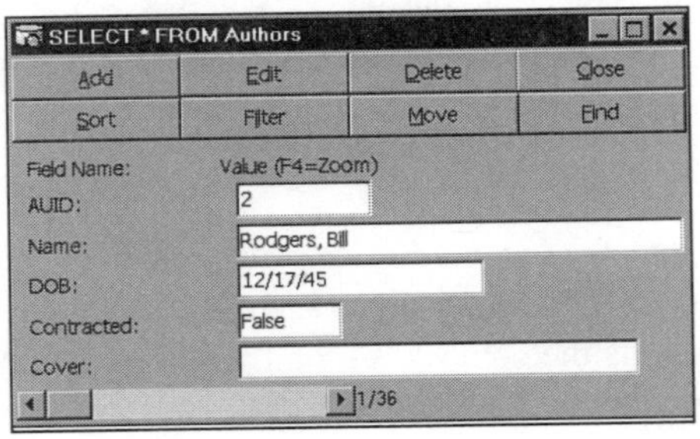

Note

You will explore SQL SELECT queries in depth in the lesson on Day 7, "Selecting Data with SQL." For now, just remember that you can write, test, and save your SQL queries using the Visdata SQL window.

You can save this query for later use within your Visual Basic 6 programs by first closing the screen that contains the result of your Select query and then clicking on the Save button in the SQL Statement window. Next, supply the query object name qryTest and click OK in the dialog box that appears (see Figure 6.8). Again, this is not an SQL Passthrough query, so answer No when the SQL Passthrough dialog appears.

FIGURE 6.8

Saving a query.

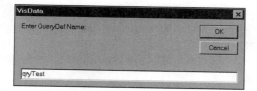

Each time you load Visdata, the program remembers the last SQL query you entered in the SQL window. You can click the Clear button to clear out the text in the SQL Statement window.

The Toolbar Buttons

Icons appear on a toolbar near the top of the Visdata main screen. You use these icons to establish the type of data object Visdata uses to access the data and the type of data entry form Visdata uses to present the selected data on the screen. You can also use these icons to assist in making changes to your database, with the option of committing the changes once made or rolling back (undoing) the change.

Selecting the Default Data Access Object

The first set of icons controls the type of data access object that Visdata uses to open the data table. The default data access object is the Visual Basic 6 Dynaset, the most flexible Visual Basic 6 data access object. You can use the Dynaset object to create updatable views of more than one table or open an existing table for read/write access.

You can also use the Snapshot data access object to open a read-only view of one or more data tables. Snapshot objects are faster than Dynasets, but require more workstation memory.

6

Finally, if you only need access to the physical base table in the database, you can select the Table radio button. Tables are fast and require little workstation memory. The disadvantage of the Table data access object is that you cannot use it to combine two or more tables into a single view.

Even though most of the work you do from Visdata is with base tables, you should set this radio button to use the Dynaset data access object. Dynasets are fast enough for almost all Visdata work, and they provide the most flexibility when dealing with multi-table views.

Selecting the Default Data Form

The second set of icons enables you to select the type of data form you see when you load your data access object. Visual Basic 6 now ships with a very nice data-bound grid tool. This grid automatically loads all the fields in the selected data access object and scrolls data records into the table as needed. This grid object may be the most useful selection of the three. Click the Use DBGrid Control on New Form icon to make this your default data form.

The other two icons select two versions of a standard data entry form. The first icon, Use Data Control on New Form, loads the records from the data access object one at a time, using the Visual Basic 6 data control tool. The second icon, Don't Use Data Control on New Form, presents a similar form, but without using the Visual Basic 6 data control tool. The advantage of the Data Control form is that it handles BIT and BINARY data type fields better than the No Data Control form. The No Data Control form, however, enables users to press F4 to display the entire contents of a data field whose contents overflow the control's display area. This zooming feature is handy when dealing with large text fields or memo fields.

You can switch the Form Type radio button after each table is opened and displayed, which enables you to open one or more tables using different data forms. Let's open three tables, each using a different data form.

First, select the Use DBGrid Control on New Form icon from the toolbar. Now double-click the Authors table. This action brings up the Authors table in a grid display. Your screen should look like Figure 6.9.

Note   Please note that the columns in this view can be resized. Simply select a column divider with your mouse and drag to the desired width.

FIGURE 6.9

Authors table using the grid data form.

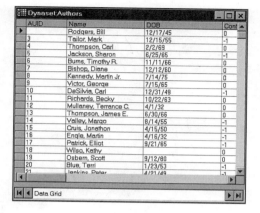

Next, select the Use Data Control on New Form button and double-click the Authors table again. Now you see the same data presented in a standard data entry form. Your screen should now look like Figure 6.10.

FIGURE 6.10

Authors table using the Data Control form.

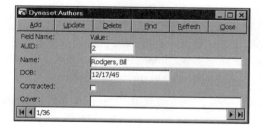

Next, select the Don't Use Data Control on New Form icon and double-click the Authors table a third time. Now you see the Authors data presented in a slightly different data entry form. Notice the differences in the way the Contracted field appears on the Don't Use Data Control on New Form (as text) form and the Data Control form (check box). Figure 6.11 shows a tiled view of the three data forms side by side.

Beginning, Rolling Back, and Committing Transactions

A basic principle in database management is the concept of begin, rollback, and commit transactions. This refers to the theory that changes are temporarily made to the database and reviewed before they are made permanent. If an error occurs as a result of the temporary change, the transaction can be undone or rolled back without causing permanent damage to the underlying data. This is a particularly handy concept when making large changes to multiple data tables. You explore this issue in detail on Day 16, "Multiuser Considerations."

FIGURE 6.11

Three data forms side by side.

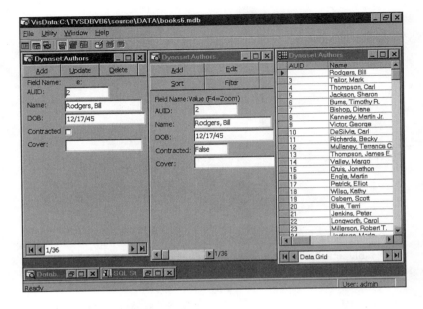

To use this concept in Visdata, simply select the Begin a Transaction icon before you make a change to your database. If you like the change, select the Commit current Transaction icon and the change becomes permanent. If you don't like the change, press the Rollback current Transaction icon to undo the changes.

Please note the use of the word *current* in the Commit and Rollback operations. This refers to all changes made since the last time the Begin icon was selected. Transactions cannot be rolled back after they are committed.

Now that you have seen the major components of the Visdata main screen, let's review each of the menu items in greater detail.

What's on the Visdata File Menu?

The Visdata File menu contains nine items. You can open, create, and close databases from the File menu; import and export data from and to the open database; log into a designated workspace; and review any errors that have been logged since you started Visdata. You can compact or repair Microsoft Jet databases from the File menu. You also exit the program from the File menu.

If you have used Visdata before, you'll also see a list of the most recently used databases in this menu. You can reload one of those databases by clicking its name in the File menu.

Open Database

Before you can begin working on an existing database, you must first load it using the Open Database menu option. This menu option enables you to load one of several database formats. Each format has a slightly different set of options in the menu tree. You can load Microsoft Access, dBASE, FoxPro, Paradox, Excel, text files, and ODBC data sources.

 Note

> You can load only one database at a time into Visdata. If you need to work on tables from more than one database, use the Utility | Attachments menu option to attach the foreign data tables (the tables that are contained within a database other than the one on which you are working) to the database you currently have open. You learn about the Attach option later today.

When you select Open Database, you see several other menu choices. You select one of the secondary items depending on the database format you want to access. The following sections cover each of the secondary menu choices and how you use them to open existing databases.

Microsoft Access

When you select the Microsoft Access option, Visdata brings up a File Open dialog box and prompts you to select the Microsoft Access database you want to load (see Figure 6.12).

FIGURE 6.12

Loading a Microsoft Access database.

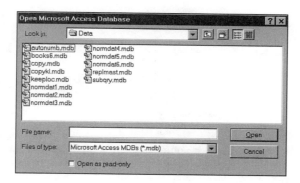

dBASE (III, IV, and 5.0)

You can also use Visdata to load dBASE-format databases. When you select the dBASE menu option, you see an additional menu that asks you to select version III, IV, or 5.0 database format.

Caution

You must tell Visdata what dBASE format you are loading so that it knows what index files and memo field formats to expect. If you load an incorrect format into Visdata, you do not see an error message right away. You may receive error messages, however, when you attempt to read or write data to the database. These errors may permanently corrupt your database. Be sure you load the FoxPro and dBASE databases using the correct menu option to avoid problems.

When you select the correct format, you see the File Open dialog box prompting you to locate and load a database. After the database is loaded, you see the list of available tables. You also see a message at the bottom of the screen suggesting that you use the Attach option to access the dBASE format data tables (see Figure 6.13).

FIGURE 6.13

Viewing a loaded dBASE database.

 Tip

When you deal with non-Microsoft Jet data formats, you get better performance speed if you access them through the Utility I Attachments menu option. You learn about the Utility I Attachments menu option later today.

FoxPro (2.0, 2.5, 2.6, and 3.0)

Loading the FoxPro format databases works the same as loading the dBASE format databases. When you select FoxPro from the menu, you see an additional menu list that asks
you to select the proper database format. When you select the format, you see the File
Open dialog prompting you to locate and load the proper database. The same warnings
mentioned in the preceding dBASE section apply here. Do not attempt to load a FoxPro
2.6 format database using the FoxPro 2.5 format menu option. Even if the file loads initially without errors, you will probably get unpredictable results and may even corrupt
your database.

Paradox (3.x, 4.x, and 5.0)

Opening Paradox files with Visdata works much like opening FoxPro or dBASE format
databases. You select the database version you wish to access and then fill out the File
Open dialog box to locate and load the database. The CD-ROM that ships with this book
contains a Paradox 4.x format database called PDSAMPLE.DB. You can locate and load this
file from the \TYSDBVB6\SOURCE\DATA\PARADOX directory.

Excel

Visdata can also directly load Microsoft Excel spreadsheet files and enable you to manipulate their contents. When you select Excel from the Open Database menu, you see the
File Open dialog box that prompts you to locate and load the Excel spreadsheet.

Visdata locates all sheets and named ranges defined in the Excel file and presents them
as table objects in the Database window (see Figure 6.14).

Figure 6.15 shows the sample Excel spreadsheet \TYSDBVB6\SOURCE\DATA\XLDATA\
EXSAMPLE.XLS as it appears in Excel. The range name box is opened in the illustration so
that you can see how the range names in Excel compare to the table names in Visdata.

Figure 6.16 shows the same Excel file opened using Visdata. In Figure 6.16, the table
object Sheet1$ has been opened as a Dynaset object.

After you open the Excel file, you can perform all data entry operations on that file
including creating new tables and editing data in existing tables in the spreadsheet.

6

> **Caution**
>
> Visdata opens Excel data files for exclusive use only. If you have an Excel
> spreadsheet open with Visdata, no other program on your workstation, or
> any other program on the network, can open the same spreadsheet. If some
> other program has an Excel spreadsheet open, you cannot open it using
> Visdata until the other program closes that file.

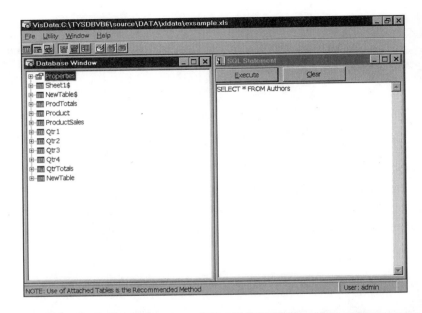

FIGURE 6.14

Using Visdata to directly load an Excel spreadsheet.

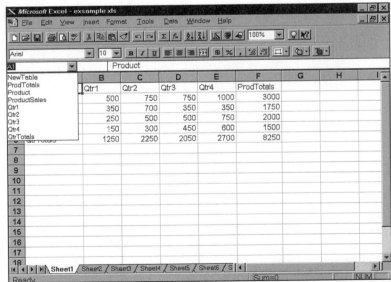

FIGURE 6.15

Viewing EXSAMPLE.XLS *with Microsoft Excel.*

FIGURE 6.16

Viewing
EXSAMPLE.XLS with
Visdata.

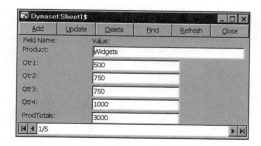

Text Files

Visdata can load various standard formats of ASCII text files for read-only access. When you select a file to load (using the File Open dialog box), you actually open the entire directory as a database. Visdata permits you to select any file with a .TXT extension from the Database window and open it as a read-only data table. Figure 6.17 shows the file \TYSDBVB\SOURCE\DATA\TEXT\TXSAMPLE.TXT opened as a read-only data file.

FIGURE 6.17

Opening a text file
with Visdata.

Visdata recognizes several types and formats of ASCII text files. The default format is comma-delimited fields with character fields surrounded by quotes.

ODBC

The ODBC menu option is slightly different from the previously discussed Open commands. This option enables you to use Visdata to open predefined ODBC data sources. When you select the ODBC menu option, you see a screen that asks you for the data source type, data source name, user ID, and password for that data source (see Figure 6.18).

After you fill out the ODBC dialog box, Visdata locates and opens the data source and updates the Database window.

Before you can open an ODBC data source, you must first define that data source using the ODBC program from the Control Panel. If you want more information on defining ODBC data sources, you can refer to the help available when you load the ODBC programs from the Control Panel.

6

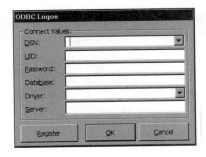

FIGURE 6.18

*Using Visdata to open
an ODBC data source.*

New

The New menu option enables you to use Visdata to create entirely new databases in several formats. This section concentrates on the Microsoft Access database format. Most of the rules for creating Microsoft Jet databases apply equally to non-Microsoft Jet formats. Although the Visdata application can create a non-Microsoft Jet database, you should not use Visdata to create non-Microsoft Jet databases very often. If you need to work in non-Microsoft Jet formats, use the native database engine to create the data files. You can then use Visdata to access and manipulate the non-Microsoft Jet databases.

Access (Version 2.0 and 7.0)

When you select the Microsoft Access menu item, Visdata asks you to select one of two versions of Microsoft Access data format: 2.0 or 7.0. The 2.0 format can be read by all versions of Microsoft Access and by Microsoft Visual Basic versions 4.0 and later. Version 7.0 format databases can be read only by the 32-bit version of Visual Basic 4 and by the 32-bit version of Microsoft Access. The advantage of the older formats is that the data can be read by most versions of the software. The advantage of the version 7.0 format is that it allows additional database properties that are not available in the older formats.

Attempting to read a version 7.0 Microsoft Access database with Access version 2.0 or Visual Basic version 3.0 results in an error that tells you your database is invalid or corrupt. If you know that you will be working only with software that can read version 7.0 files, you should select the version 7.0 format because it provides additional features. If, however, you plan to deploy your database in an environment that contains both 16- and 32-bit versions of the software (you use Visual Basic 3 or 16-bit Visual Basic 4), you should stick with the version 2.0 data format.

After you select a database format from the submenu, Visdata presents you with a dialog box that prompts you to enter a filename for the new database (refer to Figure 6.19).

FIGURE 6.19

Creating a new Microsoft Access database.

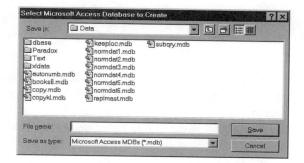

Creating a new database does not automatically create data tables; you must use the New command button in the Database window to create a new table.

dBASE, FoxPro, and Paradox

Creating dBASE, FoxPro, and Paradox format databases is similar to creating Microsoft Access databases. When you select one of these formats, you are prompted to indicate the exact version of the database you want to create. After you select a version, Visdata presents you with a simple dialog box that prompts you to enter a name for the database. This name is not a data file; it is a file directory (called a folder in Windows 95). You can include any valid drive designator and directory path you want when you create the database. See Figure 6.20 for an example of creating a FoxPro database directory.

FIGURE 6.20

Creating a FoxPro database directory.

Remember that Visdata creates directories (or folders), not data files, when you create dBASE, FoxPro, or Paradox databases. Be sure to use names that make sense as directories or folders.

6

Text

You can use Visdata to create text data files. These files are comma-delimited ASCII text files that you can open for read-only access from Visdata. Even though you can create the database files and tables, you cannot add any data to the tables or create indexes on the data tables. This might be useful if you want to create ASCII text data files for use by other applications.

When you select the text menu option, Visdata prompts you to enter a name for the database. This name is used to create a directory (Windows 95 folder) on the designated drive. You can use any valid device designator and directory path you want when you create the database.

Close Database

The Close Database menu option simply closes the open database. All tables are closed at the same time.

Import/Export

The Import/Export function enables you to move data into and out of the currently open database. To bring data in from another database, simply select Import/Export from the File menu. When this option is selected, you are presented with the dialog shown in Figure 6.21.

FIGURE 6.21

The Import/Export dialog.

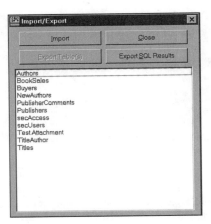

Next, select the Import command button. You are requested to select the database format from which to extract data. See Figure 6.22 for details.

FIGURE 6.22

The Import Data Format selection.

Select your database format and select OK. You are then presented with a dialog that enables you to select a database. When the database is selected, you are presented with a dialog of data tables that are available for import into your original database. (See Figure 6.23.)

FIGURE 6.23

Selecting a table to import.

Select the desired table and select the Import button to move the data into the currently open database.

To export data, select Import/Export from the File menu. Then, select the table from the dialog that appears and press the Export Table(s) button. You are then prompted to select a format and a file to hold the exported data.

Workspace

The Workspace menu item displays a login dialog that enables you to log in to the currently open database as a different user. This is handy if you want to test user IDs and passwords. When you select Workspace from the menu, you see a dialog box that requests a login ID and password (see Figure 6.24).

FIGURE 6.24

Viewing the Login dialog.

6

Workspace data objects are covered in detail on Day 9, "Creating Database Programs with the Data Environment Designer."

Errors

The Errors menu option shows the last error or set of errors reported to Visdata (see Figure 6.25).

FIGURE **6.25**

Viewing the errors collection.

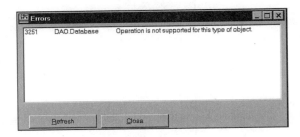

 Some data sources return more than one error message per transaction (usually ODBC data sources), which is referred to as the *errors collection*. This menu option enables you to review the errors collection in a grid listing. If no errors have been returned, this grid is empty.

 Even if you have had several successful database transactions since your last error, the most recent error remains in this grid display.

Compact MDB

You can use Visdata to compact existing Jet databases (MDB files). Compacting a database removes empty space in the data file once occupied by records that were deleted. Running the Compact menu option also reorganizes any defined indexes stored in the database.

When you select Compact MDB, you have to select a database format. If you select 7.0 MDB from this menu, the database you selected is compacted and stored as a Microsoft Jet version 3.0 database. If you select 2.0 from this menu, the database you select is compacted and stored as a Microsoft Jet version 2.0 database.

Note Although not recommended, you can use the Compact Database menu option to convert older database formats to newer ones, but you cannot use the Compact Database menu option to convert newer formats to older ones. For example, you cannot convert a 3.0 Microsoft Jet database to a 2.0 Microsoft Jet database.

When you select the target format, you see a File Open dialog box asking you to select the database you want to compact. The database you select cannot be opened by any other program while it is being compacted. After you select the source database, you have to enter the name of the destination database file. If you select the same name as the source, your current data file is overwritten with the new format. If you select a new database filename, all information is copied from the source database to the target database.

> **Caution**
>
> Even though Visdata enables you to compact a database file onto itself, this practice is not recommended. If anything happens midway through the compacting process, you could lose some or all of your data. Always compact a database to a new database filename.

Before Visdata compacts your database, you will be asked whether you want to encrypt the data. If you say Yes, Visdata copies all data and encrypts the file so that only those who have access to the security files can read the data. You learn more about data encryption on Day 21 "Securing Your Database Applications."

Repair MDB

If you get a "database corrupt" error when you attempt to open a Microsoft Jet database file, you may need to repair your database. Database files can become damaged due to power surges during read/write operations or due to physical device errors (damaged disk drive plates, and so on). You can repair an existing database by selecting Repair MDB from the File menu. You then see a File Open dialog box that asks you for the database filename. After you select the filename, Visdata loads and repairs the database to the best of its abilities. Unfortunately, you may receive a message saying some of the data could not be recovered.

> **Tip**
>
> Remember to make copies of your database on a regular basis. You should not depend on the repair routine to recover all your data. If you experience a program crash due to corrupted data, you can always restore the file from the most recent backup.
>
> You should also use the Windows 95 or DOS defragment utility on your hard drive after performing a compact or repair function to improve the overall performance of your application.

6

Exiting Visdata

The Exit item does just what you expect. When you exit Visdata, your current database closes, along with all open database objects. If you have text in the SQL window, it is saved and restored the next time you load Visdata. Visdata also remembers the windows you had open, as well as their sizes and their locations for the next time you load Visdata.

Using Visdata to Add Tables and Indexes to the Database

After you create a new database, you can add new tables and indexes to it. You can also add new tables and indexes to existing databases. To illustrate the process of managing database tables using Visdata, let's create a new Microsoft Access (Jet) database, add a new table, add a new index, and then modify the table structure.

Creating the New CH06NEW.MDB Database

If you haven't already done so, load and start Visdata. Select File | New | Microsoft Access | Version 7.0 MDB from the main menu and enter CH06NEW.MDB in the Select Microsoft Access Database to Create dialog box (see Figure 6.26). Click the Save button to create the new database.

FIGURE 6.26

Creating
CH06NEW.MDB.

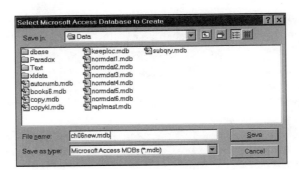

Adding a New Table to the Database

To add a new table to the database, click the alternate mouse button in an open space of the Database window and select New Table to bring up the Table Definition dialog box. Your screen should look like Figure 6.27.

FIGURE 6.27

Defining a new table.

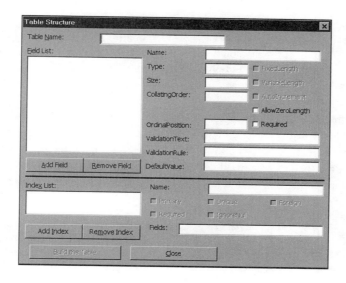

Enter NewTable in the Table Name field at the top of the dialog box. Now you can add fields to the data table. Click the Add Field command button to bring up the Add Field dialog box. Your screen should look like Figure 6.28.

FIGURE 6.28

Adding a new field to a table.

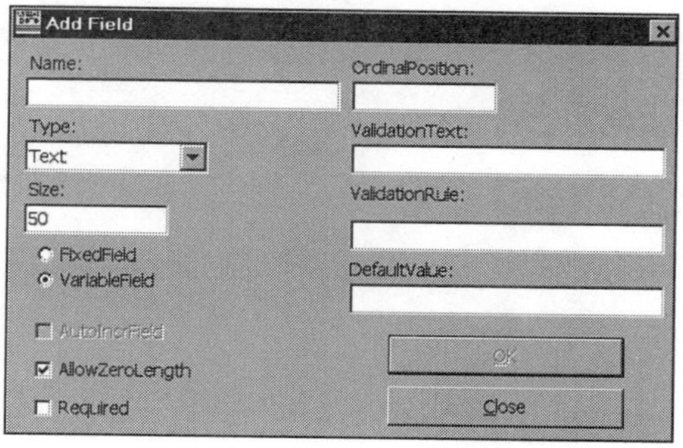

Enter the field name Field1. Set the type to Text and the Size to 10. Notice that you can set default values and validation rules here, as well. You learn about these properties on Day 8, "Visual Basic and the DAO Jet Database Engine."

After you enter the information you need to save the field, click the OK button to save the field properties to the table.

6

Caution Be sure you click the OK button after each field you define. If you just fill out the dialog box and then click the Close button, the information you entered on the form won't be saved to the table.

Now that you have defined Field1, let's define one more field. Enter `Field2` as the name and select Currency as the Field Type. Notice that you cannot set the field size. Only Text type fields enable you to set a field size. Now click the OK button to save this field definition; then exit the field definition dialog by clicking the Close button. The Table Structure dialog box should now show two fields defined. Refer to Figure 6.29 as a guide.

FIGURE 6.29

Table Structure with two fields defined.

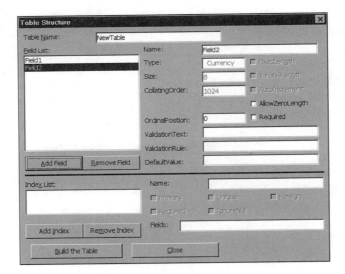

Editing an Existing Field

When you return to the Table Structure screen, notice that the same set of properties you saw in the Add Field dialog box appears to the right of the Fields list. You can edit some of these values for the field by highlighting the field in the list on the left and editing the dialog values on the right. Make Field2 required by selecting the Required check box at the right side of the dialog box.

Building the Table

Before you leave this screen, you must first click the Build Table button to actually create the table in your database. Up to this point, Visdata has stored the data table and index definitions in memory. Clicking the Build the Table button is the step that actually creates the data table.

> **Caution**
>
> If you click the Close button before you click the Build the Table button, you lose all your table definition information. You have to enter all the table definition data again before you can build the new table.

After you add data to an existing data table, you cannot use Visdata to modify the table structure. You must first remove all records from the data table before you can make any modification to the structure. You can, however, add new fields to a table after data has been entered.

Adding a New Index to the Database Using the Design Button

You can add indexes to existing tables by selecting the table, clicking the alternate mouse button, and selecting Design from the menu that appears. This option brings up the same input form you used to add fields to the database. Now let's add a Primary Key index for the NewTable you just created.

> **Caution**
>
> Even though Visdata enables you to enter New Index information during the New Tables process, you cannot build a new table and a new index for the same table at one time. Visdata must see the data table that already exists before it can create an index for that table. Use the Design mode of the Table Structure dialog box to add indexes to existing tables.

Click the Add Index command button to bring up the Add Index dialog box. Enter PKNewTable as the index name. Click Field1 in the field list to make that field the source of the Primary Key index. Your screen should look like Figure 6.30.

Be sure to click the OK button to add the index definition to the database. When you have added the index definition, click Close to exit the dialog. Your screen should now look like Figure 6.31.

6

FIGURE 6.30

Adding a new index to the database.

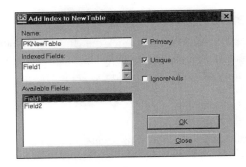

FIGURE 6.31

The Table Structure dialog after adding a new table.

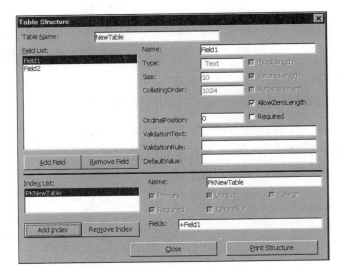

Printing the Table Structure

While you are in the Design mode of the Table Structure dialog, you can click the Print Structure button to get a hard-copy printout of the selected table and index objects you have defined. Visdata sends the information directly to the default printer defined for Windows and does not prompt you for any options. Please note that the Print Structure button does not appear when creating a New table; it appears only when you select Design after the table has been created.

Tip

If you want to save the structure to a file, you can use the printer applet in the Control Panel to define a printer as a file, and then set that print device as the default printer before you click the Print Structure button in Visdata. Be sure to reset your default printer after you send your table structures to a disk file.

What's on the Visdata Utility Menu?

The Visdata Utility menu contains several options to help you manage your data tables. You can create, test, and save query objects using the Query Builder; build data entry forms with the Data Form Designer; perform global replace routines on existing data tables; define attachments; define security; and define system preferences.

Query Builder

The Query Builder serves as a good tool for testing queries and then saving them to the database as query objects. You can later access these objects from your Visual Basic 6 programs. The Query Builder enables you to perform complex queries without having to know all the details of SQL syntax.

Note

You explore SQL SELECT queries in detail on Day 7. For now, if you are not familiar with SQL statements, just follow along with the example. The important thing to remember is that you can use the Visdata Query Builder to create, test, and store SQL queries.

Let's build a query, test it, and save it in a database.

First, make sure you have BOOKS6.MDB open (found in the TYSDBVB6\SOURCE\DATA directory created by the CD-ROM included with this book) and then select Utility | Query Builder from the main menu. You see a data entry form ready for your input (see Figure 6.32).

You have several options on this screen. It's easy to get confused if you are not quite sure of what to look for. Instead of going through all the possible options for a query, this example goes step-by-step through a rather simple SELECT query and its results. Table 6.1 shows the values to select, and Figure 6.33 shows the completed form. Refer to these items as you build your query.

6

FIGURE 6.32

*Using the Query
Builder.*

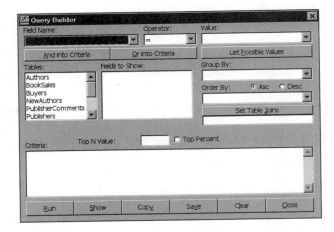

FIGURE 6.33

The completed query.

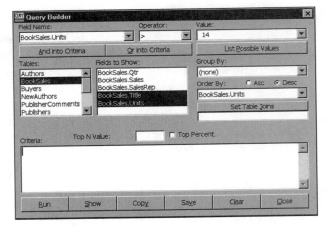

Be sure to set the values in the screen in the order they appear in Table 6.1. After you
enter the Field Name, Operator, and Value settings, click the And into Criteria button to
force the settings into the Criteria box at the bottom of the window.

TABLE 6.1 BUILDING A QUERY

Property	Setting
Tables	BookSales
Field Name	BookSales.Units
Operator	>
Value	14

Property	Setting
Fields to Show	BookSales.Title
	BookSales.Units
Order by	BookSales.Units, Desc

After you enter all the values, click Save and enter qryTest at the dialog prompt. You have just saved the query for future use. Now try running it. Click Run to get Visdata to execute the query. Click No when Visdata asks you whether this is an SQL Passthrough query. Visdata then executes the query and displays the results on your screen, as shown in Figure 6.34.

FIGURE 6.34

Results of the executed query.

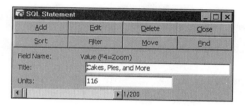

Data Form Designer

The Data Form Designer builds a data entry form complete with a data control and command buttons for data administration. The form is saved to the currently active Visual Basic project. To demonstrate, let's build a sample form with the Data Form Designer.

First, make sure you have the BOOKS6.MDB (TYSDBVB6\SOURCE\DATA) database open in Visdata. Next, select Data Form Designer from the Utility Menu. You should see the Data Form Designer dialog (see Figure 6.35).

FIGURE 6.35

The Data Form designer.

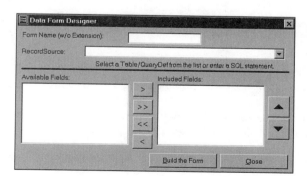

6

Enter frmAuthors in the Form Name field. Next, select Authors as the RecordSource. Note, when you select Authors, all the fields within that table appear in the Available Fields list box. Now, click the >> button to move all the fields into the Included Fields list box. Your dialog should look like Figure 6.36.

FIGURE 6.36

The completed frmAuthors design.

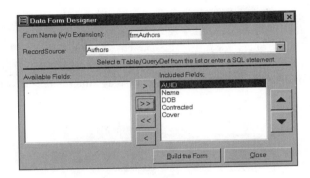

Click the Build the Form button to save the form to the currently active Visual Basic 6 project.

Now, close the Data Form Designer and Visdata and return to your Visual Basic 6 project. Open frmAuthors. You should see a form similar to the one in Figure 6.37.

FIGURE 6.37

The completed frmAuthors form.

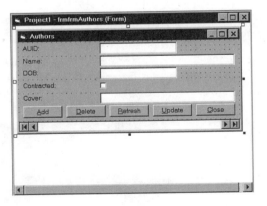

Notice how you have all the data fields, as well as a data control and command buttons. This is a quick and easy way to build forms for data entry!

Global Replace

The Global Replace menu option enables you to perform a mass update of existing tables, which comes in handy when you need to zero values in test data or need to perform mass updates on a database.

For this example, set all the fields in a data table to the same value. Load the BOOKS6.MDB database (TYSDBVB6\SOURCE\DATA) and then select Utility | Global Replace from the menu. You see the Global Replace dialog box, as shown in Figure 6.38.

Select the NewAuthors table and the Contracted field. Set the Replace With value to zero and leave the Criteria field blank. When you click the OK button, Visdata resets all the

FIGURE 6.38

Entering a Global Replace command.

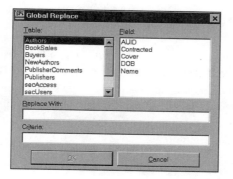

NewAuthors.Contracted fields to zero. You can limit the number of records affected by the Global Replace command by entering an appropriate logical statement in the Criteria box. For example, if you want to update only the records that have an Au_ID value of 30, you could enter the following line in the Criteria box:

```
Au_ID=30
```

You learn more about Criteria in the lesson on Day 7.

Attachments

Visdata enables you to attach external database files to an existing Microsoft Access (Jet) format database. When you create an attachment, you actually create a link between your own Microsoft Access database and another database. You don't actually import any data from the external database into your own MDB. By creating attachments, you can access

6

and manipulate external data files as if they are native Microsoft Access tables. Attached tables appear in the Database window as local table objects in your database, even though they are only links to external data files.

> Not only is the attachment method convenient, it provides the fastest way to access external data using Visual Basic 6 programs. You can load, index, and display attached external tables faster than you can if you use ODBC or directly open the external data files in their native format.

Now create an attached table in the BOOKS6.MDB database that you used earlier today.

If you like, you can create an attachment to any other Microsoft Jet format database you already have on hand.

First, if you don't have it loaded already, select File | Open Database from the main menu to load the BOOKS6.MDB (TYSDBVB6\SOURCE\DATA) database. Then select the Utility | Attachments menu option. You will see a grid that shows all the current attachments for this database. Because there are no attachments to this database, this box should be empty. Click the New command button to open the New Attached Table dialog box. Your screen should now look like Figure 6.39.

FIGURE 6.39

Adding an attachment to a Microsoft Access database.

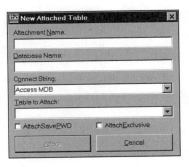

Table 6.2 shows the information you should enter in the Attachment dialog box.

TABLE 6.2 NEW ATTACHED TABLE DIALOG BOX VALUES

Dialog Field	Value
Attachment Name	Test Attachment
Database Name	\TYSDBVB6\SOURCE\DATA\NORMDAT6.MDB
Connect String	Access MDB
Table to Attach	Employees

If you are attaching to a data source that requires a password in the connect string, you could check the AttachSavePWD check box to prevent a login dialog each time you open the database. If you want to create an exclusive attachment, you could check the AttachExclusive check box. Leave both these fields blank for now.

After filling out the dialog form, click Attach to commit the attachment. After you close the Attachment dialog box, you see that the grid is updated to show the new attachment you just added to the database. Close the New Attached Tables dialog and the Attachments grid. You now see a new entry in your Database window list. This shows a new table object. Note how the icon for the attachment differs from the other tables' icons. Your screen should look something like the one in Figure 6.40.

FIGURE 6.40

The attached table object.

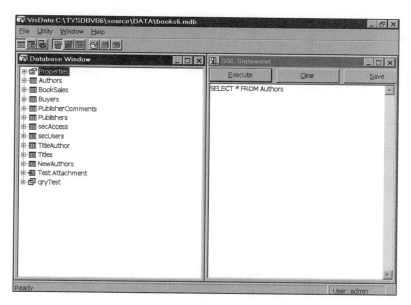

You can now access this attached table just as you would any table you created using Visdata.

Groups/Users

Selecting Utility | Groups/Users brings up the Groups/Users/Permissions dialog shown in Figure 6.41.

This dialog can be used to set all the permission rights for users and groups. In order to use this function, you must have a security file (SYSTEM.MD?) to which you belong. This function enables the setting of rights and passwords on a user and on a group level.

6

FIGURE 6.41

*The Groups/Users/
Permissions dialog.*

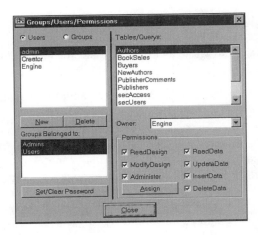

SYSTEM.MD?

Use the SYSTEM.MD? menu option to locate and load the SYSTEM.MD? security file. The
SYSTEM.MD? file contains information about Microsoft Access file security, including
defined users, groups, workspaces, passwords, and data object rights. You must create
this file using the Microsoft Access utility WRKGADM.EXE.

The Utility | SYSTEM.MD? menu option presents you with a File Open dialog so that
you can locate and load a SYSTEM.MD? file. After it is loaded, Visdata adds this information to the Registry so that you won't have to reload it in the future.

Preferences

The Preferences menu option enables you to customize the way Visdata shows you information. Two toggle settings control the way Visdata displays data, and two parameter
settings control the way Visdata performs database logins and queries.

Open Last Database on Startup

When you toggle on the Open Last Database option, Visdata remembers the last database
you had open when you last exited Visdata and automatically attempts to open that file
the next time you start Visdata.

Include System Files

When you toggle on the Include System Files option, you see several tables maintained
by Microsoft Jet to keep track of table, user, group, relation, and query definitions. Users
cannot access these tables, and the tables should not be altered or removed at any time.

Query Time-Out Value

You can use the Query Time-Out Value menu option to adjust the number of seconds Visdata waits before reporting a timeout error when attempting a query. If you work with slow external data files or ODBC connections, you can adjust this value upward to reduce the number of errors Visdata reports when you run queries.

Login Time-Out Value

You can use the Login Time-Out Value menu option to adjust the number of seconds Visdata waits before reporting a time-out error when attempting to log into a remote data source. Adjust this value upward if you get time-out errors when dealing with slow ODBC or external data sources.

What's on the Visdata Windows and Help Menus?

The last two items on the Visdata main menu are the Windows menu and the Help menu. These two items contain the usual options that all good Windows programs have.

The Windows Menu

This menu helps you control how all the child windows are displayed within the main MDI form. You can Cascade, Tile, or Arrange Icons from this menu. You can also force the focus to one of the three default Visdata windows: Database window, SQL window, or MDI form.

The Help Menu

The Help menu gives you access to the Visdata Help file included with your version of Visual Basic 6. You can also view the About box from this menu.

Summary

Today you learned how to use the Visdata sample application to perform all the basic database operations needed to create and maintain databases for your Visual Basic 6 applications.

You learned how to do the following:

- Open existing databases.
- Create new databases.

6

- Add tables and indexes to existing databases.
- Attach external data sources to existing Microsoft Access databases.
- Access data using the three data access objects: Table, Dynaset, and Snapshot.
- View data onscreen using the three data forms: form view with the data control, form view without the data control, and grid view using the data-bound grid.
- Build and store SQL queries using the Query Builder.

You learned to use Visdata to perform database utility operations, including the following:

- Copying tables from one database to another
- Repairing corrupted Microsoft Access (Jet) databases
- Compacting and converting versions of Microsoft Jet databases
- Performing global replace operations on tables

You learned to use Visdata to adjust various system settings that affect how Visual Basic 6 displays data tables and processes local and external database connections and parameters that control how Visual Basic 6 locks records at update time.

Quiz

1. Where can you find a copy of the Visdata source code?
2. How do you copy a table in Visdata?
3. When do you need to refresh the Tables/Queries window?
4. Can you manipulate spreadsheet data with Visdata?
5. What information can be obtained from the Properties object in the Database window?
6. Why would you compact a database?
7. Can you compact a database onto itself with the File | Compact MDB command?
8. Can you use Visdata to modify a table's structure after data has been entered?
9. Can you save queries in Visdata?
10. In what formats can you export data using the Visdata tool?
11. How would you use Visdata to convert an existing Access 2.0 database into an Access 7.0 format?

Exercises

You have been asked to build a database to track entities that purchase from and sell to your organization. Complete the following tasks using Visdata as your development tool:

1. Build a new database and name it Contacts. This database should have a format that can be read by Microsoft Access 7.0.

2. Build a table of customers (tblCustomers). Include the following fields:

Field	Type	Size
ID	Text	10
Name	Text	50
Address1	Text	50
Address2	Text	50
City	Text	50
StateProv	Text	25
Zip	Text	10
Phone	Text	14
Fax	Text	14
Contact	Text	50
Notes	Memo	NA

3. Build a primary key (PKtblCustomers) on the ID field for the tblCustomers table.

4. Print the table structure for tblCustomers.

5. Create and enter five sample records into the tblCustomers table.

6. Because you also need to track those from whom you purchase, copy the structure (no records) from tblCustomers to a new table, tblVendors.

7. Export the data in the tblCustomers table to a text file.

6

DAY 7

Selecting Data with SQL

Today is your first lesson in Structured Query Language (SQL). SQL is a powerful manipulation language used by Visual Basic and the Microsoft Access Jet database engine as the primary method for accessing the data in your databases. SQL statements fall into two broad categories: data manipulation language statements (DML) and data definition language statements (DDL). The DDL statements enable you to define data tables, indexes, and database relationships. DML statements are used to select, sort, summarize, and calculate the information stored in the data tables.

Today, you learn about the DML statements. When you complete this lesson, you will be able to use SQL statements to construct database queries that can be retrieved, and you will be able to reorder data in any format recognized by Visual Basic. Because SQL is used in almost all relational database systems (SQL Server, Oracle, Informix, and so on), you also will be able to apply the knowledge you gain here in almost any other relational database environment you might encounter in the future.

In this lesson, you learn how to use the SELECT_FROM statement to select data from one or more tables and present that information in a single table for update or review. You also learn how to limit the data you select to only the records that meet your criteria using the WHERE clause. You learn how to easily reorder the data in tables using the ORDER BY clause. You also learn how to create simple statements that automatically summarize and total the data using the GROUP BY_HAVING clause.

You explore typical SQL functions to manipulate numbers and strings. This lesson also covers advanced DML statements such as PARAMETERS, UNIONS, JOINS, and TRANSFORM_PIVOT.

Today, you create actual SQL queries (and in some cases, store them for later use) using the Visual Basic Visdata program you learned about on Day 6, "Using the Visdata Program."

What Is SQL?

Before jumping into specific SQL statements and their use, you should understand the definition of SQL and its uses and origins. SQL stands for Structured Query Language. It was developed in the 1970s at IBM to provide computer users with a standardized method for selecting data from various database formats. The intent was to build a language that was not based on any existing programming language, but could be used within any programming language to update and query information in databases.

Note
> The word SQL should be pronounced "ess-que-ell" instead of "sequel." The confusion about the pronunciation of the word stems from the database language's origin. The SQL language is a successor of a language called Sequel developed by IBM in the late 1960s. For this reason, many (especially those familiar with IBM's Sequel language) continued to pronounce the name of the new database language improperly.

SQL statements are just that—statements. Each statement can perform operations on one or more database objects (tables, columns, indexes, and so on). Most SQL statements return results in the form of a set of data records, commonly referred to as a *view*. SQL is not a particularly friendly language. Many programs that use SQL statements hide these statements behind point-and-click dialogs, query-by-example grids, and other user-friendly interfaces. Make no mistake, however—if the data you are accessing is stored in a relational database, you are using SQL statements, whether you know it or not.

ANSI Standard SQL Versus Microsoft Jet SQL

SQL syntax is determined by a committee that is part of the American National Standards Institute (ANSI). The ANSI-SQL committee is made up of information systems professionals who take on the job of establishing and enforcing standards on the rapidly moving computer programming industry. Although each computer programming language and database interface has its own unique version of SQL, nearly everyone has agreed to adhere to the basic standards defined by the ANSI-SQL committee. The most widely used SQL standard is SQL-89. This standard was first promulgated in 1989. An updated set of standards (SQL-92) was developed three years later.

Within each set of SQL standards, there are three levels of compliance. A database product must meet Level I compliance in order to call itself an SQL-compatible product. Levels II and III are optional levels of compliance that products can also attain in order to increase interoperability among database systems.

The Microsoft Jet database engine that is used to process all Visual Basic SQL statements is ANSI SQL-89 Level I–compliant. There are very slight differences between ANSI SQL-89 and Microsoft Jet SQL at Level II and Level III. This book won't dwell on these differences. Those who are interested in learning more about ANSI SQL standards and Microsoft Jet compliance can find additional documentation elsewhere. The lessons in this book focus strictly on the Microsoft Jet SQL syntax. Be assured that when you master the concepts covered here, you will be able to use the same skills in almost all SQL-based programming and query tools you encounter.

SQL Basics

 Now it's time to start building SQL statements. If you haven't already done so, load the Visual Basic Visdata application you learned about on Day 6. Using Visdata, select Add Ins | Visual Data Manager from the Visual Basic application. Next, load the BOOKS6.MDB (use File | Open Database | Microsoft Access) that is included in the \TYSDBVB6\SOURCE\DATA directory of the CD-ROM that ships with this book. You use this database for most of today's lesson.

 Note This book shows reserved SQL words in uppercase letters (for example, SELECT). This is not required by Visual Basic, but it is a good programming habit.

The SELECT_FROM Statement

In this section, you learn about the most commonly used SQL statement, the SELECT_FROM statement. The SELECT_FROM statement enables you to pick records from one or more tables in a database. The results of a SELECT_FROM statement are returned as a view. This view is a subset of the source data. In Visual Basic, the view can be returned

7

as a Recordset, Table, Dynaset, or Snapshot. Because today's lesson focuses on getting results you can display, views are returned as Visual Basic Snapshot data objects.

In its simplest form, a SELECT_FROM statement contains two parts:

- A list of one or more table columns to select
- A list of one or more tables that contain the requested columns

Note Standard SQL syntax uses the word column to describe a field and row to describe a record. This book uses the term field interchangeably with column and record interchangeably with row.

A simple example of a valid SQL statement is

```
SELECT AUID FROM Authors
```

This SQL statement tells the Microsoft Jet database engine to return a data object that contains the AUID from the Authors table. Enter this SQL statement into the Visdata SQL window and click the Execute button to see the returned resultset. Your screen should look similar to the one in Figure 7.1.

FIGURE 7.1

The resultset from the first SELECT statement.

SELECT AUID FROM Authors			
Refresh	Sort	Filter	Close
AUID			
1			
2			
3			
4			
5			
6			
7			
8			
9			
10			
11			
12			
13			
14			
15			
16			

Right Click for Data Control Properties

As you can see from the resultset, the SELECT_FROM statement returns all the rows in the table. Whether the table contains 10 or 10,000 records, you can get a complete resultset with just one SELECT_FROM statement. This is quite handy, but it can also be quite dangerous. If the result of your SELECT_FROM statement contains too many records, you can slow down the network, possibly run out of memory on your local workstation, and eventually lock up your PC. Later in this lesson, you will learn how to use the WHERE clause to limit the size of your view to only those records you need.

To return all the columns from a table, you can list each column in the SELECT statement. This works if you have only a few columns in the table. However, if you have several columns, it can become quite tedious. There is a shortcut. To automatically list all columns in the table in your resultset, instead of typing column names, you can type the asterisk (*). The asterisk tells SQL to return all columns in the requested table. The SELECT statement to display all columns of the Author table looks like this:

```
SELECT * FROM Authors
```

Enter the preceding SELECT statement into the Visdata SQL window and review the results. Your screen should look like the one in Figure 7.2.

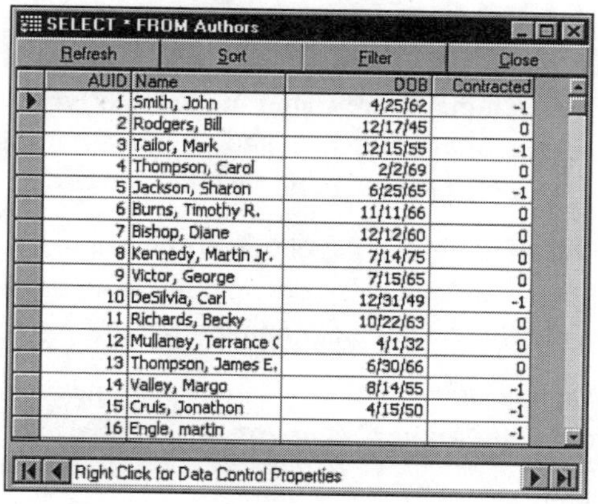

FIGURE 7.2

*The results of the SELECT * query.*

Notice that even though you listed no fields in your SELECT statement, all fields were returned in the resultset. This is very useful when you want to display a data table but do not know the names of all the columns. As long as you know a valid table name, you can use the SELECT_FROM statement to display the entire table.

The order in which you list columns in the SELECT_FROM statement controls the order in which they are displayed in the resultset. Figure 7.3 shows the results of the following SELECT_FROM statement:

```
SELECT Name, AUID FROM Authors
```

7

FIGURE 7.3

Using the
SELECT_FROM
*statement to change
column display order.*

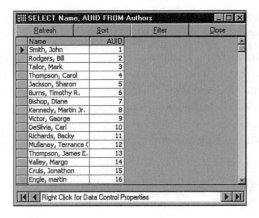

The ORDER BY Clause

When you use the SELECT_FROM statement, the records returned in the resultset are returned in the order in which they were found in the underlying table. But what if you wanted to display the results of your SELECT_FROM statement in a specialized sorted order? You can use the ORDER BY clause to do just that.

Placing ASC or DESC after each field in the ORDER BY clause indicates the order in which you want to sort the column, ascending or descending. If no order is supplied, SQL assumes that you want the set sorted in ascending order.

The following SQL example shows how you can display the records in the Authors table in descending sorted order, by Author Name:

```
SELECT * FROM AUTHORS ORDER BY Name DESC
```

Enter this statement in the SQL window of Visdata and execute it. Compare your results to Figure 7.4.

FIGURE 7.4

*The results of the
descending*
ORDER BY *clause.*

AUID	Name	DOB	Contracted
18	Wilso, Kathy		0
9	Victor, George	7/15/65	0
14	Valley, Margo	8/14/55	-1
13	Thompson, James E.	6/30/66	0
4	Thompson, Carol	2/2/69	0
3	Tailor, Mark	12/15/55	-1
27	Swanson, Patrick	3/31/2027	0
35	Smith, John		0
1	Smith, John	4/25/62	-1
2	Rodgers, Bill	12/17/45	0
11	Richards, Becky	10/22/63	0
25	Person, Joen	2/28/60	0
17	Patrick, Elliot	9/21/65	-1
19	Osbern, Scott	9/12/80	0
26	Omar, Carl	6/30/33	0
30	Norman, Chas	7/12/33	0

You can enter more than one field in the ORDER BY clause. SQL will create a resultset that reflects the aggregate sort of the ORDER BY clause. Using Visual Basic Visdata, enter and execute the following SELECT_FROM statement. Compare your results to those in Figure 7.5.

```
SELECT StateProv, City FROM Publishers ORDER BY StateProv DESC, City ASC
```

FIGURE 7.5

The results of the multiple column ORDER BY *clause.*

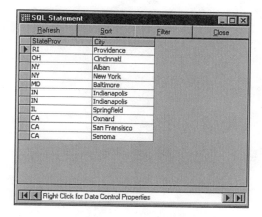

Notice in the example shown in Figure 7.5 that you have combined the ability to alter the row order of the data in the resultset with the ability to alter the column order of the data in the resultset. These are powerful tools. Now that you know how to use SQL to display complete, single-data tables, you can learn how to limit the resultset to only those records you need.

The WHERE Clause

One of the most powerful aspects of the SELECT_FROM statement is its capability of controlling the content of the resultset using the WHERE clause. There are two ways to use the WHERE clause to control the content of the resultset:

- Use WHERE to limit the contents of a resultset.
- Use WHERE to link two or more tables in a single resultset.

Using WHERE to Limit the Resultset

The WHERE clause enables you to perform logical comparisons on data in any column in the data table. In its simplest form, the WHERE clause consists of the following:

```
WHERE column = value
```

In this line, column represents the name of the column in the requested data table, and value represents a literal value such as NY or Smith. It is important to know that the

7

WHERE clause is always preceded by a SELECT_FROM statement. Use Visdata to enter and execute the following SQL statement and compare your results to those in Figure 7.6:

```
SELECT Name, StateProv FROM Publishers WHERE StateProv = 'CA'
```

FIGURE 7.6

The results of a simple WHERE *clause SQL query.*

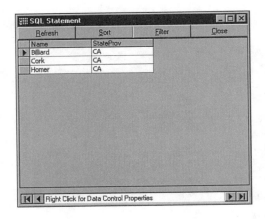

 Tip

This book uses single quotation marks (') around string literals within SQL statements. Visual Basic SQL accepts both single and double quotation marks within SQL. Because you will often be building SQL statements in Visual Basic code, using single quotation marks within SQL statements makes it easier to construct and maintain SQL statements as Visual Basic strings.

The previous SQL statement returns a subset of the data in the resultset. That is, the resulting view does not contain all the rows of the Publishers table. Only those rows that have columns meeting the WHERE clause criteria are returned in the resultset.

You can link WHERE clauses using the AND and OR operators. Enter and execute the following SQL statement and compare your results to Figure 7.7:

```
SELECT Name, StateProv, City FROM Publishers
WHERE StateProv = 'CA' AND City <> 'Senoma'
```

You can use several AND and OR operators to link valid logical comparisons together to form a single WHERE clause. You can also use more than just =, <>, >, <, <=, and >= logical comparisons. Visual Basic SQL supports the use of BETWEEN_AND, IN, and LIKE comparisons. The following SQL statement illustrates the use of BETWEEN_AND in a WHERE clause. Check your results against those shown in Figure 7.8.

```
SELECT PubID, Name, StateProv, City FROM Publishers
WHERE PubID BETWEEN 10 AND 15
```

FIGURE 7.7

The results of a complex WHERE clause.

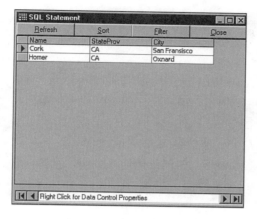

FIGURE 7.8

Using BETWEEN_AND in a WHERE clause.

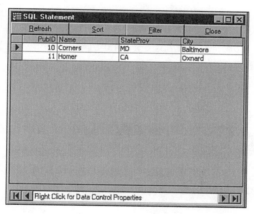

The resultset contains only rows that have a PubID value between 10 and 15. Notice that the values listed in the BETWEEN_AND clause (10 and 15) are included in the resultset.

You can also use SQL to return a resultset that contains rows that match a set of noncontiguous data. For example, if you wanted a list of all the publishers in the states of New York, California, and Alaska, you could use the IN keyword followed by the desired values, separated by commas, within parentheses, as part of the WHERE clause. Enter and execute the following SQL statement and check your results against those shown in Figure 7.9:

```
SELECT PubID, Name, City, StateProv FROM Publishers
WHERE StateProv IN ('NY','CA','RI')
```

7

FIGURE 7.9

Using the IN *keyword in the* WHERE *clause.*

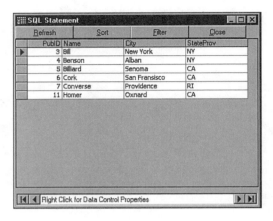

You can also use the LIKE function to return all rows whose columns' contents are similar to the literals passed in the function. For example, to return all rows with a StateProv column that has the letter *I* in any position, you use the following SQL SELECT_FROM statement (see Figure 7.10 for results):

```
SELECT PubID, Name, City, StateProv FROM Publishers
WHERE StateProv LIKE('*I*')
```

FIGURE 7.10

Using the LIKE *function in a* WHERE *clause.*

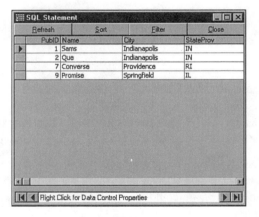

The LIKE function is a very powerful tool. It is covered in more depth in a later section of today's lesson, "SQL Aggregate Functions."

Using WHERE to Link Two or More Tables in a Resultset

You can use the WHERE clause to compare columns from different tables. In doing so, you can set up criteria that can link two or more tables in a single resultset. The syntax for this form of the WHERE clause is

```
SELECT table1.columnA, table2.columnA FROM table1, table2
WHERE table1.columnA = table2.columnA
```

table1 and table2 are different data tables in the same database. columnA represents a single column in each of the tables. Use Visdata to enter and execute the following SQL statement. Compare your resultset to the one in Figure 7.11.

```
SELECT Titles.Title, Publishers.Name
FROM Publishers, Titles
WHERE Publishers.PubID =Titles.PubID
```

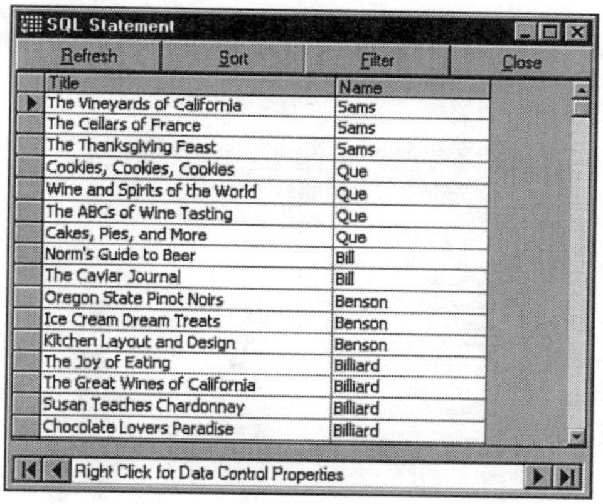

FIGURE 7.11

Using the WHERE clause to link two tables in a single resultset.

The preceding SQL statement creates a resultset that displays the book title and publisher's name. This is accomplished using the WHERE clause to tell SQL to select only those rows where the PubID values in each table match up. Keep in mind that this is done without any programming code, special indexing, or sorting commands. SQL handles all those tasks for you. Also, there are a few new items in this SQL statement that bear further review.

This is the first SQL statement you have encountered today that lists columns from two different tables. When selecting columns from more than one table, it is good programming practice to precede the column name with the table name and join the two with the period (.). As long as the column name is unique among all columns in the tables from which you are selecting, SQL does not require you to use the *table.column* syntax. But it is a good habit to do so, especially when you are building SQL statements in Visual Basic code.

You should also notice that the WHERE clause comparison columns (Publishers.PubID and Titles.PubID) were not included in the SELECT portion of the statement. You do not have to include the column in the SELECT portion of the statement to use it in the WHERE portion of the statement, as long as the column already exists in the underlying table.

7

Combining tables using the WHERE clause always returns a nonupdatable resultset. You cannot update the columns in a view created in this manner. If you want to link tables together and also be able to update the underlying tables for that view, you need to use the JOIN clause, which is covered later today.

You can combine the link-type and limit-type versions of the WHERE clause in a single SQL SELECT_FROM statement. Execute the following statement and compare your results to those in Figure 7.12:

```
SELECT Titles.PubID,Titles.Title,Publishers.Name
FROM Titles, Publishers
WHERE Titles.PubID = Publishers.PubID
AND Publishers.PubID BETWEEN 5 AND 10
```

FIGURE 7.12

Combining link-type and limit-type WHERE *clauses.*

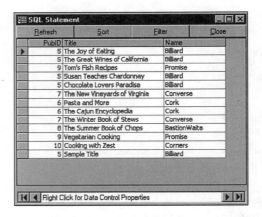

The preceding SQL statement selects only those records in which the PubID columns match and the PubID values are between 5 and 10.

You can use the WHERE clause to link more than two data tables. The linking column for table1 and table2 does not have to be the same column as for table2 and table3. Execute the following statement and review your results against those in Figure 7.13:

```
SELECT Titles.PubID,Titles.Title,Publishers.Name,Authors.Name
FROM Titles, Publishers,Authors
WHERE Titles.PubID = Publishers.PubID
AND Titles.AUID = Authors.AUID
```

In the previous example, the Publishers table and the Titles table are linked using the PubID column. The Titles table and the Authors table are linked using the AUID field. When the link is made, the selected columns are displayed in the resultset.

FIGURE 7.13

Using the `WHERE` *clause to link three tables.*

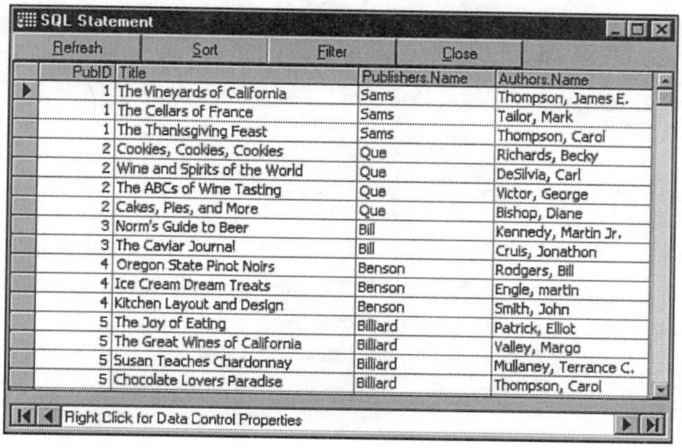

PubID	Title	Publishers.Name	Authors.Name
1	The Vineyards of California	Sams	Thompson, James E.
1	The Cellars of France	Sams	Tailor, Mark
1	The Thanksgiving Feast	Sams	Thompson, Carol
2	Cookies, Cookies, Cookies	Que	Richards, Becky
2	Wine and Spirits of the World	Que	DeSilvia, Carl
2	The ABCs of Wine Tasting	Que	Victor, George
2	Cakes, Pies, and More	Que	Bishop, Diane
3	Norm's Guide to Beer	Bill	Kennedy, Martin Jr.
3	The Caviar Journal	Bill	Cruis, Jonathon
4	Oregon State Pinot Noirs	Benson	Rodgers, Bill
4	Ice Cream Dream Treats	Benson	Engle, martin
4	Kitchen Layout and Design	Benson	Smith, John
5	The Joy of Eating	Billiard	Patrick, Elliot
5	The Great Wines of California	Billiard	Valley, Margo
5	Susan Teaches Chardonnay	Billiard	Mullaney, Terrance C.
5	Chocolate Lovers Paradise	Billiard	Thompson, Carol

You might have noticed that SQL assigns column names to the resultsets. There are times when these assigned names can be misleading or incomplete. You can use the `AS` keyword to rename the columns in the resultset. The following SQL statement is one example of using the `AS` keyword in the `SELECT` statement to rename the column headers of the resultset. This renaming does not affect the original column names in the underlying tables. Execute the following SQL statement and compare your results to those in Figure 7.14:

```
SELECT Titles.PubID AS PubCode, Titles.Title AS BookTitle,
Publishers.Name AS PubName,
Authors.Name AS AuthorName
FROM Titles, Publishers,Authors
WHERE Titles.PubID = Publishers.PubID
AND Titles.AUID = Authors.AUID
```

FIGURE 7.14

Using the `AS` *keyword to rename columns in the resultset.*

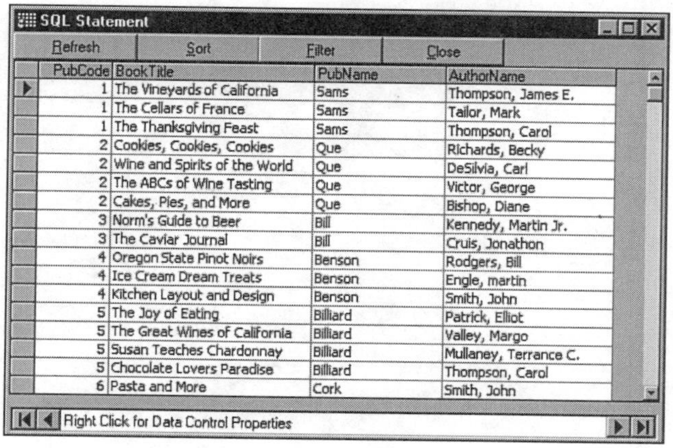

PubCode	BookTitle	PubName	AuthorName
1	The Vineyards of California	Sams	Thompson, James E.
1	The Cellars of France	Sams	Tailor, Mark
1	The Thanksgiving Feast	Sams	Thompson, Carol
2	Cookies, Cookies, Cookies	Que	Richards, Becky
2	Wine and Spirits of the World	Que	DeSilvia, Carl
2	The ABCs of Wine Tasting	Que	Victor, George
2	Cakes, Pies, and More	Que	Bishop, Diane
3	Norm's Guide to Beer	Bill	Kennedy, Martin Jr.
3	The Caviar Journal	Bill	Cruis, Jonathon
4	Oregon State Pinot Noirs	Benson	Rodgers, Bill
4	Ice Cream Dream Treats	Benson	Engle, martin
4	Kitchen Layout and Design	Benson	Smith, John
5	The Joy of Eating	Billiard	Patrick, Elliot
5	The Great Wines of California	Billiard	Valley, Margo
5	Susan Teaches Chardonnay	Billiard	Mullaney, Terrance C.
5	Chocolate Lovers Paradise	Billiard	Thompson, Carol
6	Pasta and More	Cork	Smith, John

Now that you know how to use the SELECT_FROM statement to select the desired rows and columns from data tables, read about how to use SQL functions to calculate and manipulate data within your selected columns and rows.

SQL Aggregate Functions

NEW TERM   The SQL standards define a core set of functions that are present in all SQL-compliant systems. These functions are known as *aggregate functions*. Aggregate functions are used to quickly return computed results of numeric data stored in a column. The SQL aggregate functions available through the Microsoft Access Jet database engine are

- AVG returns the average value of all the values in a column.
- COUNT returns the number of columns and is usually used to determine the total rows in a view. COUNT is the only standard SQL aggregate function that can be applied to a nonnumeric column.
- SUM returns the total of all the values in a column.
- MAX returns the highest of all the values in a column.
- MIN: returns the lowest of all the values in a column.

The following SQL statement illustrates all five SQL aggregate functions. Enter and execute this statement and check your results against Figure 7.15:

```
SELECT COUNT(Units) AS UnitCount,
AVG(Units) AS UnitAvg,
SUM(Units) AS UnitSum,
MIN(Units) AS UnitMin,
MAX(Units) AS UnitMax
FROM BookSales
```

FIGURE 7.15

Using SQL aggregate functions.

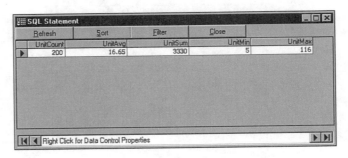

You can use the WHERE clause and aggregate functions in the same SELECT_FROM statement. The following statement shows how you can use the WHERE clause to limit rows included in the aggregate calculation. See Figure 7.16 for results. Compare these numbers to those in the view returned in the previous query (refer to Figure 7.15).

```
SELECT COUNT(Units) AS UnitCount,
AVG(Units) AS UnitAvg,
SUM(Units) AS UnitSum,
MIN(Units) AS UnitMin,
MAX(Units) AS UnitMax
FROM BookSales
WHERE Qtr = 1
```

FIGURE 7.16

Using the WHERE clause to limit the scope of aggregate functions.

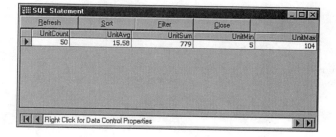

Using Visual Basic Functions in a SELECT Statement

When you call the Microsoft Access Jet database engine from within a Visual Basic program, you can use any valid Visual Basic functions as part of the SQL statement. For example, if you want to create a resultset with a column that holds only the first three characters of a field in the underlying table, you can use the Visual Basic Left$ function as part of your column list in the SELECT_FROM statement, in the following line (see Figure 7.17):

```
SELECT Left$(Name,3), Name
FROM Authors
```

You can also use Visual Basic syntax to combine several data table columns into a single column in the resultset. Enter and execute the following example and compare your results to Figure 7.18:

```
SELECT Name, City+", "+StateProv+"  "+Zip AS ADDRESS
FROM Publishers
```

7

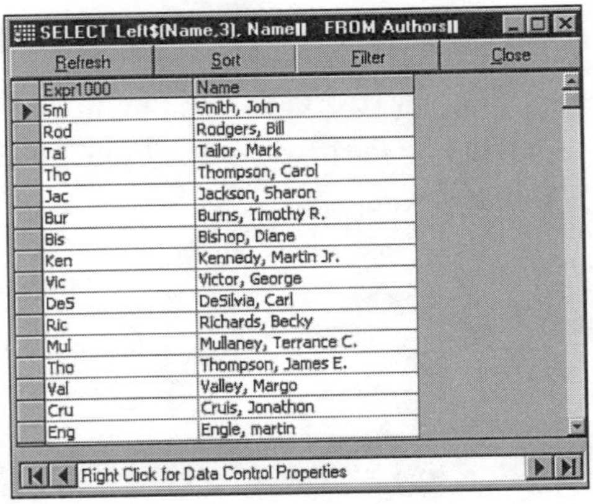

FIGURE 7.17

Using Visual Basic functions in an SQL statement.

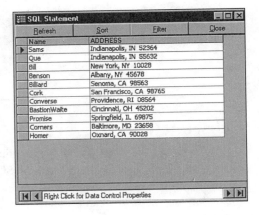

FIGURE 7.18

Using Visual Basic syntax to combine columns.

You can also use Visual Basic functions as part of the WHERE clause in an SQL statement. The following example (Figure 7.19) returns only rows that have the letter *a* as the second character in the Name column:

```
SELECT Name FROM Publishers
WHERE Mid$(Name,2,1)="a"
```

Even though using familiar Visual Basic functions and syntax is very handy, it has its drawbacks. Chief among them is the fact that after you create an SQL statement that uses Visual Basic–specific portions, your code is no longer portable. If you ever move the SQL statements to another database engine (such as SQL Server), you must remove the Visual Basic–specific portions of the SQL statements and replace them with something else that will work with the database engine you are using. This will not be an issue if you plan to stick with the Microsoft Access Jet engine for all your database access.

FIGURE 7.19

Using Visual Basic functions in an SQL WHERE clause.

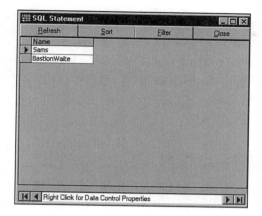

Another possible drawback that you encounter if you use Visual Basic–specific syntax in your SQL statements is that of speed. Extensive use of Visual Basic–specific code within SQL statements results in a slight performance hit. The speed difference is minor, but it should be considered.

It is better to use as few Visual Basic–specific functions in your SQL statements as possible. You will not limit the portability of your code, and you will not suffer from unduly slow processing of the SQL statements.

Note

You can't use user-defined functions within your SQL statements when you use the Microsoft Access Jet database engine from within Visual Basic. You can use only the built-in SQL functions and the predefined Visual Basic functions.

More SQL DML Statements

Now that you know how to create basic SQL SELECT_FROM statements and you know how to use the built-in SQL functions, let's return to the basic SELECT_FROM statement and add a few more enhancements to your SQL tool kit.

The DISTINCT and DISTINCTROW Clauses

There are times when you select data from a table that has more than one occurrence of the rows you are trying to collect. For example, you want to get a list of all the customers that have at least one order on file in the Orders table of your database. The problem is that some customers have several orders in the table. You don't want to see those

7

names appear more than once in your resultset. You can use the DISTINCT keyword to make sure that you do not get duplicates of the same customer in your resultset.

Enter and execute the following statement. As a test, execute the same SQL statement without the DISTINCT clause and compare the resultsets. Refer to Figure 7.20 as an example.

```
SELECT DISTINCT AUID FROM Titles
ORDER BY AUID
```

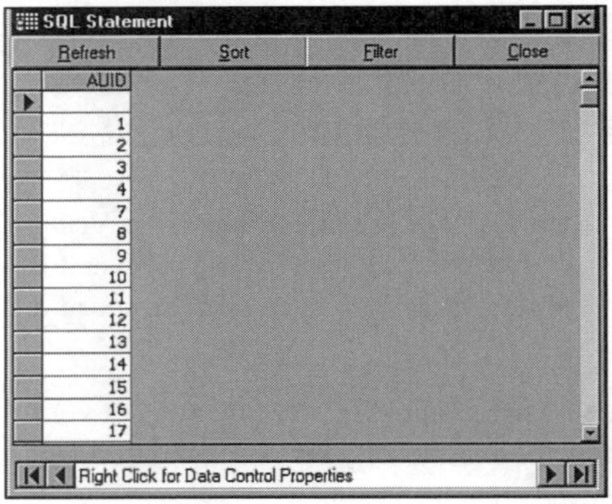

FIGURE 7.20

Using the DISTINCT keyword to remove duplicates from a resultset.

If you include more than one column in the SELECT list, all columns are used to evaluate the uniqueness of the row. Execute and compare the resultsets of the following two SQL statements. Refer to Figure 7.21 as a guide.

```
SELECT DISTINCT Title
FROM BookSales
```

```
SELECT DISTINCT Title, Units
FROM BookSales
```

Notice that the first SQL statement returns a single record for each Title in the data table. The second SQL statement returns more records for each Title because there are distinct Units values for each Title.

There are also times when you want to collect data on all rows that are distinct in any of the fields. Instead of using the DISTINCT keyword and listing all the fields in the table, you can use the DISTINCTROW keyword. The following SQL statement (see Figure 7.22) uses DISTINCTROW to return the same records as the SQL statement in the previous example:

```
SELECT DISTINCTROW *
FROM BookSales
ORDER BY Title
```

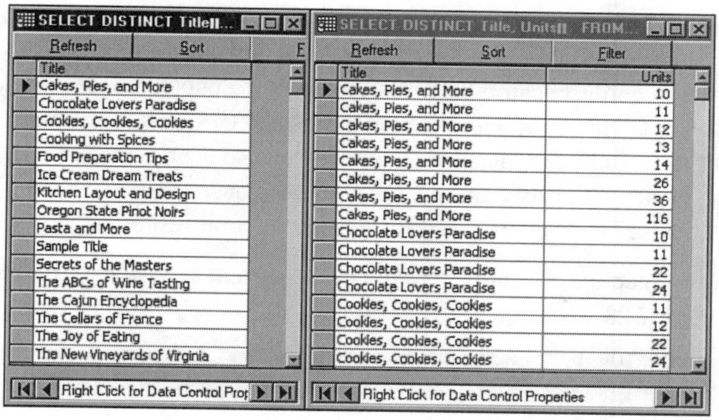

FIGURE 7.21

Using DISTINCT on multiple columns.

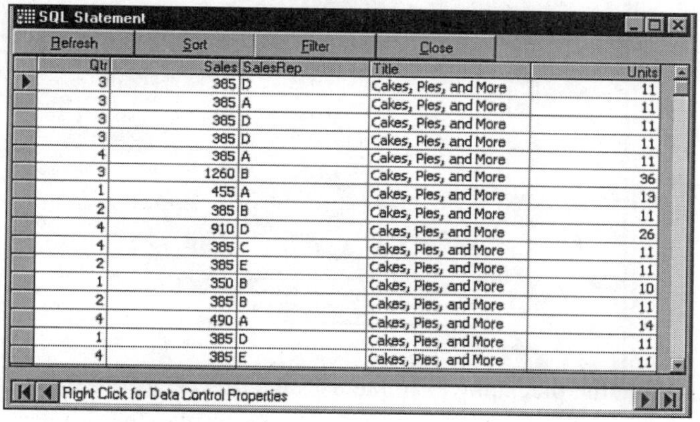

FIGURE 7.22

Using DISTINCTROW in an SQL statement.

Both the DISTINCT and DISTINCTROW keywords enable you to limit the contents of the resultset based on the uniqueness of one or more columns in the data table. In the next section, you learn how to limit the contents of the resultset to the records with the highest numeric values in selected columns.

The TOP n and TOP n PERCENT Clauses

You can use the TOP n or TOP n PERCENT SQL keywords to limit the number of records in your resultset. Suppose you want to get a list of the five top-selling books in a data table. You can use the TOP n clause to get just that. TOP n returns the first *n* number of records. If you have two records of the same value, SQL returns both records. For the previous example, if the fifth and sixth records were both equal, the resultset would contain six records, not just five.

7

When you use the TOP clause, you must also use the ORDER BY clause to make sure that your resultset is sorted. If you do not use the ORDER BY clause, you receive an arbitrary set of records, because SQL first executes the ORDER BY clause and then selects the TOP n records you requested. Without the ORDER BY clause, it is quite likely that you will not get the results you intended. If a WHERE clause is present, SQL performs the WHERE clause, the ORDER BY clause, and then the TOP n clause. As you can see, failure to use the ORDER BY clause most certainly returns garbage in your resultset.

Now enter and execute the following statement in Visdata. Compare your results to Figure 7.23.

```
SELECT TOP 5 * FROM BookSales
ORDER BY Sales DESC
```

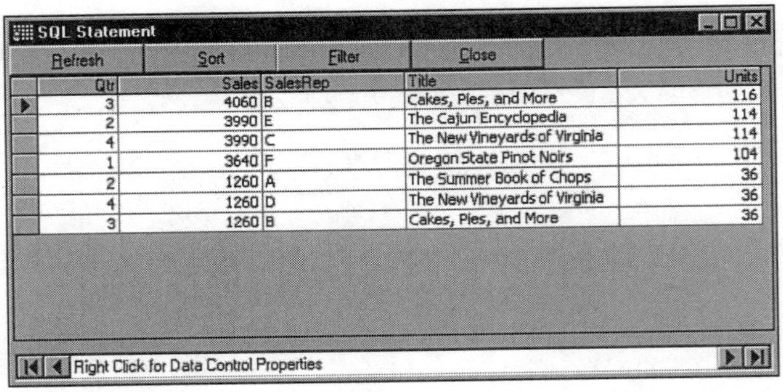
SQL Statement
Refresh
Sort
Filter
Close
Qtr
Sales
SalesRep
Title
Units
3
4060
B
Cakes, Pies, and More
116
2
3990
E
The Cajun Encyclopedia
114
4
3990
C
The New Vineyards of Virginia
114
1
3640
F
Oregon State Pinot Noirs
104
2
1260
A
The Summer Book of Chops
36
4
1260
D
The New Vineyards of Virginia
36
3
1260
B
Cakes, Pies, and More
36
Right Click for Data Control Properties

FIGURE 7.23
Using TOP n *to limit the resultset.*

Notice that the preceding example uses the DESC keyword in the ORDER BY clause. Whether you use the DESC or ASC ORDER BY format, the resultset still contains the first *n* records in the table (based on the sort). Also note that the resultset contains more than five records, because several records have the same Sales value.

The TOP n PERCENT version returns not the top five records, but the top five percent of the records in the underlying data table. The results of the following SQL statement (see Figure 7.24) contain several more records than the resultset shown previously.

```
SELECT TOP 5 PERCENT * FROM BookSales
ORDER BY Sales
```

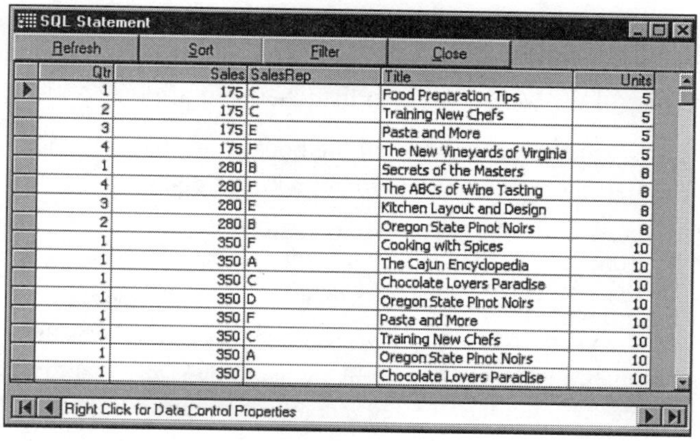

FIGURE 7.24

Using TOP n PERCENT *to limit the resultset.*

The GROUP BY_HAVING Clause

One of the more powerful SQL clauses is the GROUP BY_HAVING clause. This clause enables you to use the SQL aggregate functions discussed earlier today to easily create resultsets that contain a list of subtotals of the underlying data table. For example, you might want to be able to create a dataset that contains a list of Titles and the total Units sold, by Title. The following SQL statement (see Figure 7.25) can do just that:

```
SELECT Title, SUM(Units) AS UnitsSold
FROM BookSales
GROUP BY Title
```

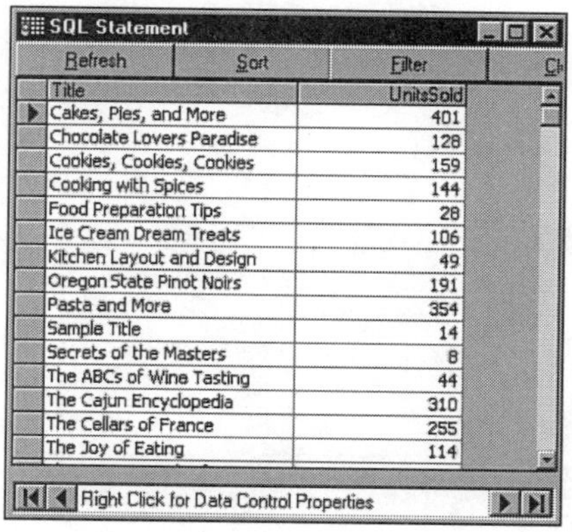

FIGURE 7.25

Using GROUP BY *to create subtotals.*

7

The `GROUP BY` clause requires that all numeric columns in the `SELECT` column list be a part of an SQL aggregate function (`SUM`, `AVG`, `MIN`, `MAX`, and `COUNT`). Also, you cannot use the `*` as part of the `SELECT` column list when you use the `GROUP BY` clause.

What if you want to get a list of all the book titles that sold more than 100 units for the year? The first thought would be to use a `WHERE` clause:

```
SELECT Titles, SUM(Units) AS UnitsSold
WHERE Sum(Units) > 100
GROUP BY Units
```

However, if you try to run this SQL statement, you discover that SQL does not allow aggregate functions within the `WHERE` clause. You really want to use a `WHERE` clause after the aggregate function has created a resulting column. In plain English, the query needs to perform the following steps:

1. Add up all the units.
2. Write the results to a temporary table.
3. Display only those rows in the temporary table that have a unit total greater than 100.

Luckily, you don't have to actually write all this in a series of SQL statements. You can get the same results by adding the `HAVING` keyword to the `GROUP BY` clause. The `HAVING` clause acts the same as the `WHERE` clause, except that the `HAVING` clause acts upon the resulting columns created by the `GROUP BY` clause, not the underlying columns. The following SQL statement (see Figure 7.26) returns only the Titles that have sold more than 100 units in the last year:

```
SELECT Title, SUM(Units) AS UnitsSold
FROM BookSales
GROUP BY Title HAVING SUM(Units)>100
```

FIGURE 7.26

Using the `HAVING` *clause with* `GROUP BY`.

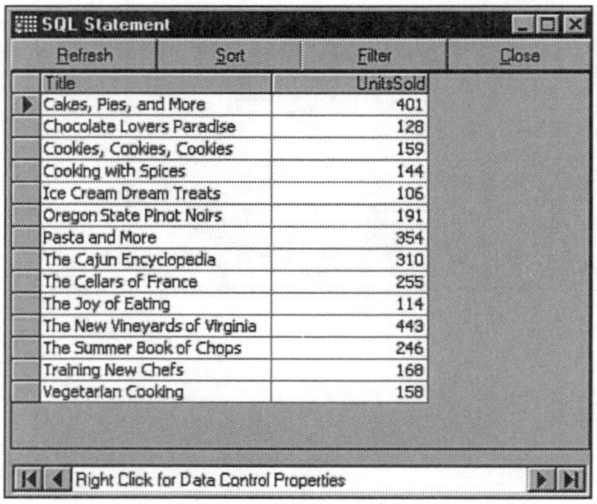
SQL Statement
Refresh
Sort
Filter
Close
Title
UnitsSold
Cakes, Pies, and More 401
Chocolate Lovers Paradise 128
Cookies, Cookies, Cookies 159
Cooking with Spices 144
Ice Cream Dream Treats 106
Oregon State Pinot Noirs 191
Pasta and More 354
The Cajun Encyclopedia 310
The Cellars of France 255
The Joy of Eating 114
The New Vineyards of Virginia 443
The Summer Book of Chops 246
Training New Chefs 168
Vegetarian Cooking 158
Right Click for Data Control Properties

The columns used in the HAVING clause do not have to be the same columns listed in the SELECT clause. The contents of the HAVING clause follow the same rules as those for the contents of the WHERE clause. You can use logical operators AND, OR, and NOT, and you can include VB-specific functions as part of the HAVING clause. The following SQL statement (see Figure 7.27) returns sales in dollars for all titles that have more than 100 units sold and whose titles have the letter *a* as the second letter in the title:

```
SELECT Title, SUM(Sales) AS SalesAmt
FROM BookSales
GROUP BY Title
HAVING SUM(Units)>100 AND Mid$(Title,2,1)="a"
```

FIGURE 7.27

Using a complex
HAVING *clause.*

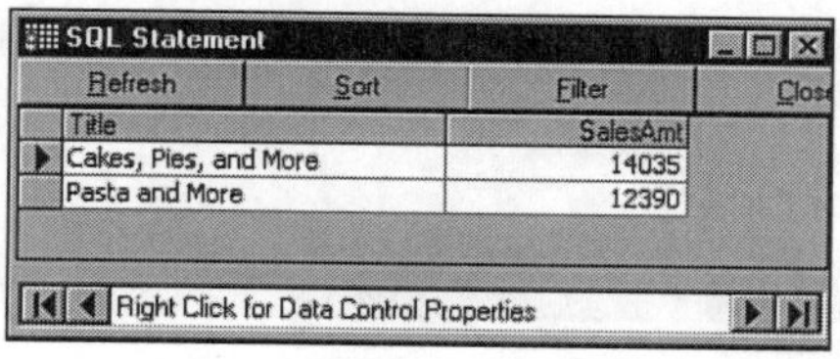

SQL JOIN Clauses

The JOIN clause is a very powerful optional SQL clause. Remember when you learned how to link two tables together using WHERE table1.column1 = table2.column1? The only problem with using the WHERE clause is that the resultset is not updatable. What if you need to create an updatable resultset that contains columns from more than one table? You use JOIN.

There are three types of JOIN clauses in Microsoft Access Jet SQL:

- INNER JOIN
- LEFT JOIN
- RIGHT JOIN

The following sections describe each form of JOIN and how it is used in your programs.

The INNER JOIN

The INNER JOIN can be used to create a resultset that contains only those records that have an exact match in both tables. Enter and execute the following SQL statement (see Figure 7.28):

```
SELECT PublisherComments.Comments,
Publishers.Name, Publishers.StateProv
FROM PublisherComments INNER JOIN Publishers
ON PublisherComments.PubID = Publishers.PubID
```

7

FIGURE 7.28

Using the INNER
JOIN *SQL clause.*

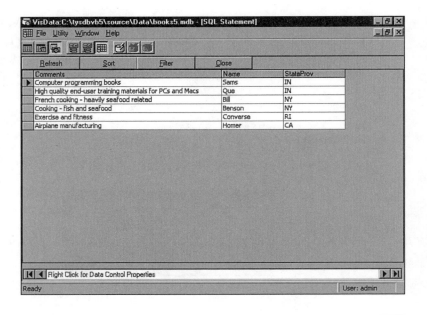

Comments	Name	StateProv
Computer programming books	Sams	IN
High quality end-user training materials for PCs and Macs	Que	IN
French cooking - heavily seafood related	Bill	NY
Cooking - fish and seafood	Benson	NY
Exercise and fitness	Converse	RI
Airplane manufacturing	Homer	CA

Note

PublisherComments was used as the name for the table used in the pre-ceding example. When creating a Microsoft Access database, you could easi-ly have named the table Publisher Comments (note the space between the two words), in which case, you would have had to enclose the table name in brackets in the preceding query:

```
[Publisher Comments]
```

This is a good time to point out that it is a bad idea to use embedded spaces in table names. Not only do you need to include brackets around the name in a query, but also the Wizard available to upsize Access data files to Microsoft SQL Server does not work successfully on tables with spaces embedded in their names.

The preceding SQL statement returns all the records from the Publisher table that have a PubID that matches a PubID in the PublisherComments table. This type of JOIN returns all the records that reside within both tables—thus, an INNER JOIN.

This is handy if you have two tables that you know are not perfectly matched against a single column and you want to create a resultset that contains only those rows that match on both sides. The INNER JOIN also works well when you have a parent table (such as a CustomerTable) and a child table (such as a ShipAddressTable) with a one-to-one rela-tionship. Using an INNER JOIN, you can quickly create a list of all CustomerTable records that have a corresponding ShipAddressTable record on file.

INNER JOINs work best when you create a JOIN on a column that is unique in both tables. If you use a table that has more than one occurrence of the JOIN column, you get a row for each occurrence in the resultset. This might be undesirable. The following example illustrates the point (see Figure 7.29):

```
SELECT Titles.Title,BookSales.Units
FROM Titles INNER JOIN BookSales
ON Titles.Title = BookSales.Title
```

FIGURE 7.29

Using the INNER
JOIN *on a non-
unique column.*

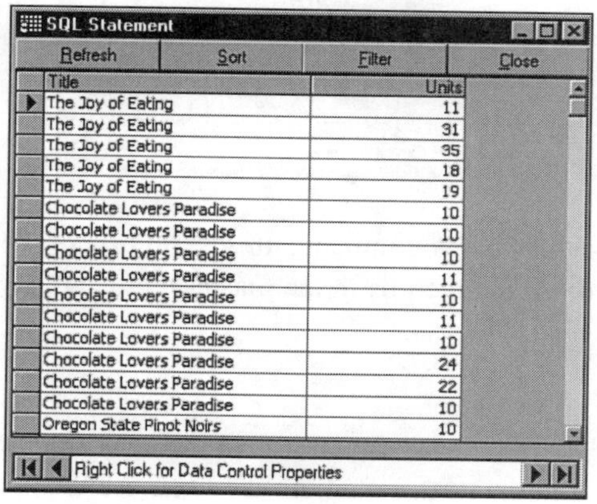

In this example, the table BookSales has numerous entries for each title (one for each quarter recorded), so the result of the INNER JOIN returns each Title multiple times.

The LEFT JOIN

The LEFT JOIN is one of the two outer joins in the SQL syntax. Although INNER JOIN returns only those rows that have corresponding values in both tables, the outer joins return all the records from one side of the join, whether or not there is a corresponding match on the other side of the join. The LEFT JOIN clause returns all the records from the first table on the list (the left table) and any records on the right side of the table that have a matching column value. Figure 7.30 shows the same SQL query that was shown in Figure 7.28, except INNER has been replaced by LEFT. Run this SQL statement and compare your results to Figure 7.30:

```
SELECT Publishers.Name,PublisherComments.Comments
FROM Publishers LEFT JOIN PublisherComments
ON Publishers.PubID = PublisherComments.PubID
```

7

FIGURE 7.30

Using the LEFT
JOIN *clause.*

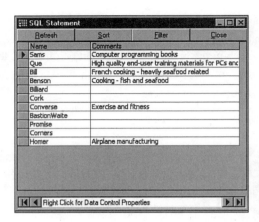

Notice that the resultset has blank comments in several places. The LEFT JOIN is handy when you want a list of all the records in the master table and any records in the dependent table that are on file.

The RIGHT JOIN

The RIGHT JOIN works the same as the LEFT JOIN except that the resultset is based on the second (right) table in the JOIN statement. You can use the RIGHT JOIN in the same manner you would use the LEFT JOIN.

UNION Queries

Another powerful SQL clause is the UNION clause. This SQL keyword enables you to create a union between two tables or SQL queries that contain similar, but unrelated, data. A UNION query is handy when you want to collate information from two queries into a single resultset. Because UNION queries return nonupdatable resultsets, they are good for producing onscreen displays, reports, and base data for generating graphs and charts.

For example, if you have a customer table and a vendor table, you might want to get a list of all vendors and customers who live in the state of Ohio. You could write an SQL statement to select the rows from the Customers table. Then write an SQL statement to select the rows from the Vendors table. Combine the two SQL statements into a single SQL phrase using the UNION keyword. Now you can get a single resultset that contains the results of both queries.

In the following SQL statement (see Figure 7.31), you are creating a resultset that contains all Publishers and Buyers located in the state of New York.

```
SELECT Name, City, StateProv, Zip FROM Publishers WHERE StateProv='NY'
UNION
SELECT Name, City, StateProv, Zip FROM Buyers WHERE StateProv='NY'
ORDER BY Zip
```

FIGURE 7.31

*An example of a
UNION query.*

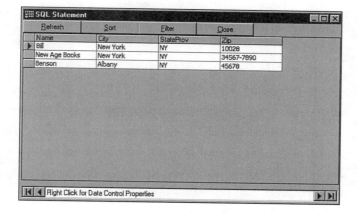

A note of caution when using the UNION query. To keep the same number of data columns, SQL does a data type override to insert results into columns that are not the same data types. The UNION query uses the column names of the first SQL query in the statement and creates a resultset that displays the data even if data types must be altered to do so.

Each portion of the UNION query must have the same number of columns. If the first query results in six displayable columns, the query on the other side of the UNION statement must also result in six columns. If there is not an equal number of columns on each side of a UNION query, you receive an SQL error message.

You can also use UNION queries on the same table. The following SQL statement (see Figure 7.32) shows how you can use SQL to return the top-selling titles and the bottom-selling titles in the same resultset:

```
SELECT SUM(Sales) AS TotSales,Title FROM BookSales
GROUP BY Title HAVING SUM(Sales)>4000
UNION
SELECT SUM(Sales) AS TotSales,Title FROM BookSales
GROUP BY Title HAVING SUM(Sales)<1000
ORDER BY TotSales
```

7

FIGURE 7.32

Using UNION on the same data table.

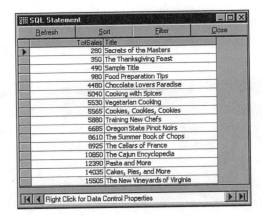

You can use Visual Basic stored queries (QueryDefs) as replacements for the complete SQL statement on either side of a UNION keyword. You can also link several SQL queries together with successive UNION keywords.

Crosstab Queries with TRANSFORM_PIVOT

The last SQL statement covered today is the TRANSFORM_PIVOT statement. This is a very powerful SQL tool that enables you to create resultsets that contain summarized data in a form known as a crosstab query. Instead of trying to explain a crosstab query, let's look at a sample problem.

Suppose you have a data table that contains information on book titles and sales by quarter (sound familiar?). You have been asked to produce a view set that lists each book title down the left side and each quarter across the top with the sales figures for each quarter to the right of the book title. The only problem is that your data table has a single record for each quarter for each book. For example, if book A has sales in three quarters this year, you have three rows in your data table. If book B has sales for four quarters, you have four rows, and so on. How can you produce a view that lists the quarters as columns instead of as rows?

You can accomplish this with a complicated set of subsequent SQL statements that produces temporary views, merges them, and so on. Thanks to the folks who invented the Microsoft Access Jet database engine, however, you can use the TRANSFORM_PIVOT statement instead. You can produce the entire resultset in one SQL statement using TRANS-FORM_PIVOT. The following SQL statement shows how this can be done. See Figure 7.33 for a sample resultset.

```
TRANSFORM SUM(BookSales.Sales)
SELECT Title FROM BookSales
GROUP BY Title
PIVOT BookSales.Qtr
```

FIGURE 7.33

The
TRANSFORM_PIVOT
example.

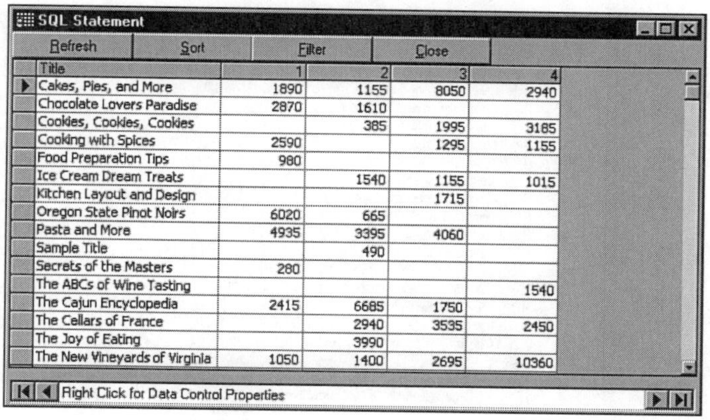

Title	1	2	3	4
Cakes, Pies, and More	1890	1155	8050	2940
Chocolate Lovers Paradise	2870	1610		
Cookies, Cookies, Cookies		385	1995	3185
Cooking with Spices	2590		1295	1155
Food Preparation Tips	980			
Ice Cream Dream Treats		1540	1155	1015
Kitchen Layout and Design			1715	
Oregon State Pinot Noirs	6020	665		
Pasta and More	4935	3395	4060	
Sample Title		490		
Secrets of the Masters	280			
The ABCs of Wine Tasting				1540
The Cajun Encyclopedia	2415	6685	1750	
The Cellars of France		2940	3535	2450
The Joy of Eating		3990		
The New Vineyards of Virginia	1050	1400	2695	10360

Notice the form of the TRANSFORM_PIVOT statement. It starts with the TRANSFORM keyword, not the SELECT keyword. Notice that a single SQL aggregate function immediately follows the TRANSFORM keyword. This is required, even if no real totaling will be performed. After the TRANSFORM aggregate function clause, you have the standard SELECT_FROM clause. Notice that the preceding example did not include the Booksales.Sales column in the SELECT statement because it will be produced by the TRANSFORM_PIVOT clause automatically. The GROUP BY clause is required in order to tell SQL how to treat the successive rows that will be handled for each BookSales.Title. Finally, add the PIVOT keyword, followed by the column that you want to use, as the set of headers that follow out to the right of the GROUP BY clause.

TRANSFORM_PIVOT uses the data in the PIVOT column as column headers in the resultset. You will have as many columns in your resultset as you have unique values in your PIVOT column. This is important to understand. Using columns that contain a limited set of data (such as months of the year) produces valuable resultsets. However, using a column that contains unique data (such as the CustomerID column) produces a resultset with an unpredictable number of columns.

The nice thing about TRANSFORM_PIVOT is that it is easy to produce several different views of the same data by just changing the PIVOT column. For example, what if you want to see the book sales results by BookSales.SaleRep instead of by BookSales.Qtr? All you have to do is change the PIVOT field. See the following code example and Figure 7.34:

```
TRANSFORM SUM(BookSales.Sales)
SELECT Title FROM BookSales
GROUP BY Title
PIVOT BookSales.SalesRep
```

7

FIGURE 7.34

*Changing the
PIVOT field.*

Title	<>	A	B	C	D
Cakes, Pies, and More	420	2100	6825	385	2800
Chocolate Lovers Paradise		770	700	700	700
Cookies, Cookies, Cookies		420	2450	1155	770
Cooking with Spices			2240	385	350
Food Preparation Tips				630	
Ice Cream Dream Treats				770	385
Kitchen Layout and Design		385			
Oregon State Pinot Noirs		700	665	350	350
Pasta and More		385	2380	1610	1820
Sample Title	490				
Secrets of the Masters			280		
The ABCs of Wine Tasting				875	
The Cajun Encyclopedia	385	1680	2100	1330	980
The Cellars of France	1120	1680	875	770	1155
The Joy of Eating		1225		630	1750

Right Click for Data Control Properties

Notice, in Figure 7.34, that you can see a column with the header <>. When Microsoft
Access Jet ran the SQL statement, it discovered some records that had no value in the
BookSales.SaleRep column. SQL automatically created a new column (<>) to hold these
records and make sure they were not left out of the resultset.

Even though TRANSFORM_PIVOT is a powerful SQL tool, there is one drawback to its
widespread use in your programs. The TRANSFORM_PIVOT clause is not an ANSI-SQL
clause. Microsoft added this clause as an extension of the ANSI-SQL command set. If
you use it in your programs, you will not be able to port your SQL statements to other
back-end databases that do not support the TRANSFORM_PIVOT SQL clause. Despite this
drawback, you will find TRANSFORM_PIVOT a very valuable SQL tool when it comes to
producing resultsets for summary reports, data graphs, and charts.

Nested SELECT Queries

Visual Basic 6 enables the use of nested SELECT queries. These are often referred to as
SQL subqueries and are literally queries contained within queries. Nested SELECT queries
can prove to be useful when you want to perform a query based upon the results of
another query.

To demonstrate the use of a SQL subquery, let's start Visdata and open the SUBQRY.MDB
database that can be found in the \\TYSDBVB6\SOURCE\DATA directory that was created
when you installed the source code from the CD-ROM that shipped with this book. This
database contains a sample listing of authors, publishers, and book sales activity (notice
that this database is very similar to the BOOKS6.MDB database) for a fictitious publisher.
Our goal in this exercise is to extract the phone numbers of all the authors who sold
more than 500 books in the first quarter.

As you examine the table structure of this database in Visdata, you notice the BookSales table contains the sales records by quarter, but the phone number is contained in the Authors table. You therefore need to query the BookSales table to find all the authors who sold more than 500 books in the first quarter, and then use that resultset to find the writers' phone numbers in the Authors table. You need to build a nested `SELECT` query.

To do this, enter the following code into the SQL Statement window of Visdata. Execute your statement. The resultset should look similar to Figure 7.35.

```
SELECT * FROM Authors WHERE AUID IN (SELECT AUID
FROM Booksales WHERE Sales>500 AND Qtr=1)
```

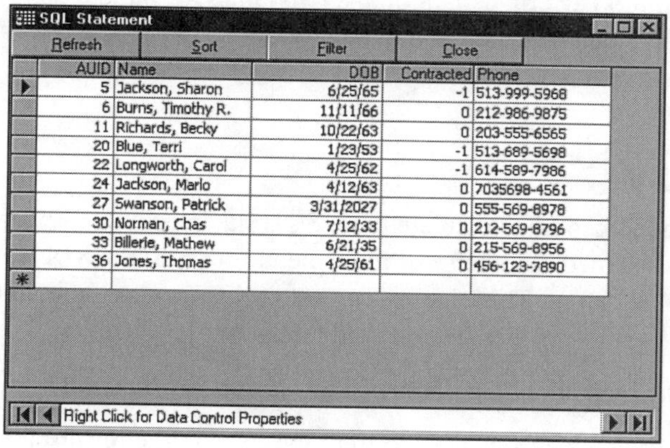

AUID	Name	DOB	Contracted	Phone
5	Jackson, Sharon	6/25/65	-1	513-999-5968
6	Burns, Timothy R.	11/11/66	0	212-986-9875
11	Richards, Becky	10/22/63	0	203-555-6565
20	Blue, Terri	1/23/53	-1	513-689-5698
22	Longworth, Carol	4/25/62	-1	614-589-7986
24	Jackson, Marlo	4/12/63	0	7035698-4561
27	Swanson, Patrick	3/31/2027	0	555-569-8978
30	Norman, Chas	7/12/33	0	212-569-8796
33	Billerie, Mathew	6/21/35	0	215-569-8956
36	Jones, Thomas	4/25/61	0	456-123-7890

FIGURE 7.35
The results of an SQL subquery.

An SQL subquery has three main components: the comparison, the expression, and the SQL statement. The comparison in our example is the `SELECT FROM Authors` query. The expression is the `IN` keyword. The SQL statement is the `SELECT` statement within the parentheses.

NEW TERM The SQL statement on which you base the comparison statement must be a `SELECT` statement. This statement must also be enclosed in parentheses and is referred to as a *subquery*.

In the exercise, the `SELECT` statement contained within the parentheses (the sqlstatement, or subquery) is executed first to determine which authors sold more than 500 books in the first quarter. The `SELECT` statement outside the parentheses (the main query) is then executed on the resultset created by the subquery. The `IN` keyword instructs the `SELECT FROM Authors` statement to take only those records that were extracted by the subquery.

7

Other keywords that can be used in the expression include ANY and ALL. Also, numeric expressions such as > and < can be used in conjunction with the keyword to make comparisons.

For example, if you use the syntax > ANY in comparing the main query with the subquery (WHERE AUID > ANY), your resultset displays all records from the main query that have a value greater than any value extracted from the subquery. Using > ALL (WHERE AUID > All) extracts only those records that are greater in value than every record extracted by the subquery.

Without the ability to use nested SQL statements, the preceding exercise would have required you to perform a JOIN on the two tables, or build a table to store the subqueries resultset, and then execute the main query on the table. The use of nested SQL SELECT statements can be a great time-saver.

Summary

Today you learned how to create basic SQL statements that select data from existing tables. You learned that the most fundamental form of the SQL statement is the SELECT_FROM clause. This clause is used to select one or more columns from a table and display the results of that statement in a resultset, or view.

You also learned about the optional clauses that you can add to the SELECT_FROM clause:

- The WHERE clause is used to limit the rows in the resultset using logical comparisons (for example, WHERE Table.Name = "SMITH") and to link two tables in a single, nonupdatable view (for example, WHERE Table1.Name = Table2.Name).
- The ORDER BY clause is used to control the order in which the resultset is displayed (for example, ORDER BY Name ASC).
- The GROUP BY clause is used to create a subtotal resultset based on a break column (for example, GROUP BY Name).
- The HAVING clause is used only with the GROUP BY clause and acts as a WHERE clause for the GROUP BY subtotal clause (for example, GROUP BY Name HAVING SUM(SalesTotal)>1000).
- The INNER JOIN clause is used to join two tables into a single, updatable resultset. The INNER JOIN returns rows that have a corresponding match in both tables.
- The LEFT JOIN and RIGHT JOIN clauses are used to join two tables into a single, updatable resultset. The LEFT JOIN includes all records from the first (left-hand) table and all rows from the second table that have a corresponding match. The RIGHT JOIN works in reverse.

- The UNION clause is used to combine two or more complete SQL queries into a single resultset (for example, SELECT * FROM Table1 UNION SELECT * FROM Table2).

- The TRANSFORM_PIVOT clause is used to create a crosstab query as a resultset (for example, TRANSFORM SUM(MonthlySales) FROM SalesTable GROUP BY Product PIVOT Month).

You also learned about additional SQL keywords that you can use to control the contents of the resultset:

- BETWEEN_AND logical operators
- DISTINCT and DISTINCTROW
- AS to rename columns in the resultset
- TOP[] and TOP[]PERCENT
- The SQL aggregate functions AVG, COUNT, MAX, MIN, and SUM

Finally, you learned about the SQL subquery, and how to nest SELECT statements to extract data from a table based upon the results of another SELECT statement.

Quiz

1. What does SQL stand for? How is SQL pronounced?
2. What SQL statement enables you to select data from table fields?
3. What wildcard character do you use in a SELECT_FROM statement to include all fields of a table in your result?
4. What clause do you use in an SQL statement to sort the displayed data?
5. Identify two functions that a WHERE clause performs in an SQL statement.
6. How do you rename the column headings in an SQL statement?
7. What are SQL aggregate functions? List the SQL aggregate functions available through the Microsoft Access Jet database engine.
8. What are the drawbacks of using Visual Basic functions in SQL statements?
9. What is the difference between the DISTINCT and DISTINCTROW SQL clauses?
10. What clause should you always use with the TOP[] or TOP[]PERCENT clause?
11. What are the three join types available in Microsoft Jet SQL? Briefly explain how each is used.
12. When would you use a UNION query?

7

Exercises

As a corporate MIS team member, you are given the task of assisting the accounting department in extracting data from its accounts payable and accounts receivable systems. As part of your analysis, you determine that these systems possess the following data tables and fields:

CustomerMaster

CustomerID

Name

Address

City

State

Zip

Phone

CustomerType

CustomerType

CustomerType

Description

OpenInvoice

InvoiceNo

CustomerID

Date

Description

Amount

Suppliers

SupplierID

Name

Address

City

State

Zip

Phone

Use this information to answer the questions that follow:

1. Write an SQL statement to list all the customers. Include their IDs, names, addresses, phone numbers, and customer types.

2. Display all the information in the Open Invoice table, but display CustomerID as Account.

3. Display the same information requested in Exercise 2, but sort the data by customer and then by invoice number within each customer.

4. Display all suppliers that can be found within New York City. Display their IDs, names, addresses, and phone numbers.

5. Display the Customer types, names, and addresses for all customers with a customer type of ABC.

6. Select and display customer IDs and names for customer names beginning with AME.

7. Display the customer ID and name of all customers who have an open invoice. Sort your information by CustomerID.

8. Select and display the five largest outstanding invoices.

9. Display a listing of names and phone numbers of all customers and vendors who reside in Ohio.

7

WEEK 1

In Review

2

In the first week, you learned about the relational database model, how to use the Visual Basic database objects to access and update existing databases, and how to use the Visual Data Manager (Visdata) program to create and maintain databases. You also learned how to design and code data entry forms, including use of the Visual Basic bound data controls, and how to create input validation routines at the keystroke, field, and form levels. You learned how to use the Visual Data Report to design simple reports. Finally, you learned the basics of SQL to extract information from databases.

Day 1: Database Programming Basics

Day 1 gave you a crash course in how to build a fully functional data entry form in Visual Basic with minimal programming code. On Day 1, you learned the following:

- How to use the data control to bind a form to a database and data table by setting the `DatabaseName` and `RecordSource` properties

- How to use the Text box bound input control to bind an input box on the form to a data table and data field by setting the `DataSource` and `DataField` properties

- How to combine standard command buttons and the `AddNew` and `Delete` methods to provide add- and delete-record functionality to a data entry form

You also learned the following about relational databases:

- A relational database is a collection of related data.
- The three key building blocks of relational databases are data fields, data records, and data tables.
- The two types of database relationships are one-to-one (which uses qualifier fields) and one-to-many (which uses pointer fields).
- There are two types of key (or index) fields: primary and foreign.

You learned the 14 basic data field types recognized by Visual Basic 6. You constructed a data entry form that enables you to test the way Visual Basic behaves when attempting to store data entered into the various data field types.

Day 2: Visual Basic Database Access Objects

On Day 2, you learned that there are three main types of Visual Basic Recordset data objects:

- *Table-type objects* are used when you have a large dataset and need to do frequent searches to locate a single record. You can use the Visual Basic Seek method and use Visual Basic Indexes with the Table object.
- *Dynaset-type objects* are used in most cases when you need read and write access to datasets. The Dynaset uses little workstation memory and enables you to create virtual tables by combining fields from different tables in the same database. The Dynaset is the only data object that enables you to read and write to ODBC data sources.
- *Snapshot-type objects* are used when you need fast read-only access to datasets. Snapshot objects are stored in workstation memory, so they should be kept small. Snapshots are good for storing validation lists at the workstation or for small reports.

You also learned about another data object: the Database object. You can use the Database object to get a list of tables in the database, a list of indexes associated with the tables, and a list of fields in each of the tables.

Day 3: Creating Data Entry Forms with Bound Controls

On Day 3, you learned about creating data entry forms with Visual Basic bound data controls.

You learned that the Visual Basic data control has five database-related properties. Three refer to the database and two refer to the Dynaset.

The following are database properties of the Visual Basic data control:

- `DatabaseName` is used to select the database to access.
- `Exclusive` is used to prevent others from opening the database.
- `ReadOnly` is used to prevent your program from modifying the data in the database.

The following are Dynaset properties of the Visual Basic data control:

- `RecordSource` is used to select the data table within the database.
- `Options` is used to set `ReadOnly`, `DenyWrite`, and `AppendOnly` properties for the Dynaset.

You learned that the Visual Basic data control has three database-related methods:

- `Refresh` is used to update the data control after setting properties.
- `UpdateControls` is used to read values from the fields in the Dynaset and write those values to the related form controls.
- `UpdateRecord` is used to read values from the form controls and write those values to the related fields in the Dynaset.

You learned that the Visual Basic data control has three database-related events:

- `Reposition` occurs each time the record pointer is moved to a new record in the Dynaset.
- `Validate` occurs each time the record pointer leaves the current record in the Dynaset.
- `Error` occurs each time a database error occurs.

You learned how to use Visual Basic–bound form controls to link form input and display controls to data fields in the database:

- The *bound text box control* is used for data entry on character and numeric data table fields.
- The *bound label control* is used for display-only character and numeric data table fields.
- The *bound check box control* is used for data entry on the `BOOLEAN` data type field.
- The *bound image control* is used to display images stored in the `BINARY` data type field.
- The *3D panel control* behaves the same as the label control, and the *3D check box control* behaves the same as a standard check box control.

You also learned several general rules for creating Visual Basic forms in the Windows 95 style:

- The default color is light gray for backgrounds.
- Use the panel3D control to create a palette on which to place all other controls.
- The default font is 8-point sans serif, regular.
- Input areas should have a background that is white; display areas should have a background that is light gray. Display areas should be recessed into the input palette.
- Use frame controls to group related items on a form.
- Left-justify all controls, including field prompts. Field prompts should be written in mixed case and followed by a semicolon.
- Standard spacing and sizing for common controls are as follows:
  - Control height is 330 twips.
  - Command button width is 1200 twips.
  - Vertical spacing between controls is 90 twips for related items and 210 twips for unrelated items.
  - Border widths (top, bottom, and side) should be 120 twips.

Finally, you learned how to write code that sets control colors to the Windows 95 default colors, how to create your own custom color scheme, and how to link your control colors to the color scheme selected with the Windows Control Panel color applet.

Day 4: Input Validation

On Day 4, you learned how to perform input validation on data entry forms. You learned that input validation tasks can be divided into three areas:

- *Key filtering* prevents unwanted keyboard input.
- *Field-level validation* validates input for each field.
- *Form-level validation* validates input across several fields.

You also learned that you should ask yourself a few basic questions when you are developing validation rules for your form.

- Is it a required field?
- What characters are valid/invalid for this field (numeric input only, capital letters only, no spaces allowed, and so on)?

- For numeric fields, is there a high/low range limit (must be greater than zero and less than 1000, can't be less than 100, and so on)?
- Is there a list of valid values for this field (can the user enter only Retail, Wholesale, or Other; Name must already be in the Customer table; and so on)?
- Is this a conditional field (if users enter Yes in field A, they must enter something in field C)?

You learned how to write keyboard filter validation functions using the Visual Basic 6 KeyPress event. You learned how to write field-level validation functions that check for valid input ranges, input that is part of a list of valid data, and input that is within minimum and maximum length requirements. You also learned how to write validation functions that make sure dependent fields have been filled out properly.

Finally, you learned how to use Visual Basic 6 to create your own custom control that incorporates all the validation techniques you learned in this chapter. You can use this ActiveX control in all your future Visual Basic projects.

You also applied your knowledge of bound data controls, Visual Basic 6 data entry form design, and validation processing to create the data entry form for the CompanyMaster data table.

Day 5: Writing Reports for Visual Basic 6 Applications

On Day 5, you learned how to design a Data Environment that can be used to create a Visual Basic 6 Data Report. You learned that a Data Environment requires you to define a connection to a data source and then a command to a data table. You learned that commands can exist in a hierarchy of relationships.

You learned that there are two properties of the Data Report that bind it to the Data Environment:

- DataSource is the name of the Data Environment.
- DataMember is the name of the command to use in the report.

You learned how quickly a report can be created by simply dragging and dropping data elements from the Data Environment directly to the Data Report. You then learned how to format the data on your reports and how to use aggregate functions to perform mathematical calculations. You learned how to use the SHOW method to display these reports from within your application.

You learned how to export data in HTML format using the Data Report. Finally, you learned that the relationships defined in the Data Environment dictate where information can be placed on the Data Report.

Day 6: Using the Visdata Program

On Day 6, you learned how to use the Visdata sample application to perform all the basic database operations needed to create and maintain databases for your Visual Basic 6 applications.

You learned how to

- Open existing databases
- Create new databases
- Add tables and indexes to existing databases
- Attach external data sources to existing Microsoft Access databases
- Access data using the three data access objects: Table, Dynaset, and Snapshot
- View data onscreen using the three data forms: form view with the data control, form view without the data control, and grid view using the data-bound grid
- Build and store SQL queries using the Query Builder

You learned to use Visdata to perform database utility operations, including

- Copying tables from one database to another
- Repairing corrupted Microsoft Access (Jet) databases
- Compacting and converting versions of Microsoft Jet databases
- Performing global replace operations on tables

You learned to use Visdata to adjust various system settings that affect how Visual Basic 6 displays data tables and processes local and external database connections and parameters that control how Visual Basic 6 locks records at update time.

Day 7: Selecting Data with SQL

On Day 7, you learned how to create basic SQL statements that select data from existing tables. You learned that the most fundamental form of the SQL statement is the SELECT_FROM clause. This clause is used to select one or more columns from a table and display the results in a resultset, or view.

You also learned about the optional clauses that you can add to the SELECT_FROM clause:

- The WHERE clause is used to limit the rows in the resultset using logical comparisons:

  ```
  WHERE Table.Name = "SMITH")
  ```

  and to link two tables in a single, nonupdatable, view:

  ```
  WHERE Table1.Name = Table2.Name
  ```

- The ORDER BY clause is used to control the order in which the resultset is displayed:

  ```
  ORDER BY Name ASC
  ```

- The GROUP BY clause is used to create a subtotal resultset based on a break column:

  ```
  GROUP BY Name
  ```

- The HAVING clause is used only with the GROUP BY clause. The HAVING clause acts as a WHERE clause for the GROUP BY subtotal clause:

  ```
  GROUP BY Name HAVING SUM(SalesTotal)>1000
  ```

- The INNER JOIN clause is used to join two tables into a single, updatable resultset. The INNER JOIN returns rows that have a corresponding match in both tables.

- The LEFT JOIN and RIGHT JOIN are used to join two tables into a single, updatable resultset. The LEFT JOIN includes all records from the first (left) table and all rows from the second table that have a corresponding match. The RIGHT JOIN works in reverse.

- The UNION clause is used to combine two or more complete SQL queries into a single resultset:

  ```
  SELECT * FROM Table1 UNION SELECT * FROM Table2
  ```

- The TRANSFORM_PIVOT clause is used to create a crosstab query as a resultset, for example:

  ```
  TRANSFORM SUM(MonthlySales) FROM SalesTable GROUP BY Product PIVOT
  Month
  ```

You also learned about additional SQL keywords that you can use to control the contents of the resultset:

- BETWEEN_AND
- DISTINCT and DISTINCTROW
- AS
- TOP[ ] and TOP[ ]PERCENT
- AVG, COUNT, MAX, MIN, and SUM

WEEK 2

At a Glance

This week, you build on the skills you developed in Week 1. Emphasis moves to developing skills that you need for application in a workgroup environment. In addition, you create tools that you use in every Visual Basic database application.

> **Note**
>
> Most of the material covered this week requires the Professional Edition of Visual Basic. However, if you are working with the Learning Edition of Visual Basic, you can still learn a great deal from this week's lessons.

There are lessons on the SQL data manipulation language and Visual Basic Data Access Objects (DAO). Other lessons cover how to use Visual Basic code to create database applications; displaying data with graphics; error trapping; and data-bound lists, combo boxes, and grids.

When you've completed this week's lessons, you will know most of the techniques needed to build solid Visual Basic database applications using Visual Basic code. You'll also have several Visual Basic custom controls that you can use in future Visual Basic projects.

Day 8: You begin the second week by delving into the database engine that ships with Visual Basic 6: Microsoft Jet. You learn the hierarchical design and use of the Data Access Object (DAO) available to you in your development. The emphasis is on the methods, properties, and events of each object.

Day 9: You temporarily abandon use of the data control in favor of writing Visual Basic code to manage data. You learn the pluses and minuses of this practice. During the lesson, you build an OLE Server library that can be used as the basis for future Visual Basic data entry projects.

Day 10: You get graphical on Day 10. Users can identify trends and deviations in data much more quickly with graphics and charts than they can with raw data. You learn how to use the graph tool that ships with Visual Basic 6 to give your applications a polished, graphical appearance. During the lesson, you work with a graphing control that you can use in all your future Visual Basic projects.

Day 11: You learn about the data-bound list boxes, combo boxes, and grids that ship with Visual Basic 6. You also learn how to use subforms to display data.

Day 12: You focus on creating databases with the SQL language. On this second day devoted to SQL, you learn how to use SQL Data Definition Language (DDML) to create and modify databases, tables, relationships, and indexes. You also work with `SQL-VB6`, a tool that can read text file scripts developed in any standard text editor or word processor to create and modify databases.

Day 13: Day 13 won't be unlucky with this chapter on error handling. No one intends to release a product with bugs in it, but it does happen. Error trapping manages these bugs and many other unforeseen kinds of problems. Emphasis is on the different kinds of errors an application can encounter and how to handle each. You work with a reusable error trapping control that can be dropped into any Visual Basic application.

Day 14: During the final day this week, you continue your study of SQL by using Data Manipulation Language to insert records into tables, append records to tables, and update records that currently exist in data tables. You also learn how to use `Make Table` queries to build tables with data from other tables. Finally, you learn how to create `Delete Table` queries that remove multiple records from a data table.

You have a great deal of information to cover—so, let's begin Week 2!

DAY 8

Visual Basic and the DAO Jet Database Engine

Today, you learn the details of the DAO Jet Database Engine. This is the default database service for Visual Basic. The letters DAO stand for database access object. The DAO object model is rich and powerful. In this lesson you learn the general layout of the DAO object model and how you can use Visual Basic code to access its features.

> **Note**
>
> DAO is just one of the data object models available to Visual Basic 6.0 programmers. You can also use RDO (Remote Data Objects) and ADO (Active Data Objects). You can learn more about RDO in Day 17, "Using the Remote Data Control and the RDO Model." ADO is covered in Day 18, "Using the ActiveX Data Objects (ADO)."

Today, you learn about several object collections that exist in Visual Basic Microsoft Jet databases. The objects covered in this chapter include the following:

- The DBEngine object
- The Workspace object
- The Database object
- The TableDef object
- The QueryDef object
- The Field object
- The Index object
- The Relation object
- The Connection object
- The Recordset object

Throughout this lesson, you build a single Visual Basic project that illustrates the various data access objects you learn about today. You can apply the Visual Basic coding techniques you learn today in future Visual Basic database projects.

What Is the DAO Database Engine?

The idea behind DAO Jet is that you can use one interface to access multiple types of data. Microsoft designed DAO Jet to present a consistent interface to the user regardless of the type of data the user is working with. Consequently, you can use the same Microsoft Jet functions that you use to access an ASCII text file or Microsoft Excel spreadsheet to also perform data operations on Microsoft Access databases.

The DAO Jet engine is not a single program; it is a set of routines that work together. The DAO Jet engine talks to a set of translation routines. These routines convert your request into a format that the target database can understand. Translation routines exist for Microsoft Access databases and for non-Microsoft Access ISAM files, such as dBASE, FoxPro, Paradox, and so on. A translation set even exists to handle ODBC data sources using the Microsoft Jet interface. In theory, you could access any data file format through the DAO Jet engine, as long as some set of translation routines is made available to the engine.

Finally, one of the most unique aspects of the DAO Jet data service is that it includes its own query engine. This means that you can use standard SQL statements to search, order, and filter the data without having to have a large, complex database server. All you need is the DAO Jet components and a compatible data file.

8

> **Note**
>
> The detailed inner workings of the Microsoft Jet engine go beyond the scope of this book. If you want to learn more about how the Microsoft Jet interface works, you can obtain copies of several white papers Microsoft has released on the topic of Microsoft Jet and the data access object layer. You can get these papers through various online sources and through the Microsoft Developers Network CD-ROMs.

Advantages and Drawbacks of DAO Jet

So far, you have learned to use the data control object to perform database administrative tasks. The data access objects (DAOs) addressed in this chapter perform all the services that the data control does, as well as many more. The data access objects give you complete control over database management.

If possible, use the data control object to manage your data. It is much easier to use, because many of the administrative functions are handled for you. You can always add DAO in your code to work with the data control object.

As mentioned earlier, another primary advantage of the DAO Jet service is that it includes its own query engine. This means that programs that use DAO Jet will not need the support of a remote or server-based database system such as SQL Server or Oracle to complete data requests. If your application will need to operate in a standalone environment (not connected to a local network or the Internet), the DAO Jet data service is your best choice.

Of course this last point—that DAO Jet includes its own query engine—can also be its greatest weakness. Because the query service runs on the local machine, any requests to remote data mean that all the data must be transported to the local workstation before processing can begin. This can be a disadvantage if you are working with large amounts of data over a slow connection. There are steps you can take to help improve DAO performance when connecting to back-end data services such as SQL Server. However, if all your data work will be against remote database servers over network connections, you might find the RDO (Remote Data Object) model better suited for your needs.

Another disadvantage of DAO is that it is not "Internet-aware." The DAO Jet service was developed for standalone machines and local area networks (LANs). This makes DAO Jet an unlikely selection for Internet or intranet applications. If your database project needs to interact with users connected via Web services, you use the ADO (active data object) model for your data programming.

Microsoft DAO Jet Data Object Model Summary

Microsoft DAO Jet is organized into a set of data access objects. Each of the objects has collections, properties, and methods:

- *Collections.* Data access objects that contain the same type of objects.
- *Properties.* The data contained within an object (control button, form, and so on) that defines its characteristics. You set an object's properties.
- *Methods.* The procedures that can be performed on an object. You invoke a method.

The Microsoft Jet data access objects exist in a hierarchy, which means that a top-down relationship exists between the objects. You learn the various Microsoft Jet data access objects in the order they reside in the hierarchy. As you push deeper into the object hierarchy, you move toward more specific data objects. For example, the first data object in the hierarchy is the DBEngine data access object. All other data access objects exist underneath the DBEngine data access objects.

| **Note** | Throughout the rest of this chapter you will see the phrases *data access objects* and *data objects*. They both refer to the data access object layer of the Microsoft Jet engine. |

Figure 8.1 shows a summary of the DAO Jet object model.

FIGURE 8.1

The DAO Jet object model.

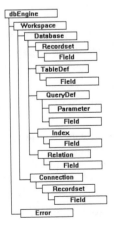

As you can see from Figure 8.1, the top-level object is called DBEngine. All other objects in the model are "child" objects of the DBEngine object. One aspect of the DAO model that is not apparent from the diagram is that all the child objects can exist as a collection. In other words, there can be more than one Workspace in the object model, more than one Database object, and so forth. These collection objects are left out of the diagram in order to simplify the figure.

Building the DAO Project

For the rest of this day's work, you build a project that demonstrates most of the objects in the DAO model. To do this, you build an application framework to hold the various dialogs you create throughout the day. After you build this framework, you can continue to build the various DAO demonstration dialogs.

If you do not already have Visual Basic up and running, start it now and begin a new Standard EXE project. Make sure that your system can reference the Microsoft Jet 3.51 Data Access Object Library.

Caution

If you don't have a reference to the data access object layer in your project, you cannot access any of the features of the Microsoft Jet database engine.

If you can't tell whether your reference to the data access object is activated, select Project | References from the Visual Basic main menu. Use Figure 8.2 as a reference.

FIGURE 8.2

Verifying the DAO 3.51 Library reference.

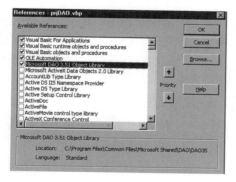

Throughout this chapter you use the Microsoft Jet 3.51 data engine. This is the most recent version of the data engine available. You can use older versions of the data engine to maintain compatibility with earlier Visual Basic projects, but it is recommended that you use Microsoft Jet 3.51 for all future projects.

You need to add an MDI form, a BAS module, and a standard form to display output results. You handle all these in this section of the chapter.

Adding the MDI Form

First, add an MDI form to the project (select Project | Add MDI Form from the main menu). This will hold all the other project dialogs. You need to add a Common Dialog control to the project, too. Select Project | Components from the main menu and locate and load the Microsoft Common Dialog Control. Then double-click on the common dialog control in the toolbox to add it to your MDI form.

Finally, you need to add several menu options to the MDI form using the Menu Editor. To call up the menu editor, select the form that will hold the menu (mdiDAO) and then select Tools | Menu Editor from the main menu.

Refer to Table 8.1 and Figure 8.3 for the various objects and their property settings for the MDI form. Notice the menu information is included in this table.

TABLE 8.1 CONTROLS FOR THE MDIDAO FORM

Control	Property	Setting
VB.MDIForm	Name	MdiDAO
	Caption	"DAO 3.51 Demonstation Project"
	ClientHeight	3540
	ClientLeft	1095
	ClientTop	1200
	ClientWidth	5505
	WindowState	2 'Maximized
CommonDialog	Name	cdlMain
	Left	0
	Top	0
VB.Menu	Name	mnuFile
	Caption	"&File"
VB.Menu	Name	mnuFileExit
	Caption	"E&xit"
VB.Menu	Name	mnuDAO
	Caption	"&DAO Objects"

Control	Property	Setting
VB.Menu	Name	mnuDAOEngine
	Caption	"DB&Engine"
VB.Menu	Name	mnuDAOWorkspace
	Caption	"&Workspace"
VB.Menu	Name	mnuDAODatabase
	Caption	"&Database"
VB.Menu	Name	mnuDAOQueryDef
	Caption	"&QueryDef"
VB.Menu	Name	mnuDAOOther
	Caption	"&Other Objects"
VB.Menu	Name	mnuWindows
	Caption	"&Windows"
	WindowList	-1 'True
VB.Menu	Name	mnuWindowsItem
	Caption	"&Cascade"
	Index	0
VB.Menu	Name	mnuWindowsItem
	Caption	"Tile &Horizontal"
	Index	1
VB.Menu	Name	mnuWindowsItem
	Caption	"Tile &Vertical"
	Index	2
VB.Menu	Name	mnuWindowsItem
	Caption	"&Arrange"
	Index	3

FIGURE 8.3

Laying out the mdiDAO form.

After laying out the MDI form, you need to add just a small bit of Visual Basic code to the form. You add some code behind the various menu click events to launch new forms, exit the application, or rearrange the open windows within the MDI.

Listing 8.1 has all the code you need for the entire MDI form.

LISTING 8.1 CODING THE MDIDAO FORM

```
 1: Option Explicit
 2:
 3: Private Sub mnuDAODatabase_Click()
 4:     ShowForm frmDatabase
 5: End Sub
 6:
 7: Private Sub mnuDAOEngine_Click()
 8:     ShowForm frmDBEngine
 9: End Sub
10:
11: Private Sub mnuDAOOther_Click()
12:     ShowForm frmOther
13: End Sub
14:
15: Private Sub mnuDAOQueryDef_Click()
16:     ShowForm frmQueryDef
17: End Sub
18:
19: Private Sub mnuDAOWorkspace_Click()
20:     ShowForm frmWorkspace
21: End Sub
22:
23: Private Sub mnuFileExit_Click()
24:     Unload Me
25: End Sub
26:
27: Private Sub mnuWindowsItem_Click(Index As Integer)
28:     Me.Arrange Index
29: End Sub
```

Adding the DAO Code Module

Now you need to create a handful of support routines that will be used throughout the project. First, add a new Code Module to the project and set its name to modDAO. This module will hold five custom methods:

- ShowType converts integer type numbers into friendly names.
- GetProperties returns a list of all the declared properties for a given DAO object.

- `GetDBFile` displays the Common Dialog control and prompts use for an MDB file.
- `ShowForm` loads the requested Windows form and sizes it appropriately for the MDI
- `DisplayResults` sends text output to a partner window that displays the results of various DAO operations.

First, add the `ShowType` method to your modDAO module. Listing 8.2 has all the code you need to add.

LISTING 8.2 CODING THE ShowType METHOD

```
1: Public Function ShowType(TypeCode As Variant) As String
2:      '
3:      ' return friendly string
4:      '
5:      Dim strReturn As String
6:      '
7:      Select Case TypeCode
8:          Case vbEmpty
9:              strReturn = "Empty"
10:         Case vbNull
11:             strReturn = "Null"
12:         Case vbInteger
13:             strReturn = "Integer"
14:         Case vbLong
15:             strReturn = "Long"
16:         Case vbSingle
17:             strReturn = "Single"
18:         Case vbDouble
19:             strReturn = "Double"
20:         Case vbCurrency
21:             strReturn = "Currency"
22:         Case vbDate
23:             strReturn = "Date"
24:         Case vbString
25:             strReturn = "String"
26:         Case vbObject
27:             strReturn = "Object"
28:         Case vbError
29:             strReturn = "Error"
30:         Case vbVariant
31:             strReturn = "Variant"
32:         Case vbDataObject
33:             strReturn = "DataObject"
34:         Case vbDecimal
35:             strReturn = "Decimal"
```

continues

LISTING 8.2   CONTINUED

```
36:            Case vbByte
37:                strReturn = "Byte"
38:            Case vbArray
39:                strReturn = "Array"
40:            Case Else
41:                strReturn = "[" & CStr(TypeCode) & "]"
42:        End Select
43:        '
44:        ShowType = strReturn
45:        '
46: End Function
```

This routine converts predefined constant values into easy-to-read strings. You use this in the next method, the GetProperties method. Enter the code from Listing 8.3 into the modDAO module.

LISTING 8.3   ADDING THE GetProperties METHOD

```
 1: Public Function GetProperties(objDAOItem As Object) As String
 2:     '
 3:     ' return list of enumerated properties
 4:     '
 5:     On Error GoTo LocalErr
 6:     '
 7:     Dim objItem As Object
 8:     Dim strReturn As String
 9:     '
10:     Screen.ActiveForm.MousePointer = vbHourglass
11:     '
12:     strReturn = ""
13:     For Each objItem In objDAOItem.Properties
14:         strReturn = strReturn & objItem.Name
15:         strReturn = strReturn & " = "
16:         '
17:         If objItem.Name = "BookMark" Then
18:             strReturn = strReturn & "?" ' skip bookmark value
19:         Else
20:             strReturn = strReturn & objItem.Value
21:         End If
22:         '
23:         strReturn = strReturn & " {"
24:         strReturn = strReturn & ShowType(objItem.Type)
25:         strReturn = strReturn & "}" & vbCrLf
26:     Next
27:     '
28:     GetProperties = strReturn
```

```
29:     '
30:     Screen.ActiveForm.MousePointer = vbNormal
31:     '
32:     Exit Function
33:     '
34: LocalErr:
35:     ' in case value gives us trouble
36:     strReturn = strReturn & "<err>"
37:     Resume Next
38:     '
39: End Function
```

The output from the GetProperties method will eventually be posted to a window where the user can review the results.

The next method to add, GetDBFile, uses a CommonDialog control to allow users to select a database for use. Add the code from Listing 8.4 to your module.

LISTING 8.4   ADDING THE GetDBFile METHOD

```
Public Function GetDBFile(Optional DefaultFileName As _
    String = "") As String
    '
    ' return an MDB file
    '
    On Error GoTo LocalErr
    '
    With mdiDAO.cdlMain
        .FileName = DefaultFileName
        .Filter = "*.mdb¦*.mdb"
        .ShowOpen
        GetDBFile = .FileName
    End With
    '
    Exit Function
    '
LocalErr:
    GetDBFile = ""
    '
End Function
```

The next method, DisplayResults, accepts the data string as input and updates a textbox in the frmResults form. You define the form later. For now, add the code from Listing 8.5 to your module.

LISTING 8.5   ADDING THE DisplayResults METHOD

```
 1: Public Sub DisplayResults(Data As String, Optional Title As String)
 2:      '
 3:      ' show results in window
 4:      '
 5:      If IsMissing(Title) Then
 6:          Title = ""
 7:      End If
 8:      '
 9:      With frmResults
10:          .Caption = Title
11:          .txtDisplay.Text = Data
12:          .Show
13:      End With
14:      '
15: End Sub
```

The last support routine is the ShowForm method. This displays the requested form along with the Results form mentioned previously. An added feature is the removal of any other open forms before loading the requested one. Add this last method to your modDAO module (see Listing 8.6).

LISTING 8.6   ADDING THE ShowForm METHOD

```
 1: Public Sub ShowForm(frmMe As Form)
 2:      '
 3:      ' render requested form
 4:      ' along with the results pane
 5:      '
 6:      Dim frm As Form
 7:      '
 8:      ' drop any current forms
 9:      For Each frm In Forms
10:          If frm.Name <> "mdiDAO" Then
11:              Unload frm
12:          End If
13:      Next
14:      '
15:      ' load requested form
16:      With frmMe
17:          .Left = 0
18:          .Top = 0
19:          .Width = mdiDAO.ScaleWidth / 2
20:          .Height = mdiDAO.ScaleHeight
21:      End With
22:      '
```

```
23:     ' load display partner
24:     With frmResults
25:         .Left = mdiDAO.ScaleWidth / 2
26:         .Top = 0
27:         .Width = mdiDAO.ScaleWidth / 2
28:         .Height = mdiDAO.ScaleHeight
29:         .txtDisplay.Text = ""
30:         .Caption = "Results for " & frmMe.Name
31:     End With
32:     '
33: End Sub
```

After adding all the support code in the modDAO module and the code in the mdiDAO form, save the form as mdiDAO.frm, the module as modDAO.bas, and the project as prjDAO.vbp.

Adding the Results Form

Now you need to create a form that will display the output of various DAO operations throughout the project. Add a new standard form to the project (select Project | Add Form from the main menu) and add a text box control to the form. Don't worry about the layout of the text box—you'll handle that at runtime. However, refer to Table 8.2 for details on the various property settings for the form and text box.

TABLE 8.2 SETTINGS FOR THE FRMRESULTS FORM

Control	Property	Setting
VB.Form	Name	frmResults
	Caption	"Results View"
	ClientHeight	3195
	ClientLeft	60
	ClientTop	345
	ClientWidth	4680
	MDIChild	-1 'True
VB.TextBox	Name	txtDisplay
	Height	495
	Left	1740
	MultiLine	-1 'True
	ScrollBars	2 'Vertical
	Top	1380
	Width	1215

You also need to add just a tiny bit of code to the project. This code will resize the text box to fill the entire form—even when users resize the form. Add the code from Listing 8.7 to your frmResults form.

LISTING 8.7 ADDING CODE TO THE FRMRESULTS FORM

```
 1: Option Explicit
 2:
 3: Private Sub Form_Resize()
 4:     '
 5:     With txtDisplay
 6:         .Left = 0
 7:         .Top = 0
 8:         .Width = Me.ScaleWidth
 9:         .Height = Me.ScaleHeight
10:         .SetFocus
11:         .ZOrder
12:     End With
13:     '
14: End Sub
```

Now save the form as frmResults.frm and save the project. You're all set. The rest of the day's work will focus on Jet DAO objects, methods, and properties.

The DBEngine Object Methods and Properties

The DBEngine data object is the default data object for all access to the database operations under Visual Basic. Even if you do not explicitly use the DBEngine object, your program is still accessing all other data objects by way of the DBEngine object, because it is invoked by default when Visual Basic begins any database work.

 Tip

> Even though Visual Basic does not require that you explicitly use the DBEngine data object, you should use the object in all your future Visual Basic projects to ensure maximum compatibility with any future versions of Visual Basic.

The DBEngine Object Collections

The DBEngine object contains three object collections. Each of these collections in turn contains other data access objects. To put it another way, the DBEngine is the top level of the DAO hierarchy, and it contains the following collections:

- Workspaces is a collection of all the defined Workspace objects. The next section of this chapter covers Workspace objects. The Workspace collection is the default collection for the DBEngine object.

- Errors is a collection of the most recent database-related errors encountered in this session. Error objects are covered later in this chapter.

- Properties is a collection of all the properties of the DBEngine object.

Building the dbEngine Form

In this section, you explore four aspects of the dbEngine object:

- The dbEngine properties.
- The Repair method, repairs corrupted MDB files.
- The Compact method optimizes MDB storage.
- The Register Method adds an ODBC entry for the workstation.

Add a new form to the project and use Table 8.3 and Figure 8.4 to lay out the new form.

TABLE 8.3 CONTROLS FOR THE DBENGINE FORM

Control	Property	Setting
VB.Form	Name	frmDBEngine
	Caption	"DBEngine"
	ClientHeight	3195
	ClientLeft	60
	ClientTop	345
	ClientWidth	4680
	MDIChild	-1 'True
VB.CommandButton	Name	cmdRegister
	Caption	"Register"
	Height	495
	Left	1500
	Top	780
	Width	1215
VB.CommandButton	Name	cmdCompact
	Caption	"Compact"

continues

TABLE 8.3 CONTINUED

Control	Property	Setting
	Height	495
	Left	120
	Top	780
	Width	1215
VB.CommandButton	Name	cmdRepair
	Caption	"Repair"
	Height	495
	Left	1500
	Top	180
	Width	1215
VB.CommandButton	Name	cmdProperties
	Caption	"Properties"
	Height	495
	Left	120
	Top	180
	Width	1215

FIGURE 8.4

Laying out the dbEngine form.

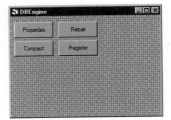

The DBEngine Object Properties

As with all Visual Basic objects, you can list the properties of the object by accessing the Properties collection. Let's write a short bit of code to list (enumerate) all the properties of the DBEngine data access object.

Because you already have a support routine (getProperties) built, you pass this routine the dbEngine object. Add the code from Listing 8.8 to the cdmProperties_Click event.

LISTING 8.8 CALLING THE getProperties METHOD FOR DBENGINE

```
Private Sub cmdProperties_Click()

    DisplayResults GetProperties(DBEngine), "DbEngine Properties"

End Sub
```

Now save the form and run the project. Select DAO Objects | DBEngine from the main menu. Then press the Properties button. This will call the GetProperties method for the dbEngine object. Visual Basic will enumerate the properties of the DBEngine data access object and display the results in the Results form. Your screen should look like Figure 8.5.

FIGURE 8.5

Viewing the dbEngine properties.

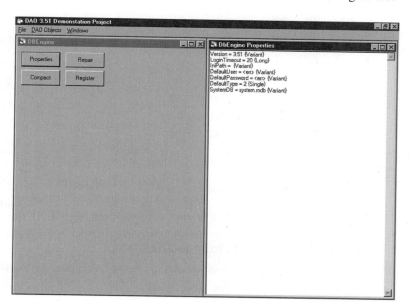

Setting the DBEngine Properties

You can set the properties of the DBEngine object in your program, too. For example, you can use the IniPath property to point to a special ISAM driver needed to process the related database:

```
DBEngine.IniPath = _"HKEY_LOCAL_MACHINE\SOFTWARE\Microsoft\Jet\3.5\ISAM
➥Formats\FoxPro 3.0"
```

Note

> In Microsoft Jet 2.5, the `IniPath` property actually points to an INI file in the `<WINDOWS>` folder on the workstation. In Microsoft Jet 3.x, the `IniPath` property is used to point to a location in the workstation's System Registry.

The `DefaultUser` and `DefaultPassword` properties are covered when you learn about the Workspace data access object.

The DBEngine Object Methods

This section covers six of the Visual Basic methods that are associated with the DBEngine data access object:

- `RepairDatabase` is used to fix corrupted Microsoft Jet database files.
- `CompactDatabase` is used to clean up, and also convert, existing Microsoft Jet databases.
- `RegisterDatabase` is used to create a link between an external data source and an existing Microsoft Jet database.
- `Idle` is used to force Visual Basic to pause processing while the DBEngine updates the contents of any existing data access objects.
- `SetOption` is used to modify one or more of the Microsoft Jet Registry settings at runtime.
- `CreateWorkspace` is used to establish a workspace for accessing one or more databases. You'll learn about this method in the section on Workspace objects later in this chapter.

Using the `RepairDatabase` Method

You can use the `RepairDatabase` method to fix corrupted Microsoft Jet database files. The default syntax to invoke this method is

`DBEngine.RepairDatabase databasename`

To see how this works, place the code from Listing 8.9 in the `cmdRepair_Click` event of the form.

LISTING 8.9   CODING THE Repair METHOD OF DBEngine

```
1: Private Sub cmdRepair_Click()
2:      '
3:      ' repair corrupted MDB
4:      '
5:      On Error GoTo LocalErr
6:      '
7:      Dim strDBName As String
```

```
 8:    '
 9:        strDBName = GetDBFile("repair.mdb")
10:    '
11:        If strDBName <> "" Then
12:            DBEngine.RepairDatabase strDBName
13:            DisplayResults strDBName & " repaired", "DbEngine Repair"
14:        End If
15:    '
16:        Exit Sub
17:    '
18: LocalErr:
19:    '
20: End Sub
```

The code in Listing 8.9 declares a local variable for the database name and then prompts the user to enter the name of a database to repair. After checking to make sure a database name was entered, the code executes the RepairDatabase method and reports the results.

 Save and run the program. When you click the Repair button, locate and select the REPAIR.MDB (shipped on the CD-ROM) database (see Figure 8.6).

FIGURE 8.6

Selecting a database to repair.

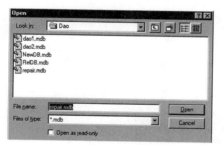

The repair method executes, and the final message box appears.

 Caution

The RepairDatabase method overwrites the existing file with the repaired database file. You should make a backup copy of your database files before you execute the RepairDatabase method.

Using the CompactDatabase Method

The CompactDatabase method cleans out empty space in Microsoft Jet databases and performs general optimization chores that improve access speed. You can also use the CompactDatabase method to convert older versions of Microsoft Jet databases to newer versions.

The syntax for this method is

DBEngine.CompactDatabase *oldDatabase*, *NewDatabase*, *locale*, *options*

In this line, *oldDatabase* is the name (including path) of the database to be compacted; *NewDatabase* is the name (including path) of the new, compacted database; and *locale* is the language in which the data is written. Options can be added to encrypt or decrypt a database, as well as to change versions. Multiple options must be joined with the plus sign (+).

Now add the code from Listing 8.10 to the cmdCompact_Click event of the dbEngine form.

LISTING 8.10 CODING THE Compact METHOD OF DBENGINE

```
 1: Private Sub cmdCompact_Click()
 2:     '
 3:     ' compact or convert MDB
 4:     '
 5:     Dim strOldDBName As String
 6:     Dim strNewDBName As String
 7:     Dim intEncrypt As Integer
 8:     Dim strVersion As String
 9:     Dim intVersion As Integer
10:     '
11:     ' get file to compact/convert
12: CompactStart:
13:     strOldDBName = ""
14:     strNewDBName = ""
15:     '
16:     strOldDBName = GetDBFile()
17:     If strOldDBName = "" Then
18:         Exit Sub
19:     End If
20:     '
21:     strNewDBName = GetDBFile(strOldDBName)
22:     If strNewDBName = "" Then
23:         GoTo CompactStart
24:     End If
25:     '
26:     ' select target version
27: SetVersion:
28:     intVersion = 0
29:     strVersion = ""
30:     '
31:     strVersion = InputBox("Select target version" & vbCrLf & _
32:     "1.1, 2.x, 3.x", "Select Version", "3.x")
33:     '
34:     Select Case LCase(strVersion)
35:         Case "1.x": intVersion = dbVersion11
36:         Case "2.x": intVersion = dbVersion20
```

```
37:          Case "3.x": intVersion = dbVersion30
38:         Case Else
39:             MsgBox "Invalid Version!", vbCritical, "Version Error"
40:             GoTo SetVersion
41:      End Select
42:      '
43:      ' select encryption mode
44: SetEncryption:
45:      intEncrypt = MsgBox("Encrypt Target?", vbInformation + vbYesNo, _
           "CompactDB")
46:      If intEncrypt = vbYes Then
47:          intEncrypt = dbEncrypt
48:      Else
49:          intEncrypt = dbDecrypt
50:      End If
51:      '
52:      'Do the Work!
53: RunCompact:
54:      DBEngine.CompactDatabase strOldDBName, strNewDBName, _
           dbLangGeneral, intVersion + intEncrypt
55:      DisplayResults "Compact completed!", "DbEngine Compact"
56:      '
57: End Sub
```

The code in Listing 8.10 declares its local variables and then prompts the user to enter the database file to compact or convert (line 16). If no filename is entered, the routine skips to the exit. If a filename is entered, the user is prompted to enter a target filename (line 21). If no name is entered, the program returns to try the whole thing again. After getting the filename, the user is prompted to supply the target Microsoft Jet version number (line 31). The value entered is checked and the user is returned to the input box if an invalid option was entered. Finally, the user is asked whether the database should be encrypted (line 45). After that, the CompactDatabase method is invoked (line 54).

Save your work and execute this program. When you press on the Compact button, you are prompted to enter the name of the database to compact. Enter the path and name for REPAIR.MDB. You then must enter a database to which to compact. Enter enc_repair.mdb as the filename. Next, enter the version (3.x). Answer Yes when you are prompted with the encryption question. The new database is now compacted, encrypted, and saved.

Caution

If you plan to run your database application using any 16-bit data tool, you need to store the database in the Microsoft Jet 2.5 version. Only Microsoft Jet 2.5 can run on both 32- and 16-bit platforms.

Using the `RegisterDatabase` Method

The `RegisterDatabase` method enables you to register an ODBC data source for Microsoft Jet access. The Visual Basic documentation encourages programmers to rely on the Windows Control Panel ODBC Setup utility rather than using the `RegisterDatabase` method. If, however, you want to perform the ODBC registration process within your Visual Basic program, you can use the `RegisterDatabase` method to do so.

The easiest way to provide ODBC registration capabilities in your program is to supply a limited number of parameters and force Windows to present the ODBC registration dialog for you—a fairly easy task. For this example, add the code in Listing 8.11 to the `cmdRegister_Click` event on your form.

LISTING 8.11   CODING THE `Register` METHOD OF DBENGINE

```
 1: Private Sub cmdRegister_Click()
 2:      '
 3:      ' register with ODBC
 4:      '
 5:      On Error Resume Next
 6:      '
 7:      Dim strDSN As String
 8:      Dim strDriver As String
 9:      Dim blnQuiet As Boolean
10:      Dim strAttributes As String
11:      Dim strDelimiter As String
12:      '
13:      strDelimiter = Chr(0)
14:      strDSN = "TDPTest"
15:      strDriver = "SQL Server"
16:      blnQuiet = False
17:      strAttributes = "SERVER=mca" & strDelimiter
18:      strAttributes = strAttributes & "DATABASE=pubs" & strDelimiter
19:      strAttributes = strAttributes & "DESCRIPTION=Sample Registration" _
         & strDelimiter
20:      '
21:      DBEngine.RegisterDatabase strDSN, strDriver, blnQuiet, strAttributes
22:      '
23: End Sub
```

The code in Listing 8.11 first tells Visual Basic to ignore any reported errors, and then it supplies a set of parameters for creating an ODBC data source. The parameters for the `RegisterDatabase` method are

- `SourceName`: The name that will be used as the database name for the `OpenDatabase` method.

- `DriverName`: The name of an ODBC driver installed and available on your workstation.

- `SilentFlag`: Setting this to `False` forces Windows to present the ODBC registration dialog box. If it is set to `True`, Windows attempts to register the ODBC data source without prompting the user with the ODBC registration dialog box.

- `AttributeList`: A list of attribute settings for the ODBC source. Examples of attributes include any server device name, database name, and any other parameters required by the back-end database server.

> **Caution**
>
> The Microsoft Visual Basic documentation tells you to create an Attributes list with each attribute separated by a CR-LF pair. This is not correct. You should delimit each attribute entry with a `CHR(0)` in order for the `RegisterDatabase` routine to work properly.

Save and run the project. When you click the Register button, you see the Windows ODBC Registration dialog box appear with some of the parameters already entered. You can complete the information and click OK to register the ODBC data source on your system (see Figure 8.7).

FIGURE 8.7

Invoking the ODBC registration dialog.

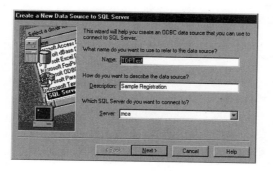

Completing an ODBC registration creates a DSN registration for the workstation. Depending on the DSN type and windows platform, this process inserts data into one of three places on the workstation. If the User or System DSN type is selected, the data is stored in the `HKEY_USERS\DEFAULT\ODBC\ODBC.INI` section of the Windows Registry. If the File DSN type is selected, the `ODBC.INI` data is stored in a file under the Program Files\Common Files\ODBC\Data Sources folder. Finally, all DSN data for 16-bit Windows systems is stored in the `ODBC.INI` file in the `<WINDOWS>` folder.

You can add features to the earlier `cmdDBRegister_Click` example by prompting the user to enter the `SourceName` and `DriverName`. You could also fill out all values within the program and set the SilentFlag to True. In this way, you could use the routine to install new ODBC connections for Visual Basic applications without requiring the user to know anything at all about ODBC or Microsoft Jet.

 Caution | Failure to register an ODBC data source properly can result in unexpected errors and possible loss of data. Be sure to test your RegisterDatabase routines completely before using them on live data.

The SetOption Method

The SetOption method of the DBEngine object enables you to override performance values in the Registry at runtime. You can use this option to perform runtime tuning of the Microsoft Jet engine. Table 8.4 shows the values you can adjust using the SetOption method.

TABLE 8.4 TUNING VALUES FOR THE SetOption METHOD OF THE DBEngine

Constant	Description
dbPageTimeout	PageTimeout key
dbSharedAsyncDelay	SharedAsyncDelay key
dbExclusiveAsyncDelay	ExclusiveAsyncDelay key
dbLockRetry	LockRetry key
dbUserCommitSync	UserCommitSync key
dbImplicitCommitSync	ImplicitCommitSync key
dbMaxBufferSize	MaxBufferSize key
dbMaxLocksPerFile	MaxLocksPerFile key
dbLockDelay	LockDelay key
dbRecycleLVs	RecycleLVs key
dbFlushTransactionTimeout	FlushTransactionTimeout key

For example, to adjust the value of the LockRetry setting, you can use the following code:

```
DBEngine.SetOption dbLockRetry = dbLockRetry * 1.5
```

Any changes made to the settings are in effect only as long as your program is running. They are not saved to the Windows Registry or INI files.

8

The `Idle` Method

The `Idle` method forces Visual Basic to pause while the DBEngine catches up on any changes that have been made to all the open data access objects. This method becomes useful when you have a lot of database traffic or a lot of data access objects in a single program. The syntax is simple:

```
DBEngine.Idle
```

The Workspace Data Object

The Workspace data object identifies a database session for a user. Workspaces are created each time you open a database using Microsoft Jet. You can explicitly create Workspace objects to manage database transactions for users and to provide a level of security during a database session. Even if you do not explicitly create a Workspace object, Visual Basic 6.0 creates a default Workspace each time you begin database operations.

Note Although you can create Workspace data objects, you can't save them. Workspace objects are temporary. They cease to exist as soon as your program stops running or as soon as you close your last data access object.

The Workspace object contains three collections, two properties, and eight methods. The `Workspaces` collection contains one property (`Count`) and one method (`Refresh`). The `Workspaces` collection enables you to access multiple Workspace objects. The Workspace object enables you to access the properties, collections, and methods of the named Workspace object.

The Workspace Object Collections

The Workspace data access object contains three object collections:

- `Databases` is a collection of all the Database objects opened for this Workspace object. This is the default collection.

- `Groups` is a collection of all the defined Group objects that have access to this Workspace.

- `Users` is a collection of all the defined User objects that have access to this Workspace.

Note You can access the Group and User objects only if the Microsoft Jet security is activated. You can activate Microsoft Jet security only through Microsoft Access. Although Visual Basic cannot initiate database security, you can manage the security features using Visual Basic 6.0. Security features are covered on Day 21, "Securing Your Database Applications."

Building the Workspaces Form

You code for examples of DAO Workspace operations in this section. To handle this, you need to add a new form to the project (frmWorkSpace) and add four buttons to the form.

Refer to Table 8.5 and Figure 8.8 for details on laying out the frmWorkspace form.

TABLE 8.5   CONTROLS FOR THE frmWORKSPACE FORM

Control	Property	Setting
VB.Form	Name	frmWorkspace
	Caption	"Workspace"
	ClientHeight	3195
	ClientLeft	60
	ClientTop	345
	ClientWidth	4680
	MDIChild	-1 'True
VB.CommandButton	Name	cmdOpenDB
	Caption	"OpenDB"
	Height	495
	Left	1620
	Top	840
	Width	1215
VB.CommandButton	Name	cmdCreateDB
	Caption	"CreateDB"
	Height	495
	Left	180
	Top	840
	Width	1215

Control	Property	Setting
VB.CommandButton	Name	cmdCreateWS
	Caption	"CreateWS"
	Height	495
	Left	1620
	Top	240
	Width	1215
VB.CommandButton	Name	cmdProperties
	Caption	"Properties"
	Height	495
	Left	180
	Top	240
	Width	1215

FIGURE 8.8

Laying out the frmWorkspace form.

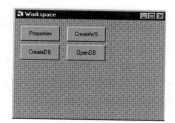

The Workspace Object Properties

Six Workspace object properties exist:

- Name
- User name
- Isolate ODBC Trans
- Login Timeout
- Default Cursor Driver
- Type

Note

ODBC connections are covered in depth in Week 3 of this book. For now, just remember that you can control the number of connections used by the session by altering the Isolate ODBC Trans property of the Workspace object.

When you begin a database operation, Visual Basic 6.0 creates a default workspace with the name #Default Workspace # and the user name admin. To see how this works, add the code from Listing 8.12 to the cmdProperties_click event of the frmWorkspace form.

LISTING 8.12   CALLING GetProperties FOR THE WORKSPACE

```
 1: Private Sub cmdProperties_Click()
 2:     '
 3:     Dim objWS As Workspace
 4:     Dim strMsg As String
 5:     '
 6:     For Each objWS In DBEngine.Workspaces
 7:         strMsg = strMsg & GetProperties(objWS)
 8:         strMsg = strMsg & vbCrLf
 9:     Next
10:     '
11:     DisplayResults strMsg, "WS Properties"
12:     '
13: End Sub
```

Notice that the code in Listing 8.12 contains a For Each...Next loop. This actually uses the Workspaces collection object to create a property report for all workspace objects currently available. You'll use this routine again to show multiple workspaces.

Save and run the program. When you click on the Property button of the Workspaces form, the program lists all the properties of the object. Your screen should look like Figure 8.9.

FIGURE 8.9

Viewing Workspace properties.

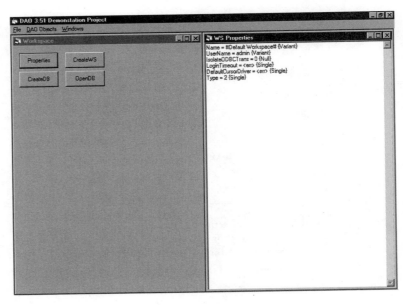

Creating a New Workspace Object

You can create new Workspace objects using the CreateWorkspace method of the DBEngine. Even though Visual Basic 6 creates and uses a default Workspace object when you first begin database operations, you should create an explicit, named Workspace from within Visual Basic. When you create a unique Workspace object, you isolate all your database operations into a single session. You can then group a set of database transactions into a single session to improve database integrity and security.

Add the code from Listing 8.13 to the cmdCreateWS_click event on your form.

LISTING 8.13   CREATING A NEW WORKSPACE OBJECT

```
 1: Private Sub cmdCreateWS_Click()
 2:     '
 3:     Dim ws As Workspace
 4:     Dim strWSName As String
 5:     Dim strWSUser As String
 6:     Dim strWSPassword As String
 7:     '
 8:     strWSName = "ws" & App.EXEName
 9:     strWSUser = "admin"
10:     strWSPassword = ""
11:     '
12:     Set ws = DBEngine.CreateWorkspace(strWSName, strWSUser, _
          strWSPassword)
13:     DBEngine.Workspaces.Append ws
14:     '
15:     cmdProperties_Click
16:     '
17: End Sub
```

The code in Listing 8.13 establishes local variables and then initializes them to the correct values. Notice that you can use any unique name you like for the Workspace object, but you must use valid User and Password parameters. These values must already exist in the system security file or as the default values if Microsoft Access security is not active. Because you do not use Microsoft Access security here, this example used the default admin user name and empty password.

After creating the new Workspace object (line 12) you add the new object to the Workspaces collection by using the Append method (line 13). After adding the new object, you can force Visual Basic to display the Workspaces collection to see your results (line 15).

Caution

It is not a good idea to append your workspace definitions to the Workspaces collection in a production environment. In rare cases, someone could "listen in" on a network connection that uses workspaces and hack one or more of the valid names, users, and passwords for secured tables. This can be done by locating and "walking through" the Workspaces collection. To prevent troubles, it is a good idea to never append workspaces to the Workspaces collection.

Save and run the project. After you click the CreateWS button, you see two workspaces displayed on the form. Check your screen against the one in Figure 8.10.

FIGURE 8.10

Viewing multiple workspaces.

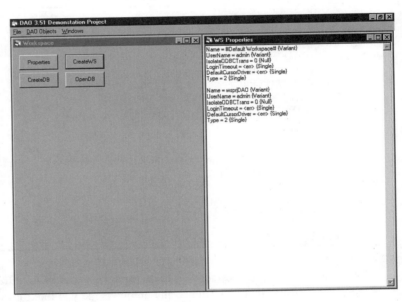

Using the Workspace Object Methods

The Workspace object methods fall into several related groups. Table 8.6 shows the Workspace methods in their respective groups.

TABLE 8.6 WORKSPACE METHODS

Group	Method
Transactions	`BeginTrans, CommitTrans, Rollback`
Security	`CreateUser, CreateGroup`

Group	Method
Microsoft Jet	`CreateDatabase`, `OpenDatabase`, `Close`
ODBCDirect	`OpenConnection`, `Close`

You learn more about the Transaction group on Day 16, "Multiuser Considerations," and the Security group is covered on Day 21. The ODBCDirect methods are covered in another section in this chapter. That leaves the Microsoft Jet database methods: `CreateDatabase`, `OpenDatabase`, and `Close`.

Using the Microsoft Jet Database Methods

The two database-related Workspace methods are `CreateDatabase` and `OpenDatabase`. You use the `CreateDatabase` method to create a new database, and you use the `OpenDatabase` method to open an existing database.

Listing 8.14 has the code to add behind the `cmdCreateDB_click` event. This will create two MDB databases. Add this code to your form.

LISTING 8.14 CREATING MDB DATABASE

```
 1: Private Sub cmdCreateDB_Click()
 2:     '
 3:     On Error Resume Next
 4:     '
 5:     Dim dbOne As Database
 6:     Dim dbTwo As Database
 7:     Dim ws As Workspace
 8:     Dim dbTemp As Database
 9:     '
10:     Dim strDBNameOne As String
11:     Dim strDBNameTwo As String
12:     Dim strWSName As String
13:     Dim strWSUser As String
14:     Dim strWSPassword As String
15:     Dim strMsg As String
16:     '
17:     strDBNameOne = App.Path & "\dao1.mdb"
18:     strDBNameTwo = App.Path & "\dao2.mdb"
19:     strWSName = App.EXEName
20:     strWSUser = "admin"
21:     strWSPassword = ""
22:     '
23:     Kill strDBNameOne
24:     Kill strDBNameTwo
25:     '
```

continues

LISTING 8.14 CONTINUED

```
26:     Set ws = DBEngine.CreateWorkspace(strWSName, strWSUser, _
          strWSPassword)
27:     '
28:     With ws
29:         Set dbOne = .CreateDatabase(strDBNameOne, dbLangGeneral, _
              dbVersion30)
30:         Set dbTwo = .CreateDatabase(strDBNameTwo, dbLangGeneral, _
              dbVersion30)
31:         '
32:         For Each dbTemp In .Databases
33:             strMsg = strMsg & "Name: " & dbTemp.Name & vbCrLf
34:         Next
35:         DisplayResults strMsg, "WS CreateDatabase"
36:         '
37:         dbOne.Close
38:         dbTwo.Close
39:         .Close
40:     End With
41:     '
42:     Set dbOne = Nothing
43:     Set dbTwo = Nothing
44:     Set ws = Nothing
45:     '
46: End Sub
```

The code in Listing 8.14 declares some variables, initializes them, and then goes on to create a workspace for this session (line 26). It then creates the new Database objects (lines 29 and 30) and, finally, shows you all the databases that are a part of the current workspace (line 35). Database objects are covered in greater detail in the next section of today's lesson. It is important to note here that you create a Workspace object before you create the database to make sure that the Database object becomes a part of the Workspace object. Now all activity on that database is a part of the Workspace. As you can see from the code, you can open more than one database in the same workspace and group the database operations together.

It is also important to note the cleanup code added at the end of the routine. When you finish using DAO objects, you need to close them and release the memory they occupied by setting the program variables to Nothing. If you do not do this, you risk running out of memory in DAO-intensive applications.

You can also open the same database in two different workspaces. This is handy when you want to provide read/write access in one operation, but want to provide read-only access in another operation. Listing 8.15 shows how this can be done.

LISTING 8.15   OPENING THE SAME DATABASE IN TWO WORKSPACES

```
 1: Private Sub cmdOpenDB_Click()
 2:      '
 3:      On Error Resume Next
 4:      '
 5:      Dim wsRW As Workspace
 6:      Dim wsRO As Workspace
 7:      Dim wsTemp As Workspace
 8:      Dim dbRW As Database
 9:      Dim dbRO As Database
10:      Dim dbTemp As Database
11:      '
12:      Dim strWSrwName As String
13:      Dim strWSroName As String
14:      Dim strDBName As String
15:      Dim strWSUser As String
16:      Dim strWSPassword As String
17:      Dim strMsg As String
18:      '
19:      strWSrwName = "wsrw"
20:      strWSroName = "wsro"
21:      strWSUser = "admin"
22:      strWSPassword = ""
23:      strDBName = App.Path & "\..\..\books6.mdb"
24:      '
25:      With DBEngine
26:          Set wsRW = .CreateWorkspace(strWSrwName, strWSUser, _
                 strWSPassword)
27:          Set wsRO = .CreateWorkspace(strWSroName, strWSUser, _
                 strWSPassword)
28:          '
29:          .Workspaces.Append wsRW
30:          .Workspaces.Append wsRO
31:      End With
32:      '
33:      Set dbRW = wsRW.OpenDatabase(strDBName)
34:      Set dbRO = wsRO.OpenDatabase(strDBName, ReadOnly:=True)
35:
36:      cmdProperties_Click
37:      '
38:      dbRW.Close
39:      dbRO.Close
40:      wsRW.Close
41:      wsRO.Close
42:      '
43:      Set dbRW = Nothing
44:      Set dbRO = Nothing
```

8

continues

LISTING 8.15 CONTINUED

```
45:     Set wsRW = Nothing
46:     Set wsRO = Nothing
47:     '
48: End Sub
```

The code in Listing 8.15 declares and initializes several variables for the two Workspace and Database object pairs (lines 19–23). Then each workspace is created and appended to the collection (lines 25–31), and the single database is opened once under each workspace session (lines 33 and 34). Finally, all the workspaces and all their databases are listed on the screen (line 36). Note that you do not have to use different user names and passwords for the two Workspace objects.

Save and run the project. When you click the OpenDB button, the program opens the database under two different workspaces and shows the results. Notice that the #Default Workspace# appears in the list. It always exists in the Workspaces collection.

Creating and Opening Non-Microsoft Jet Databases

You can create Microsoft Jet-format databases only by using the CreateDatabase method. The other ISAM-type databases (dBASE, FoxPro, Paradox, and Btreive) all use a single directory or folder as the database object. To create non-Microsoft Jet databases, you have to create a new directory or folder on the disk drive. You can then use the OpenDatabase method to open the non-Microsoft Jet database. When it is opened, you can add tables and indexes using the existing Visual Basic data objects and methods. You'll learn about opening non-Microsoft Jet databases in the next section.

The Database Data Object

The Database data object has 5 collections, 8 properties, and 16 methods. The Database object contains all the tables, queries, and relations defined for the database. It is also part of the Databases collection of the Workspace object. The Database object is created whenever you open a database with the OpenDatabase method. Database objects continue to exist in memory until you use the Close method to remove them.

Note

Do not confuse the Database object with the database file. The Database object is a Visual Basic program construct used to access the physical database file. Throughout this section, you will hear about the Database object.

The Collections of the Database Object

The Database object has five collections:

- `TableDefs` is the collection of Table objects that contain the detailed definition of each data table in the database. This is the default collection.
- `QueryDefs` is the collection of SQL queries stored in the database.
- `Relations` is the collection of database integrity relationship definitions stored in the database.
- `Recordsets` is the collection of active Recordsets opened from this database. Recordsets include any Tables, Dynasets, or Snapshots currently open. Recordsets are temporary objects and are not stored with the database file.
- `Containers` is the collection of all TableDefs, QueryDefs, and Relations stored in the physical database file. You can use the `Containers` collection to enumerate all the persistent (stored) objects in the database.

The data access objects are described in later sections of this chapter. This section focuses on the properties and methods associated with the Database data access object.

Building the Database Form

In this section, you explore eight examples of the Database object. You need to add a new form to the project and add eight command buttons to the form. Use Table 8.7 and Figure 8.11 to lay out the form.

TABLE 8.7 CONTROLS FOR THE DATABASE FORM

Control	Property	Setting
VB.Form	Name	frmDatabase
	Caption	"Database"
	ClientHeight	3930
	ClientLeft	60
	ClientTop	345
	ClientWidth	4725
	MDIChild	-1 'True
VB.CommandButton	Name	cmdAttachTable
	Caption	"Attach Table"
	Height	495
	Left	1500

continues

TABLE 8.7   CONTINUED

Control	Property	Setting
	Top	2100
	Width	1215
VB.CommandButton	Name	cmdModifyTable
	Caption	"Modify Table"
	Height	495
	Left	120
	Top	2100
	Width	1215
VB.CommandButton	Name	cmdCreateTable
	Caption	"CreateTable"
	Height	495
	Left	1500
	Top	1440
	Width	1215
VB.CommandButton	Name	cmdTableDef
	Caption	"TableDef"
	Height	495
	Left	120
	Top	1440
	Width	1215
VB.CommandButton	Name	cmdCreateProperty
	Caption	"CreateProperty"
	Height	495
	Left	1500
	Top	780
	Width	1215
VB.CommandButton	Name	cmdExecute
	Caption	"Execute"
	Height	495
	Left	120
	Top	780
	Width	1215

Control	Property	Setting
VB.CommandButton	Name	cmdOpenRS
	Caption	"OpenRS"
	Height	495
	Left	1500
	Top	120
	Width	1215
VB.CommandButton	Name	cmdProperties
	Caption	"Properties"
	Height	495
	Left	120
	Top	120
	Width	1215

FIGURE 8.11

Laying out the Database form.

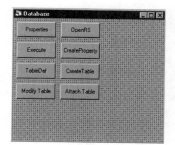

The Properties of the Database Object

The Database object has eight properties. To view these properties, add the code from Listing 8.16 to the cmdProperties_click event of the Database form.

LISTING 8.16   CALLING GetProperties FOR A DATABASE

```
1: Private Sub cmdProperties_Click()
2:     '
3:     Dim ws As Workspace
4:     Dim db As Database
5:     Dim strDBName As String
6:     '
7:     strDBName = App.Path & "\dao1.mdb"
```

continues

LISTING 8.16   CONTINUED

```
 8:        Set ws = DBEngine.Workspaces(0) ' use default
 9:        Set db = ws.OpenDatabase(strDBName)
10:        '
11:        DisplayResults GetProperties(db), "DB Properties"
12:        '
13: End Sub
```

After completing the code in Listing 8.16, save and run the project. When you select the Properties button on the Database form, you should see something similar to Figure 8.12.

FIGURE 8.12

Viewing the Database properties.

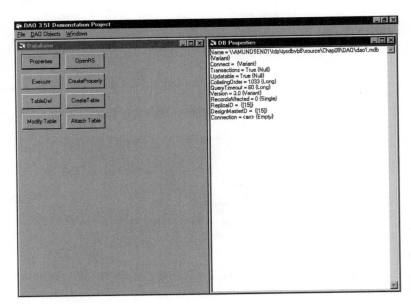

Table 8.8 lists the Database object properties and their meanings.

TABLE 8.8   DATABASE OBJECT PROPERTIES

Property	Type/Value	Meaning/Use
Name	String	The name of the physical database file or the name of the ODBC data source.
Connect	String	If the data source is not a Microsoft Jet database, this property contains additional information needed to connect to the data using Microsoft Jet.

8

Property	Type/Value	Meaning/Use
Transactions	True/False	If set to True, this data source supports the use of the BeginTrans, CommitTrans, and Rollback methods.
Updatable	True/False	If set to True, Visual Basic can provide updates to this data source. If set to False, this is a read-only data source.
Collating Order	Numeric	This value controls the order in which Microsoft Jet sorts or indexes the records. It is set by the locale parameter of the CreateDatabase method.
Query Time Out	Numeric (seconds)	This is the amount of time Microsoft Jet waits before reporting an error while waiting for the results of a query.
Version	String	Indicates the Microsoft Jet version used to create the database.
Records Affected	Numeric	Shows the number of records affected by the last database operation on this file.
ReplicaID	Numeric	This is the unique ID number of this copy of the replicated database. This is set when you initiate replication services (see Day 20, "Database Replication").
ReplicaMaster	Numeric	This is the unique ID value that identifies the Replica Master for this database (see Day 20).
Connection	Object	This is a reference to the ODBCDirect object that can be used to access this database. See the section later in this chapter on ODBCDirect data access objects.

The Methods of the Database Object

The Database object has 11 methods, but you don't explore all of them here. Table 8.9 shows the Database object methods grouped in a logical fashion.

TABLE 8.9 DATABASE OBJECT METHODS

Group	Methods
Replication	MakeReplica, PopulatePartial, Synchronize
Security	NewPassword
Child objects	CreateQueryDef, CreateTableDef, CreateRelation
Database objects	OpenRecordset, Execute, CreateProperty, Close

You'll learn about the Security methods on Day 21. The Child Object methods are covered later in this chapter. That leaves the OpenRecordset, Execute, CreateProperty, and Close methods for review here.

The OpenRecordset Method of the Database Object

You use the OpenRecordset method to access data in existing tables in the database. You can use OpenRecordset to create Dynaset, Snapshot, or Table data objects.

The format of the OpenRecordset method is as follows:

```
Set Variable = Database.OpenRecordset(Source, Type, options)
```

In this syntax, Database is the name of the database that will be used to create the Recordset. Type indicates whether the Recordset created is a Table (dbOpenTable), Dynaset (dbOpenDynaset), Snapshot (dbOpenSnapshot), or Forward-Only Cursor (dbOpenForwardOnly). A Table type is created if you don't specify a type. You can also add options for security and record viewing. See Visual Basic online help for a complete description of these options.

To see an example in action, add the code from Listing 8.17 to the cmdOpenRS_click event.

LISTING 8.17 CODING THE cmdOpenRS_Click EVENT

```
1: Private Sub cmdOpenRS_Click()
2:     '
3:     Dim ws As Workspace
4:     Dim db As Database
5:     Dim rsTable As Recordset
6:     Dim rsDynaset As Recordset
```

```
 7:        Dim rsSnapshot As Recordset
 8:        Dim rsForwardOnly As Recordset
 9:        Dim rsTemp As Recordset
10:        '
11:        Dim strDBName As String
12:        Dim strRSTable As String
13:        Dim strRSDynaset As String
14:        Dim strRSSnapshot As String
15:        Dim strRSForwardOnly As String
16:        Dim strMsg As String
17:        '
18:        strDBName = App.Path & "\..\..\data\books6.mdb"
19:        strRSTable = "Buyers"
20:        strRSDynaset = "Publishers"
21:        strRSSnapshot = "Authors"
22:        strRSForwardOnly = "BookSales"
23:        '
24:        Set ws = DBEngine.Workspaces(0) ' use default
25:        Set db = ws.OpenDatabase(strDBName)
26:        '
27:        With db
28:            Set rsTable = .OpenRecordset(strRSTable, dbOpenTable)
29:            Set rsDynaset = .OpenRecordset(strRSDynaset, dbOpenDynaset)
30:            Set rsSnapshot = .OpenRecordset(strRSSnapshot, dbOpenSnapshot)
31:            Set rsForwardOnly = .OpenRecordset(strRSForwardOnly, _
                   dbOpenForwardOnly)
32:        End With
33:        '
34:        For Each rsTemp In db.Recordsets
35:            strMsg = strMsg & GetProperties(rsTemp) & vbCrLf
36:        Next
37:        DisplayResults strMsg, "DB OpenRecordset"
38:        '
39:        For Each rsTemp In db.Recordsets
40:            rsTemp.Close
41:            Set rsTemp = Nothing
42:        Next
43:        '
44:        db.Close
45:        Set db = Nothing
46:        '
47: End Sub
```

The code in Listing 8.17 creates four Recordsets, one of each type, and then displays the properties of each of the open Recordsets. Save and run the project. Compare your results with those in Figure 8.13.

FIGURE 8.13

Viewing the open Recordsets.

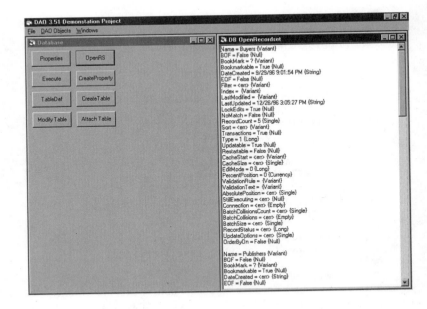

 Note

The Recordset created with this method is a very extensive object itself. You'll learn more about the Recordset object's properties and methods later in this chapter.

Using the Execute Method

You can use the Execute method on a database to perform SQL action queries. The Execute method updates the RecordsAffected property of the Database object with the total number of records found or updated by the SQL statement.

Note

An action query is an SQL statement that performs an action on a database (add, edit, or delete records; create or remove data tables; and so on). Action SQL queries are covered in detail on Day 12, "Creating Databases with SQL."

Add the code in Listing 8.18 to the cmdExecute_Click event.

LISTING 8.18 CODING THE Execute METHOD

```
 1: Private Sub cmdExecute_Click()
 2:     '
 3:     Dim ws As Workspace
 4:     Dim db As Database
 5:     '
 6:     Dim strDBName As String
 7:     Dim strSQL As String
 8:     Dim lngRecords As Long
 9:     '
10:     strDBName = App.Path & "\..\..\data\books6.mdb"
11:     strSQL = "DELETE * FROM NewAuthors WHERE AUID<10"
12:     lngRecords = 0
13:     '
14:     Set ws = DBEngine.Workspaces(0)
15:     Set db = ws.OpenDatabase(strDBName)
16:     '
17:     With db
18:         .Execute strSQL, dbFailOnError
19:         lngRecords = .RecordsAffected
20:     End With
21:     '
22:     DisplayResults "Records Affected = " & CStr(lngRecords), _
        "DB Execute"
23:     '
24:     db.Close
25:     ws.Close
26:     Set db = Nothing
27:     Set ws = Nothing
28:     '
29: End Sub
```

The code in Listing 8.18 opens a database and performs an SQL action query that deletes records from a table. The routine displays the Records Affected property to show you how many records were deleted, and then it closes the database.

You can modify the action query to add, delete, or modify existing records in the database. You can even use SQL statements that create new tables or indexes.

Using the CreateProperty Method

Microsoft Jet DAO enables you to create user-defined properties (UDPs) for most data access objects. These UDPs get stored with the database and can be read and updated by your Visual Basic program. In this example, you use the CreateProperty method to add a UDP to a database.

8

Caution

> The capability of creating and storing UDPs is available only when you use the Microsoft Jet version 3.*x*-or-later database format. If you are not using Microsoft Jet 3.*x*-or-later, you can't complete the example in this exercise.

To see how this works, add the code in Listing 8.19 to the `cmdCreateProperty_Click` window.

LISTING 8.19   CREATING USER-DEFINED PROPERTIES

```
 1: Private Sub cmdCreateProperty_Click()
 2:     '
 3:     ' add user-defined properties
 4:     '
 5:     On Error Resume Next
 6:     '
 7:     Dim ws As Workspace
 8:     Dim db As Database
 9:     Dim pr As Property
10:     '
11:     Dim strDBName As String
12:     Dim strUDPName As String
13:     Dim intUDPType As Integer
14:     Dim varUDPValue As Variant
15:     Dim strMsg As String
16:     '
17:     ' init vars
18:     strDBName = App.Path & "\dao1.mdb"
19:     '
20:     ' open ws and db
21:     Set ws = DBEngine.Workspaces(0)
22:     Set db = ws.OpenDatabase(strDBName)
23:     '
24:     ' add first UDP
25:     strUDPName = "DBAdmin"
26:     intUDPType = vbVariant
27:     varUDPValue = "D.B. Guru"
28:     '
29:     ' using params with create
30:     With db
31:         .Properties.Delete strUDPName
32:         Set pr = .CreateProperty(strUDPName, intUDPType, varUDPValue)
33:         .Properties.Append pr
34:     End With
35:     '
36:     ' add second UDP
37:     strUDPName = "Programmer"
```

```
38:        intUDPType = vbVariant
39:        varUDPValue = "V.B. Coder"
40:        '
41:        ' using properties of the object
42:        With db
43:            .Properties.Delete strUDPName
44:            Set pr = .CreateProperty(strUDPName)
45:            pr.Type = intUDPType
46:            pr.Value = varUDPValue
47:            .Properties.Append pr
48:        End With
49:        '
50:        ' now show results
51:        DisplayResults GetProperties(db), "DB CreateProperty"
52:        '
53:        ' cleanup
54:        db.Close
55:        ws.Close
56:        Set db = Nothing
57:        Set ws = Nothing
58:        Set pr = Nothing
59:        '
60: End Sub
```

The routine in Listing 8.19 adds two user-defined properties to the database. Notice that you attempt to delete the properties first (line 31). That way you can run this example several times without getting an error. Notice that you also used two different code structures to create the properties. Lines 30–34 show how you can add a user-defined property in a single line. Lines 42–48 show you how you can use multiple lines to add the user-defined property. Either one is correct.

Save and run the project. When you click the CreateProperty button, you should see a screen similar to Figure 8.14.

The TableDef Data Object

The TableDef data object contains all the information needed to define a Base table object in the Database. You can access Base table objects using the `OpenRecordset` method. You use TableDef objects to create and maintain Base tables. TableDef objects have 3 collections, 5 methods, and 10 properties.

FIGURE 8.14

*Creating user-defined
properties.*

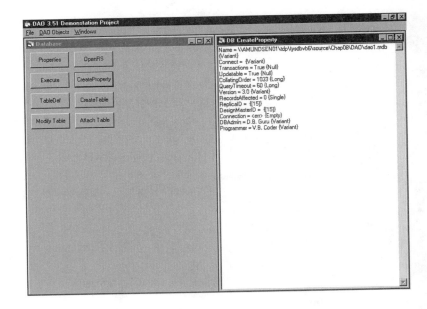

The TableDef Collections

The TableDef object has three collections:

- Fields is the collection that contains all the information about the database fields defined for the TableDef object. This is the default object.

- Indexes is the collection that contains all the information about the database indexes defined for the TableDef object.

- Properties is the collection that contains all the information about the current TableDef object.

Details of the Field and Index objects are covered later in this chapter.

The CreateTableDef Method and the TableDef Properties

The TableDef properties are set when the table is created. The values of the properties differ, depending on whether the TableDef object is a native Microsoft Jet object or an attached object. Listing 8.20 shows the properties of a native Microsoft Jet TableDef object. Add the code in Listing 8.20 to the cmdTableDef_Click event.

LISTING 8.20   CODING THE cmdTableDef_Click EVENT

```
 1: Private Sub cmdTableDef_Click()
 2:      '
 3:      ' show tabledef properties
 4:      '
 5:      On Error Resume Next
 6:      '
 7:      Dim ws As Workspace
 8:      Dim db As Database
 9:      Dim td As TableDef
10:      Dim pr As Property
11:      '
12:      Dim strDBName As String
13:      Dim strTDName As String
14:      Dim strMsg As String
15:      '
16:      ' init vars
17:      strDBName = App.Path & "\..\..\data\books6.mdb"
18:      strTDName = "NewTable"
19:      '
20:      ' open ws and db
21:      Set ws = DBEngine.Workspaces(0)
22:      Set db = ws.OpenDatabase(strDBName)
23:      '
24:      ' now enumerate the empty table defs
25:      strMsg = ""
26:      For Each td In db.TableDefs
27:          strMsg = strMsg & GetProperties(td)
28:          strMsg = strMsg & vbCrLf
29:      Next
30:      '
31:      DisplayResults strMsg, "DB TableDefs"
32:      '
33:      db.Close
34:      ws.Close
35:      Set pr = Nothing
36:      Set td = Nothing
37:      Set db = Nothing
38:      Set ws = Nothing
39:      '
40: End Sub
```

The code in Listing 8.20 opens a database and then "walks through" all the table definitions in the database, listing the properties of each table. Save and run the project. Click
the TableDef button and compare your screen with the one in Figure 8.15.

FIGURE **8.15**

Viewing the TableDef properties.

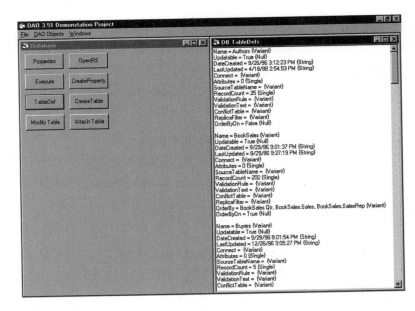

Caution

You also see several internal data tables in this listing. The tables that start with MSYS are used by Microsoft Jet to keep track of indexes, relationships, table definitions, and so on. Do not attempt to read, delete, or modify these tables. Doing so can permanently damage your database.

The actual properties you see on your screen may be different. There are many properties of the TableDef object. Most of them are easy to understand. You can search the Visual Basic online documentation for detailed listings on each of the properties.

Note

You may see one or more properties in your TableDefs that are not documented in the Visual Basic online documents. This is because the Microsoft Jet DAO language allows programmers to invent and store their own custom properties. You may be looking at properties invented by some other application (Microsoft Access, MS Project, custom applications, and so on).

The TableDef Methods

Along with the `CreateTable` method of the database, there are five methods that you can apply to the TableDef object:

- `OpenRecordset` enables you to open a Table, Dynaset, Snapshot, or Forward-Only Recordset from the TableDef object.

- `RefreshLink` updates and refreshes any attached table links for the TableDef object.

- `CreateProperty` enables you to create and store a user-defined property. See the UDP example under the Database object elsewhere in this chapter.

- `CreateIndex` enables you to add an index to the TableDef object. This method is covered in "The Index Data Object" section, later in this chapter.

- `CreateField` enables you to add a new field to an existing TableDef object. You learn more about this method in "The Field Data Object" section, later in this chapter.

Creating a New Table in the Database

The code in Listing 8.21 enables you to create a very simple database and table. Add the code in Listing 8.21 to the `cmdCreateTable_Click` event.

LISTING 8.21 CODING THE `cmdCreateTable_click` EVENT

```
 1: Private Sub cmdCreateTable_Click()
 2:     '
 3:     ' create a new table in a database
 4:     '
 5:     On Error Resume Next
 6:     '
 7:     Dim ws As Workspace
 8:     Dim db As Database
 9:     Dim td As TableDef
10:     Dim fl As Field
11:     Dim pr As Property
12:     '
13:     Dim strDBName As String
14:     Dim strTDName As String
15:     Dim strFLName As String
16:     Dim intFLType As Integer
17:     Dim strMsg As String
18:     '
19:     ' init values
20:     strDBName = App.Path & "\NewDB.mdb"
21:     strTDName = "NewTable"
22:     strFLName = "NewField"
23:     intFLType = dbText
24:     '
25:     ' erase db if it's there
26:     Kill strDBName
```

continues

LISTING 8.21   CONTINUED

```
27:        '
28:        ' open ws and create db
29:        Set ws = DBEngine.Workspaces(0)
30:        Set db = ws.CreateDatabase(strDBName, dbLangGeneral, dbVersion30)
31:        '
32:        ' create a new table
33:        Set td = db.CreateTableDef(strTDName)
34:        '
35:        ' create a new field in table
36:        Set fl = td.CreateField(strFLName, intFLType)
37:        '
38:        ' add new objects to collections
39:        td.Fields.Append fl
40:        db.TableDefs.Append td
41:        '
42:        DisplayResults GetProperties(td), "DB CreateTableDef"
43:        '
44:        ' clean up
45:        db.Close
46:        ws.Close
47:        Set pr = Nothing
48:        Set td = Nothing
49:        Set db = Nothing
50:        Set ws = Nothing
51:        '
52: End Sub
```

The code in Listing 8.21 creates a new database (erasing any old one first), creates a new table object, creates a single field object for the table, and then appends the new objects to their respective collections. Finally, the properties of the new table are displayed.

Modifying and Deleting Existing Tables

You can also use DAO Jet to add new fields or delete existing fields by using the Append or Delete methods on the TableDef object. As an example, add the code in Listing 8.22 to the cmdModifyTable_Click event.

LISTING 8.22   MODIFYING AN EXISTING TABLEDEF OBJECT

```
1: Private Sub cmdModifyTable_Click()
2:        '
3:        ' modify an existing table
4:        '
5:        On Error Resume Next
6:        '
7:        Dim ws As Workspace
```

```
 8:        Dim db As Database
 9:        Dim td As TableDef
10:        Dim fl As Field
11:        '
12:        Dim strDBName As String
13:        Dim strTDName As String
14:        Dim strFLName As String
15:        Dim intFLType As Integer
16:        Dim strMsg As String
17:        '
18:        ' init vars
19:        strDBName = App.Path & "\NewDB.mdb"
20:        strTDName = "NewTable"
21:        strFLName = "FollowDate"
22:        intFLType = dbDate
23:        '
24:        ' first create table with other subroutine
25:        cmdCreateTable_Click
26:        '
27:        ' now open ws & db & td
28:        Set ws = DBEngine.Workspaces(0)
29:        Set db = OpenDatabase(strDBName)
30:        Set td = db.TableDefs(strTDName)
31:        '
32:        ' add a new field
33:        Set fl = td.CreateField(strFLName, intFLType)
34:        td.Fields.Append fl
35:        '
36:        ' make list of fields
37:        strMsg = "Appended Field:" & vbCrLf
38:        For Each fl In td.Fields
39:            strMsg = strMsg & vbTab & fl.Name & vbCrLf
40:        Next
41:        '
42:        ' now delete the new field
43:        td.Fields.Delete strFLName
44:        '
45:        ' make list again
46:        strMsg = strMsg & "Deleted Field:" & vbCrLf
47:        For Each fl In td.Fields
48:            strMsg = strMsg & vbTab & fl.Name & vbCrLf
49:        Next
50:        '
51:        ' show list
52:        DisplayResults strMsg, "DB Table Modifications"
53:        '
54:        ' clean up
55:        db.Close
56:        ws.Close
```

continues

LISTING 8.22   CONTINUED

```
57:      Set fl = Nothing
58:      Set td = Nothing
59:      Set db = Nothing
60:      Set ws = Nothing
61:      '
62: End Sub
```

In Listing 8.22, you call the previous code section to create the table again (line 25).
Then you add a new field using the Append method and delete that field using the Delete
method. Save and run the project, and check your final results against Figure 8.16.

FIGURE 8.16

*Results of modifying
TableDef.*

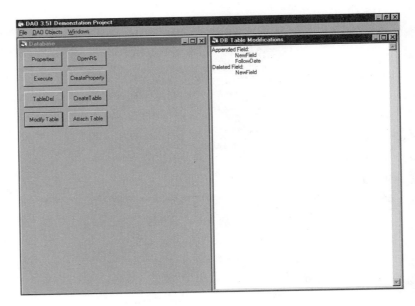

Attaching External Data

You can use Jet DAO to attach an existing external, non-Microsoft Jet database table to
an existing Microsoft Jet-format database. Attaching tables in this way gives you access
to the external data using the standard Jet DAO object model. It also enables you to mix
Microsoft Jet and non-Microsoft Jet data in the same database, which is great for handling queries that combine data from both sources.

> **Note**
> You can create and store queries on the attached external data, too. Queries are covered later in this chapter.

You cannot open a table-type Recordset on an attached table. You must use the Dynaset, Snapshot, or Forward-Only objects for accessing attached tables. Even though you cannot use Table data objects, attached tables respond faster than external data links.

Let's illustrate attachments by adding the code in Listing 8.23 to the cmdAttachTable_Click event.

LISTING 8.23   CODING THE cmdAttachTable_Click EVENT

```
 1: Private Sub cmdAttachTable_Click()
 2:      '
 3:      ' attach a non-jet table to database
 4:      '
 5:      Dim ws As Workspace
 6:      Dim db As Database
 7:      Dim td As TableDef
 8:      '
 9:      Dim strDBName As String
10:      Dim strATName As String
11:      Dim strATDBType As String
12:      Dim strATDBName As String
13:      Dim strATSrcName As String
14:      Dim strMsg As String
15:      '
16:      ' init vars
17:      strDBName = App.Path & "\NewDB.mdb"
18:      strATName = "FoxProAttachment"
19:      strATDBName = App.Path
20:      strATDBType = "FoxPro 2.5;"
21:      strATSrcName = "Customer.dbf"
22:      '
23:      ' call routine to create table
24:      cmdCreateTable_Click
25:      '
26:      ' now open ws & db
27:      Set ws = DBEngine.Workspaces(0)
28:      Set db = OpenDatabase(strDBName)
29:      '
30:      ' add a new tabldef
31:      Set td = db.CreateTableDef(strATName)
32:      '
```

continues

LISTING 8.23   CONTINUED

```
33:        ' define the new def as an attachment
34:        td.Connect = strATDBType & "DATABASE=" & strATDBName
35:        td.SourceTableName = strATSrcName
36:        '
37:        ' append attachment to collection
38:        db.TableDefs.Append td
39:        '
40:        ' show list of tables
41:        strMsg = ""
42:        For Each td In db.TableDefs
43:            strMsg = strMsg & td.Name & vbCrLf
44:        Next
45:        DisplayResults strMsg, "db AttachTable"
46:        '
47:        db.Close
48:        ws.Close
49:        Set td = Nothing
50:        Set db = Nothing
51:        Set ws = Nothing
52:        '
53: End Sub
```

The code in Listing 8.23 calls the routine that creates your test database (line 24) and then opens the created database (lines 27 and 28) and creates a new table definition (line 31). This time, instead of creating field definitions to append to the new table definition, you create an attachment to another external database (lines 33–35). Attachments always have two parts: the Connect string and the SourceTableName.

The Connect string contains all information needed to connect to the external database. For desktop (ISAM-type) databases, you need to supply the driver name (dBASE III, Paradox 3.x, and so on) and the device/path where the data file is located. For back-end database servers, you might need to supply additional parameters.

The SourceTableName contains the name of the data table you want to attach to the Microsoft Jet database. For desktop databases, this is the database filename in the device location (NAMES.DBF, CUSTOMERS.DBF, and so on). For back-end database servers, this is the data table name that already exists in the server database.

Save and run the project. When you click the Attach Table button, you will see a list of all the tables in the database (see Figure 8.17).

FIGURE 8.17

Results of
`cmdAttachTable_Click.`

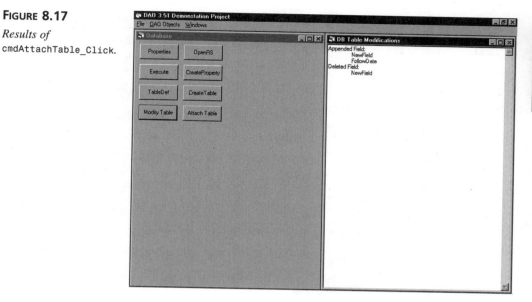

Notice that the FoxProAttachment table now appears. You can now manipulate this table as with any native Microsoft Jet data table object.

 Caution

> You also see several internal data tables in this listing. The tables that start with MSYS are used by Microsoft Jet to keep track of indexes, relationships, table definitions, and so on. Do not attempt to read, delete, or modify these tables. Doing so can permanently damage your database.

The QueryDef Data Object

The QueryDef object contains information about a stored SQL query. SQL queries can be used as record sources for the Visual Basic data control or as the first parameter in the Recordset object. QueryDef objects run faster than inline SQL queries, because Jet DAO must go through a preprocessing step before executing an inline-SQL query. QueryDef objects are stored in their preprocessed format. Using QueryDef objects means there is one less step to go through before you see your data.

Building the QueryDef Form

To test the QueryDef object, you need to add a new form. Use Table 8.10 and Figure 8.18 to lay out the new form.

TABLE 8.10   CONTROLS FOR THE QUERYDEF FORM

Control	Property	Setting
VB.Form	Name	frmQueryDef
	Caption	"QueryDef"
	ClientHeight	3195
	ClientLeft	60
	ClientTop	345
	ClientWidth	4680
	MDIChild	-1 'True
VB.CommandButton	Name	cmdQueryDef
	Caption	"QueryDef"
	Height	495
	Left	120
	Top	180
	Width	1215
VB.CommandButton	Name	cmdRunningQDs
	Caption	"Running QDs"
	Height	495
	Left	1560
	Top	180
	Width	1215
VB.CommandButton	Name	cmdParamQD
	Caption	"Param QD"
	Height	495
	Left	120
	Top	840
	Width	1215

FIGURE 8.18

Laying out the QueryDef form.

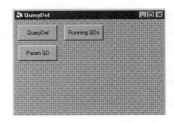

After creating the form, you must go back to the frmDatabase form and add a short routine that exposes the cmdCreateTable_Click event to other forms. Wrapping the private cmdCreateTable_Click event in a public method on the form does this. Add the following code to the frmDatabase form:

```
Public Sub CreateTable()
    cmdCreateTable_Click
End Sub
```

Now you can call the cmdCreatTable_Click event from any other form in the project:

```
frmDatabse.CreateTable
```

Creating QueryDef Objects

The example in Listing 8.24 creates a simple SELECT SQL query and stores it for later use. After creating the query, you apply it as a record source when creating a Recordset object. Finally, you enumerate the QueryDef properties. Add the code in Listing 8.24 to the cmdQueryDef_Click code window.

LISTING 8.24   CREATING A QUERYDEF OBJECT

```
 1: Private Sub cmdQueryDef_Click()
 2:         '
 3:         ' create a stored query
 4:         '
 5:         Dim ws As Workspace
 6:         Dim db As Database
 7:         Dim qd As QueryDef
 8:         '
 9:         Dim strDBName As String
10:         Dim strQDName As String
11:         Dim strQDSQL As String
12:         Dim strMsg As String
13:         '
14:         ' init vars
15:         strDBName = App.Path & "\NewDB.mdb"
16:         strQDName = "qryNewQuery"
17:         strQDSQL = "SELECT * FROM NewTable WHERE NewField<>NULL"
18:         '
19:         ' create db & table
20:         frmDatabase.CreateTable
21:         '
22:         ' open ws and db
23:         Set ws = DBEngine.Workspaces(0)
24:         Set db = ws.OpenDatabase(strDBName)
```

continues

LISTING 8.24 CONTINUED

```
25:    '
26:    ' create a new query
27:    Set qd = db.CreateQueryDef(strQDName)
28:    qd.SQL = strQDSQL
29:    '
30:    ' show properties of the querydef
31:    DisplayResults GetProperties(qd), "Create QueryDef"
32:    '
33:    db.Close
34:    ws.Close
35:    Set qd = Nothing
36:    Set db = Nothing
37:    Set ws = Nothing
38:    '
39: End Sub
```

Save and run the project. Check your final screen against the one in Figure 8.19.

FIGURE 8.19

Results of the new
`Create QueryDef`.

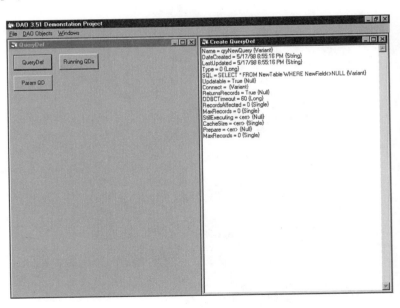

The code in Listing 8.24 exposes one very important aspect of creating QueryDef objects that you might not have noticed. There is no Append method to add the QueryDef to the QueryDefs collection. It is added automatically. As soon as you define the QueryDef with a name property, you have added it to the collection.

> **Tip**
>
> You can also create a QueryDef that is not added to the `QueryDefs` collection. Simply execute the `CreateQueryDef` method with an empty name:
>
> ```
> set qd = db.CreateQueryDef("")
> ```
>
> You can then fill the SQL property of the query and execute it to get the resulting dataset. When you close the query, it is destroyed instead of being saved to the `QueryDefs` collection. This is especially handy when you want to execute dynamic SQL statements, but do not want to create and delete QueryDefs at runtime.

Getting Results from QueryDefs

There are two basic methods for working with QueryDefs: `Execute` and `OpenRecordset`. The `Execute` method is used to perform SQL action queries. Action queries are SQL statements that perform some action on the data table. Examples of action queries are SQL statements that

- Add, modify, or remove table records
- Add indexes or relationship rules
- Add, modify, or remove tables from the database

The other method used when working with QueryDefs is the `OpenRecordset` method. This method is used to retrieve data from the tables into a programming object for manipulation.

To see how these two methods work, enter the code from Listing 8.25 into the `cmdRunningQDs_Click` event.

LISTING 8.25   CODING THE `cmdRunningQDs_Click` EVENT

```
 1: Private Sub cmdRunningQDs_Click()
 2:     '
 3:     ' running stored queries
 4:     '
 5:     Dim ws As Workspace
 6:     Dim db As Database
 7:     Dim qd As QueryDef
 8:     Dim rs As Recordset
 9:     '
10:     Dim strDBName As String
11:     Dim strQDName As String
12:     Dim strQDSQLInsert As String
```

continues

LISTING 8.25   CONTINUED

```
13:        Dim strQDSQLSelect As String
14:        Dim strMsg As String
15:        '
16:        ' init vars
17:        strDBName = App.Path & "\NewDB.mdb"
18:        strQDName = "qryNewQuery"
19:        strQDSQLInsert = "INSERT INTO NewTable VALUES('Mike')"
20:        strQDSQLSelect = "SELECT * FROM NewTable"
21:        '
22:        '
23:        ' create db & table
24:        frmDatabase.CreateTable
25:        '
26:        ' open ws & db
27:        Set ws = DBEngine.Workspaces(0)
28:        Set db = ws.OpenDatabase(strDBName)
29:        '
30:        ' create temp query and execute
31:        Set qd = db.CreateQueryDef("")
32:        qd.SQL = strQDSQLInsert
33:        qd.Execute
34:        '
35:        ' view query properties
36:        strMsg = GetProperties(qd) & vbCrLf
37:        '
38:        ' create stored query and get results
39:        Set qd = db.CreateQueryDef(strQDName)
40:        qd.SQL = strQDSQLSelect
41:        Set rs = qd.OpenRecordset(dbOpenDynaset)
42:        '
43:        strMsg = strMsg & GetProperties(qd)
44:        '
45:        DisplayResults strMsg, "Running QueryDefs"
46:        '
47:        rs.Close
48:        db.Close
49:        ws.Close
50:        Set rs = Nothing
51:        Set qd = Nothing
52:        Set db = Nothing
53:        Set ws = Nothing
54:        '
55: End Sub
```

Notice that this code creates and executes two QueryDefs. The first query is an action query—it uses the Execute method. Note also that this first query was never assigned a value for the Name property (line 31). Microsoft Jet treats it as a temporary query. This temporary query is not appended to the QueryDefs collection.

The second QueryDef selects records from the data table. Because this is not an action query, the `OpenRecordset` method is used to perform this query. Also, because this query was given a value for the `Name` property, it is appended automatically to the `QueryDefs` collection and saved with the database.

Now save and run this code. When you press the Running QDs button, you see output that lists two different queries. Note that the `Name` property of the first query has been filled by Microsoft Jet with `#Temporary QueryDef#` and that the `RecordsAffected` property has been set to 1 (see Figure 8.20).

FIGURE 8.20

Results of running two QueryDefs.

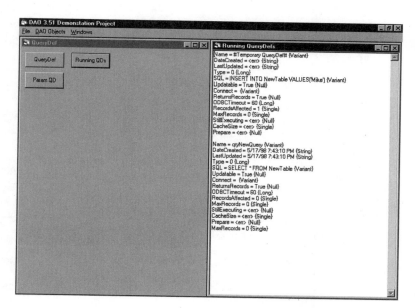

Handling Parameterized QueryDefs with DAO

Microsoft Jet DAO also has the power to create parameterized QueryDefs. These are SQL queries that have predetermined parameters that you can use at runtime. By using parameters in your QueryDefs, you can get the power of inline query building and the speed of preprocessed stored queries.

The syntax for defining parameterized queries in Jet DAO is illustrated in the following SQL query:

```
PARAMETERS FindName TEXT;
   SELECT * FROM NewTable
   WHERE NewField LIKE FindName"
```

Note that it is a standard SQL statement, but is preceded by a PARAMETERS clause. You can add any number of parameters in the PARAMETER clause as long as they follow this form:

```
<name> <type>
```

A comma separates each parameter (name, type pair). The last parameter in the list is followed by a semicolon (;).

Calling parameterized queries requires the use of the Parameters child object of the QueryDef object. For example, to call the query named qryFindName (defined previously) to look for any name that has the letter I in it, you do the following:

```
Set qd=db.QuerDefs("qryFindName")
With qd
   .Parameters.Refresh
   .Parameters("FindName").Value = "*i*"
End With
Set rs = qd.OpenRecordset(dbOpenDynaset)
```

This creates a recordset that contains all the rows in the table that match the parameter criteria.

To see how this works, add the code from Listing 8.26 to the cmdParamQD_Click event.

LISTING 8.26   CODING THE cmdParamQD_Click EVENT

```
 1: Private Sub cmdParamQD_Click()
 2:     '
 3:     ' create and run a Jet parameter querydef
 4:     '
 5:     Dim ws As Workspace
 6:     Dim db As Database
 7:     Dim qd As QueryDef
 8:     Dim rs As Recordset
 9:     '
10:     Dim strDBName As String
11:     Dim strQDName As String
12:     Dim strQDSQL As String
13:     Dim strMsg As String
14:     '
15:     ' init vars
16:     strDBName = App.Path & "\NewDB.mdb"
17:     strQDName = "qryNewQuery"
18:     strQDSQL = "PARAMETERS FindName TEXT; SELECT * FROM NewTable
        ➡WHERE NewField LIKE FindName"
19:     '
```

```
20:           ' create db & table
21:           frmDatabase.CreateTable
22:           '
23:           ' open ws and db
24:           Set ws = DBEngine.Workspaces(0)
25:           Set db = ws.OpenDatabase(strDBName)
26:           '
27:           ' add some records
28:           With db
29:               .Execute "INSERT INTO NewTable VALUES('Mike')", dbFailOnError
30:               .Execute "INSERT INTO NewTable VALUES('Ishmael')", _
                      dbFailOnError
31:               .Execute "INSERT INTO NewTable VALUES('Barney')", _
                      dbFailOnError
32:           End With
33:           '
34:           ' create a new query
35:           Set qd = db.CreateQueryDef(strQDName)
36:           With qd
37:               .SQL = strQDSQL
38:               .Parameters.Refresh
39:               .Parameters("FindName").Value = "*i*"
40:           End With
41:           '
42:           strMsg = GetProperties(qd) & vbCrLf
43:           strMsg = strMsg & GetProperties(qd.Parameters(0)) & vbCrLf
44:           '
45:           ' show properties of the querydef
46:           Set rs = qd.OpenRecordset(dbOpenDynaset)
47:           With rs
48:               .MoveLast
49:               strMsg = strMsg & "RecordCount= " & CStr(.RecordCount)
50:           End With
51:           '
52:           DisplayResults strMsg, "Run Param QueryDef"
53:           '
54:           rs.Close
55:           db.Close
56:           ws.Close
57:           Set qd = Nothing
58:           Set db = Nothing
59:           Set ws = Nothing
60:           '
61: End Sub
```

The code in Listing 8.26 combines a number of Jet DAO operations you've learned so far: Lines 24 and 25 open a database, lines 28–32 execute action queries to insert records into a table, and lines 35–40 create a parameterized QueryDef object.

Save and run the project. When you press the Param QD button, you should see results that look similar to Figure 8.21.

FIGURE 8.21

Results of running a parameterized QueryDef.

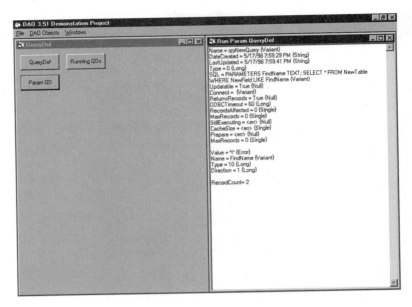

Other DAO Jet Objects

There are a number of other Jet DAO objects worth reviewing in today's lesson. This last section covers the following objects:

- The Field object is usually a child object of the TableDef, but also a child of the Recordset, Index, and Relation objects.
- The Index object is a child object of the TableDef object.
- The Recordset object is the most commonly used data object in the DAO model. This is a child of both the Database and the ODBCDirect objects.
- The ODBCDirect object is a direct connection to the ODBC service.
- The Error object is a special object that contains detailed information on database-related errors.

Building the Other Objects Form

Add one more form to the project. Use Table 8.11 and Figure 8.22 as a guide in building the form.

TABLE 8.11 CONTROLS FOR THE OTHER OBJECTS FORM

Control	Property	Setting
VB.Form	Name	frmOther
	Caption	"Other DAO Objects"
	ClientHeight	3195
	ClientLeft	60
	ClientTop	345
	ClientWidth	4680
	MDIChild	-1 'True
VB.CommandButton	Name	cmdErrors
	Caption	"Errors"
	Height	495
	Left	1620
	Top	1500
	Width	1215
VB.CommandButton	Name	cmdRelation
	Caption	"Relation"
	Height	495
	Left	180
	Top	1500
	Width	1215
VB.CommandButton	Name	cmdRecordsets
	Caption	"Recordsets"
	Height	495
	Left	1620
	Top	840
	Width	1215
VB.CommandButton	Name	cmdODBCDirect
	Caption	"ODBCDirect"
	Height	495
	Left	180
	Top	840
	Width	1215

continues

TABLE 8.11   CONTINUED

Control	Property	Setting
VB.CommandButton	Name	cmdIndex
	Caption	"Index"
	Height	495
	Left	1620
	Top	180
	Width	1215
VB.CommandButton	Name	cmdFields
	Caption	"Fields"
	Height	495
	Left	180
	Top	180
	Width	1215

FIGURE 8.22

Laying out the Other Objects form.

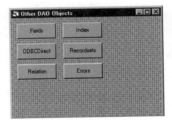

The Field Data Object

The Field object contains all the information about the data table field. In the previous section on TableDef objects, you created and deleted fields. You can also access the Field object to get information on field properties. The Field object has only one collection: the Properties collection. There are 17 properties and 4 methods.

The Field Properties

There are 17 Field properties. You can use these properties to determine the size and type of a field, and whether it is a native Microsoft Jet field object or an attached field from an external database. In version 3.0 Microsoft Jet formats, you can set the default value for the field, and define and enforce field-level validation rules.

Listing 8.27 shows all the properties for selected fields. Add the code in Listing 8.27 to the cmdFields_Click event window.

LISTING 8.27   CODING THE cmdFields_Click EVENT

8

```
 1: Private Sub cmdFields_Click()
 2:     '
 3:     ' show all the field properties of a table
 4:     '
 5:     Dim ws As Workspace
 6:     Dim db As Database
 7:     Dim td As TableDef
 8:     Dim fl As Field
 9:     Dim pr As Property
10:     '
11:     Dim strDBName As String
12:     Dim strTDName As String
13:     Dim strFLName As String
14:     Dim strMsg As String
15:     '
16:     ' init vars
17:     strDBName = App.Path & "\NewDB.mdb"
18:     strTDName = "NewTable"
19:     strFLName = "NewField"
20:     '
21:     ' build new database & table
22:     frmDatabase.CreateTable
23:     '
24:     ' now open ws and db and td
25:     Set ws = DBEngine.Workspaces(0)
26:     Set db = ws.OpenDatabase(strDBName)
27:     '
28:     ' open table and get a field
29:     Set td = db.TableDefs(strTDName)
30:     Set fl = td.Fields(strFLName)
31:     '
32:     ' show properties of the field
33:     DisplayResults GetProperties(fl), "Field Properties"
34:     '
35:     ' cleanup
36:     db.Close
37:     ws.Close
38:     Set pr = Nothing
39:     Set fl = Nothing
40:     Set td = Nothing
41:     Set db = Nothing
42:     Set ws = Nothing
43:     '
44: End Sub
```

The code in Listing 8.27 calls the `CreateTable` method of the frmDatabase form (line 22) and then opens a single table to access one of the fields (lines 25–30). The field object is then sent to the `GetProperties` method to collect the data and display the results (line 33). Check your screen against the one in Figure 8.23.

FIGURE 8.23

Field object properties.

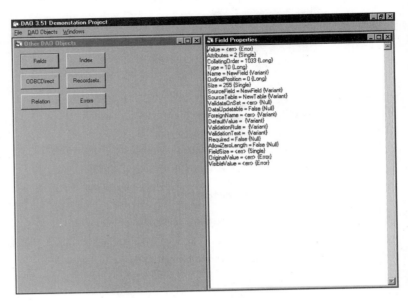

The list of field properties is quite extensive. You are encouraged to check out the Visual Basic documentation for details on some of the less obvious properties. Also remember that you may be seeing properties added by other DAO applications and that there may be no documentation for these custom properties.

The Index Data Object

The Index object is used to contain information on defined indexes for the associated table. Indexes can be built only for native Microsoft Jet data tables (no attached tables allowed). You can use indexes for two purposes: to enforce data integrity rules and to speed access for single-record lookups.

Indexes are always associated with an existing data table. You must create a native Microsoft Jet data table before you can create an index. Listing 8.28 shows how to create an index through Visual Basic code and view its properties. Add this code to the `cmdIndex_click` event.

LISTING 8.28 ADDING AN INDEX TO A TABLE

```
 1: Private Sub cmdIndex_Click()
 2:     '
 3:     ' create a new index and display its properties
 4:     '
 5:     Dim ws As Workspace
 6:     Dim db As Database
 7:     Dim td As TableDef
 8:     Dim ix As Index
 9:     Dim fl As Field
10:     '
11:     Dim strDBName As String
12:     Dim strTDName As String
13:     Dim strFLName As String
14:     Dim strIXName As String
15:     Dim strMsg As String
16:     '
17:     ' init vars
18:     strDBName = App.Path & "\NewDB.mdb"
19:     strTDName = "NewTable"
20:     strFLName = "NewField"
21:     strIXName = "PKNewTable"
22:     '
23:     ' create db and table
24:     frmDatabase.CreateTable
25:     '
26:     ' open ws, db and table
27:     Set ws = DBEngine.Workspaces(0)
28:     Set db = ws.OpenDatabase(strDBName)
29:     Set td = db.TableDefs(strTDName)
30:     '
31:     ' now create an index
32:     Set ix = td.CreateIndex(strIXName)
33:     With ix
34:         Set fl = .CreateField(strFLName)
35:         .Required = True
36:         .Primary = True
37:         .Fields.Append fl
38:     End With
39:     td.Indexes.Append ix
40:     '
41:     ' now show index properties
42:     DisplayResults GetProperties(ix), "Index Object"
43:     '
44:     ' clean up
45:     db.Close
46:     ws.Close
```

8

continues

Listing 8.28   Continued

```
47:        Set fl = Nothing
48:        Set ix = Nothing
49:        Set td = Nothing
50:        Set db = Nothing
51:        Set ws = Nothing
52:        '
53: End Sub
```

The code in Listing 8.28 seems pretty familiar, right? After creating a database and adding a table (handled by frmDatabase.CreateTable), you build and add the index. Notice that you first name the index (line 32), and then create a Field object for the target index (line 34). By adding the Field object and setting some other properties, you have completed the index definition (lines 35 and 36). Finally, you append the index to the collection of indexes for the specific table (line 37).

The ODBCDirect Connection Data Object

The ODBC Direct Connection object is was introduced to DAO Jet in Visual Basic 5.0. This object enables programmers to access ODBC data sources without first defining a Microsoft Jet data object. The ability to open a direct connection to ODBC instead of first opening a Microsoft Jet session provides added flexibility to your programs.

The process of creating and using a Connection object begins at the workspace level. When you create a new workspace, you must explicitly mark it as an ODBCDirect workspace. You can then perform an OpenConnection method to open a new connection to an ODBC data source. Once the connection has been established, you can use the OpenRecordset, Execute, CreateQueryDef, and Close methods with which you are already familiar.

To see how this works, enter the code from Listing 8.29 into the cmdODBCDirect_Click event.

Listing 8.29   Coding the cmdODBCDirect_Click Event

```
 1: Private Sub cmdODBCDirect_Click()
 2:        '
 3:        ' show use of ODBCDirect Connection object
 4:        '
 5:        On Error GoTo LocalErr
 6:        '
 7:        Dim objErr As Error
 8:        Dim errMsg As String
 9:        '
10:        Dim ws As Workspace
```

```
11:        Dim co As Connection
12:        '
13:        Dim strWSName As String
14:        Dim strCOName As String
15:        Dim strCOConnect As String
16:        Dim strDSN As String
17:        Dim strDBQ As String
18:        Dim strMsg As String
19:        '
20:        ' init vars
21:        strWSName = "wsODBCDirect"
22:        strCOName = "coODBCDirect"
23:        strDSN = "DSN=MS Access 97 Database;"
24:        strDBQ = "DBQ=\\amundsen01\tdp\tysdbvb6\source\data\books6.mdb;"
25:        strCOConnect = "ODBC;" & strDSN & strDBQ
26:        '
27:        ' create ws for ODBCDirect
28:        Set ws = DBEngine.CreateWorkspace(strWSName, "admin", "", _
           dbUseODBC)
29:        '
30:        ' open a connection
31:        Set co = ws.OpenConnection(strCOName, dbDriverNoPrompt, False, _
           strCOConnect)
32:        '
33:        ' show properties of connection object
34:        ' connection objects *do not* have a properties collection!
35:        strMsg = strMsg & "Name = " & co.Name & vbCrLf
36:        strMsg = strMsg & "Connect = " & co.Connect & vbCrLf
37:        strMsg = strMsg & "Database = " & co.Database.Name & vbCrLf
38:        strMsg = strMsg & "QueryTimeOut = " & co.QueryTimeout & vbCrLf
39:        strMsg = strMsg & "RecordsAffected = " & co.RecordsAffected & _
           vbCrLf
40:        strMsg = strMsg & "StillExecuting = " & co.StillExecuting & vbCrLf
41:        strMsg = strMsg & "Transactions = " & co.Transactions & vbCrLf
42:        strMsg = strMsg & "Updatable = " & co.Updatable & vbCrLf
43:        '
44:        DisplayResults strMsg, "ODBCDirect Connection"
45:        '
46:        ' clean up
47:        co.Close
48:        ws.Close
49:        Set co = Nothing
50:        Set ws = Nothing
51:        '
52:        Exit Sub
53:        '
54: LocalErr:
55:        '
56: End Sub
```

8

In the code in Listing 8.29, you first create a workspace object with the dbUseODBC parameter added (line 28). This creates the ODBCDirect-type workspace. Next, the code performs the Open Connection method on the workspace using the Connect string built-in program variables (line 31). This Connect string uses the default Microsoft Access driver that ships with Microsoft Office 97. Notice that you are actually pointing to the BOOKS6.MDB database used throughout this book. Another key point to notice is that you are now using Visual Basic DAO to open an Access database. This is not possible if you are using the standard Microsoft Jet ODBC connection.

> **Tip**
>
> You can now use ODBCDirect to open any ISAM-type database formats, including dBASE, FoxPro, Paradox, and so on, along with Microsoft Access and the back-end RDBMS formats, such as SQL Server and Oracle.

Finally, after successfully opening the connection to the database, the Connection object properties are displayed (lines 34–42). Unfortunately, the Connection object does not support the use of the Properties collection. This makes coding the property display a bit more labor-intensive than coding the other DAO objects.

Save and run the project. When you press the Connection button, you see the Connection property list appear on your screen (see Figure 8.24).

FIGURE 8.24

Results of the ODBCDirect Connection object.

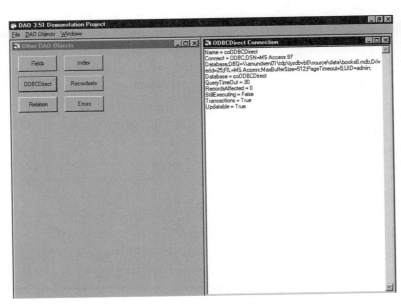

The Recordset Data Object

By far, the most commonly used objects in Visual Basic programming are the objects that contain datasets. In the Microsoft Jet object model, this object is the Recordset object. Recordset objects can be created from the Database object, the Connection Object, the QueryDef object, and even from another Recordset object. This list of parent objects speaks to the importance of the Recordset as the primary data object in the Microsoft Jet DAO.

The property and method list of the Recordset also reflects its versatility and importance. You have learned many of the Recordset's methods in previous chapters. The property list of the Recordset object is also quite extensive. Even more important, the exact methods and properties available for the Recordset depend on whether the Recordset was created within an ODBCDirect workspace or a Microsoft Jet workspace.

Rather than take up space in the book to list these methods and properties, look up the "Recordset Object, Recordset Collection Summary" topic in the Visual Basic 6 help files. This help topic lists every method and property, with extensive notes regarding the differences between ODBCDirect and Microsoft Jet. You can also use this help topic as a starting point for exploring the details of each method and property.

However, to illustrate the differences and similarities between ODBCDirect Recordsets and Microsoft Jet Recordsets, add the code from Listing 8.30 to the cmdRecordsets_Click event.

LISTING 8.30 CODING THE cmdRecordsets_click EVENT

```
 1: Private Sub cmdRecordsets_Click()
 2:     '
 3:     ' demonstrate ODBCDirect and MS Jet Recordsets
 4:     '
 5:     Dim wsDirect As Workspace
 6:     Dim wsJet As Workspace
 7:     Dim db As Database
 8:     Dim co As Connection
 9:     Dim rsDirect As Recordset
10:     Dim rsJet As Recordset
11:     '
12:     Dim strWSDName As String
13:     Dim strWSJName As String
14:     Dim strDBName As String
15:     Dim strCOName As String
16:     Dim strRSDName As String
17:     Dim strRSJName As String
18:     Dim strConnect As String
19:     Dim strMsg As String
```

continues

LISTING 8.30   CONTINUED

```
20:     '
21:     ' init vars
22:     strWSDName = "wsDirect"
23:     strWSJName = "wsJet"
24:     strCOName = "coDirect"
25:     strConnect = "ODBC;DSN=MS Access 97 _
        Database;DBQ=\\amundsen01\tdp\TYSDBVB6\Source\Data\books6.mdb"
26:     strDBName = App.Path & "\..\..\Data\books6.mdb"
27:     strRSDName = "SELECT * FROM Buyers"
28:     strRSJName = "SELECT * FROM Publishers"
29:     '
30:     ' establish ODBCDirect connection
31:     Set wsDirect = DBEngine.CreateWorkspace(strWSDName, "admin", _
        "", dbUseODBC)
32:     Set co = wsDirect.OpenConnection(strCOName, dbDriverNoPrompt, _
        False, strConnect)
33:     Set rsDirect = co.OpenRecordset(strRSDName, dbOpenForwardOnly)
34:     '
35:     ' establish MS Jet connection
36:     Set wsJet = DBEngine.CreateWorkspace(strWSJName, "admin", "")
37:     Set db = wsJet.OpenDatabase(strDBName)
38:     Set rsJet = db.OpenRecordset(strRSJName, dbOpenSnapshot)
39:     With rsJet
40:         .MoveFirst
41:         .MoveLast
42:     End With
43:     '
44:     ' now show results
45:     strMsg = "ODBCDirect Recordset:" & vbCrLf
46:     strMsg = strMsg & GetProperties(rsDirect) & vbCrLf
47:     '
48:     strMsg = strMsg & "MSJet Recordset:" & vbCrLf
49:     strMsg = strMsg & GetProperties(rsJet)
50:     '
51:     DisplayResults strMsg, "ODBCDirect & MSJet Recordsets"
52:     '
53:     ' cleanup
54:     rsDirect.Close
55:     rsJet.Close
56:     db.Close
57:     co.Close
58:     wsDirect.Close
59:     wsJet.Close
60:     '
61:     Set rsDirect = Nothing
62:     Set rsJet = Nothing
63:     Set db = Nothing
64:     Set co = Nothing
```

```
65:        Set wsDirect = Nothing
66:        Set wsJet = Nothing
67:        '
68: End Sub
```

When you save and run this routine, you see a long list of Recordset properties for each of the objects. Note that the lists are different. Even when the property names are the same, some of the values are different (see Figure 8.25).

FIGURE 8.25

Comparing the Jet and ODBCDirect Recordsets.

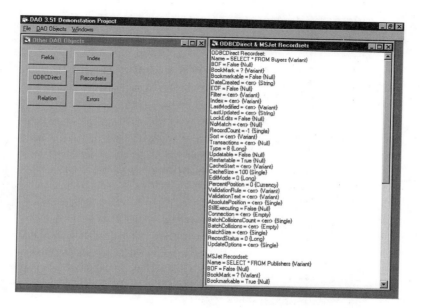

The Relation Data Object

The Relation object contains information about established relationships between two tables. Relationships help enforce database referential integrity. Establishing a relationship involves selecting the two tables you want to relate, identifying the field you can use to link the tables, and defining the type of relationship you want to establish.

Note

The details of defining relationships are covered next week in the chapters on advanced SQL (Day 12 and Day 14, "Updating Databases with SQL"). For now, remember that you can use the Relation object to create and maintain database relationships within Visual Basic code.

In the following coding example, you create a new database, add two tables, define fields and indexes for those two tables, and then define a relationship object for the table pair. This example calls on most of the concepts you have learned today. Add the code in Listing 8.31 to the cmdRelation_Click event window.

LISTING 8.31 USING DAO TO CREATE A RELATIONSHIP OBJECT

```
 1: Private Sub cmdRelation_Click()
 2:     '
 3:     ' demonstrate relationship objects
 4:     '
 5:     On Error Resume Next
 6:     '
 7:     Dim ws As Workspace
 8:     Dim db As Database
 9:     Dim td As TableDef
10:     Dim fl As Field
11:     Dim ix As Index
12:     Dim rl As Relation
13:     '
14:     Dim strDBName As String
15:     Dim strTDLookUp As String
16:     Dim strTDMaster As String
17:     Dim strIXLookUp As String
18:     Dim strIXMaster As String
19:     Dim strRLName As String
20:     Dim strMsg As String
21:     '
22:     ' init vars
23:     strDBName = App.Path & "\RelDB.mdb"
24:     strTDLookUp = "ValidUnits"
25:     strTDMaster = "MasterTable"
26:     strIXLookUp = "PKUnits"
27:     strIXMaster = "PKMaster"
28:     strRLName = "relUnitMaster"
29:     '
30:     ' erase old db if it's there
31:     Kill strDBName
32:     '
33:     ' open ws and create db
34:     Set ws = DBEngine.Workspaces(0)
35:     Set db = ws.CreateDatabase(strDBName, dbLangGeneral, dbVersion30)
36:     '
37:     ' now create the lookup list table & fields
38:     Set td = db.CreateTableDef(strTDLookUp)
39:     With td
40:         Set fl = .CreateField("UnitID", dbText, 10)
41:         .Fields.Append fl
42:         Set fl = .CreateField("Description", dbText, 50)
43:         .Fields.Append fl
```

```
44:     End With
45:     db.TableDefs.Append td
46:     '
47:     ' index the new table
48:     Set ix = td.CreateIndex(strIXLookUp)
49:     With ix
50:         .Primary = True
51:         .Required = True
52:         Set fl = .CreateField("UnitID")
53:         .Fields.Append fl
54:     End With
55:     td.Indexes.Append ix
56:     '
57:     ' now create master record table
58:     Set td = db.CreateTableDef(strTDMaster)
59:     With td
60:         Set fl = .CreateField("MasterID", dbText, 20)
61:         .Fields.Append fl
62:         Set fl = .CreateField("MasterUnitID", dbText, 10)
63:         .Fields.Append fl
64:     End With
65:     db.TableDefs.Append td
66:     '
67:     ' add index to the master table
68:     Set ix = td.CreateIndex(strIXMaster)
69:     With ix
70:         .Primary = True
71:         .Required = True
72:         Set fl = .CreateField("MasterID")
73:         .Fields.Append fl
74:     End With
75:     td.Indexes.Append ix
76:     '
77:     ' *now* do the relationship!
78:     Set rl = db.CreateRelation(strRLName)
79:     With rl
80:         .Table = strTDLookUp ' table for lookups
81:         .ForeignTable = strTDMaster ' table to verify
82:         Set fl = .CreateField("UnitID")
83:         fl.ForeignName = "MasterUnitID"
84:         .Fields.Append fl
85:         .Attributes = dbRelationUpdateCascade
86:     End With
87:     db.Relations.Append rl
88:     '
89:     ' now show relation object
90:     strMsg = "Relation Properties:" & vbCrLf
91:     strMsg = strMsg & GetProperties(rl) & vbCrLf
92:     '
```

continues

LISTING 8.31   CONTINUED

```
 93:        strMsg = strMsg & "Relation Fields:" & vbCrLf
 94:        For Each fl In rl.Fields
 95:            strMsg = strMsg & fl.Name & vbCrLf
 96:            strMsg = strMsg & fl.ForeignName
 97:        Next
 98:        '
 99:        DisplayResults strMsg, "Relation Object"
100:        '
101:        ' cleanup
102:        db.Close
103:        ws.Close
104:        '
105:        Set fl = Nothing
106:        Set ix = Nothing
107:        Set td = Nothing
108:        Set db = Nothing
109:        Set ws = Nothing
110:        '
111:        Exit Sub
112:        '
113: LocalErr:
114:        Resume Next
115:        '
116: End Sub
```

The code in Listing 8.31 performs the basic tasks. Create a database (line 35) and build two tables with two fields each (lines 37–45 and 58–65). Construct primary key indexes for both tables (lines 48–55 and 68–75). Then create the relationship object (lines 78–87).

Save and run the project. When you click the Relation command button, the program creates all the data objects and then displays the resulting Relation object in the results form.

Notice that you added an attribute to make this relationship enforce cascading updates, which means that any time a value is changed in the lookup table, all the corresponding values in the foreign table are updated automatically too. You can also set delete cascades. If the value is deleted from the lookup table, all corresponding records in the foreign table are deleted.

The Errors Object

The Final Jet DAO object you demonstrate in this chapter is the Errors object. The DAO Errors object contains added information relating to the last-known runtime database error encountered by your program. Unlike the standard Visual Basic Err object, which reports only one error message per event, the DAO Errors object is actually a collection of errors.

Often, database errors occur due to a number of factors. This is especially true if you are using Visual Basic to connect to remote databases on a server or using ODBC to handle the connection. Sometimes the error is due to trouble with the back-end database. Sometimes the error occurs within the middle tier (that is, ODBC). And there are times when the error occurs within your Visual Basic program, too.

Often, the errors occur at more than one location along the way. This results in your Visual Basic application receiving several error messages (one from each component involved in the database transaction). Unfortunately, the standard Visual Basic error reports only the last message received and throws away all the other messages.

That's where the Database Errors collection comes in. The DAO Errors collection will save *all* the messages received from *all* the components. You can then check this collection to inspect the list of messages to help diagnose your problem.

As an example, add the code from Listing 8.32 to the cmdErrors_click event on your form.

LISTING 8.32   CODING THE cmdErrors_Click EVENT

```
 1: Private Sub cmdErrors_Click()
 2:     '
 3:     ' show errors collection
 4:     '
 5:     On Error GoTo LocalErr
 6:     '
 7:     Dim objErr As Error
 8:     Dim errMsg As String
 9:     '
10:     Dim ws As Workspace
11:     Dim co As Connection
12:     '
13:     Dim strWSName As String
14:     Dim strCOName As String
15:     Dim strCOConnect As String
16:     Dim strDSN As String
17:     Dim strDBQ As String
18:     Dim strMsg As String
19:     '
20:     ' init vars
21:     strWSName = "wsODBCDirect"
22:     strCOName = "coODBCDirect"
23:     strDSN = "DSN=MS Access 97 Database;"
```

continues

LISTING 8.32   CONTINUED

```
24:        strDBQ = "DBQ=\\badserver\badshare\badfile.mdb;"
25:        strCOConnect = "ODBC;" & strDSN & strDBQ
26:        '
27:        ' create ws for ODBCDirect
28:        Set ws = DBEngine.CreateWorkspace(strWSName, "admin", "", _
           dbUseODBC)
29:        '
30:        ' open a connection
31:        Set co = ws.OpenConnection(strCOName, dbDriverNoPrompt, False, _
           strCOConnect)
32:        '
33:        ' clean up
34:        co.Close
35:        ws.Close
36:        Set co = Nothing
37:        Set ws = Nothing
38:        '
39:        Exit Sub
40:        '
41: LocalErr:
42:        '
43:        ' get regular VB error
44:        errMsg = ""
45:        errMsg = errMsg & "VB Error Object:" & vbCrLf
46:        errMsg = errMsg & "[" & CStr(Err.Number) & "] "
47:        errMsg = errMsg & Err.Description
48:        errMsg = errMsg & " from " & Err.Source & vbCrLf & vbCrLf
49:        '
50:        ' get database errors collection
51:        errMsg = errMsg & "DAO Errors Collection:" & vbCrLf
52:        For Each objErr In Errors
53:            errMsg = errMsg & "Err:"
54:            errMsg = errMsg & " [" & CStr(objErr.Number) & "] "
55:            errMsg = errMsg & objErr.Description
56:            errMsg = errMsg & " from " & objErr.Source & vbCrLf & vbCrLf
57:        Next
58:        '
59:        ' show the output
60:        DisplayResults errMsg, "Database Errors Collection"
61:        '
62: End Sub
```

You should notice that this code *purposefully* creates an error by using an invalid string for the Connect property of an ODBCDirect connection (line 24). When you run this code, you see two main outputs. The first is the error reported by the standard Visual Basic Err object. The second is the list of errors captured by the DAO Errors collection (see Figure 8.26).

FIGURE 8.26

Comparing the Visual Basic Err and DAO Errors *collection.*

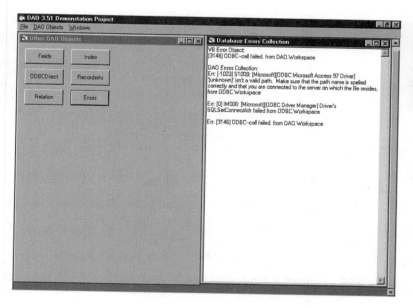

8

Summary

Today, you learned the features and functions of Visual Basic Microsoft Jet DAO data access objects. These objects are used within Visual Basic code to create and maintain workspaces, databases, tables, fields, indexes, queries, and relations. You learned the properties, methods, and collections of each object. You also learned how to use Visual Basic code to inspect the values in the properties, and how to use the methods to perform basic database operations.

Quiz

1. What does the Jet in the Microsoft Jet Database Engine stand for?
2. Describe the difference between a property and a method.
3. What is the top-level data access object (DAO)?
4. What command would you issue to repair a database? Is this a method or a property?
5. What is the syntax of the `CompactDatabase` method?
6. What happens if you don't declare a Workspace when you open a database?
7. What data object types can be created with the `OpenRecordset` method?

8. What is the difference between the `Execute` and the `ExecuteSQL` methods?

9. Which TableDef method can be used to create a table in an existing database? What syntax does this method follow?

10. Which data access object would you use to determine the data type of a table column?

11. Can you use the Index data object to build an index for a FoxPro 2.5 database?

12. What information does the QueryDef object store?

Exercise

Assume that you are a systems consultant to a large multinational corporation. You have been assigned the task of building a program in Visual Basic that creates a database to handle customer information. In this database, you need to track CustomerID, Name, Address (two lines), City, State/Province, Zip, Phone, and Customer Type.

Start a new project and add a single command button to a form that executes the code to build this database. Include the following in your code:

- A section that deletes the database if it already exists
- A table for customer information (called Customers) and a table for customer types (called CustomerTypes)
- Primary keys for both tables
- A relationship between the two tables on the Customer Type field
- A message that signifies that the procedure is complete

When you have completed the entry of this code, display the database in Visdata. Add information to both tables. Take note of how the referential integrity is enforced by deleting records from the CustomerTypes table that are used in the Customers table.

DAY 9

Creating Database Programs with the Data Environment Designer

Today, you learn how to use the new Data Environment Designer (DED) that ships with Visual Basic 6.0. This new tool provides a graphical user interface for creating ADO-based connections to databases and recordsets. You can then take this connection information and drop it on a Windows form to add the proper data-bound controls. This provides you with the power to build data-bound forms without the use of the traditional data control.

Note

Today's lesson uses the Active Data Object (ADO) model to supply data services to Visual Basic. You can learn more about the ADO data model in Day 18, "Using the ActiveX Data Objects (ADO)."

Along with learning how to use the DED to create ADO data connections, you learn how to use the underlying class module created by the DED to program additional operations against the connection and recordset objects. In the process, you build a Find dialog that enables you to locate and select any record in the dataset. You also build a simple read-only list dialog to present the recordset in a summary form.

Finally, in this chapter you build two custom controls (OCXs) that provide navigation (move first, previous, next, last) and action (add, update, delete) operations. After you build these controls, you'll be able to compile them and reuse them in any future ADO-based applications.

Introducing the Data Environment Designer (DED)

The DED is a very powerful visual interface for building data-bound forms. The DED enables you to walk through a handful of dialogs to create connections to data sources (databases) and record sources (datasets or recordsets). The process is much friendlier than the way you use the standard DAO data control. It is also a bit more complicated. Because the DED is designed to provide universal access to almost any data source (MDB files, SQL Server, Oracle, Excel, AS/400, and so forth), you have a few more decisions to make when completing your data connections. However, after you have worked through the process of building a DED data connection, you have many more options for using that connection in your programs.

The Anatomy of the DED

Before jumping into the details of using the DED to build data-bound applications, it is important to get an understanding of the inner workings of the DED and its various parts. With this understanding in hand, you are better able to use the DED to its fullest extent.

The DED ActiveX Designer Interface

The DED provides a graphical interface that shows you each of the database connections and every dataset derived from that connection (see Figure 9.1).

Unlike the standard DAO data control or other custom controls that present either the simple property window or support a custom property dialog, the DED is a special kind of interface object. In fact, the DED is just one of a class of Visual Basic objects called ActiveX Designers. ActiveX Designers are loaded into the Visual Basic IDE just like other items, such as Forms, Modules, Classes, and so forth. However, they have an active user interface instead of a passive one. For example, instead of just filling in dialogs or dropping controls on a form, you use the custom menu of the DED to build a complete set of data connections and data commands to use in your programs.

FIGURE 9.1

Viewing the DED interface.

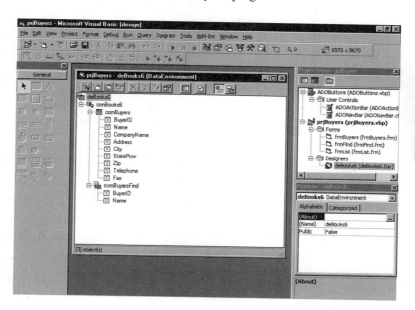

9

Tip

If you worked with the User Connection Designer in Visual Basic 5.0, you will recognize the DED. However, the User Connection Designer uses RDO for its data services. The DED uses ADO instead.

While you are working with the DED, you are prompted to add two different objects:

- The data connection object
- The data command object

The data connection object defines a connection between your program and a data source. Data source can be MDB files, dBase, FoxPro data files, and so forth. You can also use the DED to connect to an ODBC-based data source or to OLE DB data sources, such as SQL Server, Oracle, AS/400, and so forth.

The actual process of building a data connection will be covered later in this chapter. However, the important point to keep in mind is that you use a set of dialogs to build a connection between your program and the data source (see Figure 9.2).

FIGURE 9.2

Viewing the data connection dialog.

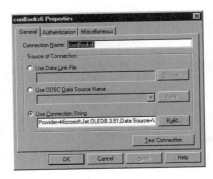

The data command object defines a set of records to retrieve from the data connection. This can be a simple base table or a recordset based on a query. Queries can be created using SQL statements (for example, SELECT * FROM MyTable). These statements can be entered directly as text or stored as QueryDefs (Access MDB) or Views (SQL Server) within the database. You can also access Stored Procedures from SQL Server or Oracle databases. Finally, data commands can be created from OLE DB connection non-SQL data sources that use some other form of selection language.

The details of building complete data commands will be covered later in this chapter. The main point to remember is that you use the DED to define data commands that will contain sets of records (see Figure 9.3).

FIGURE 9.3

Viewing the data command dialog.

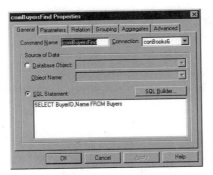

Data-Bound Forms Without Coding

One of the more powerful features of the DED is that it enables you to create data-bound input forms without writing any Visual Basic code. In fact, the DED is smart enough to enable you to simply drag a set of fields from a data command object from the DED over to a standard Windows form and drop it in place (see Figure 9.4).

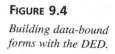

FIGURE 9.4

Building data-bound forms with the DED.

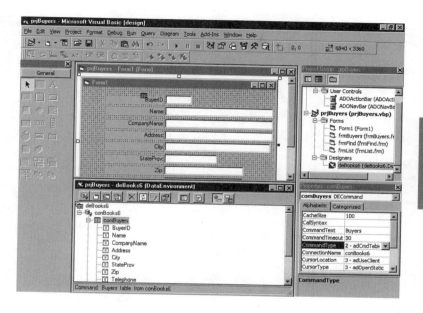

After dropping the fields onto the form you can press F5 and see a fully data-bound form in action!

However, you won't see any navigation controls (first, previous, next, last) or action buttons (update, delete, add). You need to add those yourself. The good news is the DED makes this quite easy, too.

The Class Behind the Face

Although the DED is a friendly interface, it is really turning you into a powerful object-oriented programmer! In fact, what is really happening with the DED is that while you are filling in dialogs, the DED is building a Visual Basic Class module, complete with event-handlers to support the data connections and data commands (see Figure 9.5).

After you learn how to use the DED Class module, you can add powerful features to your data-bound dialogs. The DED Class module gives you access to every connection and data command defined using the DED.

The Advantages of the DED

As mentioned previously, there are a number of obvious advantages to using the DED to build data-bound forms. First, the user interface is much more powerful. You have more options for defining data connection and data commands. You also have a friendlier interface for manipulating the connections and commands.

FIGURE 9.5

Viewing the Class module created by the DED.

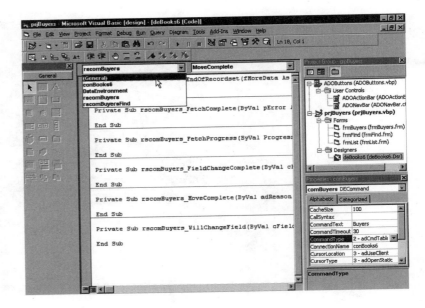

DED Is a Smart Interface

Another major advantage of the DED is that it is smart enough to create data-bound forms for you. This reduces the rather time-consuming process of adding each control and binding those controls to the data source. Of course, you can still do individual data binding and form layout as you did before.

The fact that the DED offers a Visual Basic Class module interface for programming is also another advantage. This object class provides a very rich set of methods, properties, and events for you to use when coding advanced features into your data-bound forms.

DED Uses Active Data Objects (ADO)

There are some other, less obvious, advantages to using the DED to build your data-bound forms. One of them is that DED uses the Active Data Object (ADO) model for accessing data. This new data model is much leaner and more streamlined than the traditional Data Access Object (DAO) model used by the standard data control. The ADO model is also more flexible than the Remote Data Object (RDO) model used for connecting to SQL Server and other back-end RDBMS data sources.

Microsoft designed the ADO model for data access to take advantage of the new OLE DB data connection interface. This data connection interface provides access to non-SQL data sources such as text files, email data storage, and even operating system directory services. For this reason, using DED will give you the opportunity to create applications that access new and much more varied data sources.

DED Is the Future of Visual Basic Data Programming

Microsoft has announced that all future development of data services will be geared toward expanding and improving the ADO/OLE DB object models. Although the DAO and RDO models still are quite powerful and useful, any future advances in data access will be done using ADO. Because the DED is designed to take advantage of ADO and OLE DB, any programs that use the DED will be able to take advantage of advances in ADO and OLE DB more easily than programs built using DAO or RDO.

Now that you have an idea of the power and flexibility of the DED, it's time to start using it!

Using the Data Environment Designer

Using the DED is relatively easy. You add the DED ActiveX Designer to your current project and work through its dialogs in order to add data connection and data command objects to your program. When that work is done, you can access the various connections and commands within your other Visual Basic components (forms, modules, classes, reports) without much trouble.

However, the actual process of defining the connections and commands can get a bit involved. At first, it may seem that using the DED is more trouble than it's worth—don't be fooled! Although creating your first connections and commands may take some time, you'll be able to build subsequent objects quickly and easily. If you are stymied by a bit of a learning curve at first, don't give up. After you use the DED a few times, it will all seem quite easy.

In fact, the process of building data services into your Visual Basic programs with the DED involves only three steps:

1. Select a data provider (ODBC or OLE DB).
2. Create a data connection (MDB File, SQL Server, and so forth).
3. Create a data command (SELECT * FROM Authors, and so forth).

After you get through the first two steps, you can create as many data command objects as you need for your application. These multiple data commands can all use the same data connection. If, however, you need to connect to more than one data source, you can add multiple data connections and build data commands for each connection as needed.

About Data Providers

Before you start building your connections, it is important to discuss the role of the Data Provider in completing data connections. The Data Provider is a component that handles the conversation between your program and the data source. A very familiar provider is the Open Database Connectivity (ODBC) provider. The ODBC interface is based on the idea that all data sources can be viewed with the well-known SQL query language.

There is, however, a new data provider model that has been introduced by Microsoft: the OLE DB interface. This interface does not require that the data source be addressed using the SQL query language. Instead, the OLE DB interface enables data providers to accept any query language they wish to support. This opens the list of data sources from traditional databases, such as dBase and SQL Server, to other data stores, such as Exchange mail folders and operating system directories and files.

When you use the DED, you first need to select the data provider that you will use for your connection. ODBC is still a valid and useful data provider for Visual Basic 6 applications. In fact, because the OLE DB specification is still new, you may find that you cannot find an OLE DB data provider for your target data source.

However, OLE DB is the suggested choice for your Visual Basic 6.0 data-bound applications. This is the technology that will be advanced in future versions, and this will give you the most options for attaching to various data sources. As an example, Visual Basic 6.0 ships with the following OLE DB data providers:

- Microsoft Jet 3.51 OLE DB Provider
- Microsoft OLE DB Provider for SQL Server
- Microsoft OLE DB Provider for Oracle
- Microsoft OLE DB Provider for ODBC Drivers

Note   The list of OLE DB providers continues to grow. By the time this book goes to press, there may be several more OLE DB providers available for Visual Basic 6.0. Be sure to check your installation and documentation for the most recent list of data providers.

It is important to note that the last item in the list is the OLE DB provider for ODBC Drivers. This means that you can use OLE DB to talk to the ODBC drivers, too. For example, if you wish to connect to SQL Server, you can use the OLE DB provider for SQL Server or you can use the OLE DB provider for ODBC to connect to the ODBC driver for SQL Server.

In some cases, the performance and feature support differs between the OLE DB provider and the ODBC provider for the same data source. If you have a choice, first use the OLE DB provider, because this is the most recent provider. However, you may want to check out the ODBC driver for the target data source and compare performance in order to make sure you are using the most efficient method of connecting to your data.

In summary, OLE DB is the suggested choice as the data provider for your applications. However, in some cases you may need to use ODBC because an OLE DB provider is not available. Also, it is possible that the OLE DB provider does not offer the same performance or features that the ODBC provider has. If you have a choice, you should consider both options and select the one that offers the best performance and features available.

Creating a Data Connection with DED

Enough with the preliminaries. Now it's time to start using the DED! First, start Visual Basic 6.0 and create a new Standard EXE project. This will be the project you use throughout today's lesson. Name the project prjBuyers (you'll be building a data form using the Buyers table of the BOOKS6.MDB database).

> **Tip**
>
> If you cannot locate the Data Environment Designer on your Project menu, select More ActiveX Designers from the menu instead. This will bring up a list of the remaining ActiveX Designers registered for the workstation.

Next, add the Data Environment to your project. You do this by selecting Project | Add Data Environment from the main menu. When you select this menu option, the DED will appear along with a prompt for creating the data connection object. Use the Properties window to set the Name to deBooks6. You use this data environment to connect to the BOOKS6.MDB database that ships with this book.

You're now ready to start filling in the connection properties dialog.

Filling In the Connection Properties Dialog

The first step in the process of filling in the connection properties dialog is creating a name for the data connection. In this example, use conBuyers as the connection name. You can use any name you want. This name will appear as part of the object model in the class created by DED. Thus, no spaces are allowed.

> **Tip**
>
> It is suggested that you use the prefix con to designate the item as a connection object.

The next step is to select a data source for the connection. In this example, you build an OLE DB connection to the BOOKS6.MDB database that ships with this book. To do this, you need to press the Build button at the bottom of the Connnection Properties dialog. This brings up the OLE DB Data Link Wizard.

Using the OLE DB Data Link Wizard

You use the OLE DB Data Link Wizard to select a data provider and complete a valid connection string for your Data Environment. Along the way, you can also test your connection to make sure it will work in your program.

At the first dialog, you must select a data provider. For this example, select the Microsoft Jet 3.51 OLE DB Provider and press Next to continue (see Figure 9.6).

FIGURE 9.6

Selecting an OLE DB data provider.

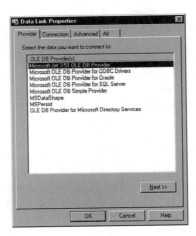

At the next page, you need to enter the exact device, folder, and filename of the MDB database you want to access. In this example, enter the drive and path that points to the BOOKS6.MDB file:

```
c:\tysdbvb6\source\data\books6.mdb
```

Next, you have the option of filling in the security information for this data connection. If opening the database required a username and password, this is where you enter it. For this example, accept the Admin default username and leave the Blank Password check box ON.

Finally, you can press the Test Connection button at the bottom-right of the dialog to make sure your data link is properly defined. If all goes well, you'll see a Test Connection Succeeded message (see Figure 9.7).

FIGURE 9.7

Checking an OLE DB data link.

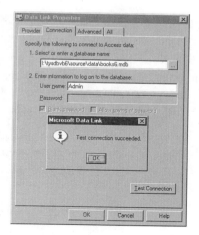

At this point you have completed your OLE DB Data Provider definition. If you need to adjust advanced settings, you can select the All tab of the dialog. This brings up a dialog that enables you access to all the OLE DB data link settings. For this example, you do not need to adjust any advanced settings.

To complete the definition, press the OK button at the bottom of the page. You will be returned to the connection properties dialog. For this example, you do not need to access the Authentication or Miscellaneous tabs on the dialog. Just press the OK button to complete the connection definition and add it to your Data Environment. Your DED interface should now look like the one in Figure 9.8.

FIGURE 9.8

Viewing the DED after adding the data connection object.

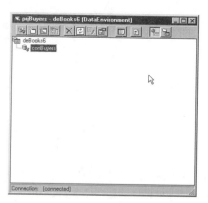

Creating a Table Data Command with DED

Now that you have a valid data connection object in the DED, you're ready to add a data command that will access the data stored within the selected database. In this example, you first build a data command that connects directly to a base table in the BOOKS6.MDB data file.

To do this, right-click over the conBuyers data connection and select Add Command from the context menu. This will bring up the data command properties dialog. Enter comBuyers as the Name property and select Table from the Database Object drop-down list. Next, select Buyers from the Object Name drop-down list. Your dialog should look similar to the one in Figure 9.3.

Before you exit this dialog, you must first switch to the Advanced tab and set the LockType to 3 - Optimistic. This will change the default setting of 1 - ReadOnly. If you fail to adjust this setting, you will not be able to update your recordset from your Visual Basic program.

After filling in the General tab as described here and setting the LockType to 3 - Optimistic, press the OK button to store the data command settings and dismiss the dialog. When you return to the DED interface, press the plus sign (+) next to the new command object to expose the list of fields in the Buyers table. Your screen should look like the one in Figure 9.9.

FIGURE 9.9

Viewing the field list for the comBuyers *data command.*

You have just completed your first DED data command. You need to add one more data command to this connection before you're ready to create the data entry form.

Creating an SQL Data Command with DED

In the data entry project you build later in today's lesson, you'll need a read-only list of the BuyerID codes and names for use in a Find dialog. To help make things easy, you need to build a new data command that will hold just the information needed for the Find dialog.

To do this, right-click over the conBooks6 connection object again and select Add Command from the context menu. Enter comBuyersFind as the command name and click on the SQL Statement radio button to activate the text box. Enter the following SQL statement in this box:

```
SELECT BuyerID, Name from Buyers
```

This produces a data command that contains just the ID codes and names of the buyers in the base table. You can press the OK button at this time to save the definition and add it to your Data Environment.

You can now complete your work with the DED. Be sure to save the Data environment (as deBooks6.dsr) before you continue to build the data entry form that will use the data commands.

Creating a Data Entry Application with DED

You're now ready to create the Windows forms that will enable you to view and update the Buyers data table. For this example project, you build three forms:

- The Buyers form will be the main display and editing form for the project.
- The List View form will be a simple, read-only list of all the records in the Buyers table.
- The Find form will be a small pop-up dialog that will enable users to double-click on a BuyerID to bring that record up in the main Buyers form.

After creating these three forms, you add some navigation and action buttons to the project. You'll get to those at the end of this chapter.

Designing the Buyers Form

Designing data entry forms with the DED is really quite simple. You bring up a blank form and drag-and-drop the data command onto the form. The DED does the rest! You see all the fields appear on the form (from top to bottom) along with an accompanying label with the field name (see Figure 9.10).

To make things as easy as possible, tile your DED and your FORM within the Visual Basic IDE. You need to view both the DED and the blank form at the same time, and this will give you the best view possible. Don't worry if it looks like the form is too small to accept the entire list of input controls; the form will automatically expand as needed.

Also, don't worry about the exact location for dropping the data command on the form. The complete control set (prompts and data-bound inputs) will appear on the form "in focus." You'll be able to use your mouse to move the entire group around the form to position it properly.

FIGURE 9.10

Using the DED to design a data entry form.

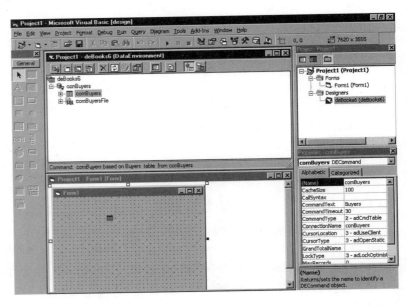

Finally, if you want to experiment with the drag-and-drop capabilities of the DED, right-click over a free space on the DED and select Options from the context menu. You see prompts for controlling which input controls appear for each data field type, and you can control whether the field names will be included in the construction of the form.

After you drop the controls on the form, you are ready to run the application. Press the Run button on the menu bar (or F5) and you should see a screen that looks close to the one in Figure 9.11.

Notice that the data form shows the values from the first record in the dataset in the data-bound inputs of the form. And you wrote no code! Of course, there's more work to do. As the form exists, users can view only the first record.

Set this form's Name property to frmBuyers and save it as frmByers.frm in the project. In the next two sections, you build other forms that use the data commands from the DED.

Before adding code that will place navigation buttons and operations, such as add, edit, and delete, you first build a simple form that shows the entire dataset in a read-only grid.

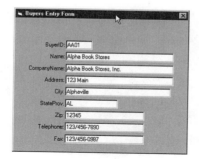

FIGURE 9.11

*Viewing the Buyers
data form.*

Adding the List View Form

In this step, you build a new form that uses the Microsoft Hierarchical Flexgrid control to produce a read-only list of all the records in a data command recordset. This will show you how you can bind visual controls to the DED data commands.

The first step is to load the Microsoft Hierarchical Flexgrid into the Visual Basic 6.0 toolbox. Select Project | Components from the main menu and locate and select Microsoft Hierarchical FlexGrid Control 6.0 from the list. Press the OK button to add this control to your toolbox.

The next step is to add a new form to the project. Set its name to `frmList` and its caption to `Data List`. Place the flexgrid control onto the form. Don't worry about sizing it or controlling its placement—you'll do that with a small bit of code.

Next, you need to bind the grid to the data command. You do this by setting the `Data Source` and `Data Member` properties of the grid. Locate these properties in the standard properties window. When you activate the pull-down list for the `Data Source` property, you see only one choice: the `conBuyers` connection. After selecting `conBuyers` as the `Data Source`, set the `Data Member` property to `comBuyers`. This tells the data grid to connect to the `Data Source` defined in the connection object called `conBuyers` and to retrieve the dataset defined in the data command object called `comBuyers`.

You need to set two more properties of the flexgrid control. First, right-click over the grid and select Retrieve Structure. This loads the field names from the Buyers table into the grid. Next, right-click again over the control and select Properties. On the first tab, set the `Fixed Cols` property to "`0`" (see Figure 9.12).

After setting the properties, press the OK button to store them with the control.

Now add just a small bit of code to the form. This code will automatically resize the grid to fill the entire frmList form. As the user adjusts the form, the flexgrid will adjust, too. Add the code from Listing 9.1 to the `Form_Resize` event.

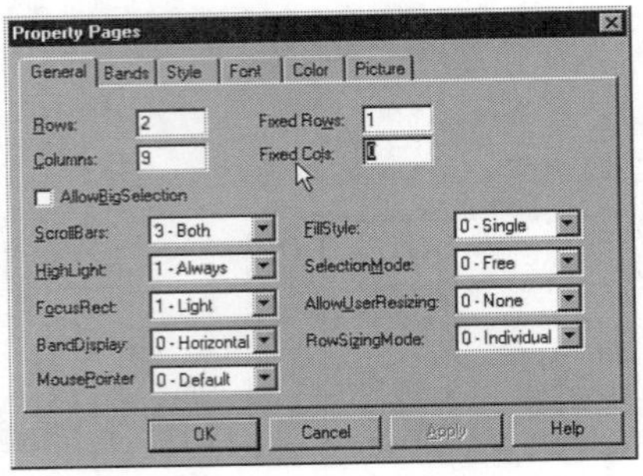

FIGURE 9.12

Setting properties of the FlexGrid control.

LISTING 9.1 CODING THE Form_Resize EVENT

```
 1: Private Sub Form_Resize()
 2:      '
 3:      ' adjust grid to form
 4:      '
 5:      With Me.MSHFlexGrid1
 6:          .Left = 0
 7:          .Top = 0
 8:          .Width = Me.ScaleWidth
 9:          .Height = Me.ScaleHeight
10:      End With
11:      '
12: End Sub
```

Finally, you add a new button to the frmBuyers form that will call the Data List form. Place a command button on the form (to the left of the input controls). Set its name to cmdListView and its caption to List View. Now add the code from Listing 9.2 to the cmdListView_click event.

LISTING 9.2 CODING THE cmdListView_Click EVENT

```
1: Private Sub cmdListView_Click()
2:      '
3:      ' call list dialog
4:      '
5:      frmList.Show vbModal
6:      '
7: End Sub
```

Save the project and run it. When you press the List View button, you should see the list of all the records in the Buyers table (see Figure 9.13).

FIGURE 9.13

Results of the List View form.

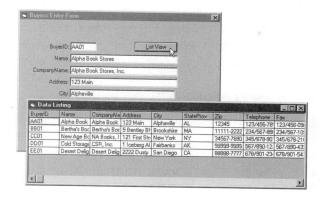

You now have used the objects built with the DED to bind to visual controls on a form. In the next step, you use Visual Basic code to perform a find operation against records in the data objects built with the DED.

Adding the Find Form

Now that you know how to bind visual inputs to the DED data objects, it's time to write some Visual Basic code against those objects, too. In this example, you create a Find dialog that presents the BuyerID code and the Buyer name in a list and, when a user double-clicks on an ID code, the find dialog forces a lookup of the selected ID and presents that record in the main Buyers Data form.

To do this work, you need another form in the project. Add a standard form. Set its Name to frmFind and its caption to Double-Click on a Buyer ID. Also set its BorderStyle to Fixed Dialog.

Add a MSFlexGrid control to this form and set the Data Source property to conBuyers and the Data Member property to comBuyersFind. Notice that you are using the second data command object you built earlier in this lesson. Finally, right-click over the grid control and select Retrieve Structure to load the fields into the grid and set the "Fixed Cols" property = 0.

There are two code pieces that must be added to this form. The first performs the same resizing you saw on the Data List form. However, notice also the two lines that set the size of the grid columns. Add the code from Listing 9.3 to the frmFind form.

LISTING 9.3 CODING THE Find Form_Resize EVENT

```
 1: Private Sub Form_Resize()
 2:        '
 3:        ' adjust grid and columns
 4:        '
 5:        With Me.MSHFlexGrid1
 6:            .Left = 0
 7:            .Top = 0
 8:            .Height = Me.ScaleHeight
 9:            .Width = Me.ScaleWidth
10:            .ColWidth(0) = .Width * 0.33
11:            .ColWidth(1) = .Width * 0.67
12:        End With
13:        '
14: End Sub
```

Next is the code that looks for a double-click event over the grid. If the user has selected a BuyerID, this value is passed back to the main Buyers form to be used as a lookup value. You add code to the Buyers form in just a bit. For now, add this last bit of code from Listing 9.4 to the Find form.

LISTING 9.4 CODING THE DOUBLE-CLICK EVENT OF THE GRID

```
 1: Private Sub MSHFlexGrid1_DblClick()
 2:        '
 3:        ' pass selected record to caller
 4:        '
 5:        With Me.MSHFlexGrid1
 6:            If .Col = 0 Then
 7:                frmBuyers.Key = .Text
 8:                Me.Hide
 9:            End If
10:        End With
11:        '
12: End Sub
```

Notice that this code sets a variable on the frmBuyers form to match the value of the selected BuyerID in the grid (line 7). You modify the Buyers form in the next set of paragraphs to accept, and use, this value.

After entering this last bit of code, save the Find form before you continue.

Now you need to modify the Buyers Data form to allow access to the Find form and to use the data from the Find form to perform a lookup on the Buyers form.

The first step is to place a command button on the form just to the right of the BuyerID input text box. Set its name to `cmdFind` and its caption to .... This will be the "find button" users can press to call up the Find form dialog box.

Next, you add a public variable to the form. This is how the Find dialog will be able to pass data back to the form. Enter the code form Listing 9.5 into the general declarations section of the Buyers form.

LISTING 9.5 ADDING A VARIABLE DECLARATION TO THE BUYERS FORM

```
1: ' for find dialog
2: Public Key As String
```

Now, as a final step, you add code to the `cmdFind_Click` event to call the Find form dialog and, upon return from the dialog, use the `Key` variable as a lookup for the data command used in the Buyers form. Add the code from Listing 9.6 to the `cmdFind_Click` event.

LISTING 9.6 CALLING THE FIND DIALOG AND RETRIEVING THE Key VALUE

```
 1: Private Sub cmdFind_Click()
 2:     '
 3:     ' call find pop-up dialog
 4:     '
 5:     Me.Key = ""
 6:     '
 7:     frmFind.Show vbModal
 8:     '
 9:     If Me.Key <> "" Then
10:         With deBooks6.rscomBuyers
11:             .MoveFirst
12:             .Find "BuyerID='" & Me.Key & "'"
13:         End With
14:     End If
15:     '
16:     Unload frmFind
17:     '
18: End Sub
```

The code in Listing 9.6 is short, but powerful. First, the form's public variable is cleared out (line 5). Next, the Find form is launched as a model form (line 7). When the user finally exits the Find form, this routine checks the `Key` variable (line 9). If it is not empty, the code first gets a pointer to the recordset built by the comBuyer data command (line 10) and then performs a `MoveFirst` and a `Find` method to locate the record (lines 11 and

12). This brings the record up in the main form. Finally, the find dialog is unloaded from memory (line 16).

That's it. You can now save and run the project. When you click on the find button, you see the find dialog and can double-click on a BuyerID and view the record in the main Buyer form (see Figure 9.14).

FIGURE 9.14

Using the new find dialog.

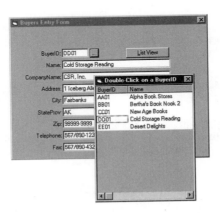

> **Caution**
>
> Unlike the `FindFirst` method for the DAO model, the `Find` method for the ADO model does not start from the first record in the dataset. For this reason, you should always use the `MoveFirst` method before executing a `Find` method on an ADO recordset.

Now you have a form that uses simple data-binding from the DED, one that you bound yourself using the Properties window, and an example of using the DED data objects in Visual Basic code.

In the next section, you learn how to build custom control OCXs that use the recordsets from the DED to provide navigation (first, previous, next, last) and action operations (add, edit, delete) on a dataset.

Creating Your Own Data-Bound Controls

Now that you have the basics of building data forms using the DED, you're ready to take the next step. In this last section of today's lesson, you learn how you can use the recordset objects from within the DED class module as a variable to pass to a custom control (OCX). In this way, you can create your own types of "bound controls."

You actually build two controls today:

- The ADONavBar control provides the familiar First, Previous, Next, and Last buttons for moving through a dataset.
- The ADOActionBar control provides the typical record modification actions (update, delete, and add) for editing records in the recordset.

Even better, because you will build these two items as custom controls, you'll be able to use them in your future Visual Basic projects that use ADO as the data service.

The Navigation Bar Custom Control

To start, you build a set of four buttons on a single OCX control that provide recordset navigation operations (first, previous, next, last). To do this, you need to first add a new project to your Visual Basic 6.0 IDE. Select File | Add Project from the main menu and select ActiveX Control from the Add Project dialog.

 Caution

> Be sure to select Add Project and not Open Project or New Project from the main menu. Only Add Project will enable you to bring up a second project in the Visual Basic 6.0 IDE. The other two options will replace the currently loaded project with your new one.

Laying Out the Navigation Bar Interface

After adding the ActiveX Control project, set its name to ADOButtons. This project will actually hold two User Control objects. For now, name the current User Control object ADONavBar. Use Table 9.1 and Figure 9.15 as a guide in laying out the User Control. Don't worry about size and placement of the command buttons—that will be fixed up at runtime.

TABLE 9.1 CONTROLS FOR THE ADONavBar USER CONTROL

Control	Property	Setting
VB.UserControl	Name	ADONavBar
	ClientHeight	1500
	ClientLeft	0
	ClientTop	0
	ClientWidth	3750
	ToolboxBitmap	"Navbar.bmp"

continues

TABLE 9.1 CONTINUED

Control	Property	Setting
VB.CommandButton	Name	CmdNavigate
	Caption	"First"
	Height	735
	Index	0
	Left	60
	Picture	"first.ico"
	Style	1 'Graphical
	Top	120
	Width	675
VB.CommandButton	Name	CmdNavigate
	Caption	"Previous"
	Height	735
	Index	1
	Left	1020
	Picture	"previous.ico"
	Style	1 'Graphical
	Top	420
	Width	735
VB.CommandButton	Name	CmdNavigate
	Caption	"Next"
	Height	675
	Index	2
	Left	1800
	Picture	"next.ico"
	Style	1 'Graphical
	Top	240
	Width	675
VB.CommandButton	Name	CmdNavigate
	Caption	"Last"
	Height	675
	Index	3
	Left	2700

Control	Property	Setting
	Picture	"last.ico"
	Style	1 'Graphical
	Top	420
	Width	675

You should notice that the command buttons are actually a control array. They all have the same name, but different index values.

Note    All the image files for this project can be found in the SOURCE\CHAP09\GRAPHICS folder on the CD-ROM that ships with this book.

FIGURE 9.15

Laying out the ADONavBar *custom control.*

Coding the Navigation Bar

Next, you add a reference to the Microsoft ActiveX Data objects 2.0 COM library to your project. Select Project | References from the main menu and locate and select the ADO Library. This adds support for the ADO recordset you will be using for these controls.

After adding the ADO library reference, you're ready to add the Visual Basic code. This control will have one public property (ADORecordset) and one public event (Error). To support this, add the following code to the general declarations section of the User Control:

```
Public Event Error(Number, Description, Source)
Private mADORecordset As ADODB.Recordset
```

Next, add the code from Listing 9.7 to the project. This creates the public property for passing the ADO recordset.

LISTING 9.7   ADDING THE ADORecordset PROPERTY TO THE ADONavBar CONTROL

```
1: Public Property Get ADORecordset() As Recordset
2:     Set ADORecordset = mADORecordset
3: End Property
4:
5: Public Property Let ADORecordset(ByVal vNewValue As Recordset)
6:     Set mADORecordset = vNewValue
7: End Property
```

Now you need to add some code that will initialize the control's size at startup and resize it to fit the host data form during runtime. Add the code from Listing 9.8 to the project.

LISTING 9.8   ADDING INITIALIZATION AND RESIZING CODE TO THE ADONavBar CONTROL

```
 1: Private Sub UserControl_Initialize()
 2:         '
 3:         With UserControl
 4:             .Height = 600
 5:             .Width = 3600
 6:         End With
 7:         '
 8: End Sub
 9:
10: Private Sub UserControl_Resize()
11:         '
12:         ' adjust navigation buttons
13:         '
14:         Dim intLoop As Integer
15:         Dim ctlTemp As Control
16:         '
17:         For intLoop = 0 To 3
18:             Set ctlTemp = cmdNavigate(intLoop)
19:             With ctlTemp
20:                 .Left = (UserControl.ScaleWidth / 4) * intLoop
21:                 .Top = 0
22:                 .Width = (UserControl.ScaleWidth / 4)
23:                 .Height = UserControl.ScaleHeight
24:             End With
25:         Next
26:         '
27: End Sub
```

There's just one more set of code to add to the control before you are done: the code to navigate through the attached recordset. The code in Listing 9.9 shows how this is done. Add this to your project.

LISTING 9.9   ADDING THE cmdNavigate_Click EVENT CODE

```
 1: Private Sub cmdNavigate_Click(Index As Integer)
 2:     '
 3:       ' handle recordset navigation
 4:       '
 5:       On Error GoTo LocalErr
 6:       '
 7:       With mADORecordset
 8:           Select Case Index
 9:               Case 0
10:                   .MoveFirst
11:               Case 1
12:                   .MovePrevious
13:                   If .BOF Then
14:                       .MoveFirst
15:                   End If
16:               Case 2
17:                   .MoveNext
18:                   If .EOF Then
19:                       .MoveLast
20:                   End If
21:               Case 3
22:                   .MoveLast
23:           End Select
24:       End With
25:       '
26:       Exit Sub
27:       '
28: LocalErr:
29:       RaiseEvent Error(Err.Number, Err.Description, Err.Source)
30:       '
31: End Sub
```

As you can see from the code in Listing 9.9, performing recordset navigation with ADO is no different than the way you do it with RDO or DAO models. You should also notice the use of the RaiseEvent method to report errors back to the calling form. This way, any errors that occur due to recordset navigation will be reported in the Data Entry form using this control instead of within this control.

Now save the User Control as ADONavBar.ctl and the project as "ADOButtons.vbp." Also be sure to close all open code windows and forms for the User Control project. When you do, you should notice an icon appear in the toolbox. This is the new OCX control you just built! Now you're ready to add the new control to the Buyers Data form.

Testing the Navigation Bar on the Buyers Form

To test the ADONavBar control, you can bring up the Buyers form and double-click on the ADONavBar control to add it to the form. Don't worry about placing the control on the form—you can do that in code at runtime.

After adding the control to the form, you need to add a few lines of code to attach the recordset, resize and locate the control, and handle any errors that might be reported.

Listing 9.10 shows the code needed to handle the location and sizing of the ADONavBar control. Add this to your project.

LISTING 9.10   LOCATING AND RESIZING THE ADONavBar CONTROL

```
 1: Private Sub Form_Resize()
 2:      '
 3:      ' adjust custom ADO button controls
 4:      '
 5:      With Me.ADONavBar1
 6:          .Width = Me.ScaleWidth
 7:          .Height = 600
 8:          .Left = 0
 9:          .Top = Me.ScaleHeight - 600
10:      End With
11:      '
12: End Sub
```

Next you need to add code to the Form_Load event that will set the recordset property of the ADONavBar control to the same recordset used by the Buyers Data form. Add the following code line to the Form_Load event:

```
ADONavBar1.ADORecordset = deBooks6.rscomBuyers
```

Finally, you add some code to the Error event of the ADONavBar control in case an error is reported. Add the following line to the ADONavBar1_Error event:

```
MsgBox CStr(Number) & vbCrLf & Description & vbCrLf & Source, vbCritical,
"ADONavBar Error!"
```

Save the project and run the form. When the form loads, you see the new navigation bars appear at the bottom of the form. You can now press on these buttons to move through the dataset (see Figure 9.16).

FIGURE 9.16

Using the ADONavBar *control.*

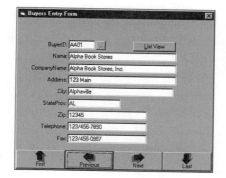

The Action Bar Custom Control

The last step today is creating an action bar that contains all the buttons needed to handle editing, deleting, and adding records to the dataset. Like the ADONavBar control, the ADOActionBar control requires that you attach a recordset to the control and then allow users to press buttons on the bar to complete requested tasks.

Laying Out the Action Bar Interface

First, add a new User Control to the ADOButtons project (select Project | Add User Control from the main menu). Set its Name property to AdOActionBar. Use Table 9.2 and Figure 9.17 to complete the layout for this control.

TABLE 9.2 CONTROLS FOR THE ADOActionBar CUSTOM CONTROL

Control	Property	Setting
VB.UserControl	Name	ADOActionBar
	ClientHeight	1065
	ClientLeft	0
	ClientTop	0
	ClientWidth	4110
	ToolboxBitmap	"actionbar.bmp"
VB.CommandButton	Name	CmdAction
	Caption	"&Delete"
	Height	495
	Index	4
	Left	3000
	Picture	"delete.bmp"

continues

TABLE 9.2 CONTINUED

Control	Property	Setting
	Style	1 'Graphical
	Top	300
	Width	675
VB.CommandButton	Name	CmdAction
	Caption	"&Update"
	Height	495
	Index	3
	Left	2220
	Picture	"udpate.bmp"
	Style	1 'Graphical
	Top	300
	Width	675
VB.CommandButton	Name	CmdAction
	Caption	"&New"
	Height	495
	Index	2
	Left	1380
	Picture	"new.bmp"
	Style	1 'Graphical
	Top	180
	Width	675
VB.CommandButton	Name	CmdAction
	Caption	"&Cancel"
	Height	495
	Index	1
	Left	720
	Picture	"cancel.bmp"
	Style	1 'Graphical
	Top	60
	Width	675

Control	Property	Setting
VB.CommandButton	Name	CmdAction
	Caption	"&Save"
	Height	495
	Index	0
	Left	0
	Picture	"save.bmp"
	Style	1 'Graphical
	Top	0
	Width	675

FIGURE 9.17

*Laying out the
ADOActionBar
custom control.*

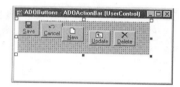

 Again, note that the cmdAction buttons are really a control array. Also remember that
you can find the image files in the SOURCE\CHAP09\GRAPHICS folder on the CD-ROM
that ships with this book.

Coding the Action Bar

Coding the ADOActionBar control is very much like the code for the ADONavBar control.
However, because this control will be a bit more complicated work (adding, editing, and
deleting records), the code is a bit more involved, too.

First, you need to add the code from Listing 9.11 to the general declarations section of
the User Control. This declares a public Error method, a private enumerated type, and
two local variables to match the public properties for this control.

LISTING 9.11 CODING THE GENERAL DECLARATIONS SECTION OF THE CONTROL

```
1: Option Explicit
2:
3: Public Event Error(Number, Description, Source)
4:
5: ' form control toggle
6: Enum ADOFormMode
7:     Add = 0
```

continues

LISTING 9.11   CONTINUED

```
 8:     Edit = 1
 9: End Enum
10: '
11: Private mADORecordset As ADODB.Recordset
12: Private mFormMode As ADOFormMode
```

Now you can add the code that exposes the two public properties, ADORecordset and FormMode. Enter the code from Listing 9.12 into the User Control.

LISTING 9.12   CODE TO EXPOSE THE PUBLIC PROPERTIES OF THE CONTROL

```
 1: Public Property Get ADORecordset() As Recordset
 2:     Set ADORecordset = mADORecordset
 3: End Property
 4:
 5: Public Property Let ADORecordset(ByVal vNewValue As Recordset)
 6:     Set mADORecordset = vNewValue
 7: End Property
 8:
 9: Public Property Get FormMode() As ADOFormMode
10:     FormMode = mFormMode
11: End Property
12:
13: Public Property Let FormMode(ByVal vNewValue As ADOFormMode)
14:     mFormMode = vNewValue
15:     Call SetFormMode(mFormMode)
16: End Property
```

Notice that the Let FormMode method contains code that calls a (yet to be completed) private method called SetFormMode. This method is used to enable and disable controls on the button bar as needed. This button bar has two modes: Add and Edit. When the control is in Add mode, only the Save and Cancel buttons will be enabled. When the control is in Edit Mode, only the New, Update, and Delete buttons will be enabled.

The code in Listing 9.13 shows you how this is done. Add this to your project.

LISTING 9.13   ADDING THE SetFormMode METHOD TO THE CONTROL

```
 1: Private Sub SetFormMode(Mode As ADOFormMode)
 2:     '
 3:     ' toggle controls
 4:     '
 5:     Dim blnFlag As Boolean
 6:     '
```

```
 7:        ' set mode flag
 8:        If Mode = Add Then
 9:            blnFlag = False
10:        Else
11:            blnFlag = True
12:        End If
13:        '
14:        ' set action buttons
15:        cmdAction(0).Enabled = Not blnFlag
16:        cmdAction(1).Enabled = Not blnFlag
17:        cmdAction(2).Enabled = blnFlag
18:        cmdAction(3).Enabled = blnFlag
19:        cmdAction(4).Enabled = blnFlag
20:        '
21: End Sub
```

After adding this custom routine, you still need to add code that will initialize the control at startup and resize it at runtime. Add the code from Listing 9.14 to the User Control.

LISTING 9.14 CODING THE Initialize AND Resize EVENTS FOR THE CONTROL

```
 1: Private Sub UserControl_Initialize()
 2:        '
 3:        ' set starting size in IDE mode
 4:        '
 5:        With UserControl
 6:            .Height = 600
 7:            .Width = 3600
 8:        End With
 9:        '
10: End Sub
11:
12: Private Sub UserControl_Resize()
13:        '
14:        ' adjust action buttons
15:        '
16:        Dim intLoop As Integer
17:        Dim ctlTemp As Control
18:        '
19:        For intLoop = 0 To 4
20:            Set ctlTemp = cmdAction(intLoop)
21:            With ctlTemp
22:                .Left = (UserControl.ScaleWidth / 5) * intLoop
23:                .Top = 0
24:                .Width = (UserControl.ScaleWidth / 5)
25:                .Height = UserControl.ScaleHeight
26:            End With
27:        Next
28:        '
29: End Sub
```

There's just one more routine left to add: the code that responds to the button clicks. This code will do the actual work of updating, deleting, or adding records in the set. Listing 9.15 has the code to accomplish this task. Add it to the cmdAction_Click event on your control.

LISTING 9.15   CODING THE cmdAction_Click EVENT

```
 1: Private Sub cmdAction_Click(Index As Integer)
 2:      '
 3:      ' handle action buttons
 4:      '
 5:      On Error GoTo LocalErr
 6:      '
 7:      Dim intAnswer As Integer
 8:      '
 9:      With mADORecordset
10:          Select Case Index
11:              Case 0 ' Save
12:                  .Update
13:                  SetFormMode Edit
14:              Case 1 'Cancel
15:                  .CancelUpdate
16:                  .MoveFirst
17:                  SetFormMode Edit
18:              Case 2 ' New
19:                  .AddNew
20:                  SetFormMode Add
21:              Case 3 ' Update
22:                  .Update
23:              Case 4 ' Delete
24:                  intAnswer = MsgBox("Delete Current Record?", _
25:                      vbYesNo + vbQuestion, "Delete")
26:                  If intAnswer = vbYes Then
27:                      .Delete
28:                      .MovePrevious
29:                  End If
30:          End Select
31:      End With
32:      '
33:      Exit Sub
34:      '
35: LocalErr:
36:      RaiseEvent Error(Err.Number, Err.Description, Err.Source)
37:      '
38: End Sub
```

Notice that after the Save, Cancel, and Add operations, the SetEditMode method is called to update the button bar. The only other code of interest is the extra confirmation dialog in the `Delete` operation. This gives users an added protection against deleting records by mistake.

That's all the coding you need to to for this new control. Save the `ADOActionBar` control and close the code and User Control windows before moving onto the last section where you test the `ADOActionBar`.

Testing the Action Bar on the Buyers Form

Now you're ready to add the new `ADOActionBar` control to the Buyers Data form. First double-click on the new control in the toolbox to add it to the form. Don't worry about positioning or resizing the control right now—you'll do that at runtime.

After adding the control, you need to add some Visual Basic code. First, update the `Form_Resize` event to include code to size and place the new `ADOActionBar` control. Listing 9.16 has the completed `Form_Resize` code. Lines 5–10 are the new lines of code.

LISTING 9.16   UPDATING THE `Form_Resize` CODE

```
 1: Private Sub Form_Resize()
 2:     '
 3:     ' adjust custom ADO button controls
 4:     '
 5:     With Me.ADOActionBar1
 6:         .Width = Me.ScaleWidth
 7:         .Height = 600
 8:         .Left = 0
 9:         .Top = 0
10:     End With
11:     '
12:     With Me.ADONavBar1
13:         .Width = Me.ScaleWidth
14:         .Height = 600
15:         .Left = 0
16:         .Top = Me.ScaleHeight - 600
17:     End With
18:     '
19: End Sub
```

Next, add some code to the `Form_Load` event. This attaches a recordset to the control and sets the intial form mode to Edit. Listing 9.17 shows the completed `Form_Load` event code.

LISTING 9.17 MODIFIED Form_Load EVENT CODE

```
 1: Private Sub Form_Load()
 2:      '
 3:      ' set starting mode
 4:      '
 5:      ADONavBar1.ADORecordset = deBooks6.rscomBuyers
 6:      '
 7:      With ADOActionBar1
 8:          .ADORecordset = deBooks6.rscomBuyers
 9:          .FormMode = Edit
10:      End With
11:      '
12: End Sub
```

Last, you need to add a single line of code to the ADOActionBar1_Error event:

```
MsgBox CStr(Number) & vbCrLf & Description & vbCrLf & Source, vbCritical, _
   "ADOActionBar Error!"
```

This will report any errors that occur during update operations.

Now save and run the Buyers Entry Form. First, you see the new action bar appear at the top of the form (see Figure 9.18).

FIGURE 9.18

Viewing the completed Buyers Entry Form.

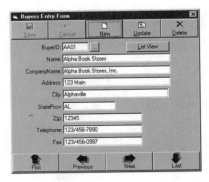

If you press the New button, you see the form inputs clear, waiting for your entries. You can cancel the entry or fill in the form and press Save. If an error occurs during the Save operation, you see the message appear in a dialog box. When you press the Delete button, you see a confirmation dialog before the record is actually deleted.

That's all there is to it! You now have two custom controls that provide navigation and update actions for ADO recordsets. You can compile these two controls in the OCX package and include them in any future Visual Basic 6.0 ADO project.

Summary

Today, you learned how to use the new Data Environment Designer (DED) that ships with Visual Basic 6.0. This new tool provides a graphical user interface for creating ADO-based connections to databases and recordsets.

In addition to learning how to use the DED to create ADO data connections, you learned how to use the underlying class module created by the DED to progam additional operations against the connection and recordset objects. You built a Find dialog that enables you to locate and select any record in the dataset, and you built a simple read-only list dialog to present the recordset in a summary form.

Finally, you built two custom controls (OCXs) that provide navigation (move first, previous, next, last) and action (add, update, delete) operations.

Quiz

1. What does DED stand for?

2. The Data Environment Designer enables you to create two different types of data objects. What are these two objects?

3. True or False: Even though ADO (Active Data Objects) can use both ODBC and OLE DB data providers, the DED allows you to use only OLE DB data providers when building database interfaces for your programs.

4. True or False: It is harder to build data-bound forms with the new Data Environment Designer.

5. If you build a data form with the DED, can you still write Visual Basic code that accesses the underlying recordsets and data objects created by the DED?

6. How is the `Find` method of the ADO recordset object different from the `FindFirst` method of the traditional DAO recordset object?

7. True or False: the Microsoft Hierarchical FlexGrid enables you to create fully updatable data grid forms.

Exercise

You have just been asked by your supervisor to build a data entry form for the Publishers Table in the `BOOKS6.MDB` database. The requirements are that the form should have a set of navigation buttons on the bottom and a set of action buttons along the top. You also need to provide a Find button next to the Primary Key field on the form to enable users to quickly bring up a list of all the publishers in the table. They should be able to double-click on a publisher ID in the listing and then see that complete data record appear in the data entry form, ready for editing.

Use the ADONavBar and ADOActionBar controls from this chapter to create a solution for the Publishers data entry form that has the following features:

- Uses a Data Environment with a connection to BOOKS6.MDB
- Uses a Table Command to connect to the Publishers Table
- Uses a SQL Statement Command to create a list of PubID and Name fields for the Find dialog
- Offers a complete data entry form for the Publishers Table
- Offers a small Find button on the form that brings up a dialog using the MSHFlexGrid control to list PubID and Name.

Use the frmBuyers and frmFind forms from the prjBuyers project as a guide in building your own solution.

DAY 10

Displaying Your Data with Graphs

Today, you learn how to add graph displays of your data to your database programs. By using the Microsoft Chart Control 6.0 that ships with Visual Basic Professional Edition, you can easily create visual displays of your database.

You also learn how to use SQL SELECT statements for creating datasets to use as the basis for your graphs. These SQL statements can be built into your code or stored as QueryDef objects in your database.

You also learn how to save the generated graphs to disk as bitmap files, how to share your graphs with other programs by placing them on the Windows Clipboard, and how to send the completed graphs to the printer.

Finally, you learn how to use a simple GraphDLL COM Component to add all this capability to any existing VB6 application.

The Advantages of Graphing Your Data

Although generating data graphs is not, strictly speaking, a database function, almost all good database programs provide graphing capabilities. Visual representations of data are much easier to understand than tables or lists. Providing graphs in your database programs also gives users the chance to look at data in more than one way. Often, users discover important information in their data simply by looking at it from another angle.

Providing graphs also gives your programs an added polish that users appreciate. Quite often, users want more than a simple data entry program with a few list reports. Many times, users take data created with a Visual Basic program and export it to another Windows application in order to develop graphs and charts. Using the techniques you learn today, you can provide your users with all the graphing tools they need to develop graphs and charts without using other programs!

Loading and Using the Microsoft Chart Control

The Microsoft Chart Control has a multitude of properties that you can manipulate in order to customize the graph display. Only the most commonly used options are covered here. (You can review the Visual Basic documentation for detailed information on all the properties of the graph control.) In this lesson, you learn how to use the Microsoft Chart Control properties to manipulate the way graphs appear on your forms by

- Setting the graph type
- Adding graph data using the Data, ChartData and DataSource properties
- Adding titles, labels, and legends

You also learn how to use the EditCopy and EditPaste methods to send the completed graph to a printer, save it as a file, or copy it to the Windows Clipboard.

Adding the Microsoft Chart Control to your Project

The Microsoft Chart Control is installed when you install Visual Basic 6.0. However, this control is not automatically added to each new project you create. You must add this one manually.

Caution

Some versions of Visual Basic may have two different versions of the Microsoft Chart Control: MSCHART.OCX and MSCHRT20.OCX. All the examples in this book use the MSCHRT20.OCX control, because it is the one that is enabled for the OLEDB/ADO data object model. Be sure you select the property Microsoft Chart Control when you add it to your Visual Basic projects.

After starting Visual Basic 6.0 and creating a new Standard EXE project, you can add the Microsoft Chart Control by selecting Project | Components from the Main Visual Basic menu and locating and choosing Microsoft Chart Control 6.0 (OLEDB)" from the list (see Figure 10.1).

FIGURE 10.1

Adding the Chart Control to your project.

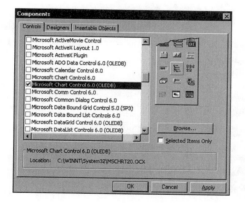

After the Microsoft Chart Control has been added to your project, you're ready to start creating data graphs.

Adding the Graph Control to Your Form

It's very easy to create a good-looking graph using the graph tool. You add the control to your form and fill it with data; the graph control does the rest. Let's create a simple graph to illustrate this point.

Start a new Standard EXE project in Visual Basic 6.0 and be sure to add the Chart Control to the project (see previous section). Next, add the Chart Control to a blank form by double-clicking the control icon in the toolbox. You see that the graph control automatically displays a two-dimensional bar graph with some data. Stretch the control so that your form looks like the one shown in Figure 10.2.

FIGURE 10.2

Adding the Chart Control to a form.

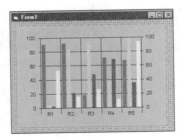

This is random data that the control automatically generates to help you get an idea of how the graph will look in your finished program. When you add your real data to the graph control, this random data disappears.

Setting the Graph Type

You determine the type of graph Visual Basic displays by setting the ChartType property. You can do this using the Properties window during design-time or through Visual Basic code at runtime. Because you already have the graph on your form, move to the Properties window and locate the ChartType property. Set the property to display a three-dimensional pie chart by clicking the property in the window and then pulling down the list box. Find and select the 3D Line option (VtChChartType3dLine). Your screen should look like the one shown in Figure 10.3.

FIGURE 10.3

Setting the ChartType property.

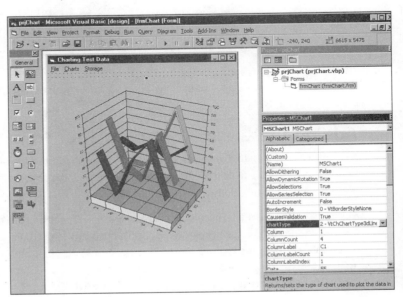

The Chart Control can display 13 different types of charts, including bar, line, area, pie, step, XY, and combination charts in both 2- and 3-D. The three most commonly used formats are covered in this lesson: bar, area, and line graphs.

How the Chart Control Organizes Your Data

Before you can display data, you have to load it into the Chart Control. Before you load it, you need to know how the Chart Control expects to see the data. The Chart Control requires that all the data be organized in rows and columns. The Chart Control also needs to know how many points of data are in each row and column you want to graph. Usually, you have a column of data with multiple rows—very much like a list of numbers. For example, if you want to graph company sales figures for the last 12 months, you would have a single column (company sales figures) with 12 rows (one for each month). If you want to create a graph that compares the actual monthly sales figures with the budgeted figures for the last 12 months, you would have two columns of data (actual and budget figures), each with 12 rows (one for each month).

You can use the ColumnCount and RowCount properties to inform the Chart Control how the data is to be organized. Now create a graph like the one just described. In design mode, use the Property box to set the ColumnCount property to 1 and the RowCount property to 1. You have just told the graph control that it should prepare for one set of data containing 12 individual points. Your graph should now look like the one in Figure 10.4.

FIGURE 10.4

Charting one column of twelve rows.

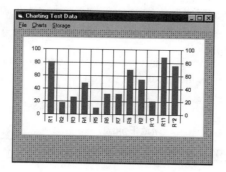

Adding Data in Design Mode

Add 12 data items at-design time so that you can see how the graph looks. To do this you must first set the AutoIncrement property of the Chart Control to TRUE. Next, Locate the Data property in the Property box. Type 1 and press the Enter key. You should see the first column of data now represents the value 1. Continue to add data by entering 2, 3, and so on until you have entered values up to 12. Your form should now look like the one in Figure 10.5.

FIGURE 10.5

Adding data at design-time.

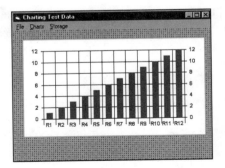

Creating the CHARTING Project

Now that you have a general idea of how to use the Microsoft Chart Control in design mode, it's time to build a Visual Basic 6.0 project that manipulates the control in run-time.

To do this, you add some menu controls to the existing form you worked with in the previous section.

Note

If you skipped the previous section, you should now load Visual Basic and create a new Standard EXE project, add the Microsoft Chart Control to the project, and drop the Microsoft Chart Control on the default form.

Refer to Table 10.1 for the controls (chart and menu) to add to the form and their property settings. You use the various menu options as you work through the examples in today's lesson.

TABLE 10.1   CONTROLS FOR THE FRMCHARTING FORM

Control Name	Property	Setting
VB.Form	Name	frmChart
	Caption	"Charting Test Data"
	ClientHeight	4215
	ClientLeft	165
	ClientTop	735
	ClientWidth	6165
	StartUpPosition	3 'Windows Default

MSChartLib.MSChart	Name	MSChart1
	Height	3135
	Left	180
	Top	240
	Width	5655
VB.Menu	Name	mnuFile
	Caption	"&File"
VB.Menu	Name	mnuFileExit
	Caption	"E&xit"
VB.Menu	Name	mnuCharts
	Caption	"&Charts"
VB.Menu	Name	mnuChartsPoints
	Caption	"Data &Points"
VB.Menu	Name	mnuChartsArray
	Caption	"&Array Data"
VB.Menu	Name	mnuChartsAutoIncr
	Caption	"Auto &Increment"
VB.Menu	Name	mnuChartsDatabase
	Caption	"&Database"
VB.Menu	Name	mnuStorage
	Caption	"&Storage"
VB.Menu	Name	mnuStorageDisk
	Caption	"&Save to Disk"
VB.Menu	Name	mnuStorageCopy
	Caption	"&Copy to Clipboard"
VB.Menu	Name	mnuStoragePrint
	Caption	"&Print"
VB.Menu	Name	mnuTest
	Caption	"&Test"

10

You also need to add a small bit of code to the form. Listing 10.1 shows the code for the Form_Resize event. This will automatically reset the chart to fill the entire form.

LISTING 10.1   CODING THE Form_Resize EVENT

```
 1: Private Sub Form_Resize()
 2:        '
 3:     With MSChart1
 4:         .Left = 0
 5:         .Top = 0
 6:         .Width = Me.ScaleWidth
 7:         .Height = Me.ScaleHeight
 8:     End With
 9:        '
10: End Sub
```

You also need to add the code from Listing 10.2 to the mnuFileExit_click event.

LISTING 10.2   CODING THE mnuFileExit_click EVENT

```
 1: Private Sub mnuFileExit_Click()
 2:        '
 3:     Unload Me
 4:        '
 5: End Sub
```

After laying out the form and adding the code, save it as frmChart.frm and the project as prjChart.vbp before continuing with the lesson.

Adding Data at Runtime

The most straightforward way to add data to the Chart Control at runtime is to use the Row, Column, and Data properties. The code in Listing 10.3 shows how this is done. Add this code to the form, open the code window and locate the mnuChartPoints item in the upper-left drop-down list, and then select the Click event in the upper-right drop-down list. Then add the code from Listing 10.3.

LISTING 10.3   CODING THE mnuChartPoints_Click EVENT

```
 1: Private Sub mnuChartsPoints_Click()
 2:        '
 3:     Dim intCol As Integer
 4:     Dim intRow As Integer
 5:        '
 6:     With MSChart1
 7:         .chartType = VtChChartType3dBar
 8:         .ColumnCount = 12
 9:         .RowCount = 12
```

```
10:               '
11:               For intCol = 1 To 12
12:                   For intRow = 1 To 12
13:                       .Column = intCol
14:                       .Row = intRow
15:                       .Data = intCol * intRow
16:                   Next
17:               Next
18:               '
19:               .ShowLegend = True
20:           End With
21:           '
22: End Sub
```

In Listing 10.3, you do a few things. First, you set the chart type to display a 3D bar chart. Next, you tell the Chart Control to prepare for 12 columns each with 12 rows of data (a total of 144 data points). Finally, you use a pair of For...Next loops to "walk" through each column and row and generate data for each point.

Save and run the project. When you select Charts | Data Points, your form looks similar to the one shown in Figure 10.6.

FIGURE 10.6

Viewing the Data Points Example.

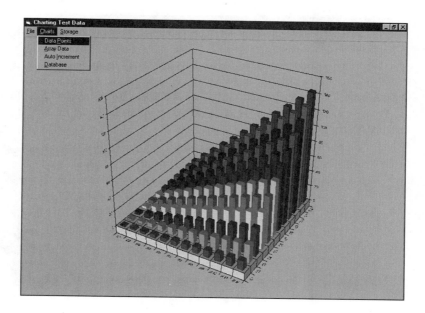

Although this method works well, there is a faster method. By setting the AutoIncrement property of the Chart Control to TRUE, the control automatically

increments the data pointer. This can simplify and speed up your code. The code in
Listing 10.4 show an example of using the AutoIncrement property. Add this code to the
mnuChartsAutoIncr_Click event of the form.

LISTING 10.4 USING AutoIncrement TO LOAD CHART DATA

```
 1: Private Sub mnuChartsAutoIncr_Click()
 2:        '
 3:        Dim intLoop As Integer
 4:        '
 5:        With MSChart1
 6:            .chartType = VtChChartType3dBar
 7:            .ColumnCount = 12
 8:            .RowCount = 12
 9:            .AutoIncrement = True
10:            '
11:            For intLoop = 1 To 144
12:                .Data = intLoop
13:            Next
14:            '
15:        End With
16:        '
17: End Sub
```

Save and run the project. When you select Charts | Auto Increment from the menu, you
see a new chart generated (see Figure 10.7).

FIGURE 10.7

*The AutoIncrement-
generated chart.*

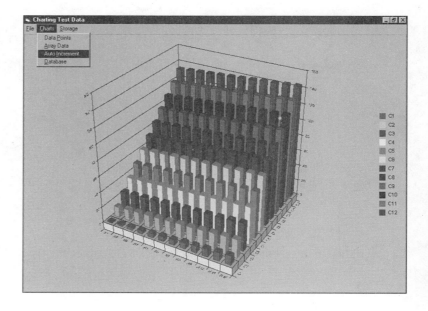

Notice that, in this example, you left out the lines of code that set the Row and Column properties. These values were handled by the graph control using the AutoIncrement property. This might not seem like a code savings, but it really is. Single-set data is relatively easy to graph. Multiple sets can get confusing. It's much easier to use the AutoIncrement property because it automatically updates the Column property, too. Not only is this approach a bit easier, it is also faster. The fewer lines of code you need to execute within the For...Next loop, the faster your program runs.

There is yet another way to add data to a graph control: using the ChartData property.

Adding Data Using the ChartData Property

You can use the ChartData property to add graphing data in a single command at runtime. The ChartData property accepts a Variant data-type array that contains all the columns and rows of data—even column legends. When you use the ChartData property to load graphing data, you do not have to set any of the properties that deal with rows or columns.

Add the code from Listing 10.5 to the mnuChartsArray_Click event.

LISTING 10.5 CODING THE ChartData EXAMPLE

```
 1: Private Sub mnuChartsArray_Click()
 2:      '
 3:      Dim aryData(0 To 3, 1 To 5)
 4:      Dim intCol As Integer
 5:      Dim intRow As Integer
 6:      '
 7:      ' now load the legends and data
 8:      For intCol = 1 To 5
 9:          For intRow = 0 To 3
10:              If intCol = 1 Then
11:                  aryData(intRow, intCol) = "Qtr" & CStr(intRow + 1)
12:              Else
13:                  aryData(intRow, intCol) = Int((50 - 10 + 1) * Rnd +
10)
14:              End If
15:          Next
16:      Next
17:      '
18:      MSChart1.ChartData = aryData
19:      '
20: End Sub
```

Notice that you first declare a variant array that will contain all the columns and rows of data. The code in Listing 10.5 declares four data columns and four rows of data for each column. The first column is used for labels. The loops are used to generate data in the array. The real action happens on line 18, where the data array is passed directly to the Chart Control in one step.

Save and run the project. When you select Charts | Array Data, you should see a chart that looks like the one in Figure 10.8.

FIGURE 10.8

Using the ChartData *method.*

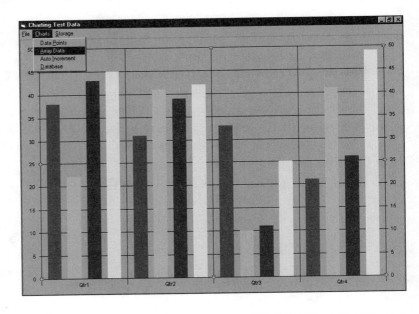

> **Note**
>
> You'll learn more coding with the ActiveX Data Objects on Day 18, "Using the Active Data Objects (ADO)."

Adding Data Using the DataSource Property

You can also load data directly from an open database into the Chart Control. To do this you must use the Active Data Object (ADO) Library. You cannot use the Microsoft Chart Control to directly access data opened using the DAO or RDO data library.

To use the Microsoft Chart Control with ADO, you need to first be sure that the ADO Library is loaded into the project. Select Project | References from the main menu and locate and check on Microsoft ActiveX Data Objects Library 2.0 (see Figure 10.9).

FIGURE 10.9

Loading the ADO Library.

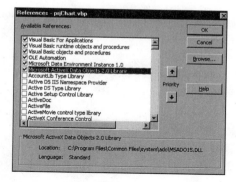

After the ADO Library is loaded, you can add the code from Listing 10.6 to the `mnuFileChartsDatabase_Click` event of your form.

LISTING 10.6   ADDING DATA USING THE DataSource PROPERTY

```
 1: Private Sub mnuChartsDatabase_Click()
 2:     '
 3:     Dim cnn As New ADODB.Connection
 4:     Dim rst As New ADODB.Recordset
 5:     '
 6:     Dim strProvider As String
 7:     Dim strDataSource As String
 8:     Dim strSQL As String
 9:     '
10:     strProvider = "Microsoft.Jet.OLEDB.3.51"
11:     strDataSource = "c:\tysdbvb6\source\data\charting.mdb"
12:     strSQL = "SELECT * FROM TestData"
13:     '
14:     cnn.Open "provider=" & strProvider & ";Data Source=" & _
          strDataSource
15:     rst.Open strSQL, cnn, adOpenStatic
16:     '
17:     With MSChart1
18:         Set .DataSource = rst
19:         .ShowLegend = True
20:         .chartType = VtChChartType2dBar
21:     End With
22:     '
23: End Sub
```

The code in Listing 10.6 first opens a data connection using the Jet OLEDB provider. Be sure to modify the `strDataSource` variable to match the location of the CHARTING.MDB file on your workstation. You can see that the act of loading data into the chart is handled in a single line of code (line 18). This is where you pass the entire recordset to the Chart Control for display.

Save and run the project. When you select Charts | Database from the menu, you should see a chart that looks like the one in Figure 10.10.

FIGURE 10.10

Using the DataSource *property to load data.*

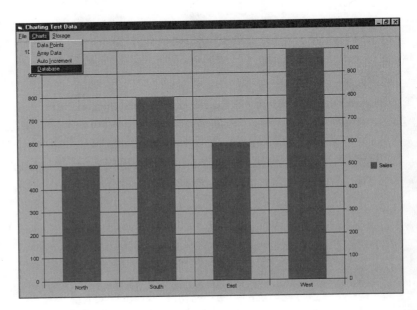

Copying, Saving, and Printing Your Charts

You can also send the completed charts to the Windows Clipboard, to a disk file, or to an attached printer. In this section, you add code to the PRJCHART project that will do just that.

Copying Charts to the Windows Clipboard

It is very easy to copy an existing chart to the Windows Clipboard. After the chart is copied to the Clipboard, you can paste it into any other compatible Windows application. To do this, add the code from Listing 10.7 to the mnuStorageCopy_Click event of the form.

LISTING 10.7 COPYING A CHART TO THE CLIPBOARD

```
1: Private Sub mnuStorageCopy_Click()
2:     '
3:     MSChart1.EditCopy
4:     '
5:     MsgBox "Chart has been copied to the clipboard", vbInformation, _
       "Copy Chart"
6:     '
7: End Sub
```

The important line in Listing 10.8 is line 3. This uses the EditCopy method of the Microsoft Chart Control to copy the chart directly to the windows Clipboard object.

After adding the code, you can run the project, select a display from the Chart menu, and then select Storage | Copy from the menu to add the chart to the Windows Clipboard. You can now load another Windows program and paste the chart into that application. Figure 10.11 shows an example chart pasted into Microsoft Paint.

10

FIGURE 10.11

Pasting a chart from the Clipboard.

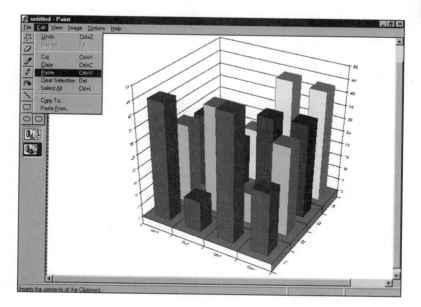

Printing Your Data Charts

You can also send the data chart directly to a printer by simply using the PrintForm method of the form that holds the chart. Add the code from Listing 10.8 to the mnuStoragePrint_Click event of the form.

LISTING 10.8   CODE TO PRINT THE CHART ON THE FORM

```
1: Private Sub mnuStoragePrint_Click()
2:        '
3:        Me.PrintForm
4:        '
5:        MsgBox "Chart has been printed", vbInformation, "Print Chart"
6:        '
7: End Sub
```

Again, line 3 is the important line in Listing 10.8. This is the line that sends the chart to the printer. Save and rn this project and select Storage | Print to print the chart to an attached printer.

Saving Your Charts to a Disk File

Saving the data chart to a disk file is a bit trickier, but not very difficult. Because the Chart Control has no Save method, you must improvise a bit. What you need to do is copy the existing chart to the Windows Clipboard and then use the Visual Basic SavePicture method to save the data from the Clipboard to a disk file.

Listing 10.9 shows how this is done. Add this to the mnuStorageDisk_Click event on your form.

LISTING 10.9   SAVING THE CHART TO A DISK FILE

```
 1: Private Sub mnuStorageDisk_Click()
 2:        '
 3:        Dim strSaveFile As String
 4:        '
 5:        strSaveFile = App.Path & "\" & App.EXEName & ".bmp"
 6:        '
 7:        MSChart1.EditCopy
 8:        SavePicture Clipboard.GetData, strSaveFile
 9:        MsgBox "Chart has been saved to " & strSaveFile, vbInformation, _
           "Save Chart"
10:        '
11: End Sub
```

Notice that this example simply saves every chart to the same filename (based on the application name) in the current directory. In a production application, you would probably want to use a Common dialog control to allow users to select their own save location and filename.

When you save and run the project, you'll be able to display a graph and then select Storage | Save to Disk to create a BMP (Bitmap) file that contains the graph image.

Creating Your Data Chart DLL Component

Now that you have learned the basic techniques of using the graph control, you are ready to build your database-graphing component. This DLL consists of a single form that contains a graph control and a menu of graphing options. It also has methods that load the form, set the graphing values using your ADO data definition, and display the results. You can pass any valid Visual Basic connection and SQL SELECT statement to the data graph OLE Server and display any dataset without any further modification of the code.

Building the Data Graph Form

First, start a new ActiveX DLL Visual Basic project. Set the name of the project to prjDataGraph and the name of the default class module to DataGraph. Add a form to the project and set its Name property to frmGraph.

Before you add the Microsoft Chart control to your project, you need to change the ActiveX DLL project property from a multithreaded version to a single-threaded version. You must do this because the MSCHRT20.OCX control will not work in a multithreaded component. To do this, select Project | Properties from the main Visual Basic menu and set the Threading Model from Apartment Threaded to Single Threaded.

Now you can load the Microsoft Chart Control into your project. Be sure to select the Microsoft Common Dialog control, too.

Note

Make sure the Microsoft Chart Control 6.0 (OLEDB) is in your Visual Basic toolbox. If not, refer to the earlier section "Loading the Graph Control into the Visual Basic Toolbox" for instructions on how to add it to your project's toolbox.

Add the Chart Control to your form. Also add the CommonDialog control to the form. You use this control to add file and print capabilities to the graphing library. You also need to add a menu to the form. Refer to Figure 10.12 and Table 10.2 as guides for laying out this form.

10

FIGURE 10.12

Laying out the Data Chart form.

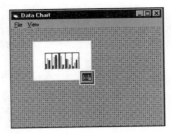

TABLE 10.2   CONTROLS FOR THE DATA CHART FORM

Control Name	Property	Setting
VB.Form	Name	frmChart
	Caption	"Data Chart"
	ClientHeight	3195
	ClientLeft	60
	ClientTop	630
	ClientWidth	4680
	StartUpPosition	1 'CenterOwner
CommonDialog	Name	cdlChart
	Left	2100
	Top	1380
MSChartLib.MSChart	Name	chtData
	Height	1275
	Left	660
	Top	420
	Width	1815
VB.Menu	Name	mnuFile
	Caption	"&File"
VB.Menu	Name	mnuFileItem
	Caption	"&Save"
	Index	0
VB.Menu	Name	mnuFileItem
	Caption	"&Copy"
	Index	1
VB.Menu	Name	mnuFileItem

continues

Control Name	Property	Setting
	Caption	" - "
	Index	2
VB.Menu	Name	mnuFileItem
	Caption	"&Print"
	Index	3
VB.Menu	Name	mnuFileItem
	Caption	"Print &Setup"
	Index	4
VB.Menu	Name	mnuFileItem
	Caption	" - "
	Index	5
VB.Menu	Name	mnuFileItem
	Caption	"E&xit"
	Index	6
VB.Menu	Name	mnuView
	Caption	"&View"
VB.Menu	Name	mnuViewItem
	Caption	"&Bar Graph"
	Index	0
VB.Menu	Name	mnuViewItem
	Caption	"&Line Graph"
	Index	1
VB.Menu	Name	mnuViewItem
	Caption	"&Pie Graph"
	Index	2
VB.Menu	Name	mnuViewItem
	Caption	"&Area Graph"
	Index	3

10

Note that you are building menu arrays with the form. Menu arrays, like other control arrays, can speed the processing of your program and simplify the coding and maintenance of your forms.

You need to add some code to this form. First, save it (FRMGRAPH.FRM) and save the project (PRJDATAGRAPH.VBP). Then add the code in Listing 10.10 to the Form_Activate event of the project. This sets the default size of the form to fill 75 percent of the screen.

LISTING 10.10 SIZING THE FORM ON THE SCREEN

```
 1: Private Sub Form_Activate()
 2:     '
 3:     With Me
 4:         If .WindowState = vbNormal Then
 5:             .Width = Screen.Width * 0.75
 6:             .Height = Screen.Height * 0.75
 7:         End If
 8:     End With
 9:     '
10: End Sub
```

Now, add the code from Listing 10.11 to the Form_Resize event. This code enables users to resize the graph by resizing the form.

LISTING 10.11 ADDING CODE TO THE Form_Resize EVENT

```
 1: Private Sub Form_Resize()
 2:     '
 3:     With chtData
 4:         .Top = 0
 5:         .Left = 0
 6:         .Width = Me.ScaleWidth
 7:         .Height = Me.ScaleHeight
 8:     End With
 9:     '
10: End Sub
```

The code in Listing 10.12 goes in the mnuFileItem_Click event. This code is executed each time the user selects one of the File menu items. The Index value returns the item number selected by the user. You code the CopyGraph and SaveGraph methods in just a moment.

LISTING 10.12 CODING THE mnuFileItem_Click EVENT

```
 1: Private Sub mnuFileItem_Click(Index As Integer)
 2:     '
 3:     ' handle file menu
 4:     '
```

```
 5:        Select Case Index
 6:            Case 0 ' save
 7:                GraphSave
 8:            Case 1 ' copy
 9:                GraphCopy
10:            Case 2 ' na
11:                ' separator
12:            Case 3 ' print
13:                Me.PrintForm
14:            Case 4 ' print setup
15:                cdlChart.ShowPrinter
16:            Case 5 ' na
17:                ' separator
18:            Case 6 ' exit
19:                Unload Me
20:        End Select
21:        '
22: End Sub
```

10

Now add the code in Listing 10.13 to the `mnuViewItem_Click` event. This enables users to select the type of graph they view.

LISTING 10.13   CODING THE `mnuViewItem_Click` EVENT

```
 1: Private Sub mnuViewItem_Click(Index As Integer)
 2:     '
 3:     ' handle graph types
 4:     '
 5:     With chtData
 6:         Select Case Index
 7:             Case 0 ' bar graph
 8:                 .chartType = VtChChartType3dBar
 9:             Case 1 ' line graph
10:                 .chartType = VtChChartType3dLine
11:             Case 2 ' pie graph
12:                 .chartType = VtChChartType2dPie
13:             Case 3 ' area graph
14:                 .chartType = VtChChartType3dArea
15:         End Select
16:     End With
17:     '
18: End Sub
```

Now you're ready to code the `GraphCopy` method. The code in Listing 10.14 is all you need to copy the graph image to the Windows Clipboard. You can then paste this image of the graph from the Clipboard to any other Windows program that allows image cut and paste operations (Microsoft Write, for example).

LISTING 10.14   CODING THE GraphCopy METHOD

```
1: Public Sub GraphCopy()
2:       '
3:       chtData.EditCopy
4:       MsgBox "Graph has been copied to the clipboard", vbInformation, _
            "Copy Graph"
5:       '
6: End Sub
```

Next, add the GraphSave method code from Listing 10.15 to the project. This code
prompts the user for a filename and saves the current graph under that filename.

LISTING 10.15   CODING THE GraphSave METHOD

```
 1: Public Sub GraphSave()
 2:        '
 3:        Dim strFileName As String
 4:        '
 5:        With cdlChart
 6:            .DefaultExt = ".bmp"
 7:            .DialogTitle = "Save Graph"
 8:            .Filter = "Bitmap Files ¦ *.bmp"
 9:            .ShowSave
10:            strFileName = .FileName
11:        End With
12:        '
13:        If Trim(strFileName) = "" Then
14:            Exit Sub
15:        Else
16:            chtData.EditCopy
17:            SavePicture Clipboard.GetData, strFileName
18:            MsgBox "Graph as been saved to " & strFileName, _
                vbInformation, "Save Graph"
19:        End If
20:        '
21: End Sub
```

That's all the code you need for the form. Save this form now. Next, you create the class
object that calls this form.

Building the DataGraph Class Object

In order to display the form you just created, you need to create a class object that
enables users to set some properties and executes a ShowGraph method. The basic properties of the DataGraph object are

- GraphType: The initial graph type for the display
- OLEDBProvider: The official OLE DB provider to use to access the DataSource
- DataSource: The official name of the database that contains the records to graph
- SQLSelect: The SQL SELECT statement that creates the Recordset to display
- GraphLegend: A Boolean property to turn charts legends on and off
- GraphTitle: The optional title of the chart
- GraphFootnote: The optional footnote of the chart

This is a simple graph tool that is capable of displaying a dataset in the most commonly used graph types. Modifications can be made to this routine to add additional labeling, legends, and text. For now, just keep the project simple. When you complete this project, you can add your own modifications.

First, you need to add some local storage variables to the class. These contain the passed properties along with a couple of local variables needed for Private methods. Add the code from Listing 10.16 to the class.

LISTING 10.16 CODING THE GENERAL DECLARATIONS FOR THE Chart CLASS

```
 1: Option Explicit
 2:
 3: ' for internal use
 4: Private cnn As New ADODB.Connection
 5: Private rst As New ADODB.Recordset
 6:
 7: ' local enum type
 8: Enum GraphType
 9:     gtBar = VtChChartType3dBar
10:     gtLine = VtChChartType3dLine
11:     gtPie = VtChChartType2dPie
12:     gtArea = VtChChartType3dArea
13: End Enum
14:
15: 'local variable(s) to hold property value(s)
16: Private mvarOLEDBProvider As String 'local copy
17: Private mvarDataSource As String 'local copy
18: Private mvarSQLSelect As String 'local copy
19: Private mvarGraphTitle As String 'local copy
20: Private mvarGraphFootnote As String 'local copy
21: Private mvarGraphType As GraphType 'local copy
22: Private mvarGraphLegend As Boolean 'local copy
```

Notice the use of the Enum..End Enum construct in the declarations section (lines 8–13). This is a special type of constant declaration that combines a user-defined type

(GraphType) with a set of predefined values (gtBar, gtLine, gtPie, gtArea). When you use this class object in your programs, you will be able to see the enumerated types in the code-complete windows that appear as you enter the source code.

Now you need to declare Public properties of the class. These properties enable users to manipulate the local storage variables of the class. Note that all five properties are included in Listing 10.17. You need to add each property individually using the Tools | Add Procedure | Property options from the main menu.

LISTING 10.17   ADDING THE Chart CLASS PROPERTIES

```
 1: Public Property Let GraphFootnote(ByVal vData As String)
 2:     mvarGraphFootnote = vData
 3: End Property
 4:
 5: Public Property Get GraphFootnote() As String
 6:     GraphFootnote = mvarGraphFootnote
 7: End Property
 8:
 9: Public Property Let GraphTitle(ByVal vData As String)
10:     mvarGraphTitle = vData
11: End Property
12:
13: Public Property Get GraphTitle() As String
14:     GraphTitle = mvarGraphTitle
15: End Property
16:
17: Public Property Let SQLSelect(ByVal vData As String)
18:     mvarSQLSelect = vData
19: End Property
20:
21: Public Property Get SQLSelect() As String
22:     SQLSelect = mvarSQLSelect
23: End Property
24:
25: Public Property Let DataSource(ByVal vData As String)
26:     mvarDataSource = vData
27: End Property
28:
29: Public Property Get DataSource() As String
30:     DataSource = mvarDataSource
31: End Property
32:
33: Public Property Let OLEDBProvider(ByVal vData As String)
34:     mvarOLEDBProvider = vData
35: End Property
36:
37:
```

```
38: Public Property Get OLEDBProvider() As String
39:     OLEDBProvider = mvarOLEDBProvider
40: End Property
41:
42: Public Property Get GraphType() As GraphType
43:     GraphType = mvarGraphType
44: End Property
45:
46: Public Property Let GraphType(ByVal vData As GraphType)
47:     mvarGraphType = vData
48: End Property
49:
50: Public Property Get GraphLegend() As Boolean
51:     GraphLegend = mvarGraphLegend
52: End Property
53:
54: Public Property Let GraphLegend(ByVal vData As Boolean)
55:     mvarGraphLegend = vData
56: End Property
```

10

Add the code from Listing 10.18 to the `Class_Initialize` event and `Class_Terminate` events. This sets the default values for the properties and cleans up any open data objects upon termination of the object.

LISTING 10.18   CODING THE `Class_Initialize` AND Terminate EVENTS

```
 1: Private Sub Class_Initialize()
 2:     '
 3:     ' setup defaults
 4:     '
 5:     mvarOLEDBProvider = "Microsoft.Jet.OLEDB.3.51"
 6:     mvarGraphTitle = App.EXEName
 7:     mvarGraphFootnote = ""
 8:     mvarGraphType = gtBar
 9:     mvarGraphLegend = False
10:     '
11: End Sub
12:
13: Private Sub Class_Terminate()
14:     '
15:     ' close any open data objects
16:     '
17:     On Error Resume Next
18:     '
19:     rst.Close
20:     cnn.Close
21:     '
22:     Set rst = Nothing
```

continues

LISTING 10.18   CONTINUED

```
23:        Set cnn = Nothing
24:        '
25: End Sub
```

Now you're ready to code the ShowGraph method. This one method collects all the property values, creates a dataset, and builds a graph based on the data. Create a Public Sub called ShowGraph in the class and add the code from Listing 10.19.

LISTING 10.19   CODING THE ShowGraph PUBLIC METHOD

```
 1: Public Sub ShowGraph()
 2:        '
 3:        ' display the results!
 4:        '
 5:        On Error GoTo LocalErr
 6:        '
 7:        Screen.MousePointer = vbHourglass
 8:        InitDB
 9:        Screen.MousePointer = vbNormal
10:        '
11:        Load frmChart
12:        With frmChart.chtData
13:            .ShowLegend = mvarGraphLegend
14:            .TitleText = mvarGraphTitle
15:            .chartType = mvarGraphType
16:            .FootnoteText = mvarGraphFootnote
17:            Set .DataSource = rst
18:        End With
19:        frmChart.Show vbModal
20:        '
21:        Exit Sub
22:        '
23: LocalErr:
24:        Err.Raise vbObjectError + 4, App.EXEName, "Error Displaying Graph"
25:        '
26: End Sub
```

This method calls a private method: InitDB. This method uses the OLEDBProvider, DataSource, and SQLSelect properties to create a dataset for the Chart Control. Create the Private Sub InitDB and add the code from Listing 10.20.

LISTING 10.20   CODING THE Private InitDB METHOD

```
1: Private Sub InitDB()
2:     '
3:     ' open the database
4:     '
5:     cnn.Open "Provider=" & mvarOLEDBProvider & ";Data Source=" & _
           mvarDataSource
6:     rst.Open mvarSQLSelect, cnn, adOpenStatic
7:     '
8: End Sub
```

That's all there is to it. You now have a reusable data graphing component. All you need to do now is save the project and compile the DLL. You can do this by selecting File | Make DataGraph.DLL from the main menu. In the next section, you test this library with a simple example.

 Caution   Be sure to compile the DLL before continuing with today's lesson. You need this DLL for the next section of the chapter. Also, compiling the DLL will ensure it is properly registered in your Windows Registry database.

Testing the DataGraph Component

You need to build a short program to test your new library. Suppose you have just been told that the marketing department needs a tool to display the year-to-date book sales by sales representative. The data already exists in a database, but there is no easy way to turn that data into a visual display that upper-level management can access on a regular basis. You have been asked to quickly put together a graphing front-end for the sales data.

In order to complete the job, you need to initialize a copy of the DataGraph.Chart object; set the database-related properties; update the title, footnote, and legend properties; and then execute the ShowGraph method. From there, users can select various graph styles and, if they want, save the graph to disk, send it to the printer, or copy it to the Clipboard to paste in other documents.

Because you already have the completed graph library, you can complete your assignment with as few as 10 lines of Visual Basic code.

First, if you don't have it running right now, start Visual Basic and create a new Standard EXE project. If you still have Visual Basic up from the last section of this chapter, select

File | Add Project to add a new Standard EXE project. Make this new project the default startup project, too.

Now, select Project | References and locate and select the DataGraph library. This links your new project with the OLE Server DLL that you built earlier in this chapter.

Add a single button to a blank form. Set its Name property to cmdRepSales and its Caption property to &RepSales. Add the code from Listing 10.21 to support the button.

LISTING 10.21   CODE TO TEST THE DataGraph.Chart OBJECT

```
 1: Private Sub cmdSalesRep_Click()
 2:       '
 3:     Dim objChart As New DataGraph.Chart
 4:       '
 5:     With objChart
 6:         .OLEDBProvider = "Microsoft.Jet.OLEDB.3.51"
 7:         .DataSource = "c:\tysdbvb6\source\data\books6.mdb"
 8:         .SQLSelect =
    "SELECT SalesRep, SUM(Units) AS UnitsSold FROM BookSales GROUP BY
    ➥SalesRep"
 9:         .GraphFootnote = "Total Units Sold"
10:         .GraphTitle = "Book Sales By SalesRep"
11:         .GraphLegend = True
12:         .GraphType = gtBar
13:         .ShowGraph
14:     End With
15:       '
16: End Sub
```

This code example sets a few properties and then calls the ShowGraph method. That's all there is to it! Save this form as FRMTEST.FRM and the project as PRJTEST.VBP. Now run the project. After you click the single command button, you see the graph displayed onscreen. Your screen should look something like the one shown in Figure 10.13.

You have just completed your first database graphing project using the new DataGraph.Chart component! You can use this component in all your future Visual Basic database projects. You can also add new features and options to the component to customize it for your own needs.

FIGURE 10.13

Viewing the results of the SalesRep chart.

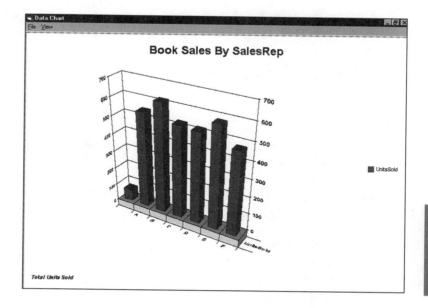

10

Summary

Today, you learned how to use the Microsoft Chart Control, which ships with Visual Basic, to create visual displays of your data tables. You learned how to add the control to your project and how to load the Chart Control with data, titles, legends, and labels.

You also built a DataGraph component that you can use to display virtually any dataset in a variety of graph formats. This library enables you to save the graph to disk, send the graph to the printer, or copy the graph to the Windows Clipboard for placement in other Windows programs by way of the Paste Special operation.

While building the graph library, you learned how to declare and use enumerated constants to improve the readability of your Visual Basic code.

Quiz

1. List the advantages of including graphics in your Visual Basic database applications.

2. Describe the purpose of the ColumnCount and RowCount properties of the Chart Control.

3. What data type must be used for the array that will be sent to the Microsoft Chart Control's ChartData property?

4. What do the following methods do?

    ```
    EditCopy
    EditPaste
    ```

5. What is an enumerated type declaration and why is it useful?

Exercise

Assume that you are an analyst for your regional airport. The Manager of Operations wants information on passenger activity throughout the year. He is an extremely busy individual who does not understand database applications. In order to help him perform his job better, you have decided to create some graphs for him to review.

Perform the following steps in completing this project:

1. Build a database using Visdata or Data Manager. Name this database Ch10Ex.MDB.

2. Build a table in this database and name it Activity. Include three fields: Airline (TEXT 10), Month (INTEGER), and Passengers (INTEGER).

3. Insert the following records into your table:

Airline	Month	Passengers
ABC	1	2562
ABC	2	4859
ABC	3	4235
ABC	4	4897
ABC	5	5623
ABC	6	4565
ABC	7	5466
ABC	8	2155
ABC	9	4455
ABC	10	5454
ABC	11	5488
ABC	12	5456
ABC	9	5468
LMN	1	1956
LMN	2	2135
LMN	3	5221

LMN	4	2153
LMN	5	2154
LMN	6	5125
LMN	7	2135
LMN	8	5465
LMN	9	5555
LMN	10	2536
LMN	11	2153
LMN	12	2168
XYZ	1	10251
XYZ	2	12123
XYZ	3	10258
XYZ	4	12000
XYZ	5	21564
XYZ	6	21321
XYZ	7	14564
XYZ	8	12365
XYZ	9	21356
XYZ	10	21357
XYZ	11	21321
XYZ	12	12365

10

4. Start a new Visual Basic project that uses the DataGraph component you created today. Build a form and add three command buttons: cmdArea, cmdLine, and cmdBar.

5. Display the following graphs when each button is pressed:

cmdArea: Displays a 3D area chart that shows comparative activity for the first month.

cmdLine: Displays a line graph that shows total passenger activity by month.
cmdBar: Displays a 3D bar graph for the activity of ABC Airlines for the entire year.

DAY 11

Data-Bound List Boxes, Grids, and Subforms

Today, you learn about the use of data-bound lists, combo boxes, and grids in your Visual Basic 6 database applications. Before Visual Basic, incorporating list boxes, combo boxes, and grids into an application was an arduous task that required a great deal of coding and program maintenance. Now, Visual Basic 6 ships with the tools you need to add lists, combo boxes, and data grids to your project with very little coding.

You learn how to add features to your data entry forms that provide pick lists that support and enforce the database relationships already defined in your data tables. You also learn the difference between data lists and combo boxes and where it's appropriate to use them.

Today, you also learn how to easily add a data grid to your form to show more than one record at a time in a table form. This grid can be used for display only or for data entry. Today, you learn how to decide which is the best method for your project.

After you learn how to use the data-bound list, combo box, and grid, you'll see an example using a custom control that provides an easy "find" dialog for all your data entry forms. Finally, you learn how to build a data entry Subform that combines all three controls on a single form.

The Data-Bound List and Combo Boxes

The data-bound list and combo controls are used in conjunction with the data control to enable you to display multiple rows of data in the same control. This provides you with a pick list of values displayed in a list or combo box. You can use these types of controls on your data entry forms to speed data entry, provide tighter data entry validation and control, and give users suggested correct values for the data entry field.

Setting up data-bound lists and combo boxes is a bit trickier than setting up standard data-bound controls. But once you get the hang of it, you'll want to use data-bound lists and combo boxes in every data entry screen you can.

Using the Data-Bound List Box

Although the data-bound list control looks like the standard list control, there are several differences between the two. The data-bound list control has properties that provide the data-binding aspects that are not found in the standard list control (for example, the data-bound list control is self-populating, and the standard list control is not). The first two of these properties are the RowSource and ListField properties of the data-bound list control:

- RowSource is the name of the Recordset object that is providing the dataset used to fill the data-bound list box.
- ListField is the name of the column in the RowSource dataset that is used to fill the list box. This is the display field for the list.

These two properties are used to bind the list control to a data control. After these two properties are set, Visual Basic 6 automatically populates the list control for you when you open the data entry form.

Let's start a new project and illustrate the data-bound list control. When you start the new project, you must make sure you have added the data-bound list controls to your project. Select the Project|Components item from the Visual Basic 6 main menu. Locate and select the Microsoft Data Bound List Controls 6.0 item. Your screen should look like the one in Figure 11.1.

FIGURE 11.1

Adding the data-bound list controls to your project.

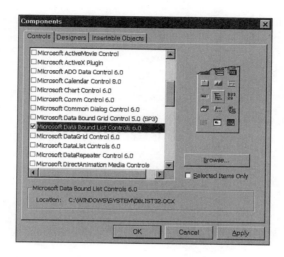

Now you need to add the data-bound list control, a standard data control, and two labels and text boxes to a form. Use Table 11.1 and Figure 11.2 as guides as you build your first data-bound list project. Be sure to save your work periodically. Save the form as LSTCNTRL.FRM and the project as LSTCNTRL.VBP.

11

FIGURE 11.2

Laying out the LSTCNTRL form.

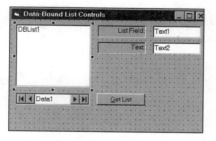

> **Tip**
>
> If you lay out the controls in the order in which they are listed in the table, you can use the down arrows of most of the property fields to get a selection list for the field names, and so on. This saves you some typing.

TABLE 11.1   THE CONTROLS FOR THE CH1301.VBP PROJECT

Controls	Properties	Settings
Form	Name	LSTCNTRL
	Caption	Data-Bound List Controls

continues

TABLE 11.1 CONTINUED

Controls	Properties	Settings
	Left	1215
	Top	1170
	Width	4995
DataControl	Name	Data1
	Caption	Data1
	DatabaseName	C:\TYSDBVB6\SOURCE\DATA\ LSTCNTRL.MDB
	Height	300
	Left	120
	RecordsetType	2 - Snapshot
	RecordSource	ValidNames
	Top	1860
	Width	1875
DBList	Name	DBList1
	Height	1620
	Left	120
	RowSource	Data1
	ListField	NameText
	Top	120
	Width	1875
Label	Name	Label1
	Alignment	1 - Right justify
	BorderStyle	1 - Fixed Single
	Caption	List Field:
	Height	300
	Left	2160
	Top	120
	Width	1200
Label	Name	Label2
	Alignment	1 - Right Justify
	BorderStyle	1 - Fixed Single
	Caption	Text:

Controls	Properties	Settings
	Height	300
	Left	2160
	Top	540
	Width	1200
Textbox	Name	Text1
	Height	300
	Left	3540
	Top	120
	Width	1200
Textbox	Name	Text2
	Height	300
	Left	3540
	Top	540
	Width	1200
Command Button	Name	cmdGetList
	Caption	&Get List
	Height	300
	Left	2160
	Top	1860
	Width	1200

11

Notice that in the preceding table, a single data control has been added to open the database and create a Snapshot object of the ValidNames table. It's always a good idea to use Snapshot objects as the RowSource for data-bound lists and combo boxes. Snapshot objects are static views of the dataset and, even though they take up more workstation memory than Dynaset objects, they run faster. Notice also that you set the ListField property of the data-bound list to NameText. This fills the control with the values stored in the NameText column of the dataset.

Now you need to add two lines of code to the project. Open the cmdGetList_Click event and enter the following lines of code:

```
Private Sub cmdGetList_Click()
Text1 = DBList1.ListField
Text2 = DBList1.TEXT
End Sub
```

These two lines of code update the text box controls each time you press the GetList button on the form. That way you are able to see the current values of the ListField and Text properties of the data-bound list control.

Save the form as LSTCNTRL.FRM and the project as LSTCNTRL.VBP. Now run the project. When the form first comes up, you see the list box already filled with all the values in the NameText column of the dataset (that is, the ListField used for the DBList). Select one of the items in the list box by clicking on it. Now press the GetList button. You see the two text controls updated with the ListField and Text values of the list control. Your screen should look like the one in Figure 11.3.

FIGURE 11.3

Running the
LSTCNTRL.VBP
project.

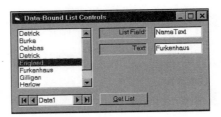

The data-bound list control has two more properties that you need to know about. These are the properties that you can use to create an output value based on the item selected from the list:

- BoundColumn is the name of the column in the RowSource dataset that is used to provide the output of the list selection. This can be the same column designated in the ListField property, or it can be any other column in the RowSource dataset.
- BoundText is the value of the column designated by the BoundColumn property. This is the actual output of the list selection.

Usually, data-bound lists present the user with a familiar set of names. The user can pick from these names, and then the program uses the selection to locate a more computer-like ID or code represented by the familiar name selected by the user. The table created for this example contains just such information.

Set the BoundColumn property of the data-bound list control to point to the NameID column of the ValidNames dataset. To do this, select the data-bound list control and then press F4 to bring up the property window if it is not already displayed. Now locate the BoundColumn property and set it to NameID.

Add two more labels and text boxes to display the new properties. Do this by selecting the existing two labels and the two text controls, all as a set. Then select Edit | Copy. This places the four selected controls on the Clipboard. Now select Edit | Paste from the Visual

Basic 6 main menu. This places copies of the controls on your new form. Answer Yes to the prompts that ask whether you want to create a control array. Set the Caption properties of the two new labels to Bound Column: and Bound Text:. Use Figure 11.4 as a guide in laying out the new controls.

FIGURE 11.4

Adding new controls to the LSTCNTRL.VBP project.

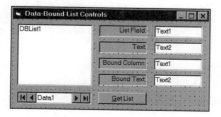

Finally, modify the code in the cmdGetList_Click event to match the following code. This shows you the results of the new BoundColumn and BoundText properties:

```
Private Sub cmdGetList_Click()
Text1(0) = DBList1.ListField
Text2(0) = DBList1.TEXT
Text1(1) = DBList1.BoundColumn
Text2(1) = DBList1.BoundText
End Sub
```

Notice that you added the array references to the code to account for the new control arrays. Now save and run the project. When you select an item from the list and click the GetList button, you'll see the BoundColumn and BoundText properties displayed in the appropriate textboxes, as shown in Figure 11.5.

FIGURE 11.5

Displaying the new BoundColumn and BoundText properties.

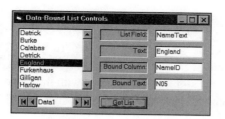

Note

You can also activate the GetList event by entering cmdGetList_Click in the Dbl_Click event of DBList. The user can get the same results by selecting the command button or by double-clicking the item in the list. This type of call provides a quick way of adding functionality to your code. You don't need to enter or maintain the code in both events.

The data that is produced by the BoundText property can be used to update another column in a separate table. The easiest way to do this is to add a second data control and link the data-bound list control to that second data control. You can do this by setting the following two properties of the data-bound list control:

- DataSource is the dataset that is updated by the output of the data-bound list control. This is the data control used to open the destination Recordset.

- DataField is the name of the column in the Recordset referred to by the DataSource property.

Now let's add a second data control to the form and a bound input control that is updated by the data-bound list. First, add a data control. Set its DatabaseName property to C:\TYSDBVB6\SOURCE\DATA\LSTCNTRL.MDB and its RecordSource property to Destination. Also, set the EOFAction property of the Data2 data control to AddNew. Now add a text control to the project. Set its DataSource property to Data2 and its DataField property to NameID. Use Figure 11.6 as a layout guide.

FIGURE 11.6

*Adding a second
data control and text
control.*

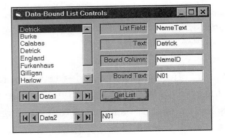

Before you save and run the project, set the DataSource and DataField properties of the data-bound list control. Set these to Data2 and NameID, respectively. This tells the list control to automatically update the Destination.NameID field. Now, each time a user selects an item in the list and then saves the dataset of the second control, the designated field of the second dataset is automatically updated with the value in the BoundColumn property of the data-bound list.

Save and run the project. This time, select the first item in the list by clicking on it. Now click on the GetList button to bring up the list properties in the text boxes. Force the second data control to save its contents by repositioning the record pointer: Click the leftmost arrow to force the second dataset to the first record in the set. You should now see that the second dataset, Destination, has been updated by the value in the BoundColumn property of the data-bound list. Your screen should look like the one in Figure 11.6.

Do this a few times to add records to the Destination table. Also notice that each time you move the record pointer of the Destination table, the data-bound control reads the value in the bound column and moves the list pointer to highlight the related NameText field. You now have a fully functional data-bound list box!

Using the Data-Bound Combo Box

The data-bound combo box works very much the same as the data-bound list control. The only difference is the way the data is displayed. The data-bound combo control can be used as a basic data entry text box with added validation. Enabling experienced users to type values they know are correct can speed up the data entry process. Also, new users are able to scan the list of valid entries until they learn them. The data-bound combo is an excellent data entry control.

Let's build a new project that shows how you can use the data-bound combo box to create friendly data entry forms. Start a new Visual Basic 6 project. Use Table 11.2 and Figure 11.7 as guides as you build your new form. Save your form as COMBO.FRM and the project as COMBO.VBP.

FIGURE 11.7

Laying out the COMBO.VBP project.

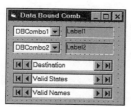

11

TABLE 11.2 THE CONTROLS FOR THE COMBO.VBP PROJECT

Controls	Properties	Settings
Form	Name	frmCombo
	Caption	Data Bound ComboBox
	Height	2500
	Left	2750
	Top	2500
	Width	3000
DataControl	Name	dtaDestination
	Caption	Destination
	DatabaseName	C:\TYSDBVB6\SOURCE\DATA\ LSTCNTRL.MDB
	EOFAction	2 - AddNew

continues

TABLE 11.2   CONTINUED

Controls	Properties	Settings
	Height	300
	Left	120
	RecordsetType	1 - Dynaset
	RecordSource	Destination
	Top	960
	Width	2535
DataControl	Name	dtaValidStates
	Caption	Valid States
	DatabaseName	C:\TYSDBVB6\SOURCE\DATA\ LSTCNTRL.MDB
	Height	300
	Left	120
	RecordsetType	2 - Snapshot
	RecordSource	"ValidStates"
	Top	1320
	Visible	False
	Width	2535
DataControl	Name	dtaValidNames
	Caption	Valid Names
	DatabaseName	C:\TYSDBVB6\SOURCE\DATA\ LSTCNTRL.MDB
	Height	300
	Left	120
	RecordsetType	2 - Snapshot
	RecordSource	ValidNames
	Top	1680
	Visible	False
	Width	2535
DBCombo	Name	DBCombo1
	DataSource	dtaDestination
	DataField	StateCode
	Height	315

Controls	Properties	Settings
	Left	120
	RowSource	dtaValidStates
	ListField	StateName
	BoundColumn	StateCode
	Top	120
	Width	1200
DBCombo	Name	DBCombo2
	DataSource	dtaDestination
	DataField	NameID
	Height	315
	Left	120
	Top	540
	Width	1200
	RowSource	dtaValidNames
	ListField	NameText
	BoundColumn	NameID
Label	Name	Label1
	BorderStyle	1 - Fixed Single
	DataSource	dtaDestination
	DataField	StateCode
	Height	300
	Left	1440
	Top	120
	Width	1200
Label	Name	Label2
	BorderStyle	1 - Fixed Single
	DataSource	dtaDestination
	DataField	NameID
	Height	300
	Left	1440
	Top	540
	Width	1200

11

You need to add two lines of code to the project before it's complete. The following lines force Visual Basic 6 to update the form controls as soon as the user makes a selection in the combo box:

```
Private Sub DBCombo1_Click(Area As Integer)
Label1 = DBCombo1.BoundText
End Sub

Private Sub DBCombo2_Click(Area As Integer)
Label2 = DBCombo2.BoundText
End Sub
```

Save the form as COMBO.FRM and the project as COMBO.VBP. Now run the project and check your screen against the one in Figure 11.8.

FIGURE 11.8

Running the COMBO.VBP
project.

You can make selections in either of the two combo boxes and see that the label controls are updated automatically. Also, you can move through the dataset using the data control arrow buttons and watch the two combo boxes automatically update as each record changes.

Deciding When to Use the List Box or Combo Box

The choice between list and combo controls depends on the type of data-entry screen you have and the amount of real estate available to your data entry form. Typically, you should use lists where you want to show users more than one possible entry. This encourages them to scroll through the list and locate the desired record. The data-bound list control doesn't allow users to enter their own values in the list. Therefore, you should not use the data-bound list control if you want to allow users to add new values to the list.

The data-bound combo box is a good control to use when you are short on form space. You can provide the functionality of a list box without using as much space. Also, combo boxes have the added benefit of enabling users to type in their selected values. This is very useful for users who are performing heads-down data entry. They type the exact values right at the keyboard without using the mouse or checking a list. Also, novices can use the same form to learn about valid list values without slowing down the more experienced users.

The Data-Bound Grid

The data-bound grid control in Visual Basic 6 adds power and flexibility to your database programs. You can easily provide grid access to any available database. You can provide simple display-only access for use with summary data and onscreen reports. You can also provide editing capabilities to your data grid, including modify only, add rights, or delete rights.

Creating Your First Data-Bound Grid Form

It's really quite easy to create a data-bound grid form. First, start a new Visual Basic 6 project. Next, make sure you add the data-bound grid tool to your list of custom controls. To do this, select Project | Components from the Visual Basic 6 main menu. Locate and select the Microsoft Data Bound Grid Control. Your screen should resemble Figure 11.9.

FIGURE 11.9

Adding the data-bound grid control to your project.

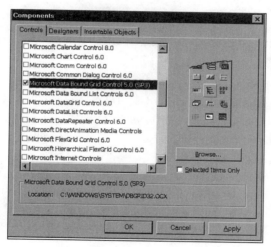

Now drop a standard data control on the form. Place it at the bottom of the form. Set the `DatabaseName` property to `C:\TYSDBVB6\SOURCE\DATA\DBGRID.MDB` and the `RecordSource` property to `HeaderTable`. Now place the data-bound grid tool on the form and set its `DataSource` property to `Data1`. That's all there is to it. Now save the form as `DBGRID.FRM` and the project as `DBGRID.VBP` and run the project. Your screen should look like the one in Figure 11.10.

You can move through the grid by clicking the left margin of the grid control. You can also move through the grid by clicking the navigation arrows of the data control. If you select a cell in the grid, you can edit that cell. As soon as you leave the row, that cell is updated by Visual Basic 6. Right now, you cannot add or delete records from the grid. You'll add those features in the next example.

FIGURE 11.10

Running the first data-bound grid project.

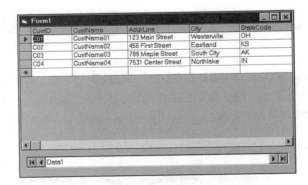

Adding and Deleting Records with the Data-Bound Grid

It's very easy to include add and delete capabilities with the data grid. Bring up the same project you just completed. Select the data grid control and press F4 to bring up the Properties window if it is not already displayed. Locate the `AllowAddNew` property and the `AllowDelete` property and set them to `True`. You now have add and delete power within the grid.

Before you run this project, make two other changes. Set the `Visible` property of the data control to `False`. Because you can navigate through the grid using scroll bars and the mouse, you don't need the data control arrow buttons. Second, set the `Align` property of the grid control to `1 - vbAlignTop`. This forces the grid to hug the top and sides of the form whenever it is resized.

Now save and run the project. Notice that you can resize the columns. Figure 11.11 shows the resized form with several columns adjusted.

To add a record to the data grid, you place the cursor at the first field in the empty row at the bottom of the grid and start typing. Use Figure 11.12 as a guide. Visual Basic 6 creates a new line for you and enables you to enter data. Note how the record pointer turns into a pencil as you type. When you leave the line, Visual Basic 6 saves the record to the dataset.

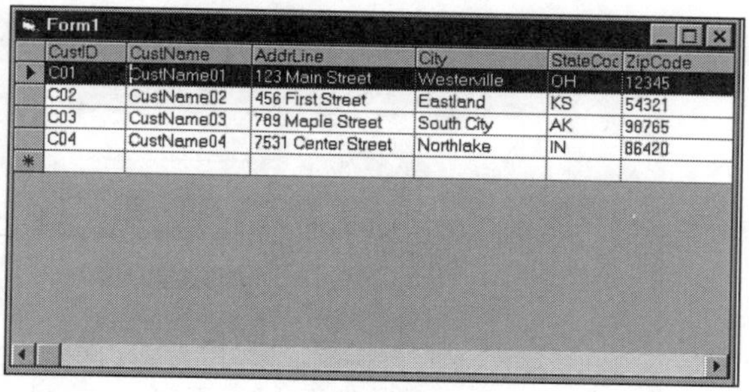

FIGURE 11.11

Resizing the form and columns of a data grid control.

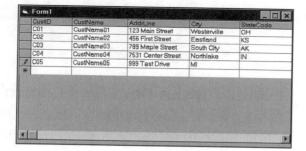

FIGURE 11.12

Adding a record to the data grid.

11

Setting Other Design-Time Properties of the Data Grid

A problem with resizing the form at runtime is that the moment you close the form, all the column settings are lost. You can prevent this problem by resizing the form at design-time. If you haven't done so, end the program and return to design mode. Next select the data grid control and press the alternate mouse button. This brings up the context menu. Select Retrieve Fields. This loads the column names of the dataset into the grid control. Next, select Edit from the context menu. Now you can resize the columns of the control. The dimensions of these columns are stored in the control and used each time the form is loaded.

You can modify the names of the column headers at design-time by using the built-in tabbed property sheet. To do this, click the alternate mouse button while the grid control is selected. When the context menu appears, select Properties from this menu. You should now see a series of tabs that enable you to set several grid-level and column-level properties. (See Figure 11.13.)

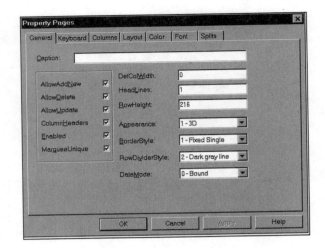

FIGURE 11.13

Using the data grid tabbed properties page.

Trapping Events for the Data Grid Control

The data grid control has several unique events that you can use to monitor user actions in your grid. The following events can be used to check the contents of your data table before you allow the user to continue:

- `BeforeInsert` occurs before a new row is inserted into the grid. Use this event to confirm that the user wants to add a new record.
- `AfterInsert` occurs right after a new row has been inserted into the grid. Use this event to perform cleanup chores after a new record has been added.
- `BeforeUpdate` occurs before the data grid writes the changes to the data control. Use this event to perform data validation at the record level.
- `AfterUpdate` occurs after the changed data has been written to the data control. Use this event to perform miscellaneous chores after the grid has been updated.
- `BeforeDelete` occurs before the selected record(s) are deleted from the grid. Use this event to perform confirmation chores before deleting data.
- `AfterDelete` occurs after the user has already deleted the data from the grid. Use this event to perform related chores after the grid has been updated.

You can use the events listed here to perform field and record-level validation and force user confirmation on critical events, such as adding a new record or deleting an existing record. Let's add some code to the `DBGRID.VBP` project to illustrate the use of these events.

The Add Record Events

First, add code that monitors the adding of new records to the grid. Select the grid control and open the DBGrid1_BeforeInsert event. Add the code in Listing 11.1.

LISTING 11.1 CODE TO MONITOR ADDITION OF NEW RECORDS TO A DATA-BOUND GRID

```
 1: Private Sub DBGrid1_BeforeInsert(Cancel As Integer)
 2: '
 3: ' make user confirm add operation
 4: '
 5: Dim nResult As Integer
 6: '
 7: nResult = MsgBox("Do you want to add a new record?", _
 8: vbInformation + vbYesNo, "DBGrid.BeforeInsert")
 9: If nResult = vbNo Then
10: Cancel = True    ' cancel add
11: End If
12: End Sub
```

In Listing 11.1, you present a message to the user to confirm the intention to add a new record to the set. If the answer is No, the add operation is canceled.

Now let's add code that tells the user the add operation has been completed. Add the following code in the DBGrid1_AfterInsert event window:

```
Private Sub DBGrid1_AfterInsert()
'
' tell user what you just did!
'
MsgBox "New record written to data set!", vbInformation, _
  "DBGrid.AfterInsert"
End Sub
```

Now save and run the project. Go to the last row in the grid. Begin entering a new record. As soon as you press the first key, the confirmation message appears. (See Figure 11.14.)

After you fill in all the columns and attempt to move to another record in the grid, you see the message telling you that the new record was added to the dataset.

The Update Record Events

Now add some code that monitors attempts to update existing records. Add Listing 11.2 to the DBGrid1.BeforeUpdate event.

11

FIGURE 11.14

Attempting to add a record to the grid.

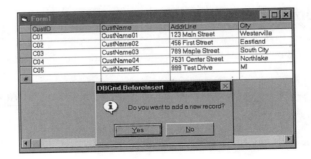

LISTING 11.2 CODE TO MONITOR FOR ATTEMPTED DATA UPDATES

```
 1: Private Sub DBGrid1_BeforeUpdate(Cancel As Integer)
 2: '
 3: ' make user confirm update operation
 4: '
 5: Dim nResult As Integer
 6: '
 7: nResult = MsgBox("Write any changes to data set?", _
 8:  vbInformation + vbYesNo, "DBGrid.BeforeUpdate")
 9: If nResult = vbNo Then
10: Cancel = True    ' ignore changes
11: DBGrid1.ReBind   ' reset all values
12: End If
13: End Sub
```

This code looks similar to the code used to monitor the add record events. The only difference is that you force the ReBind method to refresh the data grid after the canceled attempt to update the record.

Now add the code to confirm the update of the record. Add the following code to the DBGrid1.AfterUpdate event:

```
Private Sub DBGrid1_AfterUpdate()
'
' tell 'em!
'
MsgBox "The record has been updated.", vbInformation, "DBGrid.AfterUpdate"
End Sub
```

Save and run the project. When you press a key in any column of an existing record, you see a message asking you to confirm the update. When you move off the record, you see a message telling you the record has been updated.

The Delete Record Events

Add some events to track any attempts to delete existing records. Place the code in Listing 11.3 in the DBGrid1.BeforeDelete event.

LISTING 11.3 CODE TO TRACK FOR RECORD DELETES

```
 1: Private Sub DBGrid1_BeforeDelete(Cancel As Integer)
 2: '
 3: ' force user to confirm delete operation
 4: '
 5: Dim nResult As Integer
 6: '
 7: nResult = MsgBox("Delete the current record?", _
 8:   vbInformation + vbYesNo, "DBGrid.BeforeDelete")
 9: If nResult = vbNo Then
10: Cancel = True    ' cancel delete op
11: End If
12: End Sub
```

Again, no real news here. Simply ask the user to confirm the delete operation. If the answer is No, the operation is canceled. Now add the code to report the results of the delete. Put this code in the DBGrid1.AfterDelete event:

```
Private Sub DBGrid1_AfterDelete()
'
' tell user the news!
'
MsgBox "Record has been deleted", vbInformation, "DBGrid.AfterDelete"
End Sub
```

Save and run the project. Select an entire record by clicking the left margin of the grid. This highlights all the columns in the row. To delete the record, press the Delete key or Ctrl+X. When the message pops up asking you to confirm the delete, answer No to cancel. (See Figure 11.15.)

Column-Level Events

Several column-level events are available for the data grid. The following are only two of them:

- BeforeColUpdate occurs before the column is updated with any changes made by the user. Use this event to perform data validation before the update occurs.
- AfterColUpdate occurs after the column has been updated with user changes. Use this event to perform other duties after the value of the column has been updated.

FIGURE 11.15

Attempting to delete a
record from the grid.

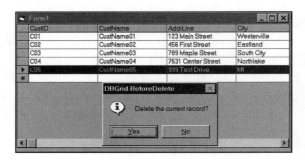

 Note   Refer to the Visual Basic 6 documentation for a list of all the events associated with the DBGrid control.

These events work just like the `BeforeUpdate` and `AfterUpdate` events seen earlier. However, instead of occurring when the record value is updated, the `BeforeColUpdate` and `AfterColUpdate` events occur whenever a column value is changed. This gives you the ability to perform field-level validation within the data grid.

Add some code in the `BeforeColUpdate` event to force the user to confirm the update of a column. Open the `DBGrid.BeforeColUpdate` event and enter the code in Listing 11.4.

LISTING 11.4   CODE TO REQUEST CONFIRMATION ON COLUMN UPDATES

```
 1: Private Sub DBGrid1_BeforeColUpdate(ByVal ColIndex As Integer, _
 2:   OldValue As Variant, Cancel As Integer)
 3: '
 4: ' ask user for confirmation
 5: '
 6: Dim nResult As Integer
 7: '
 8: nResult = MsgBox("Write changes to Column", vbInformation + vbYesNo, _
 9:   "DBGrid.BeforeColUpdate")
10: If nResult = vbNo Then
11: Cancel = False       ' cancel change & get old value
12: End If
13: End Sub
```

Now add the code that tells the user the column has been updated as requested. Place the following code in the `DBGrid1.AfterColUpdate` event:

```
Private Sub DBGrid1_AfterColUpdate(ByVal ColIndex As Integer)
'
```

```
' tell user
'
MsgBox "Column has been updated", vbInformation, "DBGrid.AfterColUpdate"
End Sub
```

Save and run the project. Now, each time you attempt to alter a column, you are asked to confirm the column update. (See Figure 11.16.)

FIGURE 11.16

Updating a grid column.

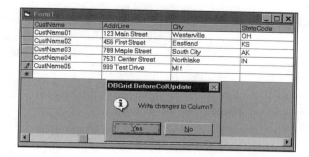

You can also see a message when you leave the column telling you that the data has been changed.

Using the `dbFind` Custom Control

A very common use of the data-bound list control is the creation of a dialog box that lists all the primary keys in a table. This dialog enables users to select an item from the list and then displays the complete data record that is associated with the primary key. In this section, you use a custom control that does just that. When you're done with this project, you'll be able to place this control on any Visual Basic form and add an instant `find` dialog to all your Visual Basic forms.

Testing the `dbFind` Custom Control

This project utilizes a Visual Basic ActiveX control. This control, named `dbFind`, shipped with the CD-ROM included with this book. This project utilizes this control to populate the elements of a data form.

The source code for the `dbFind` ActiveX control can be found on the CD-ROM and was installed on your workstation with the rest of the source code of the book. To use this control in this projects, add the `DBFIND.VBP` project to your current Visual Basic IDE.

11

Note

If you wish, you can load the DBFIND.VBP project into Visual Basic first and then compile it as an ActiveX control. Then you can use the compiled control in other Visual Basic projects, too.

Now start a new Visual Basic 6 project and build the following form. Use Table 11.3 and Figure 11.17 as guides. Please note that you are adding a dbFind control to this form. To do this, select File | Add Project from the main Visual Basic menu and locate the DBFIND.VBP project in the \TYSDBVB6\SOURCE\CHAP11\DBFIND folder. When you load the project source code into the Visual Basic editor, it is the same as loading the compiled control using the Project | Components menu option.

FIGURE 11.17

Laying out the test form.

Caution

If you fail to add the dbFind.VBP project to the Visual Basic IDE, you will not be able to use the dbFind control in this test project. Be sure to start a new Visual Basic project for the test project and then use the File | Add Project menu option to add the source code of the dbFind.VBP project to the IDE. Then the dbFind control will appear in the toolbar of the test project.

TABLE 11.3 THE TEST FORM LAYOUT

Control	Property	Setting
Form	Name	FrmTest
	Caption	"Form1"
	Height	1680
	Left	60
	Top	345
	Width	3950
	StartUpPosition	2 - CenterScreen
dbFind	Name	dbFind1

Control	Property	Setting
	Height	315
	Left	2640
	Top	240
	Width	315
Data	Name	Data1
	Align	2 'Align Bottom
	DatabaseName	C:\TYSDBVB6\Source\ Data\BOOKS6.MDB
	RecordSource	"Authors"
	Top	1464
	Width	3852
TextBox	Name	Text3
	DataSource	"Data1"
	Height	315
	Left	1380
	Top	960
	Width	1200
TextBox	Name	Text2
	DataSource	"Data1"
	Height	315
	Left	1380
	Top	600
	Width	2400
TextBox	Name	Text1
	DataSource	"Data1"
	Height	315
	Left	1380
	Top	240
	Width	1200
Label	Name	Label3
	Caption	"Date of Birth"
	Height	315
	Left	120

11

continues

TABLE 11.3   CONTINUED

Control	Property	Setting
	top	960
	Width	1215
Label	Name	Label2
	Caption	"Author Name"
	Height	315
	Left	120
	Top	600
	Width	1215
Label	Name	Label1
	Caption	"Author ID"
	Height	315
	Left	120
	Top	240
	Width	1215

You now need to add just a little code to this project. Listing 11.5 shows the code for the
Form_Load event. Add this to your project.

LISTING 11.5   CODING THE Form_Load EVENT

```
 1: Private Sub Form_Load()
 2: '
 3: ' set database control values
 4: Data1.DatabaseName = "c:\tysdbvb6\source\data\books6.mdb"
 5: Data1.RecordSource = "Authors"
 6: '
 7: ' set field binding
 8: Text1.DataField = "AUID"
 9: Text2.DataField = "Name"
10: Text3.DataField = "DOB"
11: '
12: ' set up dbfind control
13: dbFind1.DatabaseName = Data1.DatabaseName
14: dbFind1.RecordSource = "SELECT * FROM Authors ORDER BY Name"
15: dbFind1.BoundColumn = "AUID"
16: dbFind1.ListField = "Name"
17: dbFind1.Refresh
18: '
19: ' some other nice stuff
```

```
20: Me.Caption = Data1.RecordSource
21: '
22: End Sub
```

The code in Listing 11.5 sets up the data control properties, binds the text boxes to the Data1 control, and then sets up the dbFind1 control properties. Notice that the RecordSource for the dbFind1 control is the same data table used for the Data1 control. The only difference is that the dbFind1 control dataset is sorted by Name. This means that when the user presses the Find button, the dbFind dialog displays the records in Name order.

 Note | Most of the code in Listing 11.5 repeats property settings that can be performed at design-time. They are set here in order to show you how the Data1 and dbFind1 properties are closely related.

The only other code you need in this form is a list of code in the dbFind1_Selected event that repositions the data pointer to display the record selected by the user. Add the following code to the dbFind1_Selected event:

```
Private Sub dbFind1_Selected(SelectValue As Variant)
'
' re-position record based on return value
'
Data1.Recordset.FindFirst Text1.DataField & "=" & SelectValue
'
End Sub
```

Now save the form (FRMTEST.FRM) and project (PRJTEST.VBP), and then run the test form. When you press the Find button, you should see a dialog box that lists all the records in the table, in Name order (see Figure 11.18).

FIGURE 11.18

Running the test form.

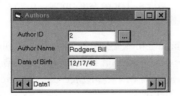

When you select a name from the list (highlight a name and press OK or double-click the name), you see that the main form returns to focus and the data pointer is moved to display the selected record. You now have a custom control that offers instant "find" features by adding just a few lines of code to your projects.

Using the Data Grid to Create a Subform

In this last section of the chapter, you use the data grid to create one of the most common forms of data entry screens, the Subform. Subforms are data entry forms that actually contain two forms within the same screen. Usually, Subforms are used to combine standard form layout data entry screens with view-only or view-and-edit lists. For example, if you want to create a form that shows customer information (name, address, and so on) at the top of the form and a list of invoices outstanding for that customer at the bottom of the form, you have a Subform type entry screen.

Typically, Subforms are used to display data tables linked through relationship definitions. In the case just mentioned, the customer information is probably in a single master table, and the invoice data is probably in a related list table that is linked through the customer ID or some other unique field. When you have these types of relationships, Subforms make an excellent way to present data.

If you spend much time programming databases, you meet up with the need for a good Subform strategy. Let's go through the process of designing and coding a Subform using Visual Basic 6 data-bound controls, especially the data grid.

Designing the Subform

For this exercise, you have a database that already exists, BOOKS6.MDB, which contains two tables. The first table is called Header. It contains all the information needed to fill out a header on an invoice or monthly statement, such as CustID, CustName, Address, City, State, and Zip. There is also a table called SalesData. This table contains a list of each invoice currently on file for the customer, and it includes the CustID, Invoice Number, Invoice Description, and the Invoice Amount. The two tables are linked through the CustID field that exists in both tables. There is a one-to-many (Header-to-SalesData) relationship defined for the two tables.

You now need to design a form that enables users to browse through the master table (Header), displaying all the address information for review and update. At the same time, you need to provide the user with a view of the invoice data on the same screen. As the customer records are changed, the list of invoices must also be changed. You need a Subform.

Laying Out and Coding the Subform with Visual Basic 6

Start a new project in Visual Basic 6. Lay out the Header table information at the top of the form and the SalesTable information in a grid at the bottom of the form. You need two data controls (one for the Header table and one for the SalesTable), one grid for the sales data, and several label and input controls for the Header data. Use Table 11.4 and Figure 11.19 as guides as you lay out the Subform.

FIGURE 11.19

Laying out the Header/Sales SubForm example.

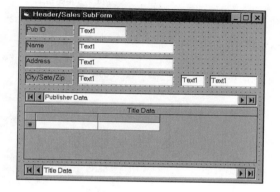

The controls table and Figure 11.19 contain almost all the information you need to design and code the Visual Basic 6 Subform. Notice that all the textbox and label controls have the same name. These are part of a control array. Lay out the first label/textbox pair. Then use the alternate mouse button to copy and repeatedly paste these two buttons until you have all the fields you need for your form.

Tip

Not only is it easier to build forms using control arrays because you save a lot of typing, but it also saves workstation resources. To Visual Basic 6, each control is a resource that must be allotted memory for tracking. Control arrays are counted as a single resource, no matter how many members you have in the array.

TABLE 11.4 THE CONTROLS FOR THE SUBFORM PROJECT

Controls	Properties	Settings
Form	Name	frmSubForm
	Caption	Header/Sales SubForm

continues

TABLE 11.4   CONTINUED

Controls	Properties	Settings
	Height	4545
	Left	1395
	Top	1335
	Width	6180
Data Control	Name	Data1
	Caption	Publisher Data
	DatabaseName	C:\TYSDBVB6\SOURCE\ DATA\BOOKS6.MDB
	EOfAction	2 - AddNew
	Height	300
	Left	120
	RecordsetType	1 - Dynaset
	RecordSource	Publishers
	Top	1800
	Width	5835
Data Control	Name	Data2
	Caption	Titles Data
	DatabaseName	C:\TYSDBVB6\SOURCE\ DATA\BOOKS6.MDB
	EOFAction	2 - AddNew
	Height	300
	Left	120
	RecordsetType	1 - Dynaset
	RecordSource	Titles
	Top	3780
	Visible	0 - False
	Width	5835
Text Box	Name	Text1
	DataSource	Data1
	DataField	PubID
	Height	300
	Left	1440

Controls	Properties	Settings
	Top	120
	Width	1200
Text Box	Name	Text1
	DataSource	Data1
	DataField	Name
	Height	300
	Left	1440
	Top	540
	Width	2400
Text Box	Name	Text1
	DataSource	Data1
	DataField	Address
	Height	300
	Left	1440
	Top	960
	Width	2400
Text Box	Name	Text1
	DataSource	Data1
	DataField	City
	Height	300
	Left	1440
	Top	1380
	Width	2400
Text Box	Name	Text1
	DataSource	Data1
	DataField	StateProv
	Height	300
	Left	4020
	Top	1380
	Width	600
Text Box	Name	Text1
	DataSource	Data1
	DataField	Zip

11

continues

TABLE 11.4   CONTINUED

Controls	Properties	Settings
	Height	300
	Left	4740
	Top	1380
	Width	1200
Label	Name	Label1
	BorderStyle	1 - Fixed Single
	Caption	PubID
	Height	300
	Left	120
	Top	120
	Width	1200
Label	Name	Label1
	BorderStyle	1 - Fixed Single
	Caption	Name
	Height	300
	Left	120
	Top	540
	Width	1200
Label	Name	Label1
	BorderStyle	1 - Fixed Single
	Caption	Address
	Height	300
	Left	120
	Top	960
	Width	1200
Label	Name	Label1
	Borderstyle	1 - Fixed Single
	Caption	City/State/Zip
	Height	300
	Left	120
	Top	1380
	Width	1200

Controls	Properties	Settings
DBGrid	Name	DBGrid1
	Height	1455
	Left	120
	Top	2222
	Width	5835

It would be nice to say that you could build a Subform without using any Visual Basic 6 code, but that's not quite true. You need just over 10 lines of code to get your data grid at the bottom of the form linked to the master table at the top of the form. Place the code in Listing 11.6 in the Data1_Reposition event of the Publishers table data control.

LISTING 11.6 CODE TO UPDATE THE SUBFORM WITH THE Reposition EVENT

```
 1: Private Sub Data1_Reposition()
 2: '
 3: Dim strSQL As String
 4: Dim strKey As String
 5: '
 6: ' create select to load grid
 7: If Text1(0).Text = "" Then
 8: strKey = "0"
 9: Else
10: strKey = Trim(Text1(0).Text)
11: End If
12: '
13: strSQL = "SELECT ISBN,Title,YearPub FROM Titles WHERE PubID=" & strKey
14: Data2.RecordSource = strSQL   ' load grid-bound data control
15: Data2.Refresh    ' refresh data control
16: DBGrid1.ReBind   ' refresh grid
17: '
18: End Sub
```

The preceding code is used to create a new SQL SELECT statement using the PubID value of the Publishers table. This SQL statement is used to generate a new dataset for the Data2 data control. This is the control that supplies the data grid. After the new record source has been created, invoke the Refresh method to update the data control and the ReBind method to update the data grid. That's it; there are only 11 lines of Visual Basic code, including the comments. Now save the form as SUBFORM.FRM and the project as SUBFORM.VBP and run the program. When the form loads, you see the first record in the Header table displayed at the top of the form and a list of all the outstanding invoices for that customer in the grid at the bottom of the form (see Figure 11.20).

11

FIGURE 11.20

Running the Header/Sales Subform example.

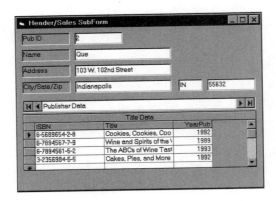

As you browse through the Publishers table, you see the data grid is updated, too. You can add records to the data grid or to the Publisher master. If this were a production project, you would add event-trapping features such as the ones mentioned in the previous section to maintain data integrity. You can also add the dbFind button to the header section of the form.

Summary

Today, you learned how to load and use three of the new data-bound controls that are shipped with Visual Basic 6:

- The data-bound list box
- The data-bound combo box
- The data-bound grid

You learned how to link these new controls to Recordsets using the Visual Basic 6 data controls and how to use these links to update related tables.

You also learned several of the important Visual Basic 6 events associated with the data grid. These events enable you to create user-friendly data entry routines using just a data control and the data grid.

You also used the dbFind custom control that uses a DBList control to build a data-bound list of all records in a table. This new control can be used to provide primary key (or some other unique value) selection dialogs to all your Visual Basic data entry forms.

Finally, you drew upon your knowledge of data grids, SQL, and form layout to design and implement a data entry Subform. This form showed a master table at the top and a related list table at the bottom of the form in a data-bound grid.

Quiz

1. What are some of the advantages of using a data-bound list or combo box?

2. What property of the data-bound list box do you set to identify the name of the Recordset object that provides the data to fill the list box?

3. What function does the BoundColumn property of the data-bound list box serve?

4. What data-bound list/combo box properties do you set to identify the destination dataset and field to be updated?

5. What properties of the data-bound grid control must be set to enable additions and removal of records?

6. What event of the data-bound grid control would you modify to prompt the user to confirm deletion of a record?

7. Why would you use the column-level events of the data-bound grid control?

8. When would you use the data-bound combo box instead of the data-bound list box?

9. What data-bound grid control method do you use to refresh the grid?

10. In what scenarios would you employ a Subform using a data grid?

Exercise

Assume that you have been assigned the responsibility of maintaining the BIBLIO.MDB database application that ships with Visual Basic 6. Your organization has determined that the information contained in this database will be of value to Help Desk personnel. The Help Desk Manager has come to you and requested a Visual Basic 6 application for Help Desk use.

Build a data form that contains a data-bound list box that displays the Name field from the Publishers table. After selection is made in this list box, text boxes should display PubID, CompanyName, Address, City, State, Zip, Telephone, and Fax of the publisher selected.

In addition, a listing of all publications of the selected publisher should appear in a data-bound grid Subform. For each entry, display the Title, Year Published, and ISBN from the Titles table.

Hint: You need to use three data controls for this form.

11

DAY 12

Creating Databases with SQL

The earlier lesson on SQL (Day 7, "Selecting Data with SQL") focused on SQL's Data Manipulation Language (DML) keywords. Today's work focuses on SQL's Data Definition Language (DDL) keywords.

On Day 7, you learned how easy it is to select and order data using the SQL `SELECT_FROM` clause. You also learned that using SQL statements to perform data selection means that your Visual Basic programs work with almost any back-end database server you might encounter in the future.

In today's lesson, you learn that you can use SQL statements to create your databases, too. Using SQL keywords to create your data tables, to set relationships, and to create indexes gives your programs an added level of portability. The SQL words you learn today work not only on Microsoft Access–formatted databases, but also on any database format that is SQL-compliant. The skills you learn today can be applied to almost every database engine on the market.

By the time you are through with today's lesson, you will be able to use SQL keywords to perform the following tasks:

- Create and delete data tables with the CREATE TABLE and DROP TABLE keywords.
- Add and delete fields in an existing data table using the ADD COLUMN and DROP COLUMN keywords.
- Create and delete indexes using the CREATE INDEX and DROP INDEX keywords.
- Define table relationships including foreign keys using the PRIMARY KEY and FOREIGN KEY_REFERENCES keywords.

Throughout today's lesson, you'll use a program called SQL-VB6. This is a Visual Basic program that processes SQL scripts. All the commands you learn today are in the form of SQL scripts. These scripts are text files that can be used in this program or ported to any other RDBMS script editor.

Using the SQL-VB6 Interpreter

Before you begin today's lesson in advanced SQL commands, you take a quick tour of the SQL-VB6 program and learn how to use SQL-VB6 to create, edit, and run SQL scripts. The SQL-VB6 Interpreter is a program that reads and executes SQL command scripts.

Loading and Running the SQL-VB6 Interpreter

 To load the SQL-VB6 Interpreter, locate the TYSDBVB6\SOURCE\SQLVB6 directory that was created from the installation CD-ROM that shipped with this book (for installation information, refer to the last page of this book). In the Windows Explorer or in File Manager, double-click on the SQLVB6.EXE file (this is a 32-bit application) to start the program. After the program loads, you should see a screen that looks similar to the one in Figure 12.1.

You can quickly run an SQL script from the opening screen. To test the system, let's load and run a simple test script. Using SQL-VB6, select the Execute icon, and at the Load SQLVB Script dialog, locate and select C:\TYSDBVB6\SOURCE\CHAP12\SQLVB01.SQV (see Figure 12.2).

When you select the script, SQL-VB6 begins to read and process the SQL commands in the file. This test script opens the BOOKS6.MDB database and then creates four resultsets and displays them on the screen (see Figure 12.3).

You can use your mouse pointer to resize individual columns and rows within a form. Figure 12.4 shows several of the ways you can alter the view of forms.

FIGURE 12.1

The opening screen for the SQL-VB6 *Interpreter.*

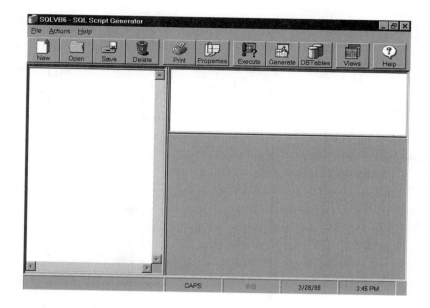

FIGURE 12.2

Loading the SQLvb01.SQV *SQL script.*

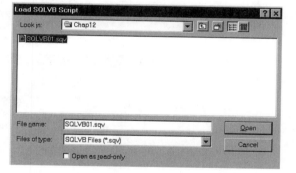

Creating and Editing SQL-VB6 Scripts

You can also use SQL-VB6 to create and edit SQL command scripts. For example, edit the SQLVB01.SQV script you tested earlier. First, load the script for editing by selecting File | Edit from the main menu. Locate and select the SQLVB01.SQV script.

Let's change the SQL script so that the first resultset includes only authors whose AUID is less than 7. To do this, add the text WHERE AUID<7; to the first SELECT statement. Be sure to place the semicolon (;) at the end of the line. SQL-VB6 needs this character to indicate the end of an SQL statement. Also, let's comment out the rest of the view sets for now. You want to see only one resultset in this test. To do this, add two slashes (//) to the start

of all the other lines that contain SELECT statements. Be sure to place a space after the / /
comment sign. Your script should now resemble Listing 12.1.

FIGURE 12.3

The completed
SQLVB01.SQV *script.*

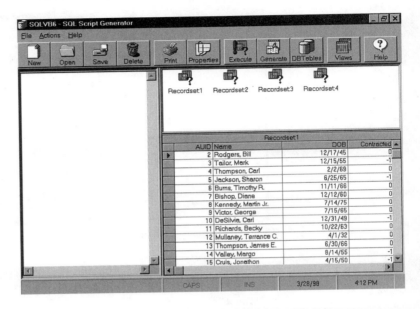

FIGURE 12.4

Altering the form views
within SQL-VB6.

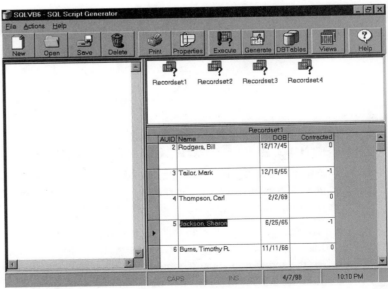

LISTING 12.1 MODIFYING AN SQL-VB6 SCRIPT

```
 1: //
 2: // test sql command file for sqlvb interpreter
 3: //
 4:
 5: // open the database
 6: dbOpen \tysdbvb6\source\data\books6.mdb;
 7:
 8: // open some tables to view
 9: SELECT * FROM Authors WHERE AUID<7;
10: // SELECT * FROM Publishers;
11: // SELECT * FROM Titles;
12: // SELECT * FROM Buyers;
13:
14: //
15: // eof
16: //
```

After you have changed the script, save it using the File | Save command. Now select Actions | Execute from the SQL-VB6 main menu to run the updated SQLVB01.SQV command script. Your results should look similar to those in Figure 12.5.

FIGURE 12.5

The results of the edited SQLVB01.SQV script.

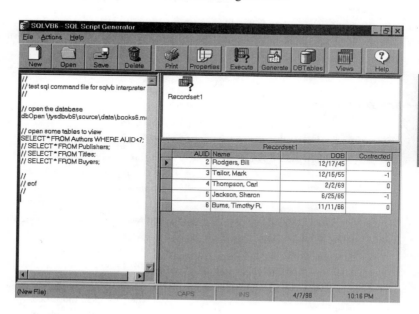

12

You can create new SQL-VB6 scripts by selecting File | New from the menu and entering any valid SQL statement into the editor. After you've created your script, save it with an .SQV file extension. Then use the Actions | Execute menu option to execute your script.

You need to know a few SQL-VB6 command syntax rules before you can create your own SQL-VB6 scripts. This is covered in the next section.

SQL-VB6 Command Syntax

The command syntax for SQL-VB6 is very similar to standard ANSI SQL syntax. In fact, any valid SQL command is a valid SQL-VB6 command. However, there are a few additional commands in SQL-VB6 that you should know about.

SQL-VB6 has three special non-SQL command words. These special commands are used to create, open, and close Microsoft Jet databases. SQL-VB6 also has a comment command. The comment command indicates to SQL-VB6 that the information on this line is for comment only and should not be executed. Finally, each command line must end with a semicolon (;). The semicolon tells SQL-VB6 where the command line ends. The special command words, their meanings, and examples are included in Table 12.1.

Note

> Any SQL editor that you use will have its own set of commands. For example, the use of two slashes (//) to indicate comments is SQL-VB6–specific and may not work in a different script editor.

TABLE 12.1 SPECIAL SQL-VB6 COMMANDS

SQL-VB6	Example	Description Command
//	// this is a comment	Any line that begins with // is treated as a comment line and is not processed by the SQL-VB6 Interpreter. Comments cannot be placed at the end of SQL command lines, but must occupy their own lines. Don't use the single quotation mark for comments as in Visual Basic because that character is a valid SQL character. Also, you must leave at least one space after the // for SQL-VB6 to recognize it as a comment marker.
dbOpen	dbOpen C:\DATA.MDB;	The dbOpen command opens a Microsoft Jet database. SQL-VB6 can open and process only Microsoft Jet-format databases. A dbOpen command must be executed before any SQL statements are processed.

SQL-VB6	Example	Description Command
dbMake	dbMake C:\NEWDATA.MDB;	The dbMake command creates a new, empty Microsoft Jet database on the drive path indicated in the command. When a database is created using the dbMake command, you do not have to issue a dbOpen command.
dbClose	dbClose;	The dbClose command closes the Microsoft Jet database that was opened using the dbOpen or dbMake command.
;	SELECT * FROM Table1;	The semicolon (;) is used to indicate the end of a command. Commands can stretch over several lines of text, but each command must always end with a semicolon (;).

You now have enough information about SQL-VB6 to use it in the rest of the lesson today. As you go through the examples, you learn more about SQL-VB6 and how you can create your own SQL scripts.

Why Use SQL to Create and Manage Data Tables?

Before you jump into the details of SQL keywords, let's talk about the advantages of using SQL statements to create and manage your data tables.

Although Visual Basic offers several powerful commands for performing the same functions within a Visual Basic program, you might find that using SQL keywords to perform database management gives you an advantage. By using SQL statements to create and maintain your database structures, you can easily create useful documentation on how your databases are structured. Are you trying to debug a problem at a client site and can't remember how the tables are laid out? If you used a set of SQL statements to create the tables, you can refer to that script when you are solving your client's problems.

It is also easy to generate, test, or sample data tables using SQL statements. If you are working on a database design and are still experimenting with table layouts and relationships, you can quickly put together an SQL DDL script, run it through SQL-VB6, and review the results. If, after experimenting, you find you need a new field in a table, you can alter your existing script and rerun it. Or you can write a short script that makes only the changes you need, preserving any data you have loaded into the existing tables.

You can even use SQL statements to load test data into your new tables. After you have created the tables, you can add SQL statements to your script that load test data into the

12

columns. This test data can exercise defined relationships, check for data table integrity, and so on. Using an SQL script to load data is an excellent way to perform repeated tests on changing data tables. As you make changes to your table structures, you can use the same data each time until you know you have the results you are looking for.

Also, you can use the same SQL statements to create data tables within other database systems, including Microsoft's SQL Server, Oracle, and others. After you create the test files using Microsoft Access Jet databases, you can then regenerate the tables for other database engines using the same SQL statements. This increases the portability of your application and eases the migration of your data from one database platform to another.

Using Table Management SQL Keywords

The type of SQL keywords you learn today are the table management keywords. These keywords enable you to create new data tables, alter the structure of existing data tables, and remove existing data tables from the database. The information you learn here can be used with any SQL-compliant database.

Designing New Tables with CREATE TABLE

The CREATE TABLE keyword enables you to create new tables in an existing database. In its most basic form, the CREATE TABLE statement consists of three parts: the CREATE TABLE clause; a TableName; and a list of column names, column types, and column sizes for each column in the new table. The following example shows a simple CREATE TABLE SQL statement.

```
CREATE TABLE NewTable (Field1 TEXT(30), Field2 INTEGER);
```

This SQL statement creates a data table called NewTable that has two columns. The column named Field1 is a TEXT column 30 bytes long. The column named Field2 is an INTEGER column. Notice that no size was designated for the INTEGER column. Microsoft Access Jet SQL statements only accept size values for TEXT columns. All other columns are set to a predefined length. See Table 1.4 in Day 1, "Database Programming Basics," for a list of the default field lengths for Microsoft Access Jet data fields.

Note

If you omit the size definition for the TEXT field, Microsoft Access Jet uses the default value of 255 bytes. Because this can result in rather large tables with empty space, it's a good habit to declare a size for all TEXT fields.

Test this SQL statement by creating the SQL script in Listing 12.2 and running it using the SQL-VB6 application. Start the application and select File | New to create a new script called SQLVB02.SQV. Enter the script in Listing 12.2.

LISTING 12.2 CREATING THE SQLVB02.SQV SCRIPT

```
 1: //
 2: // SQLVB02.SQV - Testing SQL Table Management Keywords
 3: //
 4: // create a new database for our tests
 5: dbMake sqlvb02.mdb;
 6: // create a simple table
 7: CREATE TABLE NewTable (Field1 TEXT(30), Field2 INTEGER);
 8: // show the empty table
 9: SELECT * FROM NewTable;
10: // eof (end of file)
```

This script creates a new database, creates a new table in the database, and displays the empty table in a resultset. Use SQL-VB6 to run the script by selecting Actions | Execute. Your results should appear as shown in Figure 12.6.

FIGURE 12.6

The results of the CREATE TABLE *statement.*

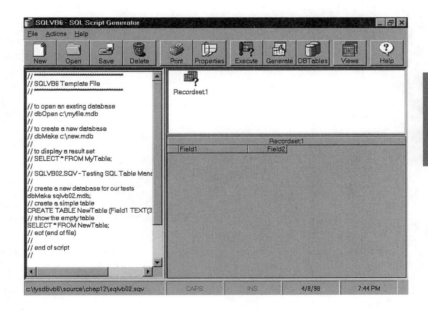

12

You can also use the PRIMARY KEY command when you CREATE a data table. This can be done by following the name of the primary key field with a CONSTRAINT clause. Use

SQL-VB6 to edit the SQLVB02.SQV script so that it sets the Field1 column as a primary key. See Listing 12.3 for an example.

LISTING 12.3 ADDING THE PRIMARY KEY CONSTRAINT

```
1:  //
2:  // testing SQL Table Management Keywords
3:  //
4:  // create a new database for our tests
5:  dbMake sqlvb02.mdb;
6:  // create a simple table
7:  CREATE TABLE NewTable
8:  (Field1 TEXT(30) CONSTRAINT PKNewTable PRIMARY KEY,
9:  Field2 INTEGER);
10: // show the empty table
11: SELECT * FROM NewTable;
12: // eof
```

Notice that the CREATE TABLE SQL statement is spread out over more than one line of text. In SQL-VB6, SQL statements can stretch over several lines, as long as each complete SQL statement ends with a semicolon. The continued lines need not be indented, but doing so makes it easier to read the SQL scripts.

You look at the CONSTRAINT clause in depth a bit later. For now, remember that you can create both primary and foreign keys in a CREATE TABLE statement.

 Note See Day 1 for a more thorough discussion of primary and foreign keys.

Modifying Tables with ALTER TABLE_ADD COLUMN and DROP COLUMN

There are two forms of the ALTER TABLE statement: the ADD COLUMN form and the DROP COLUMN form. The ADD COLUMN form enables you to add new columns to an existing table without losing any data in the existing columns. Edit the SQLVB02.SQV script using SQL-VB6 so that it matches the script in Listing 12.4.

LISTING 12.4. USING THE ADD COLUMN CLAUSE

```
1:  //
2:  // testing SQL Table Management Keywords
```

```
 3: //
 4: // create a new database for our tests
 5: dbMake sqlvb02.mdb;
 6: // create a simple table
 7: CREATE TABLE NewTable
 8: (Field1 TEXT(30) CONSTRAINT PKNewTable PRIMARY KEY,
 9: Field2 INTEGER);
10: // add a two new columns
11: ALTER TABLE NewTable ADD COLUMN Field3 DATE;
12: ALTER TABLE NewTable ADD COLUMN Field4 CURRENCY;
13: // show the empty table
14: SELECT * FROM NewTable;
15: // eof
```

Notice that you had to add two ALTER TABLE statements to add two columns to the same table. The ALTER TABLE statement can deal with only one column at a time. Run the SQLVB02.SQV script and inspect the results. Your screen should look similar to the one in Figure 12.7.

FIGURE 12.7

The results of using ALTER TABLE_ADD COLUMN *keywords.*

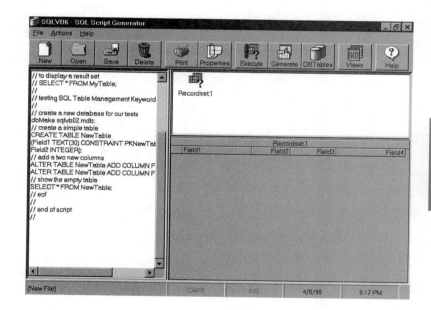

12

> **Note** Note that the ADD COLUMN clause always adds columns starting at the left col-
> umn in the table. You can always control the order of the columns in a dis-
> play using the SELECT_FROM clause (see Day 7). If you want to control the
> physical order of the fields, you must add the fields in a CREATE TABLE state-
> ment.

You can also use the ALTER TABLE statement to remove columns from an existing table
without losing data in the unaffected columns. This is accomplished using the DROP COL-
UMN clause. Edit SQLVB02.SQV to match the example in Listing 12.5.

LISTING 12.5   USING THE DROP COLUMN CLAUSE

```
 1: //
 2: // testing SQL Table Management Keywords
 3: //
 4: // create a new database for our tests
 5: dbMake sqlvb02.mdb;
 6: // create a simple table
 7: CREATE TABLE NewTable
 8: (Field1 TEXT(30) CONSTRAINT PKNewTable PRIMARY KEY,
 9: Field2 INTEGER);
10: // add two new columns
11: ALTER TABLE NewTable ADD COLUMN Field3 DATE;
12: ALTER TABLE NewTable ADD COLUMN Field4 CURRENCY;
13: // drop one of the new columns
14: ALTER TABLE newTable DROP COLUMN Field3;
15: // show the empty table
16: SELECT * FROM NewTable;
17: // eof
```

Run the SQLVB02.SQV script and check your results against the screen shown in Figure
12.8.

> **Note** You can also use the ALTER TABLE statement to add or drop constraints.
> You learn about CONSTRAINT clauses in depth later in this chapter.

Deleting Tables with DROP TABLE

You can use the DROP TABLE statement to remove a table from the database. This is often
used to remove temporary tables, or it can be used as part of a process that copies data

from one table to another or from one database to another. Edit and save SQLVB02.SQV to match the code example in Listing 12.6.

FIGURE 12.8

The results of the
ALTER TABLE_DROP
COLUMN *keyword.*

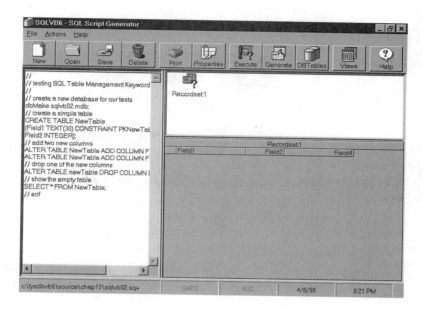

LISTING 12.6 USING THE DROP TABLE CLAUSE

```
 1: //
 2: // testing SQL Table Management Keywords
 3: //
 4: // create a new database for our tests
 5: dbMake sqlvb02.mdb;
 6: // create a simple table
 7: CREATE TABLE NewTable
 8: (Field1 TEXT(30) CONSTRAINT PKNewTable PRIMARY KEY,
 9: Field2 INTEGER);
10: // add two new columns
11: ALTER TABLE NewTable ADD COLUMN Field3 DATE;
12: ALTER TABLE NewTable ADD COLUMN Field4 CURRENCY;
13: // drop one of the new columns
14: ALTER TABLE NewTable DROP COLUMN Field3;
15: // remove the table from the database
16: DROP TABLE NewTable;
17: // show the empty table
18: SELECT * FROM NewTable;
19: // eof
```

12

Save and run the updated SQLVB02.SQV. You should see an SQL error message telling you that it could not find the table NewTable. This happened because the script executed the DROP TABLE statement just before the SELECT_FROM statement. The error message appears in Figure 12.9.

FIGURE 12.9

The results of the DROP TABLE *statement.*

Using Relationship SQL Keywords

You can create and delete indexes or constraints on a data table using the SQL keywords CREATE INDEX and DROP INDEX, and the CONSTRAINT clause of CREATE TABLE and ALTER TABLE statements. SQL constraints are just indexes with another name. However, CONSTRAINT clauses are usually used with CREATE TABLE statements to establish relationships between one or more tables in the same database. INDEX statements are usually used to add or delete search indexes to existing tables.

Managing Indexes with CREATE INDEX and DROP INDEX

The CREATE INDEX statement is used to create a search index on an existing table. The most basic form of the CREATE INDEX statement is shown in the following line:

```
CREATE INDEX NewIndex ON NewTable (Field1);
```

Several variations on the CREATE INDEX statement enable you to add data integrity to the data table. Table 12.2 shows a list of the various CREATE INDEX options and how they are used.

TABLE 12.2   THE CREATE INDEX OPTIONS

CREATE INDEX *Statement*	*Meaning and Use*
CREATE INDEX NewIndex ON NewTable(Field1) WITH PRIMARY	Creates a primary key index. A primary key index ensures that each row of the table has a unique value in the index field. No NULLs are allowed in the index field.
CREATE UNIQUE INDEX NewIndex ON NewTable(Field1)	Creates a unique index on the designated field. In this example, no two columns could have the same value, but NULL values would be allowed.

CREATE INDEX *Statement*	*Meaning and Use*
CREATE INDEX NewIndex ON NewTable (Field1) WITH DISALLOW NULL	Creates an index that is not unique, but does not allow NULL columns.
CREATE INDEX NewIndex ON NewTable (Field1) WITH IGNORE NULL	Creates a non-unique index that allows NULL records in the index column.

Use SQL-VB6 to create a new SQL script that contains the code from Listing 12.7. After you enter the code, save the script as SQLVB03.SQV.

LISTING 12.7 TESTING THE RELATIONSHIP SQL KEYWORDS

```
 1: //
 2: // sqlvb03.sqv - Test Relationship SQL keywords
 3: //
 4: // create a database
 5: dbMake sqlvb03.mdb;
 6: // create a test table to work with
 7: CREATE TABLE NewTable1
 8: (EmployeeID    TEXT(10),
 9: LastName       TEXT(30),
10: FirstName      TEXT(30),
11: LoginName      TEXT(15),
12: JobTitle       TEXT(20),
13: Department     TEXT(10));
14: // create primary key
15: CREATE INDEX PKEmployeeID
16: ON NewTable1(EmployeeID) WITH PRIMARY;
17: // create unique key column
18: CREATE UNIQUE INDEX UKLoginName
19: ON NewTable1(LoginName) WITH IGNORE NULL;
20: // create non-null column
21: CREATE INDEX IKJobTitle
22: ON NewTable1(JobTitle) WITH DISALLOW NULL;
23: // create multi-column sort key
24: CREATE INDEX SKDeptSort
25: ON NewTable1(Department,LastName,FirstName);
26: // show empty table
27: SELECT * FROM NewTable1;
28: // eof
```

12

The preceding SQL script shows several examples of the CREATE INDEX statement. You can use SQL-VB6 to run this script. Your screen should look similar to the one in Figure 12.10.

FIGURE 12.10

The results of the SQLVB03.SQV *script.*

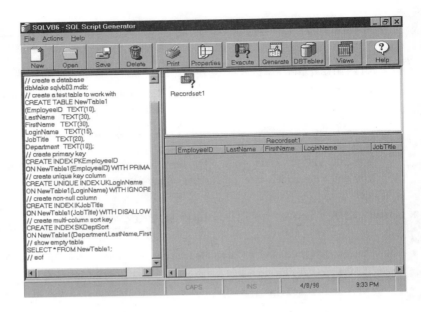

The code example in Listing 12.7 introduced a naming convention for indexes. This convention is widely used by SQL programmers. All primary key indexes should start with the letters PK (PKEmployeeID). All keys created for sorting purposes should begin with the letters SK (SKDeptSort). All index keys that require unique values should begin with UK (UKLoginName). All keys that define foreign key relationships should start with FK. (You learn more about foreign keys in the next section.) Finally, any other index keys should start with IK (IKJobTitle) to identify them as index keys.

Using the ASC and DESC Keywords in the INDEX Statement

You can control the index order by adding ASC (ascending) or DESC (descending) keywords to the CREATE INDEX SQL statement. For example, to create an index on the LastName column, but listing from Zilckowicz to Anderson, you use the following CREATE INDEX statement:

```
CREATE INDEX SKLastName ON NewTable1(LastName DESC);
```

Notice that the DESC goes inside the parentheses. If you want to control the index order on a multiple column index, you can use the following CREATE INDEX statement:

```
CREATE INDEX SKDeptSort ON NewTable1(Department ASC, LastName DESC);
```

If you omit an order word from the CREATE INDEX clause, SQL uses the default ASC order.

Using Indexes to Speed Data Access

In Listing 12.7 (line 24), the index SKDeptSort is a special index key. This is a sort key index. Sort key indexes can be used to speed data access while performing single-record lookups (using the Visual Basic Find method), or for speeding report processing by ordering the data before running a list report. Sort key indexes are not used to enforce data integrity rules or perform data entry validation.

Although sort key indexes are very common in nonrelational databases (X-base class products), they are not often used in relational databases (SQL Server or Oracle). All the related indexes in a database must be updated by the database engine each time a data table is updated. If you have created several sort key indexes, you might begin to see a performance degradation when dealing with large data files or when dealing with remote (ODBC-connected) databases. For this reason, we do not recommend extensive use of sort key indexes in your database.

Using Indexes to Add Database Integrity

You have just about all the possible indexes created in the SQLVB03.SQV example. Many of the indexes serve as database integrity enforcers. In fact, only one of the indexes is meant to be used as a tool for ordering the data (SKDeptSort). All the other indexes in SQLVB03.SQV add database integrity features to the table. This is an important point. In SQL databases, you have much more opportunity to build database editing and field-level enforcement into your database structures than you do with nonrelational desktop databases. When you use the database enforcement options of SQL databases, you can greatly decrease the amount of Visual Basic code you need to write to support data entry routines. Also, by storing the database integrity enforcement in the database itself, all other programs that access and update the database have to conform to the same rules. The rules are no longer stored in your program; they're stored in the database itself!

PRIMARY KEY Enforcement

The PRIMARY KEY index (PKEmployeeID) is familiar to you by now. By defining the index as the primary key, no record is allowed to contain a NULL value in the column EmployeeID, and every record must contain a unique value in the EmployeeID column.

IGNORE NULL UNIQUE Enforcement

The index key UKLoginName allows records in the table that have this field blank (IGNORE NULL). However, if a user enters data into this column, the database checks the other records in the table to make sure that the new entry is unique (UNIQUE keyword). This shows an excellent method for enforcing uniqueness on columns that are not required to have input. For example, if you have an input form that enables users to enter their social security number, but does not require that they do so, you can ensure that the value for the field is unique by using the IGNORE NULL and UNIQUE keywords in the INDEX definition.

DISALLOW NULL Enforcement

The index key IKJobTitle is another example of using the SQL database engine to enforce data integrity rules. By defining the IKJobTitle index as DISALLOW NULL, you have set a data rule that defines this field as a required field. No record can be saved to the data table unless it has a valid value in the JobTitle column. Notice that you have not required that the value be unique. That would require every person in the database to have a unique job title. Instead, you allow duplicate job titles in this column. In real life, you would probably want to check the value entered here against a list of valid job titles. That involves creating a foreign key relationship using the CONSTRAINT keyword. Read the next section for more on CONSTRAINTs.

Managing Relationships with CONSTRAINT

CONSTRAINT clauses are really the same as indexes from the standpoint of SQL statements. The CONSTRAINT keyword is used to create indexes that add data integrity to your database. You must use the CONSTRAINT keyword with the CREATE TABLE or ALTER TABLE SQL statement. There is no such thing in Microsoft Access Jet SQL as CREATE CONSTRAINT.

There are three forms of the CONSTRAINT clause:

- PRIMARY KEY
- UNIQUE
- FOREIGN KEY

Microsoft Access SQL syntax does not allow you to use the IGNORE NULL or DISALLOW NULL keywords within the CONSTRAINT clause. If you want to create data integrity indexes that include the IGNORE NULL or DISALLOW NULL keywords, you have to use the CREATE INDEX keyword to define your index.

Using the PRIMARY KEY CONSTRAINT

The most commonly used CONSTRAINT clause is the PRIMARY KEY CONSTRAINT. This is used to define the column (or set of columns) that contains the primary key for the table. The SQL-VB6 script in Listing 12.8 creates a new database and a single table that contains two fields, one of which is the primary key column for the table. The other field is a MEMO field. MEMO fields can contain any type of free-form text and cannot be used in any CONSTRAINT or INDEX definition.

LISTING 12.8 TESTING THE PRIMARY KEY CONSTRAINT

```
 1: //
 2: // sqlvb04.sqv - Test CONSTRAINT SQL keyword
 3: //
 4: // create a database
 5: dbMake sqlvb04.mdb;
 6: // create jobs title table
 7: CREATE TABLE JobsTable
 8: (JobTitle TEXT (20) CONSTRAINT PKJobTitle PRIMARY KEY,
 9: JobDesc  MEMO
10: );
11: // show the table
12: SELECT * FROM JobsTable;
13: // eof
```

Enter this code into the SQL-Visual Basic editor, save the script as SQLVB04.SQV, and execute it. You see a simple table that shows two fields. See Figure 12.11 for an example.

FIGURE 12.11

Defining the PRIMARY KEY CONSTRAINT.

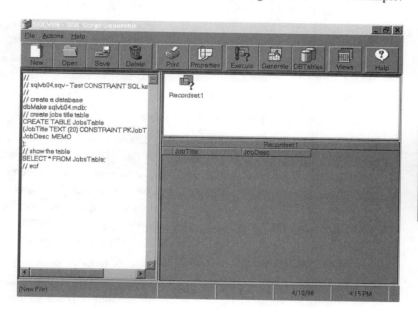

The SQL script in Listing 12.9 performs the same task, except it uses the CREATE INDEX keyword to define the primary key index.

LISTING 12.9   USING CREATE INDEX TO DEFINE THE PRIMARY KEY

```
 1: //
 2: // create index using CREATE INDEX keywords
 3: //
 4: // create database
 5: dbMake sqlvb04.mdb;
 6: // create table
 7: CREATE TABLE JobsTable
 8: (JobTitle TEXT(20),
 9: JobDesc MEMO
10: );
11: // create index
12: CREATE INDEX PKJobTitle ON JobsTable(JobTitle) WITH PRIMARY;
13: // eof
```

Although the code examples in Listing 12.8 and Listing 12.9 both perform the same task, Listing 12.8 demonstrates the preferred method for creating primary key indexes. Listing 12.8 documents the creation of the index at the time the table is created. This is easier to understand and easier to maintain over time. It is possible to create primary key indexes using the CREATE INDEX statement, but this can lead to problems. If you attempt to use the CREATE INDEX_PRIMARY KEY statement on a table that already has a primary key index defined, you get a database error. It is best to avoid this error by limiting the creation of primary key indexes to CREATE TABLE statements.

Using the UNIQUE KEY CONSTRAINT

Another common use of the CONSTRAINT clause is in the creation of UNIQUE indexes. By default, the index key created using the UNIQUE CONSTRAINT clause allows NULL entries in the identified columns. However, when data is entered into the column, that data must be unique or the database engine returns an error message. This is the same as using the IGNORE NULL keyword in the CREATE INDEX statement. You should also note that you cannot use the DISALLOW NULL keywords when creating a UNIQUE CONSTRAINT clause. By default, all keys created using the UNIQUE CONSTRAINT are IGNORE NULL index keys.

The SQL script in Listing 12.10 shows a new column in the JobsTable data table that was created in the last SQL-VB6 script. The new column, BudgetCode, is defined as an optional data column that must contain unique data. Update your version of the SQLVB04.SQV script, save it, and execute it. Your resultset should resemble the one shown in Figure 12.12.

FIGURE 12.12

Defining a UNIQUE
CONSTRAINT *index.*

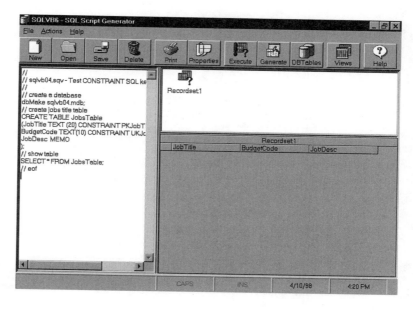

LISTING 12.10 ADDING A UNIQUE CONSTRAINT

```
 1: //
 2: // sqlvb04.sqv - Test CONSTRAINT SQL keyword
 3: //
 4: // create a database
 5: dbMake sqlvb04.mdb;
 6: // create jobs title table
 7: CREATE TABLE JobsTable
 8: (JobTitle TEXT (20) CONSTRAINT PKJobTitle PRIMARY KEY,
 9: BudgetCode TEXT(10) CONSTRAINT UKJobCode UNIQUE,
10: JobDesc   MEMO
11: );
12: // show table
13: SELECT * FROM JobsTable;
14: // eof
```

You can use the UNIQUE CONSTRAINT clause in a multicolumn index. This is especially handy if you have a data table containing more than one field that must be evaluated when deciding uniqueness. For example, what if the preceding data table, in addition to BudgetCode, had BudgetPrefix and BudgetSuffix, too? You can make sure that the combination of the three fields is always unique by building a multicolumn CONSTRAINT clause. Use the code example in Listing 12.11 as a guide. Update your SQLVB04.SQV script to match the example in Listing 12.11 and execute it to make sure you have written the syntax correctly.

12

LISTING 12.11 DEFINING A MULTICOLUMN UNIQUE CONSTRAINT

```
 1: //
 2: // sqlvb04.sqv - Test CONSTRAINT SQL keyword
 3: //
 4: // create a database
 5: dbMake sqlvb04.mdb;
 6: // create jobs title table
 7: CREATE TABLE JobsTable
 8: (JobTitle TEXT (20) CONSTRAINT PKJobTitle PRIMARY KEY,
 9: BudgetPrefix TEXT(5),
10: BudgetCode   TEXT(10),
11: BudgetSuffix TEXT(5),
12: JobDesc MEMO,
13: CONSTRAINT UKBudget UNIQUE (BudgetPrefix,BudgetCode,BudgetSuffix)
14: );
15: // show table
16: SELECT * FROM JobsTable;
17: // eof
```

Once the script has executed, your screen should look similar to the one in Figure 12.13.

FIGURE 12.13

The results of a multi-column CONSTRAINT clause.

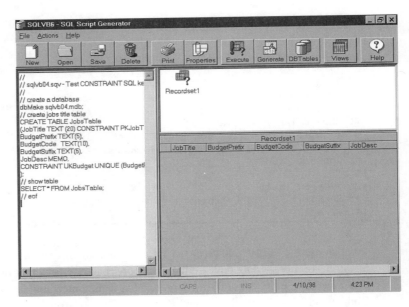

You should also be aware of an important difference between the single-column and multicolumn CONSTRAINT clause formats. Notice that when you are defining a single-column CONSTRAINT, you place the CONSTRAINT clause directly after the column definition without a comma between the column type and the CONSTRAINT keyword. In the multicolumn CONSTRAINT clause, you separate the CONSTRAINT clause with a comma and enclose the column names within parentheses. Mixing these two formats can lead to frustration when you are trying to debug an SQL script!

> **Tip**
>
> Think of it this way. In the case of a single-column CONSTRAINT, the constraint serves as an additional qualifier of the column; the constraint thus belongs within the column definition. A multicolumn CONSTRAINT, however, is a standalone definition that is not an extension of any one column definition. For this reason, multicolumn constraints are treated as if they are on an equal level with a column definition. They stand alone in the column list.

Using the FOREIGN KEY_REFERENCES Relationship

The most powerful of the CONSTRAINT formats is the FOREIGN KEY_REFERENCES format. This format is used to establish relationships between tables. Commonly, a FOREIGN KEY relationship is established between a small table containing a list of valid column entries (usually called a validation table) and another table. The second table usually has a column defined with the same name as the primary key column in the validation table. By establishing a foreign key relationship between the two files, you can enforce a database rule that says the only valid entries in a given table are those values that already exist in the primary key column of the validation table. Once again, you are using the database engine to store data integrity rules. This reduces your volume of Visual Basic code and increases database integrity.

Let's use the script from Listing 12.11 (SQLVB04.SQV) to create a foreign key relationship. You already have a table defined: JobsTable. This is an excellent example of a validation table. It has few fields and has a single column defined as the primary key. Now let's add another table: EmpsTable. This table holds basic information about employees, including their respective job titles. Listing 12.12 shows modifications to SQLVB04.SQV that include the definition of the EmpsTable data table.

LISTING 12.12 ADDING A PRIMARY KEY CONSTRAINT TO THE EMPSTABLE

```
1: //
2: // sqlvb04.sqv - Test CONSTRAINT SQL keyword
3: //
4: // create a database
5: dbMake sqlvb04.mdb;
6: // create jobs title table
```

continues

12

LISTING 12.12 CONTINUED

```
 7: CREATE TABLE JobsTable
 8: (JobTitle TEXT (20) CONSTRAINT PKJobTitle PRIMARY KEY,
 9: BudgetPrefix TEXT(5),
10: BudgetCode   TEXT(10),
11: BudgetSuffix TEXT(5),
12: JobDesc MEMO,
13: CONSTRAINT UKBudget UNIQUE (BudgetPrefix,BudgetCode,BudgetSuffix)
14: );
15: // create a test table to work with
16: CREATE TABLE EmpsTable
17: (EmployeeID   TEXT(10) CONSTRAINT PKEmployeeID PRIMARY KEY,
18: LastName      TEXT(30),
19: FirstName     TEXT(30),
20: LoginName     TEXT(15),
21: JobTitle      TEXT(20),
22: Department    TEXT(10)
23: );
24: // show empty table
25: SELECT * FROM JobsTable;
26: SELECT * FROM EmpsTable;
27: // eof
```

The SQL-VB6 script in Listing 12.12 defines the EmpsTable with only one CONSTRAINT—that of the PRIMARY KEY index. Now let's define a relationship between the EmpsTable.JobTitle column and the JobsTable.JobTitle column. You do this by using the FOREIGN KEY CONSTRAINT syntax. The modified SQLVB04.SQV is shown in Listing 12.13.

LISTING 12.13 ADDING THE FOREIGN KEY_REFERENCES CONSTRAINT

```
 1: //
 2: // sqlvb04.sqv - Test CONSTRAINT SQL keyword
 3: //
 4: // create a database
 5: dbMake sqlvb04.mdb;
 6: // create jobs title table
 7: CREATE TABLE JobsTable
 8: (JobTitle TEXT (20) CONSTRAINT PKJobTitle PRIMARY KEY,
 9: BudgetPrefix TEXT(5),
10: BudgetCode   TEXT(10),
11: BudgetSuffix TEXT(5),
12: JobDesc MEMO,
13: CONSTRAINT UKBudget UNIQUE (BudgetPrefix,BudgetCode,BudgetSuffix)
14: );
15: // create a test table to work with
16: CREATE TABLE EmpsTable
17: (EmployeeID   TEXT(10) CONSTRAINT PKEmployeeID PRIMARY KEY,
```

```
18: LastName    TEXT(30),
19: FirstName   TEXT(30),
20: LoginName   TEXT(15),
21: JobTitle    TEXT(20) CONSTRAINT FKJobTitle REFERENCES
    ➥JobsTable(JobTitle),
22: Department  TEXT(10)
23: );
24: // show empty table
25: SELECT * FROM JobsTable;
26: SELECT * FROM EmpsTable;
27: // eof
```

Notice that the exact SQL syntax for single-column foreign key indexes is

```
CONSTRAINT IndexName REFERENCES Tablename(ColumnName)
```

As long as the column name you are referencing defines the PRIMARY KEY of the referenced table, you can omit the (ColumnName) portion of the CONSTRAINT clause. However, it is good programming practice to include the column name for clarity.

Use the SQL-VB6 editor window to load SQLVB04.SQV. Modify the script to match the code in Listing 12.13, save it, and run the script. Your screen should resemble Figure 12.14.

FIGURE 12.14

A foreign key constraint cascades the related tables onscreen.

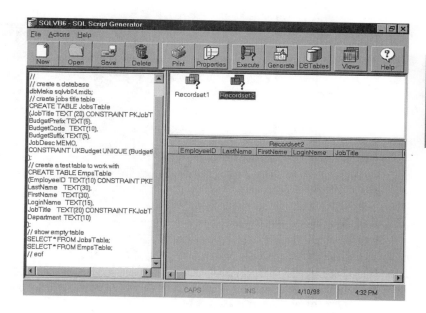

You have defined a rule that tells the Microsoft Jet database engine that any time a user enters data into the EmpsTable.JobTitle column, the engine should refer to the JobsTable.JobTitle column to make sure that the value entered in EmpsTable.JobTitle can be found in one of the rows of JobsTable.JobTitle. If not, the engine should return an error message to the user and not save the record to the data table. All that is done without writing any input validation code at all!

You can set up foreign key relations between any two columns in any two tables. They need not have the same column name, but they must have the same data type. For example, you can add a table to the `SQLVB04.MDB` database that holds information about job titles and pay grades. However, in this table the column that holds the job title is called JobName. Enter the script in Listing 12.14, save it, and execute it. See Figure 12.15 for a guide.

FIGURE 12.15

The results of a foreign key constraint on unmatched column names.

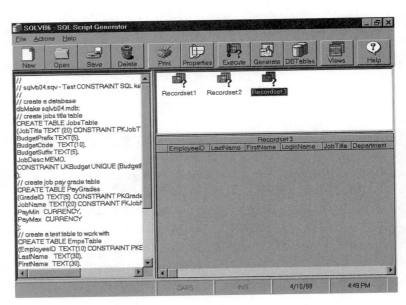

LISTING 12.14   CREATING A FOREIGN KEY RELATIONSHIP ON UNMATCHED FIELD NAMES

```
1: //
2: // sqlvb04.sqv - Test CONSTRAINT SQL keyword
3: //
4: // create a database
5: dbMake sqlvb04.mdb;
6: // create jobs title table
7: CREATE TABLE JobsTable
8: (JobTitle TEXT (20) CONSTRAINT PKJobTitle PRIMARY KEY,
```

```
 9: BudgetPrefix TEXT(5),
10: BudgetCode   TEXT(10),
11: BudgetSuffix TEXT(5),
12: JobDesc MEMO,
13: CONSTRAINT UKBudget UNIQUE (BudgetPrefix,BudgetCode,BudgetSuffix)
14: );
15: // create job pay grade table
16: CREATE TABLE PayGrades
17: (GradeID   TEXT(5)  CONSTRAINT PKGradeID PRIMARY KEY,
18: JobName   TEXT(20) CONSTRAINT FKJobName REFERENCES JobsTable(JobTitle),
19: PayMin    CURRENCY,
20: PayMax    CURRENCY
21: );
22: // create a test table to work with
23: CREATE TABLE EmpsTable
24: (EmployeeID  TEXT(10) CONSTRAINT PKEmployeeID PRIMARY KEY,
25: LastName     TEXT(30),
26: FirstName    TEXT(30),
27: LoginName    TEXT(15),
28: JobTitle     TEXT(20) CONSTRAINT FKJobTitle REFERENCES
    ➥JobsTable(JobTitle),
29: Department   TEXT(10)
30: );
31: // show empty table
32: SELECT * FROM JobsTable;
33: SELECT * FROM PayGrades;
34: SELECT * FROM EmpsTable;
35: // eof
```

Notice that the column PayGrades.JobName does not have the same name as its referenced column (JobsTable.JobTitle). You can still define a foreign key relationship for these columns. This relationship operates exactly the same as the one defined for EmpsTable.JobTitle and JobsTable.JobTitle.

It is also important to point out the order in which you must create tables when you are establishing foreign key constraints. You must always create the referenced table before you refer to it in a CONSTRAINT clause. Failure to adhere to this rule results in a database error when you run your SQL-VB6 script. SQL must see that the table exists before a foreign key reference to it can be established.

It is also possible to create a multicolumn foreign key constraint. When you create multicolumn foreign key constraints, it is important to remember that you must reference the same number of columns on each side of the relationship. For example, if you have a primary key index called PKBudgetCode that contains three columns, any foreign key constraint you define in another table that references PKBudgetCode must also contain three columns.

12

The example in Listing 12.15 shows an added foreign key constraint in the JobsTable. This constraint sets up a relationship between the Budget columns in the BudgetTrack table and JobsTable. Make the changes to the SQLVB04.SQV script and execute it to check for errors. See Figure 12.16 to compare your results.

FIGURE 12.16

The results of adding a multicolumn foreign key constraint.

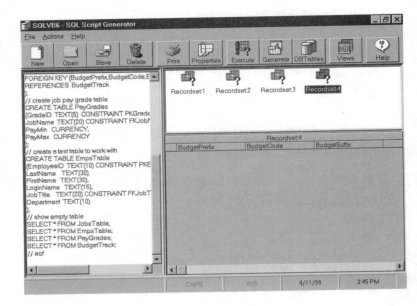

LISTING 12.15 CREATING A MULTICOLUMN FOREIGN KEY CONSTRAINT

```
 1: // create a database
 2: dbMake sqlvb04.mdb;
 3: // create budget tracking file
 4: CREATE TABLE BudgetTrack
 5: (BudgetPrefix TEXT(5),
 6: BudgetCode   TEXT(10),
 7: BudgetSuffix TEXT(5),
 8: CONSTRAINT PKBudgetCode PRIMARY KEY
    ➥(BudgetPrefix,BudgetCode,BudgetSuffix),
 9: AnnBudgetAmt CURRENCY,
10: YTDActualAmt CURRENCY
11: );
12: // create jobs title table
13: CREATE TABLE JobsTable
14: (JobTitle TEXT (20) CONSTRAINT PKJobTitle PRIMARY KEY,
15: BudgetPrefix TEXT(5),
16: BudgetCode   TEXT(10),
```

```
17: BudgetSuffix TEXT(5),
18: JobDesc MEMO,
19: CONSTRAINT FKBudget
20: FOREIGN KEY (BudgetPrefix,BudgetCode,BudgetSuffix)
21: REFERENCES  BudgetTrack
22: );
23: // create job pay grade table
24: CREATE TABLE PayGrades
25: (GradeID  TEXT(5)  CONSTRAINT PKGradeID PRIMARY KEY,
26: JobName   TEXT(20) CONSTRAINT FKJobName REFERENCES JobsTable(JobTitle),
27: PayMin    CURRENCY,
28: PayMax    CURRENCY
29: );
30: // create a test table to work with
31: CREATE TABLE EmpsTable
32: (EmployeeID  TEXT(10) CONSTRAINT PKEmployeeID PRIMARY KEY,
33: LastName     TEXT(30),
34: FirstName    TEXT(30),
35: LoginName    TEXT(15),
36: JobTitle     TEXT(20) CONSTRAINT FKJobTitle REFERENCES
    ➥JobsTable(JobTitle),
37: Department  TEXT(10)
38: );
39: // show empty table
40: SELECT * FROM JobsTable;
41: SELECT * FROM EmpsTable;
42: SELECT * FROM PayGrades;
43: SELECT * FROM BudgetTrack;
44: // eof
```

Notice that the syntax for adding multicolumn foreign key constraints differs from that used when creating single-column foreign key relationships. When creating multicolumn foreign key relationships, you have to actually use the keywords FOREIGN KEY. Also, you list the columns in parentheses in the same order in which they are listed in the referenced key for the referenced table.

Using ALTER TABLE to ADD and DROP Constraints

You can also use the ALTER TABLE statement to add constraints or drop constraints from existing data tables. The code example in Listing 12.16 adds a new constraint to an existing table and then removes it. You should be careful adding or dropping constraints outside of the CREATE TABLE statement. Although SQL allows you to do this, it can often lead to data integrity errors if data already exists within the target table. We recommend that you establish CONSTRAINTs only at the time you create the table using the CREATE TABLE statement.

12

LISTING 12.16   USING ALTER TABLE TO ADD AND DROP CONSTRAINTS

```
 1: // create a database
 2: dbMake sqlvb04.mdb;
 3: // create budget tracking file
 4: CREATE TABLE BudgetTrack
 5: (BudgetPrefix TEXT(5),
 6: BudgetCode   TEXT(10),
 7: BudgetSuffix TEXT(5),
 8: CONSTRAINT PKBudgetCode PRIMARY KEY
    ➥(BudgetPrefix,BudgetCode,BudgetSuffix),
 9: AnnBudgetAmt CURRENCY,
10: YTDActualAmt CURRENCY
11: );
12: // create jobs title table
13: CREATE TABLE JobsTable
14: (JobTitle TEXT (20) CONSTRAINT PKJobTitle PRIMARY KEY,
15: BudgetPrefix TEXT(5),
16: BudgetCode   TEXT(10),
17: BudgetSuffix TEXT(5),
18: JobDesc MEMO,
19: CONSTRAINT FKBudget
20: FOREIGN KEY (BudgetPrefix,BudgetCode,BudgetSuffix)
21: REFERENCES  BudgetTrack
22: );
23: // create job pay grade table
24: CREATE TABLE PayGrades
25: (GradeID  TEXT(5)  CONSTRAINT PKGradeID PRIMARY KEY,
26: JobName  TEXT(20) CONSTRAINT FKJobName REFERENCES JobsTable(JobTitle),
27: PayMin   CURRENCY,
28: PayMax   CURRENCY
29: );
30: // create a test table to work with
31: CREATE TABLE EmpsTable
32: (EmployeeID  TEXT(10) CONSTRAINT PKEmployeeID PRIMARY KEY,
33: LastName    TEXT(30),
34: FirstName   TEXT(30),
35: LoginName   TEXT(15),
36: JobTitle    TEXT(20) CONSTRAINT FKJobTitle REFERENCES
    ➥JobsTable(JobTitle),
37: Department  TEXT(10)
38: );
39: // use alter table to add and drop a constraint
40: ALTER TABLE EmpsTable ADD CONSTRAINT FKMoreJobs
41: FOREIGN KEY (JobTitle) REFERENCES JobsTable(JobTitle);
42: ALTER TABLE EmpsTable DROP CONSTRAINT FKMoreJobs;
43:
44: // show empty table
45: SELECT * FROM JobsTable;
46: SELECT * FROM EmpsTable;
```

```
47: SELECT * FROM PayGrades;
48: SELECT * FROM BudgetTrack;
49: // eof
```

In today's lesson, you saw SQL keywords that create and alter tables and establish table indexes and relationship constraints. Now you are ready for Day 14 ("Updating Databases with SQL"), in which you learn the SQL keywords that you can use to add data to the tables you have created. You'll also see keywords that you can use to copy tables, including the data.

Summary

Today you learned how to create, alter, and delete database table structures using DDL (Data Definition Language) SQL keywords. You also learned that using DDL statements to build tables, create indexes, and establish relationships is an excellent way to automatically document table layouts. You learned how to maintain database structures using the following DDL keywords:

- CREATE TABLE enables you to create entirely new tables in your existing database.
- DROP TABLE enables you to completely remove a table, including any data that is already in the table.
- ALTER TABLE enables you to ADD a new column or DROP an existing column from the table without losing existing data in the other columns.
- CREATE INDEX and DROP INDEX enable you to create indexes that can enforce data integrity or speed data access.
- The CONSTRAINT clause can be added to the CREATE TABLE or ALTER TABLE statement to define relationships between tables using the FOREIGN KEY clause.

12

Quiz

1. What are the benefits of using SQL to create and manage data tables?
2. What is the format of the CREATE TABLE statement?
3. What is the default size of a Microsoft Jet TEXT field?
4. What SQL statement do you use to add a column to a table? What is its format?
5. What SQL statement do you use to remove a table from a database? What is the format of this statement?
6. What SQL statement creates an index to a data table?
7. What are the three forms of the CONSTRAINT clause?

Exercise

You have been assigned the responsibility of building a database of customers for your company. After careful review of the business processes and interviews with other users, you have determined that the following data must be maintained for the Customer database:

Table	Name	Field Type
CustomerType	CustomerType	TEXT(6)
	Description	TEXT(30)
Customers	CustomerID	TEXT(10)
	Name	TEXT(30)
	CustomerType	TEXT(6)
	Address	TEXT(30)
	City	TEXT(30)
	State	TEXT(30)
	Zip	TEXT(10)
	Phone	TEXT(14)
	FAX	TEXT(14)

Use SQL-VB6 to build this structure. Include a primary key for each table and an index on Zip in the Customers table. Include any foreign key relationships that you think would increase database integrity. Name your database CH12EX.MDB. (You can use any path that you like for the MDB file.)

DAY 13

Error Handling in Visual Basic 6

Today's lesson covers a very important aspect of programming: handling runtime errors. Although you should always work to make sure your program can anticipate any problems that might occur while a user is running your software, you can't account for every possibility. That's why every good program should have a solid error-handling system.

Today, you learn just what an error handler is and why error handlers are so important. You also learn about some of the inner workings of Visual Basic and how they affect error handling.

You learn about the difference between local error-handling methods and global error-handling methods. You also learn the advantages and disadvantages of each method. You see the various types of errors your program is likely to encounter and get some guidelines on how to handle each type of error.

You also learn about the Err object and the Error collection and how to use these objects to improve the accuracy of error reporting within your application.

You also learn how to use the `Raise` method of the Err object to flag errors from within custom controls or OLE Server objects.

You learn how to create error logs to keep track of errors that occur in your program and how to create a trace log to analyze your programs. And you learn how you can write your programs to turn these features on or off without having to rewrite program code.

Finally, you build an OLE Server DLL that contains an improved error handler, an error logging facility, and a module trace routine. You can use this new OLE Server in all your future VBA-compliant programming projects.

Error Handling in General

Error handling is an essential part of any program. No program is complete unless it has good error handling. It is important to write your programs in a way that reduces the chance that errors occur, but you won't be able to think of everything. Errors do happen! Well-designed programs don't necessarily have fewer errors; they just handle them better.

Writing error handlers is not difficult. In fact, you can add consistent error handling to your program by adding only a few lines of code to each module. The difficult part of writing good error handlers is knowing what to expect and how to handle the unexpected. You learn how to do both in today's lesson.

Adding error handling to your program makes your program seem much more polished and friendly to your users. Nothing is more annoying—or frightening—to a user than seeing the screen freeze up, hearing a startling beep, or watching the program (and any file the user had been working on) suddenly disappear from the screen. This needs to happen only a few times before the user vows never to use your program again.

Polite error messages, recovery routines that enable users to fix their own mistakes or correct hardware problems, and opportunities for the user to save any open files before the program halts because of errors are all essential parts of a good error-handling strategy.

Error Handling in Visual Basic

Writing error handlers in Visual Basic is a bit trickier than in most PC languages. There are several reasons for this. First, Visual Basic follows an event-driven language model, rather than a procedure-driven model like most PC languages. Second, Visual Basic uses a call stack method that isolates local variables. This means that when you exit the routine, you can lose track of the values of internal variables, which can make resuming execution after error handling difficult. Third, in Visual Basic all errors are local. If an error occurs, it's best to handle it within the routine in which the error occurred, which means you have to write a short error handler for each routine in your Visual Basic program.

The Built-In Visual Basic Error Objects

Technically, Visual Basic does allow the use of a global error handler. However, after Visual Basic travels up the procedure stack to locate the error handler, it can't travel back down the stack to resume execution after the error has been corrected. (This is typical of most object-oriented languages.) For this reason, we highly recommend using local error handlers in your Visual Basic programs.

Visual Basic 6 has two built-in objects that can be used to track and report errors at run-time. The Err object is a built-in object that exists in all Visual Basic programs. This object contains several properties and two methods. Each time an error occurs in the program, the Err object properties are filled with information you can use within your program.

The second built-in object that helps in tracking errors is the Error object, and its associated Errors collection. These are available to any Visual Basic 6 program that has loaded one of the Microsoft data access object libraries. The Error object is a child object of the DBEngine. You can use the Error object to get additional details on the nature of the database errors that occur in a program.

The Error object is available only if you have loaded a Microsoft data access object library. If you attempt to access the Error object from a Visual Basic program that does not have a Microsoft data access object library loaded, you receive an error.

13

The advantage of the Error object over the Err object is that the Error object contains more information about the database-related errors than the Err object. In some cases, back-end database servers return several error messages to your Visual Basic application. The Err object reports only the last error received from the back-end server. However, the Errors collection can report all the errors received. For this reason, it is always a good idea to use the Error object when you are working with Visual Basic database applications.

Working with the Err Object

Visual Basic 6 has a built-in object called the Err object. This object holds all the information about the most recent error that occurred within the running application space.

Caution	There is a bit of confusion regarding the Err keyword in Visual Basic. Visual Basic 6 still supports the outdated Err and Error functions, but we do not advise you to use them in your programs. In some rare cases, the values reported by the Err and Error functions are not the same as those reported by the Err object. Throughout this book, the word *Err* refers to the Err object, not the Err function.

The Err object has several important properties. Table 13.1 shows these properties and explains their use.

TABLE 13.1   THE PROPERTIES OF THE ERR OBJECT

Property	Type	Value
Number	Long	The actual internal error number returned by Visual Basic.
Source	String	The name of the current Visual Basic file in which the error occurred. This could be an EXE, DLL, or OCX file.
Description	String	A string corresponding to the internal error number returned in the Number property, if this string exists. If the string doesn't exist, Description contains application-defined or object-defined error.
HelpFile	String	The fully qualified drive, path, and filename of the Help file. This Help file can be called to support the reported errors.
HelpContext	Long	The Help file context (topic) ID in the Help file indicated by the HelpFile property.
LastDLLError	Long	The error code for the last call to a dynamic-link library (DLL). This is available only on 32-bit Microsoft platforms.

When an error occurs in your Visual Basic program, the Err object properties are populated with the details of the error. You can inspect these values during your program execution and, if possible, use Visual Basic code to correct the error and continue the program.

For example, when an error occurs, you can inspect the properties of the object using the following code:

```
Msgbox "<" & CStr(Err.Number) & "> " & Err.Description & "[" & Err.Source
& "]"
```

After the error occurs and the Err object properties are updated, the Err object values do not change until another error is reported or the error-handling system is reinitialized.

> **Note**
>
> The error-handling system is reinitialized each time a procedure exit or end occurs, or when the special error-handling keywords Resume or On Error are executed. You learn more about these keywords later in this chapter.

If the error that was reported has an associated help file and help context ID, these properties are also filled in. You can use the HelpFile and HelpContext properties of the Err object to display an online help topic to explain the error condition to the user.

If your application has called a dynamic link library (DLL), you may be able to use the LastDLLError property of the Err object to get additional information about an error that occurred in a DLL. This property is available only on the 32-bit platform and may not be supported by the DLL you are calling.

Working with the Error Object and the Errors Collection

In addition to the built-in Err object, Visual Basic 6 also has a built-in Error object for database errors. This object is a child object of the DBEngine object. For this reason, you can access the Error object only if you have loaded a Microsoft data access object library (select Project | References from the main menu).

The primary advantage of the Error object is that it can report additional error information not included in the standard Err object mentioned earlier in this chapter. Many times, your database application needs to depend on external processes such as ODBC data connections or OLE Server modules. When an error occurs in these external processes, they may report more than one error code back to your Visual Basic application.

The Err object is able to remember only the most recent error reported. However, the Error object (and its associated Errors collection) can remember all the errors reported by external processes. It is a good idea to use the Error object for reporting errors in all your Visual Basic database programs.

The properties of the Microsoft data access Error object are almost identical to the properties of the Visual Basic Err object (see the discussion earlier in this chapter). The only difference is that the Error object does not have the optional LastDLLError property.

13

Therefore, the calling convention for the Error object is basically the same as that for the Err object:

```
Msgbox "<" & CStr(Error.Number) & "> " & Error.Description & "[" &
Error.Source & "]"
```

Although the Error and Err objects are quite similar, there is one major difference worth noting. The Err object stands alone, but the Microsoft data access Error object belongs to the Errors collection. This is very important when dealing with back-end database servers, especially when your Visual Basic program is connected to databases through the open database connectivity (ODBC) interface. When an error occurs during an ODBC transaction, the Err object always returns the same error message, ODBC failed. However, the Errors collection often contains more than one error message, which can tell you a great deal more about the nature of the problem. You can retrieve all the error information by enumerating all the Error objects in the Errors collection. The code in Listing 13.1 shows how that can be done.

LISTING 13.1   ENUMERATING THE Errors COLLECTION

```
 1: Dim objTempErr as Object
 2: Dim strMsg as String
 3:
 4: For Each objTempErr In Errors
 5:     StrMsg = "<" & CStr(objTempErr.Number) & "> "
 6:     StrMsg = strMsg & objTempErr.Description
 7:     StrMsg = strMsg & " in [" & objTempErr.Source & "]" & vbCrLf
 8: Next
 9:
10: Msgbox strMsg
```

The code in Listing 13.1 creates a single line of text (strMsg) that contains all the error messages reported by the back-end database server. You learn more about using both the Err and Error objects in the next section of the chapter.

Creating Your Own Error Handlers

Before getting into the details of using the Err and Error objects in your Visual Basic programs, let's take a look at a basic error handler in Visual Basic. Error handlers in Visual Basic have three main parts:

- The On Error Goto statement
- The error handler code
- The exit statement

The On Error Goto statement appears at the beginning of the Sub or Function. This is the line that tells Visual Basic what to do when an error occurs, as in the following example:

```
On Error Goto LocalErrHandler
```

In the preceding code line, every time an error occurs in this Sub or Function, the program immediately jumps to the LocalErrHandler label in the routine and executes the error handler code. The error handler code can be as simple or as complex as needed to handle the error. A very simple error handler would just report the error number and error message, like this:

```
LocalErrHandler:
MsgBox CStr(Err.Number) & " - " & Err.Description
```

In the preceding code example, as soon as the error occurs, Visual Basic reports the error number (Err.Number) and the error message (Err.Description) in a message box.

The third, and final, part of a Visual Basic error handler is the exit statement. This is the line that tells Visual Basic where to go after the error handler is done with its work. There are four different ways to exit an error handler routine:

- Use the Resume keyword to return to the location in the program that caused the error, in order to reexecute the same instruction.

- Use the Resume Next keywords to resume execution at the Visual Basic code line immediately following the line that caused the error.

- Use the Resume label keywords to resume execution at a specified location within the routine that caused the error. This location could be anywhere within the routine—before or after the line that caused the error.

- Use the Exit Sub or Exit Function keywords to immediately exit the routine in which the error occurred.

Which exit method you use depends on the type of error that occurred and the error-handling strategy you employ throughout your program. Error types and error-handling strategies are covered later in this chapter.

13

Now that you have the basics of error handling, you can write some error-handling routines.

Creating a Simple Error Handler

To start, let's write a simple error-handling routine to illustrate how Visual Basic behaves when errors occur. Start up a new Standard EXE project in Visual Basic 6. Add a single command button to the default form. Set its Name property to cmdSimpleErr and its

Caption property to Simple. Now add the code in Listing 13.2 to support the command button.

LISTING 13.2   WRITING A SIMPLE ERROR HANDLER

```
 1: Private Sub cmdSimpleErr_Click()
 2:      '
 3:      ' a simple error handler
 4:      '
 5:      On Error GoTo LocalErr   ' turn on error handling
 6:      '
 7:      Dim intValue As Integer ' declare integer
 8:      Dim strMsg As String     ' declare string
 9:      intValue = 10000000      ' create overflow error
10:      GoTo LocalExit           ' exit if no error
11:      '
12:      ' local error handler
13: LocalErr:
14:      strMsg = CStr(Err.Number) & " - " & Err.Description ' make message
15:      MsgBox strMsg, vbCritical, "cmdSimpleErr_Click"  ' show message
16:      Resume Next  ' continue on
17:      '
18:      ' routine exit
19: LocalExit:
20:      '
21: End Sub
```

Save the form as BASICERR.FRM and save the project as BASICERR.VBP. Then execute the program and click the command button. You see the error message displayed on the screen (see Figure 13.1).

FIGURE 13.1

Displaying the results of a simple error handler.

The example in Listing 13.2 exhibits all the parts of a good error handler. The first line in the routine tells Visual Basic what to do in case of an error. Notice that the name for the error-handling code is given as LocalErr. (Every local error handler written in this book is called LocalErr.) Next, the routine declares an integer variable and then purposely loads that variable with an illegal value. This causes the error routine to kick in.

The error routine is very simple. It is a message that contains the error number and the associated text message. The routine then displays that message along with the warning symbol and the name of the routine that is reporting the error.

The next line tells Visual Basic what to do after the error is handled. In this case, Visual Basic resumes execution with the line of program code that immediately follows the line that caused the error (Resume at the Next line).

When Visual Basic resumes execution, the routine hits the line that tells Visual Basic to go to the exit routine (Goto LocalExit). Notice again the naming convention for the exit routine. All exit jump labels in this book are called LocalExit.

Handling Cascading Errors

What happens if you get an error within your error routine? Although it isn't fun to think about, it can happen. When an error occurs inside the error-handling routine, Visual Basic looks for the next declared error routine. This would be an error routine started in the previous calling routine using the On Error Goto label statement. If no error routine is available, Visual Basic halts the program with a fatal error.

As an example, let's add a new button to the BASICERR project and create a cascading error condition. Set the button's Name property to cmdCascadeErr and its Caption property to Cascade. First, create a new Sub procedure called CreateErr. Then enter the code from Listing 13.3.

LISTING 13.3   CODING THE CreateErr ROUTINE

```
 1: Public Sub CreateErr()
 2:     '
 3:     ' create an internal error
 4:     '
 5:     On Error GoTo LocalErr
 6:     '
 7:     Dim strMsg As String
 8:     Dim intValue As Integer
 9:     '
10:     intValue = 900000 ' create an error
11:     GoTo LocalExit ' all done
12:     '
13: LocalErr:
14:     strMsg = CStr(Err.Number) & " - " & Err.Description
15:     MsgBox strMsg, vbCritical, "CreateErr"
16:     '
17:     Open "junk.txt" For Input As 1 ' create another error
18:     Resume Next
19:     '
20: LocalExit:
21:     '
22: End Sub
```

13

Notice that this routine is quite similar to the code from Listing 13.2. The biggest difference is in the lines of code in the error-handling portion of the subroutine. Notice that
Visual Basic attempts to open a text file for input. Because this file does not currently
exist, this action causes an error.

Now add the code from Listing 13.4 to the `cmdCascadeErr_Click` event. This is the code
that calls the `CreateErr` routine.

LISTING **13.4**   CODING THE cmdCascadeErr ROUTINE

```
 1: Private Sub cmdCascadeErr_Click()
 2:      '
 3:      ' create an error cascade
 4:      '
 5:      On Error GoTo LocalErr
 6:      '
 7:      Dim strMsg As String
 8:      '
 9:      CreateErr ' call another routine
10:      GoTo LocalExit ' all done
11:      '
12: LocalErr:
13:      strMsg = CStr(Err.Number) & " - " & Err.Description
14:      MsgBox strMsg, vbCritical, "cmdCascadeErr"
15:      Resume Next
16:      '
17: LocalExit:
18:      '
19: End Sub
```

Save the program and run it to see the results. When you first click the command button,
you see the error message that announces the overflow error. Notice that the title of the
message box indicates that the error is being reported by the `CreateErr` routine (see
Figure 13.2).

FIGURE 13.2

*Reporting the error
from* CreateErr.

When you click the OK button in the message box, you see another error message. This
one reports an `Error 53-File not found` message, which occurred when `CreateErr`
tried to open the nonexistent file (see Figure 13.3).

Figure 13.3

Reporting the File
not found *error.*

Here's the important point: Notice that the second error message box tells you that the error is being reported from the cmdCascadeErr routine—even though the error occurred in the CreateErr routine! The error that occurred in the CreateErr error-handling routine could not be handled locally, and Visual Basic searched upward in the call stack to find the next available error handler to invoke. This action by Visual Basic can be a blessing and a curse. It's good to know that Visual Basic uses the next available error-handling routine when things like this happen, but it's also likely to cause confusion for you and your users if you are not careful. For all you can tell in this example, an error occurred in cmdCascadeErr. You must keep this in mind when you are debugging Visual Basic error reports.

Using Resume to Exit the Error Handler

The simplest way to exit an error handler is to use the Resume method. When you exit an error handler with the Resume keyword, Visual Basic returns to the line of code that caused the error and attempts to run that line again. The Resume keyword is useful when you encounter an error that the user can easily correct, such as attempting to read a disk drive when the user forgot to insert a disk or close the drive door. You can use the Resume keyword whenever you are confident that the situation that caused the error has been remedied, and you want to retry the action that caused the error.

Let's modify the BASICERR project by adding a new button to the project. Set its Name property to cmdResumeErr and its Caption property to Resume. Now add the Visual Basic code in Listing 13.5 to support the new button's Click event.

LISTING 13.5   USING THE Resume KEYWORD

```
1: Private Sub cmdResumeErr_Click()
2:     '
3:     ' show resume keyword
4:     '
5:     On Error GoTo LocalErr
6:     '
7:     Dim intValue As Integer
8:     Dim strMsg As String
9:     '
```

13

continues

LISTING 13.5   CONTINUED

```
10:     intValue = InputBox("Enter an integer:")
11:     GoTo LocalExit
12:     '
13: LocalErr:
14:     strMsg = CStr(Err.Number) & " - " & Err.Description
15:     MsgBox strMsg, vbCritical, "cmdResumeErr"
16:     Resume ' try it again
17:         '
18: LocalExit:
19:         '
20: End Sub
```

Save and run the project. When you press the Resume button, you are prompted to enter an integer value. If you press the Cancel button or the OK button without entering data (or if you enter a value that is greater than 32,767), you invoke the error handler and receive an error message from Visual Basic (see Figure 13.4).

FIGURE 13.4

Reporting an error message from the input box.

When you click the OK button, Visual Basic redisplays the input prompt and waits for your reply. If you enter another invalid value, you see the error message, and then you see the prompt again. This is the Resume exit method in action. You can't get beyond this screen until you enter a valid value.

This can be very frustrating for users. What if they don't know what value to enter here? Are they stuck in this terrible error handler forever? Whenever you use the Resume keyword, you should give your users an option to ignore the error and move on or cancel the action completely. Those options are covered next.

Using Resume Next to Exit the Error Handler

Using the Resume Next method to exit an error handler enables your user to get past a problem spot in the program as if no error has occurred. This is useful when you use code within the error handler to fix the problem, or when you think the program can go on even though an error has been reported.

Deciding whether to continue the program even though an error has been reported is sometimes a tough call. It is usually not a good idea to assume that your program will work fine even though an error is reported. This is especially true if the error that occurs is one related to physical devices (missing disk, lost communications connection, and so on) or file errors (missing, corrupted, or locked data files, and so on). The Resume Next keywords are usually used in error-handling routines that fix any reported error before continuing.

To illustrate the use of Resume Next, add a new command button to the project. Set its Name property to cmdResumeNextErr and its Caption property to Next. Now enter the code in Listing 13.6 behind the button's Click event.

LISTING 13.6   USING THE Resume Next KEYWORDS

```
 1: Private Sub cmdResumeNextErr_Click()
 2:     '
 3:     ' show use of resume next
 4:     '
 5:     On Error GoTo LocalErr
 6:     '
 7:     Dim intValue As Integer
 8:     Dim strMsg As String
 9:     Dim lngReturn As Long
10:     '
11:     intValue = InputBox("Enter a valid Integer")
12:     MsgBox "intValue has been set to " + CStr(intValue)
13:     GoTo LocalExit
14:     '
15: LocalErr:
16:     If Err.Number = 6 Then ' was it an overflow error?
17:         strMsg = "You have entered an invalid integer value." & vbCrLf
18:         strMsg = strMsg & "The program will now set the value to 0 for
➥you." & vbCrLf
19:         strMsg = strMsg & "Select YES to set the value to 0 and
➥continue." & vbCrLf
20:         strMsg = strMsg & "Select NO to return to enter a new value."
21:         '
22:         lngReturn = MsgBox(strMsg, vbCritical + vbYesNo, _
            "cmdResumeNextErr")
23:         If lngReturn = vbYes Then
24:             intValue = 0
25:             Resume Next
26:         Else
27:             Resume
28:         End If
29:     Else ' must have been some other error(!)
30:         strMsg = CStr(Err.Number) & " - " & Err.Description
31:         MsgBox strMsg, vbCritical, "cmdResumeNext"
32:         Resume
```

13

continues

LISTING 13.6 CONTINUED

```
33:    End If
34:      '
35: LocalExit:
36:      '
37: End Sub
```

In Listing 13.6, you added a section of code to the error handler that tests for the antici-pated overflow error. You explain the options to the user and then give the user a choice of how to proceed. This is a good general model for error handling that involves user interaction. Tell the user the problem, explain the options, and let the user decide how to go forward.

Notice that this routine includes a general error trap for those cases when the error is not caused by an integer overflow. Even when you think you have covered all the possible error conditions, you should always include a general error trap.

Save and run this project. When you press the Next command button and enter an invalid value (that is, any number greater than 32,767), you see the error message that explains your options (see Figure 13.5).

FIGURE 13.5

An error message that asks for user input.

Using `Resume label` to Exit an Error Handler

There are times when you need your program to return to another spot within the routine in order to fix an error that occurs. For example, if you ask the user to enter two numbers that you use to perform a division operation, and it results in a divide-by-zero error, you want to ask the user to enter both numbers again. You might not be able to just use the `Resume` statement after you handle the error.

When you need to force the program to return to a specific point in the routine, you can use the `Resume label` exit method. The `Resume label` method enables you to return to any place within the current procedure. You can't use `Resume label` to jump to another `Sub` or `Function` within the project.

Now let's modify the BASICERR project to include an example of `Resume label`. Add a new command button to the project. Set its `Name` property to `cmdResumeLabelErr` and its

Caption property to Resume Label. Now, place the code in Listing 13.7 behind the Click event.

LISTING 13.7   USING THE Resume Label KEYWORDS

```
1: Private Sub cmdResumeLabelErr_Click()
2:    '
3:    ' show resume label version
4:    '
5:    On Error GoTo LocalErr
6:    '
7:    Dim intX As Integer
8:    Dim intY As Integer
9:    Dim intZ As Integer
10:   '
11: cmdLabelInput:
12:    intX = InputBox("Enter a Divisor:", "Input Box #1")
13:    intY = InputBox("Enter a Dividend:", "Input Box #2")
14:    intZ = intX / intY
15:    MsgBox "The Quotient is: " + Str(intZ), vbInformation, "Results"
16:    GoTo LocalExit
17:    '
18: LocalErr:
19:    If Err = 11 Then      ' divide by zero error
20:       MsgBox CStr(Err.Number) & " - " & Err.Description, vbCritical, _
             "cmdResumeLabelErr"
21:       Resume cmdLabelInput ' back for more
22:    Else
23:       MsgBox CStr(Err) & " -" & Error$, vbCritical, "cmdLabel"
24:       Resume Next
25:    End If
26:    '
27: LocalExit:
28:    '
29: End Sub
```

Save and run the project. Enter 13 at the first input box and 0 at the second input box. This causes an 11-Division by zero error, and the error handler takes over from there. You see the error message shown in Figure 13.6 and then return to the line that starts the input process.

FIGURE 13.6

Displaying the Division by zero *error message.*

13

Using the `Exit` or `End` Method to Exit an Error Handler

There are times when an error occurs and there is no good way to return to the program. A good example of this type of error can occur when the program attempts to open files on a network file server and the user has forgotten to log onto the server. In this case, you need to either exit the routine and return to the calling procedure, or exit the program completely. Exiting to a calling routine can work if you have written your program to anticipate these critical errors. Usually, it's difficult to do that. Most of the time, critical errors of this type mean you should end the program and let the user fix the problem before restarting the program.

Let's add one more button to the BASICERR project. Set its `Caption` property to `End` and its `Name` property to `cmdEndErr`. Enter the code in Listing 13.8 to support the `cmdEnd_Click` event.

LISTING 13.8   USING THE `End` KEYWORD

```
 1: Private Sub cmdEndErr_Click()
 2:     '
 3:     ' use End to exit handler
 4:     '
 5:     On Error GoTo LocalErr
 6:     '
 7:     Dim strMsg As String
 8:     Open "junk.txt" For Input As 1
 9:     GoTo LocalExit
10:     '
11: LocalErr:
12:     If Err.Number = 53 Then
13:         strMsg = "Unable to open JUNK.TXT" & vbCrLf
14:         strMsg = strMsg & "Exit the program and check your INI file" _
            & vbCrLf
15:         strMsg = strMsg & "to make sure the JUNKFILE setting is
            ➥correct."
16:         MsgBox strMsg, vbCritical, "cmdEnd"
17:         Unload Me
18:     Else
19:         MsgBox Str(Err) + " - " + Error$, vbCritical, "cmdEnd"
20:         Resume Next
21:     End If
22:     '
23: LocalExit:
24:     '
25: End Sub
```

In Listing 13.8, you add a check in the error handler for the anticipated `File not found` error. You give the user some helpful information and then tell him you are closing down the program. It's always a good idea to tell the user when you are about to exit the program. Notice that you did not use the Visual Basic `End` keyword; you used `Unload Me`. Remember that `End` stops all program execution immediately. Using `Unload Me` causes Visual Basic to execute any code placed in the `Unload` event of the form. This event should contain any file-closing routine needed to safely exit the program.

Save and run the project. When you click the End button, you see a message box explaining the problem and suggesting a solution (see Figure 13.7). When you click the OK button, Visual Basic ends the program.

FIGURE 13.7

Showing the error message before exiting the program.

So far, you have seen how to build a simple error handler and the different ways to exit error handlers. Now you need to learn about the different types of errors that you may encounter in your Visual Basic programs and how to plan for them in advance.

Types of Errors

In order to make writing error handlers easier and more efficient, you can group errors into typical types. These error types can usually be handled in a similar manner. When you get an idea of the types of errors you may encounter, you can begin to write error handlers that take care of more than one error. You can write handlers that take care of error types.

There are four types of Visual Basic errors:

- *General file errors.* These are errors you encounter when you are attempting to open, read, or write simple files. This type of error does not include errors related to internal database operations (read/write table records).

- *Physical media errors.* These are errors caused by problems with physical devices—errors such as unresponsive communications ports or printers and low-level disk errors (`Unable To Read Sector` and so on).

- *Program code errors.* These are errors that appear in your programs due to problems with your code. Errors include `Divide by zero`, `Invalid Property`, and

13

other errors that can be corrected only by changing the Visual Basic code in your programs.

- *Database errors.* These are errors that occur during database operations, usually during data read/write or data object create/delete operations.

Each of these types of errors needs to be handled differently within your Visual Basic programs. You learn general rules for handling these errors in the following sections.

General File Errors

General file errors occur because of invalid data file information, such as a bad filename, data path, or device name. Usually, the user can fix these errors, and the program can continue from the point of failure. The basic approach to handling general file errors is to create an error handler that reports the problem to the user and asks for additional information to complete or retry the operation.

In Listing 13.9, the error handler is called when the program attempts to open a control file called CONTROL.TXT. The error handler then prompts the user for the proper file location and continues processing. Start a new Standard EXE project (ERRTYPES.VBP) and add a command button to the form. Set its Caption property to Control and its Name property to cmdControl. Also, add a CommonDialog control to the project. Enter the code in Listing 13.9 into the cmdControl_Click event.

LISTING 13.9 ADDING CODE TO THE cmdControl_Click EVENT

```
 1: Private Sub cmdControl_Click()
 2:     '
 3:     ' show general file errors
 4:     '
 5:     On Error GoTo LocalErr
 6:     '
 7:     Dim strFile As String
 8:     Dim strMsg As String
 9:     Dim lngReturn As Long
10:     '
11:     strFile = "\control.txt"
12:     '
13:     Open strFile For Input As 1
14:     MsgBox "Control File Opened"
15:     GoTo LocalExit
16:     '
17: LocalErr:
18:     If Err.Number = 53 Then ' file not found?
19:         strMsg = "Unable to Open CONTROL.TXT" & vbCrLf
20:         strMsg = strMsg & "Select OK to locate CONTROL.TXT" & vbCrLf
21:         strMsg = strMsg & "Select CANCEL to exit program."
```

```
22:          '
23:              lngReturn = MsgBox(strMsg, vbCritical + vbOKCancel, _
              "cmdControl")
24:          '
25:          If lngReturn = vbOK Then
26:              CommonDialog1.filename = strFile
27:              CommonDialog1.DefaultExt = ".txt"
28:              CommonDialog1.ShowOpen
29:              Resume
30:          Else
31:              Unload Me
32:          End If
33:      Else
34:          MsgBox CStr(Err.Number) & " - " + Err.Description
35:          Resume Next
36:      End If
37:      '
38: LocalExit:
39:      '
40: End Sub
```

Save the form as FRMERRTYPES.FRM and the project as PRJERRTYPES.VBP. Now run this project. When you click on the Control button, the program tries to open the CONTROL.TXT file. If it can't be found, you see the error message (see Figure 13.8).

FIGURE 13.8

Displaying the file-not-found error.

If the user selects OK, the program calls the CommonDialog control and prompts the user to locate the CONTROL.TXT file. It can be found in the \TYSDBVB6\SOURCE\CHAP13\ERRTYPES\ directory (see Figure 13.9).

FIGURE 13.9

Attempting to locate the CONTROL.TXT file.

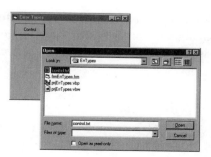

13

Tip

> Notice the use of the CommonDialog control to open the file. Whenever you need to prompt users for file-related action (open, create, or save), you should use the CommonDialog control. This is a familiar dialog for your users, and it handles all the dirty work of scrolling, searching, and so on.

Table 13.2 lists errors that are similar to the file-not-found error illustrated in Listing 13.9. Errors of this type usually involve giving the user a chance to reenter the filename or reset some value. Most of the time, you can write an error trap that anticipates these errors, prompts the user to supply the corrected information, and then retries the operation that caused the error.

TABLE 13.2   COMMON GENERAL FILE ERRORS

Error Code	Error Message
52	Bad filename or number
53	File not found
54	Bad file mode
55	File already open
58	File already exists
59	Bad record length
61	Disk full
62	Input past end of file
63	Bad record number
64	Bad filename
67	Too many files
74	Can't rename with different drive
75	Path/File access error
76	Path not found

In cases when it is not practical to prompt a user for additional information (such as during initial startup of the program), it is usually best to report the error in a message box. Then give the user some ideas about how to fix the problem before you exit the program safely.

Physical Media Errors

Another group of common errors is caused by problems with physical media. Unresponsive printers, disk drives that do not contain disks, and downed communications ports are the most common examples of physical media errors. These errors might, or might not, be easily fixed by your user. Usually, you can report the error, wait for the user to fix the problem, and then continue with the process. For example, if the printer is jammed with paper, all you need to do is report the error to the user and then wait for the OK to continue.

Let's add another button to the PRJERRTYPES.VBP project to display an example of physical media error handling. Add a new command button to the project. Set its Caption property to &Media and its Name property to cmdMedia. Enter the code in Listing 13.10 into the cmdMedia_Click event.

LISTING 13.10 TRAPPING MEDIA ERRORS

```
 1: Private Sub cmdMedia_Click()
 2:     '
 3:     ' show handling of media errors
 4:     '
 5:     On Error GoTo LocalErr
 6:     Dim strMsg As String
 7:     Dim lngReturn As Long
 8:     '
 9:     ' open a file on the a drive
10:     ' an error will occur if there
11:     ' is no diskette in the drive
12:     '
13:     Open "a:\junk.txt" For Input As 1
14:     Close #1
15:     GoTo LocalExit
16:     '
17: LocalErr:
18:     If Err.Number = 71 Then
19:         strMsg = "The disk drive is not ready." & vbCrLf
20:         strMsg = strMsg + "Please make sure there is a diskette" _
             & vbCrLf
21:         strMsg = strMsg + "in the drive and the drive door is closed."
22:         '
23:         lngReturn = MsgBox(strMsg, vbCritical + vbRetryCancel, _
             "cmdMedia")
24:         '
25:         If lngReturn = vbRetry Then
26:             Resume
27:         Else
```

continues

13

LISTING 13.10   CONTINUED

```
28:          Resume Next
29:       End If
30:
31:
32:    Else
33:       MsgBox Str(Err.Number) & " - " & Err.Description
34:       Resume Next
35:    End If
36:       '
37: LocalExit:
38:       '
39: End Sub
```

In Listing 13.10, you attempt to open a file on a disk drive that has no disk (or has an open drive door). The error handler prompts the user to correct the problem and enables the user to try the operation again. If all goes well the second time, the program continues. The user also has an option to cancel the operation.

Save and run the project. When you click on the Media button, you should get results that look like those in Figure 13.10.

FIGURE 13.10

Results of a physical media error.

Program Code Errors

Another common type of error is the program code error. These errors occur as part of the Visual Basic code. Errors of this type cannot be fixed by users and are usually due to unanticipated conditions within the code itself. Error messages such as `Variable Not Found`, `Invalid Object`, and so on, create a mystery for most of your users. The best way to handle errors of this type is to tell the user to report the message to the programmer and close the program safely.

Database Errors with the Data Control

A very common type of error that occurs in database applications is the data-related error. These errors include those that deal with data type or field size problems, table access restrictions including read-only access, locked tables due to other users, and so on. Database errors fall into two groups. Those caused by attempting to read or write invalid data to or from tables, including data integrity errors, make up the most common group. The second group includes those errors caused by locked tables, restricted access, or multiuser conflicts.

> **Note**
>
> Errors concerning table locks, restricted access, and multiuser issues are covered in depth in the last week of this book. In this chapter, you focus on the more common group of errors.

In most cases, all you need to do is trap for the error, report it to the user, and enable the user to return to the data entry screen to fix the problem. If you use the Visual Basic data control in your data forms, you can take advantage of the automatic database error reporting built into the data control. As an example, let's put together a simple data entry form to illustrate some of the common data entry–oriented database errors.

Start a new Visual Basic Standard EXE project to illustrate common database errors. Add a data control, two bound input controls, and two label controls. Use Table 13.3 as a reference for adding the controls to the form. Refer to Figure 13.11 as a guide for placing the controls.

FIGURE 13.11

Laying out the DataErr form.

13

TABLE 13.3 CONTROLS FOR THE FRMDATAERR FORM

Control	Property	Setting
VB.Form	Name	frmDataErr
	Caption	"Data Error Demo"
	ClientHeight	1335

continues

TABLE 13.3   CONTINUED

Control	Property	Setting
	ClientLeft	60
	ClientTop	345
	ClientWidth	4665
	StartUpPosition	3 'Windows Default
VB.CommandButton	Name	cmdAdd
	Caption	"&Add"
	Height	375
	Left	3300
	Top	60
	Width	1215
VB.TextBox	Name	txtName
	DataField	"Name"
	DataSource	"Data1"
	Height	315
	Left	1500
	Top	540
	Width	3015
VB.TextBox	Name	txtKeyField
	DataField	"KeyField"
	DataSource	"Data1"
	Height	375
	Left	1500
	Top	60
	Width	1515
VB.Data	Name	Data1
	Align	2 'Align Bottom
	Caption	"Data1"
	Connect	"Access"
	DatabaseName	"C:\TYSDBVB6\SOURCE\ DATA\ERRORS\ERRORDB.MDB"
	Height	360
	RecordSource	"Table1"

Control	Property	Setting
	Top	975
	Width	4665
VB.Label	Name	lblName
	Caption	"Name"
	Height	255
	Left	120
	Top	540
	Width	1215
VB.Label	Name	lblKeyField
	Caption	"Key Field"
	Height	255
	Left	120
	Top	120
	Width	1215

The only code you need to add to this form is a single line to support the Add button. Place the following code behind the cmdAdd_Click event:

```
Private Sub cmdAdd_Click()
    Data1.Recordset.AddNew
End Sub
```

Now save the new form as DATAERR.FRM and the project as DATAERR.VBP. When you run the project, you can test the built-in error trapping for Microsoft data controls by adding a new, duplicate record to the table. Press the Add button, then enter KF109 in the KeyField input box, and press one of the arrows on the data control to force it to save the record. You should see a database error message that looks like the one in Figure 13.12.

FIGURE 13.12

A sample Microsoft data control error message.

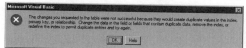

13

Are you surprised? You didn't add an error trap to the data entry form, but you still got a complete database error message! The Visual Basic data control is kind enough to provide complete database error reporting even if you have no error handlers in your Visual Basic program. Along with the automatic errors, the data control also has the Error event. Each time a data-related error occurs, this event occurs. You can add code in the Data1_Error event to automatically fix errors, display better error messages, and so on.

Let's modify the program a bit to show you how you can use the Data1_Error event. First, add a CommonDialog control to your form. Then edit the DatabaseName property of the data control to read C:\ERRORDB.MDB. Next, add the code from Listing 13.11 to the Data1_Error event.

LISTING 13.11   CODING THE Data1_Error EVENT

```
 1: Private Sub Data1_Error(DataErr As Integer, Response As Integer)
 2:     '
 3:     ' add error-trapping for data errors
 4:     '
 5:     Dim strFileName As String
 6:     '
 7:     Select Case DataErr
 8:         Case 3044, 3024 ' database not found
 9:         MsgBox "Unable to locate data file", vbExclamation, _
          "Database Missing"
10:         '
11:         CommonDialog1.DialogTitle = "Locate ERRORDB.MDB"
12:         CommonDialog1.filename = "ERRORDB.MDB"
13:         CommonDialog1.Filter = "*.mdb"
14:         CommonDialog1.ShowOpen
15:         Data1.DatabaseName = CommonDialog1.filename
16:         '
17:         Response = vbCancel ' cancel auto-message
18:     End Select
19:     '
20: End Sub
```

Notice that the code in Listing 13.11 checks to see whether the error code is 3044. This is the error number that corresponds to the "database missing" message. If the codes 3044 or 3024 are reported, the user sees a short message and then the open file dialog, ready to locate and load the database. Finally, notice line 17, which sets the Response parameter to vbCancel. This step tells Visual Basic not to display the default message.

Tip

Usually, it is not a good idea to attempt to override this facility with your own database errors. As long as you use the Visual Basic data control, you do not need to add database error-trapping routines to your data entry forms. The only time you need to add error-related code is when you want to perform special actions in the Error event of the data control.

You need to add one more bit of code to complete this error trap. Add the following lines of code to the Form_Activate event:

```
Private Sub Form_Activate()
    Data1.Refresh
End Sub
```

This code makes sure the data entry fields on the form are updated with the most recent data from the database.

Now save and run the project. You first see a message telling you that the database is missing (Figure 13.13).

FIGURE 13.13

Custom error message in the Data1_error *event.*

Next, the open file dialog waits for you to locate and load the requested database (Figure 13.14).

FIGURE 13.14

Locating the requested database.

Finally, after you load the database, the data entry screen comes up ready for your input.

Database Errors with Microsoft Data Access Objects

If you use Microsoft data access objects instead of the Visual Basic data control, you need to add error-handling routines to your project. For example, if you want to create a Dynaset using Visual Basic code, you need to trap for any error that might occur along the way.

13

Add the code in Listing 13.12 to the Form_Load event of frmData. This code opens the database and creates a Dynaset to stuff into the data control that already exists on the form.

LISTING 13.12   ADDING CODE TO THE Form_Load EVENT

```
 1: Private Sub Form_Load()
 2:      '
 3:      ' create recordset using DAO
 4:      '
 5:      On Error GoTo LocalErr
 6:      '
 7:      Dim ws As Workspace
 8:      Dim db As Database
 9:      Dim rs As Recordset
10:      Dim strSQL As String
11:      ' open bogus table
12:      strSQL = "SELECT * FROM Table2"
13:      Set ws = DBEngine.Workspaces(0)
14:      Set db = ws.OpenDatabase(App.Path & _
            "\..\..\Data\Errors\ErrorDB.mdb")
15:      Set rs = db.OpenRecordset(strSQL, dbOpenDynaset)
16:      Exit Sub
17:      '
18: LocalErr:
19:      MsgBox "<" & CStr(Errors(0).Number) & "> " & _
            Errors(0).Description, ➥vbCritical, "Form_Load Error"
20:      Unload Me
21:      '
22: End Sub
```

The code in Listing 13.12 establishes some variables and then opens the database and creates a new Dynaset from a data table called Table2.

Note

> Notice that instead of the Visual Basic Err object, the DAO Errors collection is used to retrieve the most recent database error. The Errors collection is available only if you loaded the Microsoft DAO library using the Project | References option from the main Visual Basic 6 menu.

Because there is no Table2 in ERRORDB.MDB, you see a database error when the program runs. The error message is displayed, and then the form is unloaded completely (see Figure 13.15).

FIGURE 13.15

Displaying an error message from the `Form_Load` *event.*

It is a good idea to open any data tables or files that you need for a data entry form during the `Form_Load` event. That way, if there are problems, you can catch them before data entry begins.

Reporting Errors in External Components

There are times when you will want to report errors that occur in external components, such as ActiveX DLLs and EXEs, ActiveX Controls, or ActiveX Documents. In these cases, you will not want to display a message box alerting the user of the error. Instead, you should report the error code back to the program that is using the component. This is, actually, what Visual Basic does for all the errors it encounters. It simply sets the Err object values and reports them to your program for handling.

You, too, can use the Err object to report your errors to calling programs. They can be the standard error codes and messages or you can create your own unique error codes and messages. Whatever you use, you will want to be consistent.

The key to sending error messages from your component to the calling program is to use the Err object. The Err object has a special method created just for the purpose of reporting errors back to calling programs. It is called the `Raise` method.

The `Raise` method takes up to five parameters:

- `ErrorNumber` is a unique number identifying the error that just occurred.
- `ErrorSource` is the code module that generated the error.
- `ErrorDescription` is the text message associated with the error.
- `HelpFile` is the help file that contains support information on the error.
- `HelpContextID` is the ID number of the help topic associated with this error.

When you raise your own errors, you are required to report the error number. This can be any value you wish. If you use a number already identified as a Visual Basic error code, you will automatically get the `ErrorDescription` and any associated `HelpFile` and `HelpContextID` information as well. If you generate your own error numbers, you can fill in the other parameters yourself.

13

In order to identify errors raised by your component instead of the main Visual Basic program, it is recommended that your use the vbObjectError constant as a base number for your own error codes. This guarantees that your error number does not conflict with any existing Visual Basic error code.

It's really easy to use Err.Raise. Here is a typical example:

```
Err.Raise vbObjectError + 1, "MyComponent","File Error"
```

In this example, custom error code 1—a file error—occurred in the source module "MyComponent".

You can see that this looks quite a bit like the MsgBox error messages you saw earlier in this chapter. In most cases, you can replace the MsgBox line with this line for every error report in an external component.

Of course, you can also employ the Resume, Resume Next, and Resume Label commands within an error routine in an external component. However, you should avoid using the End command in an external component. Using End may abruptly unload a component that is currently in use by one or more programs and cause the workstation to lock up.

Using Err.Raise in an External Component

As an example, start a new Visual Basic ActiveX DLL project. Set the Class Name to clsWork and the Project Name to prjWork. Create a new function called Divide and add the code from Listing 13.13.

LISTING 13.13   CODING THE Divide FUNCTION IN clsWork

```
 1: Public Function Divide(Dividend As Double, Divisor As Double) As _
    Double
 2:    '
 3:    ' produce results of division
 4:    ' or report error
 5:    '
 6:    On Error GoTo LocalErr
 7:    '
 8:    Divide = Dividend / Divisor
 9:    '
10:    Exit Function
11:    '
12: LocalErr:
13:    '
14:    ' raise error in *calling program* - don't show dialog
15:    Err.Raise vbObjectError + Err.Number, _
16:       App.EXEName & ".clsWork." & "Divide", Err.Description
17:    '
18: End Function
```

You can see that the code in the `LocalErr:` portion of the module now uses the `Err.Raise` method instead of displaying a dialog box. This will send the error code and description back to the calling program.

Note also that the `Err.Decription` value has been used. Because the local error that might occur will be a known Visual Basic error, you can use the current description and number to report back to the calling program.

Now save this project and compile it as `prjWork.DLL`. You use it in the next step when you create a standard EXE program that will use the `prjWork` component.

Receiving Error Reports from External Components

Now that you have an external component that reports errors using the `Err.Raise` method, you can create a simple Visual Basic standard EXE project that uses the component and causes the error.

First, with the `prjWork` project still loaded, select File | Add Project from the main menu and double-click on the Standard EXE template in the New project tab.

Set the form `Name` to `frmTest` and the project `Name` to `prjTest`. Use the information in Table 13.4 and Figure 13.16 to lay out the test form.

TABLE 13.4   CONTROLS FOR THE FRMTEST FORM

Control	Property	Setting
VB.Form	Name	frmTest
	BorderStyle	3 'Fixed Dialog
	Caption	"Testing External Err.Raise"
	ClientHeight	2055
	ClientLeft	5925
	ClientTop	4290
	ClientWidth	3045
	MaxButton	0 'False
	MinButton	0 'False
	ShowInTaskbar	0 'False
	StartUpPosition	2 'CenterScreen
VB.TextBox	Name	txtResults
	Height	300

13

continues

TABLE 13.4 CONTINUED

Control	Property	Setting
	Left	1680
	Text	"0"
	Top	1080
	Width	1200
VB.TextBox	Name	txtDivisor
	Height	300
	Left	1680
	Text	"0"
	Top	720
	Width	1200
VB.TextBox	Name	txtDividend
	Height	300
	Left	1680
	Text	"0"
	Top	360
	Width	1200
VB.CommandButton	Name	Command1
	Caption	"Divide"
	Height	300
	Left	1680
	Top	1560
	Width	1200
VB.Label	Name	lblResults
	Caption	"Results"
	Height	300
	Left	120
	Top	1080
	Width	1200
VB.Label	Name	lblDividend
	Caption	"Dividend"
	Height	300
	Left	120

Control	Property	Setting
	Top	360
	Width	1200
VB.Label	Name	lblDivisor
	Caption	"Divisor"
	Height	300
	Left	120
	Top	720
	Width	1200

FIGURE 13.16

Laying out the frmErrDialog form.

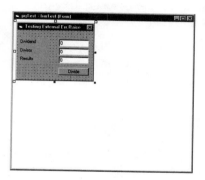

When you finish with the form layout, you can add the code. You need to add just a few lines of code to the command1_click event. Open the event and enter the code from Listing 13.14.

LISTING 13.14 ADDING CODE TO THE Command1_Click EVENT

```
 1: Private Sub Command1_Click()
 2:    '
 3:    On Error GoTo LocalErr
 4:    '
 5:    ' get instance of the class
 6:    Dim objWork As Object
 7:    Set objWork = CreateObject("prjWork.clsWork")
 8:    '
 9:    ' call method in class
10:    txtResults = objWork.Divide(txtDividend, txtDivisor)
11:    '
12:    Exit Sub
13:    '
```

13

continues

LISTING 13.14   CONTINUED

```
14: LocalErr:
15:       '
16:       ' react to error in class
17:       MsgBox Err.Description, vbCritical, Err.Source
18:       '
19: End Sub
```

You can see from Listing 13.14 that a local instance of the external object is created (lines 6 and 7), and the values from the text boxes are passed to the external component in line 10. If an error occurs in the component, it will be returned (via the Err.Raise). The error will then appear as a standard error report to be trapped in the LocalErr portion of the code (lines 14 through 17).

After adding the code from Listing 13.14, save the form as frmTest and the project as prjTest. You can then run the project and test the error handling in the external component. For example, enter 0 for the divisor and see what happens.

Caution   You need to set the error-handling options of the Visual Basic editor to Break on Unhandled Errors in order for this example to work correctly. To do this, select Tools | Options from the main menu. Then click on the General tab and select Break on Unhandled Errors in the Error Trapping section.

Using the Error Handler OLE Component

In the previous sections, you created several error handlers, each tuned to handle a special set of problems. Although this approach works for small projects, it can be tedious and burdensome if you have to put together a large application. Also, after you've written an error handler that works well for one type of error, you can use that error handler in every other program that might have the same error. Why write it more than once?

Even though Visual Basic requires error traps to be set for each Sub or Function, you can still use a generic approach to error handling by employing an external component to perform most of the "drudge work" of error handling.

In this section, you learn how to use an external component that you can install in all your Visual Basic programs: the error-handling OLE Server. This OLE Server offers some generic error-handling capabilities along with the ability to log these errors to a disk file and to keep track of the procedure call stack. These last two services can be very valuable when you encounter a vexing bug in your program and need to get additional information on the exact subroutines and functions that were executed before the error occurred.

Using Your Copy of the `prjErrHandler` Component

In this section, you use an external component to automate the handling of errors. This component, called `prjErrHandler` is included on the CD-ROM that ships with this book. It is included as source code so you can load this source into your Visual Basic editor and then compile it as a separate component later. When you compile your copy of `prjErrHandler`, it will automatically be registered on your workstation.

The examples in this chapter instruct you to load the source code as a part of a project group in the Visual Basic editor. If you choose to compile the ActiveX component first, you can simply add a reference to the compiled component for these examples.

Using the `prjErrHandler` Component

Start a new Visual Basic 6 Standard EXE project. Set the form `Name` to `frmTest` and the project `Name` to `prjTest`. Add a data control and a command button to the form. Refer to Figure 13.17 while laying out the form.

FIGURE 13.17

Laying out the `frmTest` *form.*

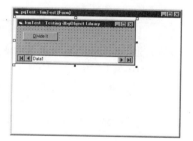

Next, you add the source code for the `prjErrHandler` component into your Visual Basic editor. To do this, select File | Add Project from the main Visual Basic menu and then locate and load the project from

`\tysdbvb6\source\chap13\errHandler\prjErrHandler.vbp`. This adds all the code for the external component into the Visual Basic environment and makes it available for your use. Figure 13.18 shows the `prjErrHandler` component source code loaded as a second project in the Visual Basic IDE.

Now you can add a bit of code to the form to set up the error handler and then cause an error to be handled. First, add the following line to the general declarations section of the form. This declares the object that contains the error handler:

```
Option Explicit
'
Public objErr As dbgObject.errHandler
```

13

FIGURE 13.18

Adding the error handler object source code to the project.

Next, add the code from Listing 13.15 to the Form_Load event of the project.

LISTING 13.15   CODING THE Form_Load EVENT

```
1: Private Sub Form_Load()
2:     '
3:     Data1.DatabaseName = "junk"
4:     Set objErr = CreateObject("dbgObject.errHandler")
5:     '
6: End Sub
```

This code creates the new error handler object and then sets up the data control with a bogus database name. Now add the code from Listing 13.16 to the Data1_Error event. This code intercepts the database error and displays the new custom dialog box.

LISTING 13.16   TRAPPING THE DATA CONTROL ERROR

```
1: Private Sub Data1_Error(DataErr As Integer, Response As Integer)
2:     '
3:     Dim lngReturn As Long
4:     Dim intAnswer As Integer
5:     '
6:     Response = 0
7:     lngReturn = objErr.errHandler(Errors, errColl)
8:     If lngReturn = errExit Then
9:       intAnswer = MsgBox("Ready to Exit program?", _
10:          vbYesNo + vbExclamation, "Data1_Error")
11:       If intAnswer = vbYes Then
12:          Unload Me
13:       End If
14:     End If
15:     '
16: End Sub
```

Now save the form (FRMTEST.FRM) and the project (PRJTEST.VBP) and run the code. You should see the new object library error dialog telling you about the database error (see Figure 13.19).

FIGURE 13.19

The new error object library in action.

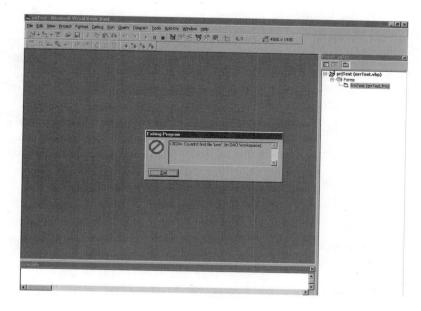

Now add some code behind the Command1_click event to create a Division by zero error. The code in Listing 13.17 does just that.

LISTING 13.17 CREATING A Division by zero ERROR IN CODE

```
 1: Private Sub Command1_Click()
 2:     '
 3:     On Error GoTo Localerr
 4:     Dim rtn as Long
 5:     '
 6:     Print 6 / 0
 7:     '
 8:     Exit Sub
 9:     '
10: Localerr:
11:     rtn = objErr.errHandler(Err, erritem, errresume, _
        "prjTest.Form1.Command1_Click")
12:     Resume Next
13:     '
14: End Sub
```

13

When you save and run this code, press the Exit button to see the new error report. You should see that the Help button is active. If you had a Windows Help file defined for this error, pressing the button would call up the associated topic (see Figure 13.20).

FIGURE 13.20

Viewing help on the Division by zero *error.*

Note

> This version of Visual Basic 6 publishes all the help files in Compressed HTML Help format instead of the standard Windows Help format. Currently, the Visual Basic Error object can call only Windows Help format files. You need to create your own Help files in Windows Help format to use this feature of the prjErrHandler object.

Now let's add an option that creates an error report file whenever the error handler is activated.

Adding Error Logs to the Error Handler

When errors occur, users often do not remember details that appear in the error messages. It's much more useful to create an error log on disk whenever errors occur. This enables programmers or system administrators to review the logs and see the error messages without having to be right next to the user when the error occurs.

It just so happens that the dbgObject component has error-logging features built right in. All you need to do is set the value of two properties to start logging errors:

- LogFileName is the name of the file that will hold the log entries.
- WriteLogFlag is set to TRUE to send all errors to the LogFile.

Now let's modify the test project to start using the error-logging features of the dbgObject component. Open the Form_Load event of the frmTest form and add two lines to set the LogFileName and WriteLogFlag properties of the errHandler object. Listing 13.18 shows how to modify the code.

LISTING 13.18   MODIFYING THE Form_Load EVENT TO INCLUDE ERROR LOGGING

```
1: Private Sub Form_Load()
2: '
```

```
3: Data1.DatabaseName = "junk"
4:    Set objErr = CreateObject("dbgObject.errHandler")
5:    '
6: objErr.WriteLogFlag = True
7: objErr.LogFileName = App.Path & "\" & App.EXEName & ".log"
8:    '
9: End Sub
```

Now, when you run the project, each error is logged to a file with the same name as the application in the same folder as the application. In the preceding example, a file called errTest.log was created in the project's home folder. Listing 13.19 shows the contents of this error log file.

LISTING 13.19   CONTENTS OF THE errTest.log FILE

```
08-Feb-98 5:27:01 AM
<3024> Couldn't find file 'junk'. (in DAO.Workspace).

08-Feb-98 5:27:08 AM
<11> Division by zero (in prjTest)
```

Adding a Module Trace to the Error Handler

NEW TERM   The final touch to add to your error-handling services is the option to keep track of and print a module trace. A *module trace* keeps track of all the modules that have been called and the order in which they were invoked. This can be very valuable when you're debugging programs. Often, a routine works just fine when it is called from one module, but it reports errors if called from another module. When errors occur, it's handy to have a module trace to look through to help find the source of your problems.

The module trace features of the dbgObject component are found in the Trace object. This object has two properties (TraceFileName and TraceFlag) and a handful of new Public methods:

- Push adds a sub or function name to the call list.
- Pop removes a sub or function name from the call list.
- List returns an array of all the names on the call list.
- Dump writes the complete call list to a disk file.
- Show displays the complete call list in a message box.
- Clear resets the call list.

With this information, you can now add module tracing to your test project.

13

First, load the frmTest form and add the following code to the general declarations area of the form:

```
Public objTrace As dbgObject.TraceObject
```

Next, update the Form_Load event as shown in Listing 13.20. This adds the use of the module trace to the project.

LISTING 13.20 UPDATING THE Form_Load EVENT TO INCLUDE MODULE TRACING

```
 1: Private Sub Form_Load()
 2: '
 3: Data1.DatabaseName = "junk"
 4: '
 5: Set objErr = CreateObject("dbgObject.errHandler")
 6: Set objTrace = CreateObject("dbgObject.TraceObject")
 7: '
 8: objTrace.Push "Form_Load"
 9: '
10: objErr.WriteLogFlag = True
11: objErr.LogFileName = App.Path & "\" & App.EXEName & ".log"
12: '
13: objTrace.Pop
14: '
15: End Sub
```

Note the use of objTrace.Push to add the name of the method onto the trace stack. This should happen as early as possible in the method code. Note, also the objTrace.Pop line at the very end of the method (line 13). This removes the name of the method from the stack just as the method is complete.

Let's also add trace coding to the Command1_click event. Update your form's command1_Click event to match the one in Listing 13.21.

LISTING 13.21 UPDATING THE Command1_click EVENT TO USE MODULE TRACING

```
 1: Private Sub Command1_Click()
 2: '
 3: On Error GoTo Localerr
 4: Dim varList As Variant
 5: Dim rtn As Long
 6: '
 7: objTrace.Push "Command1_Click"
 8: '
 9: Print 6 / 0
10: '
11: Exit Sub
```

```
12: '
13: Localerr:
14: '
15: rtn = objErr.errHandler(Err, erritem, errresume, _
      "prjTest.Form1.Command1_Click")
16: '
17: objTrace.Show
18: objTrace.Pop
19: Resume Next
20: '
21: End Sub
```

Save this code and run the project. When you press the command button, you get a trace report on the screen (see Figure 13.21).

FIGURE 13.21

Viewing the trace message.

Notice that, in order to add module tracing to a project, you add a .Push line at the start of the routine and a .Pop line at the end of the routine. This is all you need to do in order to update the procedure stack for the program. But, for this to be really valuable, you have to do this for each routine that you want to track.

In a real application environment, you wouldn't want to show the procedure stack each time an error is reported. The best place for a stack dump is at exit time due to a fatal error. You should probably use the TraceFile option to write the stack to disk rather than displaying it to the user.

Other Error Handler Options

Now that you have the basics of error handling under your belt, you can look at the source code for the prjErrHandler project and continue to add features to the generic error handler. As you add these features, your programs take on a more professional look and feel. Also, using options such as error report logs and procedure stack logs makes it easier to debug and maintain your applications.

Additional features that you can add to your error handler include:

- Add the name of the user or workstation address to the reports.

- If you have created an error trap for common errors, such as Error 53—File not found, add that recovery code to your generic handler. Now you can count on consistent handling of common errors without adding code to every project.

13

Summary

Today's lesson covered all the basics of creating your own error-handling routines for Visual Basic applications. You learned that an error handler has three basic parts:

- The On Error Goto statement
- The body of the error handler code
- The error handler exit

You learned that an error handler has four possible exits:

- Resume: Reexecutes the code that caused the error.
- Resume Next: Continues processing at the line immediately following the code line that caused the error.
- Resume label: Continues processing at the location identified by the label.
- EXIT or END: EXIT ends processing for the current routine, and END exits the program completely.

You learned how to use the Err.Raise method to flag errors without resorting to modal dialog boxes. You also learned about the major types of errors that you are likely to encounter in your program:

- *General file errors.* These include errors such as File not found and Invalid path. Errors of this type can usually be fixed by the user and then the operation retried. Use Resume as an exit for these types of errors.
- *Database errors.* These include errors related to data entry mistakes, integrity violations, and multiuser-related errors, such as locked records. Errors of this type are best handled by enabling the user to correct the data and attempt the operation again. If you use the Visual Basic data control, you do not have to write error handlers; the data control handles them for you. For operations that do not use the data control, you need to write your own error-handling routines.
- *Physical media errors.* These errors relate to device problems, such as unresponsive printers, downed communications ports, and so on. Sometimes users can fix the problems and continue (such as refilling the paper tray of the printer). Other times, users cannot fix the problem without first exiting the program. It is a good idea to give users the option of exiting the program safely when errors of these types are reported.
- *Program code errors.* These errors occur because of problems within the Visual Basic code itself. Examples of program code errors include Object variable not set and For loop not initialized. Usually, the user cannot do anything to fix

errors of this type. It is best to encourage the user to report the error to the system administrator and exit the program safely.

You also learned that you can declare a global error handler or a local error handler. The advantage of the global error handler is that it enables you to create a single module that handles all expected errors. The disadvantage is that, due to the way Visual Basic keeps track of running routines, you are not able to resume processing at the point the error occurs when you arrive at the global error handler. The advantage of the local error handler is that you are always able to use Resume, Resume Next, or Resume label to continue processing at the point the error occurs. The disadvantage of the local error handler is that you need to add error-handling code to every routine in your program.

Finally, you learned how to create an error handler object library that combines local error trapping with global error messages and responses. The error handler object library also contains modules to keep track of the procedures currently running at the time of the error, a process for printing procedure stack dumps to the screen and to a file, and a process that creates an error log on file for later review.

Quiz

1. What are the three main parts of error handlers in Visual Basic?
2. What are the four ways to exit an error handler routine?
3. When would you use Resume to exit an error handler?
4. When would you use Resume Next to exit an error handler?
5. When would you use Resume label to exit an error handler?
6. When would you use the EXIT or END command to exit an error handler?
7. List the four types of Visual Basic errors.
8. Should you use error trapping for the Visual Basic data control?
9. In what Visual Basic event should you open data tables or files in which the user enters data?
10. What is the Err.Raise method and why is it useful?

Exercises

1. Create a new project and add code to a command button that opens the file C:\ABC.TXT. Include an error handler that notifies the user that the file cannot be opened, and then terminates the program.

13

2. Modify the project started in Exercise 1 by adding a new command button. Attach code to this button that attempts to load a file named C:\ABC.TXT. Notify the user that this file cannot be opened, and give the user the option and the dialog box to search for the file. Exit the program when a selection has been made or if the user chooses not to proceed.

Run this program and elect to find the file. Cancel out of any common dialogs that appear. After this, create the file using Notepad and run the process again. Finally, move the file to a location other than the C drive and run the program. Use the common dialog to search for and select the file.

DAY **14**

Updating Databases with SQL

In today's lesson, you learn about the SQL Data Manipulation Language (DML) keywords you can use to update and modify data in existing tables. Although most of the time you use Visual Basic data entry forms and Visual Basic program code to perform data table updates, there are often times when it is more desirable to use SQL statements to update your data tables.

When you complete the examples in this chapter, you will be able to

- Alter the contents of existing tables using the UPDATE statement.
- Add new rows to existing tables with the INSERT INTO statement.
- Append rows from one table to another using the INSERT INTO_FROM clause.
- Copy one or more rows from an existing table to a new table using the SELECT_INTO keywords.
- Remove selected rows from a table using the DELETE_FROM clause.

> Throughout this chapter, you use the SQL-VB6 program to create and run
> SQL scripts. The lesson on Day 12, "Creating Databases with SQL," contains a
> short tutorial on where to locate the SQL-VB6 program and how to use it. If
> you have not worked through the lesson on Day 12 yet, now is a good time
> to review at least the first half of that chapter.

Using Data Manipulation SQL Keywords

The DML SQL keywords are used to add new data to existing tables, edit existing table
data, append data from one table to another, copy data from one table to an entirely new
table, and delete data rows from existing tables.

Most of the time, your Visual Basic programs use data-entry screens to perform these
tasks. However, sometimes the DML keywords come in handy. In some database systems, these SQL keywords are the only way you can add, edit, or delete data from tables.
At other times, these SQL keywords give you the power to produce updates to large
tables with very few lines of code and in a relatively short amount of time.

Also, many times you might need to select a small subset of data from your tables for a
report or a graphic display. Instead of creating Dynaset views of existing tables, you
might want to create a frozen Snapshot of the data to use for this purpose. You copy
some records from an existing table into a new table for use in reporting and displays.
SQL DML keywords can help create these select tables quickly without extensive Visual
Basic code.

Another example of using SQL DML keywords is when you want to append a set of
records from one table to another. Instead of writing Visual Basic code routines that read
a record from one table and then write it to another, you can use SQL DML keywords to
perform the table update—many times with just one line of SQL code.

Finally, SQL DML keywords enable you to quickly delete entire tables or subsets of data
in a single SQL statement. This reduces the amount of Visual Basic code you need to
write and also greatly speeds the processing in most cases.

Adding Rows with the INSERT Statement

The INSERT statement is used to insert values into data tables. You can use the INSERT
statement to populate data tables automatically—without the need for data-entry screens.
Also, you can perform this automatic data entry using very little Visual Basic code.

Why Use INSERT Statements?

Even though you most often perform data entry using Visual Basic–coded data-entry screens tied to Visual Basic data controls, there are times when using the INSERT statement can prove more efficient. An excellent example of using INSERT statements is the installation of a new database system. Often, several data tables need to be populated with default values before people can start using a system. You can use the INSERT statement to perform the initial data load.

Another use for the INSERT statement is in converting data from one database to another. Often, you can use INSERT statements to load existing data in one format into your newly designed relational database.

Finally, you can use INSERT statements to quickly add data to tables that would be too tedious to enter using data-entry screens.

Using the INSERT INTO Statement

The basic form of the INSERT statement is

```
INSERT INTO TableName(field1, field2) VALUES (value1, value2);
```

> **Note**
>
> INSERT and INSERT INTO statements are often used interchangeably. For the most part, this book uses the latter term.

The INSERT SQL statement has three parts. TableName identifies the table that you want to update. The (field1, field2) part of the statement identifies the columns into which you add data. The (value1, value2) part of the statement identifies the exact values you add to the fields you identified. You can name as few or as many fields as you like in the field portion of the statement. However, you must supply a list of values that has the same number of values and the same data type as those identified in the field portion of the statement. Also, you must list the values in the same order as the fields. The first value is placed in the first field, the second value in the second field, and so on.

Let's use SQL-VB6 to create a working example of the INSERT statement. Open a new .SQV script called SQLVB05.SQV using the File|New command from the main menu. Enter the script shown in Listing 14.1, save it, and run it by selecting the Execute icon. Refer to Figure 14.1 to compare your results.

14

FIGURE **14.1**

The results of the
INSERT INTO
statement.

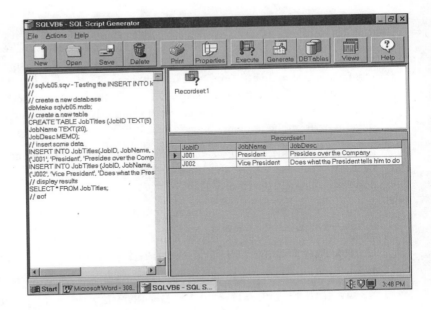

LISTING 14.1   TESTING THE INSERT INTO KEYWORD

```
 1: //
 2: // sqlvb05.sqv - Testing the INSERT INTO keyword
 3: //
 4: // create a new database
 5: dbMake sqlvb05.mdb;
 6: // create a new table
 7: CREATE TABLE JobTitles (JobID TEXT(5) CONSTRAINT PKJobTitle PRIMARY
    ➡KEY,
 8: JobName TEXT(20),
 9: JobDesc MEMO);
10: // insert some data
11: INSERT INTO JobTitles(JobID, JobName, JobDesc) VALUES
12: ('J001',
13: 'President',
14: 'Presides over the company');
15: INSERT INTO JobTitles(JobID, JobName, JobDesc) VALUES
16: ('J002',
17: 'Vice President',
18: 'Does what the President tells him to do'
19: );
20: // display results
21: SELECT * FROM JobTitles;
22: // eof
```

Notice that you must use a separate INSERT INTO statement for each row you want to add to the table. If you want to add 10 more job descriptions to the JobTitles table, you add 10 more INSERT INTO statements to the script.

Also, because you defined the JobsTitles.JobID column as the primary key, you are required to fill that field with unique, non-null data each time you execute the INSERT INTO statement. If you provide a null value or leave the JobsTitles.JobID field out of the INSERT INTO statement, you get a database error message.

If you use a COUNTER data type field in your table, you can't include that in the field list of the INSERT INTO statement. Visual Basic and the SQL engine fill the COUNTER field with an appropriate value. Also, you do not have to add data to every column in the row. If there are fields in the data table that are not required and that can be left null, you can simply omit them from the INSERT INTO statement. The code example in Listing 14.2 illustrates these last two points. Use SQL-VB6 to edit the SQLVB06.SQV script to match the one in Listing 14.2. Save and execute the script. Check your results against those in Figure 14.2.

FIGURE 14.2

The results of using INSERT INTO *with* COUNTER *and optional fields.*

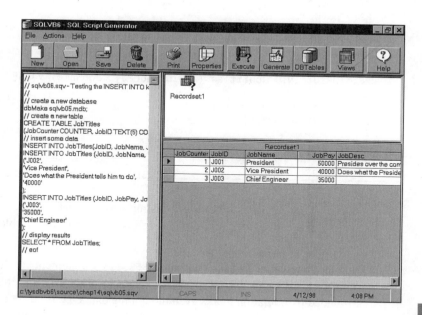

LISTING 14.2   HANDLING COUNTER AND BLANK FIELDS IN INSERT STATEMENTS

```
1: //
2: // sqlvb06.sqv - Testing the INSERT INTO keyword
```

continues

LISTING 14.2   CONTINUED

```
 3: //
 4: // create a new database
 5: dbMake sqlvb05.mdb;
 6: // create a new table
 7: CREATE TABLE JobTitles
 8: (JobCounter COUNTER,
 9: JobID TEXT(5) CONSTRAINT PKJobTitle PRIMARY KEY,
10: JobName TEXT(20),
11: JobPay CURRENCY,
12: JobDesc MEMO
13: );
14: // insert some data
15: INSERT INTO JobTitles (JobID, JobName, JobDesc, JobPay) VALUES
16: ('J001',
17: 'President',
18: 'Presides over the company',
19: '50000'
20: );
21: INSERT INTO JobTitles (JobID, JobName, JobDesc, JobPay) VALUES
22: ('J002',
23: 'Vice President',
24: 'Does what the President tells him to do',
25: '40000'
26: );
27: INSERT INTO JobTitles (JobID, JobPay, JobName) VALUES
28: ('J003',
29: '35000',
30: 'Chief Engineer'
31: );
32: // display results
33: SELECT * FROM JobTitles;
34: // eof
```

Notice that the JobTitles.JobCounter column was automatically populated by Microsoft Jet. Also, you can see that the JobTitles.JobDesc column was left blank for the third record in the table.

Two other interesting things about the INSERT INTO statement are illustrated in the code example in Listing 14.2. Notice that the values for the JobTitles.JobPay column were surrounded by quotation marks even though the data type is CURRENCY. When you use the INSERT INTO statement, all values must be surrounded by quotation marks. SQL and Visual Basic handle any type conversions needed to insert the values into the identified fields.

The second interesting thing to note in Listing 14.2 is the order in which columns are listed in the INSERT INTO statements. If you look at each of the statements, you see that the JobTitles.JobPay column appears in different places within the field list. When you use the INSERT INTO statement, you can list the columns in any order. You only need to make sure that you list the values to be inserted in the same order in which you list the columns.

You have learned how to use the INSERT INTO statement to add individual rows to a table. This is commonly called a single-record insert. In the next section, you learn about a more powerful version of the INSERT INTO statement, commonly called an Append query.

Creating Append Queries with INSERT INTO_FROM

The INSERT INTO_FROM version of the INSERT statement enables you to insert multiple records from one table into another table. This multirecord version of INSERT INTO is called an *Append query* because it enables you to append rows from one table to the end of another table. As long as the two tables you are working with have fields with the same name, you can use the INSERT INTO_FROM statement.

The basic format of the INSERT INTO_FROM statement is

INSERT INTO TargetTable SELECT field1, field2 FROM SourceTable;

There are three important parts of the INSERT INTO_FROM statement. The first part is TargetTable. This is the table that is updated by the statement. The second part is SELECT fields. This is a list of the fields that are updated in the TargetTable. These are also the fields that are supplied by the third part of the statement: SourceTable. As you can see, the INSERT INTO_FROM statement is really just a SELECT_FROM query with an INSERT INTO TargetTable in front of it.

Now, let's update the SQLVB05.SQV to provide an example of the INSERT INTO_FROM statement. First, use SQL-VB6 to load and edit the SQLVB05.SQV script. Make changes to the script so that it matches Listing 14.3. Save the script and run it. Check your results against those shown in Figure 14.3.

LISTING 14.3 USING THE INSERT INTO_FROM STATEMENT

```
1: //
2: // sqlvb05.sqv - Testing the INSERT INTO keyword
3: //
4: // create a new database
5: dbMake sqlvb05.mdb;
6: // create a new table
7: CREATE TABLE JobTitles
8:    (JobCounter COUNTER,
```

continues

14

LISTING 14.3   CONTINUED

```
 9:      JobID TEXT(5) CONSTRAINT PKJobTitle PRIMARY KEY,
10:      JobName TEXT(20),
11:      JobPay CURRENCY,
12:      JobDesc MEMO
13:      );
14: // insert some data
15: INSERT INTO JobTitles (JobID, JobName, JobDesc, JobPay) VALUES
16:      ('J001',
17:       'President',
18:       'Presides over the company',
19:       '50000'
20:      );
21: INSERT INTO JobTitles (JobID, JobName, JobDesc, JobPay) VALUES
22:      ('J002',
23:       'Vice President',
24:       'Does what the President tells him to do',
25:       '40000'
26:      );
27: INSERT INTO JobTitles (JobID, JobPay, JobName) VALUES
28:      ('J003',
29:       '35000',
30:       'Chief Engineer'
31:      );
32: // create a second table to hold some of the info from JobTitles
33: CREATE TABLE JobReport
34:      (JobID TEXT(5) CONSTRAINT PKJobReport PRIMARY KEY,
35:       JobName TEXT(20),
36:       JobDesc MEMO,
37:       DeptID TEXT(5)
38:      );
39: // now append records from JobTitles into JobReport
40: INSERT INTO JobReport
41:      SELECT JobID, JobName, JobDesc FROM JobTitles;
42: // display results
43: SELECT * FROM JobTitles;
44: SELECT * FROM JobReport;
45: // eof
```

Note

You might have noticed in Listing 14.3 that you created two indexes, each on an identical column name, but you gave the two indexes different names. SQL does not allow you to use the same name on different indexes, even if they refer to different tables. Indexes appear as independent data objects in a Microsoft Access database. Each object must have a unique name.

FIGURE 14.3

The results of the
INSERT INTO_FROM
statement.

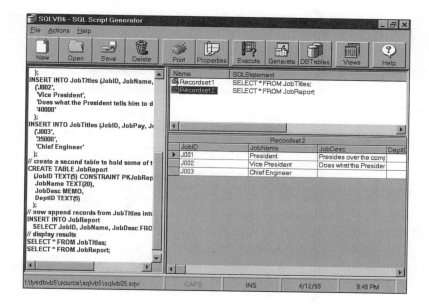

Notice that the INSERT INTO_FROM statement lists only those fields that are present in both tables. You need to list the columns by name in this example because the JobReport table does not contain all the fields that the JobTitles table contains. If both tables were an exact match, you could use the asterisk wildcard character (*) in the SELECT clause. For example, if JobTitles and JobReport shared all the same column names, you could use the following SQL statement to append data from one to the other:

```
INSERT INTO JobReport SELECT * FROM JobTitles;
```

You can also use the INSERT INTO statement to append rows to tables in another database. You accomplish this by adding an IN clause to the first part of the statement. For example, you can add rows from the JobTitles table in SQLVB05.MDB to a similar table in another database called SQLVB05B.MDB. The syntax for the IN clause of an INSERT INTO_FROM statement is

```
IN "DatabaseFileName" "DatabaseFormat"
```

DatabaseFileName is the complete database filename, including the drive identifier and the path name of the destination (or external) database. DatabaseFormat is the name of the database format of the destination database, such as FoxPro, dBASE, Paradox, and so on. For example, if you want to update TableOne in the external database called EXTERNAL.MDB on drive C in the directory called DB, you use the following IN clause for the SELECT INTO statement:

```
SELECT INTO TableOne IN "c:\db\external.mdb" "access"
```

14

Listing 14.4 shows how this is done using a real set of database files. Use SQL-VB6 to load and edit SQLVB05.SQV to match the modifications outlined in Listing 14.4. Save the script and execute it. Your results should look similar to those in Figure 14.4.

FIGURE 14.4

The results of the
INSERT INTO_FROM
statement with
the IN *clause.*

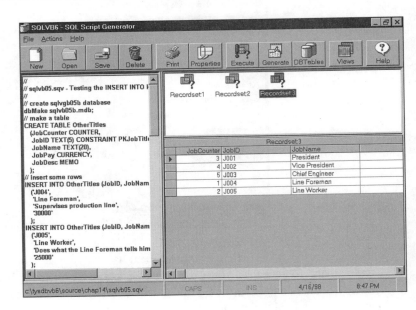

LISTING 14.4   ADDING THE IN CLAUSE

```
 1: //
 2: // sqlvb05.sqv - Testing the INSERT INTO keyword
 3: //
 4: // create sqlvgb05b database
 5: dbMake sqlvb05b.mdb;
 6: // make a table
 7: CREATE TABLE OtherTitles
 8: (JobCounter COUNTER,
 9: JobID TEXT(5) CONSTRAINT PKJobTitle PRIMARY KEY,
10: JobName TEXT(20),
11: JobPay CURRENCY,
12: JobDesc MEMO
13: );
14: // insert some rows
15: INSERT INTO OtherTitles (JobID, JobName, JobDesc, JobPay) VALUES
16: ('J004',
17: 'Line Foreman',
18: 'Supervises production line',
19: '30000'
20: );
```

```
21: INSERT INTO OtherTitles (JobID, JobName, JobDesc, JobPay) VALUES
22: ('J005',
23: 'Line Worker',
24: 'Does what the Line Foreman tells him to do',
25: '25000'
26: );
27: // show results
28: SELECT * FROM OtherTitles;
29: // now close this database
30: dbClose;
31: // *********************************************************
32: // create a new database
33: dbMake sqlvb05.mdb;
34: // create a new table
35: CREATE TABLE JobTitles
36: (JobCounter COUNTER,
37: JobID TEXT(5) CONSTRAINT PKJobTitle PRIMARY KEY,
38: JobName TEXT(20),
39: JobPay CURRENCY,
40: JobDesc MEMO
41: );
42: // insert some data
43: INSERT INTO JobTitles (JobID, JobName, JobDesc, JobPay) VALUES
44: ('J001',
45: 'President',
46: 'Presides over the company',
47: '50000'
48: );
49: INSERT INTO JobTitles (JobID, JobName, JobDesc, JobPay) VALUES
50: ('J002',
51: 'Vice President',
52: 'Does what the President tells him to do',
53: '40000'
54: );
55: INSERT INTO JobTitles (JobID, JobPay, JobName) VALUES
56: ('J003',
57: '35000',
58: 'Chief Engineer'
59: );
60: // create a second table to hold some of the info from JobTitles
61: CREATE TABLE JobReport
62: (JobID TEXT(5) CONSTRAINT PKJobReport PRIMARY KEY,
63: JobName TEXT(20),
64: JobDesc MEMO
65: );
66: // now append records from JobTitles into JobReport
67: INSERT INTO JobReport
68: SELECT JobID, JobName, JobDesc FROM JobTitles;
69: // display results
70: SELECT * FROM JobTitles;
```

14

continues

LISTING 14.4   CONTINUED

```
71: SELECT * FROM JobReport;
72: // now append data from one database to another
73: INSERT INTO OtherTitles IN "sqlvb05b.mdb" "Access"
74: SELECT JobID, JobName, JobDesc, JobPay FROM JobTitles;
75: // close this db
76: dbClose;
77: // open other db
78: dbOpen sqlvb05b.mdb
79: // show updated table
80: SELECT * FROM OtherTitles;
81: // eof
```

The script in Listing 14.4 first creates a database with a single table (OtherTitles) that has two records in the table. Then the script displays the table for a moment before the database is closed. Notice that the records in the table have OtherTitles.JobCounter values of 1 and 2. Then the script creates the JobTitles table in another database and populates that table with three records. Other tables are populated (this was done in previous examples), and eventually the JobTitles table is displayed. The three records have JobTitles.JobCounter values of 1, 2, and 3. Finally, the INSERT INTO_FROM_IN statement is executed to update the external data table. Then the external table is opened so that you can view the results.

Now look at the OtherTitles.JobCounter values. What has happened? When you append COUNTER data fields to another table, the new records are renumbered. This ensures unique counter values in the table. If you want to retain the old numbers, you can include the COUNTER field in your INSERT INTO list. To illustrate this, add the JobCounter column name to the field list (Listing 14.4, line 75) in the INSERT INTO statement that updated the external table (see Figure 14.5). Now execute the script again to see the results.

As you can see in Figure 14.5, you now have duplicate COUNTER values in your table. This can lead to data integrity problems if you are using the COUNTER data type as a guaranteed unique value. You should be careful when you use INSERT INTO statements that contain COUNTER data type columns.

 Caution The Microsoft Visual Basic documentation for the behavior of INSERT INTO with COUNTER data types states that duplicate counter values are not appended to the destination table. This is not correct. The only time duplicates are not included in the destination tables is when the COUNTER data type column is defined as the primary key.

FIGURE 14.5

The results of the
`INSERT INTO_FROM_IN`
with an updated
counter column.

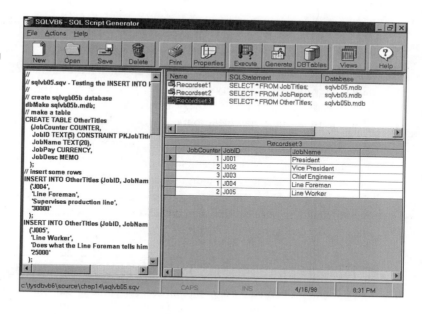

Note that if you attempt to append records to a table that has a duplicate primary key value, the new record is not appended to the table—and you receive an error message! If you edit the `SQLVB05.SQV` script to renumber the OtherTitles.JobID values to `J001` and `J002` (Listing 14.4, lines 44 and 50), you see an error message. Figure 14.6 shows what you get when you attempt to update duplicate primary key rows.

FIGURE 14.6

The results of attempt-
ing to append dupli-
cate primary key rows.

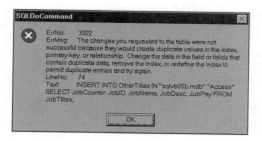

The fact that SQL does not append records with a duplicate key can be used as an advantage. You can easily merge two tables that contain overlapping data and get a single resultset that does not contain duplicates. Anyone who has worked with mailing lists can find a use for this feature of the `INSERT INTO` statement.

Now that you know how to insert rows into tables, it's time to learn how you can update existing rows using the `UPDATE_SET` statement.

14

Creating UPDATE Queries with the UPDATE_SET Statement

The UPDATE_SET statement enables you to update a large amount of data in one or more tables very quickly with very little coding. You use the UPDATE_SET statement to modify data already on file in a data table. The advantage of the UPDATE_SET statement is that you can use a single statement to modify multiple rows in the table.

For example, assume that you have a table of 500 employees. You are told by the Human Resources department that all employees are to be given a 17.5 percent increase in their pay starting immediately (wouldn't it be nice?). You could write a Visual Basic program that opens the table, reads each record, computes the new salary, stores the updated record, and then goes back to read the next record. Your code would look something like the pseudocode sample in Listing 14.5.

 Note

Listing 14.5 is not a real Visual Basic program; it is just a set of statements that read like program code. Such pseudocode is often used by programmers to plan out programs without having to deal with the details of a particular programming language. Another benefit of using pseudocode to plan programs is that people do not need to know a particular programming language to be able to understand the example.

LISTING 14.5   SAMPLE CODE FOR RECORD-ORIENTED UPDATES

```
1: OPEN EmpDatabase
2: OPEN EmpTable
3: DO UNTIL END-OF-FILE (EmpTable)
4: READ EmpTable RECORD
5: EmpTable.EmpSalary = EmpTable.EmpSalary * 1.175
6: WRITE EmpTable RECORD
7: END DO
8: CLOSE EmpTable
9: CLOSE EmpDatabase
```

This is a relatively simple process, but—depending on the size of the data table and the speed of your workstation or the database server—this kind of table update could take quite a bit of time. You can, on the other hand, use the SQL UPDATE statement to perform the same task.

```
OPEN database
UPDATE EmpTable SET EmpSalary = EmpSalary * 1.175
CLOSE database
```

The preceding example shows how you can accomplish the same task with less coding. Even better, this code runs much faster than the walk-through loop shown in Listing 14.5, and this single line of code works for any number of records in the set. Furthermore, if this statement is sent to a back-end database server connected by ODBC and not processed by the local workstation, you could see an even greater increase in processing speed for your program.

Let's start a new program that illustrates the UPDATE_SET statement. Use SQL-VB6 to create a new script file called SQLVB06.SQV and enter the commands in Listing 14.6. After you save the script, execute it and check your results against those in Figure 14.7.

FIGURE 14.7

The results of using the
UPDATE_SET *statement.*

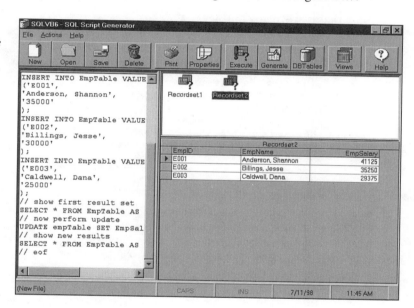

LISTING 14.6 USING THE UPDATE_SET STATEMENT

```
 1: //
 2: // sqlvb06.sqv - testing the UPDATE ... SET statement
 3: //
 4: // create a database
 5: dbMake sqlvb06.mdb;
 6: // create a table
 7: CREATE TABLE EmpTable
 8: (EmpID TEXT(5) CONSTRAINT PKEmpTable PRIMARY KEY,
 9: EmpName TEXT(30),
10: EmpSalary CURRENCY
11: );
```

14

continues

LISTING 14.6 CONTINUED

```
12: // insert some data
13: INSERT INTO EmpTable VALUES
14: ('E001',
15: 'Anderson, Shannon',
16: '35000'
17: );
18: INSERT INTO EmpTable VALUES
19: ('E002',
20: 'Billings, Jesse',
21: '30000'
22: );
23: INSERT INTO EmpTable VALUES
24: ('E003',
25: 'Caldwell, Dana',
26: '25000'
27: );
28: // show first result set
29: SELECT * FROM EmpTable AS FirstPass;
30: // now perform update
31: UPDATE empTable SET EmpSalary = EmpSalary * 1.175;
32: // show new results
33: SELECT * FROM EmpTable AS SecondPass;
34: // eof
```

Note

Notice that you did not include the column names in the INSERT INTO statements in this example. As long as you are supplying all the column values
for a table, in the same order that they appear in the physical layout, you
can omit the column names from the statement.

As you can see in Figure 14.7, all the records in the table are updated by the UPDATE_SET
statement. The SET statement works for both numeric and character fields. It can contain
any number of column updates, too. For example, if you have a table that has three fields
that need to be updated, you can use the following SQL statement:

```
UPDATE MyTable SET
CustType="RETAIL",
CustDiscount=10,
CustDate=#01/15/96#;
```

You can also add a WHERE clause to the UPDATE statement to limit the rows that are affected by the SET portion of the statement. What if you want to give anyone whose salary is
over $30,000 a 10 percent raise and anyone whose salary is $30,000 or under a 15 percent raise? You could accomplish this with two UPDATE_SET statements that each contain

a WHERE clause. Use the code in Listing 14.7 as a guide to modifying the SQLVB06.SQV script. Save your changes and run the script. Check your results against Figure 14.8.

FIGURE 14.8

The results of the UPDATE query with a WHERE clause.

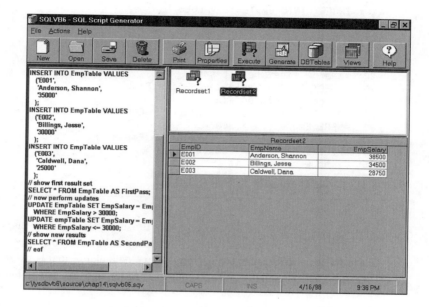

LISTING 14.7 ADDING THE WHERE CLAUSE TO THE UPDATE STATEMENT

```
 1: //
 2: // sqlvb06.sqv - testing the UPDATE ... SET statement
 3: //
 4: // create a database
 5: dbMake sqlvb06.mdb;
 6: // create a table
 7: CREATE TABLE EmpTable
 8: (EmpID TEXT(5) CONSTRAINT PKEmpTable PRIMARY KEY,
 9: EmpName TEXT(30),
10: EmpSalary CURRENCY
11: );
12: // insert some data
13: INSERT INTO EmpTable VALUES
14: ('E001',
15: 'Anderson, Shannon',
16: '35000'
17: );
18: INSERT INTO EmpTable VALUES
19: ('E002',
20: 'Billings, Jesse',
21: '30000'
```

14

continues

LISTING 14.7   CONTINUED

```
22: );
23: INSERT INTO EmpTable VALUES
24: ('E003',
25: 'Caldwell, Dana',
26: '25000'
27: );
28: // show first result set
29: SELECT * FROM EmpTable AS FirstPass;
30: // now perform updates
31: UPDATE EmpTable SET EmpSalary = EmpSalary * 1.10
32: WHERE EmpSalary > 30000;
33: UPDATE empTable SET EmpSalary = EmpSalary * 1.15
34: WHERE EmpSalary <= 30000;
35: // show new results
36: SELECT * FROM EmpTable AS SecondPass;
37: // eof
```

In Listing 14.7, you use the WHERE clause to isolate the records you want to modify with the UPDATE_SET statement. The WHERE clause can be as simple or as complicated as needed to meet the criteria. In other words, any WHERE clause that is valid within the SELECT_FROM statement can be used as part of the UPDATE_SET statement.

Creating Make Table Queries Using the SELECT_INTO_FROM Statement

The SELECT_INTO_FROM statement enables you to create entirely new tables, complete with data from existing tables. This is called a Make Table query because it enables you to make a new table. The difference between Make Table queries and the CREATE TABLE statement is that you use the Make Table query to copy both the table structure and the data within the table from an already existing table. Because the Make Table query is really just a form of a SELECT statement, you can use all the clauses valid for a SELECT statement when copying data tables, including WHERE, ORDER BY, GROUP BY, and HAVING.

Make Table queries are excellent for making backup copies of your data tables. You can also create static read-only tables for reporting and reviewing purposes. For example, you can create a Make Table query that summarizes sales for the period and save the results in a data table that can be accessed for reports and onscreen displays. Now you can provide summary data to your users without giving them access to the underlying transaction tables. This can improve overall processing speed and help provide data security, too.

The basic form of the Make Table query is

```
SELECT field1, field2 INTO DestinationTable FROM SourceTable;
```

In the preceding example, the `field1`, `field2` list contains the list of fields in the
`SourceTable` that is copied to the `DestinationTable`. If you want to copy all the
columns from the source to the destination, you can use the asterisk wildcard character
(*) for the field list. Enter the `SQL-VB6` script in Listing 14.8 as `SQLVB07.SQV`. Save and
execute the script and check your onscreen results against those in Figure 14.9.

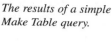

FIGURE 14.9

*The results of a simple
Make Table query.*

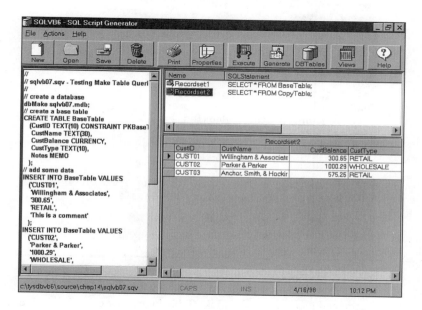

LISTING 14.8 TESTING MAKE TABLE QUERIES

```
 1: //
 2: // sqlvb07.sqv - Testing Make Table Queries
 3: //
 4: // create a database
 5: dbMake sqlvb07.mdb;
 6: // create a base table
 7: CREATE TABLE BaseTable
 8: (CustID TEXT(10) CONSTRAINT PKBaseTable PRIMARY KEY,
 9: CustName TEXT(30),
10: CustBalance CURRENCY,
11: CustType TEXT(10),
12: Notes MEMO
13: );
```

14

continues

LISTING 14.8   CONTINUED

```
14: // add some data
15: INSERT INTO BaseTable VALUES
16: ('CUST01',
17: 'Willingham & Associates',
18: '300.65',
19: 'RETAIL',
20: 'This is a comment'
21: );
22: INSERT INTO BaseTable VALUES
23: ('CUST02',
24: 'Parker & Parker',
25: '1000.29',
26: 'WHOLESALE',
27: 'This is another comment'
28: );
29: INSERT INTO BaseTable VALUES
30: ('CUST03',
31: 'Anchor, Smith, & Hocking',
32: '575.25',
33: 'RETAIL',
34: 'This is the last comment'
35: );
36: // now make a new table from the old one
37: SELECT * INTO CopyTable FROM BaseTable;
38: // show results
39: SELECT * FROM BaseTable;
40: SELECT * FROM CopyTable;
41: // eof
```

In Listing 14.8, you created a database with one table, populated the table with some test data, and then executed a Make Table query that copied the table structure and contents to a new table in the same database.

You can use the WHERE clause to limit the rows copied to the new table. Modify SQLVB07.SQV to contain the new SELECT_INTO statement and its corresponding SELECT_FROM, as shown in Listing 14.9. Save the script and execute it. Your results should look similar to those shown in Figure 14.10.

LISTING 14.9   USING THE WHERE CLAUSE TO LIMIT MAKE TABLE QUERIES

```
1: //
2: // sqlvb07.sqv - Testing Make Table Queries
3: //
4: // create a database
5: dbMake sqlvb07.mdb;
```

```
 6: // create a base table
 7: CREATE TABLE BaseTable
 8: (CustID TEXT(10) CONSTRAINT PKBaseTable PRIMARY KEY,
 9: CustName TEXT(30),
10: CustBalance CURRENCY,
11: CustType TEXT(10),
12: Notes MEMO
13: );
14: // add some data
15: INSERT INTO BaseTable VALUES
16: ('CUST01',
17: 'Willingham & Associates',
18: '300.65',
19: 'RETAIL',
20: 'This is a comment'
21: );
22: INSERT INTO BaseTable VALUES
23: ('CUST02',
24: 'Parker & Parker',
25: '1000.29',
26: 'WHOLESALE',
27: 'This is another comment'
28: );
29: INSERT INTO BaseTable VALUES
30: ('CUST03',
31: 'Anchor, Smith, & Hocking',
32: '575.25',
33: 'RETAIL',
34: 'This is the last comment'
35: );
36: // now make a new table from the old one
37: SELECT * INTO CopyTable FROM BaseTable;
38: // select just some of the records
39: SELECT * INTO RetailTable FROM BaseTable
40: WHERE CustType='RETAIL';
41: // show results
42: SELECT * FROM BaseTable;
43: SELECT * FROM CopyTable;
44: SELECT * FROM RetailTable;
45: // eof
```

As you can see from Figure 14.10, only the rows with WHERE CustType = 'RETAIL' are copied to the new table.

You can also use the GROUP BY and HAVING clauses to limit and summarize data before copying to a new table. Let's modify the SQLVB07.SQV script to produce only one record for each customer type, with each new row containing the customer type and total balance for that type. Let's also order the records in descending order by customer balance.

14

Let's rename the CustBalance field to Balance. The modifications to SQLVB07.SQV are shown in Listing 14.10. Make your changes, save and run the script, and compare your results to Figure 14.11.

FIGURE 14.10

Using a WHERE *clause to limit Make Table queries.*

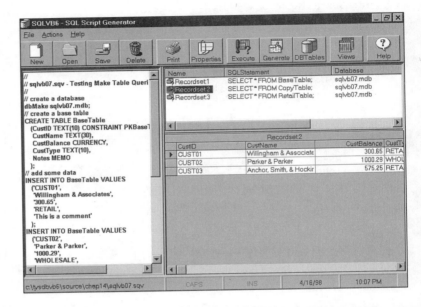

FIGURE 14.11

Using GROUP BY *and* HAVING *to summarize data.*

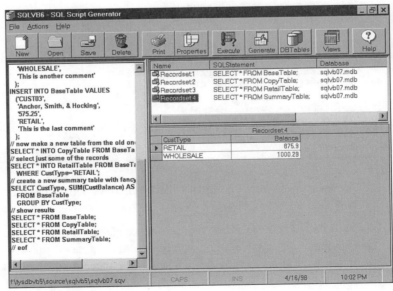

LISTING 14.10   USING GROUP BY AND HAVING TO SUMMARIZE DATA

```
 1: //
 2: // sqlvb07.sqv - Testing Make Table Queries
 3: //
 4: // create a database
 5: dbMake sqlvb07.mdb;
 6: // create a base table
 7: CREATE TABLE BaseTable
 8: (CustID TEXT(10) CONSTRAINT PKBaseTable PRIMARY KEY,
 9: CustName TEXT(30),
10: CustBalance CURRENCY,
11: CustType TEXT(10),
12: Notes MEMO
13: );
14: // add some data
15: INSERT INTO BaseTable VALUES
16: ('CUST01',
17: 'Willingham & Associates',
18: '300.65',
19: 'RETAIL',
20: 'This is a comment'
21: );
22: INSERT INTO BaseTable VALUES
23: ('CUST02',
24: 'Parker & Parker',
25: '1000.29',
26: 'WHOLESALE',
27: 'This is another comment'
28: );
29: INSERT INTO BaseTable VALUES
30: ('CUST03',
31: 'Anchor, Smith, & Hocking',
32: '575.25',
33: 'RETAIL',
34: 'This is the last comment'
35: );
36: // now make a new table from the old one
37: SELECT * INTO CopyTable FROM BaseTable;
38: // select just some of the records
39: SELECT * INTO RetailTable FROM BaseTable
40: WHERE CustType='RETAIL';
41: // create a new summary table with fancy stuff added
42: SELECT CustType, SUM(CustBalance) AS Balance INTO SummaryTable
43: FROM BaseTable
44: GROUP BY CustType;
45: // show results
46: SELECT * FROM BaseTable;
47: SELECT * FROM CopyTable;
```

continues

14

LISTING 14.10   CONTINUED

```
48: SELECT * FROM RetailTable;
49: SELECT * FROM SummaryTable;
50: // eof
```

In all the examples so far, you have used the SELECT_INTO statement to copy existing tables to another table within the database. You can also use SELECT_INTO to copy an existing table to another database by adding the IN clause. You can use this feature to copy entire data tables from one database to another, or to copy portions of a database or data tables to another database for archiving or reporting purposes.

For example, if you want to copy the entire BaseTable you designed in the previous examples from SQLVB07.MDB to SQLVB07B.MDB, you could use the following SELECT_INTO statement:

```
SELECT * INTO CopyTable IN sqlvb07b.mdb FROM BaseTable;
```

You can use all the WHERE, ORDER BY, GROUP BY, HAVING, and AS clauses you desire when copying tables from one database to another.

 Caution

When you copy tables using the SELECT_INTO statement, none of the indexes or constraints are copied to the new table. This is an important point. If you use SELECT_INTO to create tables that you want to use for data entry, you need to reconstruct the indexes and constraints using CREATE INDEX to add indexes and ALTER TABLE to add constraints.

Creating Delete Table Queries Using DELETE_FROM

The final SQL statement you learn today is the DELETE_FROM statement, commonly called the Delete Table query. Delete Table queries are used to remove one or more records from a data table. The delete query can also be applied to a valid view created using the JOIN keyword. Although it is not always efficient to use the DELETE statement to remove a single record from a table, it can be very effective to use the DELETE statement to remove several records from a table. In fact, when you need to remove more than one record from a table or view, the DELETE statement outperforms repeated uses of the Delete method in Visual Basic code.

In its most basic form, the DELETE statement looks like this:

```
DELETE FROM TableName;
```

In the preceding example, TableName represents the name of the base table from which you are deleting records. In this case, all records in the table are removed using a single command. If you want to remove only some of the records, you could add an SQL WHERE clause to limit the scope of the DELETE action.

```
DELETE FROM TableName WHERE Field = value;
```

This example removes only the records that meet the criteria established in the WHERE clause.

Now let's create some real DELETE statements using SQL-VB. Start a new script file called SQLVB08.SQV, and enter the script commands in Listing 14.11. Save the script and execute it. Check your results against those shown in Figure 14.12.

FIGURE 14.12

The results of a simple DELETE statement.

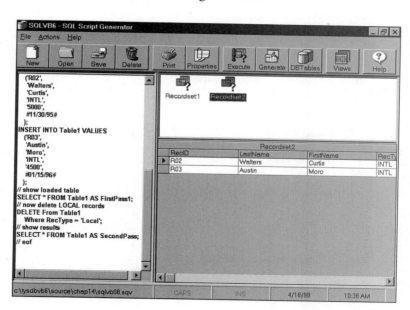

LISTING 14.11 USING THE DELETE STATEMENT

```
1: //
2: // sqlvb08.sqv - Testing DELETE statements
3: //
4: // create a new database
5: dbMake sqlvb08.mdb;
6: // create a table to work with
7: CREATE TABLE Table1
```

continues

14

LISTING 14.11 CONTINUED

```
 8: (RecID TEXT(10),
 9: LastName TEXT(30),
10: FirstName TEXT(30),
11: RecType TEXT(5),
12: Amount CURRENCY,
13: LastPaid DATE
14: );
15: // add some records to work with
16: INSERT INTO Table1 VALUES
17: ('R01',
18: 'Simmons',
19: 'Chris',
20: 'LOCAL',
21: '3000',
22: '12/15/95'
23: );
24: INSERT INTO Table1 VALUES
25: ('R02',
26: 'Walters',
27: 'Curtis',
28: 'INTL',
29: '5000',
30: '11/30/95'
31: );
32: INSERT INTO Table1 VALUES
33: ('R03',
34: 'Austin',
35: 'Moro',
36: 'INTL',
37: '4500',
38: '01/15/96'
39: );
40: // show loaded table
41: SELECT * FROM Table1 AS FirstPass;
42: // now delete LOCAL records
43: DELETE FROM Table1
44: WHERE RecType = 'LOCAL';
45: // show results
46: SELECT * FROM Table1 AS SecondPass;
47: // eof
```

The SQLVB08.SQV script in Listing 14.11 creates a database with one table in it, populates that table with test data, and then shows the loaded table. Next, a DELETE statement is executed to remove all records that have a Table1.RecType that contains LOCAL. When this is done, the results are shown onscreen.

You can create any type of WHERE clause you need to establish the proper criteria. For example, what if you want to remove all international (INTL) records where the last payment is after 12/31/95? Edit your copy of SQLVB08.SQV. Then save and run it to check your results against Figure 14.13. Our version of the solution appears in Listing 14.12.

FIGURE 14.13

The results of the DELETE *statement with a complex* WHERE *clause.*

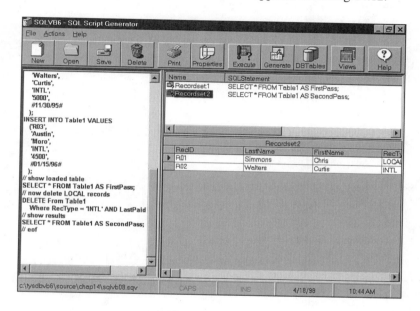

LISTING 14.12 USING A COMPLEX WHERE CLAUSE WITH A DELETE STATEMENT

```
 1: //
 2: // sqlvb08.sqv - Testing DELETE statements
 3: //
 4: // create a new database
 5: dbMake sqlvb08.mdb;
 6: // create a table to work with
 7: CREATE TABLE Table1
 8: (RecID TEXT(10),
 9: LastName TEXT(30),
10: FirstName TEXT(30),
11: RecType TEXT(5),
12: Amount CURRENCY,
13: LastPaid DATE
14: );
15: // add some records to work with
16: INSERT INTO Table1 VALUES
17: ('R01',
18: 'Simmons',
```

continues

14

LISTING **14.12**   CONTINUED

```
19: 'Chris',
20: 'LOCAL',
21: '3000',
22: #12/15/95#
23: );
24: INSERT INTO Table1 VALUES
25: ('R02',
26: 'Walters',
27: 'Curtis',
28: 'INTL',
29: '5000',
30: #11/30/95#
31: );
32: INSERT INTO Table1 VALUES
33: ('R03',
34: 'Austin',
35: 'Moro',
36: 'INTL',
37: '4500',
38: #01/15/96#
39: );
40: // show loaded table
41: SELECT * FROM Table1 AS FirstPass;
42: // now delete LOCAL records
43: DELETE FROM Table1
44: WHERE RecType = 'INTL' AND LastPaid > #12/31/95#;
45: // show results
46: SELECT * FROM Table1 AS SecondPass;
47: // eof
```

As you can see from the code in Listing 14.12, you need to change only the WHERE clause (adding the date criteria) in order to make the DELETE statement function as planned.

Note
You might have noticed that you enclose date information with the pound symbol (#). This ensures that Microsoft Jet handles the data as DATE type values. Using the pound symbol works across language settings within the Windows operating system. This means that if you ship your program to Europe, where many countries use the date format DD/MM/YY (instead of the U.S. standard MM/DD/YY), Windows converts the date information to display and compute properly for the regional settings on the local PC.

You can also use the DELETE statement to delete records in more than one table at a time. These multitable deletes can be performed only on tables that have a one-to-one relationship. The example in Listing 14.13 shows modifications to SQLVB08.SQV to illustrate the use of the JOIN clauses to create a multitable DELETE statement. Use SQL-VB6 to edit your copy of SQLVB08.SQV to match the one in Listing 14.13. Save and execute the script and refer to Figure 14.14 for comparison.

FIGURE 14.14

Results of a multitable
DELETE.

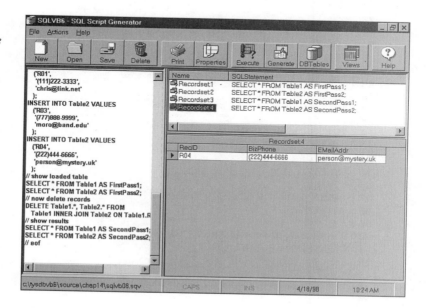

LISTING 14.13 USING JOIN TO PERFORM A MULTITABLE DELETE

```
 1: //
 2: // sqlvb08.sqv - Testing DELETE statements
 3: //
 4: // create a new database
 5: dbMake sqlvb08.mdb;
 6: // create a table to work with
 7: CREATE TABLE Table1
 8: (RecID TEXT(10),
 9: LastName TEXT(30),
10: FirstName TEXT(30),
11: RecType TEXT(5),
12: Amount CURRENCY,
13: LastPaid DATE
14: );
15: // add some records to work with
16: INSERT INTO Table1 VALUES
17: ('R01',
18: 'Simmons',
```

14

continues

LISTING 14.13   CONTINUED

```
19: 'Chris',
20: 'LOCAL',
21: '3000',
22: #12/15/95#
23: );
24: INSERT INTO Table1 VALUES
25: ('R02',
26: 'Walters',
27: 'Curtis',
28: 'INTL',
29: '5000',
30: #11/30/95#
31: );
32: INSERT INTO Table1 VALUES
33: ('R03',
34: 'Austin',
35: 'Moro',
36: 'INTL',
37: '4500',
38: #01/15/96#
39: );
40: // create a second table for JOIN purposes
41: CREATE TABLE Table2
42: (RecID TEXT(10),
43: BizPhone TEXT(20),
44: EMailAddr TEXT(30)
45: );
46: // load some data
47: INSERT INTO Table2 VALUES
48: ('R01',
49: '(111)222-3333',
50: 'chris@link.net'
51: );
52: INSERT INTO Table2 VALUES
53: ('R03',
54: '(777)888-9999',
55: 'moro@band.edu'
56: );
57: INSERT INTO Table2 VALUES
58: ('R04',
59: '(222)444-6666',
60: 'person@mystery.uk'
61: );
62: // show loaded table
63: SELECT * FROM Table1 AS FirstPass1;
64: SELECT * FROM Table2 AS FirstPass2;
65: // now delete records
66: DELETE Table1.*, Table2.* FROM
```

```
67: Table1 INNER JOIN Table2 ON Table1.RecID = Table2.RecID;
68: // show results
69: SELECT * FROM Table1 AS SecondPass1;
70: SELECT * FROM Table2 AS SecondPass2;
71: // eof
```

The results of this DELETE query might surprise you. Because there is no WHERE clause in the DELETE statement that could limit the scope of the SQL command, you might think that the statement deletes all records in both tables. In fact, this statement deletes only the records that have a matching RecID in both tables. The reason for this is that you used an INNER JOIN. INNER JOIN clauses operate only on records that appear in both tables. You now have an excellent way to remove records from multiple tables with one DELETE statement! It must be pointed out, however, that this technique works only with tables that have a one-to-one relationship defined. In the case of one-to-many relationships, only the first occurrence of the match on the many side is removed.

Note   See Day 1, "Database Programming Basics," for a discussion on one-to-one and one-to-many relationships.

Here is a puzzle for you. What happens if you list only Table1 in the first part of that last DELETE statement?

```
DELETE Table1.* FROM
Table1 INNER JOIN Table2 ON Table1.RecID = Table2.RecID;
```

What records (if any) are deleted from Table1? Edit SQLVB08.SQV (line 66), save it, and execute it to find out. Check your results against Figure 14.15.

As you can see from Figure 14.15, a DELETE query that contains an INNER JOIN removes records only from Table1 that have a match in Table2. And the records in Table2 are left intact! This is a good example of using JOIN clauses to limit the scope of a DELETE statement. This technique is very useful when you want to eliminate duplicates in related or identical tables. Note also that this INNER JOIN works just fine without the use of defined constraints or index keys.

14

FIGURE 14.15

The results of a one-sided DELETE *using an* INNER JOIN.

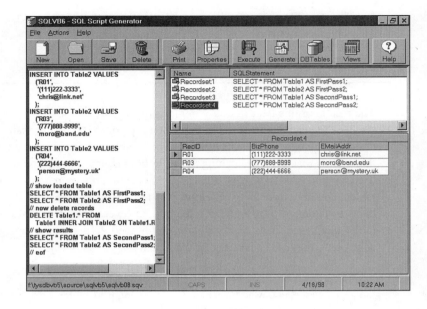

Summary

You learned how to add, delete, and edit data within tables using the DML (Data Manipulation Language) SQL keywords. You learned that, by using DML statements, you can quickly create test data for tables and load default values into startup tables. You also learned that DML statements—such as Append queries, Make Table queries, and Delete queries—can outperform equivalent Visual Basic code versions of the same operations.

You learned how to manage data within the tables using the following DML keywords:

- The INSERT INTO statement can be used to add new rows to the table using the VALUES clause.

- You can create an Append query by using the INSERT INTO_FROM syntax to copy data from one table to another. You can also copy data from one database to another using the IN clause of an INSERT INTO_FROM statement.

- You can create new tables by copying the structure and some of the data using the SELECT_INTO statement. This statement can incorporate WHERE, ORDER BY, GROUP BY, and HAVING clauses to limit the scope of the data used to populate the new table you create.

- You can use the DELETE FROM clause to remove one or more records from an existing table. You can even create customized views of the database using the JOIN clause and remove only records that are the result of a JOIN statement.

Quiz

1. What SQL statement do you use to insert a single data record into a table? What is the basic form of this statement?

2. What SQL statement do you issue to insert multiple data records into a table? What is its format?

3. What SQL statement do you use to modify data that is already in a data table? What is the form of this statement?

4. What SQL statement is used to create new tables that include data from other tables? What is the format of this statement?

5. What SQL statement do you use to delete one or more records from a data table? What is the basic format of this statement?

Exercises

1. Modify the SQL-VB6 script you created in Exercise 1 of Day 12 to add the following records:

Data for the CustomerType Table

Customer Type	Description
INDV	Individual
BUS	Business—Non-Corporate
CORP.	Corporate Entity

Data for the Customers Table

Field	Customer #1	Customer #2	Customer #3
CustomerID	SMITHJ	JONEST	JACKSONT
Name	John Smith	Jones Taxi	Thomas Jackson
CustomerType	INDV	BUS	INDV
Address	160 Main Street	421 Shoe St.	123 Walnut St.
City	Dublin	Milford	Oxford
State	Ohio	Rhode Island	Maine

14

continues

Field	Customer #1	Customer #2	Customer #3
Zip	45621	03215	05896
Phone	614-555-8975	555-555-5555	444-444-4444
Fax	614-555-5580	555-555-5555	444-444-4444

2. Create a third table that includes data from the CustomerID, City, and State fields of the Customers table. Call your table `Localities`.

3. Write an SQL statement that would delete the SMITHJ record from the Customers table. What SQL statement would you issue to delete the entire Customers table?

WEEK 2

In Review

Week 2 concentrated on topics that are of value to developers in the standalone and workgroup environments. A wide variety of topics were covered in Week 2, including

- What the Microsoft Jet engine is, and how you can use Visual Basic code to create and maintain data access objects
- How to create data entry forms with the Visual Basic Data Environment Designer
- How to use the Microsoft graph control to create graphs and charts of your data
- How to use data-bound list boxes, data-bound combo boxes, and data-bound grids to create advanced data entry forms
- How to create databases with SQL Data Definition Language (DDL) commands
- How to make applications more solid with error trapping
- How to use SQL Data Manipulation Language to manage your database

Day 8: Visual Basic and the DAO Jet Database Engine

On Day 8, you learned the features and functions of Visual Basic Microsoft Jet data access objects and ODBCDirect access objects. These objects are used within Visual Basic code to create and maintain workspaces, databases, tables, fields, indexes, queries, and relations. You learned the properties, methods, and collections of each object. You also learned how to use Visual Basic code to inspect the values in the properties, and how to use the methods to perform basic database operations.

Day 9: Creating Database Programs with the Data Environment Designer

On Day 9, you learned how to write data entry forms using Visual Basic code. These topics were covered: record search routines, the creation of a procedure library to handle all data entry processes, and creating a working data entry form for the CompanyMaster project.

You learned how to perform single-record searches using the three search methods:

- `Move` for browsing the dataset
- `Seek` for indexed table objects
- `Find` for nontable objects (Dynasets and Snapshots)

You created an OLE Server library to handle adding, editing, deleting, reading, writing, and locating records in datasets. These routines were written as a generic DLL that can be inserted into all Visual Basic programs you write in the future.

You used the new library to add a new form to the CompanyMaster database project. This new form reads a dataset and enables the user to update and browse the table. This new data entry form was built using fewer than 30 lines of Visual Basic code.

Day 10: Displaying Your Data with Graphs

On Day 10, you learned how to use the graph control that ships with Visual Basic 6 to create visual displays of your data tables. You learned how to add the control to your project and how to load the graph control with data points, titles, legends, and labels.

You also built a graph ActiveX DLL object library that you can use to display virtually any dataset in a variety of graph formats. This library enables you to save the graph to disk, send the graph to the printer, or copy the graph to the Windows Clipboard for placement in other Windows programs through the Paste Special operation.

While building the graph library, you learned how to declare and use enumerated constants to improve the readability of your Visual Basic code.

Finally, you used the new graph library to add three graphs to the CompanyMaster project.

Day 11: Data-Bound List Boxes, Grids, and Subforms

On Day 11, you learned how to load and use three of the data-bound controls that are shipped with Visual Basic 6:

- The data-bound list box
- The data-bound combo box
- The data-bound grid

You learned how to link these new controls to Recordsets using the Visual Basic 6 data controls and how to use these links to update related tables.

You also learned several of the important Visual Basic 6 events associated with the data grid. These events enable you to create user-friendly data entry routines using just a data control and the data grid.

Finally, you drew upon your knowledge of data grids, SQL, and form layout to design and implement a data entry subform. This form showed a master table at the top and a related list table at the bottom of the form in a data-bound grid.

Day 12: Creating Databases with SQL

On Day 12, you learned how to create, alter, and delete database table structures using DDL (Data Definition Language) SQL keywords. You also learned that using DDL statements to build tables, create indexes, and establish relationships is an excellent way to automatically document table layouts. You learned how to maintain database structures using the following DDL keywords:

- CREATE TABLE enables you to create entirely new tables in your existing database.
- DROP TABLE enables you to completely remove a table, including any data that is already in the table.
- ALTER TABLE enables you to ADD a new column or DROP an existing column from the table without losing existing data in the other columns.
- CREATE INDEX and DROP INDEX enable you to create indexes that can enforce data integrity or speed data access.
- The CONSTRAINT clause can be added to the CREATE TABLE or ALTER TABLE statement to define relationships between tables using the FOREIGN KEY clause.

Day 13: Error Handling in Visual Basic 6

On Day 13, you covered all the basics of creating your own error-handling routines for Visual Basic applications. You learned that an error handler has three basic parts:

- The `On Error Goto` statement
- The body of the error handler code
- The error handler exit

You learned that an error handler has four possible exits:

- `Resume`: Reexecutes the code that caused the error.
- `Resume Next`: Continues processing at the line immediately following the line that caused the error.
- `Resume label`: Continues processing at the location identified by the label.
- `EXIT` or `END`: `EXIT` ends processing for the current routine, and `END` exits the program completely.

You learned how to use the `Err.Raise` method to flag errors without resorting to modal dialog boxes.

You learned about the major types of errors that you are likely to encounter in your program:

- *General file errors.* These include errors such as `File not Found` and `Invalid Path`. Errors of this type can usually be fixed by the user and then the original procedure reattempted. Use `Resume` as an exit for these types of errors.
- *Database errors.* These include errors related to data entry mistakes, integrity violations, and multiuser-related errors, such as locked records. Errors of this type are best handled by allowing the user to correct the data and attempt the operation again. If you use the Visual Basic data control, you do not have to write error handlers—the data control handles them for you. For operations that do not use the data control, you need to write your own error-handling routines.
- *Physical media errors.* These errors relate to device problems, such as unresponsive printers, downed communications ports, and so on. Sometimes users can fix the problems and continue (for example, refilling the paper tray of the printer). Other times, users cannot fix the problem without first exiting the program. It is a good idea to give users the option of exiting the program safely when errors of these types are reported.

- *Program code errors.* These errors occur because of problems within the Visual Basic code itself. Examples of program code errors include `Object variable not Set` and `For loop not initialized`. Usually, the user cannot do anything to fix errors of this type. It is best to encourage the user to report the error to the system administrator and then exit the program safely.

You also learned that you can declare a global error handler or a local error handler. The advantage of the global error handler is that it enables you to create a single module that handles all expected errors. The disadvantage is that, because of the way Visual Basic keeps track of running routines, you are not able to resume processing at the point the error occurs when you arrive at the global error handler. The advantage of the local error handler is that you are always able to use `Resume`, `Resume Next`, or `Resume label` to continue processing at the point the error occurs. The disadvantage of the local error handler is that you need to add error-handling code to every routine in your program.

Finally, you learned how to create an error handler object library that combines local error trapping with global error messages and responses. The error handler object library also contains modules to keep track of the procedures currently running at the time of the error, a process for printing procedure stack dumps to the screen and to a file, and a process that creates an error log on file for later review.

Day 14: Updating Databases with SQL

The final lesson of the second week showed you how to add, delete, and edit data within tables using the DML (Data Manipulation Language) SQL keywords. You learned that by using DML statements you can quickly create test data for tables and load default values into startup tables. You also learned that DML statements—such as `Append` queries, `Make Table` queries, and `Delete` queries—can outperform equivalent Visual Basic code versions of the same operations.

You learned how to manage data within the tables using the following DML keywords:

- The `INSERT INTO` statement can be used to add new rows to the table using the `VALUES` clause.

- You can create an `Append` query by using the `INSERT INTO_FROM` syntax to copy data from one table to another. You can also copy data from one database to another using the `IN` clause on an `INSERT INTO_FROM` statement.

- You can create new tables by copying the structure and some of the data using the SELECT_INTO statement. This statement can incorporate WHERE, ORDER BY, GROUP BY, and HAVING clauses to limit the scope of the data used to populate the new table you create.

- You can use the DELETE FROM clause to remove one or more records from an existing table. You can even create customized views of the database using the JOIN clause and remove only records that are the result of a JOIN statement.

WEEK 3

At a Glance

Week 1 focused on developing skills necessary to build Visual Basic database applications in the desktop environment. Week 2 focused on the skills needed in the workgroup environment. This week focuses on skills needed for developing enterprise-level Visual Basic applications.

The following topics are covered:

- Using database normalization techniques to improve the organization, integrity, and performance of your databases

- Issues to consider when developing multiuser applications, including Jet locking schemes, the use of cascading updates and deletes for referential integrity, and how transaction management can improve both the speed of your programs and the quality of your data

- Using the Remote Data Control and Remote Data Objects to attach to external relational database management systems

- How to use ActiveX Data Objects (ADO) to connect to data sources

- How to attach to external data sources and use those attachments to build data forms

- Using database replication to distribute and maintain data across an entire organization.

- How to add application-level security features to your program, including user login/logout, programmable access rights for critical operations, and the use of audit trails to track database updates and all secured user activity

When you complete this week, you will have several reusable ActiveX objects that you can place into any Visual Basic application.

Day 15: You focus on using data normalization to increase database integrity and processing speed. The five rules of data normalization are covered, with logical examples that build on your knowledge of SQL.

Day 16: This lesson centers on multiuser considerations. You learn the nuances of cascading updates and cascading deletes. You spend time on transaction management using the `BeginTrans`, `CommitTrans`, and `Rollback` methods. By the time you finish, you have a good understanding of database-level, table-level, and page-level locking schemes.

Day 17: You use two alternate methods to access external database information using Visual Basic 6. You are introduced to the Remote Data Control and to Remote Data Objects. You learn to use the properties, events, and methods of these tools to attach to RDBMS data sources. You also learn some of the basics of remote data access in general.

Day 18: You learn some of the basics of the ADO model and how it can be used in your Visual Basic programs. Then you learn how to use the new ADO data control to build simple data-bound forms. Finally, you build a Visual Basic 6.0 application that shows how to use the ADO model in code to create connection objects, command objects, and recordset objects.

Day 19: You work with attachments to data outside your database. You learn the pluses and minuses of attaching to data. You also use DAO and ADO to build connections and forms that use these connections to external data sources.

Day 20: Database replication is the focus of Day 20. You learn how to use database replication to distribute data changes across a replica set. You learn to use data access objects to create Design Masters and replicas. You also use data access objects to synchronize data changes. Finally, you use data access objects to keep objects from replicating.

Day 21: The main focus of Day 21 is securing your Visual Basic database applications. All quality applications have security to protect the precious data they control. Database security, encryption, and the securing of processes are covered. You look at applying audit trails to track critical activities in your application. Throughout the day, you build security modules that you can insert into any Visual Basic project you create.

DAY 15

Database Normalization

Now that you understand the Data Definition Language (DDL) portion of SQL, it's time to apply that new knowledge to a lesson on database theory. Today you learn about the concept of data normalization. You develop a working definition of data normalization and learn about the advantages of normalizing your databases. You also explore each of the five rules of data normalization, including reasons for applying these rules. When you have completed today's lesson, you will be able to identify ways to use data normalization to improve database integrity and performance.

Throughout today's lesson, you normalize a real database using the data definition SQL statements you learned about on Day 12 ("Creating Databases with SQL") and Day 14 ("Updating Databases with SQL"), and by using Visual Basic's Visdata application, which you learned about in the first week (see Day 6, "Using the Visdata Program").

The topic of data normalization could easily take up an entire book—and there are several excellent books on it. This lesson approaches data normalization from a practical standpoint rather than a theoretical standpoint. You focus on two particular questions: What are the rules? How can these rules help me improve my Visual Basic database applications? To start, let's develop a working definition of data normalization and talk about why it can improve your Visual Basic applications.

What Is Data Normalization?

NEW TERM Data normalization is a process of refining database structures to improve the speed at which data can be accessed and to increase database integrity. This is not easy. Very often, optimizing a table for speed is not the same as optimizing for integrity. Putting a database together involves discovering the data elements you need and then creating a set of tables to hold those elements. The tables and fields you define make up the structure of the database. The structure you decide upon affects the performance of your database programs. Some database layouts can improve access speed. For example, placing all related information in a single table enables your programs to locate all needed data by looking in one place. On the other hand, you can lay out your database in a way that improves data integrity. For example, placing all the invoice line item data in one table and the invoice address information in another table prevents users from deleting complete addresses when they remove invoice line items from the database. Well-normalized databases strike a balance between speed and integrity.

Note A well-normalized database minimizes the number of times each specific bit of information (such as a company name or address) is entered into the database. Inconsistencies caused by data changes do not occur when data is located in only one place.

High-speed tables have few index constraints and can have several, sometimes repetitive, fields in a single record. The few constraints make updates, insertions, and deletions faster. The repetitive fields make it easier to load large amounts of data in a single SQL statement instead of finding additional, related data in subsidiary tables linked through those slower index constraints.

Databases built for maximum integrity have many small data tables. Each of these tables can have several indexes—mostly foreign keys referencing other tables in the database. If a table is built with high integrity in mind, it is difficult to add invalid data to the database without firing off database error messages. Of course, all that integrity checking eats precious ticks off the microchip clock.

15

> **Note** See Day 1, "Database Programming Basics," for a discussion on foreign keys.

Good data normalization results in data tables that make sense in a fundamental way. Well-normalized tables are easy to understand when you look at them. It is easy to see what kind of data they store and what types of updates need to be performed. Usually, it is rather easy to create data entry routines and simple reports directly from well-normalized tables. In fact, the rule of thumb is this: If it's hard to work with a data table, it probably needs more normalization work.

For the rest of this lesson, you use the Visdata application to build data tables. If you have not already looked at the lesson on Day 6, turn there first for information on how to use Visdata to maintain relational databases.

A Typical Database Before Normalization

 To illustrate the process of normalization, let's start with an existing database table. The database NORMDAT1.MDB can be found in the TYSDBVB6\SOURCE\DATA directory created by the CD-ROM that shipped with this book. Load this into the Visdata application and open the Table1 data table in design mode by right-clicking on Table1 in the Database window and selecting Design. Your screen should look something like the one in Figure 15.1.

> **Note** Make sure that you use the install routine to transfer the examples and the data from this book's CD-ROM. Simply copying the files from the CD-ROM will not change the file attribute from Read Only, which may lead to problems when you try to open and use these files.

This data table holds information about employees of a small company. The table contains fields for the employee ID and employee name, and the ID, name, and location of the department to which this employee is currently assigned. It also includes fields for tracking the employee's job skills, including the skill code, the name, the department in which the skill was learned, and the ability level that the employee has attained for the designated skill. Up to three different skills can be maintained for each employee.

This table is rather typical of those you find in existing record-oriented databases. It is designed to quickly give users all the available information on a single employee. It is also a fairly simple task to build a data entry form for this data table. The single form can hold the employee and department fields at the top of the form and the three skill field sets toward the bottom of the form. Figure 15.2 shows a simple data form for this table generated by Visdata.

FIGURE 15.1

Displaying Table1 before normalization.

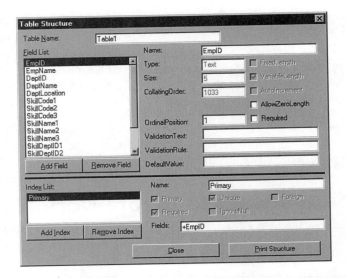

FIGURE 15.2

The data entry form for Table1.

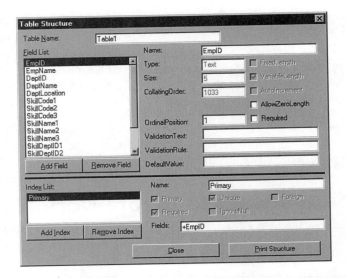

Applying the Rules of Data Normalization

Access to the information in this table is fast and the creation of a data entry screen is easy. So this is a well-normalized table, right? Wrong. Three of the five rules of normalization that you learn in the rest of this lesson are broken, and the other two are in jeopardy! Some of the problems are obvious, some are not.

In the following sections, you explore each of the five rules of data normalization, as developed by E. F. Codd, a researcher at IBM, in 1969. These rules are

- Eliminate repeating groups.
- Eliminate redundant data.
- Eliminate columns not dependent on the primary key.
- Do not store calculated data in your tables.
- Isolate related multiple relationships.

Let's now go through each of the five rules of normalization and see how applying these rules can improve the data table.

Rule 1: Eliminate Repeating Groups

The first area in which Table1 needs some work is in the repeating skill fields. Why include columns in the data table called SkillCode1, SkillCode2, SkillCode3, or SkillName1, SkillName2, SkillName3, and so forth? You want to be able to store more than one set of skills for an employee, right? But what if you want to store data on more than three skills acquired by a single employee? What if most of the employees only have one or two skills, and very few have three skills? Why waste the blank space for the third skill? Even more vexing, how easy will it be to locate all employees in the data table that have a particular skill?

> **Note**
>
> The first rule of data normalization states that you should make a separate table for each set of related columns and give each table a primary key. Databases that adhere to this first rule of normalization are said to be in the First Normal Form.

The first rule of data normalization is to eliminate repeating groups of data in a data table. Repeating groups of data, such as the skill fields (SkillCodeX, SkillNameX, SkillDeptIDX, and SkillLevelX), usually indicates the need for an additional table. Creating the related table greatly improves readability and enables you to keep as few or as many skill sets for each employee as you need without wasting storage space.

The fields that relate to employee skills need to be separated from the others in the table. You don't need to put all 12 skill fields in the new table, though. You only need one of each of the unique data fields. The new database now has not one, but two data tables. One, called Skills, contains only the skill fields. The other table, called Employees, contains the rest of the fields. Table 15.1 shows how the two new tables look.

TABLE 15.1   ELIMINATING REPEATING DATA

Skills Table	Employees Table
EmpID	EmpID
SkillCode	EmpName
SkillName	DeptID
SkillDeptID	DeptName
SkillLevel	DeptLocation

Notice that the first field in both tables is the EmpID field. This field is used to relate the two tables. Each record in the Skills table contains the employee ID and all pertinent data on a single job skill (code, name, department learned, and ability level). If a single employee has several skills, there is a single record in the Skill table for each job skill acquired by an employee. For example, if a single employee has acquired five skills, there are five records with the same employee ID in the Skills table.

Each record in the Skills table must contain a valid value in the EmpID field or it should be rejected. In other words, each time a record is added to the Skills table, the value in the EmpID field should be checked against values in the EmpID field of the Employees table. If no match is found, the Skills record must be corrected before it is written to the database. You remember from the discussion of SQL Data Definition Language statements on Day 12 that this is a FOREIGN KEY CONSTRAINT. The field EmpID in the Skills table is a foreign key that references the field EmpID in the Employees table. Also, the EmpID field in the Employees table should be a primary field to make sure that each record in the Employee table has a unique EmpID value.

Note

Resist the temptation to use string fields when numeric fields can be used when designing your data tables. For example, the EmpID field can be set up as either a string or a number field, but the database will perform much faster if you build it as a number.

15

Now that you know the fields and index constraints you need, you can use SQL DDL to create two new tables. If you have not already done so, start the Visdata application by selecting Add Ins | Visual Data Manager from the Visual Basic 6 menu and opening the NORMDAT1.MDB database. Now you create two new tables that bring the database into compliance with the first rule of data normalization.

First, create the table that holds all the basic employee data. This table has all the fields that were in the Table1 table, minus the skill fields. Using the information in Table 15.1 as a guide, enter an SQL DDL statement in the SQL window of Visdata that creates the Employees data table. Your SQL statement should resemble Listing 15.1.

Note

When you enter the following SQL statement into the Visdata SQL Statement window, you will be prompted as to whether this is a Pass Through Query. Answer No at this prompt. Afterwards, you will receive an error message 3219 from Visdata. This is an erroneous error message. Clear this message and Refresh your table listing in the Database window to reveal the created table.

LISTING 15.1 CREATING THE EMPLOYEES TABLE

```
1: CREATE TABLE Employees
2: (EmpID TEXT(5),
3: EmpName TEXT(30),
4: DeptID TEXT(5),
5: DeptName TEXT(20),
6: DeptLocation TEXT(20),
7: CONSTRAINT PKEmpID PRIMARY KEY (EmpID));
```

The EmpID field has been designated as a primary key field in line 7. This guarantees that no two records in the Employees data table can have the same EmpID value. You can use the EmpID field in the next table you create (the Skills table) as the reference field that links the two tables. Because you are using the EmpID field as a link, it must be a unique value in the Employees table in order to maintain database integrity. What you are doing here is setting up a one-to-many relationship between the Employees table (the one-side) and the Skills table (the many-side). Any time you establish a one-to-many relationship, you must make sure that the reference field (in this case, the EmpID field) is unique on the one-side of the relationship.

Now that you have built the Employees table, you can create the table that holds all the skills data. Use the information in Table 15.1 to write an SQL DDL statement that creates a table called Skills. Make sure the new table has the field EmpID and that the

EmpID field is built with the correct index constraint to enforce one-to-many database integrity. Your SQL statement should look like the one in Listing 15.2.

LISTING 15.2 CREATING THE SKILLS TABLE

```
1: CREATE TABLE Skills
2: (EmpID TEXT(5),
3: SkillCode TEXT(5),
4: SkillName TEXT(20),
5: SkillDeptID TEXT(5),
6: SkillLevel INTEGER,
7: CONSTRAINT PKSkills PRIMARY KEY (SkillCode,EmpID),
8: CONSTRAINT FKEmpID FOREIGN KEY (EmpID) REFERENCES Employees(EmpID));
```

You can see in Listing 15.2 that you have used the FOREIGN KEY_REFERENCES syntax (line 8) to establish and maintain the table relationship. As you remember from the SQL lessons on Day 12 and Day 14, the FOREIGN KEY_REFERENCES syntax makes sure that any entry in the Skills.EmpID field can be found in the related Employees.EmpID field. If users enter a value in the Skills.EmpID field that cannot be found in any Employees.EmpID field, Visual Basic automatically issues a database error message. This message is generated by Visual Basic, not by your program.

That is how you build tables that adhere to the first rule of data normalization. To see how these tables look when they have live data in them, use Visdata to load the TYSDBVB6\SOURCE\DATA\NORMDAT2.MDB database. This database contains the Employees and Skills tables with data already loaded into them. Figure 15.3 shows how Visdata displays the two new tables that have live data.

Note Before continuing with today's lesson, load the NORMDAT2.MDB database into Visdata.

Rule 2: Eliminate Redundant Data

Another aspect of the Skills table also needs attention. Although moving the repeating skills fields into a separate table improves the database, you still have work to do. The Skills table contains redundant data. That is, data is stored in several places in the database. Redundant data in your database can lead to serious database integrity problems. It's best to eliminate as many occurrences of redundant data as possible.

FIGURE 15.3

The new Employees and Skills tables from NORMDAT2.MDB.

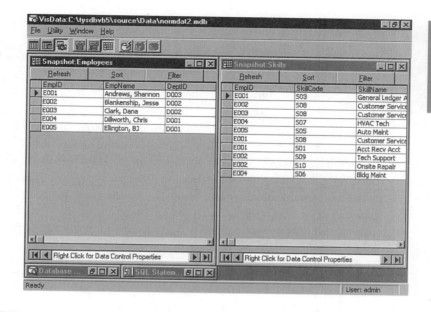

> **Note**
>
> The second rule of data normalization states that if a column depends only on part of a multivalued key, you remove it to a separate table. In other words, if you need to fill in two fields in order to truly identify the record (JobID and JobName), but only one of those fields is needed to perform a lookup in the table, you need a new table. Databases that conform to this rule are said to be in the Second Normal Form.

For example, the Skills table includes a field called SkillCode. This field contains a code that identifies the specific skill (or skills) each employee has acquired. If two employees have gained the same skill, that skill appears twice in the Skills file. The same table also includes a field called SkillName. This field contains a meaningful name for the skill represented by the value in the SkillCode field. This name is much more readable and informative than the SkillCode value. In essence, these two fields contain the same data, represented slightly differently. This is the dreaded redundant data you have to eliminate!

Before you jump into fixing things, first review the details regarding redundant data and how it can adversely affect the integrity of your database.

Update Integrity Problems

When you keep copies of data elements in several rows in the same table or in several different tables (such as job names to go with job ID codes), you have a lot of work ahead of you when you want to modify the copied data. If you fail to update one or more of these copies, you can ruin the integrity of your database. Redundant data can lead to what are known as update integrity problems.

Imagine that you have built a huge database of employee skills using the tables you built in the preceding section. All is going great when, suddenly, the Human Resources Department informs you that it has designed a new set of names for the existing skill codes. You now have to go through the entire database and update all the records in the Skills table, searching out the old skill name and updating the SkillName field with the new skill name. Because this is an update for the entire data table, you have to shut down the database until the job is complete in order to make sure no one is editing records while you're performing this update. Also, you probably have to change some Visual Basic code that you built to verify the data entry. All in all, it's a nasty job. If that isn't enough, how about a little power outage in the middle of your update run? Now you have some records with the old names, and some with the new names. Things are really messed up!

Delete Integrity Problems

Although the update integrity problem is annoying, you can suffer through most of those problems. In fact, almost all database programmers have had to face similar problems before. The more troublesome integrity problem resulting from redundant data comes not during updates, but during deletes. Let's assume you have properly handled the mass update required by the Human Resources Department. Then you discover that there is only one employee in the entire database that has the SkillCode S099 (Advanced Customer Service course). No other employee has attained this high level of training. Now that employee is leaving the organization. When you delete the employee record from the file, you delete the only reference to the Advanced Customer Service course! There is no longer any record of the Advanced Customer Service course in your entire database, which is a real problem.

The Normalization Solution

The way to reduce these kinds of data integrity problems is to pull out the redundant data and place it in a separate table. You need a single table, called SkillMaster, that contains only the SkillCode and the SkillName data fields. This table is linked to the Skills table through the SkillCode field. Now, when the Human Resources department changes the skill names, you need to update only a single record: the one in the SkillMaster table. Because the Skills table is linked to the SkillMaster table, when you delete the employee with the certification for SkillCode S099, you don't delete the last reference to the skill. It's still in the SkillMaster table.

> **Tip**
>
> Another plus to this type of table separation is in speeding data entry. With only one field to enter, and especially a brief code, data entry operators can more quickly fill in fields on the table's form.

Also, you now have a single table that lists all the unique skills that can be acquired by your employees. You can produce a Skills list for employees and managers to review. If you add fields that group the skills by department, you can even produce a report that shows all the skills by department. This would be very difficult if you were stuck with the file structure you developed in the preceding section.

So let's redefine the Skills table and the SkillMaster table to conform to the second rule of data normalization. Table 15.2 shows the fields you need for the two tables.

TABLE 15.2   THE FIELD LIST FOR THE SKILLS AND SKILLMASTER TABLES

EmpSkills	SkillMaster
EmpID	SkillCode
SkillCode	SkillName
SkillDeptID	
SkillLevel	

You can see that you rename the Skills table to EmpSkills to better reflect its contents. You also move the SkillName field out of the EmpSkills table and create SkillMaster, a small table that contains a list of all the valid skills and their descriptive names. Now you have the added bonus of being able to add a FOREIGN KEY constraint to the EmpSkills table. This improves database integrity without adding any additional programming code!

Listings 15.3a and 15.3b show the two SQL DDL statements that create the EmpSkills and the SkillMaster data tables. Note the use of FOREIGN KEY constraints in the EmpSkills table.

LISTING 15.3A   CREATING THE SKILLMASTER TABLE

```
1: CREATE TABLE SkillMaster
2: (SkillCode TEXT(5),
3: SkillName TEXT(20),
4: CONSTRAINT PKSkillMaster PRIMARY KEY (SkillCode))
```

LISTING 15.3B CREATING THE EMPSKILLS TABLE

```
 1: CREATE TABLE EmpSkills
 2: (EmpID TEXT(5),
 3: SkillCode TEXT(5),
 4: SkillDeptID TEXT(5),
 5: SkillLevel INTEGER,
 6: CONSTRAINT PKSkills PRIMARY KEY (SkillCode,EmpID),
 7: CONSTRAINT FKEmpID2 FOREIGN KEY (EmpID)
 8: REFERENCES Employees(EmpID),
 9: CONSTRAINT FKSkillCode FOREIGN KEY (SkillCode)
10: REFERENCES SkillMaster(SkillCode));
```

Use Visdata to add these two new tables to the NORMDAT2.MDB database. Please note that you must run these statements sequentially. Trying to run two CREATE statements in Visdata at one time will result in an error. The database TYSDBVB6\SOURCE\DATA\NORM-DAT3.MDB contains a complete database with the data tables Employees, EmpSkills, and SkillMaster fully populated with data. This is demonstrated in Figure 15.4.

FIGURE 15.4

The new Employees, EmpSkills, and SkillMaster tables.

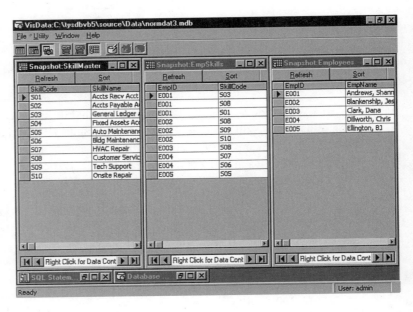

You now have a database that conforms to the first two rules of data normalization. You have eliminated repeating data and redundant data. You have one more type of data to eliminate from your tables. You handle that in the following section.

Note

Before continuing with the lesson, load the NORMDAT3.MDB database into
Visdata.

15

Rule 3: Eliminate Columns Not Dependent on the Primary Key

By now, you're probably getting the idea. You are looking for hints in the table structure that lead you into traps further down the road. Will this table be easy to update? What happens if you delete records from this table? Is it easy to get a comprehensive list of all the unique records in this table? Asking questions like these can uncover problems that are not so apparent when you first build a table.

When you are building a data table, you should also be concerned about whether a field describes additional information about the key field. In other words, is the field you are about to add to this table truly related to the key field? If not, the field in question should not be added to the table. It probably needs to be in its own table. This process of removing fields that do not describe the key field is how you make your data tables conform to the third rule of data normalization—eliminate columns not dependent on keys.

Note

The third rule of data normalization states that if a column does not fully describe the index key, that column should be moved to a separate table. In other words, if the columns in your table don't really need to be in this table, they probably need to be somewhere else. Databases that follow this rule are known to be in the Third Normal Form.

In these database examples, you have data describing the various departments in the company stored in the Employees table. Although the DeptID field is important to the Employees description (it describes the department to which the employee belongs), the department-specific data should not be stored with the employee data. Yes, you need another table. This table should contain only department-specific data and be linked to the Employees table through the DeptID field. Table 15.3 lists the modified Employees table and the new Departments table.

TABLE 15.3   THE MODIFIED EMPLOYEES TABLE AND THE NEW DEPARTMENTS TABLE

Employees	Departments
EmpID	DeptID
EmpName	DeptName
DeptID	DeptLocation

Notice that the Employees table is much simpler now that you have eliminated all unrelated fields. Use Visdata to construct SQL DDL statements that create the new Departments table and then modify the Employees table and the EmpSkills table to increase database integrity (yes, more foreign keys!). First, use the SQL DDL in Listing 15.4 to create the Departments table. Check your work against Figure 15.5.

FIGURE 15.5

The Departments table added to NORMDAT4.MDB.

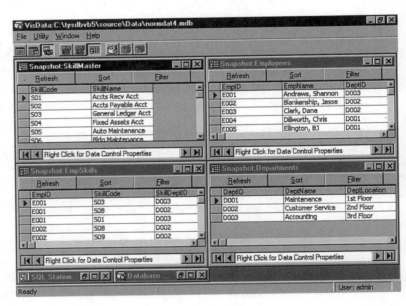

LISTING 15.4   CREATING THE DEPARTMENTS TABLE

```
1: CREATE TABLE Departments
2: (DeptID TEXT(5),
3: DeptName TEXT(20),
4: DeptLocation TEXT(20),
5: CONSTRAINT PKDeptID PRIMARY KEY (DeptID))
```

Now alter the Employees table. You need to do two things:

- Remove the DeptName column from the table.
- Add a FOREIGN KEY constraint to enforce referential integrity on the Employees.DeptID field.

Listing 15.5 contains the SQL DDL statements to create the modified Employees table.

LISTING 15.5   CREATING THE NEW EMPLOYEES TABLE

```
1: CREATE TABLE Employees
2: (EmpID TEXT(5),
3: EmpName TEXT(30),
4: DeptID TEXT(5),
5: CONSTRAINT PKEmpID PRIMARY KEY (EmpID),
6: CONSTRAINT FKEmpDept FOREIGN KEY (DeptID)
7: REFERENCES Departments(DeptID))
```

Now you need to modify the EmpSkills table to add the referential integrity check on the EmpSkills.SkillDeptID field. The new SQL DDL should look like Listing 15.6.

LISTING 15.6   CREATING THE NEW EMPSKILLS TABLE

```
1: CREATE TABLE EmpSkills2
2: (EmpID TEXT(5),
3: SkillCode TEXT(5),
4: SkillDeptID TEXT(5),
5: SkillLevel INTEGER,
6: CONSTRAINT PKEmpSkill2 PRIMARY KEY (SkillCode,EmpID),
7: CONSTRAINT FKSkillMast FOREIGN KEY (SkillCode)
8: REFERENCES SkillMaster(SkillCode),
9: CONSTRAINT FKSkillDept FOREIGN KEY (SkillDeptID)
10: REFERENCES Departments(DeptID));
```

The database NORMDAT4.MDB contains a complete set of tables that conform to the third rule of data normalization. Use Visdata to load NORMDAT4.MDB and review the data tables. Attempt to add some data that does not follow the integrity rules. Try deleting records. This shows you how Visual Basic issues database error messages when you try to save a record that breaks the referential integrity rules.

The first three rules of data normalization involve the elimination of repeating, redundant, or unrelated data fields. The last two rules involve isolating multiple relationships to improve overall database integrity. The first three rules are usually all that you need to produce well-designed databases. However, there are times when additional normalization can improve the quality of your database design. In the next two sections, you learn rules 4 and 5 of data normalization.

Do Not Store Calculated Data in Your Tables

It is important to note here that one of the results of the third rule of data normalization is that you should not store calculated fields in a data table. Calculated fields are fields that contain derived data such as year-to-date totals, a line in the invoice table that contains the totals of several other rows in the invoice table, and so forth. Calculated fields do not describe the primary key. Calculated fields are derived data. It is a bad practice to store derived data in live data tables.

Derived data can easily fall out of sync with the individual rows that make up the total data. What happens if the individual rows that add up to the total are altered or deleted? How do you make sure the row that holds the total is updated each time any line item row is changed? Storing derived data might seem to be faster, but it is not easier. And dealing with derived data opens your database to possible update and delete integrity problems each time a user touches either the prime data rows or the total data rows. Calculated data should not be stored. It should always be computed using the prime data at the time it is needed.

Note

> Before continuing with this lesson, load the NORMDAT4.MDB database into Visdata.

Rule 4: Isolate Independent Multiple Relationships

The fourth rule of data normalization concerns the handling of independent multiple relationships. This rule is applied whenever you have more than one one-to-many relationship on the same data table. The relationship between the Employees table and the EmpSkills table is a one-to-many relationship. There can be many EmpSkills records related to one Employee record. Let's add an additional attribute of employees to create a database that has more than a single one-to-many relationship.

Assume that the Human Resources Department has decided it needs more than just the skill names and skill levels attained for each employee. Human Resources also wants to add the level of education attained by the employee for that skill. For example, if the employee has an accounting skill and has an associate's degree in bookkeeping, Human Resources wants to store the degree information, too. If an employee has been certified as an electrician and works in the Maintenance Department, the Human Resources group wants to know that.

15

The first thing you might want to do is add a new column to the EmpSkills table—maybe a field called Degree, maybe even a field for YearCompleted. This makes sense because each skill might have an associated education component. It makes sense, but it is not a good idea. What about the employee who is currently working in the Customer Service Department but has an accounting degree? What happens if an employee has multiple degrees? Just because the employee has a degree does not mean that employee has the skills to perform a particular job or is working in a position directly related to his or her degree. The degree and the job skills are independent of each other. Therefore, even though the skills data and the degree data are related, they should be isolated in separate tables and linked through a foreign key relationship.

> **Note**
>
> The fourth rule of data normalization dictates that no table can contain two or more one-to-many or many-to-many relationships that are not directly related. In other words, if the data element is important (the college degree) but not directly related to other elements in the record (the customer service rep with an accounting degree), you need to move the college degree element to a new table. Databases that follow this rule are in the Fourth Normal Form.

Table 15.4 shows a sample Training table that can be used to hold the education information for each employee. Now the Human Resources department can keep track of education achievements independent of acquired job skills. Note that the EmpID directly connects the two relationships. If the Training table has only one entry per employee, the two relationships are a one-to-one relationship between the Employees table and the Training table, and a one-to-many relationship between the Employees table and the EmpSkills table. Of course, if any employee has more than one degree, both relationships become one-to-many.

TABLE 15.4   THE SAMPLE TRAINING DATA TABLE

EmpID
Degree
YearCompleted
InstitutionName

Listing 15.7 is a sample SQL DDL statement that creates the Training data table with the proper relationship constraint. Enter this statement in the SQL window of Visdata while you have the NORMDAT4.MDB database open. Check your results against Figure 15.6.

FIGURE 15.6

The Training table shows the degree achievements for the Employees table.

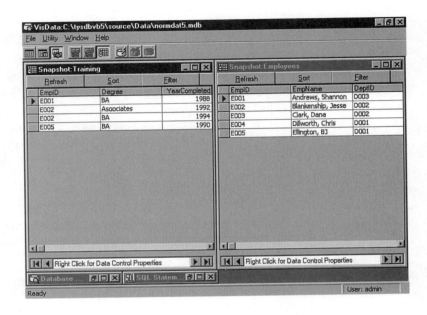

LISTING 15.7 CREATING THE TRAINING TABLE

```
1: CREATE TABLE Training
2: (EmpID TEXT(5),
3: Degree TEXT(20),
4: YearCompleted INTEGER,
5: InstitutionName TEXT(30),
6: CONSTRAINT PKTraining PRIMARY KEY (EmpID,Degree),
7: CONSTRAINT FKEmpTrn FOREIGN KEY (EmpID)
8: REFERENCES Employees (EmpID))
```

The database NORMDAT5.MDB contains a complete version of the database normalized up to the fourth rule of data normalization. Use Visdata to open the database and review the table structure.

Note

Before continuing with the lesson, load the NORMDAT5.MDB database into Visdata.

Rule 5: Isolate Related Multiple Relationships

The last remaining rule of data normalization covers the handling of related multiple relationships in a database. Unlike the fourth rule, which deals with independent,

15

one-to-many, multiple relationships, the fifth rule is used to normalize related, many-to-many multiple relationships. Related, many-to-many multiple relationships do not occur frequently in databases. However, when they do come up, these types of data relations can cause a great deal of confusion and hassle when you're normalizing your database. You won't invoke this rule often, but when you do it pays off!

Imagine that the Maintenance Department decides it wants to keep track of all the large equipment used on the shop floor by various departments. It uses this data to keep track of where the equipment is located. The Maintenance Department also wants to keep a list of suppliers for the equipment in cases of repair or replacement. When you were a novice, you might have decided to design a single table that held the department ID, equipment name, and supplier name. But, as I'm sure you have guessed by now, that is not the correct response. What if the Maintenance Department has more than one supplier for the same type of equipment? What if a single supplier provides more than one of the types of equipment used in the plant? What if some departments are restricted in the suppliers they can use to repair or replace their equipment?

Note

The fifth rule of data normalization dictates that you should isolate related multiple relationships within a database. In other words, if several complex relationships exist in your database, separate each of the relationships into its own table. Databases that adhere to this rule are known to be in the Fifth Normal Form.

The following list shows the relationships that have been exposed in this example:

- Each department can have several pieces of equipment.
- Each piece of equipment can have more than one supplier.
- Each supplier can provide a variety of pieces of equipment.
- Each department can have a restricted list of suppliers.

Although each of the preceding business rules are simple, putting them all together in the database design is tough. It's the last item that really complicates things. There is more than one way to solve this kind of puzzle. The one suggested here is just one of the many possibilities.

First, you need to expose all the tables that you need to contain the data. The preceding list describes two one-to-many relationships (department to equipment, and department to supplier, with restrictions) and one many-to-many relationship (equipment to supplier, supplier to equipment). Each of those relationships can be expressed in simple tables. Two additional tables not mentioned, but certainly needed, are a table of all the equipment in the building (regardless of its location) and a table of all the suppliers (regardless of their department affiliation). Table 15.5 shows sample field layouts for the required tables. The Equipment and Supplier tables are shortened in this example. If you were designing these tables for a real database project, you would add several other fields.

TABLE 15.5   THE FIFTH RULE SAMPLE DATA TABLES

Equipment	Supplier
EquipID	SupplierID
EquipName	SupplierName
DatePurchased	SupplierAddress

Listings 15.8a and 15.8b contain the SQL DDL statements to create these tables. Figure 15.7 shows the results of executing these statements. Please remember that when you execute a CREATE statement in Visdata, you receive an erroneous error message 3219. Simply clear this message and refresh the Database window to see the created tables.

FIGURE 15.7

Supplier and Equipment tables in NORMDAT6.MDB.

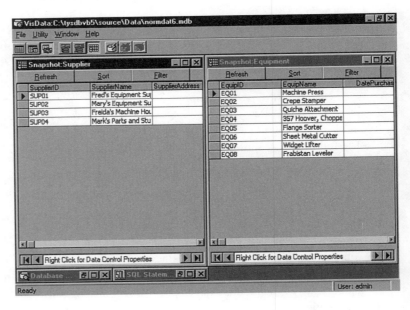

LISTING 15.8A   CREATING THE EQUIPMENT TABLE

```
1: CREATE TABLE Equipment
2: (EquipID TEXT (10),
3: EquipName TEXT(30),
4: DatePurchased DATE,
5: CONSTRAINT PKEquipID PRIMARY KEY (EquipID))
```

LISTING 15.8B   CREATING THE SUPPLIER TABLE

```
1: CREATE TABLE Supplier
2: (SupplierID TEXT (10),
3: SupplierName TEXT(30),
4: SupplierAddress MEMO,
5: CONSTRAINT PKSupplier PRIMARY KEY (SupplierID))
```

The next two data tables describe the relationships between Supplier and Equipment and between Supplier and Departments. You remember that departments can be restricted to certain suppliers when repairing or replacing equipment. By setting up a table such as the DeptSupplier table described next, you can easily maintain a list of valid suppliers for each department. Similarly, as new suppliers are discovered for equipment, they can be added to the EquipSupplier table. Refer to Table 15.6 for a sample list of fields.

TABLE 15.6   EQUIPSUPPLIER AND DEPTSUPPLIER TABLES

EquipSupplier	DeptSupplier
EquipID	DeptID
SupplierID	SupplierID

These two tables are short because they are needed only to enforce expressed simple relationships between existing data tables. Creating small tables such as these is a handy way to reduce complex relationships to more straightforward ones. It is easier to create meaningful CONSTRAINT clauses when the tables are kept simple, too. The SQL DDL statements for these two tables appear in Listing 15.9a and 15.9b. The result of executing these statements in Visdata appears in Figure 15.8.

LISTING 15.9A   CREATING THE EQUIPSUPPLIER TABLE.

```
1: CREATE TABLE EquipSupplier
2: (EquipID TEXT(10),
3: SupplierID TEXT(10),
4: CONSTRAINT PKEqSpl PRIMARY KEY (EquipID,SupplierID),
5: CONSTRAINT FKEqSplEquip FOREIGN KEY (EquipID)
6: REFERENCES Equipment(EquipID),
7: CONSTRAINT FKEqSplSupplier FOREIGN KEY (SupplierID)
8: REFERENCES Supplier(SupplierID))
```

FIGURE 15.8

The EquipSupplier and DeptSupplier tables.

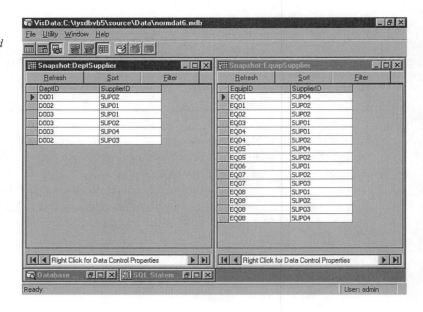

LISTING 15.9B CREATING THE DEPTSUPPLIER TABLE

```
1: CREATE TABLE DeptSupplier
2: (DeptID TEXT(5),
3: SupplierID TEXT(10),
4: CONSTRAINT PKDeptSpl PRIMARY KEY (DeptID,SupplierID),
5: CONSTRAINT FKDptSplDept FOREIGN KEY (DeptID)
6: REFERENCES Departments(DeptID),
7: CONSTRAINT FKDptSplSupplier FOREIGN KEY (SupplierID)
8: REFERENCES Supplier(SupplierID))
```

Notice that, in these two tables, the CONSTRAINT definitions are longer than the field definitions. This is common when you begin to use the power database integrity aspects of SQL databases.

Finally, you need a single table that expresses the Equipment-Supplier-Department relationship. This table shows which department has which equipment supplied by which supplier. More importantly, you can build this final table with tight constraints that enforce all these business rules. Both the Department-Supplier relationship and the Equipment-Supplier relationship are validated before the record is saved to the database. This is a powerful data validation tool—all without writing any Visual Basic code! Table 15.7 and the SQL DDL statement in Listing 15.10 show how this table can be constructed. See Figure 15.9 to review the results of executing these statements.

FIGURE 15.9

The EquipSupplier, DeptSupplier, and DeptEqpSuplr tables.

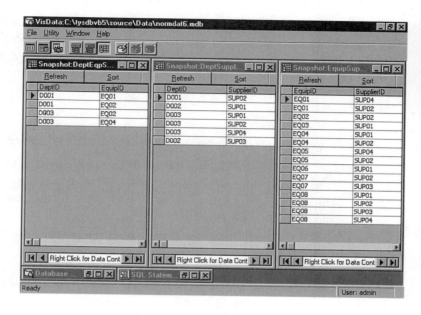

TABLE 15.7 THE DEPARTMENT-EQUIPMENT-SUPPLIER DATA TABLE

DeptID

EquipID

SupplierID

LISTING 15.10 CREATING THE DEPTEQPSUPLR TABLE

```
1: CREATE TABLE DeptEqpSuplr
2: (DeptID TEXT(5),
3: EquipID TEXT(10),
4: SupplierID TEXT(10),
5: CONSTRAINT PFDeptEq PRIMARY KEY (DeptID, EquipID),
6: CONSTRAINT FKEqSupl FOREIGN KEY (EquipID,SupplierID)
7: REFERENCES EquipSupplier(EquipID,SupplierID),
8: CONSTRAINT FKDeptSupl FOREIGN KEY (DeptID,SupplierID)
9: REFERENCES DeptSupplier(DeptID,SupplierID))
```

The Microsoft Access database NORMDAT6.MDB contains a set of live data for the tables described in this section. Use Visdata to open the database and review the table structure. Try adding or deleting records in ways that would break integrity rules. Notice that none of the last three tables defined (EquipSupplier, DeptSupplier, and DeptEqpSuplr) allow edits on any existing record. This is because you defined the primary key as having all the fields in a record. Because you cannot edit a primary key value, you must first delete the record and then add the modified version to the data table.

Summary

In today's lesson, you learned how to improve database integrity and access speed using the five rules of data normalization. You learned the following five rules:

- *Rule 1: Eliminate Repeating Groups.* If you have a set of fields that have the same name followed by a number (Skill1, Skill2, Skill3, and so forth), remove these repeating groups, create a new table for the repeating data, and relate it to the key field in the first table.

- *Rule 2: Eliminate Redundant Data.* Don't store the same data in two different locations. This can lead to update and delete errors. If equivalent data elements are entered in two fields, remove the second data element, create a new master table with the element and its partner as a key field, and then place the key field as a relationship in the locations that formerly held both data elements.

- *Rule 3: Eliminate Columns Not Dependent on Keys.* If you have data elements that are not directly related to the primary key of the table, these elements should be removed to their own data table. Store only data elements that are directly related to the primary key of the table. This particularly includes derived data or other calculations.

- *Rule 4: Isolate Independent Multiple Relationships.* Use this rule to improve database design when you are dealing with more than one one-to-many relationship in the database. Before you add a new field to a table, ask yourself whether this field is really dependent upon the other fields in the table. If not, create a new table with the independent data.

- *Rule 5: Isolate Related Multiple Relationships.* Use this rule to improve database design when you are dealing with more than one many-to-many relationship in the database. If you have database rules that require multiple references to the same field or sets of fields, isolate the fields into smaller tables and construct one or more link tables that contain the required constraints that enforce database integrity.

15

Quiz

1. Is it a good idea to optimize your database strictly for speed?
2. What is meant by the term First Normal Form?
3. Explain how the second rule of data normalization differs from the first rule of normalization.
4. Should you include fields in a data table that are the calculated results of other fields in the same table?
5. When would you invoke the fourth rule of data normalization?
6. When would you invoke the fifth rule of data normalization?

Exercises

1. As a computer consultant, you have landed a contract to build a customer tracking system for your local garage. After several days of interviews with the owner, mechanics, and staff members, you have determined that the following data fields should be included in your database. Many of the customers of this garage have more than one automobile. Therefore, you are requested to leave room for tracking two cars per customer.

   Use these fields: CustomerID, CustomerName, Address, City, State, Zip, Phone, SerialNumber, License, VehicleType1, Make1, Model1, Color1, Odometer1, VehicleType2, Make2, Model2, Color2, Odometer2.

   Optimize this data into tables using the rules of data normalization discussed in today's lesson. Identify all primary and foreign keys.

2. Write the SQL statements that create the tables you designed in Exercise 1.

DAY 16

Multiuser Considerations

Today, you look at some issues related to designing and coding applications that serve multiple users. Multiuser applications pose some unique challenges when it comes to database operations. These challenges are the main topics of this chapter:

- *Database locking schemes.* You examine the locking system used by the Microsoft Jet database engine, and you look at the differences between optimistic and pessimistic locking schemes. You learn a scheme for performing multitable locking of data tables in highly relational databases.

- *Cascading updates and deletes.* You learn how to use these features of the Microsoft Jet database engine to enforce database relations using the Cascading Updates and Deletes options.

- *Transaction management.* You see the process of transaction management, as well as how to add transaction management to your Visual Basic applications by using the BeginTrans, CommitTrans, and Rollback methods. Transaction management using the SQL pass-through method with back-end databases also is covered.

By the time you complete this chapter, you'll be able to add transaction management to your Visual Basic applications, and you'll understand using cascading updates and deletes to maintain the referential integrity of your database. You also will know how to perform database-level, table-level, and page-level locking schemes in your database applications.

Understanding Database Locking Schemes

When more than one person is accessing a single database, some type of process must be used to prevent two users from attempting to update the same record at the same time. This process is a locking scheme. In its simplest form, a locking scheme allows only one user at a time to update information in the database.

The Microsoft Jet database engine provides three levels of locking:

- *Database locking.* At this level, only one user at a time can access the database. Use this locking level when you need to perform work on multiple, related database objects (such as tables, queries, indexes, and relations) at the same time.
- *Table locking.* At this level, only one user at a time can access the locked table. Use this locking level when you need to perform work on multiple records in the same table.
- *Page locking.* At this level, only one user can access the page of records in the database table. This is the lowest locking level provided by Microsoft Jet. Page locking is handled automatically by Visual Basic whenever you attempt to edit or update a record in a dataset.

Database Locking

Database-level locking is the most restrictive locking scheme you can use in your Visual Basic application. When you open the database using the Visual Basic data control, you can lock the database by setting the Exclusive property of the data control to True. After you open the database by using Visual Basic code, you can lock the database by setting the second parameter of the OpenDatabase method to True. Here's an example:

```
Set db = DbEngine.OpenDatabase("c:mydb",True)
```

When the database is locked, no other users can open it. Other programs cannot read or write any information until you close the database. You should use database-level locking only when you must perform work that affects multiple data objects (such as tables, indexes, relations, and queries). The Visual Basic CompactDatabase operation, for example, affects all the data objects, so the database must be opened exclusively.

If you need to perform an operation to update the customer ID values in several tables and you also need to update several queries to match new search criteria, you should use database-level locking.

Take a look at a Visual Basic project to see how database-level locking works. Load Visual Basic and open a new project. Add a data control to the form. Set its `Databasename` property to `C:\TYSDBVB6\SOURCE\DATA\MULTIUSE.MDB` and its `Exclusive` property to `True`. Save the form as `MULTIUS1.FRM` and the project as `MULTIUS1.VBP`. Now create an executable version of the project by choosing File|Make `MULTIUS1.EXE` from the Visual Basic main menu. Use `MULTIUS1.EXE` as the name of the executable file.

Run the executable file. It loads and displays the data control. Run a second instance of the executable file. This is an attempt to run a copy of the same program. Because this second copy attempts to open the same database for exclusive use, you see an error message when the second program starts (see Figure 16.1).

16

FIGURE 16.1

Error message received when attempting to open a locked database.

Couldn't use 'C:\TYSDBVB6\source\DATA\multiuse.mdb'; file already in use

OK

Notice that the second program continues after the error occurs, even though the database is not opened. You can check for the error when you first load the project by adding the following code to the `Error` event of the data control:

```
Private Sub Data1_Error(DataErr As Integer, Response As Integer)
    If Err <> 0 Then
        MsgBox Error$(Err)+Chr(13)+"Exiting Program", _
         vbCritical, "Data1_Error"
    Unload Me
    End If
End Sub
```

Add this code to the `Data1_Error` event and then recompile the program. Again, attempt to run two instances of this program. This time, when you attempt to start the second instance, you receive a similar message, after which the program exits safely. (See Figure 16.2.)

FIGURE 16.2

Trapping the locked database error.

Table Locking

You can use table-level locking to secure a single table while you perform sensitive operations on the table. If you want to increase the sale price of all items in your inventory by five percent, for example, you open the table for exclusive use and then perform the update. After you close the table, other users can open it and see the new price list. Using table-level locking for an operation such as this can help prevent users from writing sales orders that contain some records with the old price and some records with the new price.

Now modify the MULTIUS1.VBP project to illustrate table-level locking. Reopen the project and set the Exclusive property of the data control to False. This setting enables other users to open the database while your program is running. Now set the RecordSource property to MasterTable and set the Options property to 3. Setting the Options property to 3 opens the Recordset with the DenyWrite (1) and DenyRead (2) options turned on. This prevents other programs from opening MasterTable while your program is running.

Save and recompile the program. Start a copy of the executable version of the program. It runs without error. Now attempt to start a second copy of the same program. You see an error message telling you that the table could not be locked because it is in use elsewhere—that is, by the first instance of the program (see Figure 16.3).

FIGURE 16.3

Attempting to open a locked database.

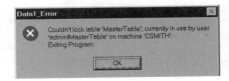

You can perform the same table-locking operation by using this Visual Basic code:

```
Sub OpenTable()
   On Error GoTo OpenTableErr
   '
   Dim db As Database
   Dim rs As Recordset
   '
   Set db = DBEngine.OpenDatabase( _
```

```
   "C:\TYSDBVB6\SOURCE\DATA\MULTIUSE.MDB")
Set rs = db.OpenRecordset("MasterTable", _
dbOpenTable,_dbDenyRead + dbDenyWrite)
'
GoTo OpenTableExit
'
OpenTableErr:
MsgBox Error$(Err) + Chr(13) + "Exiting Program" _
, vbCritical, "OpenTable"
GoTo OpenTableExit
'OpenTableExit:
'
End Sub
```

Notice the use of the `dbDenyRead` and `dbDenyWrite` constants in the `OpenRecordset` method. This is the same as setting the `Option` property of the data control to 3. Also notice that an error trap is added to the module to replace the code in the `Error` event of the data control.

Page Locking

The lowest level of locking available in Visual Basic is page-level locking. Page-level locking is handled automatically by the Microsoft Jet engine and cannot be controlled through Visual Basic code or with data-bound control properties. Each time a user attempts to edit or update a record, the Microsoft Jet engine performs the necessary page locking to ensure data integrity.

What Is Page Locking?

A data page can contain more than one data record. Currently, the Microsoft Jet data page is always 2KB. Locking a data page locks all records that are stored on the same data page. If you have records that are 512 bytes, each time Microsoft Jet performs a page lock, 4 data records are locked. If you have records that are 50 bytes, each Microsoft Jet page lock can affect 40 data records.

The exact number of records that are locked on a page cannot be controlled or accurately predicted. If your data table contains several deleted records that have not been compacted out by using the `CompactDatabase` method, you have "holes" in your data pages. These holes do not contain valid records. Also, data pages contain records that are physically adjacent to each other—regardless of any index, filter, or sort order that has been applied to create the dataset. Even though records in a dataset are listed one after another, they might not be physically stored in the same manner. Therefore, editing one of the dataset records might not lock the next record in the dataset list.

Pessimistic and Optimistic Locking

Even though page-level locking is performed automatically by Microsoft Jet, you can use the LockEdits property of a record set to control how page-locking is handled by your application. Two page-locking modes are available: pessimistic locking (LockEdits=True) and optimistic locking (LockEdits=False). The default locking mode is pessimistic.

In pessimistic locking mode, Microsoft Jet locks the data page whenever the Edit or AddNew method is invoked. The page stays locked until an Update or Cancel method is executed. When a page is locked, no other program or user can read or write any data records on the locked data page until the Update or Cancel method has been invoked. The advantage of using the pessimistic locking mode is that it provides the highest level of data integrity possible at the page level. The disadvantage of using the pessimistic locking mode is that it can lock data pages for a long period of time. This can cause other users of the same database to encounter error messages as they attempt to read or write data in the same table.

In optimistic locking mode, Microsoft Jet locks the data page only when the Update method is invoked. Users can invoke the Edit or AddNew method and begin editing data without causing Microsoft Jet to execute a page lock. When the user is done making changes and saves the record using the Update method, Microsoft Jet attempts to place a lock on the page. If it is successful, the record is written to the table. If Microsoft Jet discovers that someone else also has edited the same record and already has saved it, the update is canceled and the user is informed by an error message saying that someone already has changed the data.

The advantage of using optimistic locking is that page locks are in place for the shortest time possible. This reduces the number of lock messages users receive as they access data in your database. The disadvantage of using optimistic locking is that it is possible for two users to edit the same record at the same time. This can lead to lock errors at update time rather than at read time.

An Example of Page-Level Locking

In this section, you build a new Visual Basic project to demonstrate page-level locking as well as the differences between pessimistic and optimistic locking. Load Visual Basic and start a new project.

Place a command button on the form. Set its Name property to cmdEdit and its Caption property to &Edit. Add a frame control to the form and set its Caption property to Page Locking. Place two option button controls in the frame control. Set the Caption property of Option1 to Pessimistic and the Caption property of Option2 to Optimistic. Use Figure 16.4 as a layout guide.

FIGURE 16.4

Laying out the page locking project.

Now you need to add code to this demo. First, place the following variable declarations in the general declarations section of the form:

```
Option Explicit

Dim db As Database
Dim rs As Recordset
Dim cName As String
Dim nMax As Integer
```

Now add the following code to the Form_Load event. This code prompts you for a name for the form header. It then opens the database and data table, and it counts all the records in the table:

```
Private Sub Form_Load()
    ' get instance ID
    cName = InputBox("Enter Job Name:")
    Me.Caption = cName
    '
    ' load db and open set
    Set db = OpenDatabase("C:\TYSDBVB6\SOURCE\DATA\MULTIUSE.MDB")
    Set rs = db.OpenRecordset("mastertable", dbOpenTable, _
      dbSeeChanges)
    '
    ' count total recs in set
    rs.MoveLast
    nMax = rs.RecordCount
    '
End Sub
```

Now add the following two code pieces to the Click events of the option buttons. These routines toggle the LockEdits property of the Recordset between pessimistic locking (LockEdits=True) and optimistic locking (LockEdits=False).

This code snippet turns on pessimistic locking:

```
Private Sub Option1_Click()
    If Option1 = True Then
       rs.LockEdits = True
    Else
       rs.LockEdits = False
End If
End Sub
```

This code snippet turns on optimistic locking:

```
Private Sub Option2_Click()
    If Option2 = True Then
        rs.LockEdits = False
    Else
        rs.LockEdits = True
    End If
End Sub
```

Finally, add the following code to the `cmdEdit_Click` event of the form. While in Edit mode, this code prompts you for a record number. It then moves to that record, invokes the `Edit` method, makes a forced change in a Recordset field, and updates some titles and messages. When the form is in Update mode, this routine attempts to update the Recordset with the changed data and then resets some titles. The code is in Listing 16.1.

LISTING 16.1   THE CODE FOR THE `cmdEdit_Click` EVENT

```
 1: Private Sub cmdEdit_Click()
 2:     On Error GoTo cmdEditClickErr    ' set trap
 3:     '
 4:     Dim nRec As Integer ' for rec select
 5:     Dim X As Integer        ' for locator
 6:     '
 7:     ' are we trying to edit?
 8:     If cmdEdit.Caption = "&Edit" Then
 9:         ' get rec to edit
10:         nRec = InputBox("Enter Record # to Edit [1 - " + _
11:         Trim(Str(nMax)) + "]:", cName)
12:         ' locate rec
13:         If nRec > 0 Then
14:             rs.MoveFirst
15:             For X = 1 To nRec
16:                 rs.MoveNext
17:             Next
18:             rs.Edit ' start edit mode
19:             ' change rec
20:             If Left(rs.Fields(0), 1) = "X" Then
21:                 rs.Fields(0) = Mid(rs.Fields(0), 2, 255)
22:             Else
23:                 rs.Fields(0) = "X" + rs.Fields(0)
24:             End If
25:             ' tell 'em you changed it
26:             MsgBox "Modified field to: [" + rs.Fields(0) + "]"
27:             ' prepare for update mode
28:             cmdEdit.Caption = "&Update"
29:             Me.Caption = cName + " [Rec: " _
                + Trim(Str(X - 1)) + "]"
30:         End If
```

```
31:    Else
32:        rs.Update    ' attempt update
33:        cmdEdit.Caption = "&Edit"    ' fix caption
34:        Me.Caption = cName           ' fix header
35:        dbengine.idle dbfreelocks    ' pause VB
36:    End If
37:    '
38:    GoTo cmdEditClickExit
39:    '
40: cmdEditClickErr:
41:    ' show error message
42:    MsgBox Trim(Str(Err)) + ": " + Error$, vbCritical, _
           cName + "[cmdEdit]"
43:    '
44: cmdEditClickExit:
45:    '
46: End Sub
```

Notice that there is a new line in this routine: the DBEngine.Idle method. This method forces Visual Basic to pause for a moment to update any Dynaset or Snapshot objects that are opened by the program. It is a good idea to place this line in your code so that it is executed during some part of the update process. This ensures that your program has the most recent updates to the dataset.

Save the form as MULTIUS2.FRM and the project as MULTIUS2.VBP. Compile the project and save it as MULTIUS2.EXE. Now you're ready to test it. Load two instances of the compiled program. When it starts up, you are prompted for a job name. It does not matter what you enter for the job name, but make sure that you enter different names for each instance. The name you enter is displayed on messages and form headers so that you can tell the two programs apart. Position the two instances apart from each other on the screen. (See Figure 16.5.)

First, you'll test the behavior of pessimistic page locking. Make sure that the Pessimistic radio button in the Page Locking frame is selected in both instances of the program. Now click the Edit button of the first instance of the program; when prompted, enter 1 as the record to edit. This program now has locked a page of data. Switch to the second instance of the program, click the Edit button, and again enter 1 as the record to edit. You'll see error 3260, which tells you that the data is unavailable. (See Figure 16.6.)

FIGURE 16.5

Running two instances of the page locking project.

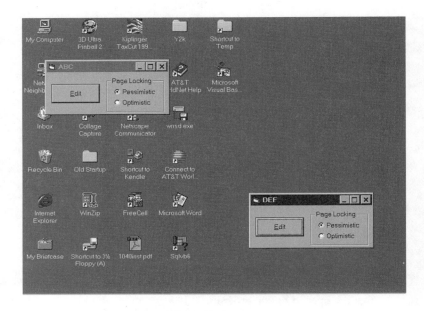

FIGURE 16.6

A failed attempt at editing during pessimistic locking.

Remember that pessimistic locking locks the data page as soon as a user begins an edit operation on a record. This lock prevents anyone else from accessing any records on the data page until the first instance releases the record by using `Update` or `UpdateCancel`. Now click the error message box and then click the Update button in the first instance of the application to release the record and unlock the data page.

Now you test the behavior of Microsoft Jet during optimistic locking. Select the Optimistic radio button on both forms. In the first form, click Edit and enter 1 when prompted. The first instance now is editing record 1. Move to the second instance and click Edit. This time, you do not see an error message. When prompted, enter 1 as the record to edit. Again, you see no error message as Microsoft Jet enables you to begin editing record 1 of the set. Now both programs are editing record 1 of the set.

Click the Update button of the second instance of the program to save the new data to the dataset. The second instance now has read, edited, and updated the same record opened earlier by the first instance. Now move to the first instance and click the Update button to save the changes made by this instance. You'll see error 3197, which tells you that data has been changed and that the update has been canceled. (See Figure 16.7.)

FIGURE 16.7

A failed attempt to update during optimistic locking.

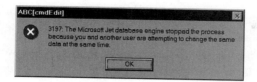

Optimistic locking occurs at the moment the Update method is invoked. Under the optimistic scheme, a user can read and edit any record he or she chooses. When the user attempts to write the record back out to disk, the program checks to see whether the original record was updated by any other program since the user's version last read the record. If changes were saved by another program, error 3197 is reported.

When to Use Pessimistic or Optimistic Page Locking

The advantage of using pessimistic locking is that after you begin editing a record, you can save your work, because all other users are prevented from accessing that record. The disadvantage of using pessimistic locking is that if you have many people in the database, it is possible that quite a bit of the file is unavailable at any one time.

The advantage of using optimistic locking is that it occurs only during an update and then only when required. Optimistic locks are the shortest in duration. The disadvantage of using optimistic locking is that, even though more than one user can edit a dataset record at one time, only one person can save that dataset record. This usually is the first person to complete the edit (not the person who opened the record first or the person who saves it last). This can be very frustrating for users who have filled out a lengthy data entry screen only to discover that they cannot update the data table! Except in rare cases where there is an extreme amount of network traffic, you probably will find that optimistic locking is enough.

Note

All ODBC data sources use optimistic locking only.

Using Cascading Updates and Deletes

In the lesson on Day 8, "Visual Basic and the DAO Jet Database Engine," you learned how to identify and define cascading updates and delete relationships by using the relation data access object. At the time, a particular aspect of relation objects was not fully covered: the capability of defining cascading updates and deletes in order to enforce referential integrity. By using cascading updates and deletes in your database definition, you can ensure that changes made to columns in one data table are distributed properly to all related columns in all related tables in the database. This type of referential integrity is essential when designing and using database applications accessed by multiple users.

Microsoft Jet can enforce update and delete cascades only for native Microsoft Jet format databases. Microsoft Jet cannot enforce cascades that involve an attached table.

> **Tip**
>
> Cascading options should be added at database design time and can be accomplished by using the Visdata program (see Day 6, "Using the Visdata Program") or by using Visual Basic code (see Day 8).

Cascading occurs when users update or delete columns in one table that are referred to (via the relation object) by other columns in other tables. When this update or delete occurs, Microsoft Jet automatically updates or deletes all the records that are part of the defined relation. If you define a relationship between the column Valid.ListID and the column Master.ListID, for example, any time a user updates the value of Valid.ListID, Microsoft Jet scans the MasterTable and updates the values of all Master.ListID columns that match the updated values in the Valid.ListID column. In this way, as users change data in one table, all related tables are kept in sync through the use of cascading updates and deletes.

Building the Cascading Demo Project

The MULTIUSE.MDB database used in the earlier exercise is also used for this exercise. This database has a one-to-many relationship, with enforced referential integrity for both cascading updates and cascading deletes. ValidTypes is the base table, and CustType is the base field. MasterTable is the foreign table, and CustType is the foreign field. You might find it helpful to open this database in the Visual Data Manager (Visdata) and explore the structure of these two tables.

> **Tip**
>
> It might seem that the terms *base table* and *foreign table* are used incorrectly in the relation definition. It might help to remember that all relation definitions are based on the values in the ValidTypes table. Also, it might help to remember that any data table related to the ValidTypes table is a foreign table.

Now you build a project that illustrates the process of cascading updates and deletes. Use the information in Table 16.1 and Figure 16.8 to build the MULTIUS3.VBP project.

FIGURE 16.8

Laying out the MULTIUS3.FRM form.

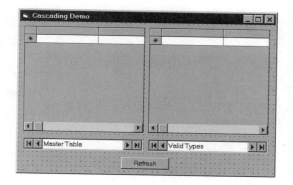

16

TABLE 16.1   THE CONTROL TABLE FOR THE MULTIUS3.VBP PROJECT

Control	Property	Setting
Form	Name	MULTIUS3
	Caption	Cascading Demo
	Left	1020
	Height	4275
	Top	1170
	Width	6480
DBGrid	Name	DBGrid1
	AllowAddNew	True
	AllowDelete	True
	DataSource	DATA1
	Height	2715
	Left	120
	Top	120
	Width	3000
DBGrid	Name	DBGrid2
	AllowAddNew	True
	AllowDelete	True
	DataSource	DATA2
	Height	2715
	Left	3240
	Top	120
	Width	3000

continues

TABLE 16.1 CONTINUED

Control	Property	Setting
Data Control	Name	Data1
	Caption	Master Table
	DatabaseName	C:\TYSDBVB6\SOURCE\
		DATA\MULTIUSE.MDB
	Height	300
	Left	120
	RecordsetType	1-Dynaset
	RecordSource	MasterTable
	Top	3000
	Width	3000
Data Control	Name	Data2
	Caption	Valid Types
	DatabaseName	C:\TYSDBVB6\SOURCE\
		DATA\MULTIUSE.MDB
	Height	300
	Left	3240
	RecordsetType	1-Dynaset
	RecordSource	ValidTypes
	Top	3000
	Width	3000
Command Button	Name	Command1
	Caption	Refresh
	Height	300
	Left	2580
	Top	3480
	Width	1200

Only two lines of Visual Basic code are needed to complete the form. Add the following lines to the Command1_Click event. These two lines update both data controls and their associated grids:

```
Private Sub Command1_Click()
    Data1.Refresh
    Data2.Refresh
End Sub
```

Save the form as MULTIUS3.FRM and the project as MULTIUS3.VBP, and then run the project. Now you're ready to test the cascading updates and deletes.

Running the Cascading Demo Project

When you run the project, you see the two tables displayed in each grid, side by side. First, test the update cascade by editing one of the records in the Valid Types table. Select the first record and change the CustType column value from T01 to T09. After you finish the edit and move the record pointer to another record in the ValidTypes grid, click the Refresh button to update both datasets. You see that all records in the MasterTable that had a value of T01 in their CustType field now have a value of T09. The update of ValidTypes was cascaded into the MasterTable by Microsoft Jet.

Now add a new record with the CustType value of T99 to the ValidTypes table (set the Description field to any text you want). Add a record to the MasterTable that uses the T99 value in its CustType field. Your screen should look something like the one shown in Figure 16.9.

FIGURE 16.9

Adding new records to the MULTIUS3.MDB database.

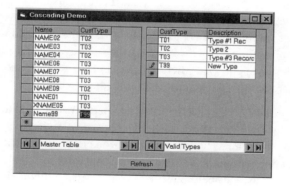

Delete the T99 record from the ValidTypes table by highlighting the entire row and pressing Delete. After you delete the record, click the Refresh button again to update both data controls. What happens to the record in the MasterTable that contains the T99 value in the CustType field? It is deleted from the MasterTable! This shows the power of the cascading delete. When cascading deletes are enforced, any time a user deletes a record from the base table, all related records in the foreign table also are deleted.

When to Use the Cascading Updates and Deletes

The capability of enforcing cascading updates and deletes as part of the database definition is a powerful tool. With this power comes some responsibility, however. Because database cascades cannot easily be undone, you should think through your database design carefully before you add cascading features to your database. It is not always wise to add both update and delete cascades to all your relationships. At times, you might not want to cascade all update or delete operations.

Whenever you define a relation object in which the base table is a validation table and the foreign table is a master table, it is wise to define an update cascade. This ensures that any changes made to the validation table are cascaded to the related master table. It is not a good idea to define a delete cascade for this type of relation. Rarely do you want to delete all master records whenever you delete a related record from the validation table. If the user attempts to delete a record from the validation table that is used by one or more records in the master table, Microsoft Jet issues an error message telling the user that it is unable to delete the record.

Whenever you define a relation object in which the base table is a master table and the foreign table is a child table (for example, CustomerMaster.CustID is the base table and CustomerComments.CustID is the foreign table), you might want to define both an update and a delete cascade. It is logical to make sure that any changes to the CustomerMaster.CustID field would be updated in the CustomerComments.CustID field. It also might make sense to delete all CustomerComments records whenever the related CustomerMaster record is deleted. This is not always the case, though. If the child table is CustomerInvoice, for example, you might not want to automatically delete all invoices on file. Instead, you might want Microsoft Jet to prevent the deletion of the CustomerMaster record if a related CustomerInvoice record exists.

The key point to remember is that cascades are performed automatically by Microsoft Jet, without any warning message. You cannot create an optional cascade or receive an automatic warning before a cascade begins. If you choose to use cascades in your database, be sure to think through the logic and the relations thoroughly, and be sure to test your relations and cascades before using the database in a production setting.

Adding Transaction Management to Database Application

Another important tool for maintaining the integrity of your database is the use of transactions to manage database updates and deletes. Visual Basic enables you to enclose all database update operations as a single transaction. Transactions involve two steps: First, mark the start of a database transaction with the `BeginTrans` keyword; second, mark the end of the database transaction with the `CommitTrans` or `RollBack` keyword. You can start a set of database operations (add, edit, and delete records) and then, if no error occurs, you can use the `CommitTrans` keyword to save the updated records to the database. If you encounter an error along the way, though, you can use the RollBack keyword to tell Microsoft Jet to reverse all database operations completed up to the point where the transaction first began.

Suppose that you need to perform a series of database updates to several tables as part of a month-end update routine for an accounting system. This month-end processing includes totaling transactions by customer from the TransTable, writing those totals to existing columns in a CustTotals table, appending the transactions to the HistoryTable, and deleting the transactions from the TransTable. The process requires access to three different tables and involves updating existing records (appending new records to a table and deleting existing records from a table). If your program encounters an error part of the way through this process, it will be difficult to reconstruct the data as it existed before the process began. In other words, it will be difficult unless you used Visual Basic transactions as part of the update routine.

Microsoft Jet Transactions and the Workspace Object

All Microsoft Jet transactions are applied to the current workspace object. (See Day 9, "Creating Database Programs with the Data Environment Designer," for a discussion of the Workspace object.) If you do not name a Workspace object, Visual Basic uses the default workspace for your program. Because transactions apply to an entire workspace, it is recommended that you explicitly declare workspaces when you use transactions. This gives you the capability of isolating datasets into different workspaces and better controlling the creation of transactions.

Here's the exact syntax for starting a transaction:

```
Workspace(0).BeginTrans    ' starts a transaction
'
If Err=0 Then
   Workspaces(0).CommitTrans    ' completes a transaction
Else
   Workspaces(0).Rollback    ' cancels a transaction
End If
```

In this code, the default workspace for the transaction area is used. In an actual program, you should name a workspace explicitly.

Building the Microsoft Jet Transaction Project

You now build a small project that illustrates one possible use for transactions in your Visual Basic applications. You create a database routine that performs the tasks listed in the previous example. You open a transaction table, total the records to a subsidiary table, copy the records to a history file, and then delete the records from the original table.

Tip

> To avoid errors when running this project, make sure that you select the appropriate DAO reference before executing the program. Do this by choosing Project|References from the Visual Basic 6 menu. Then enable the check box next to the Microsoft DAO 3.51 Object Library.

Write two main routines: one to declare the workspace and open the database, and one to perform the database transaction. First, add the following code to the general declarations section of a new form in a new project:

```
Option Explicit

Dim db As Database          ' database object
Dim wsUpdate As workspace   ' workspace object
Dim nErrFlag As Integer     ' error flag
```

These are the form-level variables you need to perform the update.

Add the following code, which creates the workspace and opens the database. Create a new Sub called OpenDB and place the code in Listing 16.2 in the routine.

LISTING 16.2   THE CODE FOR OpenDB

```
 1: Sub OpenDB()
 2:     On Error GoTo OpenDBErr
 3:     '
 4:     nErrFlag = 0 ' assume all is OK
 5:     '
 6:     Set wsUpdate = DBEngine.CreateWorkspace("wsUpdate" _
          , "admin", "")
 7:     Set db = wsUpdate.OpenDatabase( _
          "C:\TYSDBVB6\SOURCE\DATA\MULTIUS4.MDB", True)
 8:     '
 9:     GoTo OpenDBExit
10:     '
11: OpenDBErr:
12:     MsgBox Trim(Str(Err)) + " " + Error$(Err), _
          vbCritical, "OpenDB"
13:     nErrFlag = Err
14:     '
15: OpenDBExit:
16:     '
17: End Sub
```

This routine creates a new workspace object to encompass the transaction and then opens the database for exclusive use. You don't want anyone else in the system while you perform this major update. An error-trap routine has been added here in case you can't open the database exclusively.

Now you can add the code that performs the actual month-end update. Do this by using the SQL statements you learned in the lessons on Days 12, "Creating Databases with SQL," and 14, "Updating Databases with SQL." Create a new Sub called ProcMonthEnd and then add the code in Listing 16.3.

LISTING 16.3 THE CODE FOR ProcMonthEnd

```
 1: Sub ProcMonthEnd()
 2:     On Error goto ProcMonthEndErr
 3:     '
 4:     Dim cSQL As String
 5:     Dim nResult As Integer
 6:     '
 7:     wsUpdate.BeginTrans ' mark start of transaction
 8:     '
 9:     ' append totals to transtotals table
10:     cSQL = "INSERT INTO TransTotals SELECT TransTable.CustID,
    ➥SUM(TransTable.Amount) as Amount FROM TransTable
    ➥GROUP BY TransTable.CustID"
11:     db.Execute cSQL
12:     '
13:     ' append history records
14:     cSQL = "INSERT INTO TransHistory SELECT * FROM TransTable"
17:     db.Execute cSQL
18:     '
19:     ' delete the transaction records
20:     cSQL = "DELETE FROM TransTable"
21:     db.Execute cSQL
22:     '
23:     ' ask user to commit transaction
24:     '
25:     nResult = MsgBox("Transaction Completed.
    ➥Ready to Commit?",_vbInformation + vbYesNo, "ProcMonthEnd")
26:     If nResult = vbYes Then
27:         wsUpdate.CommitTrans
28:         MsgBox "Transaction Committed"
29:     Else
33:         wsUpdate.Rollback
32:          MsgBox "Transaction Canceled"
33:     End If
34:     '
35:     nErrFlag = 0
36:     GoTo ProcMonthEndExit
37:     '
```

16

continues

LISTING 16.3 CONTINUED

```
38: ProcMonthEndErr:
39:     MsgBox Trim(Str(Err)) + " " + Error$(Err), _
          vbCritical, "ProcMonthEnd"
40:     nErrFlag = Err
41:     '
42: ProcMonthEndExit:
43:     '
44: End Sub
```

This code executes the three SQL statements that perform the updates and deletes needed for the month-end processing. The routine is started with a BeginTrans. When the updates are complete, the user is asked to confirm the transaction. In a production program, you probably wouldn't ask for transaction confirmation; however, this helps you see how the process is working.

Finally, you need to add the code that puts everything together. Add the code in Listing 16.4 to the Form_Load event.

LISTING 16.4 THE Form Load EVENT

```
 1: Private Sub Form_Load()
 2:     OpenDB
 3:     If nErrFlag = 0 Then
 4:         ProcMonthEnd
 5:     End If
 6:     '
 7:     If nErrFlag <> 0 Then
 8:         MsgBox "Error Reported", vbCritical, "FormLoad"
 9:     End If
10:     Unload Me
11: End Sub
```

This routine calls the OpenDB procedure. Then, if no error is reported, it calls the ProcMonthEnd procedure. If an error has occurred during the process, a message is displayed.

Save the form as MULTIUS4.FRM and the project as MULTIUS4.VBP, and then run the project. All you'll see is a message that tells you the transaction is complete and asks for your approval. (See Figure 16.10.)

FIGURE 16.10

Waiting for approval to commit the transaction.

If you choose No in this message box, Microsoft Jet reverses all the previously completed database operations between the `Rollback` and the `BeginTrans` statements. You can confirm this by clicking No, using Visdata or Data Manager to load the `MULTIUS4.MDB` database, and then inspecting the contents of the tables.

Note

> An SQL-Visual Basic script called `MULTIUS4.SQV` is included on the CD-ROM that accompanies this book. You can use this script with the SQL-VB program (see Days 12 and 14) to create a "clean" `MULTIUS4.MDB` file. After you run `MULTIUS4.VBP` once and answer Yes to commit the transaction, you might want to run the `MULTIUS4.SQV` script to refresh the database.

Advantages and Limitations of Transactions

The primary advantage of using transactions in your Visual Basic programs is that they can greatly increase the integrity of your data. You should use transactions whenever you are performing database operations that span more than one table or even operations that affect many records in a single table. A secondary advantage of using transactions is that they often increase the processing speed of Microsoft Jet.

As useful as transactions are, there are still a few limitations. First, some database formats might not support transactions (for example, Paradox files do not support transactions). You can check for transaction support by checking the `Transactions` property of the database. If transactions are not supported, Microsoft Jet ignores the transaction statements in your code; you do not receive an error message. Some Dynasets might not support transactions, depending on how they are constructed. Usually, sets that are the result of SQL `JOIN` and `WHERE` clauses or resultsets that contain data from attached tables do not support transactions.

Transaction operations are kept on the local workstation in a temporary directory (the one pointed to by the `TEMP` environment variable). If you run out of available space on the `TEMP` drive, you'll receive error 2004. You can trap for this error. The only solution is to make more disk space available or to reduce the number of database operations between the `BeginTrans` and the `CommitTrans` statements.

Microsoft Jet enables you to nest transactions up to five levels deep. If you are using external ODBC databases, however, you cannot nest transactions.

Summary

Today, you learned about the three important challenges that face every database programmer writing multiuser applications:

- Using database-locking schemes
- Using cascading updates and deletes to maintain database integrity
- Using database transactions to provide commit/rollback options for major updates to your database

You learned that three levels of locking are available to Visual Basic programs:

- *Database level.* You can use the `Exclusive` property of the data control or the second parameter of the `OpenDatabase` method to lock the entire database. Use this option when you need to perform work that affects multiple database objects (such as tables, queries, indexes, relations, and so on).
- *Table level.* You can set the `Options` property of the data control to 3, or the third parameter of the `OpenRecordset` method to `dbDenyRead+dbDenyWrite` in order to lock the entire table for your use only. Use this option when you need to perform work that affects multiple records in a single table (for example, increasing the sales price on all items in the inventory table).
- *Page level.* Microsoft Jet automatically performs page-level locking whenever you use the data control to edit and save a record, or whenever you use Visual Basic code to perform the `Edit`/`AddNew` and `Update`/`CancelUpdate` methods. You can use the `LockEdits` property of the Recordset to set the page locking to pessimistic (to perform locking at edit time) or optimistic (to perform locking only at update time).

You learned how to use Visual Basic to enforce referential integrity and automatically perform cascading updates or deletes to related records. You learned that there are times when it is not advisable to establish cascading deletes (for example, do not use cascading deletes when the base table is a validation list and the foreign table is a master).

You learned how to use database transactions to protect your database during extended, multitable operations. You learned how to use the `BeginTrans`, `CommitTrans`, and `Rollback` methods of the workspace object. Finally, you learned some of the advantages and limitations of transaction processing.

Quiz

1. What are the three levels of locking provided by the Microsoft Jet database engine?
2. Which form of locking would you use when compacting a database?
3. Which form of locking would you use if you needed to update price codes in the price table of a database?
4. Which property of a Recordset do you set to control whether your application's data has optimistic or pessimistic page locking?
5. What is the difference between pessimistic and optimistic page locking?
6. Can you use pessimistic locking on an ODBC data source?
7. What happens to data when cascading deletes are used in a relationship?
8. Why would you use transaction management in your applications?
9. What are the limitations of transactions?
10. Do you need to declare a workspace when using transactions?

Exercises

1. Write Visual Basic code that exclusively opens a database (`C:\DATA\ABC.MDB`) during a `Form Load` event. Include error trapping.
2. Build on the code you wrote in the previous exercise to exclusively open the table Customers in `ABC.MDB`.
3. Suppose that you are building a new accounts receivable system for your company. You have saved all tables and data into a single database named `C:\DATA\ABC.MDB`. You have discovered that all invoices created must be posted to a history file on a daily basis. Because this history file is extremely valuable (it is used for collections, reporting, and so on), you don't want your posting process to destroy any of the data that it currently contains. Therefore, you decide to use transactions in your code.

   Write the Visual Basic code that takes invoice transactions from the temporary holding table, Transactions, and inserts them into a table named History, which keeps the cumulative history information.

   The History table contains four fields: HistoryItem (counter and primary key), CustID (a unique identifier for the customer), InvoiceNo (the number of the invoice issued to the customer), and Amount.

16

The Transactions table also has four fields: TransNo (counter and primary key), CustID (a unique identifier for the customer), InvoiceNo (the number of the invoice issued to the customer), and Amount.

Complete this project by starting a new project and dropping a single command button (named Post) onto a form. Clicking this button should trigger the posting process.

Include error trapping in your routines. Also, include messages to notify the user that the transaction posting is complete or that problems have been encountered.

DAY 17

Using the Remote Data Control and the RDO Model

Today, you learn about the Remote Data Control (RDC) and Remote Data object (RDO) model for accessing data with Visual Basic 6. RDC and RDO are designed for reading and updating data stored in relational database management systems (RDBMS) that are external to Visual Basic and to the Microsoft Jet data engine. Although it is possible to use the standard data control and Microsoft Jet data object collections to access data stored in RDBMS, the RDC and RDO models properties and methods make them better suited to manipulating data in remote systems.

Caution

> The RDC and RDO model is shipped as part of the Visual Basic 6 Enterprise Edition. If you do not have the Enterprise Edition of Visual Basic 6, you cannot complete the examples in this chapter

> or run the code that ships on the CD-ROM with this book. You still can get a
> lot out of this chapter by reading through the text and inspecting the code
> examples, though.

Along with the details of the RDC and the RDO model, you will learn some of the basics of remote data access in general. These basics are hidden from you when you use the DAO data control, or they do not apply unless you are accessing remote data. You'll learn the meaning and use of these elements:

- Cursor drivers
- Key sets
- Lock types

In today's lesson, you learn the properties, methods, and events of the RDC and how you can use these to develop data-entry forms using the same data-bound controls you learned about in the first week's lessons. After you learn the details of the RDC programming tool, you build a simple data-entry form based on the RDC. In this chapter, you even use an ODBC definition that links your RDC to a Microsoft Jet Access database.

You also learn the details of the RDO model. The RDO model is a set of programming objects similar to the Microsoft Jet data access objects (DAO) you learned about in Week 2. Like the RDC, the RDO collection has special properties and methods that make it better suited to accessing data from remote storage systems.

When you complete this chapter, you'll be able to create data-bound entry forms using the RDCs and to build Visual Basic programs that manipulate RDBMS data using the RDO.

The RDO Object Model Summary

Before you start creating Visual Basic programs that use RDO, it is important to spend some time learning the object model and how it relates to the DAO model you learned in Week two. Although you'll find the models are quite similar, you'll notice some important differences, too.

One of the most obvious differences is in the size of the object models. The DAO model has over twenty major objects to work with, and the RDO model has less than fifteen. This reflects the fundamental differences between the models. The DAO model is designed to give programmers complete access to both data and schema (table structure) manipulation, and the RDO model is designed to allow access only to the data itself.

Because the RDO interface was meant for use when connecting to large multiuser database systems (SQL Server, Oracle, and so forth), the details of creating and modifying tables and indexes is not the focus of the object model.

A visual representation of the RDO programming model is shown in Figure 17.1.

FIGURE 17.1

The RDO object model.

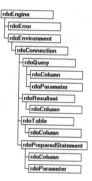

This object model is a simplified view. In fact, a collection object (rdoConnections, rdoResultsets, and so forth) can represent each one of the members in the model as well as the singular members. The model is kept simpler to focus on the different types of objects available in the RDO model.

If you are familiar with the Data Access Object (DAO) programming model (covered in Day 8, "Visual Basic and the DAO Jet Database Engine"), you will see many similarities between RDO and DAO. Even though most of the names are different, there is a close correlation between the two models. Table 17.1 shows each of the RDO objects and relates them to their DAO equivalents.

TABLE 17.1 RDO PROGRAMMING OBJECTS

Object	Description
rdoColumn	The RDO version of the Microsoft Jet Field object
rdoConnection	The RDO equivalent of the Microsoft Jet Database object
rdoEngine	The top-level data engine used to access remote data
rdoEnvironment	The RDO equivalent of the Microsoft Jet Workspace object
rdoParameters	A special collection of query parameters for the rdoQuery object
rdoQuery	The RDO version of the Microsoft Jet QueryDef object
rdoResultset	The RDO equivalent of the Microsoft Jet Recordset object
rdoTable	The RDO version of the Microsoft Jet Table object

As Table 17.1 shows, most RDO objects have a parallel in the Microsoft Jet DAO collections. If you have not read through the chapter covering the Microsoft Jet Database objects (see Day 8), you might want to review that material before you continue with this chapter.

The Basics of Remote Data Access

Before getting into the details of the RDC and RDO programming tools, it is important to review a few basic principles of remote data access. When you use the Microsoft Jet DAO or the standard data control, you usually do not need to deal with some of the issues covered here. The three concepts covered here are cursor drivers, dataset types, and lock types. Manipulating the parameters of these three properties affect the type of dataset you are working with and the types of operations you can perform on that data. By default, all remote connections to data are nonupdatable (read-only) datasets. You can change this behavior by manipulating the three properties covered here.

Cursor Drivers

You use the cursor drivers to define the way in which you can move within a set of data. When you connect to data using the standard data control or the Microsoft Jet DAO, you can, by default, move forward and backward in the dataset and move to any record in the collection. You can use any of the Move and Find methods (MoveFirst, MoveLast, MoveNext, MovePrevious, FindFirst, FindLast, FindNext, and FindPrevious), for example.

In order to have this movement capability, the database engine must be able to keep track of all the records in the collection and their place in the dataset. This process of keeping track of the location of the data pointer in the dataset is called cursor management. You can use two primary locations to keep track of the cursor location: the client workstation or the database server. Under the RDC and RDO models, the ODBC driver handles the local workstation version of cursor management. The database server that holds the data handles the server-side cursor management.

> **Note**
>
> Since the same object model is used for both the Remote Data Control (RDC) and the Remote Data Objects (RDO), it is common simply refer to the entire interface as RDO only. Throughout this book you will see RDC and RDO used. Unless otherwise noted, RDO is meant to cover both RDC and RDO.

Under RDO, there are two other possible settings for cursor management: Client Batch and None. You can use the Client Batch option with advanced data servers that allow multiple data requests to be sent simultaneously over the same connection. In this case, you can batch up multiple SQL statements in a single string and send them to the server at one time. The server manages the requests and reports results back to you as each SQL statement is completed.

You also can choose to use no cursor driver when accessing remote data. This results in the server sending you a single record from the dataset each time you request it. You cannot request previous records from the server and, if you want to start at the top of the collection, you must restart the query. This is the most limited cursor management available for a remote connection.

Tip

Although using no cursor management severely limits your capability to navigate a large set of data, it is the fastest connection possible. Even more valuable, you can use non-cursor driver sets to execute action queries such as SET UPDATE, INSERT INTO, and SELECT INTO queries. This means that you can perform multi-record updates without having to declare a cursor.

17

Cursor drivers can have five possible settings when you are working with RDC and RDO. Table 17.2 shows these values and their meanings.

TABLE 17.2 CURSOR DRIVER OPTIONS WITH RDC AND RDO

Driver Option	Integer Value	Description
rdUseIfNeeded	0	Instructs RDO to determine the best cursor driver to use for the requested operation. This is the default setting.
rdUseOdbc	1	Instructs RDO to use the client-side ODBC cursor driver to keep track of the data pointer in the dataset.
rdUseServer	2	Instructs RDO to use the remote RDBMS cursor driver to keep track of the data pointer in the dataset.
rdUseClientBatch	3	Instructs RDO to use the remote RDBMS to manage multiple cursors in response to batch requests sent from the client workstation. This is available only on advanced RDBMS systems (SQL Server 6.0 and higher).
rdUseNone	4	Instructs RDO to use no cursor driver. The result is a return on only one row, no matter how may rows are in the result-set. This option still can be used to perform action queries, such as SET UPDATE, INSERT INTO, SELECT INTO, and so on.

As you can see in Table 17.2, the default option for RDO is to allow rdoEngine to select the most appropriate cursor available. When rdUseIfNeeded is in place, RDO will attempt to use server-side cursors if they are available (rdUseServer or rdUseClientBatch if Batch mode is in force). If the RDBMS does not support server-side cursor management, RDO will use the client workstation cursor manager (rdUseOdbc). The rdUseNone option is used only if the value is explicitly selected.

Again, the important thing to remember about cursor drivers is that they govern the way you can navigate the dataset. The other important aspect of cursor drivers is that, with RDO, you can select the driver you prefer: client-side or server-side. The only caveat to all this is that the data source (RDBMS) must support your cursor request in order for you to be able to select certain server-side options.

Dataset Type

The selection of cursor drivers is just one of the options you must determine when accessing remote data. Another important parameter is the dataset type property of the connection. Several types of datasets can be returned by the remote data source. Table 17.3 outlines these types.

TABLE 17.3   DATASET TYPE OPTIONS WITH RDO

Dataset Option	Integer Value	Description
rdOpenForwardOnly	0	Creates a read-only, scroll-forward-only dataset. All members are copied to the client workstation for use. This is the default option.
rdOpenStatic	1	Creates an updatable dataset that has nonchanging membership. New records added to the set may (or may not) appear as part of the set, depending on the cursor driver. All members are copied to the client workstation for use.
rdOpenDynamic	2	Creates an updatable dataset that has changing membership. New records added to the set will appear as part of the set. Actual data records are buffered to the client workstation as needed. Record keys are not used.
rdOpenKeyset	3	Creates an updatable dataset that has changing membership. New records added to the set will appear as part of the set. Actual data records are buffered to the client workstation as needed. Record keys (the key set) are created to point to all members of the set. This enables you to use bookmarks with the dataset.

The information in Table 17.3 deserves some additional comment. Remember that the primary work of dataset management from the workstation point of view is gaining access to the actual rows of data stored in the remote system. The most efficient method for gaining access is to receive a set of row pointers from the RDBMS, not to actually receive the complete rows of data. In this way, the RDBMS can allow multiple users to have access to the same set of records without having to deal with major synchronization work if more than one user attempts to update the same row of data.

For this reason, RDO supports the use of rdOpenKeyset datasets. These are sets of data that contain not just data rows, but also key-set pointers to other rows in the requested dataset. rdOpenKeysets are the remote data access versions of Microsoft Jet Dynaset-type datasets.

The rdOpenDynamic datasets do not support keys, but they do act as dynamically changing sets of data. These dynamic datasets reflect newly added or deleted records just as rdOpenKeyset datasets, but they do not support the use of bookmarks. This is because the rdOpenDynamic datasets are kept dynamic through the use of recurring refreshes of the data membership from the remote data source. Although this method is accurate, it is hardly efficient. If you have large sets of data, using the rdOpenDynamic option can result in decreased throughput, because all data members are shipped to the client each time the set is refreshed.

It also is important to note that rdOpenStatic datasets are updatable. Even though their membership is kept static (there is no constant refresh from the remote data source), it still is possible to update the records in the set. These datasets act much like an updatable version of the Microsoft Jet Snapshot dataset.

Lock Types

The final concept that deserves special attention when dealing with remote data access is the lock type used to manage dataset updates. With Microsoft Jet data access, you have two options: pessimistic (lock at start of edit) and optimistic (lock at start of update). RDO offers a few additional variations to these two basic options. Table 17.4 shows the lock-type options with RDO.

TABLE 17.4. DATASET LOCK-TYPE OPTIONS WITH RDO

Lock-Type Option	Integer Value	Description
rdConcurReadOnly	0	Provides no row-level locking. Forces the dataset to act as a read-only set. You can use this option to perform action queries, though. This is the default option.

continues

17

TABLE 17.4   CONTINUED

Lock-Type Option	Integer Value	Description
rdConcurLock	1	Provides pessimistic locking for the entire row set. The lock occurs as soon as the data is accessed, not when an Edit operation begins.
rdConcurRowver	2	Provides optimistic locking based on internal row ID values (usually, the TimeStamp column).
rdConcurValues	3	Provides optimistic locking based on a column-by-column check of the data in each row.
rdConcurBatch	4	Provides optimistic locking based on the value in the UpdateCriteria property when using Batch Update mode. Not supported by all RDBMSs.

The type of locking mechanism used can have a great effect on the performance of your application and the capability of others to access the shared data. The rdConcurReadOnly option allows anyone else to access the same data your application is using. Your application cannot update the dataset unless you are using action queries, however. The rdConcurLock option provides the greatest degree of locking. As soon as your dataset is created, all buffered rows in the dataset are locked. Because locks occur on pages, this can result in hundreds of record locks while your application browses the dataset.

The rdConcurRowver and rdConcurValues options enable optimistic locking schemes. In the rdConcurRowver option, each record's ID value (usually, the TimeStamp column) is checked at the time the row is updated. If the ID has changed since your application retrieved the data, an error is reported. In the rdConcurValues option, each value in the row's columns is checked against the original value. If the value has changed since your application received the dataset, an error is reported.

The least intrusive form of locking for read/write datasets is the rdConcurRowver or rdConcurValues option. The most secure form of locking for read/write datasets is the rdConcurLock option. An advantage that RDO has over Microsoft Jet is that you easily can tune the number of rows in the row set by using the RowsetSize property. If you set this property sufficiently low, you can use the rdConcurLock option without adversely affecting other users who are attempting to access the remote data.

Now that you understand the basics of accessing remote data, you are ready to begin using the RDC and RDO tools to build Visual Basic programs that read and update remote data sources.

Building an ODBC Definition

 Before you can complete any of the projects in this chapter, you need to build an ODBC connection to the BOOKS6.MDB database that ships on the CD-ROM with this book. After you build this ODBC data source definition, you'll be able to use both RDC and RDO programming tools to access the BOOKS6.MDB database.

 Caution

You might have both the 32-bit and the 16-bit ODBC Administrator applets in your Control Panel group. Be sure to use the 32-bit ODBC Administrator to define your new data source. The RDC and RDO programming objects recognize only data-source definitions built with the 32-bit ODBC Administrator.

17

To build an ODBC definition, you need to call up the ODBC Administrator. Follow these steps:

1. Choose Start | Settings | Control Panel from the main Windows 95/98 (or WinNT4) menu. The Control Panel appears, as shown in Figure 17.2. Double-click the 32-bit ODBC icon to open the ODBC Administrator.

FIGURE 17.2

Accessing the 32-bit ODBC Administrator from the Control Panel.

If you are using WinNT 3.51, double-click the ODBC Administrator applet from the Control Panel group.

2. After the ODBC Data Source Administrator dialog box appears, select the User DSN tab and click Add. The Create New Data Source dialog box appears, as shown in Figure 17.3.

FIGURE 17.3

Adding a new User DSN.

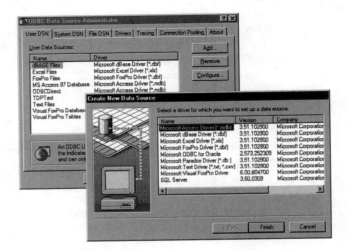

3. Double-click the Microsoft Access 7.0 Database driver. The ODBC Microsoft Access 97 Setup dialog box appears. In the Data Source Name field, enter BOOKS6. In the Description field, enter Remote Data Connection to books6.mdb. In the Database section, specify the path C:\TYSDBVB6\SOURCE\DATA\BOOKS6.MDB by clicking Select and navigating to it in the Select Database dialog box. Figure 17.4 shows what the dialog box should look like at this point.

4. Click OK to save the definition and then exit the ODBC Administrator applet. You now have an ODBC data source definition that you can use with the RDC and the RDO.

Note

Using RDO to connect to a Microsoft Jet Access database is not advisable in a production setting. The process of going through RDO to ODBC to Microsoft Access is very wasteful and limits the programming options available to the application. Using Microsoft Access tables in this way, however, is a common method of prototyping tables that will later be moved to SQL Server or some other RDBMS. If you have SQL Server or some other RDBMS available to your workstation, you can substitute the DSN built in this section for another one that uses your own remote data.

FIGURE 17.4

Filling in the Microsoft Access DSN properties.

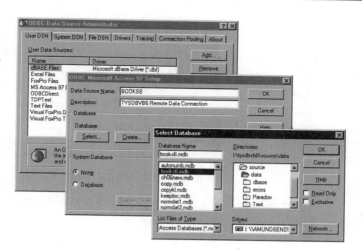

17

Programming with the Remote Data Control

Programming with the Remote Data Control (RDC) is very similar to programming with the standard data control that ships with all versions of Visual Basic 6.0. The RDC has unique property names, but these properties are quite similar to the standard data-control properties, and they provide almost the same functionality. Also notice that the RDC has methods and events that are close, if not identical, to the methods and events of the standard data control.

In the following sections, you learn the properties, methods, and events of the RDC. As you review these items, it might help to refer to the material covered in Day 2, "Visual Basic Database Access Objects."

The RDC Properties

The RDC has a number of unique properties you can use to establish and manage your connection to the remote data source. Table 17.5 shows these unique properties, their types, default settings, and short descriptions of their meaning and use.

TABLE 17.5   UNIQUE PROPERTIES OF THE RDC

Property	Type	Default Setting	Description
Connection	rdoConnection	\<none>	Contains an object reference to the RDO Connection object created by the RDC. You can use this as you use the Database property of the standard data control.
CursorDriver	Integer	rdUseIfNeeded (0)	Controls the source and behavior of the cursor manager.
DataSourceName	String	\<none>	Specifies the name of the ODBC data source you want to access. This is the RDO equivalent of the database name.
EditMode	Integer	rdEditNone (0)	Indicates whether an edit or AddNew operation is in effect. You can use this to determine whether an Update method must be used to complete a pending action.
Environment	rdoEnvironment	\<none>	Contains an object reference to the RDO Environment object created by the RDC. You can use this as you use the Workspace object in Microsoft Jet data access.
KeysetSize	Integer	100	Specifies the number of rows in the keyset buffer. Using this value and the MaxRows and RowsetSize properties can affect the way records are buffered and locked.
LockType	Integer	rdConcur ReadOnly (0)	Controls how records are locked for update.
LoginTimeOut	Integer	0	Using a value greater than zero indicates the length of time (in seconds) that RDO objects wait before reporting a time-out error when trying to log onto the remote data source. A typical LAN connection time-out value is 15 seconds. RAS/Internet connections may need a longer time-out setting.

Property	Type	Default Setting	Description
LogMessages	String	<none>	Setting this value to a valid drive/path/filename enables the creation of a trace file for ODBC conversations. This file can get quite long and should be used only for temporary debugging of questionable connections.
MaxRows	Integer	-1	Controls how many rows are affected by an action. When set to -1 (default), all rows matching the criteria are affected. You can set this value to 1 to ensure that only one record is updated when us-ing an UPDATE query.
Prompt	Integer	rdDriverPrompt (0)	Controls the behavior of the ODBC logon process. Setting this value to rdDriverNoPrompt suppresses the ODBC logon screen. You can use this setting to log onto the data source without asking the user for additional parameters. If the values set in the programmatic logon are invalid, an error is reported.
Resultset	rdoResultset	<none>	Contains an object reference to the rdoResultset object created by the RDC. you can use this as you use the Recordset object of the standard data control.
ResultsetType	Integer	rdOpenStatic (0)	Controls the type of dataset returned by the RDC. The rdOpenStatic option returns an updatable dataset with unchanging membership; the rdOpenKeyset opens an updatable dataset with changing membership.
RowsetSize	Integer	100	Controls the number of rows buffered to your application. This is also the number of rows locked when using pes-simistic locking (rdConcurLock).

17

continues

TABLE 17.5 CONTINUED

Property	Type	Default Setting	Description
SQL	String	\<none\>	Specifies the SQL statement used to populate the dataset for the RDC. This is the RDC equivalent of the RecordSource property of the standard data control.
StillExecuting	Boolean	False	Indicates whether the dataset is still in the process of being created. You can check this periodically on long data connections.
Transactions	Boolean	False	Indicates whether the remote data source supports the use of BeginTrans, CommitTrans, and RollbackTrans methods. You can check this before you attempt to use these methods.

The RDC Methods

Several methods are associated with the RDC. Most of these methods have counterparts with the standard data control. Table 17.6 lists the RDC methods.

TABLE 17.6 THE RDC METHODS

Method	Function
BeginTrans, CommitTrans, RollbackTrans	Enables programmers to provide transaction management for RDC actions. This improves data integrity on action queries and can speed up processing on single-row updates.
Cancel	Cancels any pending Query, Edit, AddNew, or Delete operation.
Refresh	Repopulates the dataset.
UpdateControls	Refreshes the data-bound controls with the contents of the dataset.
UpdateRows	Refreshes the dataset with the values in the data-bound controls.

The most important items to note in Table 17.6 are the transaction-management methods and the UpdateRows method. These methods are unique to the RDC and are not available with the standard Microsoft Jet data control.

The RDC Events

The RDC offers a set of unique events that are similar to the events supported by the Microsoft Jet data control: `Validate`, `Reposition`, and `Error`. The RDC has an additional event not supported by the Microsoft Jet data control: the `QueryCompleted` event. This event is fired after the dataset has returned successfully from the remote data source. This event can be used to alert users of the completion of delayed queries because of slow connections or a large dataset size.

The events, methods, and properties covered in the previous sections are illustrated in the RDC data-entry project in the next section.

Laying Out the RDC Data-Entry Form

In this section, you create a simple data-entry form using the RDC. This form illustrates the use of most of the properties, methods, and events covered in previous sections of this chapter. If you haven't already done so, start Visual Basic 6.0 and select a new, standard EXE project.

Before you begin laying out the data-entry form, be sure to load the RDC by choosing Project | Components. The Components dialog box appears, as shown in Figure 17.5.

FIGURE 17.5

Loading the Remote Data Control Component.

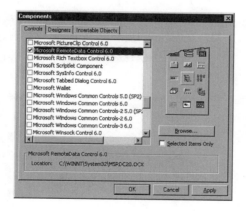

After adding the RDC to the project, create your data-entry form based on Figure 17.6 and Table 17.7.

Figure 17.6

*Laying out the RDC
data-entry form.*

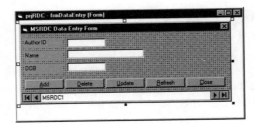

Table 17.7 Controls for the RDC Data-Entry Form

Control Name	Property	Setting
VB.Form	Name	frmDataEntry
	BorderStyle	3 'Fixed Dialog
	Caption	"MSRDC Data Entry Form"
	ClientHeight	2250
	ClientLeft	45
	ClientTop	330
	ClientWidth	6510
	MaxButton	0 'False
	MinButton	0 'False
	ShowInTaskbar	0 'False
	StartUpPosition	3 'Windows Default
VB.TextBox	Name	txtAUID
	DataSource	"MSRDC1"
	Height	285
	Left	1440
	Text	"Text2"
	Top	180
	Width	1200
VB.CommandButton	Name	cmdBtn
	Caption	"&Close"
	Height	300
	Index	4
	Left	5160
	Top	1500
	Width	1200

Control Name	Property	Setting
VB.CommandButton	Name	cmdBtn
	Caption	"&Refresh"
	Height	300
	Index	3
	Left	3900
	Top	1500
	Width	1200
VB.CommandButton	Name	cmdBtn
	Caption	"&Update"
	Height	300
	Index	2
	Left	2640
	Top	1500
	Width	1200
VB.CommandButton	Name	cmdBtn
	Caption	"&Delete"
	Height	300
	Index	1
	Left	1380
	Top	1500
	Width	1200
VB.CommandButton	Name	cmdBtn
	Caption	"&Add"
	Height	300
	Index	0
	Left	120
	Top	1500
	Width	1200
VB.TextBox	Name	txtDOB
	DataSource	"MSRDC1"
	Height	285
	Left	1440

17

continues

TABLE 17.7 CONTINUED

Control Name	Property	Setting
	Text	"Text2"
	Top	960
	Width	1200
VB.TextBox	Name	txtName
	DataSource	"MSRDC1"
	Height	285
	Left	1440
	Text	"Text1"
	Top	540
	Width	2400
MSRDC.MSRDC	Name	MSRDC1
	Align	2 'Align Bottom
	Height	330
	Left	0
	Top	1920
	Width	6510
	CursorDriver	3
	RecordsetType	1
	LockType	5
	DataSourceName	"BOOKS6"
	RecordSource	"SELECT * FROM Authors"
	UserName	"admin"
VB.Label	Name	lblDOB
	Caption	"DOB"
	Height	255
	Left	120
	Top	1020
	Width	1200
VB.Label	Name	lblName
	Caption	"Name"
	Height	255
	Left	120

Control Name	Property	Setting
	Top	600
	Width	1200
VB.Label	Name	lblAuthorID
	Caption	"Author ID"
	Height	255
	Left	120
	Top	180
	Width	1200

In addition to the main data-entry form, you need to build a second form to display status messages while the data-entry form is running. Add a new standard form to your project. Set its Name property to frmMsgs and place a single text box on the form. Set the text box Name property to txtMsg, and set its Multiline property to True and its Scrollbars property to Both (see Figure 17.7).

FIGURE 17.7

Building the frmMsgs form.

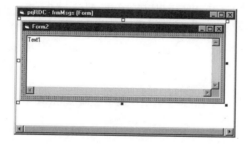

Save the project as PRJRDC.VBP, the main form as FRMDATAENTRY.FRM, and the support form as FRMMSGS.FRM. Now you're ready to add Visual Basic code to the forms.

Coding the RDC Data-Entry Forms

First, you need to add code to two events in the frmMsgs form. Listing 17.1 shows the code for the Form_Load and Form_Resize events. Add this code to your support form.

LISTING 17.1 CODING THE EVENTS FOR THE FRMMSGS SUPPORT FORM

```
1: Private Sub Form_Load()
2:     '
3:     Me.Caption = "MSRDC Event Messages"
```

continues

17

LISTING 17.1 CONTINUED

```
 4:        txtMsg.Text = ""
 5:        '
 6: End Sub
 7:
 8: Private Sub Form_Resize()
 9:        '
10:        ' make text box fill the form
11:        '
12:        If Me.WindowState <> vbMinimized Then
13:            txtMsg.Left = 1
14:            txtMsg.Top = 1
15:            txtMsg.Width = Me.ScaleWidth
16:            txtMsg.Height = Me.ScaleHeight
17:        End If
18:        '
19: End Sub
```

The code in Listing 17.1 sets up the initial caption and text box on the form and then resizes the text box to fill the entire frmMsgs form space. This form will display progress messages reported by the main data-entry form. You can save and close this form. This is all the code you need to add to the frmMsgs form.

Now open the main data-entry form (frmDataEntry) and add the code from Listing 17.2 to the Form_Load event.

LISTING 17.2 CODING THE form_Load EVENT FOR THE FRMDATAENTRY FORM

```
 1: Private Sub Form_Load()
 2:        '
 3:        ' project setup actions
 4:        '
 5:        frmMsgs.Show ' launch message window
 6:        '
 7:        ' set up RDC
 8:        With MSRDC1
 9:            .DataSourceName = "Books6"
10:            .SQL = "SELECT * FROM Authors"
11:            .CursorDriver = rdUseClientBatch
12:            .LockType = rdConcurBatch
13:            .ResultsetType = rdOpenStatic
14:            .Refresh
15:        End With
16:        '
17:        ' bind inputs to rdc
18:        txtAUID.DataField = "AUID"
19:        txtName.DataField = "Name"
```

```
20:        txtDOB.DataField = "DOB"
21:        '
22:        ' set form title
23:        Me.Caption = "Remote Data Control Demo"
24:        '
25: End Sub
```

The code in Listing 17.2 sets up the basic parameters to the RDC, uses the Refresh method to fetch the data, and then updates the DataField properties of the bound input controls in order to link them to the dataset returned in the RDC. Note that you are using the rdOpenStatic option to create an updatable, fixed-membership dataset.

Tip

> It is not a requirement for you to set the Properties of the MSRDC control at runtime. You can do this at design-time with the property box if you wish. However, it is a good programming practice to add this kind of code to the form anyway. This will make it easier to maintain the form if you ever change MSRDC settings.

17

Now add the code from Listing 17.3 to the cmdBtn_Click event of the form. This single set of code handles all the command buttons, because the buttons were added as a control array.

LISTING 17.3   CODING THE cmdBtn_Click EVENT

```
 1: Private Sub cmdBtn_Click(Index As Integer)
 2:        '
 3:        ' handle button selections
 4:        '
 5:     With MSRDC1
 6:        Select Case Index
 7:            Case 0 ' add
 8:                .Resultset.AddNew
 9:            Case 1 ' delete
10:                If MsgBox("Delete Record?", vbYesNo + vbQuestion, _
                        "Delete") = vbYes Then
11:                    .Resultset.Delete
12:                    .Resultset.MoveFirst
13:                End If
14:            Case 2 ' update
15:                .UpdateRow
16:            Case 3 ' refresh
17:                .UpdateControls
```

continues

LISTING 17.3   CONTINUED

```
18:                     Case 4 ' close
19:                         Unload Me
20:             End Select
21:         End With
22:             '
23: End Sub
```

Listing 17.4 shows the code you need to add to the four RDC-related events. Note that all four of these routines use a `PostMsg` subroutine and that the `Validate` event calls a `ShowAction` function. You build these routines in the next step of the project.

LISTING 17.4   CODING THE EVENTS OF THE RDC

```
 1: Private Sub MSRDC1_Error(ByVal Number As Long, Description As _
       String, ByVal Scode As Long, ByVal Source As String, ByVal HelpFile _
       As String, ByVal HelpContext As Long, CancelDisplay As Boolean)
 2:         '
 3:         PostMsg "MSRDC1_Error - Number=" & CStr(Number) & ", _
       Description = " & Description & ", Scode = " & CStr(Scode) & ", _
       Source = " & Source & ", HelpFile = " & HelpFile & ", _
       HelpContext = " & CStr(HelpContext) & ", CancelDisplay = " & _
       CStr(CancelDisplay)
 4:         '
 5: End Sub
 6:
 7: Private Sub MSRDC1_QueryCompleted()
 8:         '
 9:         PostMsg "MSRDC1_QueryCompleted"
10:         '
11: End Sub
12:
13: Private Sub MSRDC1_Reposition()
14:         '
15:         PostMsg "MSRDC1_Reposition"
16:         '
17: End Sub
18:
19: Private Sub MSRDC1_Validate(Action As Integer, Reserved As Integer)
20:         '
21:         PostMsg "MSRDC1_Validate - Action=" & ShowAction(Action) & _
       ", Reserved=" & CStr(Reserved)
22:         '
23: End Sub
```

After adding the code for all the events, add the code in Listing 17.5 to the form to create the `ShowAction` function. This function converts the integer value passed from the

Validate event into a friendly string name. This is used to display progress messages in the frmMsg form.

LISTING 17.5 CODING THE ShowAction FUNCTION

```
 1: Public Function ShowAction(intAction As Integer) As String
 2:     '
 3:     ' convert numeric action value
 4:     ' into friendly string value
 5:     '
 6:     Dim strMsg As String
 7:     '
 8:     Select Case intAction
 9:         Case rdActionCancel   '0
10:             strMsg = "Cancel"
11:         Case rdActionMoveFirst        '1
12:             strMsg = "MoveFirst"
13:         Case rdActionMovePrevious     '2
14:             strMsg = "MovePrevious"
15:         Case rdActionMoveNext     '3
16:             strMsg = "MoveNext"
17:         Case rdActionMoveLast     '4
18:             strMsg = "MoveLast"
19:         Case rdActionAddNew   '5
20:             strMsg = "AddNew"
21:         Case rdActionUpdate   '6
22:             strMsg = "Update"
23:         Case rdActionDelete   '7
24:             strMsg = "Delete"
25:         Case rdActionFind '8
26:             strMsg = "Find"
27:         Case rdActionBookmark '9
28:             strMsg = "Bookmark"
29:         Case rdActionClose '10
30:             strMsg = "Close"
31:         Case rdActionUnload '11
32:             strMsg = "Unload"
33:         Case rdActionUpdateAddNew '12
34:             strMsg = "UpdateAddNew"
35:         Case rdActionUpdateModified '13
36:             strMsg = "UpdateModified"
37:         Case rdActionRefresh '14
38:             strMsg = "Refresh"
39:         Case rdActionCancelUpdate '15
40:             strMsg = "CancelUpdate"
41:         Case rdActionBeginTransact '16
42:             strMsg = "BeginTrans"
43:         Case rdActionCommitTransact '17
44:             strMsg = "CommitTrans"
```

17

continues

LISTING 17.5   CONTINUED

```
45:             Case rdActionRollbackTransact '18
46:                 strMsg = "RollbackTrans"
47:             Case rdActionNewParameters '19
48:                 strMsg = "NewParameters"
49:             Case rdActionNewSQL '20
50:                 strMsg = "NewSQL"
51:         End Select
52:         '
53:         ShowAction = strMsg
54:         '
55: End Function
```

Notice that the Validate event of the RDC has several action values that are not available with the standard Microsoft Jet data control. These additional values come in handy when managing remote data connections.

Now add the PostMsg method to your data-entry form. Listing 17.6 shows the code for this support routine.

LISTING 17.6   CODING THE PostMsg SUBROUTINE

```
 1: Public Sub PostMsg(strMsg As String)
 2:     '
 3:     ' post a message to a text box
 4:     '
 5:     Static lngCounter As Long
 6:     '
 7:     lngCounter = lngCounter + 1
 8:     frmMsgs.txtMsg = Format(lngCounter, "000") & ":" & _
        strMsg & vbCrLf & frmMsgs.txtMsg
 9:     '
10: End Sub
```

As mentioned earlier, the sole purpose of this routine is to post messages to the supporting form so that you can see the progress of data requests using the RDC. Now save the form (FRMDATAENTRY.FRM) and the project (PRJRDC.VBP) before running it.

When you run the project, the message form and the data form appear. Note the messages that have been posted to the support form. Modify the first record (change the value of the Name field) and move the record pointer. You see a number of messages appear in the support form indicating the validation of the new data, the updating of the modified data, and the repositioning of the record pointer on the new record (see Figure 17.8).

FIGURE 17.8

Running the RDC data-entry project.

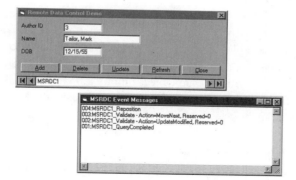

That's all there is to creating data-entry forms using data-bound controls and the RDC. The RDC can be used in just about any place where the DAO data control is used. This means you can use it to power data-bound lists and grids as well as all the standard data-bound input controls available in Visual Basic 6.0.

In the next section, you learn how to use Visual Basic to directly access the Remote Data Object (RDO) model. This will give you the skills you need to create database applications that use the RDO instead of a data-bound control set.

Programming with RDO

Creating database applications that use the RDO is quite similar to programming with the Microsoft Jet DAO. Some of the material in this section of the chapter refers to the DAO programming examples from Chapter 8. If you have not already completed that chapter, you might want to review it before you continue with this chapter.

The RDO programming objects are arranged in a hierarchy of collections. The top-level object is the rdoEngine object. This is the programmatic access to the Microsoft remote data engine used by Visual Basic 6 to gain access to all remote data. All requests using the RDO objects are handled by the rdoEngine.

The rdoEngine creates one or more rdoEnvironment objects. These objects are used to manage the details of the various connections to datasets. rdoEnvironment objects can create rdoConnection objects. These are the actual connections to existing data sources at the remote data system. Each rdoConnection can create one or more rdoResultset objects. The rdoResultset object contains the actual rows of data. You also can create and access rdoQuery objects or rdoTable objects from the rdoConnection object. The rdoQuery object also has an rdoParameter object to manage the passing of parameters during the processing of queries.

In the sections that follow, you code examples of each of the RDO objects, inspect their properties, and exercise their methods. To do this, start a new Visual Basic 6 standard EXE project. Set the project name to prjRDO and the form name to frmRDO. Save the empty form as FRMRDO.FRM and the project as PRJRDO.VBP. You also need to add a reference to the Microsoft Remote Data Object Library 2.0. To do this, select Project | References from the main menu and then locate and select the Microsoft Remote Data Object Library 2.0 component.

The rdoEngine Object

The rdoEngine object is the top-level object in the RDO collection. This object has only a handful of parameters and has no collection of its own. You can have only one rdoEngine instance in your Visual Basic programs. Add a new command button to your form. Set its Name property to cmdRDOEngine and its Caption to RDO Engine. Now add the code in Listing 17.7 to the cmdRDOEngine_Click event.

LISTING 17.7 CODING THE cmdRDOEngine_Click EVENT

```
 1: Private Sub cmdRDOEngine_Click()
 2: '
 3: ' show rdo engine properties
 4: '
 5: Dim strMsg As String
 6: Dim rdoEng As rdoEngine
 7: Dim aryCursorDriver As Variant
 8: '
 9: aryCursorDriver = Array("rdUseIfNeeded", "rdUseOdbc", "rdUseServer", _
        "rdUseClientBatch", "rduseNone")
10: '
11: Set rdoEng = rdoEngine
12: '
13: strMsg = strMsg & "rdoDefaultCursorDriver=" & _
        aryCursorDriver(rdoEng.rdoDefaultCursorDriver) & vbCrLf
14: strMsg = strMsg & "rdoDefaultErrorThreshold=" & _
        CStr(rdoEng.rdoDefaultErrorThreshold) & vbCrLf
15: strMsg = strMsg & "rdoDefaultLoginTimeOut=" & _
        CStr(rdoEng.rdoDefaultLoginTimeout) & vbCrLf
16: strMsg = strMsg & "rdoDefaultPassword=" & rdoEng.rdoDefaultPassword _
        & vbCrLf
17: strMsg = strMsg & "rdoDefaultUser=" & rdoEng.rdoDefaultUser & vbCrLf
18: strMsg = strMsg & "rdoLocaleID=" & CStr(rdoEng.rdoLocaleID) & vbCrLf
19: strMsg = strMsg & "rdoVersion=" & CStr(rdoEng.rdoVersion) & vbCrLf
20: '
21: MsgBox strMsg, vbInformation, "RDOEngine"
22: '
23: Set rdoEng = Nothing
24: '
25: End Sub
```

Save and run the project. After you click the RDO Engine command button, you should see something like the message in Figure 17.9.

FIGURE 17.9

Display the RDO Engine properties.

The rdoEnvironment Object

The rdoEnvironment object contains information about the current environment for data connections. The rdoEnvironment object is the RDO equivalent of the Microsoft Jet Workspaces object. rdoEnvironment objects can be used to group rdoConnection objects together for transaction-management purposes as well.

You can create multiple rdoEnvironment objects under the rdoEngine object. All rdoEnvironment objects are contained in the rdoEnvironments collection object.

Add a new button to the form. Set its Name property to cmdRDOEnvironment and its Caption to Environment. Now enter the code from Listing 17.8 to the cmdRDOEnvironment_Click event.

LISTING 17.8   CODING THE cmdRDOEnvironment_Click EVENT

```
 1: Private Sub cmdRDOEnvironment_Click()
 2: '
 3: ' show environment collection as properties
 4: '
 5: Dim strMsg As String
 6: Dim rdoEnv As rdoEnvironment
 7: Dim rdoNewEnv As rdoEnvironment
 8: Dim aryCursorDriver As Variant
 9: '
10: aryCursorDriver = Array("rdUseIfNeeded", "rdUseOdbc", "rdUseServer", _
    "rdUseClientBatch", "rduseNone")
11: '
12: Set rdoNewEnv = rdoEngine.rdoCreateEnvironment("rdoTEMP", "admin", "")
13: '
14: For Each rdoEnv In rdoEngine.rdoEnvironments
15: strMsg = strMsg & "rdoCursorDriver=" & _
    aryCursorDriver(rdoEnv.CursorDriver) & vbCrLf
```

continues

LISTING 17.8 CONTINUED

```
16: strMsg = strMsg & "hEnv=" & CStr(rdoEnv.hEnv) & vbCrLf
17: strMsg = strMsg & "LoginTimeOut=" & CStr(rdoEnv.LoginTimeout) & vbCrLf
18: 'strMsg = strMsg & "Password=" & rdoEnv.Password & vbCrLf
19: strMsg = strMsg & "UserName=" & rdoEnv.UserName & vbCrLf
20: strMsg = strMsg & vbCrLf
21: Next
22: '
23: MsgBox strMsg, vbInformation, "rdoEnvironment"
24: '
25: rdoNewEnv.Close
26: Set rdoEnv = Nothing
27: Set rdoNewEnv = Nothing
28: '
39: End Sub
```

After you save and run the project, click the Environment button to display a dialog box similar to the one in Figure 17.10.

FIGURE 17.10

*Viewing the
RDO Environment
properties.*

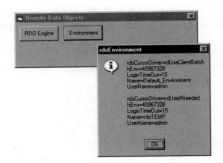

Notice that a default environment always is available to your application. It is advisable, however, to create your own environment before you attempt to establish a connection to remote data sources.

The rdoConnection Object

The rdoConnection object contains the details needed to establish a connection between your application and the remote data source. The rdoConnection object is similar to the Microsoft Jet Database object.

You can create more than one rdoConnection object under the same rdoEnvironment object. All rdoConnection objects are stored in the rdoConnections collection.

Add a new button to the form. Set its Name to cmdRDOConnection and its Caption to Connection. Then add the code in Listing 17.9 to the cmdRDOConnection_Click event.

LISTING 17.9   CODING THE cmdRDOConnection_Click EVENT

```
 1: Private Sub cmdRDOConnection_Click()
 2: '
 3: ' show resultsets
 4: '
 5: Dim strMsg As String
 6: Dim rdoEnv As rdoEnvironment
 7: Dim rdoCon As rdoConnection
 8: Dim rdoNewCon As rdoConnection
 9: Dim aryCursorDriver As Variant
10: '
11: aryCursorDriver = Array("rdUseIfNeeded", "rdUseOdbc", "rdUseServer", _
      "rdUseClientBatch", "rduseNone")
12: '
13: Set rdoEnv = rdoEngine.rdoCreateEnvironment("rdoTEMP", "admin", "")
14: Set rdoNewCon = rdoEnv.OpenConnection("Books6")
15: '
16: For Each rdoCon In rdoEnv.rdoConnections
17: strMsg = strMsg & "AsyncCheckInterval=" & _
      CStr(rdoCon.AsyncCheckInterval) & vbCrLf
18: strMsg = strMsg & "Connect=" & rdoCon.Connect & vbCrLf
19: strMsg = strMsg & "CursorDriver=" & _
      aryCursorDriver(rdoCon.CursorDriver) & vbCrLf
20: strMsg = strMsg & "hDbc=" & CStr(rdoCon.hDbc) & vbCrLf
21: strMsg = strMsg & "LoginTimeOut=" & CStr(rdoCon.LoginTimeout) & vbCrLf
22: strMsg = strMsg & "LogMessages=" & rdoCon.LogMessages & vbCrLf
23: strMsg = strMsg & "Name=" & rdoCon.Name & vbCrLf
24: strMsg = strMsg & "QueryTimeOut=" & CStr(rdoCon.QueryTimeout) & vbCrLf
25: strMsg = strMsg & "RowsAffected=" & CStr(rdoCon.RowsAffected) & vbCrLf
26: strMsg = strMsg & "StillConnecting=" & CStr(rdoCon.StillConnecting) _
      & vbCrLf
27: strMsg = strMsg & "StillExecuting=" & CStr(rdoCon.StillExecuting) & _
      vbCrLf
28: strMsg = strMsg & "Transactions=" & CStr(rdoCon.Transactions) & vbCrLf
29: strMsg = strMsg & "Updatable=" & CStr(rdoCon.Updatable) & vbCrLf
30: strMsg = strMsg & "Version=" & rdoCon.Version & vbCrLf
31: Next
32: '
33: MsgBox strMsg, vbInformation, "rdoConnection"
34: '
35: rdoNewCon.Close
36: rdoEnv.Close
37: Set rdoEnv = Nothing
38: Set rdoCon = Nothing
39: Set rdoNewCon = Nothing
40: '
41: End Sub
```

17

Save and run the project. After you click the Connection button, you'll see a display of all the default properties of an rdoConnection object, as shown in Figure 17.11.

FIGURE 17.11

Viewing the RDO Connection properties.

Note that the Version property of the rdoConnection object reports the version number of the ODBC driver used to establish the connection to the remote data source.

The rdoResultset Object

After a connection is established between your program and the remote data, you can use the rdoResultset object to create a collection of records. The rdoResultset object is the RDO equivalent of the Microsoft Jet Recordset object. rdoResultset contains a direct reference to all the rows and columns in the dataset.

You can have multiple rdoResultset objects for each rdoConnection object. All Resultset objects are stored in the Resultsets collection of the rdoConnection object.

Add a new button to the project. Set its Name property to cmdRDOResultset and its Caption to Resultset. Now add the code in Listing 17.10 to the cmdRDOResultset_Click event.

LISTING 17.10   CODING THE cmdRDOTables_Click cmdRDOResultset_Click EVENT

```
1: Private Sub cmdRDOResultset_Click()
2: '
3: ' show result set properties
4: '
5: Dim rdoEnv As rdoEnvironment
6: Dim rdoCon As rdoConnection
7: Dim rdoRS As rdoResultset
8: Dim strMsg As String
9: Dim aryEditMode As Variant
```

```
10: Dim aryLockType As Variant
11: Dim aryType As Variant
12: '
13: aryEditMode = Array("rdEditNone", "rdEditInProgress", "rdEditAdd")
14: aryLockType = Array("rdConcurReadOnly", "rdConcurLock", _
      "rdConcurRowVer", "rdConcurValues", "rdConCurBatchEdit")
15: aryType = Array("rdOpenForwardOnly", "rdOpenKeyset", _
      "rdOpenDynamic", "rdOpenStatic")
16: '
17: ' set up env/con/rs
18: Set rdoEnv = rdoEngine.rdoCreateEnvironment("rdoTEMP", "admin", "")
19: Set rdoCon = rdoEnv.OpenConnection("Books6")
20: Set rdoRS = rdoCon.OpenResultset("SELECT * FROM Authors")
21: '
22: ' show properties of the rdoRS
23: strMsg = strMsg & "AbsolutePosition=" & CStr(rdoRS.AbsolutePosition) _
      & vbCrLf
24: strMsg = strMsg & "BOF=" & CStr(rdoRS.BOF) & vbCrLf
25: strMsg = strMsg & "Bookmark=" & rdoRS.Bookmark & vbCrLf
26: strMsg = strMsg & "Bookmarkable=" & CStr(rdoRS.Bookmarkable) & vbCrLf
27: strMsg = strMsg & "EditMode=" & aryEditMode(rdoRS.EditMode) & vbCrLf
28: strMsg = strMsg & "EOF=" & CStr(rdoRS.EOF) & vbCrLf
29: strMsg = strMsg & "hStmt=" & CStr(rdoRS.hStmt) & vbCrLf
30: strMsg = strMsg & "LastModified=" & rdoRS.LastModified & vbCrLf
31: strMsg = strMsg & "LockEdits=" & CStr(rdoRS.LockEdits) & vbCrLf
32: strMsg = strMsg & "LockType=" & aryLockType(rdoRS.LockType) & vbCrLf
33: strMsg = strMsg & "Name=" & rdoRS.Name & vbCrLf
34: strMsg = strMsg & "PercentPosition=" & CStr(rdoRS.PercentPosition) & _
      vbCrLf
35: strMsg = strMsg & "Restartable=" & CStr(rdoRS.Restartable) & vbCrLf
36: strMsg = strMsg & "RowCount=" & CStr(rdoRS.RowCount) & vbCrLf
37: strMsg = strMsg & "Status=" & CStr(rdoRS.Status) & vbCrLf
38: strMsg = strMsg & "StillExecuting=" & CStr(rdoRS.StillExecuting) & _
      vbCrLf
39: strMsg = strMsg & "Transactions=" & CStr(rdoRS.Transactions) & vbCrLf
40: strMsg = strMsg & "Type=" & aryType(rdoRS.Type) & vbCrLf
41: strMsg = strMsg & "Updatable=" & CStr(rdoRS.Updatable) & vbCrLf
42: '
43: MsgBox strMsg, vbInformation, "rdoResultset"
44: '
45: rdoRS.Close
46: rdoCon.Close
47: rdoEnv.Close
48: Set rdoRS = Nothing
49: Set rdoCon = Nothing
50: Set rdoEnv = Nothing
51: '
52: End Sub
```

17

Note the use of the OpenResultset method of the rdoConnection object to create the rdoResultset. Save and run the project. After you click the Resultset button, you see a display similar to the one in Figure 17.12.

FIGURE 17.12

Viewing the RDO Resultset properties.

The rdoTable Object

You also can open an rdoTable object from the rdoConnection object. This object contains information about each of the columns in the base table that exist on the remote data source. You can use the rdoTables collection to get a listing of all the base objects available through the rdoConnection. The rdoTables collection returns more than just the defined base tables. You also receive all the stored queries (views) available at the remote data source.

Caution

The rdoTable object is included in Visual Basic 6.0 for backward compatibility with previous versions of the RDO Engine. Although the rdoTable object works as expected in this version of Visual Basic, it might not be supported in future versions of Visual Basic.

Add a new button to the project. Set its Name property to cmdRDOTables and its Caption to RDO Tables. Now add the code in Listing 17.11 to the cmdRDOTables_Click event.

LISTING 17.11 CODING THE cmdRDOTables_Click EVENT

```
1: Private Sub cmdRDOTables_Click()
2: '
3: ' get rdo table collection
4: '
```

```
 5: Dim rdoEnv As rdoEnvironment
 6: Dim rdoCon As rdoConnection
 7: Dim rdoTbl As rdoTable
 8: Dim strMsg As String
 9: '
10: ' set env/con
11: Set rdoEnv = rdoEngine.rdoCreateEnvironment("rdoTEMP", "admin", "")
12: Set rdoCon = rdoEnv.OpenConnection("Books6")
13: '
14: ' update the tables collection
15: rdoCon.rdoTables.Refresh
16: '
17: ' show table properties
18: For Each rdoTbl In rdoCon.rdoTables
19: strMsg = strMsg & "Name=" & rdoTbl.Name & vbCrLf
20: strMsg = strMsg & "RowCount=" & CStr(rdoTbl.RowCount) & vbCrLf
21: strMsg = strMsg & "Type=" & CStr(rdoTbl.Type) & vbCrLf
22: strMsg = strMsg & "Updatable=" & CStr(rdoTbl.Updatable)
23: strMsg = strMsg & vbCrLf
24: '
25: MsgBox strMsg, vbInformation, "rdoTable"
26: strMsg = ""
27: Next
28: '
29: rdoCon.Close
30: rdoEnv.Close
31: Set rdoTbl = Nothing
32: Set rdoCon = Nothing
33: Set rdoEnv = Nothing
34: '
35: End Sub
```

17

Notice the use of the Refresh method on the rdoTables collection. This is required if you want to get a list of all the table and view objects available from the data source. The rdoTables collection is not automatically refreshed when you create the rdoConnection object.

Save and run the project. After you click the RDO Tables button, you'll see a list of the tables and views available from the data source. Figure 17.13 shows one of those displays.

The rdoColumns Object

The rdoColumns object contains detailed information about the contents and properties of each data column in the rdoTable or rdoResultset object. The rdoColumn object corresponds to the Microsoft Jet Field object. Usually, more than one rdoColumn object exists for each rdoTable or rdoResultset object. All rdoColumn objects are stored in the rdoColumns collection.

FIGURE 17.13

Viewing the RDO Table properties.

Add a new button to the project. Set its Name to cmdRDOColumns and its Caption to Columns. Now add the code in Listing 17.12 to the cmdRDOColumns_Click event.

LISTING 17.12   CODING THE cmdRDOColumns_Click EVENT

```
 1: Private Sub cmdRDOColumns_Click()
 2: '
 3: ' show rdo columns collection
 4: '
 5: Dim rdoEnv As rdoEnvironment
 6: Dim rdoCon As rdoConnection
 7: Dim rdoTbl As rdoTable
 8: Dim rdoCol As rdoColumn
 9: Dim strMsg As String
10: '
11: ' set up connection
12: Set rdoEnv = rdoEngine.rdoCreateEnvironment("rdoTEMP", "admin", "")
13: Set rdoCon = rdoEnv.OpenConnection("Books6")
14: '
15: ' get table info
16: rdoCon.rdoTables.Refresh
17: Set rdoTbl = rdoCon.rdoTables("Authors")
18: '
19: ' get column info
20: For Each rdoCol In rdoTbl.rdoColumns
21: strMsg = strMsg & "AllowZeroLength=" & CStr(rdoCol.AllowZeroLength) _
        & vbCrLf
22: strMsg = strMsg & "Attributes=" & Hex(rdoCol.Attributes) & vbCrLf
23: strMsg = strMsg & "ChunkRequired=" & CStr(rdoCol.ChunkRequired) & _
        vbCrLf
24: strMsg = strMsg & "Name=" & rdoCol.Name & vbCrLf
25: strMsg = strMsg & "OrdinalPosition=" & CStr(rdoCol.OrdinalPosition) _
        & vbCrLf
26: strMsg = strMsg & "Required=" & CStr(rdoCol.Required) & vbCrLf
27: strMsg = strMsg & "Size=" & CStr(rdoCol.Size) & vbCrLf
28: strMsg = strMsg & "SourceColumn=" & rdoCol.SourceColumn & vbCrLf
29: strMsg = strMsg & "SourceTable=" & rdoCol.SourceTable & vbCrLf
30: strMsg = strMsg & "Type=" & CStr(rdoCol.Type) & vbCrLf
31: strMsg = strMsg & "Updatable=" & CStr(rdoCol.Updatable) & vbCrLf
32: '
```

```
33: MsgBox strMsg, vbInformation, "rdoColumn"
34: strMsg = ""
35: '
36: Next
37: '
38: rdoCon.Close
39: rdoEnv.Close
40: Set rdoCol = Nothing
41: Set rdoTbl = Nothing
42: Set rdoCon = Nothing
43: Set rdoEnv = Nothing
44: '
45: End Sub
```

The code in Listing 17.12 displays detailed properties for each column in the Authors table at the data source. Note that the .Value and the .OriginalValue properties have been left out of this example. You also can access these properties in your programs. The value of the .Type property maps to a set of predefined Visual Basic constants. Table 17.8 lists those values.

TABLE 17.8 VARIOUS TYPE VALUES OF THE rdoColumns.Type PROPERTY

Visual Basic Constant	Integer Value	Description
rdTypeCHAR	1	Fixed-length character string. Length set by Size property.
rdTypeNUMERIC	2	Signed, exact numeric value with precision p and scale s (1 p 15; 0 s p).
rdTypeDECIMAL	3	Signed, exact numeric value with precision p and scale s (1 p 15; 0 s p).
rdTypeINTEGER	4	Signed, exact numeric value with precision 10, scale 0 (signed: - 231[]231-1; unsigned: 0[]232-1).
rdTypeSMALLINT	5	Signed, exact numeric value with precision 5, scale 0 (signed: - 32,768[]32,767; unsigned: 0[]65,535).
rdTypeFLOAT	6	Signed, approximate numeric value with mantissa precision 15 (zero or absolute value 10-308 to 10308).
rdTypeREAL	7	Signed, approximate numeric value with mantissa precision 7 (zero or absolute value 10-38 to 1038).
rdTypeDOUBLE	8	Signed, approximate numeric value with mantissa precision 15 (zero or absolute value 10-308 to 10308).
rdTypeDATE	9	Date: Data-source dependent.

17

continues

TABLE 17.8 CONTINUED

Visual Basic Constant	Integer Value	Description
rdTypeTIME	10	Time: Data-source dependent.
rdTypeTIMESTAMP	11	TimeStamp: Data-source dependent.
rdTypeVARCHAR	12	Variable-length character string. Maximum length: 255.
rdTypeLONGVARCHAR	–1	Variable-length character string. Maximum length determined by data source.
rdTypeBINARY	–2	Fixed-length binary data. Maximum length: 255.
rdTypeVARBINARY	–3	Variable-length binary data. Maximum length: 255.
rdTypeLONGVARBINARY	–4	Variable-length binary data. Maximum data-source dependent.
rdTypeBIGINT	–5	Signed, exact numeric value with precision 19 (signed) or 20 (unsigned); scale 0 (signed: -263[]263-1; unsigned: 0[]264-1).
rdTypeTINYINT	–6	Signed, exact numeric value with precision 3, scale 0; (signed: - 128[]127; unsigned: 0[]255).
rdTypeBIT	–7	Single binary digit.

The exact data type that is returned in each column is data-source–dependent. Not all data sources support all data types listed here.

Save and run the project. After you click the RDO Columns button, you see a series of dialog boxes that show the details of each column in the Authors table. Figure 17.14 shows one of those dialog boxes.

FIGURE 17.14

Viewing the RDO Column properties.

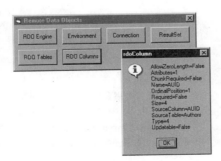

The `rdoQuery` Object

The `rdoQuery` object provides a method for creating and executing defined queries or views on the remote data source. The `rdoQuery` object is the RDO version of the Microsoft Jet QueryDef object. You can create more than one `rdoQuery` object on each `rdoConnection` object. All `rdoQuery` objects are accessed through the `rdoQueries` collection object.

Add a new button to the form. Set its `Name` to `cmdRDOQueries` and its `Caption` to `RDO Queries`. Add the code in Listing 17.13 to the `cmdRDOQueries_Click` event.

LISTING 17.13   CODING FOR THE `cmdRDOQueries_Click` EVENT

```
 1: Private Sub cmdRDOQueries_Click()
 2: '
 3: ' example rdo query
 4: '
 5: Dim rdoEnv As rdoEnvironment
 6: Dim rdoCon As rdoConnection
 7: Dim rdoQry As rdoQuery
 8: Dim rdoNewQry As rdoQuery
 9: Dim rdoRS As rdoResultset
10: Dim strMsg As String
11: Dim strSQL As String
12: Dim aryLockType As Variant
13: Dim aryType As Variant
14: Dim aryCursorDriver As Variant
15: '
16: aryCursorDriver = Array("rdUseIfNeeded", "rdUseOdbc", "rdUseServer", _
      "rdUseClientBatch", "rduseNone")
17: aryLockType = Array("rdConcurReadOnly", "rdConcurLock", _
      "rdConcurRowVer", "rdConcurValues", "rdConCurBatchEdit")
18: aryType = Array("rdOpenForwardOnly", "rdOpenKeyset", _
      "rdOpenDynamic", "rdOpenStatic")
19: '
20: strSQL = "SELECT * FROM Publishers,Titles WHERE
    ➥Publishers.PubID=Titles.PubId"
21: '
22: ' set env/con
23: Set rdoEnv = rdoEngine.rdoCreateEnvironment("rdoTEMP", "admin", "")
24: Set rdoCon = rdoEnv.OpenConnection("Books6")
25: '
26: ' build a new query & collect data set
27: Set rdoNewQry = rdoCon.CreateQuery("rdoQryTest", strSQL)
28: Set rdoRS = rdoNewQry.OpenResultset()
29: '
30: ' show details
```

17

continues

LISTING 17.13 CONTINUED

```
31: For Each rdoQry In rdoCon.rdoQueries
32: strMsg = strMsg & "BindThreshold=" & CStr(rdoQry.BindThreshold) & _
       vbCrLf
33: strMsg = strMsg & "CursorType=" & aryCursorDriver(rdoQry.CursorType) _
       & vbCrLf
34: strMsg = strMsg & "hStmt=" & CStr(rdoQry.hStmt) & vbCrLf
35: strMsg = strMsg & "KeysetSize=" & CStr(rdoQry.KeysetSize) & vbCrLf
36: strMsg = strMsg & "LockType=" & aryLockType(rdoQry.LockType) & vbCrLf
37: strMsg = strMsg & "MaxRows=" & CStr(rdoQry.MaxRows) & vbCrLf
38: strMsg = strMsg & "Name=" & rdoQry.Name & vbCrLf
39: strMsg = strMsg & "Prepared=" & rdoQry.Prepared & vbCrLf
40: strMsg = strMsg & "QueryTimeOut=" & CStr(rdoQry.QueryTimeout) & vbCrLf
41: strMsg = strMsg & "RowsAffeced=" & CStr(rdoQry.RowsAffected) & vbCrLf
42: strMsg = strMsg & "RowsetSize=" & CStr(rdoQry.RowsetSize) & vbCrLf
43: strMsg = strMsg & "SQL=" & rdoQry.SQL & vbCrLf
44: strMsg = strMsg & "StillExecuting=" & CStr(rdoQry.StillExecuting) & _
       vbCrLf
45: strMsg = strMsg & "Type=" & aryType(rdoQry.Type) & vbCrLf
46: '
47: MsgBox strMsg, vbInformation, "rdoQuery"
48: strMsg = ""
49: '
50: Next
51: '
52: rdoNewQry.Close
53: rdoCon.Close
54: rdoEnv.Close
55: Set rdoQry = Nothing
56: Set rdoNewQry = Nothing
57: Set rdoCon = Nothing
58: Set rdoEnv = Nothing
59: '
60: End Sub
```

Notice the use of the OpenResultset method on the rdoQuery object. This is the way to fetch rows from the data source using the rdoQuery object as the base. Save and run the project. After you click the RDO Queries button, you see a detailed listing of the properties of the query, as shown in Figure 17.15.

The rdoParameter Object

The rdoParameter object enables you to populate the various predefined runtime parameters of a sorted query so that you can create flexible queries that can be adjusted at runtime by programming code or user input. You can define more than one rdoParameter object for each rdoQuery object. All the parameter objects are accessed via the rdoParameters collection.

FIGURE 17.15

Viewing the RDO Query properties.

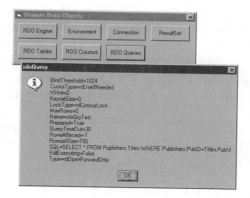

Add one last button to the project. Set its Name to cmdRDOParameter and its Caption to Parameters. Then add the code in Listing 17.14 to the cmdRDOParameter_Click event.

17

LISTING 17.14   CODING FOR THE cmdRDOParameter_Click EVENT

```
 1: Private Sub cmdRDOParameters_Click()
 2: '
 3: ' example of rdo parameters
 4: '
 5: Dim rdoEnv As rdoEnvironment
 6: Dim rdoCon As rdoConnection
 7: Dim rdoQry As rdoQuery
 8: Dim rdoRS As rdoResultset
 9: Dim rdoPrm As rdoParameter
10: Dim strMsg As String
11: Dim strSQL As String
12: '
13: strSQL = "SELECT * FROM Authors WHERE Name Like ?"
14: '
15: ' open env/con
16: Set rdoEnv = rdoEngine.rdoCreateEnvironment("rdoTEMP", "admin", "")
17: Set rdoCon = rdoEnv.OpenConnection("Books6")
18: '
19: ' create a parameter query
20: Set rdoQry = rdoCon.CreateQuery("rdoQryPrm", strSQL)
21: '
22: ' load parameter
23: rdoQry.rdoParameters(0).Value = "%s%"
24: rdoQry.rdoParameters(0).Type = rdTypeCHAR
25: '
26: ' get result from parameterized query
27: Set rdoRS = rdoQry.OpenResultset(rdOpenKeyset)
28: rdoRS.MoveLast
```

continues

LISTING 17.14   CONTINUED

```
29: '
30: ' show some details
31: strMsg = strMsg & "Name=" & rdoRS.Name & vbCrLf
32: strMsg = strMsg & "Parameter=" & rdoQry.rdoParameters(0) & vbCrLf
33: strMsg = strMsg & "RowCount=" & CStr(rdoRS.RowCount) & vbCrLf
34: '
35: MsgBox strMsg, vbInformation, "rdoParameters"
36: '
37: rdoQry.Close
38: rdoCon.Close
39: rdoEnv.Close
40: Set rdoPrm = Nothing
41: Set rdoQry = Nothing
42: Set rdoRS = Nothing
43: Set rdoCon = Nothing
44: Set rdoEnv = Nothing
45: '
46: End Sub
```

The code in Listing 17.14 first opens the data connection and then creates a parameter-ized query (note the ? that represents the parameter portion of the statement). Then the rdoParameter object is populated by using the Value and Type properties. Notice that it is not necessary to surround string parameters in single or double quotation marks. This is handled by the remote data source. Then the OpenResultset method is used to popu-late the dataset, and the MoveLast method is used to force the cursor to traverse the entire record collection. This ensures an accurate value for the Rowcount property of the rdoResultset. Finally, the results appear in a dialog box, as shown in Figure 17.16.

FIGURE 17.16

Viewing the RDO parameter.

The code in Listing 17.14 uses the Type property of the rdoParameter object. This is not a required property when creating rdoParameter objects, but it is highly recommended. If no Type property is set, the remote data source makes a guess at the data type of the parameter. This can lead to unexpected errors. If you have a CHAR column in your table that contains a shoe size (8.5, 9, and so on), for example, and use this column in a parameterized query, it is possible that passing a value of 8 will be misinterpreted by the RDBMS as an integer or long value instead of a CHAR value.

That completes your tour of the RDO programming object collection.

Summary

Today, you learned about two alternative methods for accessing remote data. You learned that you can use the RDC to create simple data-entry forms with data-bound controls. You also learned to use the RDO to create Visual Basic 6 programs that can access data from a remote RDBMS.

17

Along with the details of the RDC and the RDO, you also learned some of the basics of remote data access in general:

- *Cursor drivers.* The tools that manage the location of the Recordset pointer in a dataset. You learned that you can use client-side or server-side cursor drivers with RDO connections.

- *Dataset types.* You learned that a number of dataset types are available to you when you connect to remote data sources, including forward-only/read-only sets, static sets, key sets, and dynamic sets.

- *Lock types.* You learned that you can use several lock types when accessing data from your remote data source. You can use ConcurrentLock sets that perform locks as soon as you receive the data rows, or you can use several versions of optimistic locking that only attempt to lock the rows when you update them.

You also learned the details of the following Microsoft RDO:

- rdoColumn is the RDO version of the Microsoft Jet Field object
- rdoConnection is the RDO equivalent of the Microsoft Jet Database object
- rdoEngine is the top-level data engine used to access remote data
- rdoEnvironment is the RDO equivalent of the Microsoft Jet Workspace object
- rdoParameters is a special collection of query parameters for the rdoQuery object
- rdoResultset is the RDO equivalent of the Microsoft Jet Recordset object
- rdoQuery is the RDO version of the Microsoft Jet QueryDef object
- rdoTable is the RDO version of the Microsoft Jet Table object

Quiz

1. What is the difference between the standard data control and the Remote Data Control?

2. What is a cursor driver?

3. What are the four dataset types?

4. What are the five lock types?

5. What is the Microsoft Jet equivalent of the `rdoResultset` object?

6. What is the RDO equivalent of the Microsoft Jet Workspace object?

Exercise

You have been asked to build a quick utility that scans any RDBMS database and provides a list of all the tables and views in that database. This will be used to catalog old RDBMS databases and assist in maintenance chores.

Create a simple data entry form that enables users to select any available ODBC data source and then view all tables and views in the data source in a list box. *Hint:* Use the `rdo.connection` method with an empty DSN string to get the ODBC dialog to appear.

DAY **18**

Using the ActiveX Data Objects (ADO)

The addition of the ActiveX Data Object Library for Visual Basic 6.0 brings a whole new set of possibilities to database programming with Visual Basic. The ADO model is the smallest database object model yet. It provides a quick and effective way to build recordsets from connected databases. Even better, you can create a recordset, disconnect from the server—even save the recordset to a local disk file—and then, later, connect back to the database and send your updated recordset.

Today, you learn some of the basics of the ADO model and how it can be used in your Visual Basic programs. You also learn how to use the new ADO data control to build simple data-bound forms. Finally, you build a Visual Basic 6.0 application that shows you how to use the ADO model in code to create connections and recordsets, and to run parameter queries against both Microsoft Access and SQL Server databases.

What Is ADO?

The Microsoft ActiveX Data Object model can be thought of as a slimmed-down version of the RDO (Remote Data Object) model. Although they are not related in some special way, both models focus on providing data services to Visual Basic applications without the overhead of the full-featured DAO (Data Access Object) model. In fact, one of the important differences bewteen ADO and RDO is that ADO is built to use the OLEDB interface as the underlying data provider instead of ODBC. With OLEDB "under the covers," ADO is also able to support recordset access to non-SQL data stores, such as email, AS400, and even network directory services.

In this section of the chapter, you learn how ADO uses OLEDB and interacts with ODBC. You also learn how to use ADO cursors to manage recordset navigation.

The ActiveX Data Object Model

The ActiveX Data Object model is very lean. It is designed to enable programmers to get a set of records from the data source as quickly as possible. Because speed and simplicity is one of the key objectives of ADO, the model is designed to enable you to create a Recordset object without having to create and navigate numerous other intervening objects along the way.

In fact, there are only three key objects in the model:

- Connection represents the actual database connection.
- Command is used to execute queries against the data connection.
- Recordset represents the set of records collected from the query issued via the Command object.

The Connection object has a collection child object called Errors to hold any error information associated with the connection. The Command object has a child object collection, Parameters, to hold any replaceable parameters for queries. The Recordset also has a child collection object, Fields, to hold information about each field in the Recordset. Finally, the Connection, Command, Recordset, and Fields objects all have a Properties collection to hold detailed information about the object.

Figure 18.1 shows the ADO model diagram. The Properties collection objects have been left out of the diagram for clarity.

FIGURE 18.1

*The ActiveX Data
Object model diagram.*

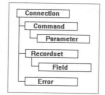

ADO and OLEDB

RDO uses ODBC to gain access to databases and DAO uses its own internal Jet engine to access database. ADO, however, is designed to use OLEDB (OLE database) instead. OLEDB is an entirely new method for connection to data storage. OLEDB can be thought of as an alternative to the ODBC method of connecting to data storage. However, OLEDB is designed to provide much more flexibility and ease than ODBC. Also, the internal design of the OLEDB service enables access to non-SQL data storage as easily as standard SQL-type data.

In the past, any time you wanted Visual Basic to access remote databases, you needed either a special API set or an ODBC interface driver. Most of the time, you could find an ODBC driver to act as a translator between your SQL requests and the data store. Although this method has been highly successful, it has its drawbacks. The rules for publishing ODBC drivers require that the SQL query language be supported and that the data store always be represented in the form of a set of tables with rows and columns. This is not always the most effective way to represent data stores. This is especially true for hierarchical stores, such as directory services and email.

To provide a more flexible method for accessing data stores, Microsoft developed the OLEDB interface. One of the key aspects of OLEDB is that it is designed to provide a process for *describing* data storage. By offering a way to describe how data is stored, OLEDB can offer a way to access data stored in any format—queried via any method. Because OLEDB does not require all data storage to be published as tables, rows, and columns, OLEDB can be used for more types of data storage than ODBC.

NEW TERM ODBC uses drivers to provide translators between Visual Basic data requests and the data store; OLEDB uses the term *provider* for the component that acts as the intermediary between your Visual Basic program and the database. There are a number of OLEDB providers available. Microsoft has published the following OLEDB providers:

- Microsoft OLE DB Provider for ODBC Drivers
- Microsoft Jet 3.51 OLEDB Provider
- Microsoft OLE DB Provider for Oracle

- Microsoft OLE DB Provider for SQL Server
- Microsoft OLE DB Provider for Directory Services

In addition, you can find several third-party OLE DB providers on the market already. More are sure to be available in the near future.

Note   The first item in the list is the OLE DB provider for ODBC. This means that you can use ADO to connect Visual Basic to existing ODBC-defined database connections. However, you should remember that when you are using ADO to connect to ODBC data sources, you will actually be using the OLE DB provider for ODBC to talk to your data.

Special ADO Properties

The ADO model has a number of unique properties not encountered with the DAO and RDO models. These properties control how the dataset is generated, the movement of the pointer within the set, and your access rights within the data connection. There are seven unique properties of the ADO model covered here:

- Connection string
- Command text
- Command types
- Cursor locations
- Cursor types
- Lock types
- Mode types

In the following sections, you'll learn what each of these properties is and how it is used when accessing data using the ADO model.

Connection String

The ADO model uses the `ConnectionString` property to indicate the OLE DB provider to use to connect to the data store, along with all the details needed to complete the data connection. A typical connection string has two parts:

```
Provider=<provider name>;Data Source=<source details>
```

For example, here is a valid connection string for connecting to a Microsoft Access database:

```
Provider=Microsoft.Jet.OLEDB.3.51;Data Source=c:\myfolder\mydata.mdb
```

Some data sources may have additional required or optional values as part of the *<source details>* portion of the connection string. Here is a valid connection string for an SQL Server database that uses additional values:

```
Provider=SQLOLEDB.1; Data Source=pubs; User ID=sa;Location=mca
```

The exact format of the details section of the connection string is governed by the provider.

Command Text

The CommandText property of the ADO model is the property that holds the actual data request query. The syntax of this data request depends on the provider you are using. For example, this request is valid when using the OLE DB Jet 3.51 provider:

```
TRANSFORM SUM(Sales)
    SELECT Title FROM Booksales GROUP BY Title
PIVOT SalesRep
```

The following request will work with the SQL Server provider:

```
CALL spMyProc(35,15)
```

It is important to keep in mind that OLE DB providers do not need to use SQL syntax as their query language. You may need to consult the documentation that ships with your provider files in order to learn the query syntax required for that provider.

Command Types

The CommandType ADO propety is used to tell ADO what type of query you are using to execute a data request. The default value is adCmdUnknown. In some cases, you can execute data requests without setting the CommandType property. However, the ADO provider may not understand how to interpret the request or may execute the request more slowly if you do not specify a CommandType. Table 18.1 shows the list of valid Command Types.

TABLE 18.1 VALID SETTINGS FOR THE CommandType PROPERTY

Setting	Value	Description
AdCmdText	1	Evaluates CommandText as a textual definition of a command.
AdCmdTable	2	Evaluates CommandText as a table name in a generated SQL query returning all columns.
AdCmdStoredProc	4	Evaluates CommandText as a stored procedure.

continues

18

TABLE 18.1   CONTINUED

Setting	Value	Description
AdCmdUnknown	8	Default. The type of command in the CommandText property is not known.
AdCommandFile	256	Evaluates CommandText as the filename of a persisted Recordset.
AdCmdTableDirect	512	Evaluates CommandText as a table name whose columns are all returned.

Cursor Locations

NEW TERM The ADO model enables you to request client-side or server-side cursor management for your recordset. In ADO a *cursor* is the collection of records that is returned to your program in response to a data request. You can use the ADO CursorLocation property to control where this collection of records is kept. Table 18.2 shows the valid settings for this property.

TABLE 18.2   VALID SETTINGS FOR THE CursorLocation PROPERTY

Setting	Value	Description
AdUseClient	3	Uses client-side cursors supplied by a local cursor library. Local cursor engines often will allow many features that driver-supplied cursors may not, so using this setting may provide an advantage with respect to features that will be enabled.
AdUseServer	2	Default. Uses data-provider– or driver-supplied cursors. These cursors are sometimes very flexible and allow additional sensitivity to changes others make to the data source. However, some features of ADO may not be available with server-side cursors.
AdUseClientBatch	3	This is the same as adUseClient and is included for backward compatibility only. You should not use this value in your Visual Basic 6.0 programs.
AdUseNone	1	No cursor services are used. This constant is obsolete and appears solely for the sake of backward compatibility. Do not use this in your Visual Basic 6.0 programs.

Notice that even though there are four possible values for the ADO CursorLocation property, only the first two (adUseClient and adUseServer) are valid. The other two are provided only for backward compatiblity with earlier versions of ADO and should not be used with your Visual Basic 6.0 programs.

Cursor Types

The ADO `CursorType` property is used to indicate the type of recordset that will be returned by the data provider. There are four valid settings for the `CursorType` property. These are shown in Table 18.3.

TABLE 18.3 VALID SETTINGS FOR THE `CursorType` PROPERTY

Setting	Value	Description
AdOpenForwardOnly	0	This provides a Forward-only cursor recordset. You can only scroll forward through records in the collection. This improves performance in situations when you need to make only a single pass through a recordset. This is the default.
AdOpenKeyset	1	This provides a Keyset cursor recordset. This recordset has a changing membership. Edits by other users are visible. Records that other users delete are inaccessible from your recordset. Records that other users add are not available.
AdOpenDynamic	2	Dynamic cursor. This recordset has a changing membership. All adds, edits, and deletes by other users are visible.
AdOpenStatic	3	This provides a Static cursor recordset. This is a static copy of a set of records that you can use to find data, move forward and back, and so forth. Any adds, edits, or deletes by other users are not visible.

Note

As you look through the descriptions in Table 18.3, you'll notice that these cursor types are very similar to the dataset types of RDO.

There are a couple of important things to keep in mind when choosing a `CursorType` for your recordset. First, if you are using a client-side cursor (`CursorLocation=adUseClient`), `adOpenStatic` is the only valid value for the `CursorType` property.

Another major issue when selecting a cursor type is knowing what the data provider supports. It is possible that the cursor type you request is not supported by your data provider. In this case, the data provider may return a recordset with a different cursor type. If you are selecting a cursor type and expecting a certain behavior (capability of seeing changes, and so forth), you should check the CursorType property *after* completing your data request to see what type of cursor was returned by the provider.

Lock Types

The ADO LockType property can be used to indicate how you wish to manage locking during edit sessions with your recordset. Table 18.4 shows the four valid options for lock types.

TABLE 18.4 VALID SETTINGS FOR THE LockType PROPERTY

Setting	Value	Description
adLockReadOnly	1	Default. Read-only—you cannot alter the data.
adLockPessimistic	2	Pessimistic record locking. This usually means the provider will lock records at the data source immediately upon editing.
adLockOptimistic	3	Optimistic record locking. The provider will lock records only when attempting to update the record.
adLockBatchOptimistic	4	Optimistic batch locking. The provider will lock the entire batch when you attempt to use the UpdateBatch method on the recordset.

Your provider may not support the locking method you request. If this is the case, the provider will substitute another locking method. You can inspect the LockType property after the recordset is returned to see the actual locking method selected by the provider.

If you are using a client-side cursor (CursorLocation=adUseClient), you cannot use pessimistic locking (LockType=adLockPessimistic).

Mode Types

The Mode property can be used to instruct the provider to limit access to the data store while you have an open recordset. Table 18.5 shows the valid settings for the ADO Mode property.

TABLE 18.5 VALID SETTINGS FOR THE ADO Mode PROPERTY

Setting	Value	Description
AdModeUnknown	0	Default. Indicates that the permissions have not yet been set or cannot be determined.

Setting	Value	Description
AdModeRead	1	Open the recordset with read-only permissions.
adModeWrite	2	Open the recordset with write-only permissions.
adModeReadWrite	3	Open the recordset with read/write permissions.
adModeShareDenyRead	4	Prevent others from opening connection with read permissions.
adModeShareDenyWrite	8	Prevent others from opening connection with write permissions.
adModeShareExclusive	12	Prevent others from opening connection.
adModeShareDenyNone	16	Prevent others from opening connection with any permissions.

If you need only a read-only recordset, you can increase the performance of your Visual Basic application by setting the Mode property to adModeRead.

Programming with the ADO Data Control (ADODC)

Programming with the ADO data control is very similar to programming with the DAO and RDO data controls. Although there are a few more properties to deal with (see previous discussion), the process of binding the data control to input controls is the same. Also, there are fewer methods associated with the ADO data control than with the DAO and RDO control. Finally, the ADO data control offers a number of new events you can use to monitor the progress of your data entry forms.

The ADO Data Control Methods

The ADO data control offers only two methods that are specific to the ADO object model:

- Use Refresh to requery the data source and rebuild the dataset.
- Use UpdateControls to refresh the data-bound controls with values from the current recordset row.

The Refresh method is most valuable when you are updating the ConnectionString or RecordSource properties of the control and want to repopulate the resulting recordset. Listing 18.1 shows an example of how you can use the ADO data control Refresh method.

LISTING 18.1   USING THE ADO Refresh METHOD

```
1: With adoDataControl
2:      .Mode = adModeReadWrite
3:      .ConnectionString = "Provider=MSDASQL.1;Data Source=ADODataDSN"
4:      .CommandType = adCmdTable
5:      .RecordSource = "MyTable"
6:      .Refresh
7: End With
```

The ADO UpdateControls method can be used as a type of "undo" method. The UpdateControls method refreshes the bound controls on a form with the values contained in the current record in the recordset associated with the ADO data control. Listing 18.2 shows an example using the UpdateControls method.

LISTING 18.2   USING THE ADO UpdateControls METHOD

```
1: If MsgBox("Undo changes?", vbYesNo + vbQuestion, "Cancel Edits") = _
   vbYes Then
2:      adoDataControl.UpdateControls
3: End If
```

The ADO Data Control Events

The ADO data control has a number of associated events. There are a total of 12 possible event messages. These twelve messages can be broken into several groups. Table 18.6 shows the ADO data control event messages.

TABLE 18.6   ADO DATA CONTROL EVENTS

Event Group	Event Name	Description
Recordset Population	FetchProgress	Fires periodically during a lengthy recordset population process. You can use this event message to report progress as the recordset is filled.
	FetchComplete	Fires when the lengthy recordset population process has finally completed. You can listen for this event and alert users when the recordset is finally ready for work.
Recordset Navigation	WillMove	Fires before the record pointer is moved from one row to another.

Event Group	Event Name	Description
	MoveComplete	Fires after the record pointer has been moved from one row to another.
	EndOfRecordset	Fires when the record pointer is moved past the last record in the dataset.
Recordset Change	WillChangeRecordset	Fires before a change is made to the recordset. You can use this event to trap unwanted changes in the dataset.
	RecordsetChangeComplete	Fires after a change is performed to the recordset. You can monitor the status parameter to verify a sucessful operation.
Row Updates	WillChangeRecord	Fires before updates for the current row are sent to the data source.
	RecordChangeComplete	Fires after updates for the current row are sent to the data source.
Field Updates	WillChangeField	Fires before the current field in the recordset is updated.
	FieldChangeComplete	Fires after the current field in the recordset has been updated.

18

You can see from Table 18.6 that most of the events exist in pairs. There is a `Will` event and and a `Complete` event. These are simliar to the `Before` and `After` events associated with the DAO and RDO data controls. The `Will` events fire before an action is about to take place. These events give you an opportunity to cancel the action, if desired. The `Complete` events fire after a process has been completed. You can use the status parameters of these events to check on the success or failure of the process.

Notice also that there are event sets for the entire recordset, the current row, and the current field. This offers a greater degree of event notification than the DAO or RDO controls.

Finally, there are events associated with the process of populating (fetching) the data for the recordset. This enables you to monitor the progress of a lengthy recordset fetch and report progress and final completion to users.

Building the ADO Data Control Project

Now that you have learned some of the details of how the ADO data control works, you're ready to build a sample data entry project. In this project, you build a typical data entry form along with a special dialog used to monitor ADO data control event messages. This will give you a better idea of how the ADO data control works. When you're done, you'll know how to build standard data-bound dialogs using the ADO data control.

Starting the ADO Data Entry Project

If you haven't done so yet, load Visual Basic 6.0 and start a new Standard EXE project. Before you can create the data entry form, you need to load the ADO data control into your Visual Basic toolbox. To do this, select Project | Components from the main menu and locate and select the Microsoft ADO Data Control 6.0 from the list (see Figure 18.2).

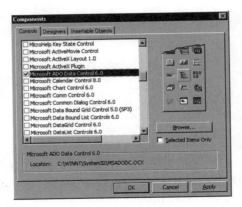

FIGURE 18.2

Adding the ADO data control to your project.

After adding the ADO data control to the project, you can lay out the sample data form. Use Table 18.7 and Figure 18.3 as a guide in laying out the form.

TABLE 18.7   CONTROLS FOR THE ADO DATA ENTRY FORM

Control Name	Property	Setting
VB.Form	Name	frmADODC
	BorderStyle	3 'Fixed Dialog
	Caption	"ADO Data Control"
	ClientHeight	1845
	ClientLeft	360
	ClientTop	1305

Control Name	Property	Setting
	ClientWidth	5310
	MaxButton	0 'False
	MinButton	0 'False
	ShowInTaskbar	0 'False
VB.CommandButton	Name	cmdAction
	Caption	"&Refresh"
	Height	315
	Index	3
	Left	4020
	Top	1080
	Width	1215
VB.CommandButton	Name	cmdAction
	Caption	"&Delete"
	Height	315
	Index	2
	Left	2700
	Top	1080
	Width	1215
VB.CommandButton	Name	cmdAction
	Caption	"&Cancel"
	Height	315
	Index	1
	Left	1380
	Top	1080
	Width	1215
VB.CommandButton	Name	cmdAction
	Caption	"&AddNew"
	Height	315
	Index	0
	Left	60
	Top	1080
	Width	1215

18

continues

TABLE 18.7 CONTINUED

Control Name	Property	Setting
VB.TextBox	Name	txtName
	DataField	"Name"
	DataSource	"adoData"
	Height	315
	Index	1
	Left	1380
	Text	"Text1"
	Top	600
	Width	1815
VB.TextBox	Name	txtIDCode
	DataField	"IDCode"
	DataSource	"adoData"
	Height	315
	Index	0
	Left	1380
	Text	"Text1"
	Top	180
	Width	615
MSAdodcLib.Adodc	Name	adoData
	Align	2 'Align Bottom
	Height	330
	Left	0
	Top	1515
	Width	5310
	ConnectMode	3
	CursorLocation	3
	CursorType	3
	LockType	3
	CommandType	2
	CursorOptions	0

Control Name	Property	Setting
	ConnectionString	"Provider=Microsoft.Jet. OLEDB.3.51;"Data Source= "c:\tdp\tysdbvb6\source\ data\ado.mdb"
	RecordSource	"ADOData"
	Caption	"ADO Data"
VB.Label	Name	lblField
	Caption	"Name"
	Height	315
	Index	1
	Left	120
	Top	600
	Width	1155
VB.Label	Name	lblField
	Caption	"IDCode"
	Height	315
	Index	0
	Left	120
	Top	180
	Width	1155

18

FIGURE 18.3

Laying out the ADO data control form.

Notice that the command buttons are built as a control array. This makes it easier to add code to the buttons.

Using the Dialogs Setting the `ConnectionString` Property

You can use a series of dialogs to set the connection information for the ADO data control. This is a bit more involved than just typing in the connection string data, but it can help you verify the proper values for all connection-related properties.

To use the dialogs associated with the ADO data control, click once on the ADO data control on the form to put it into focus. Then press the browse button on the (Custom) property entry in the Property window in the Visual Basic IDE. You'll see a dialog that looks like the one in Figure 18.4.

FIGURE 18.4

Using the ADO data control dialog.

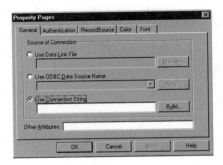

The first step is to press the Build button at the lower-left of the form. This will launch the OLE DB Provider selection Wizard. At the first screen, select the Microsoft Jet 3.51 OLE DB Provider and press the Next button (see Figure 18.5).

FIGURE 18.5

Selecting an OLE DB provider.

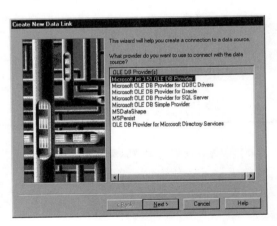

After selecting an OLE DB provider, you enter the exact path name of the Microsoft Access database for this data control. Enter c:\tysdbvb6\source\data\ado.mdb (See Figure 18.6).

After pressing the Next button, you can skip the logon data screen and press Next again to move to the Test screen. Press the Test Connection button to make sure your OLE DB connection is correct. If all is well, you see a set of status lines with a PASSED message at the end (see Figure 18.7).

FIGURE 18.6

Setting the data source location.

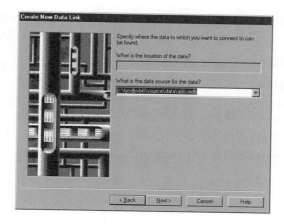

FIGURE 18.7

Testing the OLE DB connection.

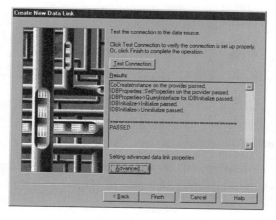

18

After you press the Finish button, you see the original connection dialog again. Now press the Record Source tab and set the Command Type to 2 - adCmdTable and the Table Name to ADOData (see Figure 18.8).

FIGURE 18.8

Setting the record source properties.

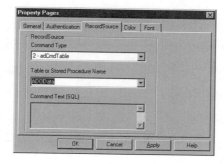

After pressing the Apply button to store the Record Source properties, you can press the OK button to exit the dialog. Your ADO data control is now ready.

Coding the ADO Data Entry Form

Now that the main form is completed, you need to add some basic support code to the form. The first step is to add some private constants and a private enumerator type to the general declarations section of the form. Listing 18.3 shows the code you need for this.

LISTING 18.3 ADDING CODE TO THE GENERAL DECLARATIONS SECTION OF THE FORM

```
1: Option Explicit
2:
3: Private Enum FormMode
4:     fmAdd = True
5:     fmEdit = False
6: End Enum
7:
8: Private Const Provider = "Provider=Microsoft.Jet.OLEDB.3.51"
9: Private Const DataSource = _
     "Data Source=c:\tysdbvb6\source\data\ado.mdb"
```

The `FormMode` enumeration type will be used to control the enabling of the command buttons on the form. The `Provider` and `DataSource` constants will be used to complete the OLE DB connection for the ADO data control.

The code in Listing 18.4 uses the `FormMode` enumerator type to manage the appearance of the command buttons. Add this code to your form.

LISTING 18.4 ADDING THE `SetFormMode` METHOD

```
1: Private Sub setFormModeTo(Mode As FormMode)
2:     '
3:     cmdAction(1).Enabled = Mode
4:     cmdAction(2).Enabled = Not Mode
5:     cmdAction(3).Enabled = Not Mode
6:     '
7: End Sub
```

Next, add the code from Listing 18.5 to the form. This local method will handle the actual population of the ADO data control.

LISTING 18.5   ADDING THE ADOControl METHOD

```
 1: Public Sub ADOConnect()
 2:     '
 3:     On Error GoTo LocalErr
 4:     '
 5:     With adoData
 6:         .Mode = adModeReadWrite
 7:         .ConnectionString = Provider & ";" & DataSource
 8:         .CommandType = adCmdTable
 9:         .RecordSource = "ADOData"
10:         .Refresh
11:     End With
12:     '
13:     Exit Sub
14:     '
15: LocalErr:
16:     MsgBox Err.Description, vbCritical, "Error: " & CStr(Err.Number)
17:     '
18: End Sub
```

Now add the ADOAdd method to the form. This code will handle the process of adding and saving a new record to the recordset. Listing 18.6 has all the code to take care of this task.

LISTING 18.6   ADDING THE ADOAdd METHOD

```
 1: Public Sub ADOAdd()
 2:     '
 3:     On Error GoTo LocalErr
 4:     '
 5:     With adoData.Recordset
 6:         If cmdAction(0).Caption = "&AddNew" Then
 7:             .AddNew
 8:             cmdAction(0).Caption = "&Save"
 9:             setFormModeTo fmAdd
10:         Else
11:             .Update
12:             cmdAction(0).Caption = "&AddNew"
13:             setFormModeTo fmEdit
14:         End If
15:     End With
16:     '
17:     Exit Sub
18:     '
19: LocalErr:
20:     MsgBox Err.Description, vbCritical, "Error: " & CStr(Err.Number)
21:     '
22: End Sub
```

18

Notice that the AddNew button is also used to provide the Save operation. This could also be done with two different buttons. Now add the code in Listing 18.7 to handle a request to cancel a pending add operation.

LISTING 18.7   ADDING THE ADOCancel METHOD

```
1: Public Sub ADOCancel()
2:      ' '
3:         If MsgBox("Undo changes?", vbYesNo + vbQuestion, _
           "Cancel Edits") = vbYes Then
4:             adoData.Refresh
5:             cmdAction(0).Caption = "&AddNew"
6:             setFormModeTo fmEdit
7:         End If
8:      '
9: End Sub
```

Now add the code from Listing 18.8. This will handle the delete task for removing records from the ADO recordset.

LISTING 18.8   ADDING THE ADODelete METHOD

```
1: Public Sub ADODelete()
2:      '
3:         On Error GoTo LocalErr
4:      '
5:         With adoData.Recordset
6:             If MsgBox("Delete Record?", vbQuestion + vbYesNo) = vbYes Then
7:                 .Delete adAffectCurrent
8:                 .MovePrevious
9:             End If
10:            setFormModeTo fmEdit
11:        End With
12:     '
13:        Exit Sub
14:     '
15: LocalErr:
16:        MsgBox Err.Description, vbCritical, "Error: " & CStr(Err.Number)
17:     '
18: End Sub
```

The last task you need to code for the ADO operations is the ADORefresh method in Listing 18.9. This will refresh the dataset from the source.

LISTING 18.9 ADDING THE ADORefresh METHOD

```
1: Public Sub ADORefresh()
2:      '
3:      adoData.Refresh
4:      setFormModeTo fmEdit
5:      '
6: End Sub
```

Now that all the support routines are done, you're ready to add some code to animate the command buttons. Listing 18.10 shows the code for the command button array. Add this to your form.

LISTING 18.10 CODE FOR THE COMMAND BUTTON ARRAY

```
1: Private Sub cmdAction_Click(Index As Integer)
2:      '
3:      With adoData
4:          Select Case Index
5:              Case 0: ADOAdd
6:              Case 1: ADOCancel
7:              Case 2: ADODelete
8:              Case 3: ADORefresh
9:          End Select
10:     End With
11:     '
12: End Sub
```

Now add the code from Listing 18.11 to handle the Form_Load and Form_Unload tasks.

LISTING 18.11 CODE FOR THE Form_Load AND Form_Unload TASKS

```
1: Private Sub Form_Load()
2:      '
3:      frmPost.Show
4:      '
5:      ADOConnect
6:      setFormModeTo fmEdit
7:      '
8: End Sub
9:
10: Private Sub Form_Unload(Cancel As Integer)
11:     '
12:     Unload frmPost
13:     '
14: End Sub
```

Notice that Listing 18.11 refers to a new form (frmPost). This form will be used to display ADO event messages for you to view. You add this form in the next section.

Adding the ADO Event Viewer Form

In order to get a better idea of how the ADO data control works, you add a new form to the project that will display all the event messages fired off by the ADO data control. Add a new form to the project and set its Name property to frmPost. Also, set the form's Caption property to ADO Events.

Next, place a single text box to the form and set its Name property to txtResults. Also set its MultiLine property to TRUE and its ScrollBars property to 3 - Both. The exact placement of the text box is not important—you'll handle that at runtime with the code from Listing 18.12.

LISTING 18.12   RESIZING THE FORM

```
 1: Private Sub Form_Resize()
 2:     '
 3:     With txtResults
 4:         .Left = 0
 5:         .Top = 0
 6:         .Width = Me.ScaleWidth
 7:         .Height = Me.ScaleHeight
 8:     End With
 9:     '
10: End Sub
```

That's all you add to the form. However, you now need to add a standard BAS module to the project and build three support methods in the BAS module. After adding the BAS module to the project (select Project I Add Module) set its Name property to modADODC. Then add the code from Listing 18.13. This will accept a line of text for posting in the text box on the form.

LISTING 18.13   ADDING THE PostMsg METHOD TO THE FORM

```
 1: Public Sub PostMsg(Message As String)
 2:     '
 3:     Static lngLine As Long
 4:     '
 5:     lngLine = lngLine + 1
 6:     '
 7:     With frmPost.txtResults
 8:         .Text = Format(lngLine, "000") & ": " & Message & vbCrLf & _
             .Text
```

```
 9:        End With
10:        '
11: End Sub
```

Next, in order to translate the status and reason codes reported by various ADO event messages, you add two support methods to the modADODC module that will turn numeric values into friendly text messages. Add the code from Listing 18.14 to modADODC.

LISTING 18.14   ADDING THE ADOStatus METHOD

```
 1: Public Function adoStatus(Status As Long) As String
 2:        '
 3:        Dim strReturn As String
 4:        '
 5:        Select Case Status
 6:            Case adStatusCancel: strReturn = "adStatusCancel"
 7:            Case adStatusCantDeny: strReturn = "adStatusCantDeny"
 8:            Case adStatusErrorsOccurred: strReturn = _
                 "adStatusErrorsOccurred"
 9:            Case adStatusOK: strReturn = "adStatusOK"
10:            Case adStatusUnwantedEvent: strReturn = _
                 "adStatusUnwantedEvent"
11:        End Select
12:        '
13:        adoStatus = strReturn
14:        '
15: End Function
```

Next, you add the method in Listing 18.15 to the same module. This turns the various reason code values into text strings.

LISTING 18.15   ADDING THE ADOReasons METHOD

```
 1: Public Function adoReasons(Reason As Long) As String
 2:        '
 3:        Dim strReturn As String
 4:        '
 5:        Select Case Reason
 6:            Case adRsnAddNew: strReturn = "adRsnAddNew"
 7:            Case adRsnClose: strReturn = "adRsnClose"
 8:            Case adRsnDelete: strReturn = "adRsnDelete"
 9:            Case adRsnFirstChange: strReturn = "adRsnFirstChange"
10:            Case adRsnMove: strReturn = "adRsnMove"
11:            Case adRsnMoveFirst: strReturn = "adRsnMoveFirst"
12:            Case adRsnMoveLast: strReturn = "adRsnMoveLast"
```

continues

18

LISTING 18.15   CONTINUED

```
13:             Case adRsnMoveNext: strReturn = "adRsnMoveNext"
14:             Case adRsnMovePrevious: strReturn = "adRsnMovePrevious"
15:             Case adRsnRequery: strReturn = "adRsnRequery"
16:             Case adRsnResynch: strReturn = "adRsnResynch"
17:             Case adRsnUndoAddNew: strReturn = "adRsnUndoAddNew"
18:             Case adRsnUndoDelete: strReturn = "adRsnUndoDelete"
19:             Case adRsnUndoUpdate: strReturn = "adRsnUndoUpdate"
20:             Case adRsnUpdate: strReturn = "adRsnUpdate"
21:     End Select
22:     '
23:     adoReasons = strReturn
24:     '
25: End Function
```

Finally, you return to the main form and add a single line of code to several ADO event
methods. By adding this code you'll be posting messages to the frmPost form each time
ADO fires off an event. Listing 18.16 has all the event methods you need to code.

LISTING 18.16   CODING THE ADO EVENT METHODS

```
 1: Private Sub adoData_EndOfRecordset(fMoreData As Boolean, adStatus As _
    ADODB.EventStatusEnum, ByVal pRecordset As ADODB.Recordset)
 2:     '
 3:     PostMsg "EndOfRecordSet"
 4:     '
 5: End Sub
 6:
 7: Private Sub adoData_Error(ByVal ErrorNumber As Long, Description As _
    String, ByVal Scode As Long, ByVal Source As String, ByVal HelpFile _
    As String, ByVal HelpContext As Long, fCancelDisplay As Boolean)
 8:     '
 9:     PostMsg "Error: " & CStr(ErrorNumber)
10:     '
11: End Sub
12:
13: Private Sub adoData_FetchComplete(ByVal pError As ADODB.Error, _
    adStatus As ADODB.EventStatusEnum, ByVal pRecordset _
    As ADODB.Recordset)
14:     '
15:     PostMsg "FetchComplete"
16:     '
17: End Sub
18:
19: Private Sub adoData_FetchProgress(ByVal Progress As Long, ByVal _
    MaxProgress As Long, adStatus As ADODB.EventStatusEnum, ByVal _
    pRecordset As ADODB.Recordset)
```

```
20:      '
21:      PostMsg "FetchProgress"
22:      '
23: End Sub
24:
25: Private Sub adoData_FieldChangeComplete(ByVal cFields As Long, _
      Fields As Variant, ByVal pError As ADODB.Error, adStatus As _
      ADODB.EventStatusEnum, ByVal pRecordset As ADODB.Recordset)
26:      '
27:      PostMsg "FieldChangeComplete " & Fields(cFields - 1).Name _
         & " - " & adoStatus(adStatus)
28:      '
29: End Sub
30:
31: Private Sub adoData_MoveComplete(ByVal adReason As _
      ADODB.EventReasonEnum, ByVal pError As ADODB.Error, adStatus As _
      ADODB.EventStatusEnum, ByVal pRecordset As ADODB.Recordset)
32:      '
33:      PostMsg "MoveComplete: " & adoReasons(adReason)
34:      '
35: End Sub
36:
37: Private Sub adoData_RecordChangeComplete(ByVal adReason As _
      ADODB.EventReasonEnum, ByVal cRecords As Long, ByVal pError As _
      ADODB.Error, adStatus As ADODB.EventStatusEnum, ByVal pRecordset _
      As ADODB.Recordset)
38:      '
39:      PostMsg "RecordChangeComplete: " & adoReasons(adReason)
40:      '
41: End Sub
42:
43: Private Sub adoData_RecordsetChangeComplete(ByVal adReason As _
      ADODB.EventReasonEnum, ByVal pError As ADODB.Error, adStatus As _
      ADODB.EventStatusEnum, ByVal pRecordset As ADODB.Recordset)
44:      '
45:      PostMsg "RecordsetChangeComplete: " & adoReasons(adReason)
46:      '
47: End Sub
48:
49: Private Sub adoData_WillChangeField(ByVal cFields As Long, _
      Fields As Variant, adStatus As ADODB.EventStatusEnum, ByVal _
      pRecordset As ADODB.Recordset)
50:      '
51:      PostMsg "WillChangeField: " & Fields(cFields - 1).Name & _
         " - " & adoStatus(adStatus)
```

18

continues

LISTING 18.16   CONTINUED

```
52:        '
53: End Sub
54:
55: Private Sub adoData_WillChangeRecord(ByVal adReason As _
        ADODB.EventReasonEnum, ByVal cRecords As Long, adStatus As _
        ADODB.EventStatusEnum, ByVal pRecordset As ADODB.Recordset)
56:        '
57:        PostMsg "WillChangeRecord: " & adoReasons(adReason)
58:        '
59: End Sub
60:
61: Private Sub adoData_WillChangeRecordset(ByVal adReason As _
        ADODB.EventReasonEnum, adStatus As ADODB.EventStatusEnum, _
        ByVal pRecordset As ADODB.Recordset)
62:        '
63:        PostMsg "WillChangeRecordset: " & adoReasons(adReason)
64:        '
65: End Sub
66:
67: Private Sub adoData_WillMove(ByVal adReason As _
        ADODB.EventReasonEnum, adStatus As ADODB.EventStatusEnum, _
        ByVal pRecordset As ADODB.Recordset)
68:        '
69:        PostMsg "WillMove: " & adoReasons(adReason)
70:        '
71: End Sub
```

That's all the coding for this project. Be sure to save the forms as frmADODC.frm and
frmPost.frm. Save the module as modADODC.bas and the project file as prjADODC.vbp.
After saving the project, press F5 to run it. You'll see the data entry form and the ADO
Event viewer. As you add, edit, and delete records, you'll see ADO event messages
appear (see Figure 18.9).

FIGURE 18.9

*Testing the ADODC
project.*

Programming with the ADO Library (ADODB)

Just as you can use DAO and RDO models to create database applications, you can use the ADO model the same way. However, unlike the DAO and RDO models, the ADO model is smaller and a bit easier to work with once you get the hang of working with it.

As mentioned at the start of this chapter, the ADO model has only three primary objects: Connection, Command, and Recordset. The Command object has a `Parameters` child object and the Recordset has a `Fields` child object. Also, most of the objects have a `Properties` collection that enables you to inspect the various settings of the objects.

Throughout the rest of this chapter, you build a test-bed project that shows you how to use each of the primary objects in the model, along with some other valuable methods and properties within the model.

Building the ADODB Project

First, start Visual Basic 6.0 and create a new Standard EXE project. Then, you add a reference to the ADO model to your project. Select Project | References and locate and select the Microsoft ActiveX Data Object Model 2.0 Library (see Figure 18.10).

FIGURE 18.10

Adding the ActiveX Data Object 2.0 Library.

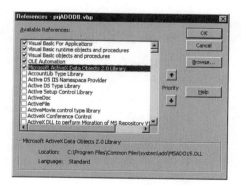

Next, you set the Name property of the default form to `frmADODB` and the Caption property to `ActiveX Data Objects`. Finally, add a single text box to the form. Set the text box's Name property to `txtResults`, the MultiLine property to `TRUE`, and the ScrollBars property to `3 - Both`.

Now use Table 18.8 and Figure 18.11 as a guide in creating the menu set for the form. You use this menu set to test the various ADO objects and methods.

18

TABLE 18.8 THE ADODB MENUS

Control Name	Property Name	Setting
VB.Form	Name	frmADODB
	Caption	"ActiveX Data Objects"
	ClientHeight	4455
	ClientLeft	165
	ClientTop	735
	ClientWidth	6855
	StartUpPosition	3 'Windows Default
VB.TextBox	Name	txtResults
	Height	4035
	Left	120
	MultiLine	-1 'True
	ScrollBars	3 'Both
	Top	180
	Width	6495
VB.Menu	Name	mnuFile
	Caption	"&File"
VB.Menu	Name	mnuFileExit
	Caption	"E&xit"
VB.Menu	Name	mnuADOCnn
	Caption	"&Connections"
VB.Menu	Name	mnuADOCnnItem
	Caption	"&SQL OLEDB"
	Index	0
VB.Menu	Name	mnuADOCnnItem
	Caption	"SQL &ODBC"
	Index	1
VB.Menu	Name	mnuADOCnnItem
	Caption	"SQL &DSNLess"
	Index	2
VB.Menu	Name	mnuADOCnnItem
	Caption	"&Jet OLEDB"
	Index	3

Control Name	Property Name	Setting
VB.Menu	Name	mnuADOCnnItem
	Caption	"Jet O&DBC"
	Index	4
VB.Menu	Name	mnuADOCnnItem
	Caption	"Jet D&SNLess"
	Index	5
VB.Menu	Name	mnuADOCmd
	Caption	"C&ommands"
VB.Menu	Name	mnuADOCmdItem
	Caption	"&SQL OLEDB"
	Index	0
VB.Menu	Name	mnuADOCmdItem
	Caption	"SQL &ODBC"
	Index	1
VB.Menu	Name	mnuADOCmdItem
	Caption	"SQL &DSNLess"
	Index	2
VB.Menu	Name	mnuADOCmdItem
	Caption	"&Jet OLEDB"
	Index	3
VB.Menu	Name	mnuADOCmdItem
	Caption	"Jet O&DBC"
	Index	4
VB.Menu	Name	mnuADOCmdItem
	Caption	"Jet D&SNLess"
	Index	5
VB.Menu	Name	mnuADORst
	Caption	"&Recordsets"
VB.Menu	Name	mnuADORstTable
	Caption	"&Table"
VB.Menu	Name	mnuADORstView
	Caption	"&View"

18

continues

TABLE 18.8   CONTINUED

Control Name	Property Name	Setting
VB.Menu	Name	mnuADORstSproc
	Caption	"&Stored Proc"
VB.Menu	Name	mnuADORstSave
	Caption	"S&ave"
VB.Menu	Name	mnuADORstFile
	Caption	"&File"
VB.Menu	Name	mnuADOPrm
	Caption	"&Parameters"
VB.Menu	Name	mnuADOPrmJetQD
	Caption	"Jet &QueryDef"
VB.Menu	Name	mnuADOPrmSQLSP
	Caption	"SQL Server &SProc"
VB.Menu	Name	mnuADOPrmSQLText
	Caption	"SQL &Text"
VB.Menu	Name	mnuSchema
	Caption	"&Schema"
VB.Menu	Name	mnuSchemaTables
	Caption	"&Tables"
VB.Menu	Name	mnuSchemaColumns
	Caption	"&Columns"
VB.Menu	Name	mnuSchemaSupports
	Caption	"&Supports"

FIGURE 18.11

*Laying out the
frmADODB form.*

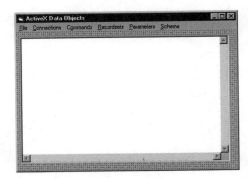

After laying out the form and adding the menus, you are ready to add some of the basic code that will support that various ADO objects and methods. First, add the code from Listing 18.17 to the general declarations section of the form.

LISTING 18.17 CODING THE GENERAL DECLARATIONS SECTION OF THE FORM

```
 1: Option Explicit
 2:
 3: ' shared ADO objects
 4: Private objCnn As New ADODB.Connection
 5: Private objCmd As New ADODB.Command
 6: Private objRst As New ADODB.Recordset
 7: Private objPrm As New ADODB.Parameter
 8:
 9: ' various connections
10: Private Const JetOLEDB = "Provider=Microsoft.Jet.OLEDB.3.51;
    ➥Data Source=c:\tysdbvb6\source\data\ado.mdb"
11: Private Const JetODBC = "DSN=ADOData"
12: Private Const JetDSNLess = "DRIVER={Microsoft Access Driver (*.mdb)};
    ➥DBQ=c:\tysdbvb6\source\data\ado.mdb"
13: Private Const SQLOLEDB = "Provider=SQLOLEDB.1;User ID=sa;Data
    ➥Source=mca;Intitial Catalog=pubs;"
14: Private Const SQLODBC = "DSN=SQLPubs"
15: Private Const SQLDSNLess = "Driver={SQL
    ➥Server};SERVER=mca;UID=sa;PWD=;DATABASE=pubs"
16:
17: ' for save/recall disk recordset
18: Private SaveFileName  As String
```

First, the code in Listing 18.17 declares form-level object variables that you use throughout the project (lines 4–7). Then the code declares a set of private constants that define various ADO connection strings. You use these throughout the project to test various types of data connections with the ADO objects. Be sure to make minor adjustments to each connection string as needed (adjust the DSNsk and pathname of the ado.mdb file, edit the names of the DSNs and names and locations of the SQL Server, and so forth).

 Caution

> These constants assume you have a Microsoft Access DSN called ADOData defined for the ado.mdb file from the CD-ROM and an SQL Server DSN called SQLPubs defined for the PUBS database that ships with SQL Server 6.5. If you do not have these defined, you need to add them before you can continue with this project.

18

Next, you add some code to handle the `Load`, `Unload`, and `Resize` events of the form. Listing 18.18 shows the code you add to your form.

LISTING 18.18   CODING THE FORM Load, Unload, AND Resize EVENTS

```
 1: Private Sub Form_Load()
 2:     '
 3:     ' set rs save/recall name
 4:     SaveFileName = App.Path & "\" & App.EXEName & ".rst"
 5:     '
 6: End Sub
 7:
 8: Private Sub Form_Resize()
 9:     '
10:     With txtResults
11:         .Left = 0
12:         .Top = 0
13:         .Width = Me.ScaleWidth
14:         .Height = Me.ScaleHeight
15:     End With
16:     '
17: End Sub
18:
19: Private Sub Form_Unload(Cancel As Integer)
20:     '
21:     On Error Resume Next
22:     '
23:     objRst.Close
24:     objCnn.Close
25:     '
26:     Set objPrm = Nothing
27:     Set objRst = Nothing
28:     Set objCmd = Nothing
29:     Set objCnn = Nothing
30:     '
31: End Sub
```

The following code shows the line you need to add to the `mnuFileExit_Click` method. This exits the form when you're done testing:

```
Private Sub mnuFileExit_Click()
    '
    Unload Me
    '
End Sub
```

You also build the `ShowProperties` method in Listing 18.19 to your form. This is used to return the properties collection values for each of the objects in the ADO model.

LISTING 18.19   ADDING THE ShowProperties METHOD

```
 1: Public Function ShowProperties(DataObject As Object) As String
 2:      '
 3:      ' output properties for an ADO Object
 4:      '
 5:      Dim intCount As Integer
 6:      Dim intLoop As Integer
 7:      Dim strMsg As String
 8:      '
 9:      strMsg = ""
10:      With DataObject
11:          .Properties.Refresh
12:          intCount = .Properties.Count
13:          '
14:          For intLoop = 0 To intCount - 1
15:              strMsg = strMsg & .Properties(intLoop).Name
16:              strMsg = strMsg & "="
17:              strMsg = strMsg & .Properties(intLoop).Value
18:              strMsg = strMsg & vbCrLf
19:          ' Next
20:      End With
21:      '
22:      ShowProperties = strMsg
23:      '
24: End Function
```

Some of the objects' tests return recordset contents. Listing 18.20 shows the code you should add to your form to handle this.

LISTING 18.20   ADDING THE ShowRecords METHOD

```
 1: Public Function ShowRecords(DataSet As ADODB.Recordset,
 2:              Optional ColumnID As Variant = 0) As String
 3:      '
 4:      Dim strMsg As String
 5:      '
 6:      Do While DataSet.EOF = False
 7:          strMsg = strMsg & DataSet.Fields(ColumnID).Name
 8:          strMsg = strMsg & ": " & DataSet.Fields(ColumnID).Value & _
                 vbCrLf
 9:          DataSet.MoveNext
10:      Loop
11:      '
12:      ShowRecords = strMsg
13:      '
14: End Function
```

18

Now that you have the support routines all built, you can start adding code to test the various ADO objects and methods.

Connecting to Databases with the ADO Connection Object

The Connection object is the topmost object in the ADO model. You use this object to connect to various data stores via the OLE DB interface. Because the OLE DB interface enables data providers to define what the various properties of the connection are and what their values should be, each provider has a slightly different set of properties in its list. You can test this by adding the code from Listing 18.21 to the form and testing the various menu options.

LISTING 18.21   CODING THE mnuADOCnnItem_Click

```
 1: Private Sub mnuADOCnnItem_Click(Index As Integer)
 2:     '
 3:     Dim strConnect As String
 4:     '
 5:     Select Case Index
 6:         Case 0
 7:             strConnect = SQLOLEDB
 8:         Case 1
 9:             strConnect = SQLODBC
10:         Case 2
11:             strConnect = SQLDSNLess
12:         Case 3
13:             strConnect = JetOLEDB
14:         Case 4
15:             strConnect = JetODBC
16:         Case 5
17:             strConnect = JetDSNLess
18:     End Select
19:     '
20:     Me.Caption = strConnect
21:     objCnn.Open strConnect
22:     txtResults.Text = ShowProperties(objCnn)
23:     '
24:     objCnn.Close
25:     '
26: End Sub
```

When you run this menu option, you see varying lists of properties that describe the details of each of the OLE DB connections (see Figure 18.12).

18

FIGURE 18.12

Viewing the ADO connection object properties.

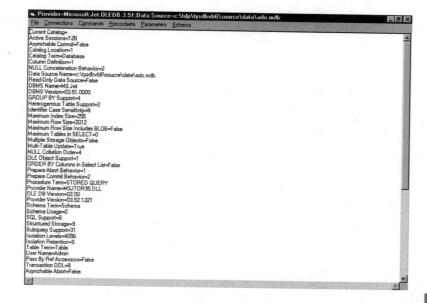

Defining Datasets with the ADO Command Object

You can use the ADO Command object to define a dataset. This dataset definition contains information about how the dataset will be populated and the details of the recordset cursor that will be used to navigate the recordset. Add the code from Listing 18.22 to your form.

LISTING 18.22   CODE TO DEFINE A DATASET

```
 1: Private Sub mnuADOCmdItem_Click(Index As Integer)
 2:     '
 3:     Dim strConnect As String
 4:     '
 5:     Select Case Index
 6:         Case 0
 7:             strConnect = SQLOLEDB
 8:         Case 1
 9:             strConnect = SQLODBC
10:         Case 2
11:             strConnect = SQLDSNLess
12:         Case 3
13:             strConnect = JetOLEDB
14:         Case 4
15:             strConnect = JetODBC
```

continues

LISTING 18.22   CONTINUED

```
16:        Case 5
17:            strConnect = JetDSNLess
18:    End Select
19:        '
20:    Me.Caption = strConnect
21:        '
22:    objCnn.Open strConnect
23:    objCmd.ActiveConnection = objCnn
24:    txtResults.Text = ShowProperties(objCmd)
25:        '
26:    objCnn.Close
27:        '
28: End Sub
```

After adding the code from Listing 18.22, save and run the form. You'll be able to select each of the options on the Command menu and view that property list in the text box (see Figure 18.13).

FIGURE 18.13

Viewing the Command object properties.

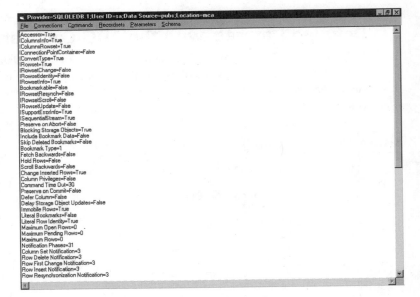

Collecting Rows with the ADO Recordset Object

You can use the Recordset object to collect a set of records from the data source. Typically, this is done using the Execute method of the ADO Command object to fill the

ADO Recordset. There are a number of ways to populate a recordset, including table name, SQL SELECT statement, and the execution of a parameter query.

Listing 18.23 shows how you can populate a recordset using a table name. Add this code to your form.

LISTING 18.23   POPULATING A RECORDSET WITH A TABLE NAME

```
 1: Private Sub mnuADORstTable_Click()
 2:     '
 3:     Me.Caption = "ADO JetOLEDB Table Recordset"
 4:     '
 5:     objCnn.Open JetOLEDB
 6:     objCmd.ActiveConnection = objCnn
 7:     objCmd.CommandType = adCmdTable
 8:     objCmd.CommandText = "Authors"
 9:     Set objRst = objCmd.Execute
10:     '
11:     txtResults.Text = ShowProperties(objRst)
12:     '
13:     objRst.Close
14:     objCnn.Close
15:     '
16: End Sub
```

You can also populate a recordset by executing a standard SQL SELECT statement. Listing 18.24 shows how this is done. Add this code to your form.

LISTING 18.24   POPULATING A RECORDSET WITH AN SQL SELECT STATEMENT

```
 1: Private Sub mnuADORstView_Click()
 2:     '
 3:     Me.Caption = "ADO JetODBC View Recordset"
 4:     '
 5:     objCnn.Open JetODBC
 6:     objCmd.ActiveConnection = objCnn
 7:     objCmd.CommandType = adCmdText
 8:     objCmd.CommandText = "SELECT SalesRep,SUM(Units) As UnitsSold FROM
        ➥BookSales GROUP BY SalesRep"
 9:     Set objRst = objCmd.Execute
10:     '
11:     txtResults.Text = ShowProperties(objRst)
12:     '
13:     objRst.Close
14:     objCnn.Close
15:     '
16: End Sub
```

18

Another option is to use a stored query, possibly one that requires input parameters, to populate a recordset. Listing 18.25 shows how this is done.

LISTING 18.25   USING STORED QUERIES OR PROCEDURES TO POPULATE A RECORDSET

```
 1: Private Sub mnuADORstSproc_Click()
 2:        '
 3:        Me.Caption = "ADO SQLOLEDB Stored Proc Recordset"
 4:        '
 5:        objCnn.Open SQLOLEDB
 6:        objCmd.ActiveConnection = objCnn
 7:        objCmd.CommandType = adCmdStoredProc
 8:        objCmd.CommandText = "byroyalty(40)"
 9:        '
10:        Set objRst = objCmd.Execute
11:        '
12:        txtResults.Text = ShowProperties(objRst)
13:        '
14:        objRst.Close
15:        objCnn.Close
16:        '
17: End Sub
```

Saving Recordsets to Disk and Recalling Them Later

One of the new features of ADO is that you can populate a recordset, then save this set to a disk file for later recall. The code in Listing 18.26 shows how you can populate a recordset and then save the results to a disk file.

LISTING 18.26   SAVING A RECORDSET TO A DISK FILE

```
 1: Private Sub mnuADORstSave_Click()
 2:        '
 3:        Me.Caption = "ADO JetOLEDB Save Recordset"
 4:        '
 5:        On Error Resume Next
 6:        Kill SaveFileName
 7:        On Error GoTo 0
 8:        '
 9:        objCnn.Open JetOLEDB
10:        objCmd.ActiveConnection = objCnn
11:        objCmd.CommandType = adCmdText
12:        objCmd.CommandText = "SELECT * FROM Authors WHERE AUID>10 AND
           ➥AUID<20"
13:        Set objRst = objCmd.Execute
14:        objRst.Save SaveFileName, adPersistADTG
15:        '
```

```
16:        txtResults.Text = "Recordset Saved to [" & SaveFileName & "]"
17:        '
18:        objRst.Close
19:        objCnn.Close
20:        '
21: End Sub
```

After saving the dataset to a disk file, you can recall that recordset with the code from Listing 18.27.

LISTING 18.27 RECALLING A STORED DATASET

```
 1: Private Sub mnuADORstFile_Click()
 2:        '
 3:        Me.Caption = "ADO JetOLEDB Open File Recordset"
 4:        objCnn.Open JetOLEDB
 5:        objRst.Open Source:=SaveFileName, ActiveConnection:=objCnn, _
           Options:=adCmdFile
 6:        '
 7:        txtResults.Text = ShowProperties(objRst)
 8:        '
 9:        objRst.Close
10:        objCnn.Close
11:        '
12: End Sub
```

You should notice that the `Recordset.Open` method is used to recall a dataset stored on a disk. You can also use this method to create standard Recordset objects.

Executing Parameter Queries with the ADO Parameters Object

You can also use ADO objects to call and execute stored parameter queries and procedures. These are routines that are stored in the database and that require one or more input parameters at runtime.

A typical Microsoft Access stored parameter query looks like this:

```
PARAMETERS IDValue Long;
  SELECT *
    FROM ADOData
      WHERE IDCode >IDValue;
```

This query returns a set of records whose `IDCode` is greater than the value of the `IDValue` that is passed into the query. Listing 18.28 shows how you can use ADO to execute this query using an input parameter.

18

LISTING 18.28 USING ADO TO EXECUTE A MICROSOFT ACCESS PARAMETER QUERY

```
 1: Private Sub mnuADOPrmJetQD_Click()
 2:         '
 3:         Dim strMsg As String
 4:         Dim objCnn As New ADODB.Connection
 5:         Dim objCmd As New ADODB.Command
 6:         Dim objRst As New ADODB.Recordset
 7:         Dim objPrm As New ADODB.Parameter
 8:         '
 9:         Me.Caption = "ADO JetODBC Parameter QueryDef"
10:         '
11:         objCnn.Open JetODBC
12:         '
13:         With objCmd
14:             .ActiveConnection = objCnn
15:             .CommandType = adCmdStoredProc
16:             .CommandText = "qryParamQD"
17:         End With
18:         '
19:         With objPrm
20:             .Name = "IDValue"
21:             .Type = adInteger
22:             .Direction = adParamInputOutput
23:             .Value = 20
24:         End With
25:         objCmd.Parameters.Append objPrm
26:         '
27:         Set objRst = objCmd.Execute
28:         '
29:         txtResults.Text = ShowRecords(objRst)
30:         '
31:         objRst.Close
32:         objCnn.Close
33:         '
34: End Sub
```

Notice that the only real difference between the code in Listing 18.28 and Listing 18.24 is the inclusion of the Parameter object to the Command object. This is the part that makes the query work. When you run this query, you should see a form that looks like the one in Figure 18.14.

You can also execute SQL stored procedures that require parameters. Listing 18.29 shows how this is done.

FIGURE 18.14

Executing a Microsoft Access parameter query.

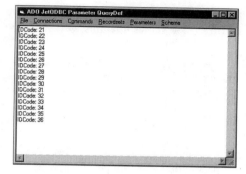

LISTING 18.29   EXECUTING SQL STORED PROCEDURES WITH PARAMETERS

```
 1: Private Sub mnuADOPrmSQLSP_Click()
 2:     '
 3:     Dim strMsg As String
 4:     Dim objCnn As New ADODB.Connection
 5:     Dim objCmd As New ADODB.Command
 6:     Dim objRst As New ADODB.Recordset
 7:     Dim objPrm As New ADODB.Parameter
 8:     '
 9:     Me.Caption = "ADO SQLOLEDB Parameter Stored Proc"
10:     '
11:     objCnn.Open SQLOLEDB
12:     '
13:     With objCmd
14:         .ActiveConnection = objCnn
15:         .CommandText = "byroyalty"
16:         .CommandType = adCmdStoredProc
17:     End With
18:     '
19:     With objPrm
20:         .Name = "percentage"
21:         .Type = adInteger
22:         .Direction = adParamInput
23:         .Value = 40
24:     End With
25:     objCmd.Parameters.Append objPrm
26:     '
27:     Set objRst = objCmd.Execute
28:     '
29:     txtResults.Text = ShowRecords(objRst)
30:     '
31:     objRst.Close
32:     objCnn.Close
33:     '
34: End Sub
```

18

Finally, you can also execute a SQL SELECT statement with question marks (?) to represent input parameters. Listing 18.30 shows how this works.

LISTING 18.30   EXECUTING AN SQL SELECT STATEMENT WITH REPLACEABLE PARAMETERS

```
 1: Private Sub mnuADOPrmSQLText_Click()
 2:      '
 3:      Dim strMsg As String
 4:      Dim objCnn As New ADODB.Connection
 5:      Dim objCmd As New ADODB.Command
 6:      Dim objRst As New ADODB.Recordset
 7:      Dim objPrm As New ADODB.Parameter
 8:      '
 9:      Me.Caption = "ADO SQLOLEDB Text Parameter Query"
10:      '
11:      objCnn.Open SQLOLEDB
12:      '
13:      With objCmd
14:          .ActiveConnection = objCnn
15:          .CommandText = "SELECT * FROM TitleAuthor WHERE royaltyper=?"
16:          .CommandType = adCmdText
17:      End With
18:      '
19:      With objPrm
20:          .Type = adInteger
21:          .Direction = adParamInput
22:          .Value = 50
23:      End With
24:      objCmd.Parameters.Append objPrm
25:      '
26:      Set objRst = objCmd.Execute
27:      '
28:      txtResults.Text = ShowRecords(objRst)
29:      '
30:      objRst.Close
31:      objCnn.Close
32:      '
33: End Sub
```

Inspecting the ADO Schema

You can use some special methods and recordset options to collect information about the tables stored in a data source. For example, the code in Listing 18.31 shows you how you can use ADO to return a set of tables names in the database (see Figure 18.15).

FIGURE **18.15**

*Using ADO to view a
list of tables.*

LISTING **18.31**   GETTING A LIST OF TABLES FROM ADO.

```
 1: Private Sub mnuSchemaTables_Click()
 2:     '
 3:     Me.Caption = "ADO Schema Tables"
 4:     '
 5:     objCnn.Open JetOLEDB
 6:     Set objRst = objCnn.OpenSchema(adSchemaTables)
 7:     '
 8:     txtResults.Text = ShowRecords(objRst, "TABLE_NAME")
 9:     '
10:     objRst.Close
11:     objCnn.Close
12:     '
13: End Sub
```

You can also use the same technique to get a set of tables and their column names.
Listing 18.32 shows how this is done (see Figure 18.16).

LISTING **18.32**   GETTING COLUMN NAMES FROM ADO

```
 1: Private Sub mnuSchemaColumns_Click()
 2:     '
 3:     Dim strMsg As String
 4:     '
 5:     Me.Caption = "ADO Schema Columns"
 6:     '
 7:     objCnn.Open JetOLEDB
 8:     Set objRst = objCnn.OpenSchema(adSchemaColumns)
 9:     '
10:     Do While objRst.EOF = False
11:         strMsg = strMsg & objRst.Fields("TABLE_NAME").Value
```

continues

18

LISTING 18.32   CONTINUED

```
12:            strMsg = strMsg & ": " & objRst.Fields("COLUMN_NAME").Value & _
               vbCrLf
13:            objRst.MoveNext
14:        Loop
15:        '
16:        txtResults.Text = strMsg
17:        '
18:        objRst.Close
19:        objCnn.Close
20:        '
21: End Sub
22:
23: Private Sub mnuSchemaTables_Click()
24:        '
25:        Me.Caption = "ADO Schema Tables"
26:        '
27:        objCnn.Open JetOLEDB
28:        Set objRst = objCnn.OpenSchema(adSchemaTables)
29:        '
30:        txtResults.Text = ShowRecords(objRst, "TABLE_NAME")
31:        '
32:        objRst.Close
33:        objCnn.Close
34:        '
35: End Sub
```

FIGURE 18.16

Viewing the columns of ADO tables.

Using the Supports Method to Inspect ADO Navigation Options

Finally, you can use a new ADO method, Supports, to see just what recordset operations are supported by the dataset returned from the data provider.

You do this by testing the Recordset object for the availability of a number of operations. Table 18.9 shows a list of the behaviors that are inspected by the Supports method.

TABLE 18.9 BEHAVIORS INSPECTED BY THE Supports METHOD

Behavior	Description
AdAddNew	You can use the AddNew method to add new records.
AdApproxPosition	You can read and set the AbsolutePosition and AbsolutePage properties.
AdBookmark	You can use the Bookmark property to gain access to specific records.
AdDelete	You can use the Delete method to delete records.
AdHoldRecords	You can retrieve more records or change the next retrieve position without committing all pending changes.
AdMovePrevious	You can use the MoveFirst and MovePrevious methods and Move or GetRows methods to move the current record position backward without requiring bookmarks.
AdResync	You can update the cursor with the data visible in the underlying database, using the Resync method.
AdUpdate	You can use the Update method to modify existing data.
AdUpdateBatch	You can use batch updating (UpdateBatch and CancelBatch methods) to transmit changes to the provider in groups.

Listing 18.33 shows the three methods needed to inspect the various behaviors of each of the OLE DB Data Providers included with the prjADODB project. Add this code to your form.

LISTING 18.33. ADDING THE CODE TO TEST THE Supports METHODS

```
 1: Private Sub mnuSchemaSupports_Click()
 2:     '
 3:     Dim strMsg As String
 4:     '
 5:     Me.Caption = "ADO Schema Supports"
 6:     '
 7:     strMsg = GetSupport(SQLOLEDB, "SQL OLEDB")
 8:     strMsg = strMsg & GetSupport(SQLODBC, "SQL ODBC")
 9:     strMsg = strMsg & GetSupport(SQLDSNLess, "SQL DSNLess/ODBC")
10:     '
11:     strMsg = strMsg & GetSupport(JetOLEDB, "Jet OLEDB")
12:     strMsg = strMsg & GetSupport(JetODBC, "Jet ODBC")
13:     strMsg = strMsg & GetSupport(JetDSNLess, "Jet DSNLess/ODBC")
```

continues

18

LISTING **18.33**   CONTINUED

```
14:         '
15:         txtResults.Text = strMsg
16:         '
17: End Sub
18:
19: Public Function GetSupport(ConnectionString As String, Title As _
       String) As String
20:         '
21:         Dim strMsg As String
22:         Dim aryCursorType As Variant
23:         Dim aryCursorName As Variant
24:         Dim intLoop As Integer
25:         '
26:         aryCursorType = Array(adOpenForwardOnly, adOpenKeyset, _
27:            adOpenDynamic, adOpenStatic)
28:         aryCursorName = Array("adOpenForwardOnly", "adOpenKeyset", _
29:            "adOpenDynamic", "adOpenStatic")
30:         '
31:         strMsg = String(10, "*") & Title & String(10, "*") & vbCrLf
32:         For intLoop = 0 To UBound(aryCursorType)
33:            With objRst
34:                .Open "Authors", ConnectionString, _
                       aryCursorType(intLoop), adLockOptimistic
35:                '
36:                strMsg = strMsg & aryCursorName(intLoop) & vbCrLf
37:                strMsg = strMsg & ShowSupports(objRst) & vbCrLf
38:                '
39:                .Close
40:            End With
41:         Next
42:         '
43:         GetSupport = strMsg
44:         '
45: End Function
46:
47: Public Function ShowSupports(DataSet As ADODB.Recordset) As String
48:         '
49:         Dim aryConstants As Variant
50:         Dim aryNames As Variant
51:         Dim intLoop As Integer
52:         Dim strMsg As String
53:
54:         ' Fill array with cursor option constants.
55:         aryConstants = Array(adAddNew, adApproxPosition, adBookmark, _
56:            adDelete, adHoldRecords, adMovePrevious, adResync, _
57:            adUpdate, adUpdateBatch)
58:         aryNames = Array("adAddNew", "adApproxPosition", "adBookmark", _
59:            "adDelete", "adHoldRecords", "adMovePrevious", _
60:            "adResync", "adUpdate", "adUpdateBatch")
```

```
61:     '
62:     For intLoop = 0 To UBound(aryConstants)
63:         strMsg = strMsg & aryNames(intLoop) & ": "
64:         If DataSet.Supports(aryConstants(intLoop)) Then
65:             strMsg = strMsg & "TRUE" & vbCrLf
66:         Else
67:             strMsg = strMsg & "FALSE" & vbCrLf
68:         End If
69:     Next
70:     '
71:     ShowSupports = strMsg
72:     '
73: End Function
```

Now, when you run the testbed project, you can see how the various recordset requests are fullfilled by the providers.

Summary

Today, you learned some of the basics of the ADO model and how it can be used in your Visual Basic programs. You also learned how to use the new ADO data control to build simple data-bound forms. Finally, you built a Visual Basic 6.0 application that shows how to use the ADO model in code to create Connection objects, Command objects, Recordset objects, and run parameter queries that work against both Microsoft Access and SQL Server databases.

You learned that the ADO model uses OLE DB as the interface between your Visual Basic programs and the data storage. You also learned about a handful of special properties of the ADO object model, including:

- Connection string
- Command text
- Command types
- Cursor locations
- Cursor types
- Lock types
- Mode types

Finally, you learned how to get a list of tables and fields from ADO data stores and how to inpect the various reordset behaviors supportd by a data connection.

18

Quiz

1. The ADO Object model does not use ODBC as the interface between your programs and databases. What is the name of the new programming interface?

2. How many primary objects are in the new ADO model? Can you name them?

3. How many cursor locations are supported by ADO? What are their names?

4. True or False: If you are using a client-side cursor, the OpenKeyset is the only valid cursor type you can request.

5. True or False: You cannot use ADO to get a list of table names from a database.

6. What new ADO Recordset method can you use to see just what recordset behaviors are supported by your current data provider?

7. If you are opening a database for read purposes only, what property can you set to possibly speed up the connection?

8. True or False: ADO enables you to save a recordset to a disk file and recall it later.

Exercise

Build an ADO-based data entry form that will enable users to enter a value and then view a set of names with IDCodes greater than the selected value. You have been told that the Microsoft Access database that holds the data table you need also has a parameter query that will return the proper dataset for you.

For this example, the ADO.MDB database (on the CD-ROM) contains the following parameter query (defined as qryParamQD):

```
PARAMETERS IDValue Long;
 SELECT *
  FROM ADOData
   WHERE IDCode >IDValue;
```

Be sure to build a valid ODBC or OLE DB connection for the ADO service. You can use the same example found in the chapter text for the ADO Data connection.

Finally, you've been asked to return the list of valid records in a list box for later use as a clickable control for calling related data.

DAY **19**

Attaching to Databases

If there is one fundamental rule in working with databases, it is that data outside your application often needs to be incorporated into the data in your database application. Many times data is on different servers, at different locations, and in different formats. Most times this data is controlled by a different organization with completely different needs.

The focus of this chapter is on how to get information out of those outside data sources and into your application. Many times, this data can be copied in with batch file transfers, but often, tables of data must be linked into your database. Today, you concentrate on attaching data using DAO and ADO.

Benefits of Attaching Tables

There are numerous benefits to using attached data in your application. The most obvious benefit is that data needs to be managed in only one source. Duplicate data entry is avoided by performing attachments. This creates more accurate data, because there is no need to reconcile two different data sources every time a change is made to the data.

Second, attachments reduce the need to train people in new applications. Many people in your organization may not be database-literate. They might prefer to enter their data in the same format they have for years. In many organizations, it is even quite common to find large amounts of data stored in spreadsheets. The use of attachments can minimize the business process changes that might otherwise have to be done if the data is not attached.

Attaching data dictates that data is managed in the same way across applications. Relational database management systems use triggers to control how records are validated and saved. The use of the attachment ensures that the same validity checks occur across applications. That is, the record validation is controlled in one spot and thus is not permitted to be handled differently by different applications.

An attachment also enables the integration of information into your application on a real-time basis. As the data changes in the original application, it's automatically updated in your application. Integrating data from other database applications into your applications with batch file transfers can work fine for data that is relatively static, but be aware that data always can change without you knowing it if others have any write access to it.

Finally, organizations benefit by having data all in one spot. This ensures that decisions are made consistently without fear that a different answer can be obtained if a different data source is used.

Note

A primary purpose of data is to use it to make decisions that improve the organization in some way. Storing data in one central location and attaching it into your application ensures that decisions are based upon consistent information. There is nothing worse than an organization struggling to make a decision when its leaders are given inconsistent data from differing sources.

Disadvantages of Attaching Data Tables

Given the numerous advantages mentioned previously, there are some disadvantages you should be aware of when attaching data. First, it is preferable to use static data at times. For example, periodic reporting is often best done with a standalone database that does not change over time. The issuance of monthly financial reporting in large organizations is a good example of this. Can you imagine how the accountants of a large organization would feel if people starting running financial statements on data from books that weren't even closed? Or if different versions of the same report started floating around the organization?

A second disadvantage of attaching tables is that it can add time to your development cycle. You need to determine how much data is stored in other applications and how often it is updated when you use it in your application. Chances are you might find that this data is fairly static and does not warrant maintaining the attachment.

Attachments might also create additional areas of maintenance concern. If you attach data across a wide area network, you need to concern yourself with communications issues. Is there contention on the line? What are the added communication charges? Is it permissible to have downtime if a router fails?

With attached data you may encounter record and file locking problems. For example, suppose you have attached an Excel spreadsheet from within your primary database. Let's also suppose that this spreadsheet is used by someone on the shop floor once per week. What happens when the user of your application that utilizes this attachment tries to access the data at the same time the spreadsheet is being used? The records will be locked, and the user of your application will receive an error message. You therefore need to be certain that you understand record and file locking for all attached data.

Attachments may also slow the execution of your application. An attachment by its very nature must read its attachment definition, go outside the database, and connect to another data source. This overhead can't be avoided, and depending upon the attached data source, can add considerable response time to your application.

You also may not be able to use the `BeginTrans`, `CommitTrans`, and `Rollback` transaction management if the attached data source does not support transactions. This can put an extremely weak link in your application if you attach to such a data source. For more on transaction management, see Day 16, "Multiuser Considerations."

You also need to watch the enforcement of relationships between the base database and the attached data source. Many times, referential integrity is not enforced, thus providing the opportunity for inconsistent data to get into your application.

Finally, security issues will most likely be a concern of attaching data tables. Are you allowed into the data? Can your users see the data? Who has access to move or delete the data source? Security needs to be controlled and thoroughly enforced in applications that use data from multiple attached sources.

> **Note**
>
> You cannot use the SEEK method with attached data sources. For more on using the SEEK method, see Day 9, "Creating Database Programs with the Data Environment Designer."

19

Even though there are some glaring weaknesses to using attached data, it does serve as a good way to build an application in many cases. Let's look at some of the ways you can make an attachment in your Visual Basic 6 application.

DAO, RDO, ADO—WHAT'S ALL THIS ALPHABET SOUP?

Visual Basic 6 offers a several of ways to work with attached data. There are Data Access Objects (DAO), Remote Data Objects (RDO) and ActiveX Data Objects (ADO). Each of these methods of access represents a different generation of data access tools. The most recent, ADO, is also the easiest to use and most powerful of the three. All new applications should use ADO.

You may be wondering why you need to learn DAO or RDO. Put simply, you may have to work on legacy applications. Though they are older technologies, Visual Basic 6 allows backward compatibility. All three methods of data access enable you to go outside the Jet database engine and use other data sources.

See the section "Comparing Database Object Models" in Day 2, "Visual Basic Database Access Objects," for a more detailed comparative analysis of DAO, RDO, and ADO.

 Note ADO is the client-side version of OLE DB.

Attaching Data with Visdata

Let's turn our attention to connecting to external data sources from within a Jet database. You might recall from Day 6, "Using the Visdata Program," how to use Visdata to build and manage databases. This section focuses on using Visdata to attach and work with external data sources. For your example, you use a Jet database (MDB file) and attach to a Microsoft Excel spreadsheet.

 Start Visual Basic 6 and open a new Standard EXE project. Now click on Add-Ins | Visual Data Manager to bring up the Visdata application. Open the Microsoft Access database \\TYSDBVB6\SOURCE\DATA\ATTACH.MDB that was installed from the CD-ROM that shipped with this book.

Now click on the Utility | Attachments menu item. This displays the Attachments dialog box. Click on New to reveal the New Attached Table dialog.

 To attach to an external data source, you need to name the connection, identify the database, identify the connection string, and then identify the data table you are attaching. In this exercise, you need to attach to the file TITLES.XLS that was installed into the \\TYSDBVB6\SOURCE\DATA directory by the CD-ROM that shipped with this book.

Set the Attachment Name to ExcelTitles. You now need to type the filename, including the path into the database name field. The full database name is `\\TYSDBVB6\SOURCE\DATA\TITLES.XLS`. Under the Connect String, select Excel 5.0. Finally, under the table to attach, select Titles$. Your screen should look similar to Figure 19.1.

FIGURE 19.1

The Visdata New Attached Table dialog.

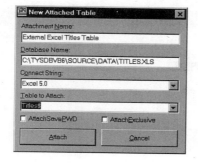

> **Note**
>
> You must type the entire path and filename of the database to attach. There is no Browse button on the Visdata Attachment dialog to help you select the appropriate database.

> **Note**
>
> You selected the Titles$ data table. The $ sign following the name of the table indicates that you are selecting the entire Titles spreadsheet in the Titles Excel workbook.

19

Click on the Attachment command button to establish the link. Now select Cancel from the dialog to display the Attachments dialog with your new connect displayed. See Figure 19.2.

FIGURE 19.2

The defined connection.

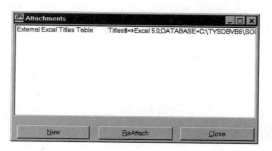

When done, select Close and you will return back to the Database window. Take note of the new connection and the icon that is used to identify that you are connecting to an external source (see Figure 19.3).

FIGURE **19.3**

How Visdata displays an attached table.

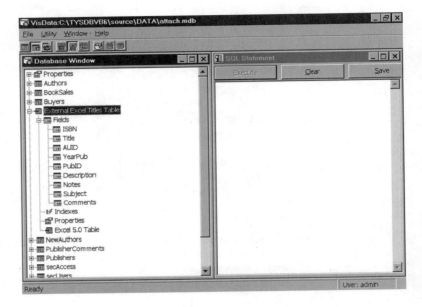

Expand the fields under the external connection in the Database window. Where do you think the field names came from? You're correct if you said the first row of the worksheet. To test this, close Visdata and open this spreadsheet in Excel. See Figure 19.4 for a picture of the worksheet if you do not have Excel on your computer.

Now that you have built your attachment to an external data source, let's build an application that shows how the attached information can be used.

Working with DAO to Attach a Table

Let's now work with the connection you created in the previous section to build a form that uses a table from the Microsoft Access database ATTACH.MDB and data from the attached spreadsheet (the ExcelTitles connection). This form will allow users to browse through the master table (Publishers), displaying all the address information contained within that table. At the same time, the user will view the titles of all books published by each publisher in a grid at the bottom of the form. As you may have guessed, the grid data is going to come from the Microsoft Excel spreadsheet TITLES.XLS.

FIGURE 19.4

The attached Excel spreadsheet.

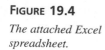

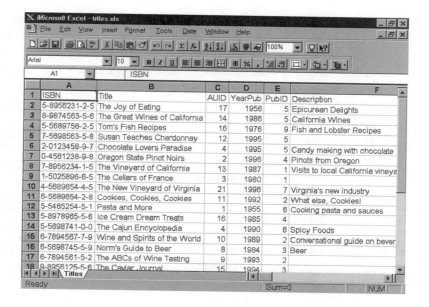

FIGURE 19.4

The attached Excel spreadsheet.

Laying Out and Coding the Master/Detail Form with Visual Basic 6

Start a new project in Visual Basic 6. Lay out the Publishers table information at the top of the form and the Titles information in a grid at the bottom of the form. You need two data controls (one for the master table and one for the detail, or Titles spreadsheet), one grid for the Titles data, and several label and input controls for the Master data. Use Table 19.1 and Figure 19.5 as guides as you lay out the Master/Detail form.

FIGURE 19.5

Laying out the Master/Detail DAO Example.

19

The controls table and Figure 19.5 contain almost all the information you need to design and code the Visual Basic 6 Master/Detail form. Notice that all the textbox and label controls have the same name. These are part of a control array. Lay out the first label/textbox pair. Then use the alternate mouse button to copy and repeatedly paste these two buttons until you have all the fields you need for your form.

Tip

Not only is it easier to build forms using control arrays because you save a lot of typing, but it also saves workstation resources. To Visual Basic 6, each control is a resource that must be allotted memory for tracking. Control arrays are counted as a single resource, no matter how many members you have in the array.

TABLE 19.1 THE CONTROLS FOR THE MASTER/DETAIL ATTACHMENT PROJECT

Controls	Properties	Settings
Form	Name	AttachDAO
	Caption	Master/Detail DAO Example
	Height	4545
	Left	1395
	Top	1335
	Width	6180
Data Control	Name	Data1
	Caption	Publisher Data
	DatabaseName	C:\TYSDBVB6\SOURCE\DATA\ATTACH.MDB
	EOfAction	2 - AddNew
	Height	300
	Left	120
	RecordsetType	1 - Dynaset
	RecordSource	Publishers
	Top	1800
	Width	5835
Data Control	Name	Data2
	Caption	Titles Data
	DatabaseName	C:\TYSDBVB6\SOURCE\DATA\ATTACH.MDB
	EOFAction	2 - AddNew
	Height	300

Controls	Properties	Settings
	Left	120
	RecordsetType	1 - Dynaset
	RecordSource	ExcelTitles
	Top	3780
	Visible	0 - False
	Width	5835
Text Box	Name	Text1
	DataSource	Data1
	DataField	PubID
	Height	300
	Left	1440
	Text	(set to blank)
	Index	0
	Top	120
	Width	1200
Text Box	Name	Text1
	DataSource	Data1
	DataField	Name
	Height	300
	Left	1440
	Text	(set to blank)
	Top	540
	Width	2400
Text Box	Name	Text1
	DataSource	Data1
	DataField	Address
	Height	300
	Left	1440
	Text	(set to blank)
	Top	960
	Width	2400

19

continues

TABLE 19.1   CONTINUED

Controls	Properties	Settings
Text Box	Name	Text1
	DataSource	Data1
	DataField	City
	Height	300
	Left	1440
	Text	(set to blank)
	Top	1380
	Width	2400
Text Box	Name	Text1
	DataSource	Data1
	DataField	StateProv
	Height	300
	Left	4020
	Text	(set to blank)
	Top	1380
	Width	600
Text Box	Name	Text1
	DataSource	Data1
	DataField	Zip
	Height	300
	Left	4740
	Text	(set to blank)
	Top	1380
	Width	1200
Label	Name	Label1
	BorderStyle	1 - Fixed Single
	Caption	PubID
	Height	300
	Left	120
	Top	120
	Width	1200

Controls	Properties	Settings
Label	Name	Label1
	BorderStyle	1 – Fixed Single
	Caption	Name
	Height	300
	Left	120
	Top	540
	Width	1200
Label	Name	Label1
	BorderStyle	1 – Fixed Single
	Caption	Address
	Height	300
	Left	120
	Top	960
	Width	1200
Label	Name	Label1
	Borderstyle	1 – Fixed Single
	Caption	City/State/Zip
	Height	300
	Left	120
	Top	1380
	Width	1200
DBGrid	DataSource	Data2
	Name	DBGrid1
	Height	1455
	Left	120
	Top	2222
	Width	5835

It would be nice to say that you could build this form without using any Visual Basic 6 code, but that's not quite true. You need just 18 lines of code to get your data grid at the bottom of the form linked to the master table at the top of the form. Place the code in Listing 19.1 in the Data1_Reposition event of the Publishers table data control.

LISTING 19.1   CODE TO UPDATE THE MASTER/DETAIL FORM WITH THE Reposition EVENT

```
 1: Private Sub Data1_Reposition()
 2: '
 3: Dim strSQL As String
 4: Dim strKey As String
 5: '
 6: ' create select to load grid
 7: If Text1(0).Text = "" Then
 8: strKey = "0"
 9: Else
10: strKey = Trim(Text1(0).Text)
11: End If
12: '
13: strSQL = "SELECT ISBN, Title, YearPub FROM ExcelTitles WHERE PubID=" _
    & strKey
14: Data2.RecordSource = strSQL  ' load grid-bound data control
15: Data2.Refresh    ' refresh data control
16: DBGrid1.ReBind  ' refresh grid
17: '
18: End Sub
```

The preceding code is used to create a new SQL SELECT statement using the PubID value of the Publishers table. This SQL statement is used to generate a new dataset for the Data2 data control. This is the control that supplies the data grid. After the new record source has been created, invoke the Refresh method to update the data control and the ReBind method to update the data grid. That's it; there are only 18 lines of Visual Basic code, including the comments. Now save the form as ATTCHDAO.FRM and the project as ATTCHDAO.VBP, and run the program. When the form loads, use the data control to view the data from the Publishers table along with all the Titles developed by each publisher (see Figure 19.6).

If you own a copy of Microsoft Excel, go into the \\TYSDBVB6\SOURCE\DATA\TITLES.XLS file and change one of the titles. Save the spreadsheet and then execute the program again. This will prove to you that the connection to the external data source is being made and updated.

As you browse through the Publishers table, you'll see the data grid is updated, too. You can add records to the data grid or to the Publisher master. If this were a production project, you would add event-trapping features such as the ones mentioned in the previous section in order to maintain data integrity. You can also add the dbFind button to the header section of the form.

FIGURE 19.6

Running the Master/Detail DAO Example.

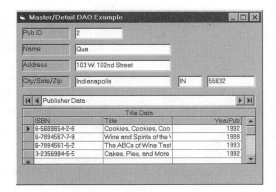

What Happens When the Attached Excel Spreadsheet Is Moved or Deleted?

You need to be very careful when working with Excel spreadsheets, because they can be easily moved or deleted. If this happens, you need to rebuild the connection by following the steps you completed in the previous section.

Note

> It is common for people to keep mission-critical data stored in spreadsheets. Many people do not use database packages due to their complexity and learning curve. Using these data sources requires a great deal of planning to secure the data and to make sure it does not move on you.

19

Attaching Data with DAO Code

From time to time you may encounter data sources that are attached to applications using DAO code. The exercise in this chapter shows you how to use code to attach an Excel spreadsheet. More specifically, this exercise attaches an Excel Workbook and returns a count of records from a given spreadsheet by using DAO code.

Start a new Standard EXE project in Visual Basic 6. This project requires the use of the DAO object, so you must first include this in your project references. To do this, click on Project | References and then find and select the Microsoft 3.51 DAO Object Library. Use Figure 19.7 as a guide.

Drop a single command button on the form in the project. Set its `Name` property to `cmdCount` and its `Caption` to `Count`. Double-click on this button to bring up the code window. Enter the code in Listing 19.2 into the `Click` event of `cmdCount`.

FIGURE 19.7

*Setting the DAO
Reference in the*
DAOCODE.VBP *project.*

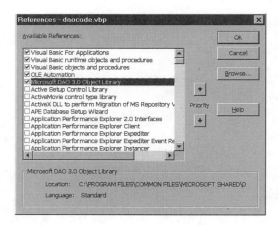

LISTING 19.2   CODE TO ATTACH AN EXCEL WORKBOOK AND COUNT THE RECORDS WITHIN A
SPREADSHEET

```
 1: Private Sub cmdCount_Click()
 2:     Dim ws As Workspace
 3:     Dim db As Database
 4:     Dim td As tabledef
 5:     Dim rsTitles As Recordset
 6:     Dim reccount As Integer
 7:
 8: 'Open the workspace
 9:     Set ws = dbengine.workspaces(0)
10:
11: 'Open the database
12:     Set db = opendatabase("c:\tysdbvb6\source\data\titles.xls", _
        False, False, "Excel 5.0;HDR=YES;")
13:
14: 'Add the tabledef
15:     Set td = db.CreateTableDef("Excel Attachment")
16:     td.Connect = "Excel
        ➥5.0;database=c:\tysdbvb6\source\data\titles.xls"
17:     td.sourcetablename = "Titles$"
18:
19: 'Create a recordset
20:     Set rsTitles = db.OpenRecordset("Titles$")
21:
22: 'Count the records in the worksheet
23:     rsTitles.MoveLast
24:     reccount = rsTitles.RecordCount
25:     MsgBox "There are " & reccount & " records in this table"
26:
27: End Sub
```

Save your form as DAOCODE.FRM and the project as DAOCODE.VBP. Execute the program and click on the Count button. You should see a message box similar to the one in Figure 19.8.

FIGURE 19.8

Display of the record count.

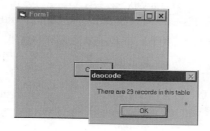

Let's now dissect the code in Listing 19.2. Put simply, this code uses the connect property of a TableDef to build a Recordset that is used for the count of the records. Take a look at the OpenDatabase command on line 12. Note how you must include the name of the database, including the path. Also note the two instances of the word False. This indicates that the Recordset is not to be opened as Read Only or Exclusively. You then define the database as an Excel workbook and indicate that the first row of the workbook contains field names (HDR=YES).

Note

> Note that in the OpenDatabase command that you separate commands by a semicolon (;) and that there are no leading or trailing spaces. Spaces before or after the semicolons will actually cause errors.

19

After the database is open, you can define the TableDef and connect to the database using the Connect and SourceTableName property of the TableDef. Notice how the Connect string includes the full path of the data source. Also notice how the SourceTableName property (line 17) contains a dollar sign ($). This defines the table to be the entire spreadsheet in the workbook, and not just a named range.

This is the way data used to be connected in previous versions of Visual Basic. Let's now turn our attention to the newest method of data access: ADO.

The New Generation:
Attaching Data with ADO

Visual Basic 6 introduces ActiveX Data Objects (ADO) for use in connecting data sources. Your next exercise builds a Master/Detail form similar to the one created earlier today, except now you will use ADO as your means of attachment to the Excel spreadsheet. As you will see, this is an easier and faster method of attaching and working with external data.

Begin a new Data Project in Visual Basic 6. As you can see from the Project Explorer window, a Data Project starts with a Data Environment, Data Report, and a form. Double-click on the Data Environment to open the Data Environment designer.

The first thing that needs to be done with any Data Environment is to create a connection. Let's now do this by connecting to the ATTACH.MDB file. Remember that this database has a connection built into it to an external data source (an Excel spreadsheet) that holds the titles of all published books. Complete the following steps to build the connection:

1. Open the Data Environment.
2. Change the Name property of the initial connection, Connection1, to cnnNAttach.
3. Right-click on cnnNAttach in the Data Environment and select Properties from the menu that appears.
4. On the Provider tab, select Microsoft OLE DB Provider for ODBC Drivers and then click the Next button.
5. Click on the Use connect string option button on the Connection tab, and then select Build.
6. Click on the New button located next to the DSN Name field on the File Data Source tab.
7. Select Microsoft Access Driver (*.mdb) and then the Next button.
8. Enter the location of the new Data Source Name (DSN) as \\TYSDBVB6\SOURCE\DATA\ATTACH.DSN (use the Browse button if you find it easier).
9. Click on the Next button, and then click on the Finish botton on the next dialog.
10. You should now see the ODBC Microsoft Access 97 Setup dialog. Click on the Select button and find and select \\TYSDBVB6\SOURCE\DATA\ATTACH.MDB. Click OK to save your work.
11. Select the ATTACH.DSN file as the connection string to use in the project.

12. Select the Test Connect button on the bottom of the Connection tab to make sure everything works properly.

13. Select OK to save the connection.

Note

You certainly are not restricted to using only the ODBC connection option. You can use any connection option you wish, but be aware that there are behavioral differences in each.

Now that the connection is created, let's save the project. Save the form as FRMDATAENV.FRM, the Data Environment designer as DEATTACH.DSR, the data report designer as DATAREPORT1.DSR, and the project as ATCHADO.VBP.

Now it is time to create the command. The command contains the information on the table and data fields that can be used in this project. Follow these steps to make a command that uses the Publishers table in the ATTACH.MDB file:

1. Right-click on Commands in the Data Environment designer and select Add Command.

2. Set the Name property to COMPublishers.

3. Set the ConnectionName property to CNNAttach.

4. Right-click on comPublishers in the Data Environment designer and select properties.

5. Set the Database object setting to Table.

6. Select Publishers as the Object Name field.

7. Click on the OK command button to save the command.

The next step in finishing the Data Environment is to add a command that uses the external attachment to the Excel spreadsheet that holds the titles. Follow these steps to build this child of the COMPublishers command:

1. Right-click on the comPublishers command in the Data Environment designer window and select Add Child Command.

2. Enter comExcelTitles as the Command Name.

3. Select Synonym as the Database Object.

Note

If you built your connection with the OLE DB Driver, you will see the ExcelTitles attachment as a table and not as a Synonym.

19

4. Select ExcelTitles as the Object Name.

5. Click on the Relation tab.

6. Add a Relation Definition that uses PubID in both the Parent Fields and Child Fields/Parameters values.

7. Select OK to save the child command.

8. Save your work.

It's now time for some fun. Open frmDataEnv and position it so that you can see all of it along with all the Data Environment. Now click on comPublishers in the Data Environment designer, hold down the left mouse button, and drag the command onto the form (see Figure 19.9).

FIGURE 19.9

Dragging the command to create a data form.

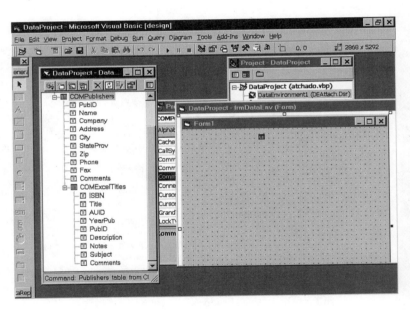

When you release the mouse button, a Master/Detail form is created from the data fields contained within the commands. The master portion comes from the Publishers table in ATTACH.MDB. This is the first connection you created. The detail in the grid comes from the TITLES.XLS file. The Data Environment automatically assumes that you want this type of Master/Detail grid form when a parent/child relationship exists.

You need to make a few changes to this form to clean it up a bit. First, select all the labels and change their Alignment property to 0 - Left Justify. Now add three command buttons to the bottom of the form. Set the Caption property of the first button to &Previous, the second to &Next, and the third to E&xit. Use Figure 19.10 as a guide.

FIGURE 19.10

Modifying the new data form.

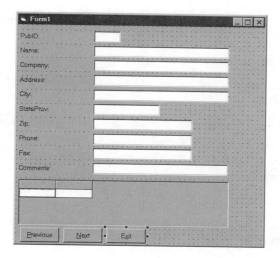

These command buttons will be used as RecordSet navigators for this form. Double-click on the Previous button and add the code in Listing 19.3 to the click event of this control.

LISTING 19.3   CODE TO MOVE TO THE PREVIOUS RECORD IN THE RECORDSET

```
1: Private Sub Command1_Click()
2:      DataEnvironment1.rsCOMPublishers.MovePrevious
3: End Sub
```

Next, enter the code from Listing 19.4 into the click event of the Next button.

LISTING 19.4   VISUAL BASIC CODE TO MOVE TO THE NEXT RECORD IN A RECORDSET

```
1: Private Sub Command2_Click()
2:      DataEnvironment1.rsCOMPublishers.MoveNext
3: End Sub
```

Finally, add the code in Listing 19.5 to the Exit button to terminate the execution of the program.

LISTING 19.5   VISUAL BASIC CODE TO STOP EXECUTION OF THE PROGRAM

```
1: Private Sub Command3_Click()
2:      Unload Me
3: End Sub
```

19

Please note that in Listings 19.3 and 19.4 you used a command in line 2 that follows this syntax:

```
<DataEnvironment.rs<DataEnvironment Command>.MoveX
```

For *MoveX* you can substitute MoveFirst or MoveLast to move to the first or last records in the RecordSet.

Now press F5 to run the program. Click on each of the navigation buttons to move forward and backward through the RecordSet. Notice how the grid PubID field is the same as the PubID above it in the Master. This shows that the program is indeed selecting the correct child records.

> You can use the same Data Environment created for this exercise for creating printed reports. For more information on creating reports, see Day 5 "Writing Reports for Visual Basic 6 Applications."

As you can see from this exercise, it is quite easy to build a Data Environment to create a form. ADO was designed as a quick means of using data from multiple data sources of different formats. You can use ADO to attach to SQL Server, Oracle, Jet, ISAM (Indexed Sequential Access Method—dBASE, FoxPro, and so forth), Text, Excel, or ODBC data sources. ADO gives you a way to attach data from just about any data source you will encounter.

> See Day 9 for more on working with the Data Environment in your applications.

ADO helps you break down the walls that exist between differing data sources. In this example, you used an attachment from within a Jet database by building a Data Environment. You can use the same procedure to attach to any external data source and combine multiple data sources in your application by simply building additional Data Environments.

Summary

Today, you learned ways to attach data to use in your database application. You perform attachments to data, because you gain the following benefits:

- Data needs to be managed by only one source.
- Reduced training time (no need to learn multiple applications).
- Consistent management of data by RDBMS triggers.
- Integration of information on a realtime basis.
- Controlled foundation for decision making.

Given these advantages, there are some disadvantages you need to guard against when attaching external data sources:

- There are times when using static data is preferable, such as in periodic financial reporting.
- Adding attachments and building connections may possibly add time to the development cycle.
- Additional maintenance issues may be created by connections that run across networks and organizations.
- Record and file locking problems may arise if the connected data is not in your control.
- The application will run slower due to the overhead of the connection.
- Transaction management may be lost if the attached data source doesn't support it.
- Many times, referential integrity is not enforceable across different data platforms.
- Security issues might become taxing, or might be out of your control.

You also learned how to use Visdata to attach external data sources. You then learned that you can use DAO to attach tables and create forms that use attached tables.

DAO code was the previously preferred method of attaching to external data sources. DAO required the user to open a database and create a TableDef to define a connection. The `Connect` and `SourceTableName` properties of the `TableDef` object are used in DAO to establish the attachment.

Finally, you learned how to use ADO to work with attachments. You learned how easy it is to define parent/child relationships among datasets. You also learned that ADO is the prescribed method to work with data and data attachments.

Quiz

1. Why would you want to create periodic financial reports from static data instead of dynamic data?
2. Explain why it is detrimental for a database application to lose transaction management as a result of connecting data.

3. Can you attach external data sources from within Visdata?

4. What is the dollar sign ($) referring to when you define a DAO attachment to an Excel spreadsheet?

5. What is the preferred data access method for building new Visual Basic 6 applications?

6. What is the first step in designing a Data Environment?

7. Can you use the same Data Environment for a form and a report?

8. What kind of form gets created when you drag a parent/child command from a Data Environment onto a form?

Exercise

Build a data project in Visual Basic 6 that utilizes a connection you build in the ATTACH.MDB database to the Titles table of the BOOKS6.MDB database. This project should contain a Master/Detail form that shows authors at the top (master) and titles in a grid at the bottom (detail). In addition, navigation buttons should be added, as well as a button that will print a report based upon the same connection used for the form.

DAY 20

Database Replication

In the 1970s, the mainframe computer was the main instrument used in the delivery of data to the enterprise. Databases were centralized, and clients were merely dumb terminals. This paradigm, however, met its partial demise because it was expensive and unfriendly to the user.

In the 1980s, the local area network (LAN) came into being, and data was distributed among groups of users tied into a common network. This reduced development costs for some, but fragmented the data into smaller databases. Enterprise data was spread out over multiple locations, which meant much data entry effort was duplicated and groups did not communicate efficiently.

The 1990s has brought the need for organizations to communicate on a much larger scale. Wide area networks (WANs) provide a means for communicating among individuals. The speed and reliability of WANs, however, are not generally enough, or too expensive to enable constant connection to databases located in other cities or countries. It is sometimes necessary to have databases located locally that communicate with one another.

The '90s have also brought the widespread use of laptop PCs. More and more workers are performing their daily chores offline. These individuals want access to data contained on WANs, but are unable to attach economically from cars, airplanes, hotels, and client offices.

The purpose of this chapter is to show you how to facilitate the environment in which you now work on a daily basis. You learn about creating databases that can be copied to other sites. You then learn how to coordinate the changes made to these databases among users at different sites. You learn about database replication.

What Is Database Replication?

NEW TERM When we refer to database replication, we are talking about the act of creating copies of a database and coordinating the changes made to the data among all copies. The original database is referred to as the *Design Master*. Each copy of the database is referred to as a *replica*. The combination of the Design Master and all the replicas of the Design Master is referred to as the *replica set*. The act of creating the components of the replica set, and keeping the data contained in it synchronized, is referred to as *database replication*.

By performing database replication, you permit users to work on the data that is most convenient for them to use. This is important in large organizations with offices in multiple sites, or among organizations with a significant population of remote or mobile users.

The Microsoft Jet engine enables several ways to perform database replication. This includes the use of the Windows 95 Briefcase and the Microsoft Access Replication Manager, and through programming using data access objects (DAO). The lesson today focuses on the use of DAO to perform replication.

Why Use Database Replication?

There are numerous reasons why you may want to consider using database replication in your Visual Basic 6 database application. If you work in a large organization, you may need to deploy your application over a wide area network environment. This typically requires you to keep the main copy of the database, the Design Master, at the central office and create replica sets across all the other offices.

You may also need to build an application for use by remote users. An example of this might be a customer contact management system for your marketing staff. Each salesperson could have a replica of the Design Master to review and update while visiting clients. All the salespeople could then update all the changes they make to the Design Master. In turn, each salesperson could receive all changes made by all other members of the sales force to the Design Master. This is referred to as synchronizing the data.

Generally, to back up a database, the data files must be closed to all users. This is sometimes not practical, however, or even possible in situations when data must be constantly available. Database replication can be used in this situation to make a replica of the original database, without having to close any files or hinder user access to the data contained in the database.

You might also want to use database replication to create a static database for reporting. In many applications, such as financial applications, data changes constantly. Mass confusion reigns if users create reports that differ each time they are generated. By using replication, you can create an unchanging copy of the data to a separate database that users can then use for reporting and analysis.

When Is Database Replication Not a Good Idea?

Though database replication can be an invaluable tool, there are scenarios where it should not be deployed. For example, you may not want to deploy replication when you are delivering data in an intranet environment. Before deploying a typical Visual Basic 6 database application in a large organization (for example, an application with a front end located on a user workstation and the data on a separate server), you may want to test the performance of a database application that uses a Web browser as the front end. This can greatly reduce the maintenance required for the application and the deployment time to individuals.

You do not want to use replication in applications that are heavily transaction-oriented. For example, an airline would not want to use replication for a reservation system. It makes little sense for users to work with a copy of a database that is unreliable, and therefore unusable, the second after the data is replicated.

You also do not want to use replication in a system where the real-time universal data updates are important, such as emergency response systems. In databases used by law enforcement or fire departments, for example, you might not be able to replicate data fast enough to be of value to the user. If, for example, a bank is robbed in Columbus, Ohio, and the criminal is fleeing toward Cincinnati, you may not have the time to perform the replication so that the police force in Cincinnati has a description of the criminal. Additionally, the mode of data transfer used in the synchronization may not be operating due to circumstances beyond your control.

20

Making a Database Replicable

 The focus of this exercise is to turn an existing database into a Design Master. You use the REPLMAST.MDB database that shipped on the CD-ROM that came with this text as your original database. Please locate this database in the \\TYSDBVB6\SOURCE\DATA directory now and place it in the directory you want to use for this project.

Before we begin, open the REPLMAST.MDB file using the Visual Data Manager (Visdata). This can be done by selecting Add Ins | Visual Data Manager from the Visual Basic 6 menu. When Visdata loads, select File | Open Database | Microsoft Access and locate REPLMAST.MDB. Your screen should resemble Figure 20.1.

FIGURE 20.1

The REPLMAST.MDB database before it becomes a Design Master.

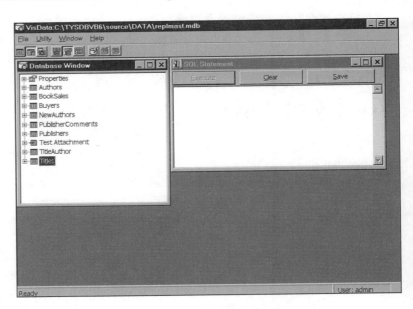

Note that there are nine tables in this database. You may also recognize this as a copy of the BOOKS6.MDB database that you used in previous lessons.

Now select Utility | Preferences | Include System Tables. This displays all the system tables for this database in the Database window. Your screen should look like Figure 20.2.

Select the Authors table and open the Fields property. Notice that there are five fields defined for this table. Open the same property for the BookSales table. Use Figure 20.3 as a reference.

FIGURE 20.2

The REPLMAST.MDB
*database and
system tables.*

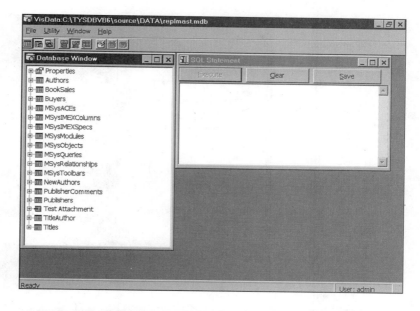

FIGURE 20.3

*The fields of the
Authors and
BookSales tables.*

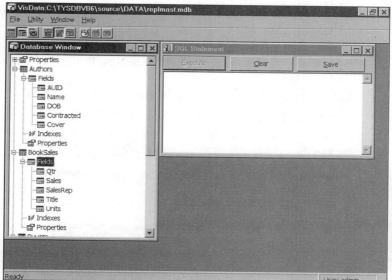

20

Finally, open the Properties object in the Database window. Take a look at the properties that currently exist for this database. Your screen should look similar to Figure 20.4.

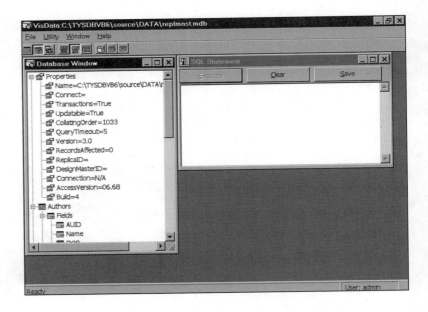

FIGURE 20.4

Database properties before the Design Master is created.

The purpose of this quick exercise was to show you what tables and fields exist within the database. You will now create a Visual Basic project that turns the REPLMAST.MDB database into a Design Master. After that, you return to Visdata and view the changes made to this database as a result of becoming a Design Master.

Creating the Design Master

Start Visual Basic 6 and begin a Standard EXE project. Add a command button to a form. Set its name property to cmdCreateMaster and its Caption property to &Create Master. Your form should look similar to Figure 20.5.

Save the form as REPLDEMO.FRM and the project as REPLDEMO.VBP.

Note

Make sure that you have set the Microsoft DAO 3.51 object library before performing the exercises in this chapter. This can be done by selecting Project from the main menu, then choosing Preferences. Find the option for the object library in the dialog that appears and then press OK.

Now, double-click the command button and enter the code from Listing 20.1 in its Click event.

FIGURE 20.5

The main form of
REPLDEMO.VBP.

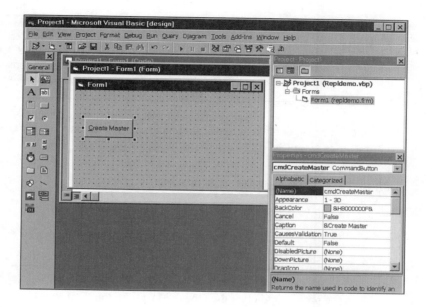

LISTING 20.1 VISUAL BASIC CODE FOR THE CREATE MASTER COMMAND BUTTON

```
 1: Private Sub cmdCreateMaster_Click()
 2:
 3: Dim dbMaster As Database
 4: Dim repProperty As Property
 5:
 6: 'Open the database in exclusive mode
 7: Set dbMaster = OpenDatabase("c:\tysdbvb6\source\data\replmast.mdb", _
    True)
 8:
 9: 'Create and set the replicable property
10: Set repProperty = dbMaster.CreateProperty("Replicable", dbText, "T")
11: dbMaster.Properties.Append repProperty
12: dbMaster.Properties("Replicable") = "T"
13:
14: 'Display a message box
15: MsgBox "You have created a Design Master!"
16:
17: End Sub
```

20

This code opens the REPLMAST.MDB database exclusively (line 7), creates the Replicable property (line 10) and appends it to the database (line 11), and then sets the Replicable property to T (line 12). Please note that you must first create this property, because it does not exist in a standard database.

Note Always make a backup copy of your database before converting it into a
Design Master. After the Design Master is created and data changes are
made, destroy the copy. Later today you will see that making and using
backup copies of the Design Master is dangerous business.

Add a second command button and name it cmdExit and use E&xit as the caption. Enter
the code from Listing 20.2 into the Click event of this project.

LISTING 20.2 THE cmdExit Click EVENT

```
1: Private Sub cmdExit_Click()
2:
3: Unload Me
4:
5: End Sub
```

Run the project and click the Create Master button. You should see a message box when
the Design Master is created. See Figure 20.6.

FIGURE 20.6

*Confirmation that the
Design Master has
been created.*

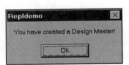

You have created the Design Master. You did not create a new file; rather, you modified
the existing file. Don't try to perform this operation on this same file a second time. A
file can be made a Design Master only once.

Select the Exit button to close the project.

What Happens to a Database When You Make It Replicable?

The simple routine you wrote and executed in the preceding example made quite a few
changes to the REPLMASTER.MDB database. This section explores these changes in detail.

Fields Added to a Replicated Database

Open the Visual Data Manager (Visdata) and load the REPLMAST.MDB database. Open the BookSales table and then expand the fields. Your screen should look like Figure 20.7. Compare Figure 20.7 and Figure 20.3 to find the fields that were added.

FIGURE 20.7

Fields added when the Design Master is created.

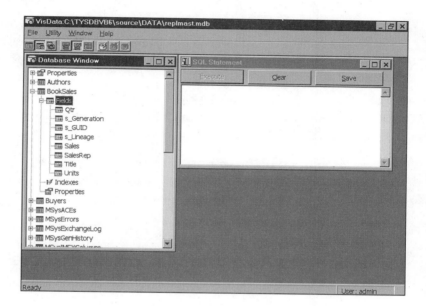

The following three fields are added to each table when the Design Master is created:

- s_Generation
- s_GUID
- s_Lineage

The s_Generation field identifies records that have been changed. All records start out with a number 1 in this field. This number changes to 0 when the record is modified in any way. During synchronization between members of the replica set (discussed later in this chapter), only the records with a 0 in this field are transferred. This speeds the synchronization process by requiring the transmission of only the records that were actually changed.

The s_GUID field is a 16-bit GUID field that serves as a unique identifier for each record. This number remains the same for each record across all members of the replica set.

20

The s_Lineage field contains the name of the last replica member to update a record. This field is not readable by the users of the database.

You learn about these fields as you make changes to the database.

System Tables Added to a Replicated Database

With the REPLMAST.MDB database still open in Visdata, let's take a look at the system tables that now exist by selecting Utility l Preferences l Include System Tables. For comparison, refer to Figure 20.2 to see a listing of the tables that existed before the creation of the Design Master.

As you can see, many new tables have been added to the REPLMAST.MDB database. The purpose of these tables is to keep track of synchronization activities to ensure that members of the replica set are updated properly.

Note   You cannot change the information contained in most of the system tables that are added when a Design Master is created. The Microsoft Jet engine makes most necessary changes during the synchronization process.

Properties Added to the Replicated Database

The creation of the Design Master added properties to the database. Open the Properties object in the Database window. Your screen should look similar to Figure 20.8.

Notice that a property named Replicable now exists and has a value of T. This means that replicas can now be made of this database.

Also note that a property called ReplicaID was added. As you might expect, this is the unique identifier for this database. Each replica receives its own ReplicaID as it is created.

A property called DesignMasterID was also created. This property identifies the Design Master of the replica set. Notice that the DesignMasterID and the ReplicaID for this database are the same.

For Microsoft Jet version 3.5, the ReplicableBool property is new. This property performs the same function as the Replicable property, but uses a Boolean data type where the Replicable property uses a TEXT data type. Note that the value of the property is set to True.

The final property added to the database was LastUpdated. This field stores the ID of the last member of the replica set to update the database.

FIGURE 20.8

Database properties after the Design Master is created.

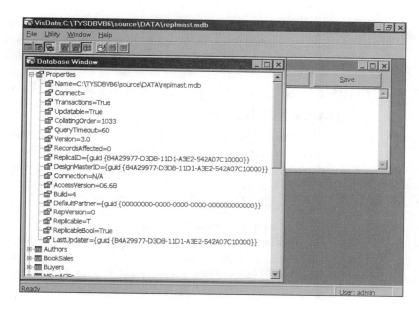

Properties Added to a Replicated Table

Open the table properties for any table in the REPLMAST.MDB database. Notice that fields were added to each table during the creation of the Design Master. See Figure 20.9.

FIGURE 20.9

Table properties after the Design Master is created.

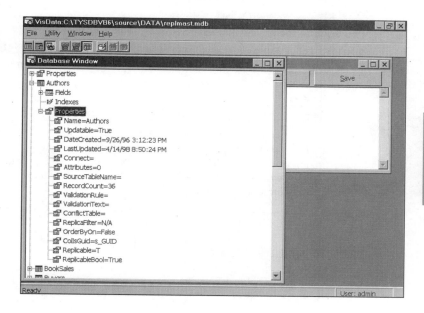

20

The `Replicable` and `ReplicableBool` properties serve the same function for the table as for database properties. When these values are set to `T`, it indicates that the table can be replicated.

Physical Size Changes Made to a Database When It Becomes Replicable

If you're thinking that the addition of these tables, fields, and properties to the Design Master will increase the size of your database, you're correct. Approximately 28 bytes are added to each record contained to allow for the replication feature. This is not much in itself, but when you consider all the tables in a typical application, and all the records in each table, it can add up to something significant.

Let's perform some mathematical calculations. Suppose that you have a database with five tables—a main table and four validation tables. Let's say there are 100,000 records in the main table and 1,000 records in each of the four validation tables. Adding replication functionality adds 2,912,000 bytes ([100,000 + 4,000] [×] 28) to the total size of each member of your replica set. As you can see, the numbers can add up quickly!

In addition to the increase for each record, replication adds many new tables, each of which takes up hard drive space. The space requirements of these tables vary dramatically depending on the frequency of synchronization, the number of members in the replica set, and the number of conflicts and errors encountered during the synchronization process.

In addition to the physical hard drive space you consume, remember that you are using up fields in each table to track replication information. The Microsoft Jet engine allows 255 fields in a table, including the replication fields. Although it may seem uncommon to have tables with 255 fields, it is possible.

Note

If you have a table in your database that is approaching 255 fields in size, you should probably be more concerned about database normalization than you are with the number of fields consumed by replication. Please refer to Day 15, "Database Normalization," for a complete discussion of database normalization issues.

The Effect of Database Replication on AutoNumber Fields

A typical AutoNumber field is incremented by 1 each time a record is added. When a database is made replicable, these fields become random numbers. Let's look at a quick example.

 Open the database AUTONUMB.MDB found in the \\TYSDBVB6\SOURCE\DATA directory created by the CD-ROM that shipped with this book. Now open the tblSupervisors table as a Dynaset. Your screen should look similar to Figure 20.10.

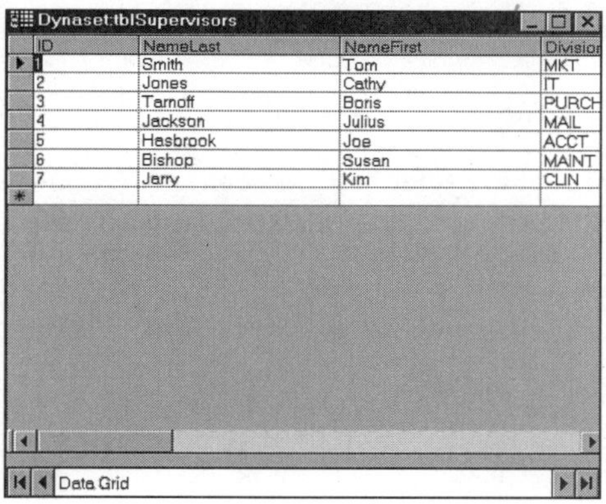

FIGURE 20.10

The AUTONUMB.MDB *file before it becomes replicable.*

ID	NameLast	NameFirst	Division
1	Smith	Tom	MKT
2	Jones	Cathy	IT
3	Tarnoff	Boris	PURCH
4	Jackson	Julius	MAIL
5	Hasbrook	Joe	ACCT
6	Bishop	Susan	MAINT
7	Jarry	Kim	CLIN

Insert a new record and watch how the ID field increments by 1. Now you can return to the Visual Basic 6 project REPLDEMO.VBP and modify the cmdCreateMaster Click event by substituting AUTONUMB.MDB for REPLMAST.MDB. Run the project and make the AUTONUMB.MDB database replicable.

Now open the database AUTONUMB.MDB in Visdata. Open the tblSupervisors table and notice what happens to the AutoNumber field when you add a new record. A random number has been inserted in the AutoNumber field. (See Figure 20.11.)

20

Note

The effects of database replication are not the only reason not to use AutoNumber fields in your application. The use of an AutoNumber, or Counter, field as a primary key in a data table should raise a red flag for the developer, indicating that the database is not properly constructed or normalized. AutoNumber fields should be used sparingly, if at all.

FIGURE 20.11

The AutoNumber field becomes random after the Design Master is created.

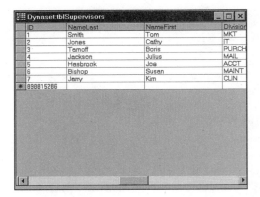

Creating Replicas

Copies of the Design Master are referred to as replicas. We now modify the REPLDEMO.VBP project to create a copy of the REPLMAST.MDB file.

If you need to, start Visual Basic 6 and load the REPLDEMO.VBP project. Add another command button to your form and name it cmdMakeReplica; insert the caption &Make Replica.

Next, insert the code from Listing 20.3 into the cmdMakeReplica_Click event.

LISTING 20.3   THE VISUAL BASIC CODE TO MAKE A REPLICA

```
1: Private Sub cmdMakeReplica_Click()
2: Dim dbMaster As Database
3:
4: 'Open the database in exclusive mode
5: Set dbMaster = OpenDatabase("c:\tysdbvb6\source\data\replmast.mdb", _
   True)
6:
7: dbMaster.MakeReplica "c:\tysdbvb6\source\data\copy.mdb", _
   "Replica of " & "dbMaster"
8:
9: dbMaster.Close
10:
11: MsgBox "You have created a copy of your database"
12:
13: End Sub
```

This code first opens the database REPLMAST.MDB (our Design Master) and then uses the MakeReplica method to create a new member of the replica set named COPY.MDB.

> **Note**
>
> Create the `COPY.MDB` file only once. Trying to create another replica named `COPY.MDB` causes the program to fail.
>
> Always make a backup copy of a database before you create a replica. This should be done whether you are creating a copy of the Design Master or another replica.

Save your project and execute it. Select the Make Replica button to create the new database.

> **Note**
>
> You can't depend on the traditional backup and restore methodology to safeguard a Design Master. Changes occur to the Design Master during the synchronization process. Restoring a backup from a tape drive might insert a database that is out of synch, and that might not be able to perform synchronization with other members of the replica set. It is a far better practice to use replication to create a backup copy that can be made the Design Master in case the original is corrupted.

Select Exit when `COPY.MDB` is created. Open your new replica in Visdata. Explore the properties of the new replica. Notice that you have all the same tables.

As you can see, it is quite easy to make a replica. A replica can be made out of any member of the replica set. For example, you could now create a third member of the set from either `REPLMAST.MDB` or `COPY.MDB`.

Synchronizing Members of a Replica Set

The act of making data in all members of the replica set identical is referred to as synchronizing data. In this exercise, you make data changes to the Design Master and the replica you created in the previous exercise and then perform a synchronization to apply the data changes to the other member of the replica set.

Open `COPY.MDB` in Visdata. Next, open the Authors table. Add a few records to this table (make them up). Take note of how the s_Generation field resets to zero when you add a record. The zero tells the Jet engine that the record is ready to be copied during the next synchronization.

Also make a change to any existing record in this table. Notice how the 1 in the s_Generation field also changes to zero. Again, this record is marked to be synchronized. Your screen should look similar to Figure 20.12.

20

FIGURE 20.12

Changes to records cause the s_Generation field to be set to 0.

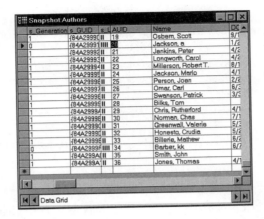

Open the REPLMAST.MDB database in Visdata and open the BookSales table. Make a change to the first record. When you perform the synchronization, notice how changes get updated in both members of the replica set.

Now close Visdata and open the REPLDEMO.VBP project in Visual Basic 6. Add one more command button to the form. Name this button cmdSynch, and set its caption to &Synchronize. Enter the code from Listing 20.4 into the cmdSynch_Click event.

LISTING 20.4 CODE TO PERFORM A BIDIRECTIONAL SYNCHRONIZATION

```
 1: Private Sub cmdSynch_Click()
 2: Dim dbMaster As Database
 3:
 4: 'Open the database
 5: Set dbMaster = OpenDatabase("c:\tysdbvb6\source\data\replmast.mdb")
 6:
 7: dbMaster.Synchronize "c:\tysdbvb6\source\data\copy.mdb"
 8:
 9: MsgBox "The synchronization is complete."
10:
11: End Sub
```

This code uses the Synchronize method to copy changes from REPLMAST.MDB to COPY.MDB, and vice versa.

Run the project and click the Synchronize button. You receive a dialog box notifying you when the synchronization is complete. Stop the program by selecting Exit.

Note

> It is a good practice to compact your database (repair it first, if necessary) before you perform a synchronization. This ensures that you are not replicating potentially damaged records that might propagate throughout the entire replica set.

Now open Visdata once more and load the COPY.MDB database. Look first at the BookSales table and notice that it now reflects the data change you made previously in the REPLMAST.MDB database. Open the Authors table. Notice how the s_Generation field has been updated for the new and the changed records. This is illustrated in Figure 20.13.

FIGURE 20.13

Data after synchronization. Notice that the s_Generation field has a new value.

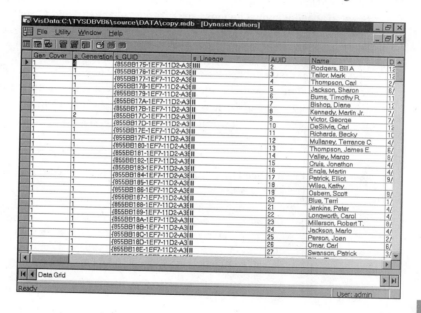

The s_Generation field is incremented by 1 each time a record is changed and a synchronization is performed. The replica keeps track of the last record sent to a particular member of the replica set and sends only records with record numbers that are greater than the last record sent, and of course, all records with an s_Generation value of zero.

Open the REPLMAST.MDB file and its BookSales table. Notice that the s_Generation field was updated on the record that was changed.

20

The `Synchronize` Method

In the preceding example, you used the `Synchronize` method to perform a bidirectional synchronization of data. This two-way synchronization is the default implementation of this method. The `Synchronize` method can also be used to import information from another database, export changes to another database, and even synchronize with databases over the Internet.

The structure of the `Synchronize` statement is

```
Database.Synchronize pathname, exchange
```

where `pathname` is a string value naming the destination of the replication, and `exchange` is one of `dbRepExportChanges`, `dbRepImportChanges`, `dbRepImpExpChanges`, or `dbRepSyncInternet`.

Use the `dbRepExportChanges` to send changes to another database without receiving updates from that database. Use `dbRepImportChanges` to bring in changes from another replica set member without sending out any changes. If you enter no exchange value, or use `dbRepImpExpChanges`, data flows both ways during a synchronization. Finally, use `dbRepSyncInternet` to perform a synchronization over the Internet.

Note

> You need the Microsoft Office 97 Developer Edition if you want to perform data synchronization over the Internet.
>
> Be aware that the `.MDB` format is used by the Microsoft Jet database engine. The Microsoft Jet engine is used by both Visual Basic and Microsoft Access. It is common practice by Access developers to store data, forms, reports, and queries in the same `.MDB` file. When you synchronize, changes to forms or reports contained within the database are also synchronized.

Resolving Synchronization Conflicts

Data conflicts are quite common among members of a replica set. They can occur when the same record gets changed in different replicas between synchronizations. This means that two users might see different values for the record. How does the Microsoft Jet engine know which value should be used? Better yet, how does it know which value to use and distribute throughout the entire replica set?

The logic that the Microsoft Jet engine uses to resolve synchronization conflicts is simple and consistent. The replica set member that changes the record the greatest number of times wins the conflict. If this number is equal for all the replica members being synchronized, the Microsoft Jet engine selects the record from the table with the lowest ReplicaID.

As you remember, the s_Lineage field stores the number of changes to a record. This is the field that the Microsoft Jet engine examines to determine which replica set member wins the conflict.

Load COPY.MDB into Visdata and open the Authors table. Change the first record by changing the name of the Author in the first record from Smith, John to Smith, Copy. Now open the REPLMAST.MDB database in Visdata, load the Authors table, and change the Name field of the first record to Smith, Curtis. Now save the record and close the table. Reopen the table and change the DOB (Date of Birth) field to 9/2/64. Save the record and close the table.

You have now changed the first record of the Authors table of COPY.MDB database once, and the same record in the REPLMAST.MDB database twice. In a synchronization, which change do you think prevails?

To find out, close Visdata and load the REPLDEMO.VBP project. Run the project and click the Synchronize button. When you are informed that the synchronization is complete, close the project by pressing Exit.

Return to Visdata and load COPY.MDB. Open the Authors table and notice that the first record is updated based upon the values that were entered into the REPLMAST.MDB database. That is, the Microsoft Jet engine knows that this record changed more times in the REPLMAST.MDB files than in COPY.MDB and therefore chooses that record as the one to use in the synchronization.

But what happened to the change made in the COPY.MDB file? To find out, close the Authors table, and you notice that a new table was added to this database during the synchronization process, the Authors_Conflict table. Open this table and you find a record with the single change. Your screen should look similar to Figure 20.14.

Open the REPLMAST.MDB database in Visdata. Notice in the Database window that the Authors_Conflict table does not exist. The error table created by a synchronization conflict is stored only in the table that lost the conflict. Open the Authors table, and you should see that both changes made to the first record were preserved.

20

FIGURE 20.14

The Authors_Conflict table.

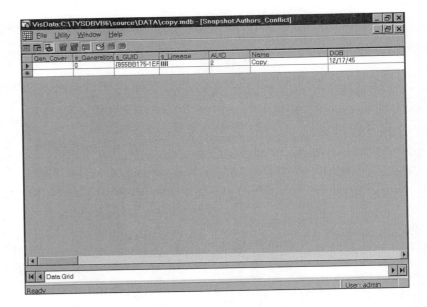

Errors That May Occur During Replication

Along with record conflicts, more serious errors can occur during synchronization. There are several actions that may cause an error during synchronization. For example, you can implement table-level validation rules after replicas have been created. This is not bad in itself, but an error occurs during synchronization if you try to replicate the rule and if a member of the replica set has entered and saved data that violates the rule.

This same type of error may occur if you change the primary key of a table. You could try replicating this change only to find that you receive an error when a replica has two equal values in two separate records in the field you tried to create as the primary key.

In both cases, you are performing serious design changes in midstream. You should therefore be careful and limit the design changes you make to members of a replica set.

An error may also occur when one replica set member deletes an entry from a validation table that has been used by another member in updating a master record. You receive an error when you try to import the master record into the replica set that deleted the validation table entry. Each member by itself doesn't violate referential integrity rules, but when combined, they do so in grand style. To avoid this situation, make validation tables read-only to all but the Design Master whenever possible.

> **Note**
>
> Try to limit users to read-only access to validation tables in a replicated environment.
>
> Try to avoid using cascading updates and cascading deletes in your application when replication is used. These features make it easy for you to cause a large number of synchronization errors.

You might also receive a synchronization error when you try to update a record that is locked by another user in a multiuser environment. An entry is written to the MSysErrors system table when you encounter such an error. To avoid this problem, it is best to have all users locked out of a database during synchronization.

You might also receive an error if you add a new table to your database and use the same name that another replica used for a different table. To avoid this, all members of the replica set need to communicate all database changes.

In summary, synchronization errors can occur as a result of design changes, as a result of violation of referential integrity rules on a consolidated basis, or as a result of record locking by users of a replica set member. You can avoid most of these errors by completing development before replication begins, by securing validation tables whenever possible, and by locking the replica members involved in a synchronization.

> **Note**
>
> Errors encountered during synchronization are stored in the MSysErrors table. This table is replicated during the synchronization process. Therefore, try to correct all encountered errors before they are passed to other members of the replica set.

Replication Topologies

When you implement database replication in your application, you most likely will make more than one replica of the original Design Master. When you do, you will be faced with the logistical question of how and when to update replica set members.

You need to implement a schema for the order in which data updates get dispersed throughout the replica set. The design of the order in which replica set members get updated is referred to as the replication topology. You explore the various topologies in this section. It is important, however, to note that there is no universal best topology. You need to investigate the needs of your application's users thoroughly before you can decide on which topology to implement.

20

NEW TERM The most commonly used topology implemented in database replication is the *star topology*. In the star topology, there is one central database, usually the Design Master, with which all members of the replica set perform a synchronization. No replication occurs directly between members of the replica set. As an example, let's assume you created a replica set with one Design Master (DM) and four replicas (A, B, C, D). To begin, A first synchronizes with DM. Next, B synchronizes with DM, then C with DM, and D with DM. A, B, C, and D don't talk to one another directly, but pass all data changes through DM.

The star topology is the simplest topology to implement. It doesn't require a strict synchronization order be maintained. Replica A could synchronize after B, and C could synchronize before B. This is therefore a good topology to use when you are working with a large number of replicas, such as in a sales force automation application. Users can synchronize in this topology without having to worry about when other members of the replica set synchronize.

There are two drawbacks to the star topology, however. First of all, the central database with which all replicas synchronize serves as a single point of failure. If this database is down, no one can talk to anyone else. You should therefore be prepared to move one of the replica set members into the central role, if necessary. Remember, though, that use of a backup is not recommended as a means of safeguarding a database in a replicated environment.

The other problem with this topology is that it permits some replicas to synchronize infrequently, or not at all. This is actually a very common problem in contact management databases, because some users don't see the need for sharing their entries with other members of the replica set, or just don't get around to performing the synchronization.

Note

> It is not realistic to believe that humans can stick to a strict replication schedule. Or that they will voluntarily perform a synchronization if it is difficult. If implemented in an end-user application, synchronization must be made extremely easy to use, or it will not be used.

NEW TERM A *linear topology* can also be used for synchronization. In this topology, replica A synchronizes with B, then B synchronizes with C, and then C synchronizes with D. To restart the process, D synchronizes with C, and then C with B, and finally B with A.

NEW TERM A *ring topology* is similar to a linear topology, except the reverse track is not performed. In this scenario, replica A synchronizes with B, B synchronizes with C, and then C synchronizes with D. Replica D then restarts the process by synchronizing with A, and then A synchronizes with B, and so on.

The linear and ring topologies are good because they do not have a single point of failure. They are bad because the synchronization can be stopped, or delayed if one member goes down. Also, the transfer to other members of the replica set is slower. In a linear topology, a change to C would have to go first to D, then back to C, and then to B before it is sent to A. This is a total of four synchronizations.

NEW TERM The fourth topology that can be used in a replicated database structure is referred to as the *fully connected topology*. In this scenario, replica A synchronizes directly with B, C, and D; replica B synchronizes directly with A, C, and D; replica C synchronizes directly with A, B, and D; and D synchronizes directly with A, B, and C. This topology requires the greatest amount of work and should be used in applications that require constant availability of data.

Note

> You might want to reconsider the use of database replication in your application if you are using the fully connected topology to guarantee data availability. Web-enabled applications with centralized data may be a better solution.

The topology you ultimately choose for your application depends on the timeline requirement of data. If this is unknown, start with the star topology and make changes as necessary.

Keeping Database Elements from Replicating

20

There might be some data tables that you do not want to replicate to other members of a replica set. This might be the case with data that is highly sensitive in nature, or data that is of little value to other replicas. For example, you might want to replicate general employee information to remote offices of your organization, but you might not want to distribute payroll information outside the main office. Or, you might not want to replicate a table of office supply vendors used by your California office to your office in Vermont.

In the following example, we create the KeepLocal property for the Authors table of a new database named KEEPLOC.MDB. This file can be found in the \\TYSDBVB6\SOURCE\DATA directory that was created by the CD-ROM that shipped with this text. We then convert this database into a Design Master and make a replica named COPYKL.MDB. This replica does not have the Authors table as part of its object collection.

Start this exercise by loading the REPLDEMO.VBP project into Visual Basic 6. Add a command button to the form REPLDEMO.FRM. Set the Name property of this button to cmdKeepLocal and its Caption to &Keep Local. Now add the code in Listing 20.5 to the cmdKeepLocal_Click event.

LISTING 20.5 THE VISUAL BASIC 6 CODE TO KEEP A TABLE OBJECT FROM REPLICATING

```
 1: Private Sub cmdKeepLocal_Click()
 2:
 3: Dim dbMaster As Database
 4: Dim LocalProperty As Property
 5: Dim KeepTab As Object
 6: Dim repProperty As Property
 7:
 8: 'Open the database in exclusive mode
 9: Set dbMaster = OpenDatabase("c:\tysdbvb6\source\data\keeploc.mdb", _
      True)
10:
11: Set KeepTab = dbMaster.TableDefs("Authors")
12: Set LocalProperty = dbMaster.CreateProperty("KeepLocal", dbText, "T")
13: KeepTab.Properties.Append LocalProperty
14: KeepTab.Properties("Keeplocal") = "T"
15:
16: MsgBox "The Authors table is set to not replicate"
17:
18: 'Create and set the replicable property
19: Set repProperty = dbMaster.CreateProperty("Replicable", dbText, "T")
20: dbMaster.Properties.Append repProperty
21: dbMaster.Properties("Replicable") = "T"
22:
23: 'Display a message box
24: MsgBox "You have created a Design Master out of KEEPLOC.MDB!"
25:
26: dbMaster.MakeReplica "c:\tysdbvb6\source\data\copykl.mdb", _
      "Replica of " &"dbMaster"
27:
28: dbMaster.Close
29:
30: MsgBox "You have created a copy of KEEPLOC.MDB"
31:
32: End Sub
```

This code first opens our database, KEEPLOC.MDB and sets the KeepLocal property of the Authors table to T. Note that the KeepLocal property must be set before the Design Master is created. The program then turns KEEPLOC.MDB into a Design Master and creates a replica named COPYKL.MDB.

Now run the application and select the Keep Local Command button. You are prompted with a Message Box when the KeepLocal property is set to T for the Authors table, when the KEEPLOC.MDB database is converted into a Design Master, and when the COPYKL.MDB file is created. Finally, select Exit to unload the project.

After the program is completed, open the KEEPLOC.MDB database in Visdata. Expand the Authors table object in the Database Window and then expand the Properties of the Authors table. Notice that the KeepLocal property is set to T. This is illustrated in Figure 20.15. Open the BookSales table. Notice that there isn't a KeepLocal property.

FIGURE 20.15

The KeepLocal *property was created and set to* T *to prevent this table from replicating.*

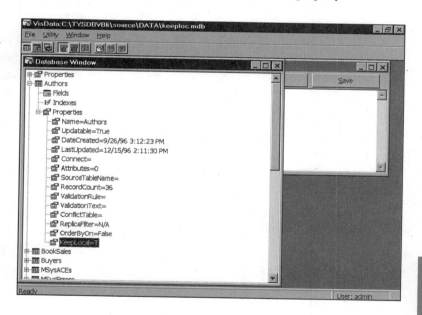

Now open the COPYKL.MDB file in Visdata. Notice that this database does not have an Authors table. You have successfully made a replica of the Design Master and excluded a table!

20

Note

Objects created after a replica is created do not flow to other members of the replica set. You must first set their Replicable property to T to replicate them.

Summary

In database replication terminology, the main, or central, database is referred to as the Design Master. A copy of the Design Master is referred to as the replica. The combination of the Design Master and all replicas is referred to as the replica set. Database replication is the process of synchronizing data so that it is the same across all members of the replica set.

Database replication is a good tool to use in the development of systems deployed across a WAN or to remote users. Replication can also be used to make copies of databases that cannot be shut down. Replication is also good for creating reporting databases.

Do not use database replication when a centralized data storage facility can be used, such as a Web-enabled application. Also, don't use replication in heavily transaction-oriented applications, or in applications where up-to-the-minute accuracy is of paramount importance.

Tables, fields, and properties are added to a database when it is made a Design Master. The addition of these items is necessary to track changes to data and to facilitate the synchronization between members of the replica set. These additions, however, consume additional hard drive space.

Creating and changing the Replicable property of a database to T creates a Design Master. Once the Design Master is created, you can use the MakeReplica method to make copies of it. Finally, you use the Synchronize method to replicate data changes to members of the replica set. Data synchronization is the act of copying data changes from one member of a replica set to another.

The Synchronize method can be used to import data changes, export data changes, perform two-way data changes, and even perform data exchanges over the Internet.

Synchronization errors occur when two members of a replica set try to synchronize records that each has changed. Errors can also occur during the synchronization process when design changes are made to a database but violated by replicas prior to synchronization of the changes. Violation of referential integrity can be encountered by replicas that add records to a database that uses validation records deleted in another replica. Record locking in a multiuser environment can also cause synchronization errors.

There are four topologies for the synchronization of replicas. These are the star, linear, ring, and fully connected topologies. The star topology is the most common, but like all the other topologies, has certain strengths and weaknesses.

There may be times when you do not want to replicate objects contained in one database to other members of the replica set. If such is the case, use the KeepLocal method before you create the Design Master. This method keeps the object from being copied to other replica set members.

Quiz

1. Define database replication.
2. Cite examples of applications that can make good use of database replication.
3. Cite examples of systems in which database replication should not be used.
4. What fields are added to all data tables when a database is turned into a Design Master?
5. What properties are added to the database during the creation of the Design Master to indicate that it can be replicated?
6. How much hard drive space is consumed by a database when it is turned into a Design Master?
7. What happens to an AutoNumber field when a database is turned into a Design Master?
8. What method do you use to create a copy of a Design Master?
9. What is the logic that the Microsoft Jet engine uses to resolve synchronization conflicts?
10. What topologies can be used for database synchronization? Which topology is the most commonly used?
11. What method do you use to keep database objects from replicating to other members of a replica set?

Exercise

Design an implementation strategy for the rollout of a database application that you built to track and deliver your company's employee information. This application needs to be installed at your corporate office in Cincinnati, and then delivered to offices in Chicago, Los Angeles, and New York. Use the following information as you design your strategy:

- The database is named EMPLOYEE.MDB and has four tables: EmployeeMaster, EmergencyInfo, Education, and SalaryInfo.
- All payroll is performed in the Cincinnati office.

20

- Updates need to be made at each site and shared with all other sites. The order in which updates are made to the database is not important.
- Cincinnati is the largest office. Chicago is the second largest, and is three times the size of the Los Angeles or the New York offices.

Include the following items as part of your implementation plan:

- Names of the tables to be distributed to each site
- Backup methodology
- Synchronization topology
- Code to keep the payroll information (SalaryInfo) from replicating
- Code to create the Design Master
- Code to create the Chicago replica
- Code to synchronize your Chicago and Cincinnati databases

DAY **21**

Securing Your Database Applications

Today, you explore topics related to securing your database and your applications. Almost all software that is deployed in a multiuser environment should use some level of security. Security schemes can be used for more than just limiting user access to the database. Security schemes can also limit user access to the applications that use the database. You can also install security features in your Visual Basic database applications to limit the function rights of users within your applications. You can even develop routines that record user activity within your applications—including user login/logout activity—each time a user updates a database record and even each time a user performs a critical operation, such as printing a sensitive report or graph, updating key data, or running restricted routines.

Throughout today, you use a new ActiveX DLL Library. You can use this library to add varying levels of security and auditing to all your future Visual Basic database applications.

Note   The source code for the `Security.DLL` file is available on the CD-ROM that comes with this book. You can use this source code as a starting point for creating your own customized COM object to provide security for your Visual Basic applications.

When you have completed this chapter, you will understand how Microsoft Access database security and encryption works and the advantages and disadvantages of both. You'll also know how to implement an application security scheme, including adding user login and logout history, implementing audit trails that show when database records have been updated, and recording each time users perform critical application operations.

Database Security

The first level of security you can employ in Visual Basic database applications is at the database level. The Microsoft Jet database format enables you to establish user and group security schemes using the Microsoft Access `SYSTEM` security file. You can also add database encryption to your Microsoft Jet databases to increase the level of security within your database.

Although the Microsoft Access `SYSTEM` security file and Microsoft Jet data encryption are powerful tools, they have some disadvantages. When adding either of these features, you should understand the limitations and pitfalls of the security features. In the following sections, you learn the most notable of these limitations, as well as some suggestions on how you can avoid unexpected results.

Limitations of the Microsoft Access SYSTEM Security

If you have a copy of Microsoft Access, you can install a database security scheme for your Visual Basic applications. The security scheme requires the presence of a single file (called `SYSTEM.MDA` or `SYSTEM.MDW`). This file must be available to your Visual Basic application either in the application path, or pointed to through the application `.INI` file or system Registry. After the `SYSTEM` security file is defined, all attempts to open the secured database cause the Microsoft Jet engine to request a user name and password before opening the database.

Note   Some 32-bit systems have a Microsoft Jet security file called `SYSTEM.MDW` (for example, Access 95). Others continue to use `SYSTEM.MDA` in both 16- and 32-bit modes (for example, Visual Basic 4). The difference between the SYS-

TEM.MDW and SYSTEM.MDA files is in name only. Throughout this lesson, you will see SYSTEM, SYSTEM.MDW, and SYSTEM.MDA. They can be used interchangeably.

You don't review the details of creating and updating the SYSTEM security file here (see Day 6, "Using the Visdata Program," for details on defining SYSTEM security). Instead, this section covers the advantages and limitations of using the SYSTEM security scheme employed by Microsoft Access and Microsoft Jet.

Microsoft Access Is Required

After you have a SYSTEM security file registered on your workstation, you can use Microsoft Access or you can use Visdata to define the system security details. However, only Microsoft Access can create the original SYSTEM file. You cannot use any Visual Basic application to create a SYSTEM file. You can, however, use Visual Basic to modify existing SYSTEM security files.

Multiple SYSTEM Files Are Possible

You can have multiple versions of the SYSTEM security file available on your workstation or network. In this way you can create unique security schemes for each of your Microsoft Jet databases. The disadvantage here is that it is possible to install the wrong SYSTEM security file for an application. This could result in preventing all users from accessing any of the data. Depending on the SYSTEM file installed, it could also result in reducing security to the point of allowing all users access to critical data not normally available to them. If you are using multiple SYSTEM security files, be sure to store these files in the same directory as the application files and include the specific path to the SYSTEM file in all installation procedures.

Removing the SYSTEM File Removes the Security

Because all security features are stored in a single file, removing SYSTEM from the workstation or network effectively eliminates all database security. You can limit this possibility by storing the SYSTEM file on a network in a directory where users do not have delete or rename rights. Setting these rights requires administrator-level access to the network and knowledge of your network's file rights utilities.

Some Applications Might Not Use SYSTEM Files

If you are using the database in an environment where multiple applications can access the database, you might find that some applications do not use the SYSTEM files at all. These applications might be able to open the database without having to go through the security features. For example, you could easily write a Visual Basic application that

21

opens a database without first checking for the existence of the SYSTEM file. By doing this, you can completely ignore any security features built into the SYSTEM security file.

Limitations of Microsoft Jet Encryption

You can also use the encryption feature of Microsoft Jet to encode sensitive data. However, you have no control over the type of encryption algorithm used to encode your data. You can only turn encryption on or off using the dbEncrypt or dbDecrypt option constants with the CreateDatabase and CompactDatabase methods.

The following list outlines other limitations to consider when using Microsoft Jet encryption:

- You cannot encrypt selected tables within a database. When you turn encryption on, it affects all objects in the database. If you have only a few tables that are sensitive, you should consider moving those tables into a separate database for encryption.
- If you are deploying your database in an environment where multiple applications access your data, it is possible that these applications might not be able to read the encrypted data.
- If you want to take advantage of the replication features of Microsoft Jet, you cannot use encrypted databases.

Application Security

Application security is quite different from database security. Application security focuses on securing not only data but also processes. For example, you can use application security to limit users' ability to use selected data entry forms, produce certain graphs or reports, or run critical procedures (such as month-end closing or mass price updates).

Any good application security scheme has two main features. The first is a process that forces users to log into your application using stored passwords. This provides an additional level of security to your Visual Basic database application. As you see later in this chapter, forcing users to log into and out of your application also gives you the opportunity to create audit logs of all user activity. These audit logs can help you locate and fix problems reported by users and give you an additional tool for keeping track of just who is using your application.

The second process that is valuable in building an application security system is an access rights scheme. You can use an access rights scheme to limit the functions that particular users can perform within your application. For example, if you want to allow only certain users to perform critical tasks, you can establish an access right for that task and check each user's rights before he or she is allowed to attempt that operation. You can establish access rights for virtually any program operation, including data form entry, report generation, even special processes such as price updates, file exports, and so on.

> Because application security works only within the selected application, it cannot affect users who are accessing the database from other applications. Therefore, you should not rely on application-level security as the only security scheme for your critical data. Still, application security can provide powerful security controls to your Visual Basic database applications.

In order to provide user login and logout and access rights checking, in this lesson you use a prebuilt set of routines in an ActiveX Component called Security. This library contains all the properties and methods needed to install and maintain application-level security for all your Visual Basic database applications.

Building a Test Application

In order to exercise the various types of application security, you need to first build a simple data entry project. This simple project will have all the parts needed to create a secured database application.

You build a basic data entry form and an MDI form to host the data entry dialog. After these are working properly, you add the following security features to the project:

- User login/logout procedures to make sure only authorized users have access to the application

- A permission-checking routine to enable only features allowed for the logged-in users (for example, update, but not delete, rights)

- Audit trails to track user login and logout and the performance of critical operations (for example, deleting a record from the database).

- Audit trails to log each record changed, including the before and after contents of fields on the form.

Building the Test MDI Form

The first step is to create a new standard EXE Visual Basic project and add a new MDI Form to the project. This form will act as the central host for both the data entry form and for providing access to the user and rights tables and the audit log you'll build later. Use Figure 21.1 and Table 21.1 as a guide in laying out the form and building the menu.

21

FIGURE 21.1

Laying out the MDI test form.

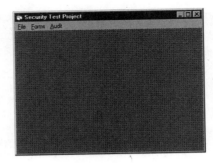

TABLE 21.1 CONTROLS FOR THE MDI TEST FORM

Control Name	Property	Setting
VB.MDIForm	Name	mdiTest
	Caption	"Security Test Project"
	ClientHeight	3990
	ClientLeft	2070
	ClientTop	1365
	ClientWidth	5835
	WindowState	2 'Maximized
VB.Menu	Name	mnuFile
	Caption	"&File"
VB.Menu	Name	mnuFileExit
	Caption	"E&xit"
VB.Menu	Name	mnuForms
	Caption	"F&orms"
VB.Menu	Name	mnuFormsBuyers
	Caption	"&Buyers"
VB.Menu	Name	mnuFormsUsers
	Caption	"&Users"
VB.Menu	Name	mnuAudit
	Caption	"&Audit"
VB.Menu	Name	mnuAuditView
	Caption	"&View Log"

After laying out the MDI form, you need to add just a small bit of Visual Basic code. This code will call the data entry form (you build that next) and exit the program safely. Add the code from Listing 21.1 to the mdiTest form.

LISTING 21.1 ADDING CODE TO THE MDITEST FORM

```
1: Private Sub mnuFileExit_Click()
2:      Unload Me
3: End Sub
4:
5: Private Sub mnuFormsBuyers_Click()
6:      frmTest.Show
7: End Sub
```

Building the Buyers Data Entry Form

The next item you need is a data entry form. For this example, you build a quick form that enables users to add, edit, and delete records from the Buyers table of the BOOKS6.MDB file on the CD-ROM that ships with this book.

Refer to Figure 21.2 and Table 21.2 for details on laying out the data-bound form. Note that this form uses the ADODC (Active Data Object Data Control) instead of the standard DAO data control. You may need to add this control to your project before you start laying out the form (select Project | Components and search for Microsoft ADO Data Control 6.0).

FIGURE 21.2

Laying out the frmTest data form.

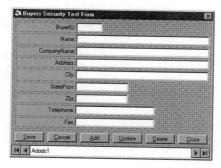

21

TABLE 21.2 CONTROLS FOR THE FRMTEST DATA FORM

Control Name	Property	Setting
VB.Form	Name	frmTest
	BorderStyle	3 'Fixed Dialog
	Caption	"Buyers Security Test Form"
	ClientHeight	4440
	ClientWidth	6240
	MaxButton	0 'False
	MDIChild	-1 'True
	MinButton	0 'False
	ShowInTaskbar	0 'False
VB.CommandButton	Name	cmdAction
	Caption	"&Close"
	Height	300
	Index	5
	Left	5220
	Top	3660
	Width	900
VB.CommandButton	Name	cmdAction
	Caption	"&Delete"
	Height	300
	Index	4
	Left	4200
	Top	3660
	Width	900
VB.CommandButton	Name	cmdAction
	Caption	"&Update"
	Height	300
	Index	3
	Left	3180
	Top	3660
	Width	900

Control Name	Property	Setting
VB.CommandButton	Name	cmdAction
	Caption	"&Add"
	Height	300
	Index	2
	Left	2160
	Top	3660
	Width	900
VB.CommandButton	Name	cmdAction
	Caption	"&Cancel"
	Height	300
	Index	1
	Left	1140
	Top	3660
	Width	900
VB.CommandButton	Name	cmdAction
	Caption	"&Save"
	Height	300
	Index	0
	Left	120
	Top	3660
	Width	900
MSAdodcLib.Adodc	Name	Adodc1
	Align	2 'Align Bottom
	Height	375
	Left	0
	Top	4065
	Width	6240
	ConnectMode	0
	CursorLocation	3
	ConnectionTimeout=	
	CommandTimeout	30
	CursorType	1

continues

21

TABLE 21.2 CONTINUED

Control Name	Property	Setting
	LockType	3
	CommandType	2
	MaxRecords	0
	BOFAction	0
	EOFAction	0
	Appearance	1
	Orientation	0
	Enabled	-1
	ConnectString	"DSN=BOOKS6"
	RecordSource	"Buyers"
VB.TextBox	Name	txtFax
	DataField	"Fax"
	DataSource	"Adodc1"
	Height	285
	Left	1980
	Top	3165
	Width	2475
VB.TextBox	Name	txtTelephone
	DataField	"Telephone"
	DataSource	"Adodc1"
	Height	285
	Left	1980
	Top	2775
	Width	2475
VB.TextBox	Name	txtZip
	DataField	"Zip"
	DataSource	"Adodc1"
	Height	285
	Left	1980
	Top	2400
	Width	1635

Control Name	Property	Setting
VB.TextBox	Name	txtStateProv
	DataField	"StateProv"
	DataSource	"Adodc1"
	Height	285
	Left	1980
	Top	2025
	Width	1650
VB.TextBox	Name	txtCity
	DataField	"City"
	DataSource	"Adodc1"
	Height	285
	Left	1980
	Top	1635
	Width	4140
VB.TextBox	Name	txtAddress
	DataField	"Address"
	DataSource	"Adodc1"
	Height	285
	Left	1980
	Top	1260
	Width	4155
VB.TextBox	Name	txtCompanyName
	DataField	"CompanyName"
	DataSource	"Adodc1"
	Height	285
	Left	1980
	Top	885
	Width	4155
VB.TextBox	Name	txtName
	DataField	"Name"
	DataSource	"Adodc1"
	Height	285

continues

21

TABLE 21.2   CONTINUED

Control Name	Property	Setting
	Left	1980
	Top	495
	Width	4155
VB.TextBox	Name	txtBuyerID
	DataField	"BuyerID"
	DataSource	"Adodc1"
	Height	285
	Left	1980
	Top	120
	Width	825
VB.Label	Name	lblFieldLabel
	Alignment	1 'Right Justify
	AutoSize	-1 'True
	Caption	"Fax:"
	Height	255
	Index	8
	Left	135
	Top	3210
	Width	1815
VB.Label	Name	lblFieldLabel
	Alignment	1 'Right Justify
	AutoSize	-1 'True
	Caption	"Telephone:"
	Height	255
	Index	7
	Left	135
	Top	2820
	Width	1815
VB.Label	Name	lblFieldLabel
	Alignment	1 'Right Justify
	AutoSize	-1 'True
	Caption	"Zip:"

Control Name	Property	Setting
	Height	255
	Index	6
	Left	135
	Top	2445
	Width	1815
VB.Label	Name	lblFieldLabel
	Alignment	1 'Right Justify
	AutoSize	-1 'True
	Caption	"StateProv:"
	Height	255
	Index	5
	Left	135
	Top	2070
	Width	1815
VB.Label	Name	lblFieldLabel
	Alignment	1 'Right Justify
	AutoSize	-1 'True
	Caption	"City:"
	Height	255
	Index	4
	Left	135
	Top	1680
	Width	1815
VB.Label	Name	lblFieldLabel
	Alignment	1 'Right Justify
	AutoSize	-1 'True
	Caption	"Address:"
	Height	255
	Index	3
	Left	135
	Top	1305
	Width	1815

21

continues

TABLE 21.2   CONTINUED

Control Name	Property	Setting
VB.Label	Name	lblFieldLabel
	Alignment	1 'Right Justify
	AutoSize	-1 'True
	Caption	"CompanyName:"
	Height	255
	Index	2
	Left	135
	Top	930
	Width	1815
VB.Label	Name	lblFieldLabel
	Alignment	1 'Right Justify
	AutoSize	-1 'True
	Caption	"Name:"
	Height	255
	Index	1
	Left	135
	Top	540
	Width	1815
VB.Label	Name	lblFieldLabel
	Alignment	1 'Right Justify
	AutoSize	-1 'True
	Caption	"BuyerID:"
	Height	255
	Index	0
	Left	135
	Top	165
	Width	1815

After laying out the frmTest form, be sure to save it before continuing with the day's lesson.

Coding the frmTest Form

Now that the data-bound form has been built, you need to add a bit of code to the form before it is fully functional. First, Listing 21.2 shows the code you need to add to the general declarations area of the form. This code declares a local enumerated type to help control the state of the data entry form.

LISTING 21.2 ADDING CODE TO THE GENERAL DECLARATIONS SECTION OF THE FORM

```
1: Option Explicit
2: '
3: Enum FormMode
4:     fmAdd = 0
5:     fmEdit = 1
6: End Enum
7: '
8: Public fmMode As FormMode
```

The next step is to build a special method that uses the enumerated type to properly enable control buttons on the form. Add the code from Listing 21.3 to your form.

LISTING 21.3 ADDING THE SetFormMode METHOD

```
 1: Public Sub SetFormMode(Mode As FormMode)
 2:     '
 3:     ' handle form mode changes
 4:     '
 5:     Dim blnMode As Boolean
 6:     '
 7:     If Mode = fmAdd Then
 8:         blnMode = False
 9:     Else
10:         blnMode = True
11:     End If
12:     '
13:     cmdAction(0).Enabled = Not blnMode
14:     cmdAction(1).Enabled = Not blnMode
15:     cmdAction(2).Enabled = blnMode
16:     cmdAction(3).Enabled = blnMode
17:     cmdAction(4).Enabled = blnMode
18:     cmdAction(5).Enabled = blnMode
19:     '
20: End Sub
```

As you can see in Listing 21.3, the SetFormMode method checks to see whether the form should be in Add or Edit mode. If the requested mode is Add, only the first two buttons

21

will be enabled (Save and Cancel). If the requested mode is Edit, only the last four buttons are enabled (Add, Update, Delete, and Close).

Now you need to add a line of code to the Form_Activate event. This calls the SetFormMode method the first time the form is activated. Add the code from Listing 21.4 to your project.

LISTING 21.4   CODING THE Form_Activate EVENT

```
1: Private Sub Form_Activate()
2:        '
3:        SetFormMode fmEdit
4:        '
5: End Sub
```

Finally, you need to add code to the cmdAction_click event of the form. This is the method that handles all the button clicks for the form. Because the command buttons were built as an array, you can add all the important code for the form in this one method. Enter the code from Listing 21.5 to your form.

LISTING 21.5   CODING THE cmdAction_Click EVENT

```
 1: Private Sub cmdAction_Click(Index As Integer)
 2:        '
 3:        ' handle buttons
 4:        '
 5:        With Adodc1.Recordset
 6:            Select Case Index
 7:                Case 0 'save
 8:                    .Update
 9:                    SetFormMode fmEdit
10:                Case 1 'cancel
11:                    .CancelUpdate
12:                    SetFormMode fmEdit
13:                Case 2 'new
14:                    .AddNew
15:                    SetFormMode fmAdd
16:                Case 3 'update
17:                    .Update
18:                    .MoveNext
19:                    .MovePrevious
20:                    SetFormMode fmEdit
21:                Case 4 'delete
22:                    If MsgBox("Delete Record?", _
23:                        vbYesNo + vbQuestion, _
24:                        "Delete") = vbYes Then
```

```
25:                          .Delete
26:                          .MoveFirst
27:                    End If
28:                    SetFormMode fmEdit
29:              Case 5 'close
30:                    Unload Me
31:        End Select
32:    End With
33:    '
34: End Sub
```

After adding this last bit of code to the form, save the project (prjTest.vbp) and the forms (mdiTest.frm and frmTest.frm).

When you run this project, you should now be able to add, edit, and delete records in the Buyers table without restriction (see Figure 21.3).

FIGURE 21.3

Running the test form.

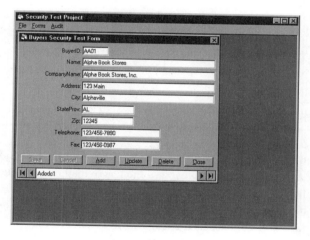

Now that you have a fully functional test form, you're ready to use the SECURITY library to add application-level security.

About the SECURITY COM Object

 Before jumping into adding all the cool security features to the test application, it is important to take a moment to describe the features of the SECURITY COM object that is on the CD-ROM that ships with this book. This is a rather simple COM library that has two objects and a handful of methods and properties. Table 21.3 shows the objects, methods, and properties of the library along with a short description for each item.

21

TABLE 21.3 THE MEMBERS OF THE SECURITY OBJECT LIBRARY

Object	Member	Type	Description
Users	AppTitle	Property	Title to display on the User Log-In Dialog box.
	CheckRights	Method	Accepts Rights Object and Security Level and returns True if the current user has sufficient rights to the object.
	ConnectString	Property	Connection string for accessing the database that holds the secUsers and secAccess data tables.
	LogIn	Method	Attempts a user login action. Accepts UserID and Password parameters. If both are supplied and are valid, no dialog is shown.
	LogOut	Method	Logs the current user out of the application.
	Maintenance	Method	Calls the dialogs that enable adding, editing, and deleting users and rights objects.
Audit	FileHeader	Property	Title string written to the top of the audit log disk file.
	FileName	Property	Disk filename used to hold the audit log entries.
	WriteLog	Method	Method to write data to the audit log. This can be a variable array of entries. The UserID and the Date And Time are automatically written for every entry and do not need to be supplied.

As you can see from Table 21.3, the SECURITY library offers a solid set of basic application-level security features. You can use the Login method to validate users upon startup of the application and the CheckRights method to verify that the current user has the proper rights to execute a command. You can also use the WriteLog method of the Audit object to track user actions, such as logging in and out of the app, and even log the changes to individual data records.

About the Required Data Tables

In order to work, the SECURITY library needs to be able to read and write to two data tables in a database. The secUsers table contains information about the valid users and their recent login history. The secRights table contains a list of default rights and rights for each user. When you use the SECURITY library, you need to add these two tables to your database and populate them with valid entries. Table 21.4 shows the table definitions for both the secUsers and the secAccess tables.

TABLE 21.4 DEFINITIONS FOR THE SECURITY DATA TABLES

Table Name	Field Name	Field Type
secUsers	UserID	TEXT(20)
	Password	TEXT(20)
	Name	TEXT(50)
	LastLogIn	Date/Time
	LastLogOut	Date/Time
secRights	UserID	TEXT(20)
	Object	TEXT(20)
	Level	Long

Caution You must be sure the secUsers and secRights tables exist in the database you are working with in order for the SECURITY library to function properly. The BOOKS6.MDB file on the CD-ROM has these tables built with default data in them. If you use this component with other databases, you need to add these tables first.

Required Startup Data

The only required data for the tables is the existence of a DEFAULT user in the secUsers table and a complete set of rights objects for the DEFAULT user in the secAccess table. Each rights object is a "security point" in the system. For example, if you wanted to secure the Add, Edit, and Delete buttons on a form, you could create an Add, Edit and Delete object in the DEFAULT rights list and set their LEVEL values to the default value for all new users (usually 0).

Although you need to create the physical data tables yourself, the SECURITY library has a special method for handling the adding, editing, and deleting of the users and rights objects: the Maintenance method.

Finally, the BOOKS6.MDB file has a complete set of records in the secUsers and secAccess tables that you can use as a starting point for building your own security data files.

Now that you have a rough idea of how the SECURITY library is designed, you're ready to start using it in the test application.

21

Adding User Login and Logout Security

The first kind of security you can add to your application is user login and logout procedures. By adding a user login and logout process, you can be sure that only authorized
users can gain access to your Visual Basic application.

The process of adding user login procedures involves two main tasks. First, you need a
login dialog that will accept a user ID and password and check this information against a
data table. The SECURITY library on the CD-ROM that ships with this book will do this
for you.

The second task you must complete in order to handle user login processing is to actually call the login routine prior to displaying the data entry forms that are secured by the
application. This is usually handled by adding a Main() startup routine to your application that will eventually launch the startup form for valid users. In other words, most
secured Visual Basic apps do not have a form as their startup object. Usually they use a
Sub Main() instead. That is how you code the example for this chapter.

Adding the Sub Main Startup Method

Instead of just starting the application with the MDI form, you use a Sub Main method.
This method will call the user login dialog and, if the user passes the login process, will
then launch the MDI form. If the user login fails, the application will end without giving
the user access to the data. To do this, you need to add a BAS module to your test project.

Before you can use the SECURITY library in your project, you need to load the ActiveX
DLL source code as a secondary project in the Visual Basic IDE. To do this, select File |
Add Project from the main Visual Basic menu and locate and load the SECURITY.VBP
project from the \TYSDBVB6\SOURCE\CHAP21\USERMGR folder. This will add the Users and
Audit objects to your Visual Basic project.

> **Tip**
>
> This example shows you how to load the source code for the SECURITY com-
> ponent. If you want, you can compile this source code into a standalone
> ActiveX DLL for use in this and other Visual Basic programs. You use the
> source code here to make it easy for you to see how the SECURITY library
> works.

After adding the SECURITY library to the project, add a BAS module (select Project | Add
Module from the main menu) and set its name to modTest. Then add the code from
Listing 21.6 to the module.

LISTING 21.6   CODING THE Sub Main METHOD FOR THE PROJECT

```
 1: Option Explicit
 2:
 3: '
 4: Public objUsers As Security.Users'
 5: Public strConnect As String
 6:
 7: Public Sub Main()
 8:     '
 9:     ' main project startup
10:     '
11:
12:     ' get connect string
13:     Load frmTest
14:     With frmTest
15:         strConnect = .Adodc1.ConnectionString
16:     End With
17:     Unload frmTest
18:
19:     ' get instance of users object
20:     Set objUsers = CreateObject("Security.Users")
21:     With objUsers
22:         .AppTitle = App.EXEName
23:         .ConnectString = strConnect
24:     End With
25:     ' login/start or fail/end
26:     If objUsers.Login = True Then
27:         frmTest.Show ' launch the data entry form
28:     Else
29:         End
30:     End If
31:     '
32: End Sub
```

Notice that you've added two declarations at the top of the module. You use these to create a complete instance of the Users object in the SECURITY library. You can also see that you must first get the connection information from the data entry form (lines 13–17) for use with the Users object. Finally, after getting an instance of the Users object and setting its properties (lines 20–24) you attempt the Login method (line 26). If it returns true, the data form is shown. If not, the program ends.

There is one more important change you need to make to this project before the user login will work correctly. You must change the Startup Object for the project to the Sub Main procedure. To do this select Project | Properties from the main menu and select Sub Main from the Startup Object drop-down list on the General tab (see Figure 21.4).

21

FIGURE 21.4

Setting the Startup Object for the project.

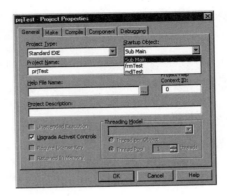

After adding the new code and setting the Startup Object for the project, save it and run it. This time, you see the login dialog appear before you are allowed access to the data entry form. Use DEFAULT for both the username and password at the login dialog. This will give you access to the data form (see Figure 21.5).

FIGURE 21.5

Logging into the test application.

You now have an application that will verify the user login and update the user data table to reflect the data and time of the login. You now need to add another bit of code to the Unload event of the MDI form. This will log the user out of the application. Add the code from Listing 21.7 to the MDIForm_Unload event of the form.

LISTING 21.7   CODING THE MDIForm_Unload EVENT

```
1: Private Sub MDIForm_Unload(Cancel As Integer)
2:     '
3:        objUsers.LogOut
4:     '
5: End Sub
```

That's all you need to do to add user login security to your Visual Basic applications. In the next section, you add permission checking within the Visual Basic application.

Adding Permission-Checking Security

After a user gains access to your Visual Basic application, you may also want to limit the user's ability to perform certain actions. For example, you may want to allow users to add new records, but not delete existing ones. You may allow them to view the data online, but not produce printed reports of critical data. For this kind of control, you need to institute a form of security sometimes called *permission checking*. Permission checking enables you to check the user's security profile to see whether that user has permission to perform a particular task.

The SECURITY library has a data table called secAccess that enables you to implement a form of permission-checking security in your Visual Basic applications. You add a list of security objects to the DEFAULT user profile. This set of objects has a permission level assigned. This is the level that new users will be granted when they are added to the secUsers table.

The secAccess table in the BOOKS6.MDB database on the CD-ROM that ships with this book contains a set of security objects to match the example in this chapter. You can use this as a starting point for creating your own security objects for your Visual Basic applications.

As an example, you can add a new method to the frmTest form that will validate each user's rights to add, update, or delete records in the table. Add the code from Listing 21.8 to the frmTest form. This code checks the user's rights for the Add, Update, Delete, and Close buttons of the form.

LISTING 21.8   ADDING THE PERMISSION-CHECKING METHOD

```
 1: Public Sub UpdateUserActions()
 2:     '
 3:     ' check user permissions for each button
 4:     '
 5:     On Error Resume Next
 6:     '
 7:     ' user should have level 3 for adds
 8:     With cmdAction(2)
 9:         .Enabled = objUsers.CheckRights(.Caption, 3)
10:     End With
11:     '
12:     ' user should have level 2 for updates
13:     With cmdAction(3)
14:         .Enabled = objUsers.CheckRights(.Caption, 2)
15:     End With
16:     '
```

continues

21

LISTING 21.8   CONTINUED

```
17:         ' user should have level 4 for deletes
18:         With cmdAction(4)
19:             .Enabled = objUsers.CheckRights(.Caption, 4)
20:         End With
21:         '
22:         ' only level 0 needed for closing the form
23:         With cmdAction(5)
24:             .Enabled = objUsers.CheckRights(.Caption, 0)
25:         End With
26:         '
27: End Sub
```

Notice that each command button object has its Enabled property set based on the results of the CheckRights method. The CheckRights method accepts two parameters: the security object in the database and the minimum required rights needed to access the object. Notice also that the caption of the button has been used as the object name. This makes it easy to check permissions for command buttons and menu items in a Visual Basic application.

You add one more bit of code to the frmTest form to call the UpdateUserActions method. Listing 21.9 shows an updated version of the SetFormMode method. Notice that several more lines (lines 20–24) of code have been added at the end of the routine. This calls the UpdateuserActions method while the form is in edit mode.

LISTING 21.9   MODIFYING THE SetFormMode METHOD

```
 1: Public Sub SetFormMode(Mode As FormMode)
 2:     '
 3:     ' handle form mode changes
 4:     '
 5:     Dim blnMode As Boolean
 6:     '
 7:     If Mode = fmAdd Then
 8:         blnMode = False
 9:     Else
10:         blnMode = True
11:     End If
12:     '
13:     cmdAction(0).Enabled = Not blnMode
14:     cmdAction(1).Enabled = Not blnMode
15:     cmdAction(2).Enabled = blnMode
16:     cmdAction(3).Enabled = blnMode
17:     cmdAction(4).Enabled = blnMode
18:     cmdAction(5).Enabled = blnMode
```

```
19:     '
20:     ' check user permissions
21:     ' for this form
22:     If Mode = fmEdit Then
23:         UpdateUserActions
24:     End If
25:     '
26: End Sub
```

After adding the new method and modifying the SetFormMode method, save and run the project. Now, when you log in with the tysdbvb6 username and password, you no longer have rights to delete records. This button is now disabled.

You can use this type of permission-checking in many different ways. You can add code to disable or hide controls on a page, including buttons, input boxes, and menus. You can also add code that will check user rights before attempting to execute an action and, if the rights fail, show a message instead:

```
If objUsers.CheckRights("SalesReport", HighLevel) = False Then
  MsgBox "You do not have rights to the Sales Report", vbExclamation,
"Print Report"
Else
  PrintSalesReport
End If
```

All you need to do is add the security objects and establish what access level is required to execute the actions.

Adding User Action Auditing

Now you are sure that only authenticated users can gain access to your applications and that you have the power to control permissions rights to individual actions within the application. The next step in security you can add is an audit trail that logs all the significant actions taken by users within your application. This includes logging in and out and executing any "secured object" within the app.

The SECURITY library offers a very simple audit-logging feature. In this example, you use the SECURITY library to add auditing for both user login and logout and for tracking secured actions (add, update, and delete).

Updating the Sub Main Method

In order to add audit tracking, you need to first add code to create an instance of the Audit object from the SECURITY library. Listing 21.10 shows the modified version of the code in the modTest module. Adjust your code to match the code in Listing 21.10.

21

LISTING 21.10   MODIFYING THE modTest MODULE

```
 1: Option Explicit
 2:
 3: '
 4: Public objUsers As Security.Users
 5: Public strConnect As String
 6: '
 7: Public objAudit As Security.Audit
 8: Public strLogFile As String
 9:
10: Public Sub Main()
11:         '
12:         ' main project startup
13:         '
14:
15:         ' get connect string
16:         Load frmTest
17:         With frmTest
18:             strConnect = .Adodc1.ConnectionString
19:         End With
20:         Unload frmTest
21:
22:         ' get instance of users object
23:         Set objUsers = CreateObject("Security.Users")
24:         With objUsers
25:             .AppTitle = App.EXEName
26:             .ConnectString = strConnect
27:         End With
28:
29:         ' get instances of audit object
30:         strLogFile = App.Path & "\" & App.EXEName & ".log"
31:         Set objAudit = CreateObject("Security.Audit")
32:         With objAudit
33:             .FileHeader = App.EXEName
34:             .FileName = strLogFile
35:         End With
36:
37:         ' login/start or fail/end
38:         If objUsers.Login = True Then
39:             objAudit.WriteLog "Login", "Succeeded"
40:             frmTest.Show
41:         Else
42:             objAudit.WriteLog "Login", "Failed"
43:             End
44:         End If
45:         '
46: End Sub
```

Most of the code in Listing 21.10 should look familiar. You should notice that lines 7 and 8 were added. These hold shared variables used throughout the application. Lines 29–35 are the ones that actually create the instance of the Audit object and set its properties. You should also notice that lines 39 and 42 have been added to create audit log entries that show the results of the user login event.

Next, you can add code to the MDIForm_Unload event to create an audit entry when the user logs out of the application. Modify your MDIForm_Unload event to match the code in Listing 21.11. Line 4 is the only new line in the code.

LISTING 21.11 MODIFYING THE MDIForm_Unload EVENT

```
1: Private Sub MDIForm_Unload(Cancel As Integer)
2:      '
3:      objUsers.LogOut
4:      objAudit.WriteLog "Logout", "Succeeded"
5:      '
6: End Sub
```

Next, you can add code to the cmdAction_click event to make audit log entries whenever a user selects the Save, Cancel, or Delete buttons on the form. The code in Listing 21.12 shows the completed cmdAction_click event.

LISTING 21.12 MODIFYING THE cmdAction_Click EVENT

```
1: Private Sub cmdAction_Click(Index As Integer)
2:      '
3:      ' handle buttons
4:      '
5:      With Adodc1.Recordset
6:          Select Case Index
7:              Case 0 'save
8:                  .Update
9:                  objAudit.WriteLog "Save New Record"
10:                 SetFormMode fmEdit
11:             Case 1 'cancel
12:                 .CancelUpdate
13:                 objAudit.WriteLog "Cancel New Record"
14:                 SetFormMode fmEdit
15:             Case 2 'new
16:                 .AddNew
17:                 SetFormMode fmAdd
18:             Case 3 'update
19:                 .Update
```

continues

21

LISTING 21.12   CONTINUED

```
20:                    .MoveNext
21:                    .MovePrevious
22:                    SetFormMode fmEdit
23:                Case 4 'delete
24:                    If MsgBox("Delete Record?", _
25:                      vbYesNo + vbQuestion, _
26:                      "Delete") = vbYes Then
27:                        .Delete
28:                        .MoveFirst
29:                        objAudit.WriteLog "Delete Existing Record"
30:                    End If
31:                    SetFormMode fmEdit
32:                Case 5 'close
33:                    Unload Me
34:            End Select
35:        End With
36:        '
37: End Sub
```

Lines 9, 13, and 29 are the only new lines in this example. Now, when you save and run the project, you won't see any outward difference in the application. However, all the audited actions will be recorded in the audit log. Listing 21.13 shows an example log created by the Audit object in the SECURITY library.

LISTING 21.13   AN EXAMPLE AUDIT LOG

```
*************************************************************
prjTest
Created: 5/21/98 1:50:40 AM
*************************************************************

"5/27/98 2:29:08 AM","mca","Login","Succeeded"
"5/27/98 2:29:58 AM","mca","Logout","Succeeded"
"5/27/98 3:50:39 PM","mca","Login","Succeeded"
"5/27/98 3:51:21 PM","mca","Logout","Succeeded"
"5/27/98 3:53:36 PM","tysdbvb6","Login","Succeeded"
"5/27/98 3:53:41 PM","tysdbvb6","Logout","Succeeded"
```

Adding Access to the Audit Log and User Maintenance

Now that you have the audit log started, this is a good time to add some code to the test project that will give you the ability to view the log and also access the User and Rights data tables.

You can access the audit log by "shelling out" to the NOTEPAD.EXE applet on the workstation and loading the document into notepad for viewing. The code in Listing 21.14 shows how this is done. Add this code to the mnuAuditView_click event in the MDIForm of the project.

LISTING 21.14 ADDING CODE TO VIEW THE AUDIT LOG

```
1: Private Sub mnuAuditView_Click()
2:     '
3:     Dim lngReturn As Long
4:     '
5:     lngReturn = Shell("notepad.exe " & strLogFile, vbNormalFocus)
6:     '
7: End Sub
```

It's even easier to gain access to the User and Rights data tables. You need call the Maintenance method of the Users object in the SECURITY library. You'll then see a complete data entry dialog for maintaining both users' and security objects (see Figure 21.6).

FIGURE 21.6

Accessing the Maintenance *method of the* SECURITY *Library.*

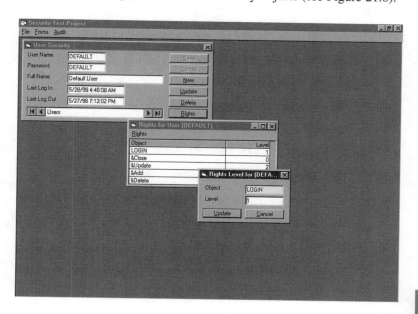

Listing 21.15 has all the code you need to access the data tables for the SECURITY library. Add this code to the mnuFormUsers_click event in the MDIForm.

21

LISTING 21.15   ADDING THE Maintenance METHOD TO THE MDI FORM

```
1: Private Sub mnuFormsUsers_Click()
2:     objUsers.Maintenance
3: End Sub
```

Now you can save your form and run it. When you select the Form | Users option from the MDI menu, you can see a screen like the one shown in Figure 21.6. If you select the Audit | View menu option, you see the current audit log in a NOTEPAD window (see Figure 21.7).

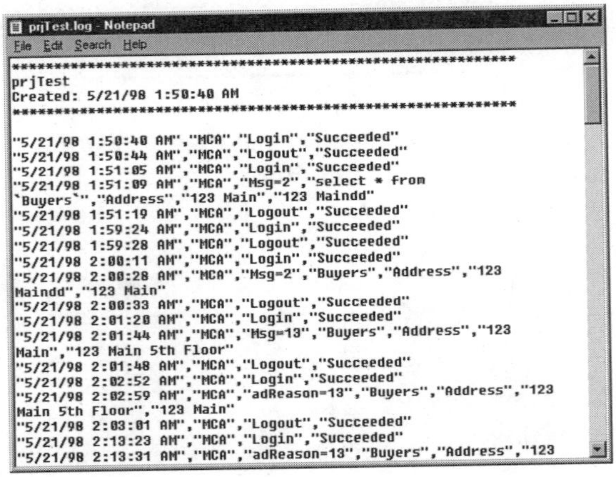

FIGURE 21.7

Viewing the audit log.

Adding Data Field Change Auditing

You add one more valuable auditing technique to the test application in this lesson: field change auditing. There are times when you need to audit the changes made to data records on a field-by-field basis. Ideally, you would like to create a log entry that shows the user, date/time, and exact field that was changed including the pre- and post- update field values.

Actually, this is not very difficult to do on a Visual Basic data-bound form. In this case, you review each of the bound text boxes and, if the data has changed, fire off an `Audit.WriteLog` method to add the information to the log.

The only "trick" is that you must execute this operation in the `WillMove` event of the ADODC (or the `Validate` event of the DAO data control). This event fires off *just before* the data is updated to the database. This gives you the opportunity to compare the values in the controls with the values currently in the database.

Another valuable item is the DataChanged property of the text box control. This is set to True if the user has made any edits to the data since it was last updated from the database. By checking this value, you'll know which fields have been changed.

Adding Code to Track Field-Level Changes

The last bit of code you need to add to the test project is shown in Listing 21.16. This code uses the techniques described above to review all the data-bound text boxes to see whether any data has changed. If so, audit information is written to the log. Add this code to the ADODC1_WillMove event in the frmTest form.

LISTING 21.16 CODING THE WillMove EVENT OF THE TEST FORM

```
 1: Private Sub Adodc1_WillMove(ByVal adReason As ADODB.EventReasonEnum, _
      adStatus As ADODB.EventStatusEnum, ByVal pRecordset As _
      ADODB.Recordset)
 2:      '
 3:      ' log field changes
 4:      '
 5:      Dim ctlTemp As Control
 6:      '
 7:      With Adodc1.Recordset
 8:          For Each ctlTemp In Controls
 9:              If TypeOf ctlTemp Is TextBox Then
10:                  If ctlTemp.DataChanged = True Then
11:                      objAudit.WriteLog "adReason=" & CStr(adReason), _
                          .Source, ctlTemp.DataField, _
                          .Fields(ctlTemp.DataField), ctlTemp.Text
12:                  End If
13:              End If
14:          Next
15:      End With
16:      '
17: End Sub
```

As you can see in Listing 21.16, each control on the form is checked to see whether it is a TextBox control (line 9). If it is, then the DataChanged property is checked (line 10). If the data has been changed, an entry is added to the audit log (line 11). This entry has the reason the WillMove event was fired, the data source (table name), the name of the field in the table, and the "before" and "after" contents of the field. Of course, this is just one example of the kind of audit log entry you can create. You can use this entry as an example for creating your own field-level change log entries.

Now save and run the project. If you change the data in the first records (for example, add Suite 501 to the Address line) and then update the record and exit the application, you'll be able to see the new log entries that reflect your changes (see Listing 21.17).

21

LISTING 21.17   LOG ENTRIES SHOWING FIELD-LEVEL AUDITING

```
"5/28/98 5:03:12 AM","mca","Login","Succeeded"
"5/28/98 5:03:19 AM","mca","adReason=13","Buyers","Address","123
Main","123 Main, Suite 501"
"5/28/98 5:03:33 AM","mca","Logout","Succeeded"
```

That's all there is to it!

Summary

Today, you learned several methods you can use to increase the level of security for your Visual Basic database applications. You learned about the limitations of using the Microsoft Access SYSTEM security file and database encryption.

You also learned how to use the SECURITY Library that was shipped with this book to add user login and logout, permission checking, action auditing, and field-level change auditing to your Visual Basic database applications.

Best of all, you have the source code for the SECURITY Library so you can modify it and add this new library to all your future Visual Basic database applications.

Quiz

1. What are the disadvantages and limitations of using the Microsoft Access SYSTEM.MDA file to secure a database?

2. What are the disadvantages of using data encryption to secure a database?

3. What is the difference between application security and database security?

4. What are the two main features of a good application security scheme?

5. Can application security schemes prevent unauthorized access to data by tools such as Visdata and Data Manager?

6. Why would you use an access rights security scheme in your application?

7. Why add audit trails to an application?

Exercise

Assume that you are a systems developer for a large corporation. Your company has had a problem keeping track of the fixed assets (desks, chairs, computers) in one of its divisions. Your manager has asked you to develop a system to help manage the tracking of these fixed assets.

These assets are a large portion of the net worth of this organization. Therefore, management wants to keep track of any changes made to the items in this database. You decide that the best way to assist them in their efforts is to place an audit log in your application.

Use the skills you developed in this chapter to modify the project built in this chapter to construct a fixed asset tracking system. Follow these guidelines in the construction of this project:

- Use Data Manager to create a new database for fixed assets. Name this database Exer21.MDB and add a table called Assets. Include the following fields in this table:

Field	Type	Length
AssetID	TEXT	12
Description	TEXT	40
Cost	CURRENCY	
DateAcq	DATE/TIME	
SerialNo	TEXT	20
Department	TEXT	10

- Be sure to also add the secAccess and secUsers tables to the MDB to provide database security. Build a user with complete access rights called USERA with a password of USERA. Populate the rights table as shown in the previous chapter examples.

- Build a form to enter and edit the data records for this table. Use an ADO data control to manage the records. Use the default (Text1, Text2, and so on) for text field's Name property. Set the Name property of the form to frmCH21Ex. Make this the first form displayed after the login process.

- Make your system write to an audit log any time a user logs in or out and any time a record is changed. Include Assets as the name of the changed object, the user who made the change, and the AssetID of the changed record in the log. Use the same log as used by the login and logout routine. (*Hint:* Use the Data Changed event.)

21

WEEK 3

In Review

The third and final week of this book covered several very important topics. This week's work focused on database issues you encounter when you develop database applications for multiple users or multiple sites. To begin the week, you learned the five rules of data normalization and how applying those rules can improve the speed, accuracy, and integrity of your databases.

You learned about Visual Basic database locking schemes for the database, table, and page level. You also learned the advantages and limitations of adding cascading updates and deletes to your database relationship definitions. You learned how to use Visual Basic keywords `BeginTrans`, `CommitTrans`, and `Rollback` to improve database integrity and processing speed during mass updates.

You were introduced to the Remote Data Control and the Remote Data Objects. You learned to use these tools to attach to RDBMS. You learned the properties, methods, and events of these useful tools.

You learned how to attach to external data sources using DAO and ADO. You learned the advantages and disadvantages of attaching data and the prescribed way to build Visual Basic 6 database applications.

You learned how to distribute data across multiple sites by using database replication. You learned how to create a Design Master and replicas and how to synchronize data changes to a member of a replica set. You also learned how not to distribute specified data tables during the synchronization process.

In the final lesson, you learned how to create application-level security schemes, such as user login and logout, program-level access rights, and audit trails to keep track of critical application operations.

Day 15: Database Normalization

On Day 15, you learned how to improve database integrity and access speed using the five rules of data normalization:

- *Rule 1: Eliminate repeating groups.*

    If you have a set of fields that have the same name followed by a number (Skill1, Skill2, Skill3, and so forth), remove these repeating groups, create a new table for the repeating data, and relate it to the key field in the first table.

- *Rule 2: Eliminate redundant data.*

    Don't store the same data in two locations. This can lead to update and delete errors. If equivalent data elements are entered in two fields, remove the second data element, create a new master table with the element and its partner as a key field, and then place the key field as a relationship in the locations that formerly held both data elements.

- *Rule 3: Eliminate columns not dependent on keys.*

    If you have data elements that are not directly related to the primary key of the table, these elements should be removed to their own data table. Store only data elements that are directly related to the primary key of the table. This particularly includes derived data or other calculations.

- *Rule 4: Isolate independent multiple relationships.*

    Use this rule to improve database design when you are dealing with more than one one-to-many relationship in the database. Before you add a new field to a table, ask yourself whether this field is really dependent upon the other fields in the table. If not, create a new table with the independent data.

- *Rule 5: Isolate related multiple relationships.*

    Use this rule to improve database design when you are dealing with more than one many-to-many relationship in the database. If you have database rules that require multiple references to the same field or sets of fields, isolate the fields into smaller tables and construct one or more link tables that contain the required constraints that enforce database integrity.

Day 16: Multiuser Considerations

On Day 16, you learned about the three important challenges that face every database programmer writing multiuser applications:

- Database locking schemes
- Using cascading updates and deletes to maintain database integrity
- Using database transactions to provide commit/rollback options for major updates to your database

You learned that there are three levels of locking available to Visual Basic programs:

- *The database level.* You can use the Exclusive property of the data control or the second parameter of the OpenDatabase method to lock the entire database. Use this option when you need to perform work that affects multiple database objects (such as tables, queries, indexes, relations, and so on).
- *The table level.* You can set the Options property of the data control to 3 or the third parameter of the OpenRecordset method to dbDenyRead+dbDenyWrite to lock the entire table for your use only. Use this option when you need to perform work that affects multiple records in a single table (for example, increasing the sales price on all items in the inventory table).
- *The page level.* Microsoft Jet automatically performs page-level locking whenever you use the data control to edit and save a record, or whenever you use Visual Basic code to perform the Edit/AddNew and Update/CancelUpdate methods. You can use the LockEdits property of the Recordset to set the page locking to pessimistic (to perform locking at edit time) or optimistic (to perform locking only at update time).

You learned how to use Visual Basic to enforce referential integrity and automatically perform cascading updates or deletes to related records. You learned that there are times when it is not advisable to establish cascading deletes (for example, do not use cascading deletes when the base table is a validation list and the foreign table is a master).

Finally, you learned how to use database transactions to protect your database during extended, multitable operations. You learned how to use the BeginTrans, CommitTrans, and Rollback methods of the workspace object. And you learned some of the advantages and limitations of transaction processing.

Day 17: Using the Remote Data Control and the RDO Model

On Day 17, you learned about two alternate methods for accessing remote data. You learned that you can use the Remote Data Control to create simple data entry forms with data-bound controls. You also learned to use the Remote Data Objects to create Visual Basic 6.0 programs that can access data from a remote RDBMS.

Along with the details of the Remote Data Control and the Remote Data Objects, you also learned some of the basics of remote data access in general:

- *Cursor drivers.* These are the tools that manage the location of the Recordset pointer in a dataset. You learned you can use client-side or server-side cursor drivers with RDC/RDO connections.
- *Dataset types.* You learned there are a number of dataset types available to you when you connect to remote data sources, including forward-only/read-only sets, static sets, keysets, and dynamic sets.
- *Lock types.* You learned there are several lock types you can use when accessing data from your remote data source. You can use ConcurrentLock sets that perform locks as soon as you receive the data rows, or you can use several versions of optimistic locking that attempt to lock the rows only when you update them.

You also learned the details of the following Microsoft Remote Data Objects:

- The rdoEngine object is the top-level data engine used to access remote data.
- The rdoEnvironment object is the RDO equivalent of the Microsoft Jet Workspace object.
- The rdoConnection object is the RDO equivalent of the Microsoft Jet Database object.
- The rdoResultset object is the RDO equivalent of the Microsoft Jet Recordset object.
- The rdoTable object is the RDO version of the Microsoft Jet Table object.
- The rdoColumn object is the RDO version of the Microsoft Jet Field object.
- The rdoQuery object is the RDO version of the Microsoft Jet QueryDef object.
- The rdoParameters object is a special collection of query parameters for the rdoQuery object.

Day 18: Using the ActiveX Data Objects (ADO)

On Day 18, you learned some of the basics of the ADO model and how it can be used in your Visual Basic programs. You also learned how to use the new ADO Data Control to build simple data-bound forms. Finally, you built a Visual Basic 6.0 application that shows how to use the ADO model in code to create connection objects, command objects, and recordset objects.

You learned that the ADO model uses OLE DB as the interface between your Visual Basic programs and the data storage. You also learned about a handful of special properties of the ADO object model.

Finally, you learned how to get a list of tables and fields from ADO data stores and how to inspect the various recordset behaviors supported by a data connection.

Day 19: Attaching to Databases

On Day 19, you learned about attaching external data and using the attachment in your database applications. You learned that attachments to external data yield the following partial list of benefits:

- Data needs to be maintained in only one source.
- There are reduced training needs because users don't have to learn multiple applications.
- Data is consistently maintained throughout the enterprise by RDBMS database triggers.

With the advantages of attachments come some major disadvantages—including, but not limited to, the following:

- Static data is sometimes preferable, such as in financial reporting processes.
- The application is slowed by having to handle the overhead of the attachment.
- Attachments create new problems, such as connectivity, security, and file locking.

You learned how easy it is to use Visdata to create an external attachment. You learned how to use a Visdata attachment to build a Master/Detail form.

You learned how to use DAO to attach to a data source. DAO requires you to open a database and create a TableDef to define a connection. The `Connect` and `SourceTableName` properties of the TableDef object are then used to establish the connection.

Finally, you learned that ADO is the prescribed method to connect to data sources. ADO is fast and easy to use. You learned that in order to create a Master/Detail form, you simply need to build a Data Environment and then drag a parent/child relationship onto a form or Data Report.

Day 20: Database Replication

Day 20 focused on database replication. In database replication terminology, the main or central database is referred to as the Design Master. A copy of the Design Master is referred to as the replica. The combination of the Design Master and all replicas is referred to as the *replica set*. Database replication is the process of synchronizing data so that it is the same across all members of the replica set.

Database replication is a good tool to use in the development of systems deployed across a WAN or to remote users. Replication can also be used to make copies of databases that cannot be shut down. Replication is also good for creating reporting databases and data marts.

Do not use database replication when a centralized data storage facility can be used, such as a Web-enabled application. Also, don't use replication in heavily transaction-oriented applications, or in applications where up-to-the minute accuracy is of paramount importance.

Tables, fields, and properties are added to a database when it is made a Design Master. The addition of these items is necessary to track changes to data and to facilitate the synchronization between members of the replica set. These additions, however, consume additional physical hard drive space.

Creating and changing the Replicable property of a database to T creates a Design Master. After the Design Master is created, you can use the `Make Replica` method to make copies of it. Finally, you use the `Synchronize` method to replicate data changes to members of the replica set. Data synchronization is the act of copying data changes from one member of a replica set to another.

The `Synchronize` method can be used to import data changes, export data changes, perform "two-way" data changes, and even perform data exchanges over the Internet.

Synchronization errors occur when two members of a replica set try to synchronize records that both have changed. Errors may also occur during the synchronization process when design changes are made to a database that are violated by replicas prior to synchronization of the changes. Violation of referential integrity can be encountered by a replica that added records to its database that uses validation records deleted in another replica. Record locking in a multiuser environment can also cause synchronization errors.

There are four topologies for the synchronization of replicas: star, linear, ring, and fully connected. The star is the most common, but like all the other topologies it has certain strengths and weaknesses.

There may be times when you do not want to replicate objects contained in one database to other members of the replica set. If such is the case, use the KeepLocal method before you create the Design Master. This method keeps the object from being copied to other replica set members.

Day 21: Securing Your Database Applications

In your final lesson in this book, you learned several methods that can improve user and application-level security for your Visual Basic database applications. You learned about the limitations of using the Microsoft Access SYSTEM security file and database encryption.

This lesson also showed you how you can add application-level security to your Visual Basic programs by adding user login/logout routines and creating a user access rights scheme for your applications. In this lesson, you designed and implemented an OLE Server DLL library that you can use for all your Visual Basic applications, and you created several screens for maintaining user lists and managing access rights for each user.

You also learned how to add an audit trail option to your programs. You added routines to a new OLE Server DLL library that logs all critical user activity to an audit trail file, including user logins, database modifications, and all critical program operations, such as running reports or processing mass database updates.

APPENDIX

Answers to Quizzes and Exercises

Day 1, "Database Programming Basics"

Answers to Day 1 Quiz

1. The two data control properties you must set when you link a form to a database are the `DatabaseName` property and the `RecordSource` property.

2. Set the `Caption` property of the data control to display a meaningful name between the record pointer arrows.

3. You must set the `DataSource` property of the input control to the data table, and the `DataField` property of the input control to the field name in the data table.

4. You need only one line of Visual Basic code (not including the `Sub...End Sub` statements) to add delete functionality to a data entry form when using the Visual Basic data control. An example of this code is

```
datTitles.Recordset.Delete   ' delete the current record
```

5. Select either the Save Changes or Prompt to Save Changes option from the Program Starts environmental variable option group. This can be found by selecting the menu option Tools | Options and then selecting the Environment tab. After one of these choices is selected, you save, or will be prompted to save, your project each time you run it.

6. The three main building blocks of relational databases are data fields, data records, and data tables.

7. The smallest building block in a relational database is the data field.

8. A data record is a collection of related data fields.

9. The main role of a primary key in a data table is to maintain the internal integrity of a data table.

10. A data table can have any number of foreign keys defined. It can, however, have only one primary key defined.

11. There are only two values that can be stored in a BOOLEAN data field: –1 (true) and 0 (false).

12. The highest value that can be stored in a BYTE field is 255. Visual Basic allows users to enter up to 32767 without reporting an error, but any value higher than 255 is truncated to a single-byte value.

13. Any attempt to edit and update a counter field results in a Visual Basic error.

14. The CURRENCY data type can store up to four places to the right of the decimal. Any data beyond the fourth place is truncated by Visual Basic without reporting an error.

15. You can use the International applet from the Windows Control Panel to determine the display format of DATE data fields.

Answers to Day 1 Exercises

1. While in design mode, select the form by clicking anywhere on the form that doesn't have a control. Press F4 and select the Caption property. Type The Titles Program and press Enter. Note that the title appears on the title bar of the form as you type.

2. Complete the following steps to build an Exit button:

   - Double-click the Command Button control on the Visual Basic toolbox to add a new button to the form.
   - Set the Name property to cmdExit for the new button.
   - Drag the new button to align it with the Add and Delete buttons.

- Set the `Caption` property to `E&xit`.
- Enter the following code in the `cmdExit_Click` procedure:
  ```
  Private Sub cmdExit_Click()
  End
  End Sub
  ```
- Save your changes and execute your program.
- Click the Exit button to stop the program.

3. Modify the `cmdAdd_Click` procedure as shown in the following to set the focus on the ISBN field when the Add button is pressed:
```
Private Sub cmdAdd_Click()
datTitles.Recordset.AddNew   ' Add a new record to the table
txtISBN.SetFocus  ' Set the focus to the txtISBN control
End Sub
```

4A. There are three records in the table.

4B. The SSN (Social Security Number) would make an excellent primary key for this table because it would be unique for all records entered.

4C. The answer to part C appears in the following table:

Field	Data Type	Visual Basic Type
SSNo	Text	String
Last	Text	String
First	Text	String
Age	Byte	Integer
City	Text	String
St	Text	String
Comments	Memo	String

5. Perform the following steps to add the check box: First, double-click the check box control. Second, position the check box in an aesthetically pleasing position on the form. Third, set these properties:

Property	Setting
DataSource	datFieldTypes
DataField	BOOLEAN
Name	chkBoolean

Run your program and check the BOOLEAN box. Notice that nothing happens to the BOOLEAN text field. Now move to the subsequent record, and then return. You should see –1 displayed in the BOOLEAN text field.

This example shows how to use a check box to enter values into fields. Your program can now reference this field and get the value as –1 (yes) or 0 (no), which are the only two values that can be in a BOOLEAN type data field.

Day 2, "Visual Basic Database Access Objects"

Answers to Day 2 Quiz

1. Visual Basic database objects are dataset-oriented. You work with a set of records at one time, not one record at a time as you would with a record-oriented database.

2. The Dynaset is the most common Visual Basic data object. It is the object created when you open a form with a data control.

3. Dynasets use minimal RAM resources. Visual Basic stores only the pointer to the records in the underlying table, not the actual data.

4. The weaknesses of using Dynasets include the following:

   - You can't specify an index with a Dynaset. Dynasets are only a portion of the underlying table, whereas indexes are for the entire table.

   - You can't use the SEEK method with Dynasets.

   - Errors can occur if records in the underlying table have been altered or deleted between the time that the Dynaset is created and the time that a record is updated.

5. Table objects allow you to use indexes and the SEEK method.

6. You do not use the Refresh method with the Table data object because this object is the one that links you directly to the underlying data itself.

7. A Snapshot stores all the data in the workstation's memory, whereas the Dynaset stores only pointers to the data. The Snapshot is also read-only and can't be updated. A Dynaset can be updated.

8. You use the Database and TableDefs objects to extract field and table names from a database.

Answers to Day 2 Exercises

1. You use the Dynaset-type data object, because this will give you both read and write capabilities and consume minimal workstation memory. The code might look like this:

```
Private Sub cmdOpenDynaset_Click()
    '
    Dim objDB As Database
    Dim objRS As Recordset
    '
    Dim strDBName As String
    Dim strDataSet As String
    '
    strDBName = "c:\data\acctpay.mdb"
    strDataSet = "Vendors"
    '
    Set objDB = OpenDatabase(strDBName)
    Set objRS = objDB.OpenRecordset(strDataSet, dbOpenDynaset)
    '
End Sub
```

2. The Snapshot data object should be used for reporting purposes because it does not change after it is created. This prevents data used in your report from being updated while your report is generated. Snapshots also enable you to collect a subset of the data instead of opening the entire dataset. Your code might look like this:

```
Private Sub cmdOpenSnapshot_Click()
    '
    Dim objDB As Database
    Dim objRS As Recordset
    '
    Dim strDBName As String
    Dim strDataSet As String
    '
    strDBName = "c:\data\acctpay.mdb"
    strDataSet = "SELECT * FROM Vendors WHERE OverDueAmount > 1000"
    '
    Set objDB = OpenDatabase(strDBName)
    Set objRS = objDB.OpenRecordset(strDataSet, dbsnapshot)
    '
End Sub
```

3. You use the Table object to give you instant information about each record in the collection as it is changed. Your code might look like this:

```
Private Sub cmdOpenTable_Click()
    '
    Dim objDB As Database
    Dim objRS As Recordset
    '
```

```
        Dim strDBName As String
        Dim strDataSet As String
        '
        strDBName = "c:\data\acctpay.mdb"
        strDataSet = "Vendors"
        '
        Set objDB = OpenDatabase(strDBName)
        Set objRS = objDB.OpenRecordset(strDataSet, dbOpenTable)
        '
    End Sub
```

Day 3, "Creating Data Entry Forms with Bound Controls"

Answers to Day 3 Quiz

1. You can establish a database for a data control by setting the `DatabaseName` property of the data control to the name of the database (including the path), or to a defined variable that points to the database. For example, to attach the data control `Data1` to a Microsoft Access database `C:\DATAPATH\XYZ.MDB`, you can enter the following:

    ```
    Data1.DatabaseName = "C:\DATAPATH\XYZ.MDB"
    ```

2. You use the `RecordSource` property to establish the name of a table for a data control in Visual Basic. For example, to set the data control `Data1` to a table of vendors in an accounts payable application, you can type the following:

    ```
    Data1.RecordSource = "Vendors"
    ```

    It is better form, however, to assign the `RecordSource` to a variable that has been defined and points to the data table. Here's an example:

    ```
    Dim cTable as String' Declare the variable
    cTable = "Vendors" ' Establish the name of the table
    Data1.RecordSource = cTable ' Set the data control
    Data1.Refresh ' Update the data control
    ```

3. The `UpdateControls` method takes information from the underlying database table and places it in the form controls; whereas the `UpdateRecord` method takes information entered into the form controls and updates the attached table.

4. Check boxes should be bound only to Boolean fields and can produce only values of 0 (No or False) and -1 (Yes or True).

5. You use the `DataField` property to bind a control to a table field.

6. The standard color for a Windows 95 form is light gray. Input areas are white. Display-only controls are light gray. Labels are left-aligned.

Answers to Day 3 Exercises

1. You should enter the following code as a new procedure in the general declarations section:

```
Sub OpenDB()
 'Declare the variable for the name of the database
Dim cDBName as String
 'Assign the variable to a database, including the path
cdbName = App.Path + " \Students.MDB"
 'Set the name of the database used by the data control
Data1.DatabaseName = cDBName
 'Refresh and update the data control
Data1.Refresh
End Sub
```

2. Your code should look like this:

```
Sub OpenDB()
 'Declare the variable for the name of the database
Dim cDBName as String
 'Declare the variable for the table
Dim cTable as String
 'Assign the variable to a database, including the path
cdbName = App.Path + "\Students.MDB"
 'Assign the variable to the appropriate table
cTable = "Addresses"
 'Set the name of the database used by the data control
Data1.DatabaseName = cDBName
 'Set the name of the table used by the data control
Data1.RecordSource = cTable
 'Refresh and update the data control
Data1.Refresh
End Sub
```

3. Your code should look like this:

```
Sub OpenDB()
Dim cDBName as String
Dim cTable as String
Dim cField1 as String
Dim cField2 as String
Dim cField3 as String
Dim cField4 as String
Dim cField5 as String
 'Assign variables
cdbName = App.Path + "\Students.MDB"
```

```
cTable = "Addresses"
cField1 = "StudentID"
cField2 = "Address"
cField3 = "City"
cField4 = "State"
cField5 = "Zip"
 'Set the data control properties
Data1.DatabaseName = cDBName
Data1.RecordSource = cTable
 'Bind the text fields
txtStudentID.DataField = cField1
txtAddress.DataField = cField2
txtCity.DataField = cField3
txtState.DataField = cField4
txtZip.DataField = cField5
 'Refresh and update the data control
Data1.Refresh
End Sub
```

Day 4, "Input Validation"

Answers to Day 4 Quiz

1. Input validation occurs as the data is entered, whereas error trapping occurs after the data is entered. Input validation is used to guarantee uniformity in the data that is saved.

2. The KeyPress event occurs whenever a key is pressed.

3. No, a validation list can be entered in any order.

4. The txtUpper field is being trimmed of trailing and leading spaces and then tested to see whether the length is anything other than zero. This code is used to test whether any values are entered into a field.

5. Conditional field validation should be performed at the form level. User may skip around on the form using the mouse, thus making field-level conditional validation impractical.

6. Validation lists should be loaded early in the Form_Load or Form_Initialize events.

7. The first section is the format of a positive number. The second section is the format of a negative number. The third section is the format of a zero value. Each section is separated by a semicolon (;).

Answers to Day 4 Exercises

1. Here's a keypress filter that allows control codes and any alpha character. All alpha characters are converted to uppercase; any others are rejected:

```
Private Sub Text1_KeyPress(KeyAscii As Integer)
'
    If KeyAscii > 26 Then
        If KeyAscii >= Asc("A") And KeyAscii <= Asc("z") Then
            KeyAscii = Asc(UCase(Chr(KeyAscii)))
        Else
            KeyAscii = 0
        End If
    End If
'
End Sub
```

2. Place the following code in the Format property of the MaskedEdit control:

```
#,##0.00;-#,##0.00
```

3. Here's an example of validating a field input before exiting the form:

```
Private Sub cmdOK_Click()
'
    If Len(Trim(txtDate)) = 0 Then
        MsgBox "You must enter a valid Date before you exit this
form"
        txtDate.SetFocus
    Else
        Unload Me
    End If
'
End Sub
```

4. The following code fills a combo box with names at runtime. You must first set the Sorted property of the control to TRUE in design-time:

```
Public Sub FillEmployees()
'
    ' set the Sorted Property = TRUE
    '
    With cboEmployees
        .AddItem "Mitchell"
        .AddItem "Albright"
        .AddItem "Cox"
    End With
'
End Sub
```

Day 5, "Writing Reports For Visual Basic 6 Applications"

Answers to Day 5 Quiz

1. A Command actually identifies the data fields that can be placed on your data report.

2. You must set the DataSource (the Data Environment) and DataMember (the Data Environment's Command) property of the Data Report in order for it to know what data is used in the report.

3. Row spacing is determined by the amount of empty space left above and below the fields in the Detail Section of the Data Report.

4. SQL statements can be used in a data report. In fact, the use of SQL statements is probably the best way to define a Command.

5. Use the SHOW method of the data report to display the report to the screen. After the report is displayed to the screen, it can be printed or exported. The structure of the command is <REPORT NAME>.SHOW.

6. You use the ORDER BY clause in the SELECT statements of a data report to sort records on a report.

7. The DataMember must be changed to the name of the grouping rather than the command for the grouping to display properly. Be very careful, because setting the wrong DataMember often does not yield an error message, even if incorrect values are displayed.

8. No, an aggregate function can be created only to return the sum, average, minimum, maximum, standard deviation, and count of a record set. There are no capabilities of displaying the median value of a record set.

9. No, data can be exported only into HTML and Text formats. You can, however, export the information into the Text format and then import that into Microsoft Excel.

Answer to Day 5 Exercise

Perform the following steps to complete this project:

1. Create a new Data Project.

2. Build the connection. Use the BOOKS6 connection created in this chapter.

3. Add a command that uses the Authors table.

4. Add a child command to the Authors table command. This child should use the

Titles table as its source. The two tables should relate on the AUID field.

5. Add a child command to the previous child. This command should use the Publishers table as the data source. It should be related to the Titles table by the PubID field.

6. Set the `DataSource` of the data report to the connection.

7. Set the `DataMember` of the report to the Authors table command.

8. Right-click on the report and select Retrieve Structure.

9. Drag the AUID and Name fields from the Authors table, the Title and PubID from the Titles table, and the Name field from the Publishers table. This will give you the Author, that Author's title, and the name of the publisher.

10. Format the report appropriately. Add a report header, page header, and report footer, at a minimum.

11. Set the startup object in the `DataProject` properties to the data report you just created.

12. Run the report and make any necessary adjustments.

Day 6, "Using the Visdata Program"

Answers to Day 6 Quiz

1. The Visdata project can be found in the `Samples\Visdata` subdirectory on the Visual Basic CD-ROM.

2. To copy a table, simply select the table from the Table/Queries window, press the alternate mouse button, and select Copy Structure.

3. You need to refresh the Tables/Queries window each time you enter an SQL statement to create a new table.

4. You can open and edit Excel spreadsheets in Visdata.

5. The `Properties` object in the Database window shows the complete name and path of the database, the version of the database engine in use, the connect property, the login time-out, the Microsoft Access version, the replica ID, and several other update settings.

6. You compact databases to remove empty spaces where deleted records used to reside and to reorganize any defined indexes that are stored in the database.

7. You can compact a database onto itself with the File|Compact MDB command. This action is not advisable, however, because problems can occur during the compacting process.

8. You cannot modify a table's structure after data has been entered. You must delete

all records before you can modify the structure.

9. You can save queries in Visdata for future use. You do this by building a query with the Query Builder and saving the results or by entering an SQL statement and saving its resultset.

10. Visdata can export data in the following formats:

- Microsoft Access (Jet)
- dBASE IV, III
- FoxPro 2.6, 2.5, 2.0
- Paradox 4.*x*, 3.*x*
- Btrieve
- Excel 5, 4, 3
- Text
- ODBC

11. You can use the Files | Compact Database option to convert existing Microsoft Access 2.0 databases to newer versions by selecting the new data format at the Compact Database submenu. Do not do this, however, because this is not the same converter used by Microsoft Access, and some objects in the database will be unusable by Access after the conversion.

Answers to Day 6 Exercises

1. To create the new database, select File | New | Microsoft Access | Version 7.0 MDB. Next, enter the path and the name of the database and save.

2. Click the alternate mouse button in the Database window and select New from the menu that appears to build the new table. Insert the name tblCustomers in the Table Name field. Next, select Add to insert the fields. Enter the name, type, and size for each field, clicking OK after you complete each one. When all fields are entered, select Close. When you return to the Table Structure form, select Build Table.

3. To build the primary key, first make sure that tblCustomers is highlighted in the DatabaseQueries window and select Design from the menu that appears when you click the alternate mouse button in the Database window. Select the Add Index button from the Table Structure window. Enter the name of the primary key (PKtblCustomers) and click the ID field in the Available Fields list box. Make sure that the Primary and Unique check box have been checked. Finally, click OK to build the primary key index.

4. Select the tblCustomers table from the Database window and click the alternate

A

mouse button. Select Design from the menu that appears. Next, select Print Structure in the bottom-right corner of the Table Structure window.

5. To enter records, first double-click tblCustomers. You can enter data in any Form type you want; however, you can only enter Notes data in the Grid form.

6. To copy a table structure, highlight the table, click the alternate mouse button, and select Copy Structure. Leave the Target Connect String empty and make sure that neither the Copy Indexes nor the Copy Data check boxes are checked. Enter the table name tblVendors when prompted for the name of the new table. Select the OK button to create the table.

After the table is copied, you should then go into the table design and add a primary key. Build this index the same way you built the primary key for the tblCustomers table.

7. To export, select File | Import/Export. Select the tblCustomers table and then press Export Table(s). Next choose the text format as the data source and click OK. You are then prompted to enter a path and a name. Select Save, and the file is created.

Review the file. Notice that empty fields in a record are denoted by the use of two commas (, ,).

Day 7, "Selecting Data with SQL"

Answers to Day 7 Quiz

1. SQL stands for Structured Query Language. You pronounce SQL by saying the three individual letters ("ess-que-ell"). It is not pronounced "sequel."

2. Use the SELECT_FROM statement to select information from table fields.

3. Use the asterisk (*) in a SELECT_FROM statement to select all the fields in a data table. For example, to select all fields in a table of customers, you can enter the following SQL statement:

```
SELECT * FROM Customers
```

4. Use the ORDER BY clause to sort the data you display. For example, to sort the data from quiz answer 3 by a field contained within the table CustomerID, you enter the following:

```
SELECT * FROM Customers ORDER BY CustomerID
```

5. A WHERE clause can be used to limit the records that are selected by the SQL statement, as well as to link two or more tables in a resultset.

6. Use the AS clause to rename a field heading. For example, issue the following SQL

statement to rename the field CustomerID in the Customers table to `Customer`:

```
SELECT CustomerID AS Customer FROM Customers
```

7. SQL aggregate functions are a core set of functions available in all SQL-compliant systems used to return computed results on numeric data fields. The functions available through Jet include `AVG`, `COUNT`, `SUM`, `MAX`, and `MIN`.

8. Chief among the drawbacks of using Visual Basic functions in your SQL statement is the loss of portability to other database engines. There is also a slight performance reduction when Visual Basic functions are used in your SQL statement.

9. Both the `DISTINCT` and `DISTINCTROW` clauses extract unique records. The `DISTINCTROW` command looks at the entire record, whereas `DISTINCT` looks at the fields you associate with it.

10. You should always use the `ORDER BY` clause when you use the `TOP[]` or `TOP[]` `PERCENT` clauses. The `ORDER BY` clause ensures that your data is sorted appropriately to enable the `TOP[]` clauses to select the appropriate data.

11. The three types of joins found in Microsoft Access Jet SQL are `INNER`, `LEFT`, and `RIGHT`. An `INNER JOIN` is used to create updatable resultsets whose records have an exact match in both tables. The `LEFT JOIN` is used to return an updatable resultset that returns all records in the first table in your SQL statement and any records in the second table that have matching column values. The `RIGHT JOIN` is just the opposite of the `LEFT JOIN`; it returns all records in the second table of your SQL statement and any records in the first table that have matching column values.

12. `UNION` queries are used to join tables that contain similar information but are not linked through a foreign key. An example of a `UNION` query would be listing all your company's customers and suppliers located in the state of Iowa. There won't be any foreign key relationships between a data table of supplier's information and a table of customer's information. Both tables will, however, contain fields for names, addresses, and phone numbers. This information can be joined through a `UNION` query and displayed as one result.

Answers to Day 7 Exercises

1. `SELECT * FROM CustomerMaster`

2. `SELECT InvoiceNo, CustomerID AS Account, Description, Amount FROM OpenInvoice`

3. `SELECT InvoiceNo, CustomerID AS Account, Description, Amount FROM OpenInvoice ORDER BY CustomerID, InvoiceNo`

4. `SELECT * FROM Suppliers WHERE City LIKE ("New York *") and State =`

"NY"

5. SELECT CustomerMaster.CustomerType, CustomerMaster.Name,
   CustomerMaster.Address, CustomerMaster.City, CustomerMaster.State,
   CustomerMaster.Zip FROM CustomerMaster WHERE
   CustomerMaster.CustomerType = "ABC"

6. SELECT CustomerID, Name FROM CustomerMaster WHERE Left(Name,3) =
   "AME"

7. SELECT DISTINCT OpenInvoice.CustomerID, CustomerMaster.Name FROM
   OpenInvoice INNER JOIN CustomerMaster ON OpenInvoice.CustomerID =
   CustomerMaster.CustomerID ORDER BY OpenInvoice.CustomerID

8. SELECT TOP 5 * FROM OpenInvoice ORDER BY Amount Desc

9. SELECT Name, Phone FROM CustomerMaster WHERE State = "OHIO" UNION
   SELECT Name, Phone FROM Suppliers WHERE State = "Ohio"

Day 8, "Visual Basic and the DAO Jet Database Engine"

Answers to Day 8 Quiz

1. A property is data within an object that describes its characteristics, whereas a method is a procedure that can be performed upon an object. You set a property and invoke a procedure.

2. The top level DAO object is the DBEngine object.

3. You use the RepairDatabase method to repair an MDB database. This command uses the following syntax:

   DBEngine.RepairDatabase databasename

4. The syntax for the CompactDatabase method is the following:

   DBEngine.CompactDatabase olddatabasename,newdatabasename, locale,
   options

5. Visual Basic creates a default workspace if you fail to define one when you open a database.

6. The OpenRecordset method can create three types of datasets: Table, Dynaset, and Snapshot.

7. The CreateTableDef method builds a new table in an existing MDB database. The

syntax of this method is the following:

```
ObjTableDef = ObjDatabase.CreateTableDef(tablename)
```

8. You can determine the data type of a database table column using the `Type` property of the `Field` object.

9. You can use only the `Index` object to create indexes for MDB format databases.

10. The QueryDef object stores a Structured Query Language (SQL) statement. Using QueryDefs to collect records from MDB databases into recordsets is slightly faster than using plaintext SQL.

Answer to Day 8 Exercise

The following code builds two tables, establishes their primary keys, and defines a relationship between the two tables:

```
Public Sub CreateNewDB()
    '
    On Error Resume Next
    '
    ' *** objects needed
    Dim objDB As Database
    Dim objTD As TableDef
    Dim objFLD As Field
    Dim objIDX As Index
    Dim objREL As Relation
    '
    ' *** variables needed
    Dim strDBName As String
    Dim strCustTbl As String
    Dim strCustTypesTbl As String
    Dim strCustIdx As String
    Dim strCustTypesIdx As String
    Dim strRelName As String
    '
    ' *** init variables
    strDBName = App.Path & "\newdb.mdb"
    strCustTbl = "Customers"
    strCustTypesTbl = "CustomerTypes"
    strCustIdx = "PKCustomers"
    strCustTypesIdx = "PKCustTypes"
    strRelName = "RELCustType"
    '
    ' *** build mdb database
    Kill strDBName
    Set objDB = CreateDatabase(strDBName, dbLangGeneral)
    '
    ' *** create customer table
    Set objTD = objDB.CreateTableDef(strCustTbl)
```

```
'
' add fields
With objTD
    Set objFLD = .CreateField("CustomerID", dbText, 10)
    .Fields.Append objFLD
    Set objFLD = .CreateField("Name", dbText, 50)
    .Fields.Append objFLD
    Set objFLD = .CreateField("Address1", dbText, 50)
    .Fields.Append objFLD
    Set objFLD = .CreateField("Address2", dbText, 50)
    .Fields.Append objFLD
    Set objFLD = .CreateField("City", dbText, 25)
    .Fields.Append objFLD
    Set objFLD = .CreateField("StateProv", dbText, 25)
    .Fields.Append objFLD
    Set objFLD = .CreateField("PostalCode", dbText, 20)
    .Fields.Append objFLD
    Set objFLD = .CreateField("Phone", dbText, 20)
    .Fields.Append objFLD
    Set objFLD = .CreateField("CustomerType", dbText, 10)
    .Fields.Append objFLD
End With
'
' add primary key index
Set objIDX = objTD.CreateIndex(strCustIdx)
With objIDX
    .Primary = True
    .Required = True
    Set objFLD = objTD.CreateField("CustomerID")
    .Fields.Append objFLD
End With
objTD.Indexes.Append objIDX
'
' add table to database
objDB.TableDefs.Append objTD
'
' *** build customer types table
Set objTD = objDB.CreateTableDef(strCustTypesTbl)
'
' add fields
With objTD
    Set objFLD = .CreateField("CustomerType", dbText, 10)
    .Fields.Append objFLD
    Set objFLD = .CreateField("Description", dbText, 50)
    .Fields.Append objFLD
End With
'
' add primary key index
Set objIDX = objTD.CreateIndex(strCustIdx)
With objIDX
    .Primary = True
```

```
        .Required = True
        Set objFLD = objTD.CreateField("CustomerType")
        .Fields.Append objFLD
    End With
    objTD.Indexes.Append objIDX
    '
    ' add table to database
    objDB.TableDefs.Append objTD
    '
    ' *** build relationship
    Set objREL = objDB.CreateRelation(strRelName)
    With objREL
        .Table = strCustTypesTbl
        .ForeignTable = strCustTbl
        Set objFLD = .CreateField("CustomerType")
        objFLD.ForeignName = "CustomerType"
        .Fields.Append objFLD
    End With
    objDB.Relations.Append objREL
    '
    ' *** issue completion msg
    MsgBox "Database is built!"
    '
End Sub
```

Day 9, "Creating Database Programs with the Data Environment Designer"

Answers to Day 9 Quiz

1. Data Environment Designer

2. The two types of data objects are Data Connections to connect to databases and Data Commands to define recordsets.

3. True. This is a tricky question. The ADO model uses OLE DB for all its data store interface. There is, however, an OLE DB interface for accessing existing ODBC data drivers. You use this special OLE DB interface to access the ODBC-defined data.

4. False. It is actually much easier. This is because the DED allows you to use drag-and-drop methods to build the Textbox and Labels for a form. You *do* need to add code for handling recordset navigation and action items (add, delete, and so forth), but that can be handled with some reusable class objects.

5. Yes, you can use the object model created by the DED to directly access all the

parts of the Data Connection and recordsets. You can find this object model by selecting the View Code option in the DED.

6. The ADO `Find` method enables you to use only a single field in the find phrase. You cannot, for example, use the following phrase with the ADO Find:

```
"NAME='Mike' AND Size=13.
```

You can, however, create a Data Command that defines a special recordset that includes all the search fields in a single returned column.

7. False. You cannot use the `MSHFlexGrid` to create an updatable grid on the form. The `MSHFlexGrid` is a read-only grid. You can, however, listen for mouse-down events on the `MSHFlexGrid` and then pop up a complete user dialog for editing a member of the grid.

Answer to Day 9 Exercise

The first step is to add a Data Environment Designer to the project and set its name to `dePublishers`. Next, add a Data Connection to the designer called `cnnPublishers` that connects to the `BOOKS6.MDB` database.

Add two data commands to the designer. The first should be called `comPublishers`; it uses a Table database object that connects to the Publishers table. Then add another data command called `comPubsFind` that uses the following SQL statement:

```
SELECT PubID, Company FROM Publishers
```

Now you're ready to build the main data entry form. To do this, bring the default form up in the IDE beside the Data Environment Designer. Set its name to `frmPublishers` and drag the `comPublishers` data command over the form and drop it. This will add all the columns from the Publishers table to your form. Position the items to leave room for button bars at the top and bottom of the form.

Next, add a new form to the project to act as the Find dialog for the project. Set its name to `frmFind` and add an `MSHFlexGrid` to the form (you may need to load it from the Project|Components menu option first).

 Add the `ADOButtons.VBP` project (from the CD-ROM) to your IDE. Be sure to *add* the project, not *open* it. This will result in two projects available in the IDE. You should now see two new controls in your toolbox window. Drag the `ADONavBar` and the `ADOActionBar` from the toolbox onto your form.

Now you're ready to add code to the two forms in your project. First, add the following code to the frmFind form:

```
Option Explicit
```

```
Private Sub Form_Resize()
    '
    ' adjust grid and columns
    '
    With Me.MSHFlexGrid1
        .Left = 0
        .Top = 0
        .Height = Me.ScaleHeight
        .Width = Me.ScaleWidth
        .ColWidth(0) = .Width * 0.33
        .ColWidth(1) = .Width * 0.67
    End With
    '
End Sub

Private Sub MSHFlexGrid1_DblClick()
    '
    ' pass selected record to caller
    '
    With Me.MSHFlexGrid1
        If .Col = 0 Then
            frmPublishers.Key = .Text
            Me.Hide
        End If
    End With
    '
End Sub
```

Now bring the frmPublishers form up and add a command button named cmdFind next to the PubID field on the form. This will be used to call up the frmFind form. Add code to several events on the frmPublishers form. You also need to add a Public variable to support the frmFind form. Use the following code as a guide:

```
Option Explicit
'
' for find dialog
Public Key As String

Private Sub ADOActionBar1_Error(Number As Variant, Description As Variant,
➡Source As Variant)
    '
    MsgBox CStr(Number) & vbCrLf & Description & vbCrLf & Source,
    ➡vbCritical, "ADOActionBar Error!"
    '
End Sub

Private Sub ADONavBar1_Error(Number As Variant, Description As Variant,
➡Source As Variant)
    '
```

```
        MsgBox CStr(Number) & vbCrLf & Description & vbCrLf & Source, _
            vbCritical, "ADONavBar Error!"
        '
End Sub

Private Sub cmdFind_Click()
    '
    ' call find pop-up dialog
    '
    Me.Key = ""
    '
    frmFind.Show vbModal
    '
    If Me.Key <> "" Then
        With dePublishers.rscomPublishers
            .MoveFirst
            .Find "PubID='" & Me.Key & "'"
        End With
    End If
    '
    Unload frmFind
    '
End Sub

Private Sub Form_Load()
    '
    ADONavBar1.ADORecordset = dePublishers.rscomPublishers
    '
    With ADOActionBar1
        .ADORecordset = dePublishers.rscomPublishers
        .FormMode = Edit
    End With
    '
End Sub

Private Sub Form_Resize()
    '
    ' adjust custom ADO button controls
    '
    With Me.ADOActionBar1
        .Width = Me.ScaleWidth
        .Height = 600
        .Left = 0
        .Top = 0
    End With
    '
    With Me.ADONavBar1
        .Width = Me.ScaleWidth
        .Height = 600
```

A

```
        .Left = 0
        .Top = Me.ScaleHeight - 600
    End With
    '
End Sub
```

Finally, save and test your project!

Day 10, "Displaying Your Data with Graphs"

Answers to Day 10 Quiz

1. The use of charts and graphs in your Visual Basic database application offers the following advantages:

    - Visual representation of data is easier to understand than tables and lists.

    - Graphics offer a different view of the same data.

    - Graphics give your applications a polished appearance

2. The `ColumnCount` and `RowCount` properties of the `MSCHART` control determine how many columns and rows are in the dataset to be charted.

3. You must use a `VARIANT` type array to send data to the `MSCHART` control using the `ChartData` property.

4. The `EDITCOPY` method copies the current chart image from the `MSCHART` control to the Windows Clipboard object. The `EDITPASTE` method copies the current data from the Windows Clipboard object to the `MSCHART` control.

5. Enumerated data types are used to provide a "friendly" set of values for parameters of methods or properties. You use the `ENUM...END ENUM` construct to create enumerated data types.

Answer to Day 10 Exercise

Start a new VB6 Standard EXE project and add three command buttons on the form. Set their names to `cmdArea`, `cmdLine`, and `cmdBar`. Next, add the `GraphDLL.VBP` project to your IDE. Be sure to *add* the project, not *open* it. This will bring both projects into your IDE at the same time and make the `GraphDLL` available to your exercise.

Behind the `cmdArea_click` event, add the following code:

```
Public Sub cmdArea_Click()
    '
    Dim objChart As New DataGraph.Chart
    '
```

```
    With objChart
        .OLEDBProvider = "Microsoft.Jet.OLEDB.3.51"
        .DataSource = "i:\tysdbvb6\source\chap10\exercises\ch10ex.mdb"
        .SQLSelect = "SELECT Airline, SUM(Passengers) AS Seats FROM
        ➥Activity WHERE Month=1 GROUP BY Airline"
        .GraphFootnote = "Seats Sold"
        .GraphTitle = "Comparative Activity for Month 1"
        .GraphLegend = True
        .GraphType = gtArea
        .ShowGraph
    End With
    '
    Set objChart = Nothing
    '
End Sub
```

Behind the `cmdLine_click` event, add the following code:

```
Public Sub cmdLine_Click()
    '
    Dim objChart As New DataGraph.Chart

    With objChart
        .OLEDBProvider = "Microsoft.Jet.OLEDB.3.51"
        .DataSource = "i:\tysdbvb6\source\chap10\exercises\ch10ex.mdb"
        .SQLSelect = "SELECT SUM(Passengers) AS Seats FROM Activity GROUP
        ➥BY Month"
        .GraphFootnote = "Seats Sold"
        .GraphTitle = "Total Actvity By Month"
        .GraphLegend = True
        .GraphType = gtLine
        .ShowGraph
    End With
    '
    Set objChart = Nothing
    '
End Sub
```

Finally, add the following code behind the `cmdBar_click` event:

```
Public Sub cmdBar_Click()
    '
    Dim objChart As New DataGraph.Chart

    With objChart
        .OLEDBProvider = "Microsoft.Jet.OLEDB.3.51"
        .DataSource = "i:\tysdbvb6\source\chap10\exercises\ch10ex.mdb"
        .SQLSelect = "SELECT Passengers AS Seats FROM Activity WHERE
        ➥Airline='ABC' ORDER BY Month"
        .GraphFootnote = "Seats Sold"
        .GraphTitle = "Monthly Activity for ABC Airline"
        .GraphLegend = True
```

```
        .GraphType = gtBar
        .ShowGraph
    End With
    '
    Set objChart = Nothing
    '
End Sub
```

Save and test your project.

Day 11, "Data-Bound List Boxes, Grids, and Subforms"

Answers to Day 11 Quiz

1. Using a data-bound list or combo box increases the speed of data entry, gives you added control over data validation, and provides suggested values to use for entry.

2. You set the `RowSource` property to identify the data source for the list box.

3. The `BoundColumn` property sets the column that is saved in the new data record. Put another way, it's the field that is extracted from the source and placed in the destination. Remember that the bound column does not have to equal the `ListField` property of the control.

4. You set the `DataSource` property to the name of the dataset that should be updated by the contents of the data-bound list/combo box. You set the `DataField` property to identify the field in the dataset determined by the `DataSource` property that will be updated.

5. You must set the `AllowAddNew` property to `True` to permit users to add records. You must set the `AllowDelete` property to `True` to permit removal of records.

6. Use the `BeforeDelete` event to confirm deletion of records.

7. The column-level events of the data-bound grid control provide field-level validation functionality.

8. You would use the data-bound combo box, rather than the data-bound list box, when you want to allow the user to type the entry or when space on the data entry form is limited.

9. You use the ReBind method to refresh a data-bound grid.

10. Subforms are typically used to display data from two different data tables that are linked through a common key. For example, subforms can display invoice details of a customer linked by customer ID, or work orders that have been performed on a fixed asset linked by asset ID.

Answer to Day 11 Exercise

Complete the following steps to build this form:

1. Add a data control (Data1) and a data-bound list box to a new form.

2. Set the following properties of Data1:

   DatabaseName   C:\VB6\BIBLIO.MDB   Publishers
   (include appropriate path)
   RecordSource

3. Set the DataSource property to Data1 and the ListField property to Name for the data-bound list.

4. Add a second data control (Data2) and set its Database property to BIBLIO.MDB and its RecordSource property to Publishers.

5. Add text fields in an array to the form. Set their DataSource properties to Data2 and their DataField properties to their respective fields.

6. Add a third data control to the form. Set its DatabaseName to BIBLIO.MDB (include path) and its RecordSource property to Titles.

7. Set the Visible property of all three data controls to False.

8. Add a data-bound grid to the form. Set its DataSource property to Data3.

9. Load the dataset column names into the grid by selecting Retrieve Fields from the context menu of the DBGrid. Then select Properties from the context menu of the DBGrid and click the Columns tab. Make sure that the Visible checkbox is selected only for the Title, Year Published, and ISBN columns.

10. Use the context menu again on the DBGrid and select Edit. Resize the columns as needed.

11. Set the BoundColumn property of the data-bound list control to PubID. Blank out the DataField and DataSource properties.

12. Enter the following code in the DBList1_click event:

```
Private Sub DBList1_Click()

Dim cFind As String
```

```
cFind = "PubID=" + Trim(DBList1.BoundText)
Data2.Recordset.FindFirst cFind

End Sub
```

13. Enter the following code in the Data2_Reposition event:

```
Private Sub Data2_Reposition()

Dim cSQL As String

cSQL = "Select * from Titles WHERE PubID=" + Trim(Text1(0))

Data3.RecordSource = cSQL ' filter the data set
Data3.Refresh ' refresh the data control
DBGrid1.ReBind ' refresh the data grid

End Sub
```

14. Save and execute your program.

Day 12, "Creating Databases with SQL"

Answers to Day 12 Quiz

1. These are the benefits of using SQL to create and manage data tables:

   - SQL statements can serve as documentation for your table layouts.
   - It's easy to produce test or sample data tables with SQL statements.
   - You can easily load test data into new tables with SQL statements.
   - You can utilize SQL for multiple data platforms.

2. The syntax is

   CREATE TABLE TableName (Field1 TYPE(SIZE), Field2 TYPE(SIZE), _);

   You first enter CREATE TABLE, followed by the name of the table, and then the fields in parentheses. The field types and sizes (sizes apply to TEXT columns only) are entered after each field.

3. The default size of a Microsoft Jet TEXT field is 255 bytes.

4. You use the ALTER TABLE_ADD COLUMN statement to add a column to a table. The ALTER TABLE_ADD COLUMN statement uses the following format:

   ALTER TABLE <Name of Table> ADD COLUMN <Name of column> <Type> <Size>;

5. You use the DROP TABLE statement to remove a table from a database. The DROP

TABLE statement uses the following format:

```
DROP TABLE <Table Name>;
```

6. You create indexes to data tables with the `CREATE INDEX SQL` statement.

7. The following are the three forms of the `CONSTRAINT` clause:

- `PRIMARY KEY`
- `UNIQUE`
- `FOREIGN KEY`

A

Answer to Day 12 Exercise

Enter the following code to build the CustomerType and Customers tables. Please note that the CustomerType table must be built before the Customers table because of the foreign key constraint on CustomerType in the Customers table:

```
// Create the database
dbmake C:\CUSTOMER\CH12EX.MDB;
// Build the Customer Types Table
CREATE TABLE CustomerType(
CustomerType TEXT(6) CONSTRAINT PKCustomerType PRIMARY KEY,
Description TEXT(30));
// Build the Customers table
CREATE TABLE Customers(
CustomerID TEXT(10) Constraint PKCustomerID PRIMARY KEY,
Name TEXT(30),
CustomerType TEXT(6) CONSTRAINT FKCustomerType
_REFERENCES CustomerType(CustomerType),
Address TEXT(30),
City TEXT(30),
State TEXT(30),
Zip TEXT(10),
Phone TEXT(14),
Fax TEXT(14));
// Build the index on Zip
CREATE INDEX SKZip on Customers(Zip);
//Display the results
SELECT * FROM CustomerType;
SELECT * FROM Customers;
```

Day 13, "Error Handling in Visual Basic 6"

Answers to Day 13 Quiz

1. The three main parts of Visual Basic error handlers are

   - The `ON ERROR GOTO` statement
   - The error handler code at the end of the method
   - The `EXIT` statement just before the error handler code

2. The four ways to exit an error handler are

   - `RESUME` (returns to execute the code that caused the error).
   - `RESUME NEXT` (resumes execution of the Visual Basic code at the line immediately following the one that caused the error).
   - `RESUME <LABEL>` (resumes execution at a specified location in the method that caused the error).
   - `EXIT SUB` or `EXIT FUNCTION` (exit the current method in which the error occurred. You can also use `END` to exit the program completely.

3. You use `RESUME` to exit an error handler when users have done something that they can easily correct. For example, a user may have forgotten to insert a disk into drive A or close the drive door.

4. You use `RESUME NEXT` to exit an error handler when the program runs properly, even though an error has been reported, or if code within the program can correct the problem.

5. You use `RESUME <LABEL>` to exit an error handler when you want the program to return to a portion of code that allows correction of an invalid entry. For example, if the user enters numeric data that yields improper results (for example, division by zero) you may want the code to redisplay the input screen so the entry can be corrected.

6. You use `EXIT` or `END` to exit an error handler when there is no good way to return to the program processing after the error has occurred. This might happen if the user forgot to log into a network or if there is insufficient disk space to run the program.

7. The four types of Visual Basic errors are

   - General File Errors, which occur when you try to open, read, write, or close disk files.
   - Database Errors, which occur when you try to perform database operations such as open, read, write, delete, execute, and so forth.

- Physical Media Errors, which occur when physical devices (such as printers, disk drives, input devices, and so forth) do not respond.

- Program Code Errors, which occur when your Visual Basic source code has errors in the text itself.

8. The Visual Basic data controls provide their own error trapping. You should use the ERROR event for the data controls to catch errors that occur due to data control operations.

9. It is a good idea to open data tables in the FORM_LOAD, FORM_INITIALIZE, or FORM_ACTIVATE events. This enables you to capture most database errors prior to any actual data entry work being done.

10. The Err.Raise method enables you to create your own error messages and conform to the Visual Basic standard, including the ability to "post" an error message to another component through the COM object model interface.

Answers to Day 13 Exercises

1. Create a new VB6 Standard EXE Project and add two command buttons to the form. Set one button's name to cmdOpenText and its caption to OpenText. Set the name of the other button to cmdFindText and its caption to FindText.

   Add the following CONST definition to the general declarations of the form:

   ```
   Option Explicit
   '
   Private Const TEXTFILE = "c:\abc.txt"
   ```

   Next, add the following code to the cmdOpenText_Click event:

   ```
   Private Sub cmdOpenText_Click()
       '
       On Error GoTo LocalErr
       '
       Open TEXTFILE For Input As 1
       '
       Exit Sub
       '
   LocalErr:
       MsgBox "Error opening file [" & TEXTFILE & "]" & vbCrLf & _
       "Exiting Program.", vbCritical, "File Error"
       End
       '
   End Sub
   ```

2. Add the following code to the cmdFindText_Click event:

   ```
   Private Sub cmdFindText_Click()
       '
   ```

```
        On Error GoTo LocalErr
        Dim strFile As String
        '
        Open TEXTFILE For Input As 1
        '
        Exit Sub
        '
LocalErr:
    If Err.Number = 53 Then
        If MsgBox("Unable to open file. Do you wish to find it
        ➥yourself?", vbCritical + vbYesNo, "File Error") = vbYes Then
            strFile = GetFile(TEXTFILE)
            If strFile <> "" Then
                Open strFile For Input As 1
            End If
        End If
    End If
    '
    End
    '
End Sub
```

This code uses a custom method called GetFile. The following is the code for the
GetFile method. Be sure to add the CommonDialog control to your project before
adding this method to the form, and set its Name property to cdlFile.

```
Public Function GetFile(Name As String)
    '
    On Error GoTo LocalErr
    '
    Dim strTemp As String
    '
    With cdlFile
        .CancelError = True
        .DialogTitle = "Open " & TEXTFILE
        .FileName = TEXTFILE
        .ShowOpen
        strTemp = .FileName
    End With
    '
    If strTemp <> "" Then
        GetFile = strTemp
    Else
        GetFile = ""
    End If
    '
    Exit Function
    '
LocalErr:
    GetFile = ""
    '
End Function
```

Day 14, "Updating Databases with SQL"

Answers to Day 14 Quiz

1. You use the INSERT statement to insert data into tables. The basic form of this statement is

   ```
   INSERT INTO TableName(field1, field2,...) VALUES(value1, value2,...);
   ```

2. You use the INSERT INTO_FROM statement to insert multiple records into a data table. The format of this statement is

   ```
   INSERT INTO TargetTable SELECT field1, field2 FROM SourceTable;
   ```

3. You use the UPDATE_SET statement to modify existing data. This statement uses the following form:

   ```
   UPDATE <table name> SET <field to update> = <New Value>;
   ```

4. You use the SELECT_INTO_FROM SQL statement to create new tables and insert existing data from other tables. The format of this statement is

   ```
   SELECT field1, field2 INTO DestinationTable FROM SourceTable;
   ```

   In this statement, field1 and field2 represent the field names in the source table.

5. You use the DELETE_FROM statement to remove records from a data table. The form of this statement is

   ```
   DELETE FROM TableName WHERE field = value;
   ```

Answers to Day 14 Exercises

1. Enter the following INSERT_INTO statements after your CREATE INDEX statement to insert the data:

   ```
   INSERT INTO CustomerType VALUES('INDV', 'Individual');
   INSERT INTO CustomerType VALUES('BUS', 'Business - Non-corporate');
   INSERT INTO CustomerType VALUES('CORP', 'Corporate Entity');
   INSERT INTO Customers VALUES('SMITHJ', 'John Smith', 'INDV',
   '160 Main Street', 'Dublin', 'Ohio', '45621',
   '614-569-8975', '614-569-5580');
   INSERT INTO Customers VALUES('JONEST', 'Jones Taxi', 'BUS',
   '421 Shoe St.', 'Milford', 'Rhode Island', '03215',
   '401-737-4528', '401-667-8900');
   INSERT INTO Customers VALUES('JACKSONT', 'Thomas Jackson', 'INDV',
   '123 Walnut Street', 'Oxford', 'Maine', '05896',
   '546-897-8596', '546-897-8500');
   ```

2. Your script should now look like this:

   ```
   // Create the database
   dbmake C:\CUSTOMER\CH14EX.MDB;
   // Build the Customer Types Table
   ```

```
CREATE TABLE CustomerType(
CustomerType TEXT(6) CONSTRAINT PKCustomerType PRIMARY KEY,
Description TEXT(30));
// Build the Customers table
CREATE TABLE Customers(
CustomerID TEXT(10) Constraint PKCustomerID PRIMARY KEY,
Name TEXT(30),
CustomerType TEXT(6) CONSTRAINT FKCustomerType REFERENCES
_CustomerType(CustomerType),
Address TEXT(30),
City TEXT(30),
State TEXT(30),
Zip TEXT(10),
Phone TEXT(14),
Fax TEXT(14));
// Build the index on Zip
CREATE INDEX SKZip on Customers(Zip);
// Insert Data
INSERT INTO CustomerType VALUES('INDV', 'Individual');
INSERT INTO CustomerType VALUES('BUS', 'Business - Non-corporate');
INSERT INTO CustomerType VALUES('CORP', 'Corporate Entity');
INSERT INTO Customers Values('SMITHJ', 'John Smith', 'INDV',
'160 Main Street', 'Dublin', 'Ohio', '45621',
'614-569-8975', '614-569-5580');
INSERT INTO Customers Values('JONEST', 'Jones Taxi', 'BUS',
'421 Shoe St.', 'Milford', 'Rhode Island', '03215',
'401-737-4528', '401-667-8900');
INSERT INTO Customers Values('JACKSONT', 'Thomas Jackson', 'INDV',
'123 Walnut Street', 'Oxford', 'Maine', '05896',
'546-897-8596', '546-897-8500');
// Copy data into the localities table
SELECT CustomerID, City, State INTO Localities FROM Customers;
// Display the results
SELECT * FROM CustomerType;
SELECT * FROM Customers;
SELECT * FROM Localities;
```

3. You issue the following SQL statement to delete the SMITHJ record from the Customers table:

```
DELETE FROM Customers WHERE CustomerID = 'SMITHJ';
```

You use the DROP TABLE command to delete an entire table. To delete the Customers table, you issue the following statement:

```
DROP TABLE Customers;
```

Day 15, "Database Normalization"

Answers to Day 15 Quiz

1. It is not necessarily a good idea to look at database optimization strictly from the point of view of processing performance. Other factors, such as data integrity, are also important. The role of data normalization is to strike a balance between speed and integrity.

2. If the term "First Normal Form" is applied to a database, it means that the first rule of data normalization—eliminate repeating groups—has been achieved.

3. The first rule of data normalization is to delete repeating groups, whereas the second rule of normalization requires the deletion of redundant data. Rule one requires the separation of fields that contain multiple occurrences of similar data into separate tables. Rule two requires that fields that must maintain constant relationships with other fields (for example, the name of a customer as associated with the customer ID) should be placed in a separate table.

4. Do not include calculated fields in a data table. Not only does the calculated data take up disk space, but problems can arise if one of the fields used in the calculation is deleted or changed. Calculations are best saved for forms and reports. Placing a calculated field in your data table violates the third rule of data normalization: eliminate columns not dependent on keys.

5. You invoke the fourth rule of data normalization if you have multiple independent one-to-many relationships within the same table. You need to use this rule when you unwittingly create relationships that do not necessarily exist. For example, if you included educational degree in the Employee skills table in the examples used in this lesson, you mistakenly aligned skills with degrees that do not necessarily match.

6. You invoke the fifth rule of data normalization if you have multiple dependent many-to-many relationships. To resolve any potential conflict under this rule, you might need to break the different components of the relationships into separate tables and link them through another table.

Answers to Day 15 Exercises

1. To achieve First Normal Form, you must delete repeating groups. In this exercise, this includes the fields for the multiple automobiles (VehicleType1, Make1, Model1, Color1, Odometer1, VehicleType2, Make2, Model2, Color2, Odometer2). This requires that you create two tables. The first tracks the customers (Customers), and the second tracks their vehicles (Vehicles).

Customers Table	Vehicles Table
CustomerID (primary key)	SerialNumber (primary key)
CustomerName	CustomerID (foreign key)
License	VehicleType
Address	Make
City	Model
State	Color
Zip	Odometer
Phone	

Please note that by separating the VehicleTypes into a separate table, you can have any number of vehicles for a customer. Also note that SerialNumber makes a better primary key than License, because the serial number of an automobile does not change, whereas a license plate can change on an annual basis.

Next, you need to reach Second Normal Form. This requires you to take the Customer and Vehicle tables and remove any redundant data. There is no redundant data in the Customers table. The Vehicles table, on the other hand, has redundant data describing the VehicleType. You should move the type information into a separate table to yield the following structure:

Customers	Vehicles	VehicleTypes
CustomerID	SerialNumber	VehicleType
(Primary Key)	(Primary Key)	(Primary Key)
CustomerName	CustomerID	Make (Foreign Key)
Address	License	Model
City		VehicleType (Foreign Key)
State	Color	
Zip	Odometer	
Phone		

To reach Third Normal Form, you must delete any fields that do not describe the primary key. A review of all fields shows that you have already eliminated any fields that do not describe the entire primary key.

To achieve Fourth Normal Form, you need to separate any independent one-to-many relationships that can potentially produce unusual answers when you query the data. The Vehicles table does have several one-to-many relationships with the

CustomerID and the VehicleType fields. The combination of these two fields in the same table would not, however, lead to misleading results further down the line. Therefore, you do not need to make any changes to reach Fourth Normal Form.

Similarly, no changes need to be made to reach Fifth Normal Form because you have no dependent many-to-many relationships in your tables. Most data structures do not require you to use the fourth and fifth rules of normalization to optimize your structure.

As a final point, you might want to add a Comments field to each table. This enables users to store any miscellaneous data they choose to track. Adding a memo field to track comments is a good idea in almost every table, because memo fields do not take up room when empty, and they provide great flexibility to your system.

2. The following SQL code builds these tables:

Note

> Please note that you need to create the VehicleTypes table before the Vehicles table. This is required because the Vehicles table has a foreign key constraint to the VehicleTypes table. In such situations, the foreign key must be defined prior to its use in another table, or an error occurs.

```
Create Table Customers
(CustomerID TEXT (10),
CustomerName TEXT (40),
Address TEXT (40),
City TEXT (40),
State TEXT (20),
Zip TEXT (10),
Phone TEXT (14),
Comments MEMO,
CONSTRAINT PKCustomers Primary Key (CustomerID));

Create Table VehicleTypes
(VehicleType TEXT (10),
Make TEXT (25),
Model TEXT (25),
Comments MEMO,
CONSTRAINT PKVehicleTypes Primary Key (VehicleType));

Create Table Vehicles
(SerialNumber INTEGER,
CustomerID TEXT (10),
License TEXT (10),
VehicleType TEXT (10),
Color TEXT (15),
Odometer INTEGER,
```

```
Comments MEMO,
CONSTRAINT PKVehicles Primary Key (SerialNumber),
CONSTRAINT FKCustomer Foreign Key (CustomerID)
_REFERENCES  Customers(CustomerID),
CONSTRAINT FKType Foreign Key (VehicleType)
_REFERENCES VehicleTypes(VehicleType));
```

Day 16, "Multiuser Considerations"

Answers to Day 16 Quiz

1. The Microsoft Jet database engine provides three levels of locking: database locking, which locks the entire database for exclusive use; table locking, which locks a table for exclusive use; and page locking, which locks data pages 2KB in size.

2. You use database locking when compacting a database, because compacting affects all the objects in a database.

3. You use table locking when doing a mass update of a single table. You want exclusive use of the data to be changed, but you do not necessarily have to have exclusive use of the entire database when performing field update functions.

4. You use the LockEdits property of a recordset to control how page locking is handled by your application. Setting this property to True means you have pessimistic locking. Setting this property to False means you have optimistic locking.

5. Pessimistic locking prohibits two users from opening a data page at the same time (that is, when the Edit or AddNew method is invoked). Optimistic locking permits two users to open the same page, but allows updates to be saved only by the first user to make the changes.

6. You cannot use pessimistic locks on an ODBC data source. ODBC data sources use optimistic locking only.

7. When cascading deletes are used in a relationship, each time a base table element is deleted, all foreign table records that contain that element are deleted.

8. You use transaction management in your applications to provide an opportunity to reverse a series of database updates if your program fails to complete all requested data changes. This is particularly useful if you have processes that affect multiple tables within the database. Failure to fully complete such a transaction could lead to a database that has lost or inaccurate data. This can also result in a database that is difficult or impossible to repair.

9. The limitations of transactions include the following:

- Some database formats do not support transactions.

- Datasets that are the result of some SQL JOIN or WHERE clause, and datasets that contain data from attached tables do not support transactions.

- Transaction operations are kept on the local workstations, which could lead to errors if the process runs out of space in the TEMP directory.

10. Declaring a unique workspace object is not required; however, it is highly recommended that you do so because transactions apply to an entire workspace.

Answers to Day 16 Exercises

1. Enter the following code to load a database exclusively when you bring up a form:

```
Private Sub Form_Load()

    Dim DB As Database
    Dim dbName As String

    On Error GoTo FormLoadErr

    dbName = App.Path + "\abc.mdb"
    Set DB = DBEngine.OpenDatabase(dbName, True) _
    ' Open database exclusive
    MsgBox "Database opened successfully"
    GoTo FormLoadExit

FormLoadErr:
    MsgBox "Unable to load database ABC.MDB"
    GoTo FormLoadExit

FormLoadExit:
    Unload Me

End Sub
```

2. Enter the following code in the Form_Load event to load a table exclusively:

```
Private Sub Form_Load()

    Dim db As Database
    Dim rs As Recordset
    Dim dbName As String
    Dim tabName As String

    dbName = App.Path + "\abc.mdb"
    tabName = "Customers"

    On Error GoTo FormLoadErr
```

```
        Set db = DBEngine.OpenDatabase(dbName)
        Set rs = db.OpenRecordset(tabName, dbOpenTable, _
         _dbDenyRead + dbDenyWrite) ' table opened exclusively
        MsgBox "Table opened exclusively"
        GoTo FormLoadExit

    FormLoadErr:
        MsgBox "Unable to load table exclusively"
        GoTo FormLoadExit

    FormLoadExit:
        Unload Me

    End Sub
```

3. To start the project, insert the following code into the general declarations section:

```
Option Explicit

        'Declaration of global variables
        Dim DB As Database
        Dim wsUpdate As Workspace
        Dim nErrFlag As Integer
```

Next, start a new procedure and insert the following code. This code creates a workspace and opens the database:

```
Public Sub OpenDB()

    On Error GoTo OpenDBErr

    Dim dbName As String

    nErrFlag = 0 'Reset the error flag
    dbName = App.Path + "\abc.mdb"

    'Open the workspace and database
    Set wsUpdate = DBEngine.CreateWorkspace( _
    "WSUpdate", "admin", "")   Set DB = wsUpdate.OpenDatabase(dbName,
    ➡True)
    GoTo OpenDBExit

OpenDBErr:
    MsgBox Trim(Str(Err)) + " " + Error$(Err), _
      vbCritical, "OpenDB"   nErrFlag = Err

OpenDBExit:

End Sub
```

Now build the following procedure to perform the posting:

```
Public Sub Post()

    On Error GoTo PostErr
```

```
    Dim cSQL As String

    wsUpdate.BeginTrans

    'Create the SQL statement to insert the records. _
     'Note that we do not use the TransNo field _
     'as it is a counter field necessary only _
     'for the Transactions table
    cSQL = "INSERT INTO History Select CustID, _
    InvoiceNo,_Amount FROM Transactions"
    DB.Execute cSQL

    'Delete the temporary transactions data
    cSQL = "DELETE FROM Transactions"
    DB.Execute cSQL

    'Commit the transactions
    wsUpdate.CommitTrans
    MsgBox "Transactions have been committed"

    'Set the error flag and exit the program
    nErrFlag = 0
    GoTo PostExit

PostErr:
    'Display the error and rollback the transactions
    MsgBox Trim(Str(Err)) + " " + Error$(Err), _
     vbCritical, "Post"
    wsUpdate.Rollback
    MsgBox "Post routine has been aborted"

PostExit:

End Sub
```

Finally, insert the following code into the cmdPost_Click event:

```
Private Sub cmdPost_Click()

    OpenDB
    If nErrFlag = 0 Then
        Post
    End If

    If nErrFlag <> 0 Then
        MsgBox "Error Reported", vbCritical, "cmdPost"
    End If

    Unload Me

End Sub
```

You can test this program by building the database in Visdata or Data Manager and then inserting some sample records into the Transactions table.

Day 17, "Using the Remote Data Control and the RDO Model"

Answers to Day 17 Quiz

1. The standard data control uses the DAO model to access data. The RDO data control uses the RDO model instead. The RDO model is designed for optimal performance with remote databases on a live network connection.

2. Cursor drivers are tools that manage the location of the recordset pointer in a dataset. RDO and RDC connections can use client-side or server-side cursors.

3. The four dataset types available when you use RDO and RDC are

   - OpenForwardOnly creates a scroll-forward-only dataset. This is the default option.

   - OpenStatic creates an updatable set that has nonchanging membership.

   - OpenDynamic creates an updatable set that has changing membership. Record keys are not used, and you cannot use bookmarks.

   - OpenKeyset creates an updatable set that has changing membership. Record keys are used, and you can create bookmarks with this dataset.

4. The five lock types available with RDO and RDC are

   - ConcurReadOnly provides no row-level locking. This is the default option.

   - ConcurLock provides pessimistic locking for the entire row set. Locks occur as soon as the dataset is accessed and remain until the dataset is released.

   - ConcurRowVer provides optimistic locking based on an internal row ID number (usually the TimeStamp column).

   - ConcurValues provides optimistic locking based on a column-by-column check of the data in each row.

   - ConcurBatch provides optimistic locking based on the value in the UpdateCriteria property when using BatchUpdate mode. Not supported by all RDBMSs.

5. The Microsoft Jet (DAO) equivalent of the `rdoResultSet` object is the Recordset object. These objects both contain the actual records collected from the data source.

6. The RDO equivalent of the Workspace object is the `rdoEnvironment`. Both these objects are used to encapsulate multiple databases and recordsets in transactions and security management.

Answer to Day 17 Exercise

Start a new VB6 Standard EXE project and add the Microsoft Remote Data Object Library to the project (select Project|References to locate and load the library). Add a list box and two command buttons to the project. Set one command button's name to `cmdTables` and its caption to `Select DB`. Set the other command button's name to `cmdClear` and its caption to `Clear List`.

Now add the following code to the form:

```
Option Explicit

Private Sub cmdTables_Click()
    '
    ' get rdo table collection
    '
    On Error GoTo LocalErr
    '
    Dim rdoEnv As rdoEnvironment
    Dim rdoCon As rdoConnection
    Dim rdoTbl As rdoTable
    '
    ' set env/con
    Set rdoEnv = rdoEngine.rdoCreateEnvironment("rdoTEMP", "admin", "")
    Set rdoCon = rdoEnv.OpenConnection("")
    '
    ' update the tables collection
    rdoCon.rdoTables.Refresh
    '
    ' show table properties
    List1.Clear
    For Each rdoTbl In rdoCon.rdoTables
        List1.List(List1.ListIndex) = rdoTbl.Name & " [" & rdoTbl.Type & "]"
    Next
    '
    rdoCon.Close
    rdoEnv.Close
    Set rdoTbl = Nothing
    Set rdoCon = Nothing
    Set rdoEnv = Nothing
```

```
'
    Exit Sub
'
LocalErr:
    MsgBox Err.Description, vbExclamation, "RDOTables"
'
End Sub

Private Sub cmdClear_Click()
    List1.Clear
End Sub

Private Sub Form_Load()
'
    Me.Caption = "RDBMS Tables Lister"
'
End Sub
```

Save and test your project.

Day 18, "Using the ActiveX Data Objects (ADO)"

Answers to Day 18 Quiz

1. The ADO object model uses OLE DB as the data interface. However, even though OLE DB is the data interface, you can use the OLE DB Provider for ODBC data sources to gain access to existing ODBC-defined databases.

2. There are three primary objects in the ADO model. They are the Connection, Command, and Recordset objects.

3. ADO only supports two different cursor locations: client-side (adUseClient) and server-side (adUserServer). Two other properties (adUseNone and adUseClientBatch) are no longer valid and should not be used.

4. True. You cannot use OpenForwardOnly, OpenDynamic, or OpenStatics cursor types with client-side cursor.

5. False. You can use the OpenSchema method to return a list of values, fields, or other interesting information about the recordset.

6. You can use the Supports method of the Recordset object to see just what methods it supports.

7. Setting the Mode property to adModeRead may provide an increase in speed when populating a read-only recordset.

8. True. You can now use the Save method to save a recordset to a disk file and use the Source:=diskfile to recall the saved set at a later time.

Answer to Day 18 Exercise

Start a new VB6 project and add a list box, a command button, and a text box to the form. Now add the following code to the Command1_Click event of the form:

```
Private Sub Command1_Click()
    '
    ' *** execute Jet QueryDef using ADO
    '
    Dim objCnn As New ADODB.Connection
    Dim objCmd As New ADODB.Command
    Dim objRst As New ADODB.Recordset
    Dim objPrm As New ADODB.Parameter
    Dim JetODBC As String
    '
    ' open connection
    objCnn.Open "DSN=ADOData"
    '
    ' build command object
    With objCmd
        .ActiveConnection = objCnn
        .CommandType = adCmdStoredProc
        .CommandText = "qryParamQD"
    End With
    '
    ' create parameter object
    With objPrm
        .Name = "IDValue"
        .Type = adInteger
        .Direction = adParamInputOutput
        .Value = Val(Text1.Text)
    End With
    objCmd.Parameters.Append objPrm
    '
    ' collect records
    Set objRst = objCmd.Execute
    '
    ' populate list control
    List1.Clear
    Do While objRst.EOF = False
        List1.AddItem objRst.Fields(0) & " - " & objRst.Fields(1)
        objRst.MoveNext
    Loop
    '
    ' close open items
    objRst.Close
    objCnn.Close
```

```
'
' release memory space
Set objCnn = Nothing
Set objCmd = Nothing
Set objPrm = Nothing
Set objRst = Nothing
'
End Sub
```

Save and test your project.

Day 19, "Attaching to Databases"

Answers to Day 19 Quiz

1. For many reporting needs, including financial reporting, it is preferable to have a snapshot of the data to base reports upon. This enables consistent reporting across time and prevents people from creating reports too soon in the reporting cycle (that is, before the data is deemed usable by the creator).

2. It is possible that transaction management capabilities are lost if an attached external data source does not support it. This can be detrimental, because processes that can affect data cannot be controlled and undone or reversed if they are not allowed to complete properly. Partially changed data may take substantial effort to repair. Worse yet, the user might not know the process did not complete, and thus erroneous data may be stored.

3. Yes, you can attach data from within Visdata by using the Utility | Attachments menu option.

4. The dollar sign ($) signifies that you are using the entire spreadsheet as the data source for your connection.

5. ADO is the preferred data access method for all new development.

6. Building the connection to the data is the first step in designing a Data Environment.

7. Yes, you can use the same Data Environment for both a data form and a data report.

8. A Master/Detail form gets created when you drag a parent/child command from a Data Environment onto a data form.

Answer to Day 19 Exercise

A

Complete the following steps to perform this exercise:

1. Start a Visual Basic 6 data project.

2. Open Visdata and load `ATTACH.MDB`.

3. Select Utility | Attachments and then define a new attachment to the Titles table of `BOOKS6.MDB` in the `\\TYSDBVB6\SOURCE\DATA` directory.

4. Return to the Visual Basic 6 project and open the Data Environment.

5. Build a connection to the `ATTACH.MDB` database.

6. Add a command to attach the Authors table of the `ATTACH.MDB` database.

7. Add a child command that uses the attachment to the Titles table in `BOOKS6.MDB` by right-clicking on the command created in the previous step and selecting Add Child Command.

8. Open the data form and drag and drop the parent command onto the form. This will create your Master/Detail form.

9. Add four command buttons onto the form for navigation. Insert the following code into each button:

   `<DataEnvironment>.rs<Command>.MoveX`

   where `DataEnvironment` is the name of your Data Environment, `Command` is the name of the parent command, and x is either `First`, `Last`, `Previous`, or `next`.

10. Open the Data Report and set its `DataSource` property to your Data Environment and its `DataMember` property to the parent command.

11. Right-click anywhere on the Data Report and select Retrieve Structure.

12. Drag the parent command into the group header of the Data Report.

13. Drag the child command into the detail section of the report.

14. Open the data form again and add another command button that uses the following command in its click event to display the report:

    `<Report Name>.show`

    where `Report Name` is the name you assigned to your data report.

15. Save your work and run the program.

Day 20, "Database Replication"

Answers to Day 20 Quiz

1. Database replication refers to the act of creating a master database (the Design Master) and copies of the master (replicas), and synchronizing data contained in all members of the replica set (the Design Master and all replicas).

2. You may want to use database replication in systems deployed on a wide area network or to remote users. Replication can also be useful for making backups of databases that cannot be shut down to make a copy. Replication is also good for building datasets that must be "frozen," which is a reason for building static databases and reporting systems.

3. You do not want to use replication in an application that can be better deployed as an intranet application. Also, replication should not be considered in systems that are heavily transaction-oriented (such as reservation systems), or where data accuracy and timeliness are of the utmost importance (such as emergency response systems).

4. Three fields are added to each table when a database is turned into a Design Master. The first field, s_Generation, identifies records that changed during data entry. The second, s_GUID, serves as a unique identifier for each record. The third field, s_Lineage, stores the name of the last replica set to update the record.

5. The `Replicable` and the `ReplicableBool` properties are added to the database during creation of the Design Master to indicate that replicas can be made of the Design Master.

6. A replicable database consumes an additional 28 bytes per record, plus the space required to accommodate the additional system tables added when the database is made replicable.

7. An AutoNumber field stops incrementing by 1 and starts inserting random numbers for each new record added to a table. This is but one reason why AutoNumber data types should not be used in your application.

8. You use the `MakeReplica` method to create a copy of the Design Master. You can also use the `MakeReplica` method to create a copy of any member of the replica set (that is, you can use a replica other than the Design Master). In fact, you are better off using a copy of a replica set member as a backup of the Design Master than you are using a tape backup.

9. In a synchronization conflict, the Microsoft Jet engine takes the record that has been changed the greatest number of times. In the case of a tie, the Microsoft Jet engine takes the record from the replica set member with the lowest `ReplicaID`.

10. You can use the star, linear, ring, and fully connected topology synchronization schemes. The star is the most commonly used.

11. Use the `KeepLocal` method to keep database objects from replicating to other members of the replica set. This method must be used before the Design Master is created.

Answer to Day 20 Exercise

You should keep the Design Master at your Cincinnati office. Distribute all tables, except for the SalaryInfo table, to the Los Angeles, Chicago, and New York offices.

For backup, each office should synchronize often with the Cincinnati Office. The Chicago office, given its size, should synchronize more often than the other two remote offices. In case of failure of the Cincinnati database, the Chicago database is probably the best choice to use as a backup. Do not keep a tape backup of the Cincinnati database. The use of a backup copy of the Design Master could be disastrous for the entire replica set.

You should use the star topology in your synchronization strategy. This is the easiest to understand and use, as well as being the most logical, because the order in which databases synchronize is unimportant.

The following code can be attached to a command button (in this case cmdKeepLocal) to keep the SalaryInfo table from replicating. It then goes on to turn the EMPLOYEE.MDB database into a Design Master, and creates a replica named COPYCHI.MDB:

```
Private Sub cmdKeepLocal_Click()

Dim dbMaster As Database
Dim LocalProperty As Property
Dim KeepTab As Object
Dim repProperty As Property


'Open the database in exclusive mode
Set dbMaster = OpenDatabase("c:\tysdbvb6\source\data\employee.mdb", True)

Set KeepTab = dbMaster.TableDefs("SalaryInfo")
Set LocalProperty = dbMaster.CreateProperty("KeepLocal", dbText, "T")
KeepTab.Properties.Append LocalProperty
KeepTab.Properties("Keeplocal") = "T"

MsgBox "The SalaryInfo table is set to not replicate"

'Create and set the replicable property
Set repProperty = dbMaster.CreateProperty("Replicable", dbText, "T")
```

```
dbMaster.Properties.Append repProperty
dbMaster.Properties("Replicable") = "T"

'Display a message box
MsgBox "You have created a Design Master out of EMPLOYEE.MDB!"

dbMaster.MakeReplica "c:\tysdbvb6\source\data\copychi.mdb", "Replica of "
➥& "dbMaster"

dbMaster.Close

MsgBox "You have created a copy of EMPLOYEE.MDB"

End Sub
```

Use the following code from the `Click` event of a command button (cmdSynch) to synchronize the Chicago and the Cincinnati databases:

```
Private Sub cmdSynch_Click()
Dim dbMaster As Database

'Open the database
Set dbMaster = OpenDatabase("c:\tysdbvb6\source\data\employee.mdb")

dbMaster.Synchronize "c:\tysdbvb6\source\data\copychi.mdb"

MsgBox "The synchronization is complete."

End Sub
```

Day 21, "Securing Your Database Applications"

Answers to Day 21 Quiz

1. The disadvantages and limitations of the Microsoft Access SYSTEM.MDA include

   - You must own Microsoft Access to create the SYSTEM.MDA file.

   - It is possible to have multiple SYSTEM.MDA files, which could lead to problems if the wrong file is used with your database.

   - System security can be removed by replacing or sometimes deleting the SYTEM.MDA file.

   - Some applications do not use the SYSTEM.MDA file at all. These applications will not be affected by restrictions placed in the SYSTEM.MDA data file.

2. Disadvantages of using data encryption are

   - MDB encryption affects the entire database, not selected tables or fields.

   - Other programs cannot read encrypted databases. This limits the distribution of your database.

   - Encrypted MDB databases cannot be replicated using the Microsoft Replication Manager tools.

3. Application security focuses on processes, not just data. Application security enables you to grant permissions for forms, reports, and procedures within an application.

4. The two main features of a good application security scheme are

   - It has a user login/logout process to verify that only valid users gain access to the application

   - It has an access rights scheme that limits the tasks that users can perform within the application.

5. No. Application security schemes can't prevent unauthorized access of your data. Application security works only with the application that implements the security model.

6. Access rights security schemes build an added level of security into your application. This type of security enables you to define a set of secured operations within the application that can be accessed only by validated users.

7. Some reasons for adding audit trails to your application are

   - To track when users log in and out of your application

   - To provide detailed information on the status of the application when errors occur

   - To create a record of all major operations within the application, including the printing of reports and any changes made to existing data tables.

Answer to Day 21 Exercise

Start a new VB6 Standard EXE project and add the ADO Data Control to the toolbox (select Project | Components from the main menu). Add the SECURITY.VBP project to the Visual Basic IDE. Be sure to *add* the project, not *open* it. This will enable both your new EXE project and the SECURITY.VBP project to exist in the Project Explorer window.

Add the ADO Data control to the form and, using the (Custom) button in the properties box, set its Data Connection property to Provider=Microsoft.Jet.OLEDB.3.51;Data Source=i:\tysdbvb6\source\chap21\exercises\exer21.mdb and the RecordSource property to point to the Assets table.

Add an array of six command buttons (all named cmdAction) in a row at the bottom of the form. Set their captions to (in order from left to right): Save, Cancel, Addnew, Update, Delete, and Close.

Next, add six text boxes to the form, arranged from top to bottom. Set their DataSource property to point to the ADO data control, and set their data field properties to match the columns in the data control.

Finally, add an array of six label controls (all named label1) and align them to the left of each text box to act as the prompt for data entry.

Add the following code to the Form_Load event to the form:

```
Private Sub Form_Load()
    '
    With Adodc1
        .ConnectionString = "Provider=Microsoft.Jet.OLEDB.3.51;Data
        ➥Source=i:\tysdbvb6\source\chap21\exercises\exer21.mdb"
        .RecordSource = "Assets"
        .CommandType = adCmdTable
        .LockType = adLockOptimistic
        .CursorLocation = adUseClient
        .CursorType = adOpenStatic
        .Refresh
    End With
    '
    FillLabels
    SetFormModeTo fmEdit
    '
End Sub
```

This code uses two custom methods to handle setting the label captions and managing the input mode of the form. The following code shows how to build these two methods and how to add the enumerated data type used in the SetFormModeTo method:

```
Option Explicit

Private Enum FormMode
    fmAdd = 0
    fmEdit = 1
End Enum

Private Sub SetFormModeTo(Optional fmMode As FormMode = fmEdit)
    '
    Dim blnFlag As Boolean
    '
    If fmMode = fmAdd Then
        blnFlag = True
    Else
        blnFlag = False
```

```
        End If
        '
        cmdAction(0).Enabled = blnFlag
        cmdAction(1).Enabled = blnFlag
        cmdAction(2).Enabled = Not blnFlag
        cmdAction(3).Enabled = Not blnFlag
        cmdAction(4).Enabled = Not blnFlag
        cmdAction(5).Enabled = Not blnFlag
        '
End Sub

Public Sub FillLabels()
    '
    Dim intCount As Integer
    Dim intLoop As Integer
    '
    intCount = Adodc1.Recordset.Fields.Count
    '
    For intLoop = 0 To intCount - 1
        With Adodc1.Recordset
            Label1(intLoop).Caption = .Fields(intLoop).Name
        End With
    Next
    '
End Sub
```

Add the following code to the cmdAction_Click event to handle the various buttons on the form:

```
Private Sub cmdAction_Click(Index As Integer)
    '
    With Adodc1.Recordset
        Select Case Index
            Case 0 'save
                .Update
                objAudit.WriteLog "Save New Record"
                SetFormModeTo fmEdit
            Case 1 'cancel
                .CancelUpdate
                objAudit.WriteLog "Cancel New Record"
                SetFormModeTo fmEdit
            Case 2 'new
                .AddNew
                SetFormModeTo fmAdd
            Case 3 'update
                .Update
                .MoveNext
                .MovePrevious
                SetFormModeTo fmEdit
            Case 4 'delete
                If MsgBox("Delete Record?", _
```

```
                    vbYesNo + vbQuestion, _
                    "Delete") = vbYes Then
                      .Delete
                      .MoveFirst
                      objAudit.WriteLog "Delete Existing Record"
                  End If
                  SetFormModeTo fmEdit
              Case 5 'close
                  Unload Me
          End Select
      End With
      '
  End Sub
```

The last bit of code to add to the form is the code that will update the change log each time a user changes the contents of a record. Add this code to the adodc1_WillMove event:

```
Private Sub Adodc1_WillMove(ByVal adReason As ADODB.EventReasonEnum, _
adStatus As ADODB.EventStatusEnum, ByVal pRecordset As ADODB.Recordset)
    '
    ' log field changes
    '
    On Error Resume Next
    '
    Dim ctlTemp As Control
    '
    With Adodc1.Recordset
        For Each ctlTemp In Controls
            If TypeOf ctlTemp Is TextBox Then
                If ctlTemp.DataChanged = True Then
                    objAudit.WriteLog "adReason=" & CStr(adReason), _
                      .Source, ctlTemp.DataField, _
                      .Fields(ctlTemp.DataField), ctlTemp.Text
                End If
            End If
        Next
    End With
    '
End Sub
```

Next, add a code module to the project and enter the following code into that module. This will declare project-level variables and handle the login/logout process for the application.

```
Option Explicit

    '

Public objUsers As Security.Users
Public strConnect As String
```

```
'
Public objAudit As Security.Audit
Public strLogFile As String

Public Sub Main()
    '
    ' main project startup
    '

    ' get connect string
    Load frmCH21Ex
    With frmCH21Ex
        strConnect = .Adodc1.ConnectionString
    End With
    Unload frmCH21Ex

    ' get instance of users object
    Set objUsers = CreateObject("Security.Users")
    With objUsers
        .AppTitle = App.EXEName
        .ConnectString = strConnect
    End With

    ' get instances of audit object
    strLogFile = App.Path & "\" & App.EXEName & ".log"
    Set objAudit = CreateObject("Security.Audit")
    With objAudit
        .FileHeader = App.EXEName
        .FileName = strLogFile
    End With

    ' login/start or fail/end
    If objUsers.Login = True Then
        objAudit.WriteLog "Login", "Succeeded"
        frmCH21Ex.Show
    Else
        objAudit.WriteLog "Login", "Failed"
        End
    End If
    '
End Sub
```

The last step is to use the Project|Properties dialog to set the Startup Object to
Sub Main. This ensures that the Main() subroutine is launched before the form. Now
save and run your project.

INDEX

The Waite Group's Visual Basic 6 Database How-To

Eric Winemiller, Jason T. Roff, Bill Heyman, and Ryan Groom

With the release of Visual Basic 6, database development in Visual Basic moves to a new level of sophistication. With *The Waite Group's Visual Basic 6 Database How-To,* you can keep abreast of the new developments. It contains more than 120 step-by-step solutions to challenging, real-world problems, presented in the Waite Group's award-winning "How-To" format, tackling even the most complex issues with easily understood solutions. You will discover how to use the power of SQL Server in your own apps and learn how to use Open Database Connectivity to create powerful high-end programs quickly. If you're a Visual Basic developer, this complete, easy-to-use guide provides the information and resources needed to write high-quality database applications, no matter which database management system you use. *Visual Basic 6 How-To* has sold over 50,000 copies to date and won the *Visual Basic Programmer's Journal* Reader's Choice Award in 1995. This book includes expanded coverage of Visual Basic 98, including Internet topics and lots of all-new How-To's.

$39.99 US $56.95 CDN   *Intermediate—Advanced*
1-57169-152-9   *1,100 pp.*

Roger Jennings' Database Developer's Guide with Visual Basic 6

Roger Jennings

Roger Jennings' Database Developer's Guide with Visual Basic, Third Edition offers complete coverage of the following database topics: Data Access Objects and Data-Aware Controls; Database and Query Design Concepts; An Introduction to Database Front-End Design; Advanced Programming for Data Access and Automation; Multiuser and Client/Server Database Front-Ends; Databases, Intranets, and the Internet; Enterprise-Level Development Techniques; and Finishing a Production Database Application. This book also covers the following new Microsoft Technologies: ActiveX Controls (VB/database-related), Microsoft Transaction Server, OLE DB, Active Data Objects (ADO), and Advanced Data Connector (ADC). Over 70% of all Visual Basic applications involve databases. The primary focus of this book is on VB 6 ActiveX controls; Microsoft's new Internet database technologies; and Microsoft's newest client/server technology, Microsoft Transaction Server. *Roger Jennings' Database Developer's Guide with Visual Basic, Third Edition* includes updated coverage of OLE DB and ADO.

$59.99 USA $85.95 CDN   *Accomplished—Expert*
0-672-31063-5   *1,100 pp.*

The Waite Group's Visual Basic 6 Client/Server How-To

Noel Jerke, et al.

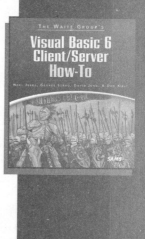

The Waite Group's Visual Basic 6 Client/Server How-To is a practical step-by-step guide to implementing three-tiered distributed client/server solutions, using the tools provided in Microsoft's Visual Basic 6. It addresses the needs of programmers looking for answers to real-world questions and assures them that what they create really works. It also helps simplify the client/server development process by providing a framework for solution development. This book saves you hundreds of hours of programming time by providing step-by-step solutions to more than 75 Visual Basic 6 client/server problems. *Visual Basic 6 Client/Server How-To* covers topics such as OOP, ODBC, OLE, RDO, distributed computing, and three-tier client/server development, and addresses the issues associated with deploying business rules on an intermediate, centralized server.

$49.99 US $71.95 CDN
1-57169-154-5

Intermediate—Advanced
1,000 pp.

Visual Basic 6 Unleashed

Rob Thayer

Visual Basic 6 Unleashed provides comprehensive coverage of the most sought-after topics in Visual Basic programming. This book provides a means for a casual-level Visual Basic programmer to quickly become productive with VB 6. You explore a comprehensive reference to virtually all the topics that are used in today's leading-edge Visual Basic applications. The integration of the text and the CD-ROM makes this an invaluable tool for accomplished Visual Basic programmers—it includes everything you need to know, as well as the tools and utilities to make it all work. *Visual Basic 6 Unleashed* includes topics important to developers, including creating and using ActiveX controls, creating Wizards, adding and controlling RDO, tuning and optimization, and much more. It is targeted toward the programmer who is at the beginning-to-intermediate level and who needs additional step-by-step guidance in learning the more advanced features of Visual Basic. You can use this book as a building block to step to the next level from *Sams' Teach Yourself Visual Basic 6 in 21 Days*.

$49.99 US $71.95 CDN
0-672-31309-X

Intermediate—Advanced
1,000 pp.

Doing Objects in Visual Basic 6

Deborah Kurata

Doing Objects in Visual Basic 6 is an intermediate-level tutorial that begins with the fundamentals of OOP. It advances to the technical aspects of using the VB IDE to create objects and interface with databases, Web sites, and Internet applications. This revised edition features more technical information and specifically highlights the features of VB 6. This is a revised edition of *Doing Objects in Microsoft Visual Basic 5*, the #1 OOP title for Visual Basic programmers and developers. The text focuses on the technical aspects of developing objects and covers the Internet and database programming aspects of VB 6.

$49.99 US $46.18 CDN
1-56276-577-9

Intermediate—Expert
560 pp.

Add to Your Sams Library Today with the Best Books for Programming, Operating Systems, and New Technologies

To order, visit our Web site at www.mcp.com or fax us at

1-800-835-3202

ISBN	Quantity	Description of Item	Unit Cost	Total Cost
1-57169-152-9		The Waite Group's Visual Basic 6 Database How-To	$39.99	
0-672-31063-5		Roger Jennings' Database Developer's Guide with Visual Basic 6	$59.99	
1-57169-154-5		The Waite Group's Visual Basic 6 Client/Server How-To	$49.99	
0-672-31309-X		Visual Basic 6 Unleashed	$49.99	
1-56276-577-9		Doing Objects in Visual Basic 6	$49.99	
		Shipping and Handling: See information below.		
		TOTAL		

Shipping and Handling

Standard	$5.00
2nd Day	$10.00
Next Day	$17.50
International	$40.00

201 W. 103rd Street, Indianapolis, Indiana 46290   1-800-835-3202 — FAX

Book ISBN 0-672-31308-1

What's on the Disc

The companion CD-ROM contains all the authors' source code and samples from the book and some third-party software products.

Windows NT 3.5.1 Installation Instructions

1. Insert the CD-ROM disc into your CD-ROM drive.
2. From File Manager or Program Manager, choose Run from the File menu.
3. Type `<drive>\AUTORUN.EXE` and press Enter, where `<drive>` corresponds to the drive letter of your CD-ROM. For example, if your CD-ROM is drive D:, type `D:\AUTORUN.EXE` and press Enter.
4. Follow the onscreen instructions to finish the installation.

Windows 95, Windows 98, and Windows NT 4.0 Installation Instructions

1. Insert the CD-ROM disc into your CD-ROM drive.
2. From the Windows 95 desktop, double-click on the My Computer icon.
3. Double-click on the icon representing your CD-ROM drive.
4. Double-click on the icon titled `AUTORUN.EXE` to run the installation program.
5. Follow the onscreen instructions to finish the installation.

 Note

If Windows 95, Windows 98, or Windows NT 4 is installed on your computer, and you have the AutoPlay feature enabled, the `AUTORUN.EXE` program starts automatically when you insert the disc into your CD-ROM drive.
